Principles of Supply Chain Management

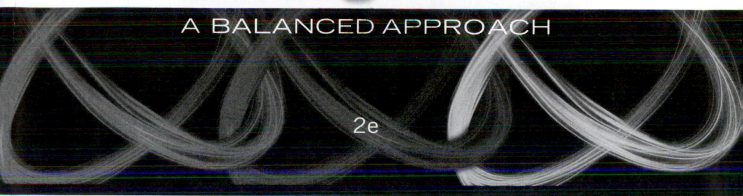

A BALANCED APPROACH

2e

JOEL D. WISNER
University of Nevada, Las Vegas

•

KEAH-CHOON TAN
University of Nevada, Las Vegas

•

G. KEONG LEONG
University of Nevada, Las Vegas

SOUTH-WESTERN
CENGAGE Learning™

Australia • Brazil • Japan • Korea • Mexico • Singapore • Spain • United Kingdom • United States

SOUTH-WESTERN
CENGAGE Learning™

Principles of Supply Chain Management, 2nd edition
Joel Wisner, Keah-Choon Tan,
G. Keong Leong

Vice President of Editorial, Business:
Jack W. Calhoun

Editor-in-Chief: Alex von Rosenberg

Sr. Acquisitions Editor: Charles McCormick, Jr.

Associate Developmental Editor: Julie Klooster

Editorial Assistant: Bryn Lathrop

Marketing Manager: Bryant Chrzan

Content Project Manager: Jennifer A. Ziegler

Production Technology Analyst: Erin Donohoe

Technology Project Editor: John Rich

Senior Manufacturing Buyer: Diane Gibbons

Production Service: Newgen Publishing Services

Art Director: Stacy Jenkins Shirley

Internal Designer: Joseph Pagliaro
Design: Patti Hudepohl

Cover Designer: Lou Ann Thesing

Cover Image: Getty Images

For product information and technology assistance, contact us at
Cengage Learning Academic Resource Center, 1-800-423-0563

For permission to use material from this text or product, submit all requests online at **www.cengage.com/permissions**

Further permissions questions can be emailed to
permissionrequest@cengage.com.

Exam*View*® and Exam*View* Pro® are registered trademarks of FSCreations, Inc. Windows is a registered trademark of the Microsoft Corporation used herein under license. Macintosh and Power Macintosh are registered trademarks of Apple Computer, Inc. used herein under license.

© 2008 Cengage Learning. All Rights Reserved.

Library of Congress Control Number: 2008921349

Student edition ISBN-13: 978-0-324-37508-4

Student edition ISBN-10: 0-324-37508-5

South-Western Cengage Learning
5191 Natorp Boulevard
Mason, OH 45040
USA

Cengage Learning products are represented in Canada by Nelson Education, Ltd.

For your course and learning solutions, visit
academic.cengage.com

Purchase any of our products at your local college store or at our preferred online store **www.ichapters.com**

Printed in the United States of America
3 4 5 6 7 12 11 10

Brief Contents

Contents

Preface

Welcome to the second edition of *Principles of Supply Chain Management: A Balanced Approach.* The practice of supply chain management is becoming widespread in all industries around the globe today, and both small and large firms are realizing the benefits provided by effective supply chain management. We think this text is unique in that it uses a novel and logical approach to present discussions of this topic from four perspectives: purchasing, operations, logistics, and the integration of processes within these three vitally important areas of the firm. We think this book is somewhat different than the other supply chain management texts available, because we present a more balanced view of the topic—many of the texts available today concentrate primarily on just one of the three areas of purchasing, operations, or logistics.

The objective of the book is to make readers think about how supply chain management impacts all of the areas and processes of the firm, and to show how managers can improve their competitive position by employing the practices we discuss throughout the text. Junior or senior level undergraduate business students, beginning MBA students, as well as practicing managers can benefit from reading and using the text.

There are a number of additions to this second edition that we hope you will find interesting and useful. You might have noticed the green vertical ribbon on the textbook's cover—this signifies the environmental sustainability emphasis throughout the text. In addition, each chapter contains new Supply Chain Management in Action, e-Business Connection, and Global Perspective boxed features, along with new references throughout and new end-of-chapter discussion questions and exercises. Other specific additions and changes to the text are described below.

The textbook also comes packaged with a student disk containing teaching cases for each section of the book. Some of the case companies and situations are real, while others are fictional, and the cases are varied from easy to difficult and short to long. In the Chapter 1 Appendix, there is a discussion of the Beer Game, with inventory tracking sheets to allow instructors to actually play the game with their students. Finally, there are quantitative as well as qualitative problems and questions, Internet exercises, and spreadsheet problems at the ends of the chapters.

Part 1 is the overview and introduction of the topic of supply chain management. This chapter introduces the basic understanding and concepts of supply chain management, and should help students realize the importance of this topic. Core concepts such as the bullwhip effect, supplier relationships, forecasting and demand management, enterprise resource planning, logistics management, and customer relationship management are discussed. There is also a new section on current trends in supply chain management.

Part 2 presents supply management issues in supply chain management. This very important topic is covered in three chapters, building from an introduction to purchasing management, to employing strategic concepts aimed at increasing supply chain management success. Within these chapters can be found new sections on government purchasing, Web purchasing, software applications, vendor managed inventory, and green purchasing.

Part 3 includes four chapters regarding operations issues in supply chain management. This section progresses from topics on forecasting, resource planning and inventory management to lean production and Six Sigma. New sections in Part 1 include a greater emphasis on collaborative planning, forecasting, and replenishment (CPFR), discussions of distribution requirements planning (DRP) and radio frequency identification (RFID), and finally discussions of the latest lean production and Six Sigma programs.

Part 4 presents distribution issues in supply chain management and consists of four chapters. Chapter 1 is a review of domestic U.S. and international logistics and contains new sections on transportation security and reverse logistics. This is followed by chapters on customer relationship management, global location decisions, and service response logistics. New content in these chapters includes new software application discussions, environmental issues in logistics, China's role in the global economy, and supply chain management in services.

The final section is Part 5, which presents discussions of integration issues in supply chain management and performance measurement along the supply chain. While cooperation and integration are frequently referred to in the text, this section brings the entire text into focus, tying all of the parts together, first by discussing process integration in detail, followed by a discussion of traditional and world-class performance measurement systems. New material here includes the topics of supply chain risk and security management, and expanded coverage of performance measurement models.

We think we have compiled a very interesting set of supply chain management topics that will keep readers interested and we hope you enjoy it. The disk that comes with the teacher's edition contains sample syllabi, Power Point slides, sample tests, answers to all chapter questions and problems, and case notes for each of the cases on the disk. We welcome your comments and suggestions for improvement. Please direct all comments and questions to any of the authors:

Joel Wisner: joel.wisner@unlv.edu

Keah-Choon Tan: kctan@unlv.nevada.edu

G. Keong Leong: keong.leong@unlv.edu

Acknowledgments

We greatly appreciate the efforts of a number of fine and hard-working people at Cengage Learning/South-Western College Publishing. Without their feedback and guidance, this text would not have been completed. The team members are Charles E. McCormick, Jr., Senior Acquisitions Editor; Bryant Chrzan, Marketing Manager; Jennifer Ziegler, Content Project Manager; and most importantly, Julie Klooster, our Associate Developmental Editor and day-to-day contact person. Thanks, Julie, for listening and sorting all our details out. A number of other people at Cengage Learning and South-Western also need to be thanked including Erin Donohoe, Stacy Shirley, John Rich, and Bryn Lathrop. We also would like to thank Arunesh Shukla and his people at Newgen who put the manuscript into final copy form.

Additionally, we wish to thank all of the reviewers who graciously added their time to this effort, greatly improving our final product. These people are:

Yavuz Agan	*Western Illinois University*
Sudip Bhattacharjee	*University of Connecticut*
Steven Brown	*Arizona State University*
Zhi-Long Chen	*University of Maryland*
Adam Conrad	*Penn State—Altoona*
Deborah Cook	*Virginia Tech*
Richard Crandall	*Appalachian State University*
Sime Curkovic	*Western Michigan University*
Eddie Davila	*Arizona State University*
K. Kathy Dhanda	*DePaul University*
Krishna Dhir	*Berry College*
Ike Ehie	*Kansas State University*
Ray Eldridge	*Freed-Hardeman University*
Mark Ferguson	*Georgia Institute of Technology*
Mark Goudreau	*Johnson & Wales University*
Gregory Graman	*Michigan Technological University*
Marsha Haasch	*Milwaukee Area Technical College*
John Hebert	*The University of Akron*
Richard Hoffmann	*The Pennsylvania State University, Berks Campus*
Michael Jones	*Southeastern Louisiana University*
Anil Kukreja	*Xavier University of Louisiana*
Robert Landeros	*Western Michigan University*
Kathy Lewis-Payne	*Mountain State University*
Michael McGinnis	*Penn State University*
Mark Moosbrugger	*Wright State University*
Philip Musa	*The University of Alabama at Birmingham*
Barb Osyk	*The University of Akron*
Daewoo Park	*Xavier Univeristy*

Sue Perrott Siferd	*Arizona State University*
Gerald Pineault	*Northeastern University*
Tony Polito	*East Carolina University*
Alfred Quinton	*The College of New Jersey*
Michael Smith	*Western Carolina University*
Andrew Stapleton	*University of Wisconsin*
James Stephens	*Emporia State University*
Sri Talluri	*Michigan State University*
Billy Thornton	*Colorado State University*
Larry Weinstein	*Wright State University*
Theresa Wells	*University of Wisconsin—Eau Claire*
George Zsidisin	*Colorado State University.*

Finally, we would like to thank all of the case writers who contributed to this text-book. Their names are printed with each of the cases on the disk. As with any project of this size and time span, there are certain to be a number of people who gave their time and effort to this textbook and yet, their names were inadvertently left out of these acknowledgments. We apologize for this and wish to thank you here.

About the Authors

Joel D. Wisner is professor of Supply Chain Management at the University of Nevada, Las Vegas. He earned his BS in Mechanical Engineering from New Mexico State University in 1976 and his MBA from West Texas State University in 1986. During that time, Dr. Wisner worked as an engineer for Union Carbide at their Oak Ridge, Tennessee facility and then worked in the oil industry in various extremely wet and green Louisiana Gulf Coast locations and in desolate, dry and sandy West Texas areas. In 1991, he earned his PhD in Operations and Logistics Management from Arizona State University. He is certified in transportation and logistics (CTL) and in purchasing management (C.P.M.).

He is currently keeping busy with international travels and lectures, and with other textbook projects, while teaching undergraduate and graduate courses in supply chain management at the University of Nevada, Las Vegas. His research interests are in process assessment and improvement strategies along the supply chain. His articles have appeared in numerous journals including *Journal of Business Logistics, Journal of Operations Management, Journal of Supply Chain Management, Journal of Transportation, Production and Operations Management Journal,* and *Quality Management Journal.* More information about Dr. Wisner can be found at his Web site: www.scsv.nevada.edu/~wisnerj

Keah-Choon Tan is professor of Operations and Supply Chain Management at the University of Nevada, Las Vegas. He received a BS degree and an MBA from the University of South Alabama, and his PhD in Production and Operations Management from Michigan State University. He is a Certified Purchasing Manager (C.P.M.) of the Institute for Supply Management (ISM), and is certified in production and inventory management (CPIM) by the Association for Operations Management (APICS).

Dr. Tan's publications appear in academic journals such as *Decision Sciences, International Journal of Operations and Production Management, International Journal of Production Research, Journal of Supply Chain Management, Omega,* and *Quality Management Journal,* among others. Prior to academia, Dr. Tan was the hospital administrator of a specialist hospital and the account comptroller of a listed manufacturing firm.

G. Keong Leong is professor and Chair of the Management Department in the College of Business at the University of Nevada, Las Vegas. He received an undergraduate degree in Mechanical Engineering from the University of Malaya and an MBA and PhD from the University of South Carolina. He was previously a member of the faculty at Ohio State University and held a visiting faculty position at the Thunderbird School of Global Management.

His publications appear in academic journals such as *Journal of Operations Management, Decision Sciences, Interfaces, Journal of Management, European Journal of Operational Research,* and *International Journal of Production Research,* among others. He has coauthored three books including *Operations Strategy: Focusing Competitive Excellence* and *Cases in International Management: A Focus on Emerging Markets* and received research and teaching awards including an Educator of the Year award from the Asian Chamber of Commerce in Las Vegas. He has been active in the Decision Sciences Institute, serving as Editor of *Decision Line,* At-Large Vice-President, Chair of the Innovative Education Committee, Chair of the Doctoral Student Affairs Committee, and Manufacturing Management Track Chair. In addition, he served as Chair of the Professional Development Workshop and Chair of the Operations Management Division, Academy of Management. Professor Leong is listed in *Who's Who Among American Teachers,* Marquis *Who's Who in the World, Who's Who in America,* and *Who's Who in American Education.*

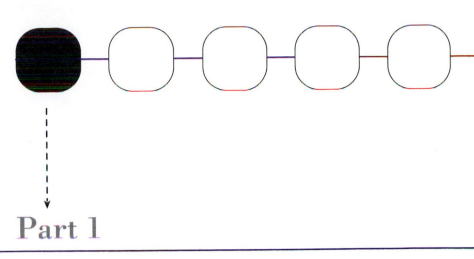

Part 1

Supply Chain Management: An Overview

Chapter 1   Introduction to Supply Chain Management

Chapter 1

INTRODUCTION TO SUPPLY CHAIN MANAGEMENT

Businesses are beginning to recognize the potential of going beyond the historical view of the supply chain as a cost center to its emerging role as a strategic enabler of increased sales and margins.[1]

There is a need to recognize the reality of relationships within supply chain management. It's a risk and a revenue sharing relationship.[2]

Learning Objectives

After completing this chapter, you should be able to

- Describe a supply chain and define supply chain management.
- Describe the objectives and elements of supply chain management.
- Describe local, regional, and global supply chain management activities among services and manufacturing companies.
- Describe a brief history and some of the trends of supply chain management.
- Understand how the bullwhip effect impacts supply chain members.

Chapter Outline

Supply Chain Management in Action

P&G's Global Supply Chain Starts with the Consumer

Since the beginning of this decade, The Procter & Gamble Company (P&G) has followed three primary growth strategies: (1) focus on P&G's biggest brands, countries, and retail customers; (2) develop faster-growing, higher-margin businesses such as beauty, health, and home; and (3) serve more of the world's consumers by accelerating growth in developing markets.

Each of these strategies has contributed to P&G's ability to deliver topline growth at or above the company's targets for the past five consecutive years. And each of these strategies has implications for P&G's supply chain operations.

The third strategy—growing P&G's business in developing markets—puts supply chain operating strategy to one of its biggest tests. P&G calls this strategy the "Consumer-Driven Supply Network." It is based directly on P&G's purpose: to improve the lives of the world's consumers. And it is tied directly to a deeply held belief at P&G that "the consumer is boss."

With the Consumer-Driven Supply Network, P&G is building and operating supply chains "from the shelf back." Today's consumers have more choices than ever, and those choices offer a broader range of value. The consumer-goods companies that win with consumers will be those who perform the best at two critical "moments of truth." The first moment of truth is when a consumer stands at the shelf and chooses a brand to purchase. The second moment of truth is at home, when the consumer uses the P&G brand and decides whether it lives up to his or her expectations.

The implications for the supply chain are clear. Historically, P&G supply chains have been internally focused on meeting cost and productivity targets. Externally, the focus was limited almost entirely to the second moment of truth—how the finished product design and quality performed with consumers when they used it.

The challenge for today's supply chain leaders is to continue to deliver at the second moment of truth, while designing supply chains to better meet consumers' and customers' needs at the first moment of truth. The most important measure of how the supply chain works is whether products are always there, always affordable, and always preferred by the consumer when he or she stands at the shelf and decides what to buy.

As P&G has grown, so have its supply chains, with more supply chains in more places around the world delivering an increasing number of products. Today, P&G is facing several competing priorities:

- Rising supplier costs versus the need to meet the consumer value equation.
- Reaping the benefits of global scale versus the need for local differentiation.
- Meeting the unique challenges of developed and developing markets.
- Serving large, global retailers versus small, local high-frequency stores.

P&G is addressing these challenges by building a set of capabilities that create value for retail customers and consumers and drive growth for P&G's businesses. These capabilities fall into three areas: reliable service, agile, demand-driven supply, and affordable differentiation.

In terms of reliable service, P&G wants to measure performance through the eyes of the consumer as he/she experiences our products at the first moment of truth. This means getting the right product at the right place—on the shelf—at the right time. It also means understanding the quality of the product on the shelf (not just the quality when it left the manufacturing facility or distribution center) and ensuring products are priced to represent a good value to the consumer. Consistent, reliable service everyday is an essential building block for any supply network.

With agile, demand-driven supply, P&G is focusing on reducing end-to-end supply network time by building a flexible and responsive supply network that is capable of producing what is actually selling, not what is forecast to sell. P&G believes it can dramatically reduce supply network time, which has significant cash benefits for P&G and retail customers. Furthermore, it translates to speed to shelf for promotional events and new product initiatives.

The third new area of capability P&G is building into its supply network is affordable differentiation—product, packaging, or supply chain solutions that help our retail customers better serve their shoppers. Pringles Prints is one example. P&G has created the ability to print a message on each chip, which can be customized for different retailers.

These new capabilities—reliable service, agile, demand-driven supply, and affordable differentiation—are allowing P&G to better meet consumers' needs while creating new growth opportunities for its retail customers and P&G brands.

P&G's Consumer-Driven Supply Network strategy has sparked a fundamental culture change in P&G's supply chain operations. P&G has transformed from an internal focus to an external, end-to-end focus. Today, product supply consists of 70,000 P&G employees who each understand how their piece of the supply network affects the end consumer.

The most effective supply chains are those that are built around the company's business strategies and purpose. At P&G, all employees share a common purpose—winning with consumers by improving their lives.

Source: Harrison, K. "P&G's Global Supply Chain Starts with the Consumer." *Supply Chain Management Review*, 10, no. 7 (2006): 8. Reprinted with permission of *Supply Chain Management Review*, © 2006.

Introduction

Operating successfully in any business environment today requires companies to become much more involved in how their suppliers and customers do business. As global markets expand and competition increases, making products and services that customers want to buy means that businesses must pay closer attention to where materials come from, how their suppliers' products and services are designed and assembled, how finished products are transported and stored, and what their direct consumers and end-product users are really asking for. The chapter-opening feature, Supply Chain Management in Action, describes the role that customers play in Proctor & Gamble's supply chain management (SCM) efforts.

Over the past fifteen years, many large firms or conglomerates have found that effectively managing all of the business units of a **vertically integrated firm**—a firm whose business boundaries include one-time suppliers and/or customers—is quite difficult. Consequently, firms are selling off business units and otherwise paring down their organization to focus more on core capabilities, while trying to create alliances or **strategic partnerships** with suppliers, transportation and warehousing companies, distributors, and other customers who are good at what they do. This collaborative approach to making and distributing products and services to customers is becoming the most effective and efficient way for businesses to stay successful—and is central to the practice of supply chain management.

Several factors require today's firms to work together more effectively than ever before. Communication and information exchange through computer networks using **enterprise resource planning (ERP)** systems (discussed further in Chapter 6) and the Internet has made global teamwork not only possible but necessary for firms to compete in most markets. Communication technology continues to change rapidly, making global partnerships and teamwork much easier than ever before. Competition is expanding rapidly in all industries and in all markets around the world, bringing new materials, products, people, and resources together, making it more difficult for the local, individually owned, "mom-and-pop" shops to keep customers. New markets are opening up as governments change and as consumers around the world learn of new products from television, the Internet, radio, and contact with tourists. It is an exciting time for companies seeking to develop new products, find new customers, and compete more successfully. New jobs and opportunities are opening up in the areas of purchasing, operations, logistics, and supply chain management as firms build a better competitive infrastructure.

As you read this textbook, you will be introduced to the concepts of supply chain management and how to use these concepts to become better managers in today's global economy. We use examples throughout the text to illustrate the topics discussed; and we provide cases on the student disk for each section of the textbook to enable you to test your problem solving, decision making, and writing skills in supply chain management. We hope that by the end of the text you will have gained an appreciation of the value of supply chain management and will be able to apply what you have learned, both in your profession and in future courses in supply chain management.

In this chapter, the term *supply chain management* is defined, including a discussion of its importance, history, and developments to date. The chapter ends with a look at some of the current trends in supply chain management, followed by directions for playing the supply chain-oriented Beer Game in Appendix 1.1.

Supply Chain Management Defined

There are many definitions of supply chain management in the literature today, but we start with a discussion of a **supply chain**, as shown in Figure 1.1. The supply chain shown in the figure starts with firms extracting raw materials from the ground—such as iron ore, oil, wood, and food items—and then selling these to raw material suppliers such as lumber companies and raw food distributors. These firms, acting on purchase orders and specifications they have received from component manufacturers, turn the raw materials into materials that are usable by these customers (materials such as sheet steel, aluminum, copper, lumber, and inspected foodstuffs). The component manufacturers, responding to orders and specifications from their customers (the final-product manufacturers), make and sell intermediate components (electrical wire, fabrics, plumbing items, nuts and bolts, molded plastic components, processed foods). The final-product manufacturers (companies such as Boeing, General Motors, and Coca-Cola) assemble finished products and sell them to wholesalers or distributors, who then resell these products to retailers as their product orders are received. Retailers in turn sell these products to us, the end-product consumers.

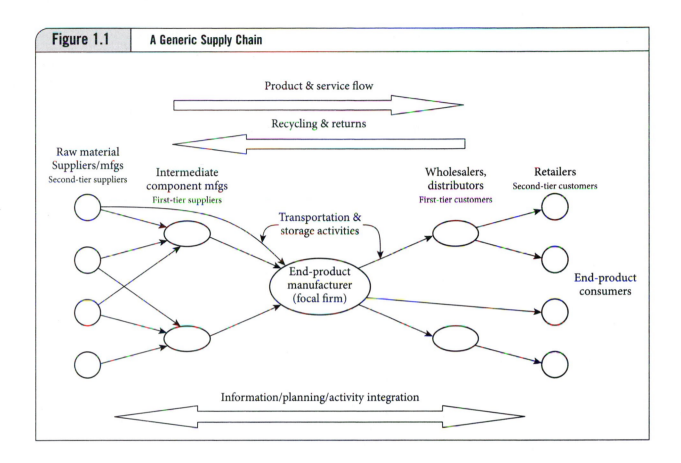

Figure 1.1 | **A Generic Supply Chain**

Consumers buy products based on a combination of cost, quality, availability, maintainability, and reputation factors, and then hope the purchased products satisfy their requirements and expectations. The companies, along with their supply chains, that can provide these desired things will ultimately be successful. Along the supply chain, intermediate and end customers may need to return products, obtain warranty repairs, or may just throw products away or recycle them. These **reverse logistics activities** are also included in the supply chain, and are discussed further in Chapter 9.

Referring again to Figure 1.1, the firm in the middle of the figure is referred to as the **focal firm**, while companies on either side of the focal firm are the first-tier, second-tier (or further removed) suppliers and customers. While the focal firm is presented here and in other chapter discussions as an end-product assembly firm, it can be any of the firms involved in the supply chain, depending on the frame of reference of the manager viewing the diagram.

Thus, the series of companies eventually making products and services available to consumers, including all of the functions enabling the production, delivery, and recycling of materials, components, end products, and services, is called a supply chain. Companies with multiple products likely have multiple supply chains. All products and services reach their customers via some type of supply chain—some much larger and more complex than others. With this idea of a supply chain in mind, then it is easy to come to the realization that there really is only one true source of income for all supply chain organizations—the end customer. Steve Darendinger, vice president of advanced sourcing and supply chain strategy for Cisco Systems of

California, says the key to developing effective supply chain management programs is keeping the customer in mind. "The things that we do within our supply chain are driven around customer success," he says. "We provide opportunities and solutions for customers."[3] When individual firms in a supply chain make business decisions that ignore the interests of the end customer and other chain members, these suboptimal decisions transfer risks, costs, and additional waiting time along the supply chain, ultimately leading to higher end-product prices, lower supply chain service levels, and eventually lower end customer demand.

A number of other companies are also indirectly involved in most supply chains, and they play a very important role in the eventual delivery of end products to customers. These are the many service providers, such as trucking, rail, and airfreight shipping companies, information system providers, public warehousing firms, freight forwarders, agents, and consultants. These service providers are extremely useful to the firms in most supply chains, since they can get products where they need to be in a timely fashion, allow buyers and sellers to communicate effectively, allow firms to serve outlying markets, enable firms to save money on domestic and global shipments, and in general allow firms to adequately serve their customers at the lowest possible cost.

So, now that a general description of a supply chain has been provided, what is **supply chain management (SCM)**? A number of similar definitions are available in the literature and among various professional associations. For example,

- The Institute for Supply Management describes supply chain management as *"[t]he design and management of seamless, value-added processes across organizational boundaries to meet the real needs of the end customer."*[4]
- The Supply-Chain Council's definition of supply chain management is *"[m]anaging supply and demand, sourcing raw materials and parts, manufacturing and assembly, warehousing and inventory tracking, order entry and order management, distribution across all channels, and delivery to the customer."*[5]
- The Council of Supply Chain Management Professionals defines supply chain management as *"[t]he planning and management of all activities involved in sourcing and procurement, conversion, and all logistics management activities. Importantly, it also includes coordination and collaboration with channel partners, which can be suppliers, intermediaries, third-party service providers, and customers."*[6]

Consistent across these definitions is the idea of coordinating or integrating a number of product-related activities among supply chain participants to improve operating efficiencies, quality, and customer service in order to gain a sustainable competitive advantage for all of the collaborating organizations. Thus, for supply chain management to be successful, firms must work together by sharing information on things like demand forecasts, production plans, capacity changes, new marketing strategies, new product and service developments, new technologies employed, purchasing plans, delivery dates, and anything else impacting the firm's purchasing, production, and distribution plans.

In theory, supply chains work as a cohesive, singularly competitive unit, accomplishing what many large, vertically integrated firms have tried and failed to accomplish. The difference is that independent firms in a supply chain are relatively free to enter and leave supply chain relationships if these relationships are no longer proving beneficial; it is this free market organization that helps supply chains operate more effectively than vertically integrated conglomerates.

For example, when a particular material or product is in short supply accompanied by rising prices, a firm may find it beneficial to align itself with one of these suppliers to ensure continued supply of the scarce item. This alignment may become beneficial to both parties—new markets for the supplier, leading to new, future product opportunities; and long-term continuity of supply and stable prices for the buyer. Later, when new competitors start producing the scarce product or when demand declines, the supplier may no longer be valued by the buying firm; instead, the firm may see more value in negotiating with other potential suppliers for its purchase requirements and may then decide to dissolve the original buyer/supplier alignment. As can be seen from this example, supply chains are often very dynamic or fluid, which can also cause problems in effectively managing them.

While supply chain management may allow organizations to realize the advantages of vertical integration, certain conditions must be present for successful supply chain management to occur. Perhaps the single most important prerequisite is a change in the corporate cultures of all participating members in the supply chain to make them conducive to supply chain management. More traditional organizational cultures that emphasize short-term, company-focused performance in many ways conflict with the objectives of supply chain management. Supply chain management focuses on positioning organizations in such a way that all participants in the supply chain benefit. Thus, effective supply chain management relies on high levels of trust, cooperation, collaboration, and honest, accurate communications.

Purchasing, operations, logistics, and transportation managers must not only be equipped with the necessary expertise in these critical supply chain functions but must also appreciate and understand how these functions interact and affect the entire supply chain. Rebecca Morgan, president of Fulcrum Consulting Works, an Ohio-based supply chain management consulting firm, says too many companies go into agreements they call partnerships, then try to control the relationship from end to end. "A lot of the automotive companies did this in the beginning," she says. "They issued a unilateral ultimatum: 'You will do this for me if you want to do business with me, no matter what it means for you.'"[7] This type of supply chain management approach can lead to distrust, poor performance, and ultimately loss of suppliers and customers.

Boundaries of supply chains are also dynamic. It has been often said that supply chain boundaries extend from "the firm's suppliers' suppliers to its customers' customers." Today, most firms' supply chain management efforts do not extend beyond those boundaries. In fact, in many cases, firms find it very difficult to extend coordination efforts beyond a few of the firms' most important direct or **first-tier suppliers** and **first-tier customers** (in one survey, a number of firm representatives stated that most of their supply chain efforts were with the firm's *internal* suppliers and customers only!).[8] However, with time and successful initial results, many firms are extending the boundaries of their supply chains to include **second-tier suppliers** and **customers** (these are the suppliers' suppliers and the customers' customers), as well as nondomestic suppliers and customers.

The Importance of Supply Chain Management

While all firms are part of a chain of organizations bringing products and services to customers (and most firms operate in a number of supply chains), certainly not all supply chains are managed in any truly coordinated fashion. Firms continue to operate independently in many industries (particularly small firms). It is often easy for managers to be focused solely on their immediate customers and their internal daily operations. After all, with customers complaining, employees to train, late supplier deliveries, creditors to pay, and equipment to repair, who has time for relationship building and other supply chain management efforts?

Many firms, though, have worked through their daily problems and encountered value-enhancing, long-term benefits from their supply chain management efforts. Firms with large system inventories, many suppliers, complex product assemblies, and highly valued customers with large purchasing budgets have the most to gain from the practice of supply chain management. For these firms, even moderate supply chain management success can mean lower purchasing and inventory costs, better product quality, and higher levels of customer service and sales. According to the U.S. Census Bureau's Annual Survey of Manufacturers, the cost of inventories exceeded $2.5 trillion among U.S. manufacturers in 2005, up from $2.2 trillion in 2000. In addition, transportation and inventory carrying costs in the U.S. totaled $1.1 trillion in 2005, up 77 percent over the past decade, due to rising fuel prices and interest rates.[9] Thus it can easily be seen that purchasing, inventory, and transportation cost savings can be quite sizable for firms utilizing effective supply chain management strategies.

Managers must realize that their supply chain management efforts can start small—for instance, with just one key supplier—and build through time to include more supply chain participants—such as other important suppliers, key customers, and logistics services—and, then eventually, second-tier suppliers and customers. So why is this integration activity important? As alluded to earlier, when a firm, its customers, and its suppliers all know each others' future plans and are willing to work together, the planning process is easier and much more productive, in terms of cost savings, quality improvement, and service enhancement. A fictitious example is provided in Example 1.1.

Example 1.1 illustrates some of the costs of independent planning and lack of supply chain information sharing and coordination. Grebson's safety stock, which they have built in to their roller bearing purchase orders, has resulted in still additional safety stock production levels at the Pearson plant. In fact, some of the erratic purchasing patterns of Grebson are probably due to their left-over safety stocks causing lower purchase quantities for those periods. This in turn, creates greater demand variability, leading to a decision at Pearson to produce an even higher level of safety stock. This same scenario plays out between Pearson and Fawcett Steels, resulting in erratic buying patterns by Pearson and further safety stock production by Fawcett Steels. If the supply chain was larger, this magnification of safety stock, based on erratic demand patterns and forecasts derived from demand already containing safety stock, would continue as orders pass to more distant suppliers up the chain. This supply chain safety stock, forecasting, and production problem is known as the **bullwhip effect**. If Grebson Manufacturing knew its customers' purchase plans for the coming quarter along with their forecasting methods and the way their purchase plans were derived, it would need to add little, if any, safety stock to its own purchase plan for roller bearings. In turn, if Grebson purchased its roller bearings from only Pearson and further, told Pearson what their quarterly purchase plans were and if Pearson did likewise with Fawcett Steels, safety stocks throughout the supply chain would be reduced drastically, driving down the costs of purchasing, producing, and carrying roller bearings at each stage. This discussion also sets the stage for a supply chain management concept called **collaborative planning, forecasting,** and **replenishment (CPFR)**, discussed further in Chapter 5.

Example 1.1   Grebson Manufacturing's Supply Chain

Pearson Bearings makes roller bearings for Grebson Manufacturing on an as-needed basis. For the upcoming quarter, they have forecasted Grebson's roller bearing demand to be 25,000 units. Since Grebson's demand for bearings from Pearson has been somewhat erratic in the past due to the number of bearing companies competing with Pearson and also the fluctuation of demand from Grebson's customers, Pearson's roller bearing forecast includes 5,000 units of safety stock. The steel used in Pearson Bearings' manufacturing process is usually purchased from Fawcett Steels, Inc. Fawcett Steels has, in turn, forecasted Pearson's quarterly demand for the high-carbon steel it typically purchases for roller bearings. The forecast also includes safety stock of about 20 percent over what Fawcett Steels expects to sell to Pearson over the next three months.

This short description has exposed several problems occurring in most supply chains. Because Pearson does not know with any confidence what Grebson's roller bearing demand will be for the upcoming quarter (it could be zero, or it could exceed 25,000 units), Pearson will incur the extra cost of producing and holding 5000 units of safety stock. In addition, Pearson risks having to either scrap, sell, or hold onto any units not sold to Grebson, as well as losing current and future sales to Grebson if their demand exceeds 25,000 units over the next quarter. Fawcett Steels faces the same dilemma—extra materials, labor costs, and warehouse space for safety stock along with the stockout costs of lost present and future sales. In addition, Grebson's historical demand pattern for roller bearings from its suppliers already includes some safety stock, since it uses roller bearings in one of the products it makes for a primary customer.

The result includes lower supply chain costs and better customer service (remember, there would be few, if any, stockouts if purchase quantities were decided ahead of time and shipping companies delivered on time; additionally, production quantities would be less, reducing purchase costs and production time). Trade estimates suggest that the bullwhip effect results in excess costs on the order of 12–25 percent at each firm in the supply chain, which can be a tremendous competitive disadvantage.

Lower costs resulting from reducing the bullwhip effect can also result in better quality, since potentially higher profit margins mean more investment into materials research, better production methods, and use of more reliable transportation and storage facilities. In addition, as working relationships throughout the supply chain mature, firms will feel more comfortable investing capital in better facilities, better products, and better services for their customers. With time, customers will share more information with suppliers and suppliers will be more likely to participate in their key customers' new product design efforts, for instance. These, then become some of the more important benefits of a well-integrated supply chain. In the following chapters of the text, other associated benefits will also become apparent.

The Origins of Supply Chain Management in the U.S.

During the 1950s and 1960s, U.S. manufacturers were employing mass production techniques to reduce costs and improve productivity, while relatively little attention was typically paid to creating supplier partnerships, improving process design

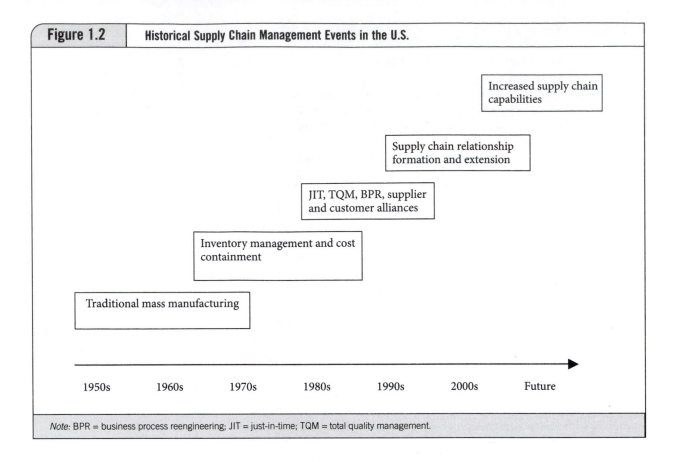

| Figure 1.2 | Historical Supply Chain Management Events in the U.S. |

Note: BPR = business process reengineering; JIT = just-in-time; TQM = total quality management.

and flexibility, or improving product quality (see Figure 1.2). New product design and development was slow and relied exclusively on in-house resources, technologies, and capacities. Sharing technology and expertise through strategic buyer–supplier partnerships was essentially unheard of back then. Processes on the factory floor were cushioned with inventory to keep machinery running and maintain balanced material flows, resulting in large investments in work-in-process inventory.

In the 1960s and 1970s, material requirements planning (MRP) systems and manufacturing resource planning (MRP-II) systems were developed, and the importance of effective materials management was recognized as manufacturers became aware of the impact of high levels of inventories on manufacturing and storage costs. As computer capabilities grew, the sophistication of inventory tracking software also grew, making it possible to further reduce inventory costs while improving internal communication of the need for purchased parts and supplies.

The 1980s were the breakout years for supply chain management. One of the first widely recorded uses of the term *supply chain management* came about in a paper published in 1982.[10] Intense global competition beginning in the 1980s (and continuing today) provided an incentive for U.S. manufacturers to offer lower-cost, higher-quality products along with higher levels of customer service. Manufacturers utilized just-in-time (JIT) and total quality management (TQM) strategies to improve quality, manufacturing efficiency, and delivery times. In a JIT manufacturing environment with little inventory to cushion scheduling and/or production problems, firms began to realize the potential benefits and importance of strategic and cooperative supplier–buyer–customer relationships. The concept of these partnerships or alliances emerged as manufacturers experimented with JIT and TQM.

As competition in the U.S. intensified further in the 1990s accompanied by increasing logistics and inventory costs and the trend toward market globalization, the challenges associated with improving quality, manufacturing efficiency, customer service, and new product design and development also increased. To deal with these challenges, manufacturers began purchasing from a select number of certified, high-quality suppliers with excellent service reputations and involved these suppliers in their new product design and development activities as well as in cost, quality, and service improvement initiatives. In other words, companies realized that if they started giving only their best suppliers most of their business, then, in return, they could expect these suppliers to help generate more sales through improvements in delivery, quality, and product design and to generate cost savings through closer attention to the processes, materials, and components they used in manufacturing their products. Many of these buyer–supplier alliances have proven to be very successful.

Interestingly, the general idea of supply chain management had been discussed for many years prior to the chain of events shown in Figure 1.2. Back in 1915, Arch W. Shaw of the Harvard Business School wrote the textbook, *Some Problems in Market Distribution,* considered by many to be the first on the topic of what we now refer to as supply chain management. The text included discussions of how best to purchase raw materials, transport products, locate facilities, and analyze productivity and waste. He espoused a "laboratory point of view" or systematic study of many relevant supply chain management issues.[11] And business school professors today continue to discuss these topics with students and business managers. According to C. John Langley, Jr., professor of supply chain management at the Georgia Institute of Technology, "The idea that companies ought to work together and coordinate activities has always been around, but ask people today what one of the biggest problems with supply chains are today, and they say companies don't work very well together." And Langley continues, "It takes a period of time to identify new ideas. It takes a lot longer to implement them."[12]

Business process reengineering (BPR), or the radical rethinking and redesigning of business processes to reduce waste and increase performance, was introduced in the early 1990s and was the result of a growing interest during this time in the need for cost reductions and a return to an emphasis on the key competencies of the firm to enhance long-term competitive advantage. As this "fad" died down in the mid- to late-1990s (the term became synonymous with downsizing), supply chain management rapidly increased in popularity as a source of competitive advantage for firms.

Also during this time, managers, consultants, and academics began developing an understanding of the differences between logistics and supply chain management. Up until then, supply chain management was simply viewed as logistics outside the firm. As companies began implementing supply chain management initiatives, they began to understand the necessity of integrating all key business processes among the supply chain participants, enabling the supply chain to act and react as one entity. Today, logistics is viewed as one important element of the much broader supply chain management concept.

At the same time, companies also saw benefits in the creation of alliances or partnerships with their customers. The focal firm became a highly valued and heavily used supplier to its customers. Developing these long-term, close relationships with customers meant holding less finished product safety stock (as discussed earlier in the bullwhip effect example) and allowed firms to focus their resources on providing better products and services to these customers. In time, when market share improved for its customers' products, the result was more business for the focal firm.

Thus, supply chain management has evolved along two parallel paths: (1) the purchasing and supply management emphasis from industrial buyers and (2) the transportation and logistics emphasis from wholesalers and retailers. The increasing popularity of these alliances with suppliers and customers (and suppliers' suppliers and customers' customers) in the later part of the 1990s and continuing today has also meant a greater reliance on the shipping, warehousing, and logistics services that provide transportation, storage, documentation, and customs-clearing services to many firms within a typical supply chain. Relationship building has also occurred increasingly with many of these **third-party logistics providers (3PLs)** and the firms that use them to ensure a continuous, uninterrupted supply of goods. The need to assess the performance of these relationships periodically has also accompanied the growth of supply chain management. One of the challenges faced today by many firms involved in supply chain management is how to adequately assess overall performance in often extremely complex, **global supply chains**.

For the wholesaling and retailing industries, the supply chain management focus is on location and logistics issues more often than on manufacturing. Supply chain management in these industries has often been referred to as **quick response (QR)**, **service response logistics**, or **integrated logistics**. The advancement of electronic data interchange (EDI) systems, bar coding, Internet systems, and radio frequency scanning technologies over the past two decades has greatly aided the evolution of the integrated supply chain concept. Organizations in the retail industry have utilized supply chain management to meet the ever-increasing uncertainty and complexity of the marketplace and to reduce inventory throughout their supply chains.

Most recently, the rapid development of client/server supply chain management software that typically includes integrated supply chain management and electronic commerce components has aided in the evolution and adoption of supply chain management. Sharing information with supply chain partners through EDI and the Internet has enabled firms to integrate stocking, logistics, materials acquisition, shipping, and other functions to create a more proactive and effective style of business management and customer responsiveness. The e-Business Connection feature profiles Wal-Mart and its use of information technology (IT) to facilitate its supply chain management efforts.

The Foundations of Supply Chain Management

The foundation elements within the topic of supply chain management are introduced in this section. These elements essentially make up the table of contents for this textbook and are shown in Table 1.1 along with the chapters where they are discussed.

Supply Management Elements

Traditional purchasing strategies emphasize the use of many suppliers, competitive bidding, and short-term contracts; this often creates adversarial buyer–supplier relationships with a focus primarily on the product's purchase price instead of the capabilities

e-Business Connection

Collaboration and Use of IT at Wal-Mart

In retailing, Wal-Mart is the world champion of lean. Its inventory turnover, 4.1 in 1990, had risen to 7.6 in 2005, an improvement rate of 3.1 percent per year over that 15-year time span. That betterment took place while Wal-Mart was branching out into 15 countries, greatly extending its supply pipelines. Wal-Mart's SCM practices have served as a model for other major retailers. As a retailer, Wal-Mart has no work-in-process or finished-goods inventories. It is all purchased materials. Behind Wal-Mart's sharp trimming of those stocks is a continuing series of innovations that, for other retailers, become the next thing to learn.

A movement called quick response (QR) got its start in 1986 when textile manufacturer Milliken brought together key department stores and apparel houses to agree to share demand, production, and shipping data. While a manufacturer got QR going, retailer Wal-Mart soon took it over, placing new requirements on its suppliers, such as vendor-managed inventory. Under VMI, suppliers were obliged to manage Wal-Mart's inventory replenishment via electronic access to the retailer's point-of-sale data.

Next, Wal-Mart elected to phase out of dealing with middlemen, requiring that producers ship direct to Wal-Mart distribution centers or to stores. Instead of large-batch shipping to fill downstream warehouses, the new mode became continuous replenishment: shipments synchronized to daily barcode-scanned retail sales. For manufacturers, the system calls for extending the synchronization to their production schedules and purchasing. Upping the ante, Wal-Mart is the current world leader in upgrading to radio frequency identification (RFID), opening up more ways of tightening supply and synchronizing to real demand.

For its own distribution centers, Wal-Mart pioneered cross-docking, in which a truckload of an incoming item goes not into storage, but directly into multiple trucks in small lots for immediate transfer to retail stores. Wal-Mart reportedly delivers 85 percent of its merchandise using cross-docking. Topping all this off, more than 2000 of Wal-Mart's suppliers have seen fit to relocate empowered staff to the mega-retailer's Bentonville, Arkansas home base, to collaborate on both strategic and tactical issues. The ring of 20 office parks housing these suppliers has acquired the nickname "Vendorville."

Wal-Mart's contributions to SCM are best summed up in terms of collaboration, which includes, but only secondarily, collaboration IT systems. As has been widely reported, Wal-Mart, along with such manufacturers as Dell and IBM, employs leading-edge information technology in their supply chains. One Wal-Mart IT system, according to *Business Week,* allows 2000 vendors to immediately see how their merchandise is selling. But any company can install software. The effectiveness of information technology at Wal-Mart and its successful imitators follows from extensive formation of collaborative agreements.

High-performing collaboration develops in two stages: the first is internal, requiring breaking down the company's departmental silos. The most successful Wal-Mart suppliers, Proctor & Gamble and Johnson & Johnson, for example, have managers in Vendorville from a mix of functions. That mix would at least include marketing, operations, and finance. Together they can, with counterparts at Wal-Mart, cover the essential bases: joint impacts on sales and market share, effects on operational and supply chain capacities, and projected changes in cost and cash flows. This is quite unlike the usual approach in which, separately at each company, sales booking orders are thrown over the wall, clashing with operational realities; and, later, finance sees if they made money or not. Or, alternatively, to keep capacity busy, production makes product in large lots and sends it into storage. Sales offers price and other inducements to move the excesses; and, again, finance sees if money was made.

However collaboration has developed, it cannot resolve many supply chain problems without astute uses of information technology. Again, Wal-Mart is masterful. Though the company spends less on IT per sales dollar than major competitors, it leads them in results. Part of the reason may be that Wal-Mart develops most of its IT in-house, rather than using off-the-shelf systems. Moreover, Wal-Mart's IT personnel commonly have prior experience in merchandising and, later, are frequently promoted out of IT and into an IT-using function. This connectivity helps ensure that it is not IT for technology's sake, but for furthering the company's multiple ambitions.

The lesson here for manufacturing is not that they must develop their own software; that may not be feasible, except in small measure. Bringing functional expertise into IT, however, makes good sense for manufacturers. (The idea has often been addressed in the systems development community. Usually, though, it has involved much talk, but little change.) Bringing outside experience into IT is one more step in breaching internal silos, thus paving the way for effective external collaboration.

of the suppliers and how they can contribute to the long-term competitiveness of the buying organization. Over the past fifteen years, there has been a gradual shift toward a more strategic approach to purchasing, and this broader approach is more commonly referred to as supply management. Effective supply management has resulted generally in smaller supply bases and the development of more long-term supplier

Table 1.1	Important Elements of Supply Chain Management	
SUPPLY CHAIN MANAGEMENT ELEMENTS	**IMPORTANT ISSUES**	**CHAPTERS**
Purchasing	Supply base reduction, supplier alliances, SRM, strategic sourcing, green sourcing, VMI	2,3,4
Operations	Demand management, CPFR, inventory management, MRP, ERP, RFID, lean systems, Six Sigma quality	5,6,7,8
Distribution	Logistics management, CRM, security, network design, global supply chains, service response logistics, green logistics	9,10,11,12
Integration	Integration activities and problems, risk management, performance measurement	13,14

Note: CPFR = collaborative planning, forecasting, and replenishment; CRM = customer relationship management; ERP = enterprise resource planning; MRP = materials requirements planning; RFID = radio frequency identification; SRM = supplier relationship management; VMI = vendor-managed inventory.

relationships to achieve the competitive benefits described earlier. Purchasing and the strategic concepts of supply management are one of the foundations of supply chain management, since incoming material quality, delivery timing, and purchase price are impacted by the buyer–supplier relationship and the capabilities of suppliers. Chapters 2, 3, and 4 cover the topics associated with supply management.

Harvey Kaylie, president of Mini-Circuits, a New York-based manufacturer of microwave components, sees the supply chain as a relay team, with each link like a runner handing off a baton to the next in line. "It's a challenge, having a process to work with suppliers as partners to achieve the goal of a smooth hand-off," he says. "If we truly want to be world-class, we have to be in tune with our suppliers. If we cannot respond because we don't have the right materials at the right time, we will fail," he adds.[13] Problems with suppliers will ultimately cause end-product customers to get less and pay more. For instance, TaylorMade Golf, maker of the number one rated golf clubs on the PGA Tour, began instituting strict rules for its supplier partnerships a few years back when its customers began complaining that their orders were often late. "We are big enough to drive what our supply chain looks like and how it performs," says Mark Leposky, vice president of global operations for TaylorMade. "But we try to establish partnerships with our suppliers that work to our mutual benefit."[14]

One of the most crucial issues within the topic of supply management is **supplier management**. Simply put, this means encouraging or helping the firm's suppliers to perform in some desired fashion, and there are a number of ways to do this. This involves assessing suppliers' current capabilities and then figuring out how they need to improve them. Thus, one of the key activities in supplier management is **supplier evaluation**, or determining the current capabilities of suppliers. This occurs both when potential suppliers are being evaluated for a future purchase and when existing suppliers are periodically evaluated for ongoing performance purposes. A closely related activity is **supplier certification**. Certification programs can either be company-designed and administered, or they can be internationally recognized and standardized programs like the ISO 9000 series of quality certifications. Supplier certification allows buyers to assume the supplier will meet certain product quality and service requirements covered by the certification, thus reducing duplicate testing and inspections and the need for extensive supplier evaluations.

Over time, careful and effective supplier management efforts allow firms to selectively screen out poor-performing suppliers and build successful, trusting relationships with the remaining top-performing suppliers. These suppliers can provide tremendous benefits to the buying firm and the entire supply chain. As discussed in greater detail in Chapter 2, higher purchase volumes per supplier typically mean lower per unit purchase costs (causing a much greater impact on profits than a corresponding increase in sales), and in many cases higher quality and better delivery service. These characteristics are viewed as strategically important to the firm because of their impact on the firm's competitiveness. Suppliers also see significant benefits from these relationships in terms of long-term, higher-volume sales. These trading partner relationships have come to be termed strategic partnerships and are emphasized throughout this text as one of the more important aspects of supply chain management. One of the network equipment maker Cisco Systems' key improvement initiatives of the past few years has been supply base reduction. In 2001, it had 1500 suppliers, and 80 percent of its spend was with 200 suppliers. By the end of 2006, Cisco was using 600 suppliers and 90 percent of its spend was with 95 suppliers.[15] Chapters 3 and 4 present these and other topics associated with the buyer–supplier relationship.

Operations Elements

Once materials, components, and other purchased products are delivered to the buying organization, a number of internal operations elements become important in assembling or processing the items into finished products, ensuring that the right amount of product is produced, and that finished products meet specific quality, cost, and customer service requirements. After supply management, operations management is considered the second foundation of supply chain management and is covered in Chapters 5 through 8.

During a calendar year, seasonal demand variations commonly occur. Firms can predict when these variations occur, based on historical demand patterns, and use forecasting techniques to guide weekly or monthly production plans. If demand does not materialize as forecasted, then the firm is left with either too much inventory (or service capacity) or not enough. Both situations cost the firm money and can even cause permanent loss of future business if a stockout has occurred. To minimize these costs, firms often rely on **demand management** strategies and systems, with the objective of matching demand to available capacity, either by improving production scheduling, curtailing demand, using a back-order system, or increasing capacity. Rapid-Line of Grand Rapids, Michigan, uses a package called SyteLine APS from Frontstep to schedule production of the metal parts it supplies for customers in the office furniture, appliance, and automotive industries. Rapid-Line typically has two weeks to turn around its customers' orders, and some want as little as seven-day or less turnaround. Their scheduling system works like an airlines reservation system. They get preliminary order information and use this information to reserve capacity for their bigger customers. "We want to be able to reserve capacity for our customers' orders, then hold off on the actual production of those orders until the last possible minute, while still ensuring that all orders will reach their destinations at the right time," says Mark Lindquist, Rapid-Line's president.[16]

Controlling or managing inventory is one of the most important aspects of operations and is certainly value enhancing for the firm. Firms can and typically do have some sort of **material requirements planning (MRP)** software application for managing their inventory. These applications can be linked throughout the organization and its supply chain partners using enterprise resource planning (ERP) systems, providing real-time sales data, inventory, and production information to all business units and to key supply chain participants. These system configurations vary considerably, based on the number and complexity of products and the design of the supply chain. Retailers like Wal-Mart, for example, scan the bar codes of the products purchased, causing the local store's MRP system to deduct units from inventory until a preset re-order point is reached. When this occurs, the local computer system automatically contacts Wal-Mart's regional distribution center's MRP system and generates an order. At the distribution center, the order is filled and sent along with other orders to the particular Wal-Mart. Eventually, the inventory at the distribution center needs replenishing; and, at that time, the distribution center's MRP system automatically generates an order with the manufacturer who sells the product to Wal-Mart. This order communication and **inventory visibility** may extend farther back up the supply chain, reducing the likelihood of stockouts or excess inventories.

However, inventory visibility may be difficult to achieve along the supply chain. Ohio-based Sterling Commerce, a subsidiary of AT&T and one of the world's largest providers of business process management software, points out that in order to convert point-of-sale data into valuable intelligence along the supply chain it must be cleansed, harmonized, contextualized, unified, and connected with business operations data from the customer relations management, enterprise resources planning, and SCM applications. In addition, the data, hardware and software configuration of trading partners has to be recognized, aligned, and optimized to achieve any strategic advantage.[17]

Another common form of inventory management is through the use of a lean or **just-in-time (JIT) production system** (**lean production** is also commonly referred to as the **Toyota Production System**). Implementing this type of system usually results in faster delivery times, lower inventory levels, and better quality. An example here would be Texas-based computer maker Dell Inc. A customer calls or contacts Dell through its Web site and custom-configures his computer. Once the computer is ordered, Dell assembles the computer from in-stock, mass-produced components and delivers the computer in just a few days. Thus, Dell can mass-manufacture computer components and still be able to offer customized products to its customers.

An important aspect of a lean production system is the quality of the incoming purchased items and the quality of the various assemblies as they move through the various production processes. This is due to the characteristically low inventory levels of purchased goods and work in process in lean-oriented facilities. Thus, firms and supply chains employing concepts of lean usually have a **Six Sigma** quality or total quality management (TQM) strategy in place to ensure continued quality compliance among suppliers and with internal production facilities. The type of inventory control system used (MRP or ERP versus lean) is especially important when considering the design of the supply chain (for instance, where to construct distribution centers, what transportation services to use, and how big to make the various production facilities and warehouses).

Distribution Elements

When products are completed, they are delivered to customers through a number of different modes of transportation. Delivering products to customers at the right time, quality, and volume requires a high level of planning and cooperation between the firm, its customers, and the various distribution elements or services employed (such as transportation, warehousing, and break-bulk or repackaging services). For services, products are produced and delivered to the customer simultaneously in most cases, so services are extremely dependent upon server capacity and successful service delivery to meet customer requirements. Distribution is the third foundation of supply chain management and these topics are presented in Chapters 9 through 12.

Distribution decisions typically involve a trade-off between cost and delivery timing or customer service. Motor carriers (trucks), for example, are typically more expensive than rail carriers but offer more flexibility and speed, particularly for short routes. Air carriers are yet more expensive but much faster than any other transportation mode. Water carriers are the slowest but are also the least expensive. Finally, pipeline transportation is used to transport oil, water, natural gas, and coal slurry. Many transportation services offer various modal combinations, as well as warehousing and customs-clearing services. In a typical integrated supply chain environment where JIT deliveries are the norm, logistics services or 3PLs are critical to the overall success of the supply chain. In many cases, these services are considered supply chain partners and are viewed as key value enhancers for the supply chain.

Anchor Blue, for example, a teen fashion retailer headquartered in California, was having many problems with its distribution center and inventory management system, leading to problems stocking its retail stores in 2004. Consequently, they outsourced their logistics function to UPS Supply Chain Solutions, resulting in a 40 percent decrease in unit processing costs and a 37 percent increase in merchandise pieces moved per year. According to Richard Space, senior vice president for logistics at Anchor Blue, "We have increased delivery to stores and seen better fill rates. What used to take ten days from DC to stores now takes two. And that means improved cash flow." In the end, Space says the keys to a successful outsourcing arrangement are communication and trust.[18]

The desired outcome of distribution is customer service. In order to provide the desired level of customer service, firms must identify customer requirements and then provide the right combination of transportation, warehousing, packaging, and information services to successfully satisfy those requirements. Through frequent contact with customers, firms develop **customer relationship management (CRM)** strategies regarding how to meet delivery due dates, how to successfully resolve customer complaints, how to communicate with customers, and how to determine the distribution services required. From a supply chain management perspective, these customer activities take on added importance, since second-tier, third-tier, and final-product customers are ultimately dependent on the distribution outcomes at each stage within the supply chain.

Designing and building a **distribution network** is one method of ensuring successful product delivery. Again, there is typically a trade-off between the cost of the distribution system's design and customer service. For example, a firm may utilize a large number of regional or local warehouses in order to deliver products quickly to customers. The transportation cost from factory to warehouse, the inventory holding cost, and the cost to build and operate warehouses would be quite high, but the payoff would be better customer service flexibility. On the other hand, a firm may choose to operate only a few highly dispersed warehouses, saving money on the inbound transportation cost, the inventory holding cost, and the warehouse construction and operating cost but then having to be content with limited customer service capabilities. Customer desires and competition levels play important roles in this network design decision. Building a dependable distribution network can often mean higher profits. A study performed by AMR Research, an independent company of supply chain experts headquartered in Massachusetts, found that a 3 percent improvement in **perfect order fulfillment** (orders arriving on time, complete, and damage free) led to a 1 percent improvement in profits.[19]

When firms operate globally, their supply chains are more complex, making global location decisions, the topic of Chapter 11, a necessary aspect of supply chain management. The increasing demand for products in emerging global markets and the growing foreign competition in domestic markets, along with low production costs in locations such as China, have made overseas business commonplace for many companies. Firms must understand both the risks and advantages of operating on a global scale and the impact this may have on their global supply chains. Some of the advantages include a larger market for products, economies of scale in purchasing and production, lower labor costs, a supply base of potentially cheaper, higher-quality suppliers, and the generation of new product ideas from nondomestic suppliers and employees. Some of the risks include fluctuating exchange rates affecting production, warehousing, and purchasing and selling prices, or **operating exposure**; government intervention or political instabilities causing changes in subsidies, tariffs, taxes, or corporate operating laws; and, finally, failure to identify particular foreign customer needs and local reactions to products.

Firms can successfully react to these problems by building flexibility into their global supply chains. This is accomplished by using a number of suppliers, manufacturing, and storage facilities in various foreign locations. As product demand and economic conditions change, the supply chain can react to take advantage of opportunities or cost changes to maximize profits.

For service products, the physical distribution issue is typically much less complex. Making sure services are delivered in a timely fashion is the topic of Chapter 12—service response logistics. Services are, for the most part, delivered by a server when customers request service. For instance, consider an example in which a customer walks into a bank in search of a loan for a used automobile. He may contact three separate bank employees during this transaction but eventually will complete a loan application, wait for loan approval, and then receive funds, assuming his loan is approved. He will leave, satisfied with the service products he received provided that a number of things occurred: he got what he came for (the loan); he got the type of service he expected to get (reasonable amount of waiting, knowledgeable servers); and he got his product at a reasonable price (a good interest rate for the right period of time).

Thus, successful service delivery depends on service location (service providers must be close to the customers they are trying to serve), service capacity (customers will leave if the wait is too long), and service capability (customers must be able to trust what servers are telling them or doing for them). Hard goods producers must also be concerned with the delivery of service products for their customers, such as providing warranty repairs and information, financing, insurance, and equipment troubleshooting and operating information. An interesting example of financial supply chain management in the banking industry is provided in the Global Perspective feature.

Global Perspective

Globalization Drives Banks to Implement Financial Supply Chain Management

Financial supply chain management is an outgrowth of the long-established concept of the physical supply chain in the trade business. Rather than dealing solely with the actual physical/logistical aspects of trade, however, financial supply chain management, as the name implies, covers the payments side of trade, from the moment a purchase order is cut, to the time of settlement and everything in between.

"It's the layer atop the physical supply chain," explains Michael Sugirin, product specialist for financial supply chain management with Frankfurt-based Deutsche Bank. "It spans the planning and execution of payments between trading partners, whether they're the buyer or a supplier managing cash flow, working capital and key risk factors."

"It's visibility into the movement of information that has a financial impact across all the participants in a supply chain so that informed decisions can be made efficiently," adds La Hulpe, Belgium-based SWIFT's regional solutions manager. "There are a lot of parallels between the physical and financial supply chain. You're creating synergies by combining all this information into one service set."

Financial supply chain management also is a means to further eliminate paper from the world of international trade. "A lot of these payments are still done with paper, in addition to the paper that follows these transactions around," explains Richard Winston, director of payments and processing at Accenture (Chicago). "Automation stops at the interface point between counterparties. Corporates want an electronic facilitation of the process so you can use imaging and workflow engines, not paper and checks."

Once again, banks are being driven to reevaluate some long-established paper-based processes to make life easier for their clients. "The goal is to create benefits for corporates around operational efficiency and working capital management," says Tim House, director, global supply chain strategy, for Charlotte, N.C.-based Wachovia. "You want to give them the ability to squeeze more cash out of their supply chain."

Of course, when the paper is cut out of the process, so too is a good deal of cost, relates National City's Craig Schurr, SVP, global trade and treasury. "There's a cost every time someone makes a payment," Schurr comments. "There are costs for the whole trade cycle. The current thinking [among banks] is to find ways to drive that cost to the lowest point possible for clients."

And beyond the financing costs, continues Schurr, is the cost associated with the transport of physical paper in the trade process. "With international trade, there's a documentary/paper component that involves the movement of paper among couriers," he says. By employing imaging technology, banks such as National City are attempting to capture the paper at the earliest point possible in the process in an attempt to cut out one of the middlemen—in this case, the courier service. "We capture an image of the documents at our Hong Kong partner, for example, and make that available to the buyer in the U.S. so the purchase order information can be viewed as it becomes available," relates Schurr.

According to Wachovia's Chris Ward, SVP and manager, payables and receivables solutions, this kind of real-time, actionable data availability is just what banks' corporate clients desire. "Our customers are driving toward speeding up their supply chains to get more transparency and visibility into them," he says. "Payments are key to understanding what's going on in the financial supply chain. Corporate treasurers are keen on this because, traditionally, a lot of the processes have been very manual. They want to digitize trade information so they can more aggressively handle their business. Banks want to provide this real-time synchronicity to their clients. This is very powerful for corporates."

Such timely financing is made possible by the manner in which banks and corporates interact in this new process. Part of financial supply chain management involves banks more intimately linking their systems with the enterprise resource planning (ERP) systems of their corporate clients in order to provide certain just-in-time services, according to SWIFT's Christopher Conn (Regional Solution Manager) "First, we had just-in-time inventory management. Now we can have just-in-time financing arrangements," he says. "As banks become more attuned to what's going on in clients' supply chains, they can make better financing decisions for them. They can see the transaction flow around the merchandise that's being manufactured and sold. So instead of providing a general working capital loan, you can offer a transaction-by-transaction loan."

There is no standard way of implementing financial supply chain management; there is no one key technology. Rather, integration is what really matters. "It's about integration and collaboration of technology," says Deutsche Bank's Sugirin. "We see integration as the key because it all comes down to the seamlessness of the connectivity to trading partners."

Wachovia's Ward confirms the importance of systems integration: "Customers deploy different technologies. Although traditional ERP systems are popular, some are using homegrown solutions. We focus a lot of time on integrating our solutions with clients' ERP solutions. The one common element is probably the move to Web-based technology."

In the end, both corporates and banks need to resign themselves to the fact that the new kind of collaboration enabled by financial supply chain management is the key to their mutual survival. National City's Schurr says this is especially vital for banks as use of letters of credit declines. "As the world moves away from letters of credit, a revenue stream goes away for the banks," he observes. "This is about preservation. Banks make the payment at the end, and we want to provide other value-added services to clients." "If banks don't effectively deliver a strategy on this, they'll be disintermediated," warns Accenture's Winston. "Banks' treasury management operations are at risk if they can't figure out how to be more open in the supply chain. If banks don't facilitate the part of the supply chain around the movement of paper and checks, they will be relegated to settlement entities, a low-value area. The winner will be someone who can bring a seamless infrastructure to facilitate payment exchange between parties. Banks will have quite an opportunity here."

Source: Bruno-Britz, M. "As the World Turns— Globalization Is Driving Banks to Examine New Ways to Cater to Corporate Clients, Including Financial Supply Chain Management." *Bank Systems & Technology*, 44, no. 1 (2007): 28. © CMP Media LLC Jan. 2007. Used with permission.

Integration Elements

Thus far, three of the foundations of supply chain management have been discussed: supply management, operations, and distribution process activities occurring among the firm and its various tiers of customers and suppliers. The final foundation topic—and certainly the most difficult one—is to coordinate and integrate these processes among the focal firm and its key supply chain participants. Supply chain **process integration** is discussed in the final two chapters of the text.

Processes in a supply chain are said to be coordinated or integrated when members of the supply chain work together when making delivery, inventory, production, quality, and purchasing decisions that impact the profits of the supply chain. If one activity fails or is performed poorly, then supplies moving along the chain are disrupted, jeopardizing the effectiveness of the entire supply chain. Successful **supply chain integration** occurs when the participants realize that supply chain management must become part of the firms' strategic planning processes, where objectives and policies are jointly determined based on the end-consumers' needs and what the supply chain as a whole can do well.

Ultimately, firms act together to maximize total supply chain profits by determining optimal purchase quantities, product availabilities, service levels, lead times, production quantities, and technical and product support at each tier within the supply chain. This integration process also requires better internal functional integration of activities within each of the participating firms, such that the supply chain acts as one entity. This idea of supply chain integration can run contrary to the notion among many potential supply chain participants of their firm's independent profit-maximizing objectives, making supply chain integration a very tough sell in many supplier–buyer–customer situations. Thus, continued efforts are required to break down obstacles, change cultural norms, change adversarial relationships, reduce conflict, and bridge various functional barriers within and between companies if supply chain integration is to become a reality.

One additional integration topic is the use of a **supply chain performance measurement** system. Performance measurements must be utilized along supply chains to help firms keep track of their supply chain management efforts. It is crucial for firms to know whether certain strategies are working as expected—or not—before they become financial drains on the organizations. Firms work together to develop long-term supply chain management strategies and then devise short-term tactics to implement these strategies. Performance measurements help firms decide the value of these tactics and should be developed to highlight performance within the areas of purchasing, operations, distribution, and integration.

Performance measures should be designed around each important supply chain activity and should be detailed performance descriptors instead of merely sales or cost figures. High levels of supply chain performance occur when the strategies at each of the firms fit well with overall supply chain strategies. Thus, each firm must understand its role in the supply chain, the needs of the ultimate customer, the needs of its immediate customers, and how these needs translate into internal operations requirements and the requirements being placed on suppliers. Once these needs and the products and services themselves can be communicated and transported through the supply chain effectively, successful supply chain management and its associated benefits will be realized. Best Buy, a consumer electronics retailer based in Minnesota, has installed an integrated business intelligence system called MicroStrategy Web that provides internal users and external supply chain partners with visibility into its business performance. Using Best Buy's Business and Vendor Performance application allows its users to view performance data; perform trending analyses on sales, inventory, advertising, pricing; and view other financial metrics such as revenue and operating margin, using a single Web interface.[20]

Some Current Trends in Supply Chain Management

The practice of supply chain management is a very recent phenomenon, as many organizations are just now beginning to realize the benefits and problems that accompany an integrated supply chain. Supply chain management is an incredibly complex and time-consuming undertaking, involving cultural change among most or all of the participants, investment and training in new software and communication systems, the building of trust between supply chain members, and a change or realignment of the competitive strategies employed among the participating firms. As competitive situations, products, technology, and customers change, the priorities for the supply chain also must change, requiring supply chains to be ever more flexible to respond quickly to these changes. As we look at the most recent practices and trends in supply chain management, a number of issues present themselves as areas that need to be addressed including the expansion of the supply chain, increasing supply chain responsiveness, creating a green supply chain, and reducing total supply chain costs.

Expanding the Supply Chain

As markets for the supply chain grow, so too must the supply chain. Today, firms are increasing their partnerships with foreign firms and building foreign production facilities to accommodate their market expansion plans and to increase their responsiveness to global economic conditions and demand. The supply chain dynamic today is changing, and companies are now working with firms located all over the globe to coordinate purchasing, manufacturing, and logistics activities. While this global expansion of the supply chain is occurring, firms are also trying to expand their influence and control of the supply chain to include second- and third-tier suppliers and customers. Thus, supply chain expansion is occurring on two fronts: increasing the *breadth* of the supply chain to include foreign manufacturing, office, and retail sites, along with foreign suppliers and customers; and increasing the *depth* of the supply chain to include second- and third-tier suppliers and customers.

With advances and improvements in communication technology, manufacturing, and transportation, more and more companies around the globe have the capability to produce and sell high-tech parts and products and move these quickly to world markets as demand develops. Trade agreements such as the European Union, the World Trade Organization, and the North American Free Trade Agreement have also facilitated the production and movement of goods between countries; and this has enabled firms to easily expand their supply bases and their markets. New software tools and "market makers" bring buyers and suppliers together in e-marketplace settings, helping to expand supply chains considerably and more easily, using the Internet. A rapid expansion of the global marketplace is occurring, and this pace should continue as new market enablers, producers, customers, and transportation infrastructures come into the global picture. Expanding the breadth of the supply chain is covered in more detail in Chapter 11.

In addition, as firms become more comfortable and experienced with their supply chain relationships with immediate suppliers and customers, there is a tendency to expand the depth or span of the supply chain by creating relationships with second- and third-tier suppliers and customers. This span expansion phenomenon is now occurring in many industries and should continue to increase as the practice of supply chain management matures. In a survey of firms already practicing supply chain management, about one-third of the respondents stated that they practiced supply chain management with second-tier suppliers, while somewhat fewer practiced supply chain management with second-tier customers.[21] Expanding a firm's influence to second- and third-tier suppliers and customers is discussed in more detail in Chapters 4 and 10.

Increasing Supply Chain Responsiveness

Agile manufacturing, JIT, lean production, mass customization, efficient consumer response, and quick response are all terms referring to concepts that are intended to make the firm more flexible and responsive to customer requirements and changes. Particularly with the tremendous levels of competition in almost all avenues of business, firms (and their key supply partners) are looking today at ways to become more responsive to customers. To achieve greater levels of responsiveness, supply chains must identify the end customers' needs, look at what the competition is doing and position the supply chain's products and services to successfully compete, and then consider the impact of these requirements on each of the supply chain participants. Once these requirements have been adequately identified among the firms in the supply chain, additional improvement in responsiveness comes from designing more effective information and communication systems, and faster product and service delivery systems as products and information are passed through the supply chain. Supply chain members must also continuously monitor changes occurring in the marketplace and then use this information to reposition the entire supply chain to stay competitive.

Saying these things is easy, but improving customer responsiveness requires firms to reevaluate their supply chain relationships to utilize business process reengineering, reposition and automate warehouses, design new products and services, reduce new product design cycles, standardize processes and products, empower and train workers in multiple skills, build customer feedback into daily operations, and, finally, link together all of the supply chain participants' information and communication systems. So, very quickly, it is seen that achieving high levels of customer satisfaction through responsiveness requires potentially significant changes not only in firm culture but also in the technical aspects of providing products, services, and information throughout the supply chain. This remains a significant and ongoing challenge for supply chain effectiveness. Automotive sector companies, for instance, have been heavy users of product life-cycle management systems to connect supply chain management members. "Tires used in specific models may need to be recalled, for example," explains Sath Rao, industry manager at Texas-based research and consulting company Frost & Sullivan. "So, systems must be able to find customers who need to be informed of the recall. And managers want to determine if the problem can be traced back to a design flaw or a manufacturing error."[22] These topics are discussed in Chapters 6 through 10.

The Greening of Supply Chains

Producing, packaging, moving, storing, repackaging, delivering, and then returning or recycling products can pose a significant threat to the environment in terms of discarded packaging materials, scrapped toxic products, carbon monoxide emissions, noise, traffic congestion, and other forms of industrial pollution. As the practice of supply chain management matures, governments along with firms and their supply chain partners are working harder to reduce these environmental problems. Many governments, for example, are enacting environmental regulations that restrict inbound shipments of products containing hazardous materials. Following Europe, which enacted restrictions in July of 2006, China established the first stage of their restrictions in March of 2007. Eventually, exporters to China will be prohibited from shipping any items containing lead, mercury, cadmium, and several other hazardous materials. David Wilson, a global supply chain consultant at New York-based JPMorgan Chase Vastera, says that many existing products will have to be redesigned to meet the new Chinese requirements. This, in turn, will cause disruptions in some supply chains, excess inventories of toxic substances, and the need for supply chain managers to work closely with engineers to identify and communicate prohibited parts. Several other countries have also enacted or proposed similar legislation including Canada, Japan, South Korea, Switzerland, and Taiwan.[23]

In fact, relationships between companies in an integrated supply chain are much more conducive to taking a more proactive approach to reducing the negative environmental consequences of producing, moving, and storing products as they wend their ways through supply chains. Over time, consumer sentiment toward environmentally friendly processes and the prevention of global warming has increased, making this topic one of concern for companies managing their supply chains. As mentioned in one study, 75 percent of U.S. consumers say their purchasing decisions are impacted by a firm's environmental reputation.[24] In addition, companies are finding that pollution control activities and waste reduction can reduce costs and attract environmentally conscious customers.

Added to this increasing concern and awareness among the general public for environmentally friendly business processes is the growing cost of natural resources such as wood products, oil, and natural gas. Strategies to successfully compete under these conditions include using recyclable materials in products; using returnable and reusable containers and pallets; using recyclable and reusable packaging materials; managing returns along the supply chain efficiently; designing effective transportation, warehousing, and break-bulk/repackaging strategies; and using environmental management systems from initial producer to final consumer in the supply chain. The benefits of these activities will include lower system-wide costs, fewer duplicate activities, marketing advantages, less waste, and, ultimately, better customer satisfaction. Global retail giant Wal-Mart has exhaustively tested green initiatives in experimental stores for more than fourteen years. Their goal of reducing energy costs and greenhouse gas emissions in new stores by 30 percent by the end of 2010 may actually be surpassed, says Charles Zimmerman, Wal-Mart's vice president of prototype and new format design. Wal-Mart has also directed its suppliers to share green designs specifically developed for Wal-Mart with other interested retailers.[25] More discussion of **green supply chain management** can be found in Chapters 4 and 9.

Reducing Supply Chain Costs

Considering again the objectives of supply chain management, cost reduction is clearly high on this list of priorities. Cost reduction can be achieved throughout the supply chain by reducing waste as already described, by reducing purchasing and product distribution costs, and by reducing excess inventories and non-value-adding activities among the supply chain participants. As supply chains become more mature, they tend to improve their performance in terms of these cost reduction activities through use of continuous improvement efforts, better supply chain communication and inventory visibility, and a further integration of processes. Interestingly, a recent survey of Chicago Illinois CEOs found that while 75 percent said their company's overall focus was on topline growth, 82 percent said their company's current supply chain initiatives were directed at cost reduction. "Cutting costs via the supply chain and being much more closely connected, umbilically connected, to customers are absolutely the driving principles of our supply chain," says Doug Ramsdale, CEO of Home Products International, a consumer housewares product manufacturer based in Illinois.[26]

As time passes, supply chain costs continue to decrease due to trial and error, increased knowledge of the supply chain processes, use of technology to improve information flow and communication, **benchmarking** other successful supply chains to copy what they are doing well, and continued performance measurement and other process improvement efforts. The purchasing function among supply chain participants will continue to be viewed as a major strategic contributor to cost reduction through better supplier evaluation techniques, value engineering and analysis in product design and production, standardization and reduction of parts and materials, and through make-or-buy decisions. Finally, the transportation and logistics functions will also play major roles in cost reduction along the supply chain through better design of the distribution networks and more efficient use of third-party logistics service providers. The various topics of cost reduction along the supply chain are spread throughout the entire text.

SUMMARY

Supply chain management is the integration of key business processes from initial raw material extraction to the final or end customer, including all intermediate processing, transportation, and storage activities and final sale to the end-product customer. Today, the practice of supply chain management is becoming extremely important to achieve and maintain competitiveness. Many firms are just now becoming aware of the advantages of supply chain process integration. Supply chain management is an outgrowth and expansion of logistics and purchasing activities and has grown in popularity and use since the 1980s. The foundation of supply chain management can be found in the areas of purchasing, operations, distribution, and process integration. Finally, as markets, political forces, technology, and competition change around the world, the practice of supply chain management must also change.

KEY TERMS

benchmarking, 27

bullwhip effect, 10

Business process reengineering (BPR), 13

collaborative planning, forecasting, and replenishment (CPFR), 10

customer relationship management (CRM), 20

demand management, 18

distribution network, 20

enterprise resource planning (ERP), 6

first-tier customers, 9

first-tier suppliers, 9

focal firm, 7

global supply chains, 14

green supply chain management, 27

integrated logistics, 14

inventory visibility, 18

just-in-time (JIT) production system, 19

lean production, 19

material requirements planning (MRP), 18

operating exposure, 20

perfect order fulfillment, 20

process integration, 23

quick response (QR), 14

reverse logistics activities, 7

second-tier suppliers and customers, 9

service response logistics, 14

Six Sigma, 19

strategic partnerships, 5

supplier certification, 17

supplier evaluation, 17

supplier management, 17

supply chain, 6

supply chain integration, 23

supply chain management (SCM), 8

supply chain performance measurement, 24

third-party logistics providers (3PLs), 14

Toyota Production System, 19

vertically integrated firm, 5

DISCUSSION QUESTIONS

1. Define the term "supply chain management" and list its most important activities.

2. Can a small business like a local sandwich or bicycle shop benefit from supply chain management? How?

3. Describe and draw a supply chain for a small sandwich shop.

4. What roles do "collaboration" and "trust" play in the practice of supply chain management?

5. What are the four foundation elements of supply chain management? Describe some activities within each element.

6. What does the "bullwhip effect" refer to?

7. What are the benefits of supply chain management?

8. Can nonprofit, educational, or government organizations benefit from supply chain management? How?

9. What does the term, "third-tier supplier" mean? What about "third-tier customer"? What about the "focal firm"? Provide examples.

10. Could a firm have more than one supply chain? Explain.

11. When did the idea and term, "supply chain management," first begin to be thought about and discussed?

12. Do you think supply chain management is simply the latest trend in management thinking, and will die out in a few years? Why or why not?

13. Is the use of a large number of suppliers a good idea? Why?

14. Why don't firms just buy out their suppliers and industrial customers, forming conglomerates, instead of practicing supply chain management?

INTERNET QUESTIONS

1. Visit the Web sites of companies such as Wal-Mart, Dell, and Home Depot and see if you can find discussions of their supply chain management activities. List what you can find, in terms of purchasing/supplier issues, transportation, warehousing, purchased item quality, and customer service.

2. Go to a good Internet search engine such as Google and search on the term *supply chain management*. How many hits did you get? Describe five of the Web sites found in your search.

3. Go to http://www.agrichain-centre.com (or a similar Web site found when searching on *New Zealand supply chain management*) and discuss the current state of supply chain management in New Zealand.

INFOTRAC QUESTIONS

Access http://academic.cengage.com/infotrac to answer the following questions:

1. Search for the term "bullwhip effect" and write a paper on the impacts of the bullwhip effect and the companies profiled in the papers you find.

2. Search for the terms "supply chain management" and "software applications" and write a paper about how companies use these to improve their financial performance.

3. Search on "green supply chains" and write a paper regarding the global regulatory status of environmental legislation and how it is impacting supply chain management.

APPENDIX 1.1

The Beer Game[27]

The Beer Game has become a very popular game played in operations management and supply chain management courses since being developed by MIT in the 1960s. The game simulates the flow of product and information in a simple supply chain consisting of a retailer, a wholesaler, a distributor, and a manufacturer. One person takes the role of each supply chain partner in a typical game. The objective is to minimize total supply chain inventory and back-order costs. In this way, a class can be separated into any number of four-person supply chains—each supply chain competing against the others. The game is used to illustrate the bullwhip effect, and the importance of timely and accurate communications and information with respect to purchases along the supply chain.

© 2007 Ted Goff

"Do you know anything about the system resources being overloaded by some kind of game?"

Each supply chain participant follows the same set of activities:

1. The participant fills customer orders from current inventory and creates back orders if demand cannot be met.

2. The participant forecasts customer demand and then orders beer from their supplier (or schedules beer production if the participant is the manufacturer), which then takes several weeks to arrive.

3. The participant manages inventories in order to minimize back-order costs (stockouts) and inventory carrying costs.

Figure A1.1 illustrates the beer game supply chain, showing the transportation and information delays. There is no product transportation or order delay between the retailer and the end customers. For the other supply chain members, there is a one-week delay between customer order and supplier acceptance, and a two-week transportation delay from the time a customer's order is received, until that order reaches the customer. It also takes two weeks to complete a production order at the factory, such that beer will be ready to fill customer orders.

Figure A1.1	The Beer Game Supply Chain

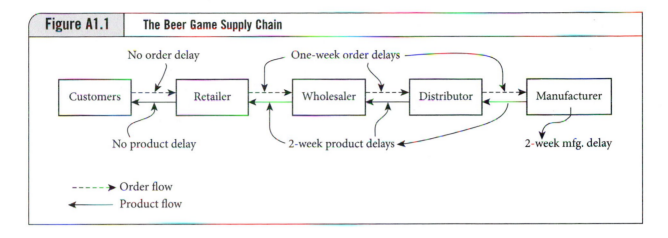

Here is how the game progresses:

Starting conditions: At the start of the game (Week 0), each supply chain member (except the manufacturer) has twelve cases of beer in ending inventory (see Table A1.1), four cases in the second week of inbound transportation delay, four cases in the first week (updated) of inbound transportation delay and four cases in the beginning of the first week of inbound transportation delay. The manufacturer has twelve cases of beer in ending inventory, four cases of beer in the second week of production lead time, four cases in the first week of production lead time and four cases at the beginning of the first week of production lead time. Each player also has an *outgoing order* of four cases sitting in their outgoing order box (or production order box). The retailer must begin with twenty weeks of customer demand slips, provided by the game coordinator or instructor, such that the retailer can only view one week's demand at a time (these can be written underneath each of the twenty sticky note pads for each retailer, for example).

Step 1: Each member *updates their beer inventories.*

- Move the cases of beer from the second week of inbound delay for the previous period and add to the ending inventory of the previous period, putting the total in the beginning inventory column of the current period (see Week 0/ Week 1 of Table A1.1). For the manufacturer, this is a production delay.
- Move inventory from the first week of inbound delay (updated column) to the second week of delay (see Table A1.1).
- Move inventory from the first week of inbound delay (beginning column) to the first week of inbound delay (updated column) (see Table A1.1).

Step 2: Each member *fills their customer orders.*

- The retailer uncovers and reads the current week's customer demand slip, then places the slip face down in the discard area, **such that it cannot be seen by the wholesaler.**
- The retailer then fills this order (after first satisfying any back orders) and subtracts demand from beginning inventory. This amount then becomes the ending inventory amount. If ending inventory is negative, then a back order of this amount is created, and ending inventory becomes zero.
- Next, the retailer places last week's outgoing order on the wholesaler's incoming demand order box.

Table A1.1	Inventory Record Sheet

Your supply chain role:

Your name: Team name:

Incoming demand from supply chain customer	Discard area		Outgoing orders to supply chain supplier, OR production orders for manufacturer

Week	Ending Inventory	Beginning Inventory	Back Orders	Second Week Inbound Delay	First Week Inbound Delay	
					Updated	Beginning
0	12		0	4	4	4
1		16		4	4	
2						
3						
4						
5						
6						
7						
8						
9						
10						
11						
12						
13						
14						
15						
16						
17						
18						
19						
20						
Totals						

Amount of outgoing order received

Note: Ending inventories must be zero when you have a back order. If ending inventory is greater than zero, back orders must equal zero. Back orders equal previous period back orders plus incoming order minus current inventory.

At end of game: Sum <u>ending inventory</u> column and <u>back-orders'</u> column and determine total cost as − [Total ending inventories × $1] + [Total back orders × $2] = $_____. Then sum total costs for all supply chain members. Total supply chain costs = $_____.

- Finally, the retailer forecasts future demand and orders beer from the whole-saler by writing an order on the slip provided and places it face down in the re-tailer's outgoing order box, **such that it cannot be seen by the wholesaler.**

The wholesaler follows the same steps as above: it reads the incoming demand order slip, discards it, satisfies any back orders and fills as much of the incoming order as pos-sible from beginning inventory. At this point, the wholesaler must tell the retailer how much of the order it can satisfy, and the retailer records this amount in the first week beginning delay for the current period. The wholesaler then updates its ending inven-tory and back-order quantities, it sends last week's outgoing order to the distributor's in-coming demand, and then it decides how much to order and places the order sheet face down in the wholesaler's outgoing order box, **such that it cannot be seen by the distributor.**

The distributor goes through the same steps as the wholesaler when it gets an in-coming order from the wholesaler.

The manufacturer follows the same steps also, except instead of sending last week's outgoing order somewhere, it reads the outgoing order and fills the production request by transferring that number of cases from its raw materials storage area to the first week's beginning production delay (it simply creates the cases needed for the order).

Step 3: Repeat Steps 1 and 2 until the game limit is reached. Calculate total costs at game's end.

A typical game progresses in this fashion for twenty weeks. The game is played with sticky note pads for beer orders, using Table A1.1 to keep track of inventories, or-ders, and back orders. Players must take care **not to talk** to the other players during the game **or to show what orders they are receiving or planning** for the next week. The retailer must **not look at future customer demand data,** provided by the instruc-tor. Remember, this game is meant to illustrate what happens when no communica-tion about future orders or order strategies occurs between supply chain members.

At the end of twenty weeks (or shorter if time does not permit), players deter-mine the total cost of their inventories and back orders on the inventory record sheet (back orders cost $2 per unit per week, and inventories cost $1 per unit per week). Given these costs, the basic strategy should be to attempt to avoid back or-ders, while minimizing total inventory carrying costs. This requires attempting to forecast future demand accurately (as time progresses, firms should use their inven-tory record sheet demand information for forecasting purposes). The winning team is the team with the lowest total supply chain costs.

BEER GAME QUESTIONS AND EXERCISES

1. All players but the retailer should answer this question. What did you think the re-tailer's customer demand pattern looked like? How did your customer orders vary throughout the game?

2. What happened to the current inventory levels as we move backward, up the sup-ply chain from retailer to manufacturer? Why?

3. How could the supply chain members reduce total inventory and back-order costs in the future?

4. Go to http://beergame.mit.edu and try playing the Internet version of the game. Report on your experiences playing the game.

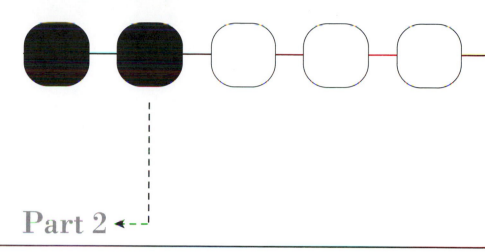

Part 2

Supply Management Issues in Supply Chain Management

Chapter 2

PURCHASING AND SUPPLY MANAGEMENT

The title, Chief Procurement Officer, is taking hold in corporations, reflecting the increasing influence purchasing has on attainment of corporate objectives.[1]

While cost is a big reason to involve purchasing in design, it is not the only one. Many OEMs do so to make sure their company's technology roadmaps are tracking with suppliers' roadmaps and vice versa. Purchasers who are involved in design also need to make sure that new, robust technologies that will eventually become mainstream get designed into new products, rather than older technology parts, which may soon [become obsolete].[2]

It's no secret that electronics OEMs are increasingly turning to purchasing to reduce cost. After all about 60–70% of a typical electronics company's revenue is spent with the production suppliers that purchasing manages.[3]

Learning Objectives

After completing this chapter, you should be able to

- Describe purchasing, procurement, and supply management.
- Understand the role of supply management and its strategic impact on an organization's competitive advantage.
- Have a basic knowledge of the manual purchasing process, e-procurement, public procurement, and green purchasing.
- Understand and know how to handle small value purchase orders.
- Understand sourcing decisions and the factors impacting supplier selection.
- Understand the pros and cons of single sourcing versus multiple sourcing.
- Describe centralized, decentralized, and hybrid purchasing organizations and their advantages.
- Describe and understand how globalization impacts supply management, and describe and understand the opportunities and challenges of global sourcing.
- Understand total cost of ownership and be able to select suppliers using more than unit price alone.

Chapter Outline

Introduction

A Brief History of Purchasing Terms

The Role of Supply Management in an Organization

The Purchasing Process

Sourcing Decisions: The Make-or-Buy Decision

Roles of the Supply Base

Supplier Selection

How Many Suppliers to Use

Purchasing Organization

International Purchasing/Global Sourcing

Procurement for Government and Nonprofit Agencies

Summary

Supply Chain Management in Action

Strategic Supply Management at Harrah's Entertainment Inc.

Las Vegas-based Harrah's Entertainment Inc. (HET), founded in 1937, is the world's largest gaming company by revenue. The company has expanded rapidly through the development of new properties, expansions, and acquisitions. HET operates 48 casinos worldwide, employs more than 85,000 workers in three countries, and has a total revenue in excess of $9.67 billion for the fiscal year ending December 31, 2006. HET owns eight properties in Las Vegas—Bally's, Caesars Palace, Flamingo, Harrah's, Paris, Rio, Bill's, and Imperial Palace.

HET operates multiple restaurants in each property. Since foods and beverages account for at least 25 percent of the costs of restaurant sales, it is imperative that HET has a well-designed supply management system that maintains tight control of the purchasing process and yet provides maximum service to the chefs and other users of the system. Moreover, the system must ensure that suppliers are treated fairly and professionally. Effectiveness of supply management impacts not only the operating costs of a restaurant, but more importantly its quality, customer service, and its ability to introduce new menus quickly.

The Las Vegas division of HET uses a centralized–decentralized or hybrid purchasing structure that emphasizes contemporary management philosophy to enable buyers to purchase foods, beverages, and operating supplies efficiently and effectively. This purchasing system stresses long-term, mutually beneficial buyer–supplier relationships, trust, and single sourcing to achieve lowest total acquisition cost, instead of forcing the suppliers to bid on each purchase or contract that tends to focus on short-term, suboptimizing performance, such as unit purchase price.

The company uses a centralized structure to negotiate blanket orders at the national and regional level, whereas a decentralized structure is used to release orders by buyers at each property. The regional purchasing office selects the best supplier and negotiates a blanket order for each item based on quality, reliability, delivery, and total costs of acquisition. Estimated usage, price, and delivery terms along with the corresponding tolerance for each performance measure are negotiated for each blanket order. The blanket orders are then made available to the buyers at each property, called property buyers, via a computer database. Property buyers purchase goods by issuing order releases against the appropriate blanket orders without the need to renegotiate prices and delivery terms. Once an order is released, suppliers must deliver the products according to specified terms.

According to Mr. Larry Peterson, vice president of procurement, HET uses a single source for most of its products because it is more efficient and cost-effective in the long run. However, competing suppliers' terms are listed side-by-side to the single source so that the single source's performance can be monitored and compared against current market conditions. Moreover, this information allows the company to locate alternate sources quickly if problems arise with its single source.

The hybrid purchasing system has many benefits, including cost and time savings by eliminating duplicate bidding by each property for the same product. Moreover, the system allows the regional purchasing office to fully utilize its contracted suppliers, national contracts, regional contracts, and other programs. Most notably, the regional office preserves the four fundamental purchasing rights to select the supplier, use whichever pricing method is appropriate, question the specifications, and monitor contacts with potential suppliers.

Note: Some parts of this feature came from Tan, K. C. "Effective Purchasing System: Is It Technology or Supplier Relationship Management?" *Practix: Best Practices in Purchasing & Supply Chain Management,* 11 (September 2007): 1–8.

Introduction

In the context of supply chain management (SCM), purchasing can be defined as the act of obtaining merchandise, capital equipment, raw materials, services, or maintenance, repair, and operating (MRO) supplies in exchange for money or its equivalent. Purchasing can be broadly classified into two categories: **merchants** and **industrial buyers**. The first category, merchants, includes the wholesalers and retailers, who primarily purchase for resale purposes. Generally, merchants purchase their merchandise in volume to take advantage of quantity discounts and other incentives such as transportation economy and storage efficiency. They create value by consolidating merchandise, breaking bulk, and providing the essential logistical services. The second category is the industrial buyers, whose primary task is to purchase raw materials for conversion purposes. Industrial buyers also purchase services, capital equipment, and maintenance, repair, and operating supplies. The typical industrial buyers are the manufacturers, although some service firms such as restaurants, landscape gardeners, and florists also purchase raw materials for conversion purposes.

An effective and efficient purchasing system is crucial to the success of a business. Indeed, the *Annual Survey of Manufactures*[4] shows that the cost of materials exceeds value added through manufacturing. Thus, it is not surprising that purchasing concepts and theories that evolved over the last two decades focused on industrial buyers' purchases of raw materials and how purchasing can be exploited to improve competitive success.

The primary focus of this chapter is the industrial buyer. This chapter describes the role of purchasing in an organization, the processes of a traditional manual purchasing system and the common documents used, how an electronic purchasing system works, various strategies for handling small order problems, the advantages and disadvantages of centralized versus decentralized purchasing systems, purchasing for nonprofit and government agencies, sourcing issues including supplier selection, and other important topics affecting the role of purchasing and supply management in supply chain management.

A Brief History of Purchasing Terms

Purchasing is a key business function that is responsible for acquisition of the required materials, services, and equipment. However, acquisition of services is widely called *contracting*. The increased strategic role of purchasing in today's business setting has brought a need for higher levels of skill and responsibility on the part of the purchasing professionals. Consequently, the term **supply management** is increasingly being used in place of purchasing to describe the expanded set of responsibility of the purchasing professionals. The traditional purchasing function of receiving requisitions and issuing orders is no longer adequate, but a holistic and comprehensive acquisition strategy is required to meet the organization's strategic objectives.

The Institute of Supply Management defines supply management as the "identification, acquisition, access, positioning, and management of resources an organization needs or potentially needs in the attainment of its strategic objectives."[5] Key activities of supply management has expanded beyond the basic purchasing function to include negotiations, logistics, contract development and administration, inventory control and management, supplier management and other activities.

However, purchasing remains the core activity of supply management. Although *procurement* is frequently used in place of purchasing, procurement typically includes the added activities of specifications development, **expediting**, supplier quality control and some logistics activities; hence procurement is widely used by government agencies due to the type of purchases and frequent service contracting they make with government suppliers. However, it is difficult to clearly distinguish where purchasing activities end and the supply management function begins. Moreover, many organizations are still using these terms interchangeably. In many parts of this book, we have retained the traditional term "purchasing" to emphasize its origin in place of "supply management."

The Role of Supply Management in an Organization

Traditionally, purchasing was regarded as being a service to production, and corporate executives paid limited attention to issues concerned with purchasing. However, as global competition intensified in the 1980s, executives realized the impact of large quantities of purchased material and work-in-process inventories on manufacturing cost, quality, new product development, and delivery lead time. Savvy managers adopted new supply chain management concepts that emphasized purchasing as a key strategic business process rather than a narrow specialized supporting function to overall business strategy.

The *Annual Survey of Manufactures* (Table 2.1), conducted by the U.S. Census Bureau, shows that manufacturers spent more than 50 percent of each sales dollar (shown as "value of shipments") on raw materials (shown as "cost of materials") from 1977 to 2005. Purchases of raw materials actually exceeded value added through manufacturing (shown as "manufacture"), which accounted for less than 50 percent of sales. Purchases as a percent of sales dollars for merchants are expected to be much higher since merchandise is primarily bought for resale purposes. Unfortunately, aggregate statistics for merchants are not readily available.

However, individual information can easily be obtained from the annual reports of publicly traded companies, either directly or from the U.S. Securities and Exchange Commission (SEC). For example, Wal-Mart Stores, Inc., reported that its cost of sales was more than 76 percent of its net sales for the three most recent fiscal years that ended January 31, 2005, 2006, and 2007. This ratio shows the potential impact of purchasing on a company's profits. Therefore, it is obvious that many successful businesses are treating purchasing as a key strategic process.

The primary goals of purchasing are to ensure uninterrupted flow of raw materials at the lowest total cost, to improve quality of the finished goods produced, and to optimize customer satisfaction. Purchasing can contribute to these objectives by actively seeking better materials and reliable suppliers, working closely with and exploiting the expertise of strategic suppliers to improve the quality of raw materials, and involving suppliers and purchasing personnel in new product design and development efforts. Purchasing is the crucial link between the sources of supply and the organization itself, with support coming from overlapping activities to enhance manufacturability for both the customer and the supplier. The involvement of purchasing and strategic suppliers in concurrent engineering activities is essential for selecting components and raw materials that ensure that requisite quality is designed into the product and to aid in collapsing design-to-production cycle time.

Table 2.1	Cost of Materials as a Percentage of the Value of Shipments						
YEAR	VALUE OF SHIPMENTS $ MILLIONS	COST OF MATERIALS $ MILLIONS	%	MANUFACTURE $ MILLIONS	%	CAPITAL EXPENDITURES $ MILLIONS	%
2005	$4,735,384	$2,555,492	54.0%	$2,204,095	46.5%	$128,325	2.7%
2004	$4,308,971	$2,283,144	53.0%	$2,041,434	47.4%	$113,793	2.6%
2003	$4,015,387	$2,095,279	52.2%	$1,923,415	47.9%	$112,176	2.8%
2002	$3,914,719	$2,022,158	51.7%	$1,889,291	48.3%	$123,067	3.1%
2001	$3,967,698	$2,105,338	53.1%	$1,850,709	46.6%	$142,985	3.6%
2000	$4,208,582	$2,245,839	53.4%	$1,973,622	46.9%	$154,479	3.7%
1999	$4,031,885	$2,084,316	51.7%	$1,954,498	48.5%	$150,325	3.7%
1998	$3,899,810	$2,018,055	51.7%	$1,891,266	48.5%	$152,708	3.9%
1997	$3,834,701	$2,015,425	52.6%	$1,825,688	47.6%	$151,510	4.0%
1996	$3,715,428	$1,975,362	53.2%	$1,749,662	47.1%	$146,468	3.9%
1995	$3,594,360	$1,897,571	52.8%	$1,711,442	47.6%	$134,318	3.7%
1994	$3,348,019	$1,752,735	52.4%	$1,605,980	48.0%	$118,665	3.5%
1993	$3,127,620	$1,647,493	52.7%	$1,483,054	47.4%	$108,629	3.5%
1992	$3,004,723	$1,571,774	52.3%	$1,424,700	47.4%	$110,644	3.7%
1991	$2,878,165	$1,531,221	53.2%	$1,341,386	46.6%	$103,153	3.6%
1990	$2,912,227	$1,574,617	54.1%	$1,348,970	46.3%	$106,463	3.7%
1989	$2,840,376	$1,532,330	53.9%	$1,325,434	46.7%	$101,894	3.6%
1988	$2,695,432	$1,444,501	53.6%	$1,269,313	47.1%	$ 84,706	3.1%
1987	$2,475,939	$1,319,845	53.3%	$1,165,741	47.1%	$ 85,662	3.5%
1986	$2,260,315	$1,217,609	53.9%	$1,035,437	45.8%	$ 80,795	3.6%
1985	$2,280,184	$1,276,010	56.0%	$1,000,142	43.9%	$ 91,245	4.0%
1984	$2,253,429	$1,288,414	57.2%	$ 983,228	43.6%	$ 80,660	3.6%
1983	$2,045,853	$1,170,238	57.2%	$ 882,015	43.1%	$ 67,480	3.3%
1982	$1,960,206	$1,130,143	57.7%	$ 824,118	42.0%	$ 77,046	3.9%
1981	$2,017,543	$1,193,970	59.2%	$ 837,507	41.5%	$ 83,767	4.2%
1980	$1,852,668	$1,093,568	59.0%	$ 773,831	41.8%	$ 74,625	4.0%
1979	$1,727,215	$ 999,158	57.8%	$ 747,481	43.3%	$ 65,797	3.8%
1978	$1,522,937	$ 877,425	57.6%	$ 657,412	43.2%	$ 58,346	3.8%
1977	$1,358,526	$ 782,418	57.6%	$ 585,166	43.1%	$ 51,907	3.8%

Source: "Statistics for Industry Groups and Industries: 2005." *Annual Survey of Manufactures*, U.S. Census Bureau (November 2006): 1.

The Financial Significance of Supply Management

Undoubtedly, purchasing has become more global and has gained a strategic corporate focus over the last two decades. The increasing use of outsourcing noncore activities has further elevated the role of purchasing in a firm. In addition to affecting the competitiveness of a firm, purchasing also directly affects profitability. Next, we discuss the financial significance of purchasing on a firm.

Profit-Leverage Effect

The **profit-leverage effect** of purchasing measures the impact of a change in purchase spend on a firm's profit before taxes, assuming gross sales and other expenses remain unchanged. The measure is commonly used to demonstrate that a dollar decrease in purchase spend directly increases profits before taxes by the same amount. However, it is important to remember that a decrease in purchase spend must be achieved through a better purchasing strategy that enables the firm to acquire materials of similar or better quality and yield at a lower total acquisition cost. The profit-leverage effect example in Table 2.2 shows that if a firm manages to lower its purchase spend by $20,000, profits before taxes increase by $20,000 because purchase spend on materials is a part of the cost of goods sold. Indeed, the reduction in purchase spend has an identical impact on gross profits. Table 2.2 shows that gross profits also increased by $20,000 from $500,000 to $520,000. The direct effect of purchasing on a firm's profitability is a key reason that drives business executives to continually refine the sourcing function. Boosting sales and cutting costs are not the only ways to increase profits. An often overlooked, but very efficient means to improve profits is through smarter purchasing.

Return on Assets Effect

Return on assets (ROA) is a financial ratio of a firm's net income in relation to its total assets. The ratio is also referred to as **return on investment** (ROI). In the context of accounting, total assets consist of current and fixed assets. Current assets include cash, accounts receivable, and inventory, whereas fixed assets include equipment, buildings, and real estate. ROA indicates how efficient management is using its total assets to generate profits. A high ROA suggests that the management is capable of generating large profits with little investment.

Assuming the firm in Table 2.2 has a total assets of $500,000, its ROA is 10 percent ($50,000 ÷ $500,000). If the firm reduces its purchase spend on materials by $20,000 through a more effective purchasing strategy, its ROA increases to 14 percent ($70,000 ÷ $500,000). The $20,000 reduction in purchase spend on materials is also likely to result in a lower raw material inventory (and thus lower total assets). However, its effect on ROA is difficult to quantify because the portion of a firm's

Table 2.2	Profit-Leverage Effect		
		SIMPLIFIED PROFIT AND LOSS STATEMENT	REDUCE MATERIAL COSTS BY $20,000
Gross sales/net revenue		$1,000,000	$1,000,000
Cost of goods sold (materials + manufacturing cost)		−$500,000	−$480,000
Gross profits		$500,000	$520,000
General and administrative expenses (45%)		−$450,000	−$450,000
Profits before taxes		$50,000	$70,000

raw material inventory to its total assets, and the ratio of materials cost to its total cost of goods sold vary widely depending on the firm and industry.

Inventory Turnover Effect

Inventory turnover shows how many times a firm's inventory is utilized and replaced over an accounting period, such as a year. There are numerous ways to compute the inventory turnover ratio, but a widely used formula is the ratio of the cost of goods sold over average inventory at cost. In general, low inventory turnover indicates poor sales, overstocking, and/or obsolescence. Through more effective sourcing strategy, purchasing can help reduce inventory investment, and thus improve the firm's inventory turnover.

The Purchasing Process

The traditional purchasing process is a manual, paper-based system. However, with the advent of information technology, personal computers, local area networks, and the Internet, many companies are moving toward a more automated, electronic-based system. The goal of a proper purchasing system is to ensure the efficient transition of information from the users to the purchasing personnel and, ultimately, to the suppliers. Once the information is transmitted to the appropriate suppliers, the system must also ensure the efficient flow of the purchased materials from the suppliers to the users, and the flow of invoices from the suppliers to the accounting department. Finally, the system must have an internal control mechanism to prevent abuse of the system. For example, **purchase orders (POs)** should be prenumbered and issued in duplicate, and buyers should not be authorized to pay invoices. Prenumbered purchase orders make it easier to trace any missing or unaccounted-for purchase order. A duplicate purchase order should be issued to the accounting department for internal control purposes and to inform the department of a future payment or commitment of resources.

The Manual Purchasing System

Figure 2.1 shows a simplified traditional manual purchasing system. While some manual systems may look slightly different than what is shown in Figure 2.1, it captures the essential elements of a good purchasing system that is easy to use and yet exerts adequate control of the process. The manual purchasing system is slow and prone to errors due to duplications of data entries during various stages of the purchasing process. For example, similar information on the material requisition, such as the product description, is reproduced on the purchase order.

The Material Requisition

The purchasing process starts when the material user initiates a request for a material by issuing a **material requisition (MR)** in duplicate. A **purchase requisition**, instead of a material requisition, is used in some firms. The product, quantity, and delivery due date are clearly described on the material requisition. The number of duplicates issued depends on the internal accounting control system of the organization. Generally, the issuer retains a copy and the warehouse receives the original plus a duplicate. The duplicate accompanies the material as it moves from the warehouse to the user. This copy also provides the essential information for the accounting department to charge the appropriate user or department for the material.

While most requisitions are transmitted through the generic material requisition, a **traveling requisition** is used for materials and standard parts that are requested on a

Figure 2.1	Traditional Manual Purchasing System

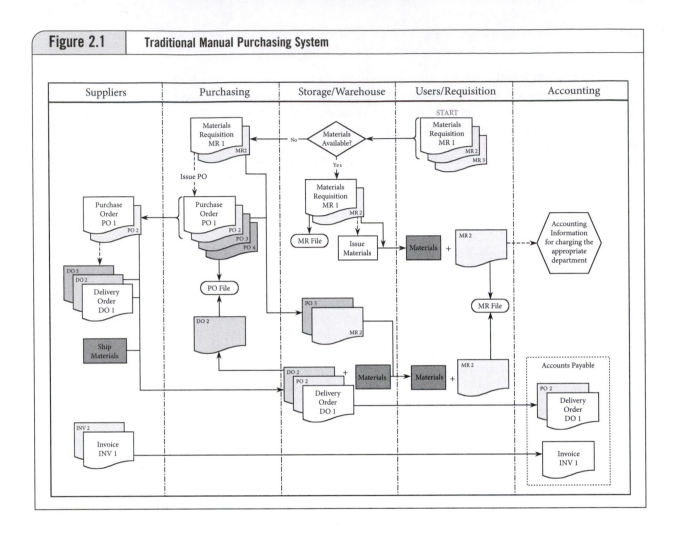

recurring basis. Instead of describing the product on the generic material requisition, the product description and other pertinent information, such as delivery lead time and lot size, are preprinted on the traveling requisition. When a resupply is needed, the user simply enters the quantity and date needed and submits it to the warehouse. Once the resupply information is recorded, the traveling requisition is returned to the user for future requests.

Planned order releases from the material requirements planning (MRP) and/or a bill of materials (BOM) can also be used to release requisitions or to place orders directly with the suppliers. This approach is appropriate for firms that use the same components to make standard goods over a relatively long period of time.

If the requested material is available in the warehouse, the material is issued to the user without going through the purchasing department. Otherwise, the requisition is assigned to a buyer who is responsible for the material. If there is a better substitute for the material, the purchasing department recommends to and works with the user to see if it is a viable substitute. However, the purchasing personnel cannot change the specifications of the materials or parts without the user's knowledge and agreement. While it is the right and responsibility of the purchasing personnel to select the appropriate supplier, the user in many cases may suggest a list of potential suppliers when requesting new material. A sample material requisition is shown in Figure 2.2.

The Request for Quotation and the Request for Proposal

If the material is not available in the warehouse, the material requisition is channeled to the purchasing department. If there is no current supplier for the item, the buyer must identify a pool of qualified suppliers and issue a **request for quotation (RFQ)**. A **request for proposal (RFP)** may be issued instead for a complicated and highly technical component part, especially if the complete specification of the part is unknown. A request for proposal allows suppliers to propose new material and technology, thus enabling the firm to exploit the expertise of suppliers.

Figure 2.2	Sample Material Requisition

BabiHutan Inc.   **Purchase Requisition**   RX #: 6334554
523 Las Vegas Blvd
Las Vegas, NV89154
Tel: 702-123-4567

Requestor: _____   Department: _____

Phone #: _____   Account #: _____   Date: _____

Suggested Vendor:_____

Address: _____   Phone: _____

No.	Description	Price	Quantity

Special instructions: _____
_____
_____

Approval Authority: _____   Date: _____

Distribution: White-Purchasing/Yellow-Purchasing (return to requestor)/Pink-Department

A growing trend among firms that practice supply chain management is **supplier development**. When there is a lack of suitable suppliers, firms may assist existing or new suppliers to improve their processing capabilities, quality, delivery, and cost performance by providing the needed technical and financial assistance. Developing suppliers in this manner allows firms to focus more on core competencies, while **outsourcing** noncore activities to suppliers.

The Purchase Order

When a suitable supplier is identified, or a qualified supplier is on file, the buyer issues a purchase order (PO) in duplicate to the selected supplier. Generally, the original purchase order and at least a duplicate are sent to the supplier. An important feature of the purchase order is the terms and conditions of the purchase, which is typically preprinted on the back. The purchase order is the buyer's offer and becomes a legally binding contract when accepted by the supplier. Therefore, firms should require the supplier to acknowledge and return a copy of the purchase order to indicate acceptance of the order. A sample purchase order is shown in Figure 2.3.

The supplier may offer the goods at the supplier's own terms and conditions, especially if it is the sole producer or holds the patent to the product. Then, a supplier's **sales order** will be used. The sales order is the supplier's offer and becomes a legally binding contract when accepted by the buyer.

Once an order is accepted, purchasing personnel need to ensure on-time delivery of the purchased material by using a **follow-up** or by expediting the order. A follow-up is considered a proactive approach to prevent late delivery, whereas expediting is considered a reactive approach that is used to speed up an overdue shipment.

The **Uniform Commercial Code (UCC)** governs the purchase and sale of goods. The UCC applies only to legal situations arising in the U.S., except in the state of Louisiana, which has a legal system based on the Napoleonic Code.

Electronic Procurement Systems (e-Procurement)

Electronic data interchange (EDI) was developed in the 1970s to improve the purchasing process. However, its proprietary nature required significant up-front investments. The rapid advent of Internet technology in the 1990s spurred the growth of more flexible Internet-based e-procurement systems. Proponents of e-commerce argued that Internet-based systems would quickly replace the manual system, as we saw many e-commerce service providers rise rapidly in the late 1990s. Since then, there has been a shake-up among these companies as they have struggled to find a sustainable market. A large number of e-commerce firms saw their share values plummet in the early 2000s, and many are no longer in business after the dot-com bubble burst in 2000. Critics argued that growth in e-commerce had been overinflated, and the savings for users were inadequate to justify their time and investments. Today though, many well-managed e-commerce firms are beginning to thrive as users realize the benefits of their services.

Figure 2.4 describes an actual Internet-based business-to-business (B2B) electronic purchasing system used by some prominent resorts in Las Vegas, Nevada, to handle their purchases, ranging from low-cost office supplies to perishable foods and beverages and high-cost engineering items.[6] An e-commerce service provider provided the software and technology for the B2B purchases.

Figure 2.3	Sample Purchase Order

BabiHutan Inc.
523 LasVegas Blvd
Las Vegas, NV89154
Tel: 702-123-4567

Purchase Order

PO#: 885729

Date: _____

Vendor:

Required Delivery Date: _____
Payment Terms: _____
FOB Terms: _____
Price Agreement No.: _____

Ship To:

Include PO # in all packages, invoice,
shipping papers & correspondence.
Mail original and one copy of invoice
attached to second copy of Purchase
Order for payment.

No.	Description	Unit Price	Quantity	Total Price
		Total $ of Order		

Buyer: _____ Phone: _____ Fax: _____

Buyer Signature: _____ Requisition No.: _____

SEE REVERSE FOR TERMS & CONDITIONS

Distribution: White-Vendor/Yellow-Vendor(return with invoice)/Pink & Blue-Purchasing/Green-Fixed Assets

The material user initiates the e-procurement process by entering a materials request and other pertinent information, such as quantity and date needed, into the material requisition module. Next, the materials requisition is transmitted electronically to a buyer at the purchasing department. The buyer reviews the materials requisition for accuracy and appropriate approval level. Upon satisfactory verification of the requisition, the buyer transfers the materials requisition data to the Internet-based e-procurement system and assigns qualified suppliers to bid on the requisition. The product description, closing dates, and bid conditions are specified on the requisition. Suppliers connected to the e-commerce system receive the bid instantaneously, while others can receive a faxed bid from the service provider. The purchasing department maintains a list of preferred suppliers for each category of material. The list

Figure 2.4	Internet-Based Electronic Purchasing System

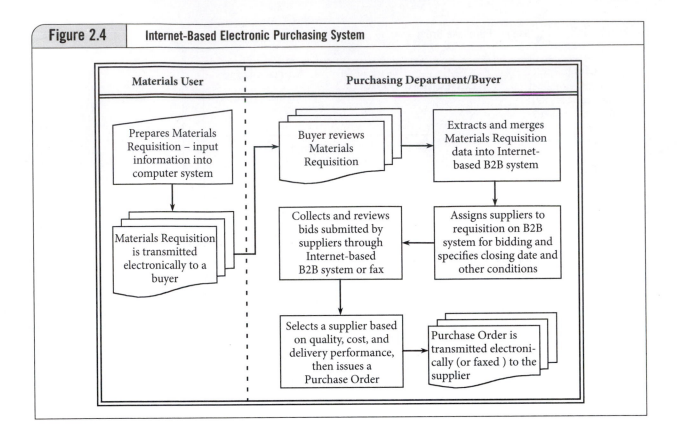

can be edited and shared with other buyers. Using this list, the buyer can submit bid requests to numerous suppliers within seconds.

Upon closing of the bids, the buyer reviews all the bids tendered through the Internet-based e-procurement system or fax and selects a supplier based on quality, cost, and delivery performance. Next, a purchase order is submitted electronically to the selected supplier if it is connected to the e-procurement system. Otherwise, a purchase order is printed and mailed to the supplier.

Advantages of the e-Procurement System

The traditional manual purchasing system is a tedious and labor-intensive task of issuing material requisitions and purchase orders. Although EDI solved some of these problems, its proprietary nature requires a high start-up cost, making it inaccessible to small firms with limited budgets. Internet-based e-procurement systems have changed the infrastructure requirement, making it readily affordable to most firms. Benefits derived from implementing an e-procurement system include:

1. *Time savings:* E-procurement is more efficient when (1) selecting and maintaining a list of potential suppliers, (2) processing requests for quotation and purchase orders, and (3) making repeat purchases. Individual buyers can create preferred supplier lists for each category of products and services. For example, a small tools supplier group may consist of fifteen suppliers of small tools. The buyer uses this group to purchase small tools. The list can be edited and shared with all buyers in the firm. Supplier performance data can be updated quickly and made available online in real time. Collecting, sorting, reviewing,

and comparing requests for quotation are labor-intensive and time-consuming processes. Using the manual purchasing system, a typical firm may have to sort and match hundreds of bids on a daily basis. E-procurement eliminates these nonvalue-adding collection and sorting activities. Duplicate data entry on the purchase order is eliminated since the information is extracted from the request for quotation, originally entered by the user.

The system can be programmed to handle automatic bidding of frequently ordered items on a fixed interval, such as daily or weekly. The ability to submit automatic bidding is invaluable for handling perishable goods, which must be ordered in small lot sizes, and other frequently purchased items where the specifications are known.

2. *Cost savings:* Buyers can handle more purchases, and the manual task of matching bids to materials requisitions is eliminated. Other cost savings include lower prices of goods and services since more suppliers can be contacted, reduced inventory costs due to the ability to purchase on a more frequent basis, fewer purchasing staff, lower administrative costs, and faster order fulfillment.

3. *Accuracy:* The system eliminates double-key inputs—once by the material users and then once again by the buyers. The system also enhances the accuracy of communications between buyers and suppliers. More up-to-date information on goods and services are readily available online.

4. *Real time:* The system enables buyers to initiate bids and suppliers to respond in real time on a 24-hour, 7-days-per-week basis. Once the material requisition is processed, the buyer can post the bid immediately, instead of waiting to contact all the suppliers individually to alert them of the bids.

5. *Mobility:* The buyer can submit, process, and check the status of bids, as well as communicate with suppliers regardless of the buyer's geographical location and time of day. Thus, the e-procurement system is highly flexible.

6. *Trackability:* Audit trails can be maintained for all transactions in electronic form. Tracing an electronic bid and transaction is much easier and faster than tracking paper trails. Buyers and suppliers can ask for additional information online, leave comments, or indicate whether they are interested in bidding.

7. *Management:* The system can be designed to store important supplier information, including whether suppliers are minority or locally owned, thus allowing the buyers to support such businesses. Summary statistics and supplier performance reports can be generated for management to review and utilize for future planning.

8. *Benefits to the suppliers:* Benefits include lower barriers to entry and transaction costs, access to more buyers, and the ability to instantly adjust to market conditions, thus making e-procurement attractive to most suppliers.

The e-Business Connection feature highlights some of the key results of the 2006 e-Procurement Benchmark Report conducted by Arizona-based CAPS Research.

Small Value Purchase Orders

The administrative costs to process an order can be quite substantial. It has been estimated that the cost of placing an order using the manual purchasing system could be as high as $175.[7] The figure could be higher when we consider the salary of senior purchasing personnel and other indirect costs incurred by purchasing personnel. It is not

e-Business Connection

2006 e-Procurement Benchmark Report

CAPS Research recently conducted an e-procurement benchmark study by surveying 195 manufacturers and service organizations to look at the impact of e-procurement on purchasing efficiency and effectiveness. Participants of the study came from a wide range of industry sectors, including aerospace, automotive, chemical, electronics, government agencies, pharmaceuticals, retail, and utilities. This study provides the supply community with details of e-procurement usage and key performance indicators, and allows purchasing managers to compare their e-procurement systems to others. The report is also very useful for companies that are considering implementing e-procurement systems.

Some of the key benchmarks/findings of the study are

1. The primary spend analysis tool was Microsoft Excel, followed by an Enterprise Resource Planning (ERP) module. More than 80 percent of the survey participants used Excel, and less than 30 percent of the participants engaged third-party providers for spend analysis. The two most widely used third-party providers were Ariba and SAP.

2. Sixty-four percent of the survey participants used software and/or Internet-based applications for their eRFx (**e**lectronic **R**equest **F**or **x**, where x can be **P**roposal, **Q**uote, **I**nformation, or **T**ender) activity. The top three eRFx providers were Ariba, Procuri, and Emptoris.

3. About 61 percent of the survey participants used e-Reverse auctions, primarily hosted by third-party providers. The average spend per e-Reverse auction was slightly more than $1 million, but the size of the firms has no impact on the number of auctions conducted. Overall, purchases awarded through e-Reverse auctions were 3.1 percent of total spend, and participants reported that they achieved 14 percent of cost savings through e-Reverse auctions.

4. Although e-marketplaces have been touted as the next wave of e-commerce, only 17 percent of the participants used electronic marketplaces or exchanges.

5. Seventy percent of the participants used some form of e-procurement systems, suggesting that e-procurement systems have gained wider acceptance across different industry sectors. The most widely used e-procurement system is ERP modules (50 percent), followed by third-party providers (25 percent).

Note: Some parts of this feature came from Wade, S. D. "Executive Summary: 2006 eProcurement Benchmark Report." *CAPS Research* (July 14, 2006).

uncommon to find that the cost to process a purchase order exceeds the total dollar value of the order itself. While small dollar value is a relative term depending on the size of the firm, purchase orders of $500 to $1,000 can be considered a reasonable cutoff point.

Small value purchases, particularly in a manual system, should be minimized to ensure that buyers are not overloaded with unnecessary purchases that may compromise the firm's competitive position. Owing to the efficiency of the e-procurement system, buyers are less likely to be overburdened by small value purchases. Nevertheless, all firms should have a system in place to handle small value purchases. To control unnecessary administrative costs and reduce order cycle time, purchasing managers have various alternatives to deal with small value purchases. Generally, the alternatives are used for purchase of office supplies and other indirect materials. Let us review the alternatives.

Procurement Credit Card/Corporate Purchasing Card

Procurement credit cards or **corporate purchasing cards** are credit cards with a pre-determined credit limit, usually not more than $1000 depending on the organization, issued to authorized personnel of the buying organization. American Express, Diners Club, Mastercard, and Visa cards are commonly used for this purpose. The card allows the material user to purchase the material directly from the supplier, without going through purchasing. Usually, the user must purchase the needed materials from a list of authorized suppliers. The use of procurement credit cards has gained popularity over the last decade, especially among government agencies, because of its ease of use and flexibility.

When authorized, the card can also be used to pay for meals, lodging, and other traveling expenses, thus eliminating the need to process travel expenses in advance for the user. At the end of the month, an itemized statement is sent to purchasing, to the cardholder's department, or directly to the accounting department. Generally, the purchasing department is responsible for managing the overall program, but each individual unit is responsible for managing its cardholder accounts. To ensure appropriate internal control of the procurement credit card system, a supervisor should be assigned to review the monthly statement of each cardholder to determine if there has been any unauthorized use of the procurement card. In addition, cardholders should maintain proper supporting documents and records for each purchase.

Blanket or Open-End Purchase Orders

A **blanket purchase order** covers a variety of items and is negotiated for repeated supply over a fixed time period, such as quarterly or yearly. The subtle difference of an **open-end purchase order** is that additional items and expiration dates can be renegotiated. The price and estimated quantity for each item, as well as delivery terms and conditions, are usually negotiated and incorporated in the order. A variety of mechanisms, such as a **blanket order release** or production schedule, may be used to release a specific quantity against the order. Blanket or open-end purchase orders are suitable for buying maintenance, repair, and operating (MRO) supplies and office supplies. At a fixed interval, usually monthly, the supplier sends a detailed statement of all releases against the order to the buying firm for payment.

While blanket purchase orders are frequently used to handle small value purchases, the company discussed in the Supply Chain Management in Action feature at the beginning of this chapter demonstrates that when used in conjunction with blanket order releases, cooperative supplier relationships, and single sourcing, blanket purchase orders are a formidable tool to handle the complex purchasing needs of a large, multidivision corporation.

Blank Check Purchase Orders

A **blank check purchase order** is a special purchase order with a signed blank check attached, usually at the bottom of the purchase order. Owing to the potential for misuse, it is usually printed on the check that it is not valid for over a certain amount, usually $500 or $1000. If the exact amount of the purchase is known, the buyer enters the amount on the check before passing it to the supplier. Otherwise, the supplier enters the amount due on the check and cashes it after the material is shipped. Nevertheless, purchasing managers are embracing the use of procurement credit cards and phasing out blank check purchase orders.

Stockless Buying or System Contracting

Stockless buying or **system contracting** is an extension of the blanket purchase order. It requires the supplier to maintain a minimum inventory level to ensure that the required items are readily available for the buyer. It is considered stockless to the buyer because the burden of keeping the inventory is on the supplier. Some firms require suppliers to keep inventory at the buyer's facilities to minimize order cycle time.

Petty Cash

Petty cash is a small cash reserve maintained by a midlevel manager or clerk. Material users generally purchase needed materials and then claim the purchase against the petty cash by submitting the receipt to the petty cashier. A benefit of this system is that the exact reimbursement is supported by receipts.

Standardization and Simplification of Materials and Components

Where appropriate, purchasing should work with design, engineering, and operations to seek opportunities to standardize materials, components, and supplies to increase the usage of standardized items. For example, a car manufacturer could design different models of automobiles to use the same starter mechanism, thus increasing its usage and reducing the need for multiple item storage space, while allowing for large quantity price discounts. This will also reduce the number of small value purchases for less frequently used items.

Simplification refers to reduction of the number of components, supplies, or standard materials used in the product or process during product design. For example, an engine starter manufacturer could design all of its starter models to use a single type of housing or solenoid. Thus, simplification can further reduce the number of small value purchases while reducing storage space requirements, as well as allowing for quantity purchase discounts.

Accumulating Small Orders to Create a Large Order

Numerous small orders can be accumulated and mixed into a large order, especially if the material request is not urgent. Otherwise, purchasing can simply increase the order quantity if the ordering cost exceeds the inventory holding cost. Larger orders also reduce the purchase price and unit transportation cost.

Using a Fixed Order Interval for Specific Categories of Materials/Supplies

Another effective way to control small orders is to group materials and supplies into categories and then set fixed order intervals for each category. Order intervals can be set as biweekly or monthly depending on usage. Instead of requesting individual materials or supplies, users request the appropriate quantity of each item in the category on a single requisition to be purchased from a supplier. This increases the dollar value and decreases the number of small orders.

Sourcing Decisions: The Make-or-Buy Decision

While the term "outsourcing" popularly refers to buying materials or components from suppliers instead of making them in-house, it also refers to buying materials or components that were previously made in-house. In recent years, the trend has been moving toward outsourcing combined with the creation of supply chain relationships, although traditionally firms preferred the make option by using backward and forward vertical integration. **Backward vertical integration** refers to acquiring upstream suppliers, whereas **forward vertical integration** refers to acquiring downstream customers. For example, an end-product manufacturer acquiring a supplier's operations that supplied component parts is an example of backward integration. Acquiring a distributor or other outbound logistics providers would be an example of forward integration.

Whether to **make or buy** materials or components is a strategic decision that can impact an organization's competitive position. It is obvious that most organizations buy their MRO and office supplies rather than make the items themselves. Similarly, seafood restaurants usually buy their fresh seafood from fish markets. However, the decision on whether to make or buy technically advanced engineering parts that impact the firm's competitive position is a complicated one. For example, consider this question: Do you think automaker Honda Motor Company would rather make or buy the engines for its automobiles? Why?

Traditionally, cost has been the major driver when making sourcing decisions. However, organizations today focus more on the strategic impact of the sourcing decision on the firm's competitive advantage. In answer to the previous question, Honda would not **outsource** the making of its engines because it considers engines to be a vital part of its automobiles' performance and reputation. However, Honda may outsource the production of brake drums to a high-quality, low-cost supplier that specializes in brake drums. Generally, organizations outsource noncore activities while focusing on core competencies. Finally, the make-or-buy decision is not an exclusive either-or option. Firms can always choose to make some components or services in-house and buy the rest from suppliers.

Reasons for Buying or Outsourcing

Organizations buy or outsource materials, components, and/or services from suppliers for many reasons. Let us review these now:

1. *Cost advantage:* For many firms, cost is an important reason for buying or outsourcing, especially for supplies and components that are nonvital to the organization's operations and competitive advantage. This is usually true for standardized or generic supplies and materials for which suppliers may have the advantage of **economies of scale** because they supply the same item to multiple users. In most outsourcing cases, the quantity needed is so small that it does not justify the investment in capital equipment to make the item. Some foreign suppliers may also offer a cost advantage because of lower labor and/ or materials costs.

2. *Insufficient capacity:* A firm may be running at or near capacity, making it unable to produce the components in-house. This can happen when demand grows faster than anticipated or when expansion strategies fail to meet demand. The firm buys parts or components to free up capacity in the short term to focus on vital operations. Firms may even subcontract vital components and/or operations under very strict terms and conditions in order to meet demand. When managed properly, **subcontracting**, instead of buying, is a more effective means to expand short-term capacity because the buying firm can exert better control over the manufacturing process and other requirements of the component parts or end products.

3. *Lack of expertise:* The firm may not have the necessary technology and expertise to manufacture the item. Maintaining long-term technological and

economical viability for noncore activities may be affecting the firm's ability to focus on core competencies. Suppliers may hold the patent to the process or product in question, thus precluding the make option, or the firm may not be able to meet environmental and safety standards to manufacture the item.

4. *Quality:* Purchased components may be superior in quality because suppliers have better technology, process, skilled labor, and the advantage of economies of scale. Suppliers may be investing more in research and development. Suppliers' superior quality may help firms stay on top of product and process technology, especially in high-technology industries with rapid innovation and short product life cycles.

Reasons for Making

An organization also makes its own materials, components, services, and/or equipment in-house for many reasons. Let us briefly review these reasons:

1. *Protect proprietary technology:* A major reason for the make option is to protect proprietary technology. A firm may have developed an equipment, product, or process that needs to be protected for the sake of competitive advantage. Firms may choose not to reveal the technology by asking suppliers to make it, even if it is patented. An advantage of not revealing the technology is to be able to surprise competitors and bring new products to market ahead of competition, allowing the firm to charge a price premium. For example, global computer component manufacturers Intel Corporation and Advanced Micro Devices are not likely to ask suppliers to manufacture their latest central processing units.

2. *No competent supplier:* If the component does not exist, or suppliers do not have the technology or capability to produce it, the firm may have no choice but to make an item in-house, at least for the short term. The firm may use supplier development strategies to work with a new or existing supplier to produce the component in the future as a long-term strategy.

3. *Better quality control:* If the firm is capable, the make option allows for the most direct control over the design, manufacturing process, labor, and other inputs to ensure that high-quality components are built. The firm may be so experienced and efficient in manufacturing the component that suppliers are unable to meet its exact specifications and requirements. On the other hand, suppliers may have better technology and processes to produce better-quality components. Thus, the sourcing option ensuring a higher quality level is a debatable question and must be investigated thoroughly.

4. *Use existing idle capacity:* A short-term solution for a firm with excess idle capacity is to use the excess capacity to make some of its components. This strategy is valuable for firms that produce seasonal products. It avoids laying off skilled workers and, when business picks up, the capacity is readily available to meet demand.

5. *Control of lead-time, transportation, and warehousing cost:* The make option provides easier control of lead time and logistical costs since management controls all phases of the design, manufacturing, and delivery processes. Although raw materials may have to be transported, finished goods can be produced near the point of use, for instance, to minimize holding cost.

6. *Lower cost:* If technology, capacity, and managerial and labor skills are available, the make option may be more economical if large quantities of the component are needed on a continuing basis. Although the make option has a higher fixed cost due to initial capital investment, it has a lower variable cost because it precludes suppliers' profits.

Make-or-Buy Breakeven Analysis

The current sourcing trend is to buy equipment, materials, and services unless in-house manufacturing provides a major benefit such as protecting proprietary technologies, achieving superior characteristics, or ensuring adequate supplies. However, buying or outsourcing has its own shortcomings, such as loss of control and exposure to supplier risks. While cost is rarely the sole criterion in strategic sourcing decisions, **breakeven analysis** is a handy tool for computing the cost-effectiveness of sourcing decisions, when cost is the most important criterion.

Several assumptions underlie the analysis: (1) all costs involved can be classified under either fixed or variable cost, (2) fixed cost remains the same within the range of analysis, (3) a linear variable cost relationship exists, (4) the fixed cost of the make option is higher because of initial capital investment in equipment, and (5) the variable cost of the buy option is higher because of supplier profits.

| Figure 2.5 | Breakeven Analysis |

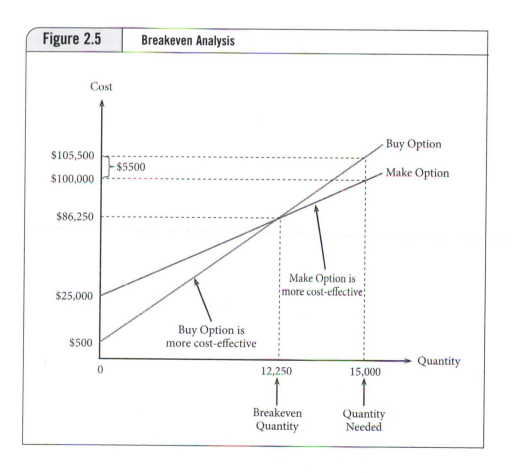

Consider a hypothetical situation in which a firm has the option to make or buy a component part. Its annual requirement is 15,000 units. A supplier is able to supply the part at $7 per unit. The firm estimates that it costs $500 to prepare the contract with the supplier. To make the part, the firm must invest $25,000 in equipment and the firm estimates that it costs $5 per unit to make the part. The quantities are shown in the table below, and are illustrated in Figure 2.5.

COSTS	MAKE OPTION	BUY OPTION
Fixed Cost	$25,000	$500
Variable Cost	$5	$7
Annual Requirement = 15,000		

The Breakeven Point, Q

The breakeven point, Q is found by setting the two options equal to one another and solving for Q (see Figure 2.5):

$$\text{Total Cost to Make} = \text{Total Cost to Buy}$$
$$\Rightarrow \$25,000 + \$5Q = \$500 + \$7Q$$
$$\Rightarrow 7Q - 5Q = 25,000 - 500$$
$$\Rightarrow 2Q = 24,500 \text{ units}$$
$$\Rightarrow \text{Breakeven point}, Q = 12,250 \text{ units}$$
$$\text{Total Cost at the Breakeven Point}, TC_{BE} = \$25,000 + (\$5 \times 12,250)$$
$$= \$86,250$$

For an annual requirement of 15,000 units:

$$\text{Total Cost for the Make Option}, TC_{Make} = \$25,000 + (\$5 \times 15,000)$$
$$= \$100,000.$$
$$\text{Total Cost for the Buy Option}, TC_{Buy} = \$500 + (\$7 \times 15,000)$$
$$= \$105,500$$
$$\text{The Cost Difference} = TC_{Buy} - TC_{Make}$$
$$= \$105,500 - \$100,000$$
$$= \$5,500$$

The analysis shows that the breakeven point is 12,250 units. The total cost at the breakeven point is $86,250. If the annual requirement is less than 12,250 units, it is cheaper to buy. It is cheaper to make the parts if the firm needs more than 12,250 units. With small purchase requirements (less than 12,250 units), the low fixed cost of the buy option makes this option attractive. With larger purchase requirements (greater than 12,250 units), the low variable cost of the make option makes this option more attractive. The analysis shows that the firm should make the item since the quantity is large enough to warrant the capital investment.

Roles of the Supply Base

The **supply base** or **supplier base** refers to the list of suppliers that a firm uses to acquire its materials, services, supplies, and equipment. Firms engaging in supply chain management emphasize long-term strategic supplier alliances by reducing the variety of purchased items and consolidating volume into one or fewer suppliers, resulting in a smaller supply base. For example, global document management company Xerox Corp. and automaker Chrysler LLC reduced their supply bases by about 90 percent in the 1980s. An effective supply base that complements and contributes to a firm's competitive advantage is critical to its success. Savvy purchasing managers develop a sound supply base to support the firm's overall business and supply chain strategies, based on an expanded role for the supplier. It is thus vital to understand the strategic role of suppliers.

Besides supplying the obvious purchased items, key or preferred suppliers also supply the following:

1. Product and process technology and knowledge to support the buyer's operations, particularly in new product design, termed *early supplier involvement* or *concurrent engineering.*

2. Information on the latest trends in materials, processes, or designs.

3. Information on the supply market, such as shortages, price increases, or political situations that may threaten supplies of vital materials.

4. Capacity for meeting unexpected demand.

5. Cost efficiency due to economies of scale, since the supplier is likely to produce the same item for multiple buyers.

When developing and managing the supply chain, preferred suppliers are found or developed to provide these services and play a very important role in the success of the supply chain.

Supplier Selection

The decision of which supplier to use for office supplies or other noncritical materials is likely to be an easy one. However, the process of selecting a group of competent suppliers for important materials, components, and services which can potentially impact the firm's competitive advantage, is a complex one and should be based on multiple criteria. In addition to cost and delivery performance, firms should also consider how suppliers can contribute to product and process technology. Factors that firms should consider while selecting suppliers include

1. *Product and process technologies:* Suppliers should have up-to-date and capable products and process technologies to produce the items needed.

2. *Willingness to share technologies and information:* With the current trend that favors outsourcing to exploit suppliers' capabilities and to focus on core competencies, it is vital that firms seek suppliers that are willing to share their technologies and information. Suppliers can assist in new product design and development through **early supplier involvement (ESI)** or **concurrent engineering** to ensure cost-effective design choices, develop alternative conceptual solutions, select the best components and technologies, and help in design assessment. By increasing the involvement of the supplier in the design process, the buyer is free to focus more attention on core competencies.

3. *Quality:* Quality levels of the purchased item should be a very important factor in supplier selection. Product quality should be high and consistent since it can directly affect the quality of the finished goods.

4. *Cost:* While unit price of the material is not typically the sole criterion in supplier selection, total cost of ownership is an important factor. **Total cost of ownership** or **total cost of acquisition** includes the unit price of the material, payment terms, cash discount, ordering cost, carrying cost, logistical costs, maintenance costs, and other more qualitative costs that may not be easy to assess. Example 2.1 of a total cost of ownership analysis is provided at the end of this section. A total cost analysis demonstrates how other costs beside unit price can affect the purchase decision.

5. *Reliability:* Besides reliable quality levels, reliability refers to other supplier characteristics. For example, is the supplier financially stable? Otherwise, it may not be able to invest in research and development or stay in business. Is the supplier's delivery lead time reliable? Otherwise, production may have to be interrupted due to shortage of material.

6. *Order system and cycle time:* How easy to use is a supplier's ordering system, and what is the normal order cycle time? Placing orders with a supplier should be easy, quick, and effective. Delivery lead time should be short, so that small lot sizes can be ordered on a more frequent basis to reduce inventory holding costs.

7. *Capacity:* The firm should also consider whether the supplier has the capacity to fill orders to meet requirements and the ability to fill large orders if needed.

8. *Communication capability:* Suppliers should also possess a communication capability that facilitates communication between the parties.

9. *Location:* Geographical location is another important factor in supplier selection, as it impacts delivery lead time, transportation, and other logistical costs. Some organizations require their suppliers to be located within a certain distance from their facilities.

10. *Service:* Suppliers must be able to back up their products by providing good services when needed. For example, when product information or warranty service is needed, suppliers must respond on a timely basis.

There are numerous other factors, some strategic while others tactical, that a firm must consider when choosing suppliers. The days of using competitive bidding to identify the cheapest supplier for strategic items are long gone. The ability to select competent strategic suppliers directly impacts a firm's competitive success. Strategic suppliers are trusted partners and become an integral part of the firm's design and production efforts.

How Many Suppliers to Use

The issue of how many suppliers to use for each purchased item is a complex one. While numerous references propose the use of a **single source** for core materials and supplies to facilitate cooperative buyer–supplier partnerships, single sourcing can be a very risky proposition. Although Xerox and Chrysler had substantially reduced their supply base in the 1980s, it was not documented that the firms resorted to single sourcing for their vital materials and components. However, the company featured in the chapter opening Supply Chain Management in Action relied on a single source for most of its materials. Nonetheless, current trends in sourcing favor using fewer sources, although not necessarily a single source. Theoretically, firms should use single or a few sources whenever possible to enable the

Example 2.1   The Total Cost of Ownership Concept

Total cost of ownership is more than just the purchase price—other qualitative and quantitative factors, including freight and inventory costs, tooling, tariffs and duties, currency exchange fees, payment terms, maintenance, and nonperformance costs must be considered. Firms can use a total cost analysis as a negotiation tool to inform suppliers regarding areas where they need to improve.

EXAMPLE

Kuantan ATV, Inc., assembles five different models of all-terrain vehicles (ATVs) from various ready-made components to serve the Las Vegas, Nevada, market. The company uses the same engine for all its ATVs. The purchasing manager, Ms. Jane Kim, needs to choose a supplier for engines for the coming year. Owing to the size of the warehouse and other administrative restrictions, she must order the engines in lot sizes of 1000 each. The unique characteristics of the standardized engine require special tooling to be used during the manufacturing process. Kuantan ATV agrees to reimburse the supplier for the tooling. This is a critical purchase, since late delivery of engines would disrupt production and cause 50 percent lost sales and 50 percent back orders of the ATVs. Jane has obtained quotes from two reliable suppliers but needs to know which supplier is more cost-effective. She has the following information:

Requirements (annual forecast)	12,000 units
Weight per engine	22 pounds
Order processing cost	$125/order
Inventory carrying rate	20% per year
Cost of working capital	10% per year
Profit margin	18%
Price of finished ATV	$4500
Backorder cost	$15 per unit

Two qualified suppliers have submitted the following quotations:

UNIT PRICE	SUPPLIER 1	SUPPLIER 2
1 to 999 units/order	$510.00	$505.00
1000 to 2999 units/order	$500.00	$498.00
3000 + units/order	$490.00	$488.00
Tooling cost	$22,000	$20,000
Terms	2/10, net 30	1/10, net 30
Distance	125 miles	100 miles
Supplier quality rating (defects)	2%	3%
Supplier delivery rating (late delivery)	1%	2%

Jane also obtained the following freight rates from her carrier:

Truckload (TL $\geq$ 40,000 lbs): $0.80 per ton-mile

Less-than-truckload (LTL): $1.20 per ton-mile

(Note: per ton-mile = 2000 pounds per mile)

The total cost analysis (see Figure 2.6) shows that Supplier 1 is more cost-effective, although its unit price and tooling costs are slightly higher than those of Supplier 2. The cash discount, quality cost, and delivery performance set Supplier 1 apart from Supplier 2. Using unit cost as the sole criterion to select a supplier would have cost the company $138,926.67 ($6,265,060.00 − $6,126,133.33).

Figure 2.6	Total Cost Analysis	

Description	Supplier 1		Supplier 2	
1. Total Engine Cost	12,000 units × $500	$6,000,000.00	12,000 units × $498	$5,976,000.00
2. Cash Discount				
n/30	$6,000,000 × 10% × 30/360 $50,000.00		$5,976,000 × 10% × 30/360 $49,800.00	
1/10	N/A		$5,976,000 (10% × 10/360 + 1%) $76,360.00	
2/10	$6,000,000 (10% × 10/360 + 2%) $136,666.67		N/A	
Largest discount		$(136,666.67)		$(76,360.00)
3. Tooling Cost		$22,000.00		$20,000.00
4. Transportation Cost (22,000 lb LTL)	125 miles × 12,000 units × 22 lb × $1.20/2000	$19,800.00	100 miles × 12,000 units × 22 lb × $1.20/2000	$15,840.00
5. Ordering Cost	(12,000/1000) × $125	$1,500.00	(12,000/1000) × $125	$1,500.00
6. Carrying Cost	(1000/2) × $500 × 20%	$50,000.00	(1000/2) × $498 × 20%	$49,800.00
7. Quality Cost	$6,000,000 × 2%	$120,000.00	$5,976,000 × 3%	$179,280.00
8. Delivery Rating				
Backorder (50%)	12,000 × 1% × 50% × $15	$900.00	12,000 × 2% × 50% × $15	$1,800.00
Lost Sales (50%)	12,000 × 1% × 50% × $4500 × 18%	$48,600.00	12,000 × 2% × 50% × $4500 × 18%	$97,200.00
TOTAL COST		$6,126,133.33		$6,265,060.00

development of close relationships with the best suppliers. However, by increasing reliance on one supplier, the firm increases its risk that poor supplier performance will result in plant shutdowns or poor quality finished products. Although **sole sourcing** and single sourcing have been used interchangeably, sole sourcing typically refers to the situation when the supplier is the *only available source,* whereas single sourcing refers to the deliberate practice of concentrating purchases of an item with *one source from a pool of many potential suppliers.* A comparison follows for some of the reasons favoring the use of a single supplier versus using two or more suppliers for a purchased item.

Reasons Favoring a Single Supplier

1. *To establish a good relationship:* Using a single supplier makes it easier for the firm to establish a mutually beneficial strategic alliance relationship, especially when the firm can benefit from the supplier's technology and capabilities.

2. *Less quality variability:* Since the same technology and processes are used to produce the parts when using a single source, variability in the quality levels is less than if the parts are purchased from multiple suppliers.

3. *Lower cost:* Buying from a single source concentrates purchase volume with the supplier, typically lowering the purchase cost per unit. Single sourcing also avoids duplicate fixed costs, especially if the component requires special tooling or expensive setups.

4. *Transportation economies:* Because single sourcing concentrates volume, the firm can take advantage of truckload (TL) shipments, which are cheaper per unit than the less-than-truckload (LTL) rate. By moving up to full truckloads, the firm has the option of using both rail and motor carriers. Rail carriers are more efficient for hauling heavy loads over long distances.

5. *Proprietary product or process purchases:* If it is a proprietary product or process, or if the supplier holds the patents to the product or process, the firm has no choice but to buy from the sole source.

6. *Volume too small to split:* If the requirement is too small, it is not worthwhile to split the order among many suppliers. Single sourcing is also a good approach for acquiring nonvital supplies and services.

Reasons Favoring Multiple Suppliers

1. *Need capacity:* When demand exceeds the capacity of a single supplier, the firm has no choice but to use multiple sources.

2. *Spread the risk of supply interruption:* Multiple sources allow the firm to spread the risk of supply interruptions due to a strike, quality problem, political instability, or other supplier problems.

3. *Create competition:* Using multiple sources encourages competition among suppliers in terms of price and quality. While modern supplier management philosophy discourages the use of multiple sources simply to create competition, this may still be the preferred approach for sourcing nonvital items that do not affect the firm's competitive advantage. Using a single source to develop alliances for these types of purchases may not be cost-effective.

4. *Information:* Multiple suppliers usually have more information about market conditions, new product developments, and new process technologies. This is particularly important if the product has a short product life cycle.

5. *Dealing with special kinds of businesses:* The firms, particularly government contractors, may need to give portions of their purchases to small, local, or women- or minority-owned businesses, either voluntarily or as required by law.

The number of suppliers to use for one type of purchase has changed from the traditional multiple suppliers to the more modern use of fewer, reliable suppliers and even to the extent of using a single supplier. Relationships between buyers and suppliers were traditionally short term, adversarial, and based primarily on cost, resulting in mutual lack of trust. Buyer–supplier relationships, particularly in integrated supply chain settings, have evolved today into trusting, cooperative, and mutually beneficial long-term relationships. Firms today reduce their supply base to only the best suppliers.

Purchasing Organization

Purchasing organization within the firm has evolved over the years as the responsibilities of the purchasing function of firms changed from a clerical, supporting role to an integral part of corporate strategy that directly affects the competitiveness of the firm. In addition to the actual buying process, purchasing is now involved in product design, production decisions, and other aspects of a firm's operations. The decision of how to organize purchasing to best serve its purpose is firm, industry specific, and dependent on many factors, such as market conditions and the types of materials required. Purchasing structure can be viewed as a continuum, with centralization at one extreme and decentralization at the other. While there are few firms that adopt a pure centralized or decentralized structure, the benefits of each are worth a closer examination. The current trend is toward purchasing centralization for the vital materials where firms can take advantage of economies of scale and other benefits.

Centralized purchasing is where a single purchasing department, usually located at the firm's corporate office, makes all the purchasing decisions, including order quantity, pricing policy, contracting, negotiations, and supplier selection and evaluation. **Decentralized purchasing** is where individual, local purchasing departments, such as at the plant or field-office level, make their own purchasing decisions. A discussion of advantages and disadvantages to each of these purchasing structures follows.

Advantages of Centralization

1. *Concentrated volume:* An obvious benefit is the concentration of purchase volume to create quantity discounts, less costly volume shipments, and other more favorable purchase terms. This is often referred to as **leveraging purchase volume**. A centralized system also provides the buying firm more clout and bargaining power. Suppliers generally are more willing to negotiate, give better terms, and share technology due to the higher volume.

2. *Avoid duplication:* Centralized purchasing eliminates the duplication of job functions. A corporate buyer can research and issue a large purchase order to cover the same material requested by all units, thus eliminating duplication of activities. This also results in fewer buyers, reducing labor costs.

3. *Specialization:* Centralization allows buyers to specialize in a particular group of items instead of being responsible for all purchased materials and services. It allows buyers to spend more time and resources to research materials for which they are responsible, thus becoming specialized buyers.

4. *Lower transportation costs:* Centralization allows larger shipments to be made to take advantage of TL shipments, and yet smaller shipments still can be arranged for delivery directly from suppliers to the points of use.

5. *No competition within units:* Under the decentralized system, when different units purchase the same material, a situation may be created in which units are competing among themselves, especially when scarce materials are purchased from the same supplier. Centralization minimizes this problem.

6. *Common supply base:* A common supply base is used, thus making it easier to manage and to negotiate contracts.

Advantages of Decentralization

1. *Closer knowledge of requirements:* A buyer at the individual unit is more likely to know its exact needs better than a central buyer at the home office.

2. *Local sourcing:* If the firm desires to support local businesses, it is more likely that a local buyer will know more about local suppliers. The proximity of local suppliers allows materials to be shipped more frequently in small lot sizes, and is conducive to the creation of closer supplier relationships.

3. *Less bureaucracy:* Decentralization allows quicker response, due to less bureaucracy, and closer contact between the user and the buyer. Coordination and communication with operations and other divisions are more efficient.

Thus, while centralized purchasing may result in lower costs and better negotiating power, the centralized system may also be too rigid and even infeasible for large, multiunit organizations consisting of several unrelated business operations. For these reasons, a **hybrid purchasing organization** may be warranted. For example, large multiunit organizations may use a **decentralized–centralized purchasing structure** to decentralize purchasing at the corporate level, but centralize the procurement function at the business unit level. Conversely, a firm may utilize a **centralized–decentralized purchasing structure** to negotiate national contracts at the corporate level, but decentralize buying at the business unit level, like the example discussed in the Supply Chain Management in Action feature. The hybrid purchasing organization allows the firm to exploit the advantages of both the centralized and decentralized systems.

International Purchasing/Global Sourcing

International agreements aimed at relaxing trade barriers and promoting free trade have provided opportunities for firms to expand their supply bases to participate in **international purchasing**, also referred to as global sourcing. Indeed, world merchandise trade and commercial services trade reached $11.762 trillion and $2.710 trillion, respectively, in 2006.[8] That year, the U.S. was the world's largest importer for merchandise trade ($1.920 trillion), and the world's largest importer and exporter for commercial services (imports were $307 billion; exports were $387 billion). The world's top two exporters of merchandise trade were Germany ($1.112 trillion) and the U.S. ($1.037 trillion). While global sourcing provides opportunities to improve quality, cost, and delivery performance, it also poses unique challenges for purchasing personnel. Engaging in global sourcing requires additional skills and knowledge to deal with international suppliers, logistics, communication, political, cultural, and other issues not usually encountered in domestic sourcing. Example 2.1 (The Total Cost of Ownership Concept) provides an excellent means to evaluate all the costs involved in global sourcing.

Various methods are employed for global sourcing. It is not limited to setting up an international purchasing office or using the firm's existing purchasing personnel to handle the transactions in-house. Instead, an **import broker** or **sales agent**, who will perform transactions for a fee, can be used. Import brokers do not take title to the goods. Instead, title passes directly from the seller to the buyer. International purchasers can also buy foreign goods from an **import merchant**, who will buy and take title to the goods, and then resell them to the buyer. Purchasing from a **trading company**, which carries a wide variety of goods, is another option.

There are numerous international trade organizations designed to reduce tariff and nontariff barriers among member countries. A **tariff** is an official list or schedule showing the duties, taxes, or customs imposed by the host country on imports or exports. **Nontariffs** are import quotas, licensing agreements, embargoes, laws, and other regulations imposed on imports and exports. A discussion of some of the major international trade organizations and agreements follows.

1. The *World Trade Organization (WTO)* is the largest and most visible international trade organization dealing with the global rules of trade between nations. It replaced the General Agreement on Tariffs and Trade (GATT) on January 1, 1995. Its primary goal is to ensure that international trade flows smoothly, predictably, and freely among member countries. The WTO Secretariat is based in Geneva, Switzerland. It had 150 member countries as of January 11, 2007.

2. The *North American Free Trade Agreement (NAFTA)* was implemented on January 1, 1994. Its goal was to remove trade and investment barriers among the U.S., Canada, and Mexico. Under NAFTA, all nontariff agricultural trade

barriers between the U.S. and Mexico were eliminated and many tariffs were either eliminated or to be phased out in fifteen years. All tariffs affecting agricultural trade between the U.S. and Canada (with the exception of items covered by tariff-rate quotas) were removed by January 1, 1998. Ten years after its implementation (from 1994 to 2004), studies showed that NAFTA had only a modest positive effect on the U.S. and Mexican economies.[9]

3. The *European Union (EU)* was set up on May 9, 1950, and comprised Belgium, France, Luxembourg, Italy, the Netherlands, and Germany. The United Kingdom, Denmark, and Ireland joined the EU in 1973. It had 27 member countries as of May 2007. One of the primary goals of EU is to create a single market without internal borders for goods and services, allowing member countries to better compete with markets such as the U.S.

Reasons for Global Sourcing

Firms expand their supply bases to include foreign suppliers for many reasons. These can include lower price, better quality, an overseas supplier holding the patent to the product, faster delivery to foreign units, better services, and better process or product technology.

A primary reason that many firms purchase from foreign suppliers is to lower the price of materials. As stated earlier, price generally is an important factor when purchasing standard materials and supplies that do not impact the competitive position of the firm. Many reasons can contribute to cheaper materials from overseas suppliers—for example, cheaper labor costs and raw materials, favorable exchange rates, more efficient processes, or intentional dumping of products by foreign suppliers in overseas markets.

In addition, the quality of overseas products may be better due to newer and better product and process technologies. Further, while foreign suppliers may be located farther away, they may be able to deliver goods faster than domestic suppliers due to a more efficient transportation and logistical system. Foreign suppliers may even maintain inventory and set up support offices in the host country to compete with domestic sources and to provide better services.

Firms may buy from foreign suppliers to support the local economy where they have subsidiaries, or they may be involved in **countertrade**, in which the contract calls for the exchange of goods or services for raw materials from local suppliers. While foreign purchasing may provide a number of benefits to the buyer, some problems may also be encountered when buying from foreign firms.

Potential Challenges for Global Sourcing

Over the last few decades, global sourcing has surged due to many factors, such as the improvement of communication and transportation technologies, the reduction of international trade barriers, and deregulation of the transportation industry. However, global sourcing poses additional challenges that purchasing must know how to handle effectively. For example, the complexity and costs involved in selecting foreign suppliers and dealing with duties, tariffs, custom clearance, currency exchange, and political, cultural, labor, and legal problems present sizable challenges for the international buyer. The importer discussed in the Global Perspective feature reveals the potential problems of global sourcing.

Unlike dealing with domestic suppliers, the costs involved in identifying, selecting, and evaluating foreign suppliers can be prohibitive. If the foreign supplier is located at a distant location, custom clearance, transportation, and other logistical issues may render delivery lead time unacceptable, especially for perishable goods.

In addition to the Uniform Commercial Code (UCC), which governs the purchase and sale of goods in the U.S. (except the state of Louisiana), global purchasers must also know the United Nations' **Contracts for the International Sale of Goods (CISG)**. The CISG applies to international purchases and sales of goods, unless both parties elect to opt out. The UCC allows either party to modify the terms of acceptance for the purchase contract, but the terms of acceptance cannot be modified under the CISG.

Global purchasers must also deal with more complex shipping terms than domestic buyers. The International Chamber of Commerce created a uniform set of rules, called **incoterms (International Commercial Terms)**, to simplify international transactions of goods with respect to shipping costs, risks, and responsibilities of buyer, seller, and shipper. However, incoterms do not deal with transfer of title of the goods. Incoterms are often used in conjunction with a geographical location. There are thirteen incoterms, grouped into four categories.

Global Perspective

May You Live in Interesting Times

In March 2007, the U.S. Food and Drug Administration (FDA) announced that they had found the chemical melamine in samples of the wheat gluten, a pet food ingredient, imported by a Las Vegas, Nevada-based company from its supplier in China. Melamine is a chemical used in plastics, fertilizers, and other industrial products. The discovery prompted the largest recall of pet foods in the United States. The FDA linked the deaths of a dog and 16 cats to the tainted pet foods and asked the Chinese government to help with the investigation of the contaminated wheat gluten.

The importer was concerned and troubled about the purity of its imported ingredient, although the *certificate of analysis* provided by its foreign supplier did not report the presence of melamine. After the discovery of the tainted ingredient, a representative of the importer visited the foreign supplier, but was taken to a most unusual meeting. The supplier's representative spread out newspapers on a parking lot so that they could sit on the newspapers to talk. The supplier was sorry and promised to look into the matter. Unfortunately, bulldozers razed the supplier's factory before the Chinese officials could investigate the wheat gluten plant. It was later reported that the supplier was in jail. This incident is likely to change the pet food industry on how ingredients are tested and the reliability of suppliers' *certificates of analysis.*

Global sourcing has many benefits, but the potential problems should not be underestimated. Contemporary supply chain management practices encourage the use of supplier certifications to ensure that the supplier's product and processes conform to specifications and requirements. Although the supplier may furnish a *certificate of analysis*, an independent laboratory analysis should be conducted on random samples of the imported product until the product and processes are certified. Once certified, a recertification program needs to be employed.

Note: Some parts of this feature came from Edwards, J. G. "LV Importer Totally Stunned by Tainted Pet Food Ingredient." *Las Vegas Review Journal* (May 19, 2007): P1.

Countertrade

Global sourcing may involve countertrade, in which goods and/or services of domestic firms are exchanged for goods and/or services of equal value or in combination with currency from foreign firms. This type of arrangement is sometimes used by countries where there is a shortage of hard currency or as a means to acquire technologies. Countertrade transactions are more complicated than currency transactions because goods are exchanged for goods.

The various forms of countertrade include barter, offset, and counterpurchase. Barter is the complete exchange of goods and/or services of equal value without the exchange of currency. The seller can either consume the goods and/or services or resell the items. **Offset** is an exchange agreement for industrial goods and/or services as a condition of military-related export. It is also commonly used in the aerospace and defense sectors. Offset can be divided into direct and indirect offsets. **Direct offset** usually involves coproduction, or a joint venture, and exchange of related goods and/or services; whereas **indirect offset** involves exchange of goods and/or services unrelated to the aerospace or defense sector. **Counterpurchase** is an arrangement whereby the original exporter either buys or finds a buyer to purchase a specified amount of unrelated goods and/or services from the original importer. Many developing countries mandate the transfer of technology as part of a countertrade or offset arrangement.

Procurement for Government and Nonprofit Agencies

Public procurement or **public purchasing** refers to the management of the purchasing and supply management function of the government and nonprofit sector, such as educational institutions, charitable organizations, and the federal, state, and local governments. Although public procurement is subjected to political pressure and public scrutiny, the goals of public procurement are basically similar to the private sector. However, public procurement is subjected to special rules and regulations that are established by the federal, state, and local governments. For example, all U.S. federal government purchases must comply with the **Federal Acquisition Regulation (FAR)**. Consequently, the procedures for public procurement differ from the public sector—in addition to ensuring that purchases for goods and services are in strict compliance with statute and policies, public procurement procedures are generally designed to **maximize competition**.

The U.S. **General Services Administration (GSA)**, passed by the eighty-first Congress and signed into law by President Harry Truman in 1949, is responsible for most federal purchases. The GSA, based in Washington, D.C., has 11 regional offices in Boston, New York, Philadelphia, Atlanta, Chicago, Kansas City, Fort Worth, Denver, San Francisco, Auburn (Washington), and Washington, D.C. It is one of the world's largest purchasing entities. The **Department of Defense (DOD)** is the other major public procurement entity in the U.S.

Characteristics of Public Procurement

A unique characteristic of public procurement is the preference to use competitive bidding to encourage competition among suppliers. For example, a government agency may implement procurement procedures that require a written quote for purchases that are more than $2500 but less than $10,000, two written quotes for purchases that are less than $25,000, and three written quotes for purchases less than $100,000; purchases over $100,000 must be competitively bid.

In **competitive bidding**, the contract is usually awarded to the *lowest priced bidder,* determined to be responsive and responsible by the buyer. A **responsive bid** is a submitted bid that conforms to the invitation to bid, and a **responsible bid** is one that is capable and willing to perform the work as specified.

The bidding process is usually very time consuming and costly for small purchases. On October 13, 1994, President Bill Clinton signed the **Federal Acquisition Streamlining Act (FASA)** to remove many restrictions on government purchases that do not exceed $100,000. Instead of using full and open competitive bidding, government agencies can now use simplified procedures that require less administrative details, lower approval levels, and less documentation for soliciting and evaluating bids up to $100,000. **Micro-purchases**, government purchases of $2500 and below, can now be made without obtaining competitive quotes. In addition, all federal purchases between $2500 and $100,000 are now reserved for small businesses, unless the buyer cannot obtain offers from two or more small businesses that are competitive on price, quality, and delivery. A small business is defined as a business with less than 100 employees in the U.S.

Government agencies are required to advertise all planned purchases over $25,000. When the requirements are clear, accurate, and complete, the government agency usually uses an **invitation for bid (IFB)** to solicit sealed bids. The specifications for the proposed purchase, instructions for preparation of bids, and the conditions of purchase, delivery, and payment schedule are usually included with the IFB. The IFB also designates the date and time of bid opening. Sealed bids are opened in public at the purchasing office at the time designated in the invitation, and facts about each bid are read aloud and recorded. A contract is then awarded to the lowest responsible and responsive bidder.

Generally, bidders are also required to furnish **bid bonds** to ensure that the successful bidder will fulfill the contract as stated. There are three basic types of bid bonds— bid or **surety bonds** guarantee that the successful bidder will accept the contract; **performance bonds** guarantee that the work of the successful bidder meets specifications and will be completed in the time specified; and **payment bonds** protect the buyer against any third-party liens not fulfilled by the bidder.

Another characteristic of U.S. public procurement is the **Buy American Act** that mandates U.S. government purchases and third-party purchases that utilize federal funds to buy domestically produced goods if the price differential between the domestic product and an identical foreign-sourced product does not exceed a certain percentage amount. However, the U.S. President has the authority to waive the Buy American Act.

While **green purchasing** is not a new sourcing concept, there is a push to expand green purchasing requirements in the pubic sector. There are at least five federal statutes and more than a dozen Presidential Executive Orders requiring federal purchasing officials to include environmental considerations and human health when making purchasing decisions.[10] Public procurement advocates the purchase of more energy efficient products, bio-based products, recycled content products, alternative fuel vehicles, alternative fuels, nonozone depleting substances, and other environmentally preferable products and services. More on green purchasing can be found in Chapter 4.

SUMMARY

Over the last decade, the traditional purchasing function has evolved into an integral part of supply chain management. Purchasing is an important strategic contributor to overall business competitiveness. It is the largest single function in most organizations, controlling activities and transactions valued at more than 50 percent of sales. Every single dollar saved due to better purchasing impacts business operations and profits directly. Purchasing personnel talk to customers, users, suppliers, and internal design, finance, marketing, and operations personnel, in addition to top management. The information they gain from all this exposure can be used to help the firm provide better, cheaper, and more timely products and services to both internal and external customers. Savvy executives are thus turning to purchasing to improve business and supply chain performance.

KEY TERMS

backward vertical integration, 53

bid bonds, 67

blank check purchase order, 51

blanket order release, 51

blanket purchase order, 51

breakeven analysis, 55

Buy American Act, 67

centralized purchasing, 62

centralized–decentralized purchasing structure, 63

competitive bidding, 67

concurrent engineering, 57

contracts for the international sale of goods (cisg), 65

corporate purchasing cards, 51

counterpurchase, 66

countertrade, 64

decentralized purchasing, 62

decentralized–centralized purchasing structure, 62

Department of Defense (DOD), 66

direct offset, 66

early supplier involvement (ESI), 57

economies of scale, 53

expediting, 40

Federal Acquisition Regulation (FAR), 66

Federal Acquisition Streamlining Act (FASA), 67

follow-up, 46

forward vertical integration, 53

General Services Administration (GSA), 66

green purchasing, 67

hybrid purchasing organization, 62

import broker, 63

import merchant, 63

incoterms (international commercial terms), 65

indirect offset, 66

industrial buyers, 39

international purchasing, 63

inventory turnover, 43

invitation for bid (IFB), 67

leveraging purchase volume, 62

make or buy, 53

material requisition (MR), 43

maximize competition, 66

merchants, 39

micro-purchases, 67

nontariffs, 63

offset, 66

open-end purchase order, 51

outsource, 53

outsourcing, 46

payment bonds, 67

performance bonds, 67

petty cash, 52

planned order releases, 44

procurement credit cards, 51

profit-leverage effect, 42

public procurement, 66

public purchasing, 66

purchase orders (POs), 43

purchase requisition, 43

request for proposal (RFP), 45

request for quotation (RFQ), 45

responsible bid, 67

responsive bid, 67

return on assets, 42

return on investment, 42

sales agent, 63

sales order, 46

simplification, 52

single source, 58

sole sourcing, 60

DISCUSSION QUESTIONS

1. Describe the steps in a traditional manual purchasing system.

2. Describe the e-procurement system and its advantages over the manual system. Are there any disadvantages to the electronic system? Do you think the e-procurement system will ultimately replace the manual system? Why or why not?

3. How can purchasing help to improve the competitive edge of an organization?

4. What is the profit-leverage effect of purchasing? What is the return on assets effect of purchasing?

5. How does a merchant differ from an industrial buyer?

6. Describe the purpose of a material requisition, a purchase order, a request for quotation, and a request for proposal. Is the material requisition serving the same purpose as the purchase order?

7. Why are small value purchase orders problematic? How can purchasing more effectively deal with this problem?

8. Should unit price be used as the sole criterion for selecting suppliers? Why or why not?

9. Explain backward vertical integration. What are the advantages of outsourcing compared to backward vertical integration?

10. When should a firm outsource instead of making the items in-house?

11. What factors should be considered while choosing suppliers?

12. What are the reasons to use a single supplier? Is this the most efficient way to purchase materials in general?

13. Describe centralized and decentralized purchasing and their advantages.

14. Describe how the hybrid purchasing organization works.

15. Describe how blanket orders and blanket order releases can be used to manage the procurement system of a business that owns a dozen large restaurants in a city.

16. How does public procurement differ from corporate purchasing?

17. Describe the different types of bid bonds.

18. What are micro-purchases? How can they be used to improve public procurement?

19. Why do firms purchase from foreign suppliers? What are the risks involved in global sourcing?

20. What is countertrade? Describe the various types of countertrade.

INTERNET QUESTIONS

1. Go to the World Trade Organization's Web site, and use the information to write a report that includes (a) the functions of the WTO, (b) the latest number of membership countries, (c) its relationship with GATT, (d) the number of countries that had originally signed the GATT by 1994, and (e) the last five countries that became members of the WTO.

2. Go to the Institute of Supply Management's Web site and use their "ISM Glossary of Key Supply Management Terms" to explain the terms: (a) supply management, (b) materials management, (c) procurement, (d) purchasing, (e) sourcing, (f) acquisition, (g) sole sourcing, and (h) single sourcing.

3. Go to the European Union's Web site, and use the information to write a report that includes its brief history, membership countries, and the euro.

4. Utilize the Internet to search for the thirteen incoterms. Write a report to explain the primary purpose of the terms in general, and then describe each of the thirteen terms individually.

5. Go to the General Services Administration's Web site and use the information to write a brief report to summarize the roles of GSA. In addition, discuss the roles of the Federal Acquisition Regulation (FAR), Federal Management Regulation (FMR), and the Federal Travel Regulation (FTR).

6. Use resources available on the Internet to write a report on the results achieved by NAFTA in promoting trades among the U.S., Canada, and Mexico since its implementation in 1994.

7. Use resources available on the Internet to write a report on green purchasing efforts in public procurement.

8. Use resources available on the Internet to write a report on green purchasing efforts in the private sector.

INFOTRAC QUESTIONS

Access http://academic.cengage.com/infotrac to answer the following questions:

1. Search on the term "strategic alliances" and write a paper on the impacts of strategic alliances on the buying firm's competitive edge.

2. Search on the term "outsourcing" and write a report on the current stage of outsourcing in North America.

3. Search on the term "global sourcing" and write a report on how global sourcing can enhance a firm's competitiveness.

4. Search on the term "global sourcing" and write a report on how global sourcing can adversely affect a firm's competitiveness.

5. Report on some of the companies that have successfully used global sourcing to enhance competitiveness.

6. Write a report to show how the government bidding process is conducted.

7. Write a report to show the current state of government green procurement, using a country of your choice.

SPREADSHEET PROBLEMS

1. If a firm's net income (profits before taxes) is $120,000, and the firm has total assets of $1.5 million, what is its return on assets?

2. If a firm is able to sustain the same level of operations in terms of sales and administrative expenses but reduces its materials cost by $50,000 through smarter purchases, what is the profit-leverage effect on gross profits? What is the profit-leverage effect on profits before taxes?

3. If a firm's cost of goods sold is $2.5 million and its average inventory is $500,000, what is the inventory turnover?

4. You are given the following information:

COSTS	MAKE OPTION	BUY OPTION
Fixed cost	$125,000	$5000
Variable cost	$15	$17

   a.   Find the breakeven quantity and the total cost at the breakeven point.

   b.   If the requirement is 150,000 units, is it more cost-effective for the firm to buy or make the components? What is the cost savings for choosing the cheaper option?

5. You are given the following information:

COSTS	MAKE OPTION	BUY OPTION
Fixed cost	$25,000	$3000
Variable cost	$8	$12

   a.   Find the breakeven quantity and the total cost at the breakeven point.

   b.   If the requirement is 4500 units, is it more cost-effective for the firm to buy or make the components? What is the cost savings for choosing the cheaper option?

   c.   If the requirement is 6000 units, is it more cost-effective for the firm to buy or make the components? What is the cost savings for choosing the cheaper option?

6. Ms. Jane Kim, purchasing manager of Kuantan ATV, Inc., is negotiating a contract to buy 20,000 units of a common component part from a supplier. Ms. Kim has done a preliminary cost analysis on manufacturing the part in-house and concluded that she would need to invest $50,000 in capital equipment and incur a variable cost of $25 per unit to manufacture the part in-house. Assuming the total fixed cost to draft a contract with her supplier is $1000, what is the maximum purchase price that she should negotiate with her supplier? What other factors should she negotiate with the suppliers?

7. A Las Vegas, Nevada, manufacturer has the option to make or buy one of its component parts. The annual requirement is 20,000 units. A supplier is able to supply the parts for $10 per piece. The firm estimates that it costs $600 to prepare the contract with the supplier. To make the parts in-house, the firm must invest $50,000 in capital equipment, and the firm estimates that it costs $8 per piece to make the parts in-house.

   a.   Assuming that cost is the only criterion, use breakeven analysis to determine whether the firm should make or buy the item. What is the breakeven quantity, and what is the total cost at the breakeven point?

b. Calculate the total costs for both options at 20,000 units. What is the cost savings for choosing the cheaper option?

8. Given the following information, use a total cost analysis to determine which supplier is more cost-effective. Late delivery of raw material results in 60 percent lost sales and 40 percent back orders of finished goods.

Order lot size	1000
Requirements (annual forecast)	120,000 units
Weight per engine	22 pounds
Order processing cost	$125/order
Inventory carrying rate	20% per year
Cost of working capital	10% per year
Profit margin	15%
Price of finished goods	$4500
Backorder cost	$15 per unit

UNIT PRICE	SUPPLIER 1	SUPPLIER 2
1 to 999 units/order	$50.00	$49.50
1000 to 2999 units/order	$49.00	$48.50
3000 + units/order	$48.00	$48.00
Tooling cost	$12,000	$10,000
Terms	2/10, net 30	1/10, net 30
Distance	125 miles	100 miles
Supplier quality rating	2%	2%
Supplier delivery rating	1%	2%

Truckload (TL $\geq$ 40,000 lb): $0.85 per ton-mile

Less-than-truckload (LTL): $1.10 per ton-mile

(Note: per ton-mile = 2,000 pounds per mile)

9. A buyer received bids and other relevant information from three suppliers for a vital component part for its latest product. Given the following information, use a total cost analysis to determine which supplier should be chosen. Late delivery of the component results in 70 percent lost sales and 30 percent back orders of finished goods.

Order lot size	2000
Requirements (annual forecast)	240,000 units
Weight per engine	40 pounds
Order processing cost	$200/order
Inventory carrying rate	20% per year
Cost of working capital	10% per year
Profit margin	15%
Price of finished goods	$10,500
Backorder cost	$120 per unit

UNIT PRICE	SUPPLIER 1	SUPPLIER 2	SUPPLIER 3
1 to 999 units/order	$200.00	$205.00	$198.00
1000 to 2999 units/order	$195.00	$190.00	$192.00
3000 + units/order	$190.00	$185.00	$190.00
Tooling cost	$12,000	$10,000	$15,000
Terms	2/10, net 30	1/15, net 30	1/10, net 20
Distance	120 miles	100 miles	150 miles
Supplier quality rating	2%	1%	2%
Supplier delivery rating	1%	1%	2%

Truckload (TL $\geq$ 40,000 lb): $0.95 per ton-mile

Less-than-truckload (LTL): $1.20 per ton-mile

(Note: per ton-mile $=2,000$ pounds per mile)

Chapter 3

CREATING AND MANAGING SUPPLIER RELATIONSHIPS

At The Boeing Company, we realize that in today's global economy, the relationships we forge with our supplier partners are key to our team's agility, integrity and competitiveness, and our ability to meet our customers' needs. At Boeing, we work with our suppliers as One Team, with One Future.[1]

We're like any technology company in recognizing that our suppliers and partners will play an increasingly more critical role in our business strategies. SRM provides the enabling mechanism for selecting, developing and leveraging the supplier capabilities we need to deliver superior customer value today and, more important, tomorrow. It's vital to our success.[2]

Learning Objectives

After completing this chapter you should be able to

- Explain the importance of supplier partnerships.
- Understand the key factors for developing successful partnerships.
- Develop a supplier evaluation and certification program.
- Explain the importance of a supplier recognition program.
- Understand the capabilities of supplier relationship management (SRM).
- Explain the benefits of using SRM software to manage suppliers.

Chapter Outline

Introduction

Developing Supplier Partnerships

Supplier Evaluation and Certification

Supplier Development

Supplier Recognition Programs

Supplier Relationship Management

Summary

Supply Chain Management in Action

McDonald's Applies SRM Strategy to Global Technology Buy

"A successful supplier relationship management (SRM) strategy requires dedicated supplier managers, effective processes to create standardized best practices, and tools to track and evaluate the results. The success of an SRM plan can dramatically impact the value of a supply contract."

Those words of advice come from Joseph Youssef, director of global technology supplier management for McDonald's of Oak Brook, IL. Youssef detailed the worldwide restaurant chain's SRM strategy at the June Best Practices Xchange forum on global strategic sourcing and supply chain management, a quarterly event hosted by The Mpower Group, of Oak Brook, IL.

"You need to segment your suppliers; you need to measure your suppliers; then you need to manage your suppliers based on those measurements," Youssef told *Purchasing*. McDonald's kicked off its global SRM initiative in May 2004, soon after the worldwide restaurant chain began a new contract to outsource its IT infrastructure with Dallas-based Affiliated Computer Services (ACS). As the company's business relationship with ACS evolved, Don Chapman, senior director of global technology sourcing at McDonald's, says it "realized the concepts and principles used to manage [the contract with] ACS were applicable to our other strategic suppliers."

Youssef outlined four prime measurements as best practices to manage its supplier relationships. First are performance measurements, which evaluate a supplier's efficiency in delivery and service. Second is contract administration, which ensures an agreement is followed and double-checks for any changes or variations, always with an eye on additional business prospects. The third element is financial management administration, which confirms that invoices are correct and the buyer is paying for the agreed-upon services under the contract. And, fourth, relationship management keeps both parties in close contact to maintain, as Youssef describes it, a healthy relationship and to ensure that the purchaser's end users also are benefiting from the supplier contracts.

McDonald's also utilized the expertise of the Procurement Strategy Council, which provides best practices research and executive education to senior procurement executives, for what Chapman called the company's "get what you pay for strategy."

Approximately 80 percent of McDonald's restaurants in the U.S. are run as franchises, while the remaining 20 percent are owned or operated by the company. Outside of the U.S., there are additional ownerships models, such as joint ventures and developmental licensees.

In the U.S., McDonald's has eight people who are actively involved in the company's technology supplier management, with similar teams in other regions of the world. The group's global leadership participates in a weekly conference call to discuss issues they are facing, share information on suppliers and their performances, and coordinate global initiatives. "For instance, Panasonic supplies point-of-sale terminals worldwide," Chapman says, "so we need to coordinate our efforts in working with a key supplier like Panasonic."

McDonald's also has an ongoing effort to evaluate, or "scorecard," its restaurant-level, or point-of-sale (POS), suppliers. All the people on the global IT supplier management group are part of the process. "It is a single initiative that brings all those folks together to get a clear global picture of what the supplier's performance is like," says Youssef.

As McDonald's began to see positive results from applying SRM methodologies and measurements to its relationship with ACS, the company took the next logical step to extend the strategies to other IT contracts. The SRM plan included segmenting its suppliers, based, in part, on contract size, strategic value and risk. McDonald's proceeded to group network vendors, such as Verizon and MCI, and restaurant-level IT suppliers to its restaurants (or POS, point-of-sale), which include Panasonic, ParTech, and NCR. The company also created an executive sponsorship program, through which McDonald's assigns executives to keep in close touch with all of its major suppliers.

Once the company is satisfied with the application of its SRM strategy with IT suppliers, it plans to move to other indirect materials suppliers. McDonald's will proceed in that direction with the help of the Procurement Strategy Council and other sources. The company plans to work with procurement services provider IQNavigator, of Denver, to implement a reporting tool to assess the performance of suppliers' help desk operations, should, for example, a McDonald's restaurant manager call with a problem or question about a vendor's product or technology.

Youssef emphasized that SRM must be coordinated at all levels within a company, from sourcing executives to business unit staff to senior executives. In addition, as a company moves from transitional relationships with suppliers to strategic partnerships, the number of vendors designated as strategic will decrease.

"Typically, in most organizations, you have maybe 10% of the suppliers you do the majority of business and the majority of the spend," he says. At the same time, "the number of resources you have to dedicate to those relationships increases. In order to drive the value out of the supplier relationship, you need to increase the time you spend managing those suppliers."

Although Chapman says McDonald's can cite some cases where costs were avoided and money saved, the company has not come to the point where it can put a specific dollar amount on its two-year initiative. "That's one of the challenges of this program, when you don't have the easy metric of cost savings of a contract," he says.

Youssef concurred, adding that it is too early to judge how well the measurements and methodologies have worked financially, because the results are not easily quantifiable in dollars and cents. "We are still early in the maturity of this process," he adds. "I think next year we will be able to measure that and provide a dollar savings."

Until then, McDonald's is confident that it is heading in the right direction.

Source: Wayne Forrest "McDonald's applies SRM strategy to global technology buy." *Purchasing* (September 7, 2006). Used with permission of *Purchasing* magazine.

Introduction

In today's competitive environment, as companies focus on their core competencies, the level of outsourcing will continue to rise. Increasingly, companies are requiring their suppliers to deliver innovative and quality products not only in just-in-time fashion, but also at a competitive price. In the last two decades the Japanese have proven that good supplier relations can provide many benefits such as flexibility in terms of delivery, better quality, better information, and better material flows between buyers and suppliers. For example, Boeing recognizes that "the relationships we forge with our supplier partners are key to our team's agility, integrity and competitiveness, and our ability to meet our customers' needs" (see the opening quote at the beginning of this chapter). However, the recent delay in delivering Boeing's latest Dreamliner 787 could be traced to problems at one of its smallest suppliers. This shows that companies should not focus only on major suppliers but on the smaller suppliers as well, to avoid any type of production and delivery problems.

Many companies believe strongly that better **supplier partnerships** are important to achieving competitive corporate performance. As such, companies are realizing the importance of developing win-win, long-term relationships with suppliers. It is critical that customers and suppliers develop stronger relationships and partnerships based on a strategic rather than a tactical perspective and then manage these relationships to create value for all participants. Successful partnerships with key suppliers can contribute to innovations and have the potential to create competitive advantage for the firms involved. Selecting the right supply partners and successfully managing these relationships over time is thus strategically important, and it is often stated that "a firm is only as good as its worst suppliers."

According to the Institute for Supply Management's glossary of terms, a supplier partnership is defined as

> *A commitment over an extended time to work together to the mutual benefit of both parties, sharing relevant information and the risks and rewards of the relationship. These relationships require a clear understanding of expectations, open communication and information exchange, mutual trust and a common direction for the future. Such arrangements are a collaborative business activity that does not involve the formation of a legal partnership.*[3]

Automaker Ford has introduced the Aligned Business Framework program which involves supplier relations projects and includes "intensified annual reviews of commodity suppliers, which are made available to all car making organizations; a supplier evaluation system of 11 financial and nonfinancial metrics by which potential suppliers can be judged by buyers; a five-year supplier training plan that will provide a basis for ongoing cooperation in areas of corporate social responsibility."[4] This new framework is beneficial to Ford since it enables the company to reduce costs and obtain suppliers' innovative technologies. At the same time this arrangement also benefits the suppliers who get a long-term commitment that will significantly improve their forecasting and planning. Good supplier relationships are just one ingredient necessary for developing an end-to-end integrated supply chain.

Developing Supplier Partnerships

According to Kenichi Ohmae, globally acclaimed speaker and founder and Managing Director of Japan-based Ohmae & Associates, "Companies are just beginning to learn what nations have always known: in a complex, uncertain world filled with dangerous opponents, it is best not to go it alone."[5] Building strong supplier partnerships requires a lot of hard work and commitment by both buyers and sellers. Developing true partnerships is not easily achieved and much has to be done to get the partnership to work. Several key ingredients for developing successful partnerships are discussed below.

Building Trust

Trust is critical for any partnership or alliance to work. Trust enables organizations to share valuable information, devote time and resources to understand each other's business, and achieve results beyond what could have been done individually. Jordan Lewis, in his book *Trusted Partners,* points out that "Trust does not imply easy harmony. Obviously, business is too complex to expect ready agreement on all issues. However, in a trusting relationship conflicts motivate you to probe for deeper understandings and search for constructive solutions. Trust creates goodwill, which sustains the relationship when one firm does something the other dislikes."[6] With trust, partners are more willing to work together, find compromise solutions to problems, work toward achieving long-term benefits for both parties, and in short, go the extra mile. In addition, there is goodwill developed over time between the partners. This can be beneficial when one partner gets into a difficult situation and the other partner is willing to help out.

Shared Vision and Objectives

All partnerships should state the expectations of the buyer and supplier, reasons and objectives of the partnership, and plans for the dissolution of the relationship. According to Lenwood Grant, sourcing expert with Bristol-Meyers-Squibb, "You don't want a partnership that is based on necessity. If you don't think that the partnership is a good mix, but you do it because you have to—possibly because that supplier is the only provider of that material in the market, because you've signed an exclusive contract in the past, or for some other reason—it's not a true partnership and is likely to fail."[7] Both partners must share the same vision and have objectives that are not only clear but mutually agreeable. Many alliances or partnerships have failed because objectives are not well aligned or are overly optimistic. The focus must move beyond tactical issues and toward a more strategic path to corporate success. When partners have equal decision-making control, the partnership has a higher chance of success.

Personal Relationships

Interpersonal relationships in buyer-supplier partnerships are important since it is people who communicate and make things happen. According to Leonard Greenhalgh, author of *Managing Strategic Relationships,* "An alliance or partnership isn't really a relationship between companies, it's a relationship between specific individuals. When you are considering strategic alliances of any kind, the only time the company matters is in the status associated with it [strategic alliance]. Whoever is interfacing with the other company, they are the company."[8]

Mutual Benefits and Needs

Partnering should result in a win-win situation, which can only be achieved if both companies have compatible needs. Mutual needs create not only an environment conducive for collaboration but opportunities for increased innovation. When both parties share in the benefits of the partnership, the relationship will be productive and long lasting. An alliance is much like a marriage, and if only one party is happy, then the marriage is not likely to last.

Commitment and Top Management Support

First, it takes a lot of time and hard work to find the right supplier partner. Having done so, both parties must dedicate their time, best people, and resources to make the partnership succeed. According to author Stephen R. Covey, "Without involvement, there is no commitment. Mark it down, asterisk it, circle it, and underline it. No involvement, no commitment."[9] Commitment must start at the highest management level. Partnerships tend to be successful when top executives are actively supporting the partnership. The level of cooperation and involvement shown by the organization's top leaders is likely to set the tone for joint problem solving further down the line.

Successful partners are committed to continuously looking for opportunities to grow their businesses together. Management must create the right kind of internal attitude needed for alliances to flourish. Since partnerships are likely to encounter bumps along the way, it is critical that management adopt a collaborative approach to conflict resolution instead of assigning blame.

Change Management

With change comes stress, which can lead to a loss of focus. As such, companies must avoid distractions from their core businesses as a result of the changes brought about by the partnership. Companies must be prepared to manage change that comes with the formation of new partnerships. According to author Stephen Covey, "The key to successful **change management** is remaining focused on a set of core principles that do not change, regardless of the circumstances."[10] Whirlpool attributed the success of their global outsourcing initiative to the change management involved. Steven Rush, Whirlpool's vice president of North American region procurement, noted that "since outsourcing was a politically charged term, the department needed an effective communication program in order to build alignment within the organization; not only at the senior management level, but to make sure that there was buy-in throughout the organization."[11] Thus a company must ensure that the reasons why certain processes are being outsourced are communicated to those affected by the change. Thus effective internal communications is one of the keys to successfully managing change.

Information Sharing and Lines of Communication

Both formal and informal lines of communication should be set up to facilitate free flows of information. When there is high degree of trust, information systems can be customized to serve each other more effectively. Confidentiality of sensitive financial, product, and process information must be maintained. Any conflict that occurs can be resolved if the channels of communication are open. For instance, early communication to suppliers of specification changes and new product introductions are contributing factors to the success of purchasing partnerships. Buyers and sellers should meet regularly to discuss any changes of plans, evaluate results, and address issues critical to the success of the partnerships. Since there is free exchange of information, nondisclosure agreements are often used to protect proprietary information and other sensitive data from leaking out. It is not the quantity but rather the quality and accuracy of the information exchanged that indicates the success of information sharing.

Although collaboration has many positives, there is also the fear of the loss of **trade secrets** when sensitive information is shared between partners. According to the Economic Espionage Act of 1996, 18 U.S.C. § 1839 (3), the definition of trade secrets is:

All forms and types of financial, business, scientific, technical, economic, or engineering information, including patterns, plans, compilations, programmed devices, formulas, designs, prototypes, methods, techniques, processes, procedures, programs, or codes, whether tangible or intangible, and whether or how stored, compiled, or memorialized physically, electronically, graphically, photographically, or in writing.[12]

Trade secrets tend to be more critical in the high technology sector where the unique technique or process used in the company's business can provide it with tremendous competitive advantage. Vendors have been known to steal or misappropriate trade secrets, terminate the partnership, and become competitors. One of the most basic and successful approaches for protecting trade secrets is to require employees and vendors to sign a nondisclosure agreement. According to Dave Drab, Director, Information Content Security Services, Xerox Global Services, "Fostering a sense of trust and loyalty in the workplace helps to galvanize a security culture and establish enterprise-wide best practices."[13]

Developing Relationship Capabilities

Organizations must develop the right capabilities for developing long-term relationships with their suppliers. In a recent study on world-class procurement organizations, the Georgia-based strategic advisory firm Hackett Group found that one of the two best practices for top-performing companies is using cross-functional teams to achieve common objectives.[14] As such, companies aspiring to be world-class must develop cross-functional team capabilities. In addition, the employees must not only be able to collaborate successfully within the company in a cross-functional team setting but have the skills to do so externally. Key suppliers must have the right technology and capabilities to meet cost, quality, and delivery requirements. In addition, suppliers must be sufficiently flexible to respond quickly to changing customer requirements. Before entering into any partnership, it is imperative for an organization to conduct a thorough investigation of the supplier's capabilities and core competencies. Organizations prefer working with suppliers who have the technology and technical expertise to assist in the development of new products or services that would lead to a competitive advantage in the marketplace. In another study, global consulting firm Accenture found that by developing expert capabilities in **supplier relationship management (SRM)**, the existing benefits could increase from 1 to 20 percent.[15]

Performance Metrics

The old adage, "You can't improve what you can't measure," is particularly true for buyer-supplier alliances. Measures related to quality, cost, delivery, and flexibility have traditionally been used to evaluate how well suppliers are doing. Supplier performance information can be used to improve performance in the entire supply chain. Thus, the goal of any good performance evaluation system is to provide metrics that are understandable, easy to measure, and focused on real value-added results for both the buyer and supplier.

By evaluating supplier performance, organizations hope to identify suppliers with exceptional performance or developmental needs, improve supplier communication, reduce risk, and manage the partnerships based on an analysis of reported data. FedEx not only has **performance scorecards** for their suppliers but has also developed a Web-based "reverse scorecard" that allows suppliers to provide constructive performance feedback to the company to enhance the customer/supplier relationship.[16] After all, it is not unusual that the best customers want to work with the best suppliers. In addition, the best suppliers are commonly rewarded and recognized for their achievements. Supplier awards will be discussed later in this chapter.

Although the purchase price is an important factor when selecting suppliers, other criteria such as technical expertise, lead-times, environmental awareness, and market knowledge must also be considered. In the electronics industry, which pioneered the Six Sigma revolution (discussed in Chapter 8), quality is the prime selection criteria due to its strategic importance. In this case, cost is not the key driver but rather quality and the ability of suppliers to bring new technologies and innovations to the table. Thus it is seen that a multi-criteria approach is needed to measure performance. Examples of broad performance metrics are shown in Table 3.1.

Table 3.1   **Examples of Supplier Performance Metrics**

1. **Cost/Price**
   - Competitive price
   - Availability of cost breakdowns
   - Productivity improvement/cost reduction programs
   - Willingness to negotiate price
   - Inventory cost
   - Information cost
   - Transportation cost
   - Actual cost compared to historical (standard) cost, target cost, cost-reduction goal, benchmark cost
   - Extent of cooperation leading to improved cost

2. **Quality**
   - Zero defects
   - Statistical process controls
   - Continuous process improvement
   - Fit for use
   - Corrective action program
   - Documented quality program such as ISO 9000
   - Warranty
   - Actual quality compared to historical quality, specification quality, target quality
   - Quality improvement compared to historical quality, quality-improvement goal
   - Extent of cooperation leading to improved quality

3. **Delivery**
   - Fast
   - Reliable/on-time
   - Defect free deliveries
   - Actual delivery compared to promised delivery, window (i.e., two days early to zero days late)
   - Extent of cooperation leading to improved delivery

Table 3.1	Examples of Supplier Performance Metrics (continued)

4. Responsiveness and Flexibility

- Responsiveness to customers
- Accuracy of record keeping
- Ability to work effectively with teams
- Responsiveness to changing situations
- Participation/success of supplier certification program
- Short-cycle changes in demand/flexible capacity
- Changes in delivery schedules
- Participation in new product development
- Solving problems
- Willingness of supplier to seek inputs regarding product/service changes
- Advance notification given by supplier as a result of product/service changes
- Receptiveness to partnering or teaming

5. Environment

- Environmentally responsible
- Environmental management system such as ISO 14000
- Extent of cooperation leading to improved environmental issues

6. Technology

- Proactive improvement using proven manufacturing/service technology
- Superior product/service design
- Extent of cooperation leading to improved technology

7. Business Metrics

- Reputation of supplier/leadership in the field
- Long-term relationship
- Quality of information sharing
- Financial strength such as Dunn & Bradstreet's credit rating
- Strong customer support group
- Total cash flow
- Rate of return on investment
- Extent of cooperation leading to improved business processes and performance

8. Total Cost of Ownership

- Purchased products shipped cost effectively
- Cost of special handling
- Additional supplier costs as the result of the buyer's scheduling and shipment needs
- Cost of defects, rework, and problem solving associated with purchases

During the past several years, total cost of ownership (TCO), a broad-based performance metric, has been widely discussed in the supply chain literature. TCO is defined as "The combination of the purchase or acquisition price of a good or service and additional costs incurred before or after product or service delivery." Costs are often grouped into **pretransaction**, transaction and **posttransaction costs**.[17] These three major cost categories are discussed below.

- *Pretransaction costs.* These costs are incurred prior to order and receipt of the purchased goods. Examples are cost of certifying and training suppliers, investigating alternative sources of supply, and delivery options for new suppliers.
- *Transaction costs.* These costs include the cost of the goods/services and cost associated with placing and receiving the order. Examples are purchase price, preparation of orders, and delivery costs.
- *Posttransaction costs.* These costs are incurred after the goods are in the possession of the company, agents, or customers. Examples are field failures, the company's goodwill/reputation, maintenance costs, and warranty costs.

TCO provides a proactive approach for understanding costs and supplier performance leading to reduced costs. However, the challenge is to effectively identify the key cost drivers needed to determine the total cost of ownership.

Continuous Improvement

The process of evaluating suppliers based on a set of mutually agreed upon performance measures provides opportunities for **continuous improvement**. The Japanese have demonstrated through the just-in-time philosophy that continuously making a series of small improvements over time results in the elimination of waste in a system. Both buyers and suppliers must be willing to continuously improve their capabilities in meeting customer requirements of cost, quality, delivery, and technology. Partners should not focus on merely correcting mistakes, but work proactively toward eliminating them completely. For continuous improvement to work, employees must first identify areas that are working, to understand the improvements made. These improvements provide the basis for implementing improvements in other processes, which in turn will lead to even more achievements. In today's dynamic environment, staying ahead of change means that firms have to practice continuous improvement. Companies must work continuously with suppliers on continuous improvement programs to ensure that products and services are meeting customer requirements (more on continuous improvement can be found in Chapter 8).

It must be noted that developing supplier partnerships is not easy. All the ingredients mentioned in this section have to be in place for supplier relationships to be successful. Although there are numerous instances where supplier partnerships work well, there are also examples where the relationship did not turn out as expected. In 2007 for example, Mattel pulled more than 18 million toys off the shelves due to product safety concerns.[18] A failure on the part of the organization to properly monitor the quality of the goods that they purchased created a "moral hazard" for their Chinese suppliers. In China, production costs are increasing and intense pressures to reduce prices are making it more difficult for suppliers to maintain their profit margin. As a result, without a good quality verification program, it is easy for the suppliers to compromise on quality and to deliver substandard products. The importance of relationships cannot be overstated and cultivating relations is an essential part of doing business in China. According to Ryan Finstad, director of operations at California-based import/export advisory company Cathay Solutions, "Companies that have long-standing relationships with their manufacturers have naturally become more lax over time. As these firms searched for ways to cut costs, they may have reduced or eliminated monitoring of manufacturers that had historically performed well."[19] However, problems can be avoided if trading partners have better two-way communications, a quality assurance program in place, sound performance metrics, and trust built into the relationship.

Supplier Evaluation and Certification

Only the best suppliers are targeted as partners. Companies want to develop partnerships with the best suppliers to leverage suppliers' expertise and technologies to create a competitive advantage. Learning more about how an organization's key suppliers are performing can lead to greater visibility, which can provide opportunities for further collaborative involvement in value-added activities. A recent *Purchasing* magazine survey[20] shows that 85 percent of purchasing organizations are tracking product and service quality, on-time deliveries, customer service efforts and cost-control programs as part of their supplier rating system. However, only 52 percent use the information to develop supplier programs that will help eliminate problems or improve supply chain performance (see Supplier Development Program in the next section).

A supplier evaluation and certification process must be in place so that organizations can identify their best and most reliable suppliers. In addition, sourcing decisions are made based on facts and not perceptions of a supplier's capabilities. Providing frequent feedback on supplier performance can help organizations avoid major surprises and maintain good relationships. For example, Honeywell has developed their *Supply Line* Web site, www.cas.honeywell.com/ssm, where suppliers can access monthly "report cards," containing supplier performance information such as quality, timeliness of deliveries, conformity to specifications, and service.[21] In addition, the Web site contains supplier profiles, quality and shipping codes, critical documents such as specifications and drawings, and general information relevant to all approved suppliers. The *Supply Line* Web site also enhances supplier relationships since the Web-based technology has resulted in improvements in efficiency and productivity for Honeywell and the suppliers. The Web site enables both Honeywell and their suppliers to be more efficient by spending less time on administrative work involving faxes and mail, or manually tracking supplier performance. Improved productivity is achieved because fewer employees are needed and decisions can be made faster as a result of speedier transmission of information between the companies involved. Findings from a major survey of supply chain executives regarding supplier relationships are detailed in the Global Perspective feature.

Global Perspective

Effective Supplier Relationship Management— Accenture Researches the Correlation with High Performance Businesses

Accenture research has shown that high-performance businesses outrun the competition by successfully positioning their supply chains as a strategic capability. More than ever before, leading companies are using supplier relationship management* (SRM) to differentiate themselves, increase sales, and penetrate new markets and channels.

For six consecutive years, Accenture has evaluated the performance and challenges of supply chain executives in the procurement arena. In 2005, Accenture surveyed 229 senior procurement executives from across Europe and the United States to discover how companies can successfully manage supplier relationships to deliver sustainable benefits in the long term.

According to the Head of a sourcing practice at a global banking giant: "Senior supply chain executives take note—the 'differentiate or die' philosophy is alive and well. As this report shows, the question is not whether SRM is happening, but how much more value we can realise."

SOUTH AFRICANS AGREE

For many chief procurement officers SRM represents an opportunity to build more robust post-contract award capabilities and ensure that the savings promised during the sourcing process are achieved and even surpassed.

Mike Mitchley, vice president of commercial services at South African gold producer Gold Fields, agrees. "We have moved away from a short-term approach towards longer term partnerships with suppliers. In essence, we've started saying to vendors: 'We want a long-term, mutually beneficial relationship with you. Let's work together to see how we can improve each other's bottom lines,' " he said.

"With the South African government placing a focus on economic growth and capital investment for infrastructure through its Accelerated and Shared Growth Initiative, organizations cannot afford to ignore SRM—it will be the chief factor in determining an organization's ability to deliver," said Hayley Walters, supply chain lead at Accenture, South Africa. "Accenture experience has shown that, successfully harnessed, SRM can channel innovation into an organization and help businesses move one step closer toward achieving high performance."

FINDINGS

The findings of the study not only illustrate the cost benefits of SRM but indicate that in order to extract the best value, a company must use a holistic approach to align procurement capabilities, technologies and processes. SRM leaders are organizations that achieve more than 50 percent of their procurement benefits from postcontract award activities. By analyzing the activities adopted by SRM leaders, we can draw conclusions as to how other companies might successfully implement SRM to reduce operational costs, influence the bottom line and, ultimately, achieve high performance.

Specific findings of the study included:

1. There is a tangible prize for those that focus on sourcing and SRM. Looking across the total benefits achieved, 3 to 5 percent savings can be achieved by both sourcing and postcontract activities against total procurement operating spend. SRM leaders achieved savings of 3 percent on their total annual procurement spend.

2. Companies' focus on SRM is set to increase. When questioned about their future focus on SRM, 64 percent of all respondents believed the importance of postcontract activities would increase or remain the same. Some respondents were even more bullish—an additional 12 percent reported that their SRM focus would increase.

3. SRM activities span departments. All survey respondents split their procurement activities between the procurement function and other departments within their business—37 percent of all respondents ranked the ability to work cross-functionally as most important. Interestingly, the procurement department tended to focus on administrative activities such as logging of contract information, whereas other departments spent more time on value-adding activities such as joint product development.

4. Superior results are achieved by those that focus on collaboration with suppliers. SRM leaders not only recognize the importance of value-added collaboration with suppliers, but they also assign greater resources against these activities. For example, they dedicate (on average) nine full-time employees to joint product development compared with all respondents, which dedicate only three full-time employees. However, SRM leaders also ensure they master the basics, such as monitoring and reporting suppliers' performance.

5. There is a SRM skills gap. SRM requires supply chain skills that appear to be lacking inside and outside of the procurement department. This is illustrated by the fact that those who succeed at improving supplier relationships consider the most important activity to be monitoring supplier performance, yet only 15 percent consider themselves to be experts in this activity.

6. SRM leaders use collaborative technology. High performing SRM practitioners demonstrate higher levels of technology adoption across all functional areas of procurement technology. The difference between the SRM leaders and all respondents is greatest for contract management, business-to-business integration/collaboration, and e-sourcing.

7. SRM varies across different industries. Amongst the global survey population, the greatest percentage of SRM leaders were found in the following sectors: media and entertainment (50 percent); automotive (38 percent), and pharmaceutical, medical products and health (32 percent). The lowest corresponding percentages were found in the sectors of property and facilities management (0 percent), banking and insurance (5 percent), and industry and manufacturing (8 percent).

The path of partnership is never an easy one. Leaders that have embraced SRM from a more strategic and holistic standpoint, however, are clearly winning in the marketplace—and not purely through cost reductions. Companies can realize other benefits beyond savings, including reduced risk, increased speed-to-market and access to new technology and solutions.

*Accenture defines SRM as "the systematic management of supplier relationships to optimise the value delivered through the relationship over their life cycle."

Source: http://www.accenture.com/Countries/South_Africa/About_Accenture/Newsroom/News _Releases/EffectiveHPBusiness.htm. Used with permission of Accenture.

One of the goals of evaluating suppliers is to determine if the supplier is performing according to the buyer's requirements. An extension of supplier evaluation is **supplier certification**, defined by the Institute of Supply Management as "an organization's process for evaluating the quality systems of key suppliers in an effort to eliminate incoming inspections."[22] The certification process implies a willingness on the part of customers and suppliers to share goals, commitments, and risks to improve their relationship. This would involve making visits to observe the operations at the supplier organizations. For example, easily visible things such as dirty bathrooms could indicate that the attitude toward quality is lacking in the supplier's production facility. A supplier certification program also indicates long-term mutual commitment. For example, a certification program might provide incentives for suppliers to deliver parts directly to the point of use in the buyer firm, thus reducing costs associated with incoming inspection and storage of inventory.

Implementing an effective supplier certification process is critical to reducing the supplier base, building long-term relationships, reducing time spent on incoming inspections, improving delivery and responsiveness, recognizing excellence, developing a commitment to continuous improvement, and improving overall performance. Supplier certification allows organizations to identify the suppliers who are most committed to creating and maintaining a partnership and who have the best capabilities. Table 3.2 presents criteria generally found in many certification programs.

The Weighted Criteria Evaluation System

One approach of evaluating and certifying suppliers is to use the weighted criteria evaluation system described below.

1. Select the key dimensions of supplier performance mutually acceptable to both customer and supplier.

2. Monitor and collect supplier performance data.

3. Assign weights to each of the dimensions of performance based on their relative importance to the company's objectives. The weights for all dimensions must sum to 1.

4. Evaluate each of the performance measures on a rating between zero (fails to meet any intended purpose or performance) and 100 (exceptional in meeting intended purpose or performance).

5. Multiply the dimension rating by the importance weight and sum to get an overall score.

6. Classify suppliers based on their overall score. An example of a supplier classification guideline might be as follows:
   - Unacceptable (less than 50)—supplier dropped from further business.
   - Conditional (between 50 and less than 70)—supplier needs development work to improve performance but may be dropped if performance continues to lag.
   - Certified (between 70 and less than 90)—supplier meets intended purpose or performance.
   - Preferred (90 and above)—supplier will be considered for involvement in new product development and opportunities for more business.

7. Perform an on-going supplier evaluation process review.

An example of the above evaluation and certification process is shown in Table 3.3.

Table 3.2	Criteria Used in Supplier Certification Programs[23]

- No incoming product lot rejections (e.g., less than 0.5 percent defective) for a specified time period
- No incoming nonproduct rejections (e.g., late delivery) for a specified time period
- No significant supplier production-related negative incidents for a specified time period
- ISO 9000/Q9000 certified or successfully passing a recent, on-site quality system evaluation
- Mutually agreed set of clearly specified quality performance measures
- Fully documented process and quality system with cost controls and continuous improvement capabilities
- Supplier's processes are stable and in control

Table 3.3	Supplier Scorecard Used for the XYZ Company			
PERFORMANCE MEASURE	**RATING**	× **WEIGHT**	=	**FINAL VALUE**
TECHNOLOGY	80	0.10		8.00
QUALITY	90	0.25		22.50
RESPONSIVENESS	95	0.15		14.25
DELIVERY	90	0.15		13.50
COST	80	0.15		12.00
ENVIRONMENTAL	90	0.05		4.50
BUSINESS	90	0.15		13.50
Total score		1.00		88.25

Note: Based on the total score of 88.25, the XYZ Company is considered a certified supplier.

Federal-Mogul has their Global SupplyNet Scorecard Web site, http://www .federal-mogul.com/en/Suppliers/SupplyNet/Scorecard/, which provides the Supplier Rating Criteria and rates suppliers on three main categories of evaluating the suppliers, with the weights shown in parenthesis: quality (40%), delivery (40%), and supplier cost-saving suggestions (SCSS; 20%). The quality score is based on two equally weighted components: parts per million (ppm) defective and quality of supplier corrective action requests (SCARs) issued. The delivery score is computed as "line items received on time divided by the number of line items due by the supplier for the month." The total score ranges from 0 to 100. Suppliers are considered "preferred" if they score between 90 and 100. Preferred suppliers are those that Federal-Mogul will work with on new product development, approve for new business, and assist these suppliers in maintaining a competitive position. An acceptable supplier rating is between 70 and 89. In this category, the supplier is required to provide a plan to Federal-Mogul on how to achieve preferred status. A score of 0 to 69 means that the supplier has a developmental supplier rating. Here, Federal-Mogul "requires corrective action if the supplier is rated at this level for three consecutive months during the calendar year" (see Figure 3.1).

Ford Motor Company's Q1 program assesses a supplier's excellence in the important areas of systems capability, performance, manufacturing process, and customer satisfaction. In developing the program, Ford worked closely with suppliers to get their feedback. Ford's Q1 program has now been recognized as the global industry standard. Ford now works closely with suppliers on all issues related with quality. After suppliers are Q1 certified, they re-validate their status every six months. The suppliers are expected not only to maintain excellence but also to continue to improve every year. Ford Q1 suppliers are preferred suppliers to Ford, provide technical assistance, and are recognized worldwide as having exceptional quality.

Today, external certifications such as **ISO 9000** and **ISO 14000** have gained popularity globally as a natural extension of an organization's internal supplier evaluation and certification program. These are briefly discussed next.

Figure 3.1	**Federal-Mogul's Supplier Rating Criteria**

Road to Supplier Performance Excellence
2007 Supplier Rating Criteria
Overview

Introduction
Federal-Mogul Corporation uses the following criteria to rate the performance of their suppliers for all Federal-Mogul manufacturing and distribution facilities.

Purpose
Identification of continuous improvement and cost-savings opportunities.
Promote and encourage improved communication on performance issues.
Provide objective data for use in supplier management and sourcing decisions.
Recognition of exceptional supplier performance.

Terminology
Category: These are the main groupings by which suppliers will be measured. The initial set of categories for which measurements will be compiled are **Delivery, Quality,** and **Supplier Cost-Saving Suggestions (SCSS).** Each category has assigned weighting, which is rolled into the overall score. Category scores range from 0 to 100 points.

Overall Rating: The Overall Rating is a description of the performance level of supply as viewed by Federal-Mogul. Scores for each category are multiplied by the weighting, and the summation entails the overall score for the supplier. Overall Ratings associated to the overall score are as follows:

Overall Rating Weighted Point Score:
Preferred: 90 to 100
Acceptable: 70 to 89
Developmental: 0 to 69

"Preferred" Supplier Rating:
  1. Federal-Mogul will work with these suppliers on new product development.
  2. Federal-Mogul will assist these suppliers in maintaining a competitive position.
  3. Federal-Mogul will maintain a listing of "Approved for New Business" suppliers.

"Acceptable" Supplier Rating:
  1. Federal-Mogul will require a plan from the supplier outlining how to achieve preferred status.
  2. Federal-Mogul will monitor supplier improvement.

"Developmental" Supplier Rating:
  1. Federal-Mogul requires corrective action if the supplier is rated at this level for three consecutive months during the calendar year.
  2. The supplier must provide plans to improve performance to an acceptable level.
  3. Federal-Mogul will look at alternative sources if performance does not improve.

Supplier Rating Qualifications:
The rating system will entail any supplier deemed appropriate by the Federal-Mogul Manufacturing/Distribution Purchasing Team.

Supplier Scores and Category Weighting

Figure 3.1	(continued)

As illustrated above, there are three main categories by which suppliers are measured:

> Delivery—40 percent
> Quality—40 percent
> Supplier Cost-Saving Suggestions (SCSS)—20 percent

A value is displayed in each category on the Global Scorecard for every Federal-Mogul facility receiving product(s) or service(s) from the supplier.

Quality Category: Rating Criteria
The Quality category comprises two components:

> Parts per million (PPM)—50 percent
> Quantity of supplier corrective action requests (SCARs) issued—50 percent

PPM is based on SCARs. Both the number of SCARs and PPM are reported monthly. SCAR responsiveness does not factor into the supplier's Overall Score. Currently, it is only displayed on the Scorecard.

PPM	COUNTPOINTS	# OF SCARS	POINTS
0	100	0	100
1–25	90	1	70
26–50	80	2–4	40
51–100	60	5+	0
101–250	40		
251–500	20		
501+	0		

Delivery Category: Rating Criteria
Ontime delivery: The delivery score is based on the average percentage across using plants for the current month. Ontime delivery percentage has a window of one day early and zero days late to the due date and +/–5 percent of order quantity. The ontime delivery percentage is determined by line items received ontime divided by the number of line items due by the supplier for the month.

Consignment programs receive a 100 percent delivery percentage unless a stockout is caused. The score is reduced by 10 percent for each day of the stockout.

SCSS (Supplier Cost-Saving Suggestions): Rating Criteria
5 percent target performance: SCSS are targeted at 5 percent of the year's forecasted dollars spent. The supplier must make SCSS submittals to the plant or the commodity manager.

SCORE	SCSS MEASUREMENT
100	5% and above
85	4% to 4.9%
70	3% to 3.9%
40	2% to 2.9%
20	1% to 1.9%
0	0.9% and below

Source: http://www.federal-mogul.com/en/Suppliers/SupplyNet/Scorecard/. Reproduced with permission from Federal-Mogul.

ISO 9000

In 1987 the International Organization for Standardization (ISO) developed ISO 9000, a series of management and quality assurance standards in design, development, production, installation, and service. The European Union in 1992 adopted a plan that recognized ISO 9000 as a third-party certification; the result is that many European companies today prefer suppliers with an ISO 9000 certification. Thus,

U.S. companies wanting to sell in the global marketplace are compelled to seek ISO 9000 certification. The ISO survey of 2005[24] showed that 776,608 ISO 9000 certificates had been awarded in 161 countries up to the end of December 2005. This represents an increase of 17.6 percent over the number of certificates issued during the same period in 2004. In the U.S., 44,270 certificates had been issued up to the end of 2005, representing 5.7 percent of the worldwide numbers. The ANSI (American National Standards Institute)/ISO/ASQC (American Society for Quality Control) Q9000 standards are the U.S. equivalent of ISO 9000. Obtaining the ISO 9000 certification provides further verification that the supplier has an established quality management system in place. For example, Ford's Q1 process requires suppliers to be ISO 9000 certified.

A recent study found that ISO 9000 certification and Total Quality Management practices (discussed in Chapter 8) had a significant positive relationship.[25] This result suggests that organizations should seriously consider ISO 9000 as the first step to total quality management.

ISO 14000

In 1996, ISO 14000, a family of international standards for environmental management, was first introduced. In 2004, ISO 14000 was revised to make the standards easier to understand and emphasized compliance and compatibility with ISO 9000 for businesses that wanted to combine their environmental management and quality management systems. Companies that implemented ISO 14000 found benefits from cost savings (conserving materials, reduced water and energy use), better public image, and decreased liability due to reduced waste clean-up costs. According to a study by ISO, by the end of 2005 there were 5061 ISO 14000 certificates in the U.S., representing only 4.5 percent of the 111,162 certificates issued globally in 138 countries.[26] The number of ISO 14000 certifications pales in comparison with those for ISO 9000.

The benefits of investing in an environmental management system (EMS) based on ISO 14000 standards include reduced energy and other resource consumption, decreased environmental liability and risk, reduced waste and pollution, and improved community goodwill. As such, investment in environmental management systems is likely to increase in the future. In addition, as more organizations are certified in ISO 14000, they are likely to pass this requirement on to their suppliers in the future. A recent study shows that the successful adoption of an ISO 14000-based environmental management system provides the driving force for sustainable development and value creation.[27] The U.S. federal government also played a role in improving the environment when President George W. Bush signed Executive Order 13148, "Greening the Government through Leadership in Environmental Management," in April 2000, which requested all federal facilities to implement an EMS by December 2005.

Supplier Development

Supplier development is defined as "any activity that a buyer undertakes to improve a supplier's performance and/or capabilities to meet the buyer's short- and/or long-term supply needs."[28] Supplier development requires financial and human resource investments by both partners and includes a wide range of activities such as training of the supplier's personnel, investing in the supplier's operations, and ongoing performance assessment. As noted earlier, a little more than 50 percent of suppliers have supplier development programs, even though more than 85 percent have supplier rating systems.[29] This indicates that there are still many companies that do not practice supplier development. As companies outsource more and more parts, a larger portion of costs lie outside the company in a supply chain, and it becomes increasingly difficult to achieve further cost savings internally. One way out of this dilemma is for companies to work with their suppliers to lower the total cost of materials purchased. Companies that are able to leverage their supply base to influence their total cost structure will have a competitive advantage in their markets. A seven-step approach to supplier development is outlined below.[30]

1. *Identify critical products and services.* Assess the relative importance of the products and services from a strategic perspective. Products and services that are purchased in high volume, do not have good substitutes, or have limited sources of supply are considered strategic supplies.

2. *Identify critical suppliers.* Suppliers of strategic supplies that do not meet minimum performance in quality, on-time delivery, cost, technology, or cycle time are targets for development.

3. *Form a cross-functional team.* Next, the buyer must develop an internal cross-functional team with a clear agreement for the development initiative.

4. *Meet with top management of supplier.* The buyer's cross-functional team meets with the supplier's top management team to discuss details of strategic alignment, supplier performance measurement, improvement, and professionalism.

5. *Identify key projects.* After the promising opportunities have been identified, they are evaluated in terms of feasibility, resource and time commitment, and expected return on investment. The most promising projects are selected.

6. *Define details of agreement.* After agreement has been reached on the development projects, the partners must jointly decide on the metrics to be monitored such as percent improvement in quality, delivery, and cycle time.

7. *Monitor status and modify strategies.* To ensure continued success, management must actively monitor progress, promote exchange of information, and revise the strategy as business conditions warrant.

Intel's Supplier Continuous Quality Improvement (SCQI) Program is a "corporate wide program that utilizes critical Intel supplier management tools and processes to drive continuous improvements in a supplier's overall performance and business."[31] The SCQI program was started in 1987 with the objective of improving supplier quality and minimizing the time needed to inspect incoming products. According to Intel, the SCQI program accomplishes the following[32]:

- Establishes aligned goals, indicators, and metrics.
- Enables benchmarking of supplier's performance.
- Identifies potential quality issues before they affect Intel.
- Drives supplier's agility and ability to provide leading-edge products and services.
- Matures critical Intel-supplier relationships.
- Encourages collaborative agreements, team problem resolution, two-way continuous learning.

- Encourages continuous improvement throughout the year.
- Provides data to support supplier recognition.

With the SCQI program, Intel was able to reap great benefits from the suppliers. Further, as the quality of their suppliers' products improved, greater opportunities existed for making further improvement.

By tracking supplier performance over time, New Jersey-based Honeywell is able to observe trends and to catch problems early. Honeywell has implemented their Six-Sigma-plus program aimed at eliminating variations in processes to meet required specifications with no more than 3.4 parts per million (ppm) defective and to apply lean manufacturing techniques to eliminate waste and to synchronize suppliers' activities. Recently, Honeywell implemented the Six-Sigma-plus initiatives with their suppliers. For example, Wong's-CMAC, a supplier of Honeywell based in Mexicali, Mexico, was experiencing chronic quality and lead-time problems. With Honeywell's assistance the supplier was able to improve its quality from 3.2 sigma (or 44,565 ppm defective) to six sigma (approximately 4 ppm defective).[33]

In summary, it is critical that an organization has an active supplier development program. The program should be managed such that it can meet both current and future needs. With a proactive supplier development program, suppliers are forced to stay on top of today's dynamic environment, so that customers are not stuck with products or services that are not leading edge.

Supplier Recognition Programs

A recent *Purchasing* survey[34] found that although a large percentage of companies tracked supplier performance, only approximately half recognized excellent performance with supplier awards and appreciation banquets. Today, it is not sufficient just to reward a firm's best suppliers with more business but to also recognize and celebrate the achievements of their best suppliers. As award winning suppliers, they serve as role models for other suppliers. Phillip Morris USA, for example, has a Crown of Excellence Supplier Recognition Program. The program has a statement of purpose given below[35]:

> The future is up to us. In the coming weeks and years, we will anticipate, not react to, the opportunities in our markets. In our world, we recognize the forces we cannot control. But even more important, we know the depth of our own talent and commitment, as well as the loyalty of our suppliers. We are focusing our potential on leading the markets we serve, and we're counting on our suppliers' performance to help us achieve our goals.

The above statement shows that Phillip Morris is proactively looking into the future. The company recognizes that it will have to depend on their suppliers to help them achieve organizational goals. Philip Morris benefits from their suppliers, continuously improving all aspects of their business relationships. The awards program also enables Philip Morris to strengthen the company's relationships with suppliers. Suppliers also benefit from the program because they are motivated to achieve excellence in quality, cost, security and technology, and delivery and service, the four areas that suppliers are judged for their awards program. The award indicates commitment to quality and customer service, which the suppliers can showcase to their customers. In essence, it is a win-win situation for both the organization and its suppliers.

Ford Motor Company's World Excellence Award is a comprehensive global supplier awards program that annually recognizes their global suppliers for their exemplary performance. These metrics are jointly developed with their suppliers. In 2007, Ford presented fifty-five World Excellence Awards to global suppliers for their exemplary performance in 2006. Examples of winners of the Gold Award (suppliers that excel in quality, cost, and delivery) are ArvinMeritor, Inc., Spain (Exhaust Systems), Fujikura Ltd., Japan (Wiring Harnesses), Intier Automotive Seating, England (Seats), Ronal Polska Sp., Poland (Wheels), and Superior Industries International, Inc., USA (Wheels). The Silver Award is given to suppliers that meet the quality excellence requirement and either the cost or delivery excellence requirement. Past winners in the quality and cost category include Getrag S.P.A. (Germany) and J. Walter Thompson Publicidade Ltda. (Brazil). Recognition of Achievement Awards are given to suppliers who have made a significant contribution in Ford's key initiatives of New Consumer-Focused Technology, Durability and Reliability Performance, Corporate Responsibility, Diversity and Community Service, Consumer-Driven Six-Sigma, and New Consumer-Focused Technology.[36]

As part of Intel's CQSI Program (see the earlier discussion in the preceding section), there are three recognition awards: Certified Supplier Award (CSA), Preferred Quality Supplier (PQS) Award, and Supplier Continuous Quality Improvement (SCQI) Award. The CSA is given to suppliers who consistently meet Intel's expectations and have a proven commitment to continuous improvement. Intel's Preferred Quality Supplier (PQS) award is for outstanding commitment to quality, excellent performance, and excellence at meeting and exceeding high expectations and tough performance goals. According to Bob Bruck, vice president Technology and Manufacturing Group and general manager of Technology Manufacturing Engineering at Intel, "The Preferred Quality Supplier award winners have an excellent and ongoing focus on technology innovation, manufacturing support and customer satisfaction. The suppliers we're recognizing today are role models for our industry, achieve higher levels of performance than their peers and is key to Intel's delivery of new products to our customers worldwide."[37] The SCQI Award, which is the most prestigious of Intel's three recognition awards, is given to suppliers who consistently perform at world-class levels, provide outstanding strategic contribution, and deliver cost reductions.

Spam lunchmeat producer Hormel Food Corporation's No. 1 Award program differs from other programs because they only give out awards once every five years. Hormel gave out its first award in 1996 for suppliers whose relationships span from 1991 to 1995; the second award was given in 2001 for suppliers from 1996 to 2001, and the last award recognizes partners from 2001 to 2005. According to Hormel, suppliers must meet the following criteria to qualify for the Hormel No. 1 Award[38]:

- *Supplier must have a Supplier Rating Index of 98 percent or better in the fourth calendar quarter of the reporting year.*
- *The average of the five-year Supplier Rating Index must be equal to or greater than 98 percent.*
- *Supplier must be a recipient of the Spirit of Excellence Award—an annual award given by Hormel Foods—for a minimum of four times during the past five consecutive years.*
- *The trend of the Supplier Rating Index must be even or positive during the five-year period.*
- *Suppliers must meet certain requirements, such as number of products sold by the supplier to Hormel Foods, dollars of exposure and deliveries to*

Hormel Foods, number of Hormel Foods locations serviced, and stage of Hormel Foods' Quality Improvement Process.

To receive their Spirit of Excellence Award, suppliers must achieve a minimum Supplier Rating Index score of 92 during a twelve-month period. The criteria for the Supplier Rating Index include an ability to meet requirements, make timely deliveries, provide accurate administrative support, and maintain inventories. Additional criteria such as customer support, awareness of environmental concerns, and sales representative performance are considered but are not requirements for the award.

According to a *Purchasing* magazine survey,[39] the following shows how award-wining suppliers are rated: Quality (83%), Delivery (78%), Service (44%), Cost (39%) and Value-add (22%). As can be seen here, quality and not cost is cited as the top criterion for supplier recognition awards.

Supplier Relationship Management

Supplier relationship management (SRM) has garnered increasing attention from firms practicing supply chain management. SRM is an umbrella term that includes "extended procurement processes, such as sourcing analytics (e.g., spend analysis), sourcing execution, procurement execution, payment and settlement, and—closing the feedback loop—supplier scorecarding and performance monitoring."[40] Accenture defines SRM as "the systematic management of supplier relationships to optimize the value delivered through the relationship over their life cycle."[41] According to business analytics software manufacturer SAS, SRM "strives to help companies determine their most important suppliers. It also reveals how best to focus time and energy to create and maintain more effective, strategic relationships with suppliers, thus maximizing the positive impact the supply base has on costs, quality, delivery and innovation within an organization."[42] In a nutshell, SRM involves streamlining the processes and communication between the buyer and supplier and using software applications that enable these processes to be managed more efficiently and effectively.

Definitions of what is included in these SRM modules vary widely with i2 Technologies claiming to have coined the term, SRM, in collaboration with AMR Research. The success of e-procurement, which has a predominantly internal focus, created the need for SRM solutions for managing the supply side of an organization's supply chain. According to Nick Ford, European vice president of e-procurement with i2, "The automation that SRM brings creates efficiencies which are clearly a source of sustainable competitive advantage. With shrinking product life cycles, it becomes critical to design, source, plan and manufacture materials right the first time to take advantage of market trends. By making the scope of supplier relationships broader, more flexible and more responsive, enterprises can achieve new areas of growth and build profitable new business models."[43] SRM software automates the exchange of information among several layers of relationships that are complex and too time consuming to manage manually and results in improved procurement efficiency, lower business costs, real-time visibility, faster communication between buyer and seller, and enhanced supply chain collaboration.

Many organizations are investing in SRM software modules due to the wealth of information that can be derived from these systems. SRM software can organize supplier information and provide answers to questions such as

- Who are our vendors? Are they the right set of suppliers?
- Who are our best suppliers and what are their competitive rankings?
- What is our suppliers' performance with respect to on-time delivery, quality, and costs?
- Can we consolidate our buying to achieve greater scale economies?
- Do we have consistency in suppliers and performance across different locations and facilities?
- What products/services do we purchase?
- What parts can be re-used in new designs?

According to SAS, an effective SRM solution "provides real supplier intelligence—the ability to understand and predict the value of supplier relationships—through an enterprisewide, integrated view of a company's suppliers and the commodities or services they provide. It enables businesses to collect, analyze and leverage all aspects of their supplier data and purchasing history, providing vital insights into the supply base and purchasing history."[44]

In general, SRM software varies by vendors in terms of capabilities offered. AMR Research has identified five key tenets of an SRM system.[45]

- *Automation* of transactional processes between an organization and its suppliers.
- *Integration* that provides a view of the supply chain that spans multiple departments, processes, and software applications for internal users and external partners.
- *Visibility* of information and process flows in and between organizations. Views are customized by role and aggregated via a single portal.
- *Collaboration* through information sharing and suppliers' ability to input information directly into an organization's supply chain information system.
- *Optimization* of processes and decision making through enhanced analytical tools such as data warehouse and On-Line Analytical Processing (OLAP) tools with the migration toward more dynamic optimization tools in the future.

Table 3.4 is a listing of a number of SRM software suppliers and some of their customers.

There are two types of SRM: transactional and analytic.[46] Basically, **transactional SRM** enables an organization to track supplier interactions such as order planning, order payment, returns, and so on. The volume of transactions involved may result in independent systems maintained by geographic region or business lines. Transactional SRM tends to focus on short-term reporting and are event driven such as: What did we buy yesterday? What supplier did we buy from? What is the cost of the purchase? On the other hand, **analytic SRM** allows the company to analyze the complete supplier base. The analysis provides answers to questions such as: Which suppliers should the company develop long-term relationships with? Which supplier would make the company more profitable? Analytic SRM attempts to answer more difficult and important questions about supplier relationships. Thus we can see that transactional SRM addresses tactical issues such as size of order whereas analytic SRM focuses on long-term procurement strategy. With analytic SRM, an organization can assess where it was yesterday, where it stands today, and where it wants to go in the future to meet its strategic purchasing goals.[47]

Table 3.4	Examples of SRM Software Suppliers and Their Customers

EcVision (http://www.ecvision.com/)

Customers: J. C. Penney Company, Inc., MAST Industries, Inc. (buying arm for The Limited family of stores including Express, Lerner New York, Lane Bryant, Limited Stores, Structure, and Henri Bendel)

i2 Technologies, Inc. (http://www.i2.com/)

Customers: eLSG SkyChefs, Airbus, PEMSTAR Inc., Nippon Steel Corporation, Hitachi, Toshiba Corporation's Semiconductor Company, Honeywell

Oracle (http://www.oracle.com/)

Customers: Dartmouth-Hitchcock Medical Center, Aquila Inc., Boise, Beth Israel Deaconess Medical Center

SAP (http://www.sap.com/)

Customers: Lockheed Martin, Mercedes-Benz Espana (Spain), Deutsche Bank, Kimberly Clark, Proctor and Gamble, Royal Dutch/Shell

SAS Institute (http://www.sas.com/)

Customers: BayerCropScience, Schneider Electric.

SupplyWorks (http://www.supplyworks.com/)

Customers: BorgWarner Morse TEC, Barnes & Noble, Ingersoll-Rand, Plasti-Line, Inc.

The challenge in any SRM software implementation is assembling all the data needed for an SRM application to work and providing effective employee training. For example, analysis of supplier information requires access to applications containing data about suppliers, as well as enterprise resource planning (ERP), material requirements planning (MRP), accounting, and existing supplier information databases. Prior to SRM implementation, buyers typically spend 10 percent of their time on supplier relationship development, 40 percent on expediting, and 50 percent on order processing/tracking. After SRM implementation, the buyer's time allocation is estimated to be 50 percent on collaborative planning, 30 percent on supplier relationship development, 10 percent on expediting, and 10 percent on exception management.[48]

Until recent years, purchasing professionals did not have the right technologies to help them accomplish their jobs effectively. Automating procurement activities can lead to significant cost savings as buyers move toward managing processes by exception. This effectively frees buyers to focus on more strategic and value-added activities such as collaborative planning. In addition, purchasing professionals can work effectively on maximizing the return on their relationships with suppliers. The greater procurement visibility from using SRM software also translates into smoother processes, faster cycle times, reduced new product development, improved time to market, streamlined purchasing, and reduced inventory costs.

Internally, SAS has used its own SAS® Supplier Relationship Management solution to "develop cost-effective strategies for purchasing, to determine the best vendors and to secure the most beneficial deals for SAS."[49] According to Dan Southwick, director of Procurement and Business Services for SAS, the investment in SRM is expected to pay for itself from savings accrued through the skilled management of supplier relationships. Procurement is not just about getting the lowest price for the product but also ensuring that firms get on-time delivery, quality, and favorable payment terms. The SAS solution allows for greater visibility of the vendors and the amount of business conducted. SAS was also able to identify minority- and

e-Business Perspective

Delta Uses e-Auctions as a Tool, SRM as a Process

With the rise of new technology focused on sourcing and supplier management, buyers are more often faced with the decision of which tool to take out of the toolbox. Typically, it's thought that the decision comes down to e-sourcing tools or supplier relationship management (SRM) tools. But, SRM and e-auctions are not exclusive. They often work hand-in-hand. Which tool and strategy a procurement organization selects depends on the individual contract, commodity, and a multitude of other market factors.

Delta Air Lines of Atlanta is a good example of this process. Although in 2006 the company continued to plan its emergence from Chapter 11 bankruptcy protection, procurement's strategic role (and the tools it picks to support that strategy) had perhaps never been more important.

Delta's procurement managed $9.4 billion in spend and nearly $6.2 billion of that was spent on fuel in 2005. The remaining $3.2 billion was spent on direct and indirect materials, which is where Delta has been targeting its reverse auction strategy.

"You should leverage [e-auctions] where there is a very healthy and robust supply base to make sure you get the best deal," says Bob Currey, general manager of sourcing innovation and supply management for Delta, in a recent interview with *Purchasing*. Delta's early experience with e-auctions came in handy in negotiating contracts for hotel rates and has progressed to other indirect spend areas such as office supplies, while using technology from Verticalnet. Currey says to "absolutely reverse auction those products" based on supplier competitiveness as well as supplier switching cost.

But it's not just indirect materials—Delta has used e-auctions in more complex spend categories. Currey recently detailed an e-auction Delta held for IT professional services. Prior to the auction, RFPs were sent to 30 suppliers of IT services, listing the descriptions of requirements for the contract. Each supplier had the opportunity to hear the expectations in detail, an opportunity to ask questions, and respond to the RFP. Based on the responses of the 30 suppliers, Delta selected 15 to participate in the on-line reverse auction.

For direct spend areas at Delta, there is typically a more narrow supply base or even some cases where Delta uses single-sourcing. Some parts on an airplane will be replaced only once every 15 to 20 years. "If you have to go to Boeing to get those parts, because they are licensed and there are no alternatives in the supply base, then an RFP isn't an option," says Currey. "That's when SRM is so important to us. In some cases we may need [those suppliers] more than they need us."

Delta focuses its SRM strategy on its top 200 suppliers. In these close relationships, Currey works with suppliers in ways that will create incremental value. For instance, where better prices may not be accomplished, purchasing at Delta might look toward working with its suppliers to manage inventory better or manage areas of warranty recovery.

Currey makes an important distinction, however, in separating supplier performance from SRM. Although both are part of supplier management, supplier performance can be defined and measured with key metrics. "The great thing about this is it forces us to define success," says Currey. Supplier performance is tied to a scorecard while SRM strategy depends on what tier that supplier is in. "Because I know they are in the top tier, I have a scorecard for those suppliers and top management meetings," says Currey.

Source: Karen Prema. "SRM + E-AUCTIONS: Tools in the Toolbox." *Purchasing* (April 6, 2006). Used with permission of *Purchasing* magazine.

women-owned vendors to support the company's diversity goals. As SAS expands sourcing globally, SRM will become even more important as it will have more contracts with vendors around the world. One SRM tool, the use of e-auctions to obtain supplies, is discussed in the e-Business Connection feature.

Trends in Supplier Relationship Management

As companies source globally, the supply base can become more challenging. Companies are faced with more complex supplier relationships associated with greater distances and cultural differences. Companies need help in managing these complexities. How is supplier relationship management evolving today? A recent benchmarking study on supplier relationship management by ASUG (America's SAP Users' Group), found four trends:[50]

1. The sourcing and procurement functions are increasing in prominence within the organization and considered of strategic importance instead of back-office partners. The study found that in 25 percent of companies surveyed, the procurement function reported directly to the CEO or CFO.

2. More companies are expecting cost reductions to come from the procurement organization. The study found that 76 percent of companies have formal strategic sourcing programs focusing on cost reduction.

3. Companies recognize that reducing headcount in transactional activities and allocating staff to strategic activities are more cost effective. The study found that for top performers, only 27 percent of procurement employees are allocated for transactional activities while 73 percent are for strategic, value-added functions.

4. Companies with the most effective procurement and sourcing functions have the highest spend or purchased cost reduction. These companies have strategic sourcing programs and use technology to achieve best practices.

Overall, the study finds that the procurement and purchasing function in best-in-class companies have an increasing role and importance within the organization. These companies have gained a competitive advantage by managing suppliers strategically, implementing the latest technology, outsourcing strategically, building stronger supplier relationships, and adopting best practices.

SUMMARY

During the past two decades, the buyer-supplier relationship has evolved from an arm's-length/adversarial approach to one favoring the development of long-term partnerships. Significant competitive advantage can be achieved by organizations working closely with their suppliers. Without a shared vision, mutual benefits, and top management commitment, partnerships are likely to be short-lived. Other ingredients necessary for developing and managing lasting supplier relationships are trust, creating personal relationships, effective change management, information sharing, and using performance metrics to create superior capabilities. Mutually agreeable measures to monitor supplier performance provide the basis for continuous improvement to enhance supplier quality, cost, and delivery. Supplier certification ensures that buyers continue to work with their best suppliers to improve cost, quality, delivery, and new product development to gain a competitive advantage. Finally, supplier relationship management software automates the exchange of information and allows for improved efficiency and effectiveness in managing supplier relationships and improving performance. Organizations that successfully implement supplier relationship management can improve quality, reduce cost, access new technologies from their suppliers, increase speed-to-market, reduce risk, and achieve high performance.

KEY TERMS

analytic SRM, 96

change management, 79

continuous improvement, 83

ISO 9000, 88

ISO 14000, 88

performance scorecards, 80

posttransaction costs, 82

pretransaction, 82

supplier certification, 86

supplier development, 91

supplier partnerships, 77

supplier relationship management (SRM), 80

trade secrets, 79

transactional SRM, 96

DISCUSSION QUESTIONS

1. Why should an organization be concerned with supplier relationships?

2. Compare and contrast the arm's-length/adversarial approach to partnership approaches to the customer-supplier relationship.

3. How can an organization manage its suppliers effectively?

4. What are the key factors that contribute to a lasting supplier partnership?

5. It has often been pointed out that 60 percent of strategic alliances fail. What are the reasons for this?

6. What are the criteria used in evaluating a supplier?

7. Discuss how an organization develops a supplier evaluation and certification program.

8. Why should an organization invest in supplier development programs? What are the challenges of supplier development activities?

9. What are the benefits of ISO 9000 certification?

10. Are environmental concerns influencing purchasing decisions? What are the benefits of ISO 14000 certification?

11. Research ISO's Web site (www.iso.ch) and discuss the growth of ISO 9000 and 14000 certification by regions of the world such as Africa/West Asia, Central and South America, North America, Europe, Far East, and Australia/New Zealand.

12. What are the key capabilities of supplier relationship management software?

13. Why do organizations have supplier awards programs?

14. Why do organizations use supplier certification? What are the benefits of supplier certification?

15. What are the similarities and differences in capabilities of SRM software offered by i2, Oracle, and SAP?

16. What are the advantages of using SRM solutions to manage suppliers?

17. What are the differences between transactional and analytic SRM?

INTERNET QUESTIONS

1. Go to the SAS and SAP Web sites and compare the different features of SRM software provided by these companies.

2. Go to the Internet and find three companies that have supplier recognition programs. Compare and contrast the criteria and the award programs.

3. Go to the Internet and find three companies that have supplier development programs. Compare and contrast these programs.

INFOTRAC QUESTIONS

Access http://academic.cengage.com/infotrac to answer the following questions:

1. Search for the term "supplier relationship management" and write a report on the key areas included in the SRM software.

2. Search for the term "supplier development programs" and write a report on how companies can use supplier development programs to help them improve supplier performance.

3. Report on how companies use better supplier relationships to enhance competitiveness.

4. Write a report to show the current state of supplier relationship management technology.

SPREADSHEET PROBLEMS

1. The Margo Manufacturing Company is performing an annual evaluation of one of its suppliers, the Mimi Company. Bo, purchasing manager of the Margo Manufacturing Company, has collected the following information.

PERFORMANCE CRITERIA	SCORE	WEIGHT
Technology	85	0.10
Quality	95	0.25
Responsiveness	90	0.15
Delivery	80	0.15
Cost	90	0.20
Environment	75	0.05
Business	95	0.10
Total score		1.00

A score based on a scale of 0 (unsatisfactory) to 100 (excellent) has been assigned for each of the performance categories considered critical in assessing the supplier. Different weights are assigned to each of the performance criteria based on its relative importance. How would you evaluate the Mimi Company's performance as a supplier?

Chapter 4

STRATEGIC SOURCING FOR SUCCESSFUL SUPPLY CHAIN MANAGEMENT

Ask yourself what the pressures and priorities of the business are, and how that fits with your supply strategy. Strategic means you are important. If you are not being strategic then you are just being annoying.[1]

Stiff competition for skilled purchasers is spawning a thriving market for interim professionals across all industry sectors.[2]

Learning Objectives

After completing this chapter, you should be able to

- Describe the difference between purchasing and strategic sourcing.
- Describe how strategic sourcing plans are developed and implemented.
- Define and describe the terms green sourcing, VMI, JIT II, insourcing, co-sourcing, and co-managed inventories.
- Describe the role of sourcing personnel in managing key supplier relationships.
- Describe the performance criteria used in assessing suppliers.
- Describe how strategic supplier relationships can impact the firm.
- Describe how a reverse auction works.
- Understand the importance of sharing the benefits of strategic partnerships.
- Understand the strategic role played by the purchasing function in developing and improving the supply chain.

Chapter Outline

Introduction

Developing Successful Sourcing Strategies

Supply Base Rationalization Programs

Evaluating and Selecting Key Suppliers

Strategic Alliance and Supplier Certification Programs

Green Sourcing

Outsourcing Products and Services

Early Supplier Involvement

Strategic Alliance Development

Negotiating Win–Win Strategic Alliance Agreements

Managing and Developing Second-Tier Supplier Relationships

Use of e-Procurement Systems

Rewarding Supplier Performance

Benchmarking Successful Sourcing Practices

Using Third-Party Supply Chain Management Services

Assessing and Improving the Firm's Purchasing Function

Summary

Supply Chain Management in Action	*Green Purchasing in Office Supplies*

With some commodities, the immediate financial value of using green products may be difficult to decipher. But when it comes to office products, the value is easy to quantify, say office supplies distributors Staples and Corporate Express.

To many buyers, the most obvious office supply product to begin sustainability practices with is office paper. But sustainability practices extend beyond simply paper and can translate into longer-term savings. Mark Buckley, vice president of environmental affairs at Massachusetts-based Staples, says sustainable purchasing is not as simple as being green—it is also the life cycle of the product, how it is used, and how it is recycled at the end of its life.

"There's a misconception that green [purchasing] is in conflict with traditional purchasing, but sustainable business uses resources more efficiently," Buckley says. He says that while there may be a larger up-front investment to buy a recycled product, for instance, the overall cost savings to the buyer manifests over time.

Office supplies distributors want to make it easy for buyers to go green with minimal changes to their regular purchasing practice. Currently one-quarter of Colorado-based Corporate Express' overall catalog—not just paper products—uses recycled material that has 30–100 percent post-consumer waste (PCW) content. Even items like office furniture and cleaning chemicals can use recycled materials.

Buyers showing the highest interest in green products are in healthcare, banking, education, and government—all of which use large amounts of paper. But both Corporate Express and Staples say they see increased demand for sustainable products across the board. Buckley says some of Staples' customers emphasize the "triple bottom line" when buying for the office—environmental impact, social implication, and, of course, financial impact/cost. Distributors increasingly disclose the PCW content as well as diversity supplier information of products right on their catalog. They also encourage buyers to include sustainable purchasing criteria as part of their office supply request for proposals.

Both Corporate Express and Staples emphasize the benefits of making the buying process itself green too. Both see an increase in paperless transactions through e-procurement and Web-based services. About 80 percent of transactions with Corporate Express now occur online, and the company also uses electronic delivery tools to minimize delivery truck miles. This cuts down on overall "soft" procurement costs for a buyer, such as paperwork and delivery costs. Tom Heisroth, senior vice president of the Staples National Advantage division, estimates that 90 percent of its contract division transactions arrive via e-commerce tools, in addition to a large pickup in use of electronic payments as well, reducing overall implementation costs for buyers.

Source: Varmazis, M. "Office Distributors Give Buyers Greater Access to Green Products." *Purchasing,* 136, no. 6 (2007): 24. © 2007, *Purchasing,* reprinted by permission.

Introduction

As you have read in Chapter 2 and Chapter 3 of this text, purchasing departments are increasingly seen as highly valued, strategic contributors to the organization because of their ability to impact product design and quality, cost of goods sold, cycle time, and, hence, the firm's reputation, profitability, and competitive position. The influence of the purchasing or supply management department both within the organization and outside its boundaries is quite unique, in that it interacts with internal and external customers and suppliers, and with internal design, production, finance, marketing, and accounting personnel, as well as the firm's executive managers. As companies move toward taking a more proactive role in managing their supply chains, purchasing departments are seen as one of the primary designers and facilitators of these efforts. In fact, in many leading organizations today, and as discussed in Chapter 2, managers prefer using the broader terms *supply management* or *sourcing* rather than *purchasing* to refer to the many strategic activities beyond the mere purchase of services and materials undertaken by supply management departments or sourcing departments. **Sourcing** is thus defined here as all of the activities involved in managing the firm's external resources. In many firms, though (as well as in this textbook), the terms sourcing, purchasing, and supply management tend to be used interchangeably.

The ever-changing global economic climate has acted to hasten many organizations' plans to institute supply chain management strategies to reduce costs and delivery cycle times while improving quality, leading to improvements in long-term competitiveness and financial performance. Additionally, the increasing number of global competitors, demands by customers for firms to become more environmentally focused, the rising costs of fuel and materials, and the desire to deliver more innovative products more frequently and cheaply than competitors have also combined to place added pressures on firms to achieve breakthrough performance in supply chain management.

Today, these trends have become the drivers of **strategic sourcing** and supply chain initiatives. Taking the notion of sourcing one step further, strategic sourcing can be thought of as managing the firm's external resources in ways that support the long-term goals of the firm. This includes the make-or-buy decision, identification and selection of suppliers, managing and improving supplier relationships and capabilities, monitoring and rewarding supplier performance, developing and managing second- and third-tier supplier relationships, and the use of technology to benefit sourcing activities. Some of these topics have been introduced in earlier chapters and will only be lightly touched upon here, while other strategic sourcing topics will be covered in greater detail in this chapter.

Today, supply management personnel must be much more adept at locating and developing good suppliers, integrating them into the firm's business processes and strategies, achieving greater levels of purchased item quality, developing cost-saving sourcing plans, and achieving acceptable supplier delivery performance, as well as ensuring that purchased materials and products are consistent with internal and external customer requirements. Furthermore, because of corporate downsizing and the emphasis on cost containment, purchasing departments often must conduct these strategic sourcing activities with fewer people. These are some high expectations for purchasing managers. As a matter of fact, in an effort to save money, many firms are choosing to **outsource** the entire purchasing function. A report by the British outsourcing advisory body Everest Research Institute states that this trend is growing at 30 percent per year in the United Kingdom.[3]

On the other hand, demand for talented sourcing personnel is currently very high, as suggested by one of the chapter opening quotes. As of mid-2006, the average basic salary excluding bonuses, for a purchasing director in the United Kingdom was £66,267, or approximately \$135,000 per year.[4] And other surveys have found the demand for sourcing personnel to be so great that employers are being forced to offer higher salaries, extra perks, flexible hours, home working, and job sharing to attract buyers.[5]

Developing sourcing strategies to support a sustainable competitive advantage is no easy task. Building, maintaining, and improving supplier alliances pose many benefits for the firms involved; but many buyer–supplier relationships end in failure because of misaligned strategies, lack of commitment, unrealized goals, and loss of trust in the relationships. Purchasing managers proactively managing their firms' supply chains must also come to understand that some sourcing strategies are better suited to some supply chains than to others. Indeed, firms may have dozens of supply chains associated with their most important inbound purchased items and outbound finished products. Some of these supply chains may be driven by a low-cost overall strategy, while others may have quality or service as the overriding objective. Even different parts and components used in one product may have diverging supply chain strategies. In this chapter, we discuss the development of successful supply chain and sourcing strategies and the specific elements that constitute these strategies.

Developing Successful Sourcing Strategies

To achieve the supply chain management objectives we have described thus far in this and previous chapters, a number of sourcing strategies must be considered and implemented. Care must be taken, though, when developing these plans. Failure to align sourcing strategies with supply chain objectives, for example, may result in considerable resources being expended to design and manage a set of sourcing activities, with the resulting impact on the firm and its supply chains being much less than desired. In one of the more important papers written on this topic, Martin Fisher describes two types of supply chains: those for **functional products,** and those for innovative products.[6]

Examples of functional products are maintenance, repair, and operating (MRO) items and other commonly purchased items and supplies. These items are characterized by low profit margins, relatively stable demands, and high levels of competition. Thus, companies purchasing functional products most likely concentrate on using sourcing strategies based on securing a dependable supply at the lowest cost. Many of Wal-Mart's purchases, for example, might fall into this category. Examples of recent innovative consumer goods have been the Apple iPod and the Toyota Prius; in industrial settings, innovations might be new types of control mechanisms, new software applications, or a new piece of communications equipment. Innovative products are characterized by short product life cycles, volatile demand, high profit margins, and relatively less competition. Consequently, the sourcing criteria for these products may be more closely aligned with the supplier's quality reputation, delivery speed and flexibility, and the supplier's communication capabilities. Many of Illinois-based Motorola's purchases, for example, might fall into the innovative product category.

Many of the commonly used sourcing strategies of thirty years ago do not work well today. For instance, "squeezing" or hard-bargaining suppliers to generate a lower annual **purchasing spend** (or expense) may ultimately prove harmful to buyer–supplier relationships, eventually leading to deteriorations in quality and service, as

"Repeat after me: 'Your price is too high.' 'Your price is too high.' 'Your price is too high.'"

suppliers seek ways to cut corners in order to keep their profit margins at desired levels. If long-term sourcing plans are to be successful, they must support the firm's long-term supply chain and business strategies; and suppliers must also see some benefit from the initiatives implemented. The cost-cutting efforts of Chrysler, for example, include working with their existing suppliers to find cost-saving product alternatives, instead of resorting to hard bargaining.[7] A six-step framework for supply chain strategy development is shown in Figure 4.1.

In Step 1, the firm's suppliers and the items they supply are classified as belonging to the innovative or functional category. In Step 2, the goals of the inbound portion of the firm's supply chains are developed. Sourcing strategies derived from these goals should then ensure that purchased products are consistent with the long-term

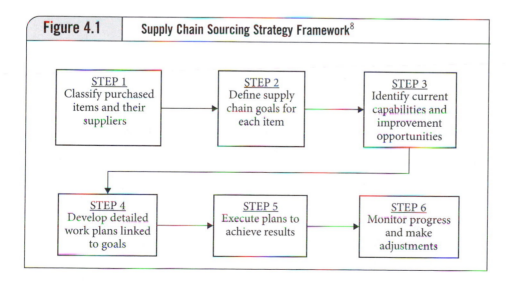

| Figure 4.1 | Supply Chain Sourcing Strategy Framework[8] |

STEP 1
Classify purchased items and their suppliers

STEP 2
Define supply chain goals for each item

STEP 3
Identify current capabilities and improvement opportunities

STEP 4
Develop detailed work plans linked to goals

STEP 5
Execute plans to achieve results

STEP 6
Monitor progress and make adjustments

objectives of the firm. For example, if the firm's overall reputation and strategy are to be the quality leaders in the firm's markets, then sourcing strategies for most of the *innovative* products, components, and parts that make up the finished products must concentrate on assuring high levels of quality, flexibility, and service as well. In Step 3, supply chain capabilities are evaluated and compared to the performances necessary to achieve the sourcing strategies from Step 2, thus identifying areas for improvement. For a company geared toward quality leadership, key suppliers will be evaluated based on their quality and service capabilities and commitment toward contributing to the firm's long-term sourcing strategies. In Step 4, the areas for improvement identified in Step 3 are taken and goals set for improving capabilities and closing these gaps. The goals must be specific and measurable, and may be the result of industry benchmarking. Measurement or performance targets are then determined to identify success in achieving these goals. The second objective of Step 4 is to develop specific work plans to meet these goals. The work plans are broken down into smaller project tasks, with target implementation dates for each of the tasks. For example, if we extend the quality thread through these last few steps, the firm may institute a goal to develop a quality certification program and then may require certification of all **key suppliers**. Thus, the certification process must be designed and communicated to all key suppliers, and then a time-phased certification implementation plan should be developed. Step 5 involves implementing the work plan successfully. This may involve an initial pilot study at one plant, for instance, to gauge the ability of the certification program to improve incoming supply quality. Finally, Step 6 is to monitor the progress and outcomes and adjust the work plans to more adequately meet the original supply chain goals. In this example, it may be that certain elements in the certification program need to be revised to more adequately meet desired quality goals.

As personnel in design, marketing, production, and other departments begin working with purchasing to develop various sourcing strategies, a number of initiatives, some of which have already been introduced in earlier chapters, may be used separately or in some combination to support the organization's long-term goals. These proactive sourcing initiatives, when combined with internal operations and customer relationship initiatives, form the foundation for successful supply chain management and, ultimately, the competitive advantage for the firm. The remainder of the chapter discusses a number of these strategic sourcing initiatives.

Supply Base Rationalization Programs

As first mentioned in Chapter 2, firms taking an active role in supply chain management seek to reduce purchases from marginal or poor-performing suppliers while increasing and concentrating purchases among their top-performing key suppliers. These firms have thus been practicing **supply base rationalization**, also referred to as **supply base reduction** or **supply base optimization**, and this has been a common occurrence since the late 1980s. Indeed, activities aimed at fostering buyer–supplier partnerships and increasing the performance and value of suppliers are simply easier when fewer suppliers are involved. Thus, supply base rationalization programs have the benefits of reduced purchase prices, fewer supplier management problems, closer and more frequent interaction between buyer and supplier, and greater overall levels of quality and delivery reliability, since only the best suppliers remain in the supply base.

At automaker Ford, Paul Wood, manager of global purchasing, describes their sourcing framework—"The framework is designed to develop long-term, closer relationships with significantly fewer suppliers. The theory is that developing closer relationships will result in better quality, lower cost, and improved innovation." The project began with Ford identifying twenty items that accounted for about 50 percent of Ford's annual production spend. "We saw that for each of these items, we might have seven, eight, nine or even more different suppliers. We want to reduce this to three or four suppliers who will supply 100 percent of that commodity." Thus, the suppliers benefit from increased business, and Ford benefits from shared innovation, increased quality, and lower cost.[9] Even if the goal in a supply chain is predominantly spend minimization, there are still typically enough competing suppliers such that only the best-performing, highest-quality, low-cost suppliers constitute an organization's supply base. Supply base rationalization is a straightforward, simple sourcing strategy, and is often the initial supply chain management effort, usually preceding the formation of long-term buyer–supplier strategic relationships.

In some cases, the focal firm must restructure its supply base while optimizing its size, by identifying new and better suppliers in addition to the firms in its supply base. This can result in even greater levels of supply base performance and possibly even increase the total number of firms in the supply base. A supply base should also be viewed as a dynamic or evolving entity. Suppliers come and go, and they often develop new and better capabilities; thus, revisiting supply bases annually or as purchasing contracts expire makes good economic sense. Obviously, monitoring the performance of existing suppliers also helps in assuring that the supply base is meeting quality, cost, and service standards.

Evaluating and Selecting Key Suppliers

Supplier evaluation and selection, as discussed in general in Chapter 2 and more specifically in Chapter 3, involve the careful use of multiple criteria for supplier screening and evaluation purposes. Rationalizing the supply base, as discussed in the previous section, requires use of performance criteria that relate to the competitive strategies of the firm and each particular supply chain.

When evaluating suppliers for potential strategic partnering or **collaborative relationships**, these criteria take on added importance. In these cases, purchase cost becomes relatively less important, although it is likely that over time, long-term buyer–supplier agreements will allow suppliers to concentrate more resources on reducing their costs, resulting in lower selling prices. As the reliance on these key suppliers increases, firms must manage their supply base as an extension of their internal operations.

Supplier evaluation and selection criteria, described in detail in Chapter 3, can initially allow firms to screen out undesirable suppliers but are also used to build better ongoing supplier relationships, improve the overall performance of the supply base, and, ultimately, provide competitive advantage to the organization and its supply chain. Studies indicate that only about half of the firms in the United States formally evaluate suppliers using evaluation forms or **scorecards** that have been created for this purpose.[10] The U.S. defense contractor Lockheed Martin Corporation of Maryland, for instance, has some of the toughest supplier performance standards in the industry. Their supplier performance evaluation system has measurements in four categories—quality, delivery, affordability, and management/administration. In 1999, they developed their STAR Supplier Program to recognize their top-performing suppliers with the additional objective of developing stronger supply chain relationships. Less than one-half of 1 percent of Lockheed's suppliers have been designated as STAR suppliers.[11]

Communicating supplier evaluation criteria and minimum performance expectations to existing and potential suppliers communicates the firm's expectations and creates performance standards that, in turn, become strategic goals for the suppliers. Incremental improvements can thus be achieved by increasing supplier performance expectations over time. These criteria, then, act to further integrate key suppliers with the organization.

Once the buyer–supplier relationship is established, firms periodically monitor supplier performance using essentially the same criteria, which might have been modified based on purchase contract requirements. Contracts with strategic suppliers are increasingly becoming long-term, resulting in even closer relationships, more effective two-way communication, a greater willingness to share information, and even better supplier performance. These important channel partnerships provide continuous and increasing value for all of the participants, and this is termed **channel equity**.[12] Many firms are requiring their supply bases pursue the same continuous improvement strategies they have created for themselves. Motorola does this by requiring suppliers to satisfy improvement goals in four areas: progressing toward attaining perfect product quality, remaining on the leading edge of product and process technology, practicing just-in-time manufacturing and delivery, and offering cost-competitive service. To these ends, Motorola uses a comprehensive performance evaluation system to keep track of suppliers' progress.[13]

When selecting key suppliers to use for important purchased items or services, a cross-functional team selection approach is used, wherein purchasing staff, primary users, product designers, and manufacturing personnel are involved in designing the supplier evaluation instrument and its distribution to various suppliers. Once evaluations are completed, suppliers are selected and agreements are discussed and finalized between this group and the suppliers. Ongoing evaluations are also frequently administered using the same or a similar group.

Strategic Alliance and Supplier Certification Programs

Proactively seeking and creating **strategic supplier alliances** have become important objectives of firms seeking to manage their supply chains, as we read in Chapter 3. Strategic alliances are a more formalized type of collaborative relationship, involving commitments to long-term cooperation, shared benefits and costs, joint problem solving, continuous improvement, and information sharing. Because of these relationships, suppliers are able to invest more of their resources toward becoming specialized in areas required by the buyer, to establish production and/or storage facilities close to the buyer's facilities, to purchase compatible communication and information systems, and to invest in better technology that will ultimately improve product quality and delivery time.

Supplier certification programs are one way to identify strategic alliance candidates. In many cases, certification programs are simply based on internationally recognized certifications like the Switzerland-based International Organization for Standardization's ISO 9000 series of quality certifications.[14] For the organization actively managing its supply chain, this type of certification requirement is good, but may not be specific enough in areas of importance to the firm. In these cases, firms develop their own formal certification programs, most of which require ISO 9000 or similar quality certifications as one element of the certification process.

An extensive site audit may be performed using a cross-functional team to identify a supplier's process capabilities, materials and methods used, and to assure that a certain level of management control exists. Buyers can monitor quality assurance methods, for instance, and identify the type of **acceptance sampling** and **statistical process control (SPC)** methods used.

Certification teams can also detect potential weaknesses and areas in need of improvement during these site audits, which can mean the difference between a successful and an unsuccessful supplier relationship. Formal certification programs require this type of physical contact, as well as visits of supplier representatives to the buyer facility to discuss buyer requirements, production characteristics, and other typical buyer–supplier interactions or sourcing elements. Additionally, certification programs typically include surveys given to the supplier and meetings with a sample of the supplier's current customers to obtain feedback on the supplier's performance.

For existing suppliers, certification procedures can be somewhat different, since much of the information is already known to the buyer. Still, certifications and re-certifications of existing suppliers most likely contain periodic surveys, site visits, and reviews of performance.

Formal certification programs thus assure a level of capability among suppliers and act as a way to communicate performance requirements and areas in need of improvement to the supplier or supply base. Taken in a positive way, strategic suppliers can see this feedback as an extremely important tool for improving their performance and competitiveness. In this environment, certification programs are viewed as win–win exercises. Automaker Chrysler LLC is on a mission to prove to the world that it can build reliable vehicles. To accomplish this, representatives of Chrysler's supply base are encouraged to attain Six Sigma Black Belt quality certifications, and so far, over 40 suppliers have taken part in the process. In fact, five of Chrysler's top executives have attained Black Belt certifications.[15]

Green Sourcing

Also termed **sustainable procurement**, **green sourcing** has become the current buzz-word of strategic sourcing, and for good reason. In recent years, the growing awareness about global warming and the need to protect the environment has been helped along by the likes of former U.S. vice president and longtime environmentalist Al Gore, who wrote the bestselling book *Earth in the Balance* in 1992 and, more recently, starred in the award-winning 2006 film documentary *An Inconvenient Truth*. Additionally, awards such as the Goldman Environmental Prize have served to encourage environmental reform and provided global publicity for specific environmental problems. The Goldman Prize began in 1990 and, since its inception, has awarded 113 people from 67 countries $125,000 each. Eight winners have gone on to become appointed or elected officials, and the 1991 prize winner, Wangari Maathai, also won the 2004 Nobel Peace Prize (Al Gore won the Nobel Peace Prize in 2007 for his environmental work).[16] Finally, many organizations and their supply chain trading partners are obtaining environmental certifications such as ISO 14000 as a way to show potential buyers that their systems meet certain environmental standards.[17] Perhaps just as important, and as shown in the discussion on green retailing in the chapter opening feature Supply Chain Management in Action, businesses today are discovering that significant additional profits can be realized from acting environmentally responsible.

Worldwide leading retailer Wal-Mart, already one of the global leaders in supply chain management, has recently taken a leading role in terms of **sustainability**. Wal-Mart president and CEO Lee Scott, in a speech in October 2005, described how sustainability permeates Wal-Mart and has become an integral part of their decision making. One of Wal-Mart's goals, for example, is to reduce packaging by 5 percent by 2013. This will prevent approximately 667 metric tons of carbon dioxide from entering the atmosphere each year. Prior to Christmas 2005, the company "right-sized" packaging on 277 SKUs (stock keeping units) of its Kid Connection toys, resulting in the use of 727 fewer shipping containers and the harvesting of 5100 fewer trees that year. They also, by the way, saved $3.5 million in transportation costs. Now, Wal-Mart wants to be supplied 100 percent by renewable energy, create zero waste, and sell products that sustain resources and the environment. Starting in 2008, Wal-Mart's 2000 private brand suppliers will be graded on things like cube utilization, recycled content, recovery value of materials used, transport distance, and carbon dioxide emissions. Wal-Mart expects these actions will reduce their costs considerably.[18]

The topics of green sourcing, sustainable procurement, and sustainability can be the source of much confusion, though, in various industries and even within an organization. In a survey of 100 U.K. buyers in both the public and private sectors, only 17 percent said they thought the concepts were fully understood. "The problem is the terms sustainable, green, ethical and fair trade are used interchangeably and in a confusing way," said one survey respondent. "The issue does not just cover what we buy, but how we buy, and this is the area that suffers a lack of understanding," said another.[19] According to the globally recognized Institute for Supply Management, green sourcing is defined as:

> *Making environmentally conscious decisions throughout the purchasing process, beginning with product and process design, and through product disposal.*

Additionally, sustainability is defined as:

> *The ability to meet current needs without hindering the ability to meet the needs of future generations in terms of economic, environmental and social challenges.*

Thus, green sourcing or sustainable procurement can be seen as a subset of the broader term sustainability.[20]

Governments and leading businesses are now getting involved, to set some clear targets for organizations to achieve. For example, in 2005, U.K. Prime Minister Tony Blair set up a business-led group called the Sustainable Procurement Task Force (SPTF) to examine how funds can be spent in a sustainable manner. The aim of the group was to show how sustainable purchases could benefit organizations, help society, boost the economy, and support the natural environment. Some examples of sustainable procurement where the SPTF has assisted include:

- Manchester City's Eastlands Stadium has built a wind turbine on site that produces three megawatts of power, and they purchase most things locally to insure use of local suppliers and reduced emissions;
- Dorset County Council reviewed its fleet vehicles to reduce emissions,
- Warwickshire County Council recycled demolition materials into road paving materials, and
- Brighton & Hove City Council developed a library with little impact on the environment.[21]

Another problem is the perceived conflict between higher sourcing costs caused by adherence to green sourcing policies, and the need to keep costs under control. "If a buyer was asked why he had not saved any money this year, a response of 'well, I didn't save any money, but I helped save the planet,' is hardly going to impress the CEO," says Adam Smith, a senior buyer at Ceramaspeed, a U.K.-based manufacturer of electronic heating and control systems.[22] Matt Kissler, vice president of package and product innovation at Wal-Mart's membership warehouse affiliate Sam's Club, may have gotten to the heart of the matter when he said "Sustainability is not just about the environment. No matter how good we do things for the environment, if they are not sustainable for our business, sustainability will not work. If what we are doing is not sustainable financially for our business entities, we should not be doing it."[23]

From the supplier's perspective, there are tools available to help determine what buyers want, in terms of environmentally friendly goods. The EcoMarkets Survey, created by the Canadian environmental marketing agency TerraChoice, for example, surveys up to 6000 business and government buyers annually, to learn how organizations are greening their supply chains. Some of their general findings are:

- The number of organizations buying green is increasing.
- Energy conservation is the most popular aspect of green sourcing.
- The market for environmentally friendly products is large and growing rapidly.[24]

Firms, their supply chains, and government agencies alike are coming to realize that every purchase has a global environmental impact, and with careful sourcing, money can be saved. Collection, transport, manufacturing, and scrapping of raw materials and finished products require the use of fossil fuels; products purchased from distant suppliers require greater amounts of fuel for transportation; use of ships or rail for transporting products use less fuel than trucks or airlines; plant-based products generally have a smaller environmental impact than petroleum-based ones; factories powered by solar or wind power have a smaller environmental impact than factories powered by oil or coal; and energy-efficient products consume less energy. The City of Portland, Oregon, for instance, has been busy tracking its greenhouse gas emissions since 1993, when it became the first U.S. city to launch a global warming action plan. In 2001, they replaced all of their traffic lights with LEDs, cutting annual energy use by 4.9 million kilowatt hours, reducing annual CO_2 emissions by 2300 tons, and saving $500,000 annually.

As of early 2007, thirty-five states in the United States were requiring use of hybrid vehicles, and over 4000 were in use in government fleets. Buying recycled paper means that less energy is used to make paper, and fewer trees are cut down. Buying one pound of recycled paper, for instance, also eliminates one pound of atmospheric pollutants.[25] Buyers today can thus have an impact on their environment as well as on their organizations' costs. Table 4.1 describes some steps organizations can take to utilize green sourcing.

Table 4.1	**Greening Your Firm's Sourcing**
STEPS	**EXPLANATION**
1. Establish corporate green sourcing policies.	Legitimizes the change from traditional procedures, verifies top management support, establishes a vision and direction, enforces the importance of green sourcing, reduces confusion.
2. Start with a focus on a small basket of items.	Get used to purchasing with an environmental mindset. Look at what trading partners are doing. Look at your firm's environmental interests. Pick the "low hanging fruit" that will have the greatest impact. Get comfortable with the process before expanding and going corporatewide.
3. Educate the users.	Provide training for employees that must use the policies—janitors, maintenance and clerical workers, and anyone who doesn't believe in "green." Use information from outside sources like the North American Green Purchasing Initiative.
4. Develop a green performance measurement system.	Measurement provides accountability and a way to improve over time. Track even the smallest actions to build pride in being green. Revisit measures periodically.
5. Use certified green products and services.	Ask questions of suppliers. Get copies of suppliers' green policies, standards, and testing procedures. Require certifications done by third parties like GreenSeal or ISO.
6. Expand the focus toward sustainability.	Use the purchasing department's internal and external influence to grow awareness and use in other departments and among the firm's customers. Introduce purchasing based on ethical, human rights, community involvement, or other social considerations.

Source: Based in part on Newman, D. "Steps You Can Take to 'Green' Your Procurement." *Summit,* 9, no. 4 (2006): 10.

Outsourcing Products and Services

Purchasing spend as a percentage of sales has been growing over the years, as firms have opted to outsource materials, parts, services, and assembled components to concentrate more of their resources and energy on core business activities. Simply put, many manufacturing firms are buying more and making less these days. In managed supply chains where a high level of trust permeates the buyer–supplier relationship, the use of outsourcing is even higher. In the Arizona-based Center for Advanced Purchasing Studies (CAPS) Cross-Industry Benchmarking Report combining both service and manufacturing firms, annual purchase spend as a percentage of sales in the United States was approximately 43 percent for 2006.[26] Firms are outsourcing noncore products and service functions (i.e., maintenance, janitorial, or other support services) and, in some supply chain situations, more strategic products or services are outsourced, which can impact the competitiveness of the firm. Notably, outsourcing gives firms the potential to leverage larger purchase volumes to gain quantity discounts, particularly if purchases are concentrated among fewer suppliers. Additionally, industrial buyers can typically negotiate better associated supply services as well when purchasing in larger quantities.

Aside from allowing firms to concentrate more on core capabilities while potentially reducing their costs, outsourcing can also result in reduced staffing levels or the redeployment of staff, accelerated reengineering efforts, reduced management problems, and gains in manufacturing flexibility. These benefits must be weighed against the risks associated with outsourcing, including loss of control, increased need for supplier management, and an increased reliance on suppliers. When outsourcing strategically important products or services, these risks can be very significant. Consequently, supplier selection can be an extremely important activity when outsourcing.

Outsourcing typically occurs as the result of a make-or-buy analysis, as addressed in Chapter 2. At this point, an outsourcing team is created with representation from all stakeholder areas in the firm. The team leader is most often a staff member from purchasing. The team's objective is to identify the organization's long-term needs for the outsourcing project, identify and select the supplier, negotiate and finalize the outsourcing agreement with the supplier based on the identified long-term needs, and then plan the transition and execution of the outsourcing project.

In cases where firms are actively managing their supply chains, firms often outsource products and services to suppliers who are already or are on the verge of becoming strategic partners or key suppliers. These outsourcing arrangements can be used to further solidify a trading relationship, to gain additional negotiating leverage, and to minimize the outsourcing risks mentioned in the preceding paragraph. In these cases, outsourcing to highly capable and reliable suppliers can lead to improved quality as well as lower prices, particularly when the outsourced product or service is a core product of the supplier. In some trading relationships, outsourcing is done in both directions if the supplier and buyer both have core competencies in product areas desired by the other.

Insourcing

Unfortunately, some firms do not adequately study the decision to outsource, and experience problems with a supplier's product quality, late deliveries, or services not living up to expectations. In these cases, the outsourcing arrangement is unsuccessful and can result in **insourcing**, also referred to as **backsourcing**. One study found that approximately one-third of outsourcing contracts are eventually canceled. Some of the recent outsourcing failures have received significant attention in the press. For example, global financial giant JPMorgan Chase & Co. rescinded its IT outsourcing agreement with IBM after only two years of what was expected to be a seven-year, $5 billion arrangement.[27] Global energy company Chevron also recently arranged to bring back in-house some activities that had been previously outsourced. This created a need in Chevron to develop a careful long-term strategy for evaluating insourcing and outsourcing activities. "When you completely outsource as a 'black box,' you can't rely on a third party to understand how your organization works," says Richard Nitz, telecommunications infrastructure manager at Chevron. Now, Chevron uses their strategic retention model to help them decide what functions to retain at Chevron and what less-strategic functions it makes sense to outsource.[28]

Insourcing, though, does not always mean that a firm has reversed a decision to outsource. When one firm outsources, another firm must, in turn, insource that product or service. With financial services, for instance, banks seeking to expand their market share often offer their clients a wide array of financial products and services, branding them as their own, while in reality other larger, global banks such as Wachovia are most likely performing the services. In this case, Wachovia has insourced these services.

Some companies are turning outsourcing on its head. Jeff Meehan of R.T. London, a furniture manufacturing company headquartered in Michigan, explains, "If we can insource it, we will. Our goal is to shrink the lead time and increase the throughput. The way to do that is by insourcing." R.T. London used to primarily do the final assembly while outsourcing all their components. Through insourcing and attention to lean manufacturing principles, they have reduced product lead times by 50 percent, increased output, improved customer service, and enabled employees to think more like owners.[29]

Co-sourcing

In yet another variation of the outsourcing theme, and in many cases the most popular outsourcing arrangement, is to use **co-sourcing**, also referred to as **selective sourcing**. Co-sourcing refers to the sharing of a process or function between internal staff and an external provider. Typically, firms will retain the more strategic activities, while outsourcing the more resource intensive, non-value-adding activities. The firm is thus able to retain control over the most vital parts of a product or service. Co-sourcing gives a firm the flexibility to decide what areas to outsource, when, and for how long. This also can be an appealing option for companies that have yet to create long-term supplier relationships, are in transition because of a merger or acquisition, or are facing financial problems.

For some IT services, co-sourcing has been shown to result in the most successful outsourcing arrangements. One research study found that firms choosing to completely outsource their IT application development efforts experienced lower overall levels of product quality, relationship quality, and service quality, as well as higher costs, when compared to firms that co-sourced.[30] For customer contact centers, firms may opt to retain some contact capabilities while outsourcing others. Tom Johnson, managing director at BearingPoint, a global management consulting firm based in Virginia, explains, "Co-sourcing for extended hours, multilingual capabilities, [and] level-two problems or even level-one, are certainly ways to drive your cost out…[and] give you expanded capabilities and competencies without taking on the fixed costs." AAA Arizona, for example, uses virtual contact center service provider Arise, based in Florida, to incorporate telecommuting agents to handle their call overflow during busy periods in the morning and late afternoon.[31]

Early Supplier Involvement

As the adoption of concurrent engineering and design for manufacturability techniques become more commonplace and relationships with suppliers become more trusted, reliable, and long-term in nature, key suppliers become more heavily involved in the internal operations of their industrial customers, including managing inventories of their products at the customers' points of use and participating in their customers' new product and process design processes. Key suppliers can become contributors to these efforts by serving in a decision-making capacity for purchase timing and quantities, and on new product and process design teams within the firm. They become involved managing the buyer firm's inventories and participating in product part and assembly design, new product materials usage, and even the design of the processes to be used in manufacturing new products. Thus, strategic suppliers play a greater role in their customers' decision-making processes as the trading relationships mature, which in turn further solidifies the supply chain.

While serving on a customer's new product development team, a supplier representative's input can help the firm to reduce material cost, improve new product quality, and reduce product development time. Cost reductions come about through use of more standardized parts, fewer parts, and less expensive materials. Cost, quality, and delivery timing improvements all come about when suppliers use the information gained through **early supplier involvement** to design parts and processes at their own facilities to match the buyer's specifications. Additionally, since they have been involved early on, in the buyer's new product design process, these part and process changes can be timed to be in place and available when first needed by the buyer. Use of these **value engineering** techniques with help from the supplier allows firms to design better quality and cost savings into the products from the time a product first hits the shelves. Over the product's life, this can generate significant savings and revenues while reducing the need for cost-savings initiatives later on.

Early supplier involvement is perhaps one of the most effective supply chain integrative techniques. Buyers and suppliers working together—sharing proprietary design and manufacturing information that their competitors would love to see—establishes a level of trust and cooperation that results in many future collaborative and potentially successful projects. Discussions of several other early supplier involvement activities follow.

Vendor Managed Inventories

Vendor managed inventory (VMI) services for key customers is perhaps one of the more value-enhancing activities performed by suppliers when their past performance allows buyers to develop trust in the supplier's ability to manage buyer inventories, such that inventory carrying costs are minimized and stockouts are avoided. From the buying firm's perspective, allowing a supplier to track inventories and determine delivery schedules and order quantities saves time, which may be better spent on more strategic sourcing activities. Additionally, buyers can delay taking ownership of product until it reaches the stocking location, reducing inventory carrying costs. For the supplier, it means they avoid ill-advised orders from buyers, they get to decide how inventory is set up, when to ship it, how to ship it, where it goes, and they have the opportunity to educate their customers about their other products. According to an *Industry Week* 2006 survey, fourteen of the top twenty-five U.S. manufacturing plants between 2002 and 2006 used suppliers to track and replenish inventories. On a dollar volume basis, about 14 percent of the purchased materials of these firms were vendor managed.[32]

Ideally, these valued suppliers manage their customers' inventories using real-time visibility of inventory movements in their customers' storage areas or at the point of assembly or sale. This can be accomplished with bar code labels and scanners that instantly update computer counts of inventories as the items are used or sold. This data is stored and made available to trusted suppliers using for instance, **electronic data interchange (EDI)** or a secured Web site. This allows a supplier to profile demand and determine an accurate forecast and then to ship an order quantity when the inventory levels become low enough—the **reorder point (ROP).** Electronic data interchange, an XML format that lets buyers and suppliers exchange information via computer-to-computer Internet communications, is helpful for VMI situations as well as for exchanging pricing, product availability, and catalog and order status information.

Wal-Mart is generally given credit for popularizing the use of VMI in the mid-1990s when it initiated a relationship with Proctor & Gamble to manage its diaper inventories. A similar arrangement with Rubbermaid soon followed.[33] Lake Erie Screw, a fastener and bolt manufacturer located in Indiana, uses a local supplier to manage its inventory of bar code labels. Once a week, bar code inventory data is automatically transmitted to the supplier's inventory tracking system, where it is compared to the reorder point and established order quantities are shipped when the reorder point is reached.[34] Michigan-based Dow Chemical uses office supply giant Staples as a sole supplier to manage office supplies across all of its U.S. and Canadian manufacturing sites. "They're on-site with their trucks every day and they're using a Staples system to manage that inventory effectively to pre-established minimum and maximum levels," says Tary Schumacher, global supply manager for Dow. For low-turnover items, Dow employees order whatever they need, using a dedicated Staples Web site.[35]

A somewhat more collaborative form of VMI is termed **co-managed inventories**. In this case, the buyer and supplier reach an agreement regarding the buyer's periodic demand forecasts, how information is shared, the order quantity, when an order is generated, and the delivery timing and location. This type of controlled VMI may be preferable for very high value, strategic item purchases, where the customer desires more input into the day-to-day supply activities, or perhaps as a precursor to a sole-source VMI where the buyer is still assessing the supplier's ability to take full responsibility for the order fulfillment process.

JIT II

Also referred to as **supplier co-location**, JIT II is an extension of the vendor managed inventory concept (recall that JIT is an abbreviation for just-in-time, a much broader concept than JIT II, and is discussed at length in Chapter 8). Mr. Lance Dixon, who at the time was a purchasing manager at the Massachusetts-based Bose Corp., is credited with creating the JIT II concept in 1987. The concept refers to a situation wherein a supplier's employee is permanently located in the purchasing department of the buyer's organization, acting as both buyer and supplier representative. This person is given all the rights and duties of an employee for the purchasing organization—they forecast demand, monitor inventory levels, and place purchase orders, and they have access to all of the files and records of the firm.

Back in 1987 this idea was very controversial; Bose had a somewhat typical view of suppliers at the time—apply pressure on them to achieve lower prices. But Dixon realized that the costs of poor supplier performance far exceeded potential purchase spend savings, so he pushed ahead with his idea of co-location. Within five years, Bose reported a savings of $1 million in overhead alone. Lance Dixon noted, "On parts from G&F Industries, moreover, the new system has allowed a reduction in inventories to one-seventh or even one-ninth the already low levels we had reached with our conventional Just-In-Time program."[36] Within a few years, many firms had adopted supplier co-location, including Harley-Davidson, Honeywell, IBM, Intel, DuPont, Ford, Motorola, and AT&T. "One of the real bangs for the buck of JIT II is that suppliers, who have more expertise on the parts they supply than their customers do, can suggest modifications during the design phase that customers would not know about on their own," says Bill Grimes, a former vice president of global supply for Honeywell.[37]

Several advantages exist for both sides of a JIT II relationship. The purchasing organization gets the use of a cost-free employee who understands their particular problems and requirements and who can easily communicate these needs to the supplier. The supplier gets the security of future purchases and the "first mover" advantage of having someone on-site when new items need to be purchased. Communication between both firms also improves with this arrangement. The supplier representative learns very quickly about new products and design changes occurring at the customer's firm that are going to impact the supplier. This person also learns about production problems potentially caused by the supplier's products and customer service performance, and can help to more quickly alleviate these problems. The arrangement serves both sides, and creates a much closer working relationship between the two companies. At the Chrysler Group's automobile plant in Toledo, Ohio, three suppliers are co-located within the plant to manage and operate body, paint, and chassis operations. "At the Chrysler Group, we love to defy conventional wisdom," says Thomas LaSorda, of Chrysler. The savings accrued to these partnerships is enough to pay for the design and manufacture of an additional vehicle, according to LaSorda.[38] At Bose, the team of co-located supplier personnel handling just Bose's transportation function represent a less-than-truckload carrier, a truckload carrier, an import/export brokerage firm, and a major ocean carrier. These representatives are each linked to their respective firm's information system, and work daily with Bose's transportation group and each other to assure parts and products arrive at Bose facilities when they are needed. The system has reduced late shipments by 50 percent, transportation costs by 37 percent, and shipping errors by 87 percent.[39]

Strategic Alliance Development

As the growth of supply chain management continues, firms must also become more adept at managing their suppliers and more willing to assist them in improving their production and service capabilities. Simply put, **supplier management**, as first defined in Chapter 1 and then further discussed in Chapter 3, is concerned with getting suppliers to do what firms need them to do, while **strategic alliance development,** an extension of supplier development (covered in Chapter 3), refers to increasing a *key or strategic supplier's* capabilities. A number of activities already discussed in this textbook such as supply base reduction, supplier evaluation, and certification programs, constitute forms of supplier management. As supply bases become smaller, more opportunities for creating collaborative relationships with buyers also occur. As a whole, then, supply bases become more manageable. Supplier management activities tend to become somewhat less time-consuming as strategic supplier alliances begin to constitute more and more of the supply base, while alliance development begins to occupy more of the purchasing function's time and resources.

Business owners and executives are beginning to realize that strategic supplier alliances, if successful, can result in better market penetration, access to new technologies and knowledge, and higher returns on investment than competitors with no such alliances. Massachusetts-based defense contractor Raytheon, for example, uses the formation of strategic supplier alliances as part of its Six Sigma quality initiative.[40] Managing these alliances, though, can result in expensive failures and unrealized goals perhaps as much as 60 to 70 percent of the time, and thus require a significant effort on both sides to assure that these relationships stay beneficial to both parties.[41]

As discussed in Chapter 3, a number of supplier development activities exist, and these become more vital to the firm as outsourcing continues and as the firm comes to depend more on a smaller group of vital suppliers. Alliance development will eventually even extend to a firm's second-tier suppliers, as the firm's key suppliers begin to form their own alliance development activities. Alliance development among the firm and its key suppliers tends to be much more of a collaborative activity, requiring both sides to commit time, people, communication, and monetary resources to achieving goals that will benefit both parties. Instead of simply providing one-time assistance to help solve a particular problem, or presenting a seminar that will soon be forgotten, alliance development results in retained learning because of the commitment of relationship management personnel from both trading partners. The focal firm and its key suppliers jointly decide on improvement activities, resources required, and the means to measure progress. As the improvements and learning take place, suppliers eventually become capable of passing these same capabilities on to their key suppliers and extending these capabilities up the supply chain.

Strategic alliance development requires companies to improve relationship value systems within their organizations' cultures, learn from their mistakes and from the successes of other alliances within their firms, and make investments to enable collaborative problem solving. Many firms are hiring strategic relationship managers, whose sole job is to build trust, commitment, and mutual value within the alliance. These relationship managers work on negotiating win–win collaborations resulting mutual benefits, such that alliances become the norm among the various business units in the organization. Strategic supplier alliances, like products, have their own life cycles, requiring ongoing management, development, and negotiating activities to monitor success, manage conflict, evaluate the current fit with partners, revisit the ground rules for working together, and make adjustments through mutual problem solving and information sharing.

Some of the more successful alliance-generating companies like Hewlett-Packard, Oracle, and Eli Lilly & Co. have directors of strategic alliances. They function as the coordinators of the strategic alliance programs and facilitators of other alliance-related activities, like providing educational programs, developing guidelines for alliance management, finding alliance partners, and creating alliance teams. These alliances also create external visibility for the firm, affect the firm's reputation, and create significant value for the firm. In fact, in their study on strategic alliances, Dyer, Kale, and Singh found that a firm's stock price jumped 1 percent for each announcement of a new alliance.[42] Organizing and managing a successful alliance program is thus very important to the firm's competitiveness. Table 4.2 describes the strategic alliance organization process.

To make strategic alliance programs successful, firms must determine how to organize a program that can cut across firm functions; disseminate program information

Table 4.2	Maintaining a Successful Strategic Alliance Program
STEPS	**DISCUSSION**
1. Determine the key strategic parameters to organize around.	Can be based on business units, geographic areas, industries, key alliance partners, or combinations of these.
2. Facilitate the dissemination of information.	Alliance management and development information should be centrally controlled and available through internal Web sites, pamphlets, internal experts, workshops.
3. Elevate the importance of the strategic alliance program.	Assign a director or vice president of alliance programs, reporting to top management. Establish consistent procedures for alliance programs throughout the organization.
4. Provide continuous evaluation of alliance performance, visibility, and support.	Management can increase the value and acceptance of alliance programs when successes are made visible to the firm's lower-level managers and employees. Alliance management requires resources and ongoing reevaluation.
5. Reward suppliers as performance merits.	Rewards typically include increased business and other nonmonetary awards.

Source: Adapted from Dyer, J., P. Kale, and H. Singh. "How to Make Strategic Alliances Work." *Sloan Management Review*, 42, no. 4 (2001): 37–43.

quickly and effectively throughout the organization; acquire the necessary resources; create program acceptance by the line managers and their employees; achieve concrete, measurable success; and reward supplier performance. Some firms have chosen to organize their key alliance partners by assigning alliance managers to each of these partners. Others have decided to create an alliance board to oversee alliances and coordinate alliance managers in various divisions within the organization or in different geographic regions of the world. An extremely important responsibility of the alliance managers is to facilitate the distribution of alliance development information throughout the organization.

The alliance function can act as a clearinghouse for information regarding all types of alliance needs, from negotiation strategies to problem-solving assistance to outreach programs and workshops. To give the alliance function credibility, the program director should report to the organization's top management. This facilitates the use of company resources and provides internal visibility to the function. Alliance strategies, goals, policies, and procedures can then be generated and communicated across the entire organization. Finally, since alliance goals change over time, they must be evaluated periodically. Some alliances may no longer be performing adequately, and should be discontinued. Performance evaluation metrics must be established, and as alliances show signs of success, strategies can be shared across the various alliance boundaries. As briefly mentioned earlier, continued alliance success depends on both the supplier and the buyer getting value from the alliance; the topic of negotiations with strategic alliance relationships follows.

Negotiating Win–Win Strategic Alliance Agreements

When negotiating with strategic alliances, the most advantageous outcome occurs when both parties utilize **collaborative negotiations**. This is sometimes also referred to as **integrative negotiations**. In other words, both sides work together to maximize the joint outcome, or to create a win–win result. The belief is that there is more to gain from collaborating, rather than trying to seek an outcome that favors primarily one side's interests (referred to as **distributive negotiations**). For collaborative negotiations to succeed, members from both parties must trust each other, believe in the validity of each other's perspective, and be committed to working together. From the perspective of key supply chain trading partners, these requirements should already be present so that collaborative negotiations may be easier to achieve in actively managed supply chains.

Successful integrative negotiations or bargaining also requires open discussions and a free flow of information between parties. In contrast, distributive bargaining usually means that some information will be withheld, distorted, delayed, or completely misrepresented. The likelihood that one or the other or some combination of the two methods occurs depends on the nature of the trading relationship, the strategic nature of the item(s) being negotiated, and potentially the balance of power in the relationship. In the automotive sector, particularly at Toyota, collaborative negotiations are described to be part of a *lean thinking* approach to supplier relationships, although automobile manufacturers typically enjoy high levels of buyer dominance, which may tilt the negotiating scales somewhat in the buyer's favor.

To maximize the likelihood of achieving equitable collaborative negotiations, supply chain partners should first develop a collaborative negotiation infrastructure and then facilitate a negotiating approach that supports a win–win outcome. Table 4.3 describes the steps in developing a collaboration infrastructure. Over time, purchasing representatives will get better at collaborative negotiations as they become more familiar with their trading partners' interests, learn from previous negotiations, and determine how best to work with each trading partner. Managers or negotiating team leaders can also aid in this process by maximizing exchanges of information, dealing fairly with negotiating problems, creating an environment of information sharing, and brainstorming options for achieving mutual gains.

Table 4.3	Developing a Collaborative Negotiation Infrastructure
STEPS	**DESCRIPTION**
1. Build a preparation process.	Gain an understanding of both parties' interests; brainstorm value-maximizing solutions and terms; identify objective criteria wherein both sides evaluate fairness of an agreement.
2. Develop a negotiation database.	Review previous negotiations to catalog standards, practices, precedents, metrics, creative solutions used, and lessons learned.
3. Design a negotiation launch process.	Create an environment allowing parties to first focus on how they will work together to create a shared vocabulary, build working relationships, and map out a shared decision-making process.
4. Institute a feedback mechanism.	Create a debriefing process to provide feedback to negotiating teams and capture lessons learned.

Source: Adapted from Kliman, S. "Enabling Win-Win." *Executive Excellence,* 17, no. 4 (2000): 9–11.

Managing and Developing Second-Tier Supplier Relationships

As already alluded to, developing effective alliances with key suppliers tends to create effective second-tier supplier relationships as key suppliers embark on alliance development programs of their own. A study by Drs. Park and Hartley confirms this. They showed that supplier management practices adopted by first-tier suppliers impacted second-tier supplier performance, which then, in turn, impacted the first-tier suppliers' quality and delivery performance to the focal firm.[43]

Thus, successful alliance development can indirectly create successful, high-performing second-tier and, eventually, even third-tier relationships as well, as supplier management and development practices are implemented and sequentially passed back up the supply chain from tier to tier. This becomes yet another benefit of long-term supplier alliance building efforts.

Organizations can also take a more direct approach to second-tier supplier management and development by requiring direct suppliers to acquire goods and services from specific suppliers and under specific conditions. They can also work directly with supplier alliance partners in solving second-tier supplier problems, designing supplier selection and certification programs, and implementing alliance development strategies. Doing the math, though, shows that a firm's influence is substantially reduced among second- and third-tier suppliers (e.g., if each firm in the supply chain has twenty suppliers, the focal firm will have 400 suppliers in its second-tier network and 8000 suppliers in its third-tier network).

However daunting these numbers may seem, managing these more distant members of the supplier networks will significantly impact the overall cycle time, cost, and quality for the supply chain members, creating even greater competitive advantage. Information technology often plays a role in achieving successful second-tier supplier management. Wal-Mart and the U.S. Department of Defense for example, are mandating that second-tier suppliers become RFID-enabled to add visibility of product movement as it passes through their supply chains.[44]

Use of e-Procurement Systems

As discussed in Chapter 2, using the Internet in procurement can create enormous benefits to organizations with mostly paper-based procurement systems and a large volume of standard, functional item, or maintenance, repair, and operating (MRO) supplies purchases. The primary strategic benefits of **e-procurement** include significant cost savings and the freeing up of time for purchasing staff to concentrate on more of the firm's core business activities. This comes about because e-procurement systems enable the concentration of a large volume of small purchases with a few suppliers in electronic catalogs, which are made available to the organization's users. The users then select items directly from the catalogs and buy on contracts that allow repeat purchases. The firm's computer system automatically routes transactions for approvals, sends the information along to the accounting system, and routes the purchase order directly to the supplier.

Another form of e-procurement is the use of the Internet to conduct **reverse auctions.** Reverse auctions utilize the Internet to allow suppliers to enter a reverse auction Web site supported by one of many application service providers (ASPs). At a designated time and date, qualified suppliers try to underbid their competitors and can monitor bid prices until the session is over (company identities are known only by the buyer). These third-party reverse auction services charge a fee in many cases to both the buyer and the suppliers to participate.

Many ASPs sell reverse auction software to companies and offer technical support for a monthly fee; the costs vary tremendously based on security required, the number of sellers, reporting features, buyer–supplier communication capabilities, and other desired customized services. Self-serve reverse auction sites are also very easy to find on the Internet and are extremely low cost. A quick Web search on the term "reverse auction providers" resulted in hundreds of company sites, most offering similar services. A few examples of these ASPs are global business software giant SAP AG, California-based Ariba, and HedgeHog, with headquarters in Indiana. As we can see here, the Internet can be an extremely useful sourcing tool, in that it allows firms to efficiently screen and select suppliers and then automate the buying activity, greatly reducing the time required to manage these activities while creating significant opportunities for cost savings. The e-Business Connection feature describes the use of reverse auctions for transportation services.

Rewarding Supplier Performance

Rewarding suppliers for improving or maintaining high levels of performance accomplishes several objectives: it provides a continuous incentive to all suppliers to meet and surpass specific performance goals; it provides an incentive for marginal (unrewarded) suppliers to achieve a level of performance that will allow their supplier status to be upgraded, resulting in rewards; and, finally, it gives suppliers an incentive to create and share rewards, in turn, with *their* suppliers. Sharing the benefits of performance in this way is one of the central foundations of building effective supply chains. As we mentioned at the start of the chapter, suppliers, in addition to buyers, must be able to realize benefits from supply chain relationships. Without this incentive, suppliers may keep any improvements realized within their operations quiet, while keeping the benefits as well. With time, this lack of information and benefit sharing stunts the growth of relationships within the supply chain and results in lower overall supply chain performance.

As many may remember from their childhoods, performance motivation can come in several forms, including punishment and various reward mechanisms. With suppliers, motivational tools can be used as an integral part of supplier management and supplier development programs. Punishment may take the form of reduced future business with the focal firm; a downgrade of the supplier's status from key to marginal, for instance, or a **billback penalty** equal to the incremental cost resulting from a late delivery or poor material quality. On the other hand, when performance meets or exceeds expectations, suppliers can be rewarded in some way.

Many formal strategic supplier agreements allow suppliers to benefit in the following ways:

- a share of the cost reductions resulting from supplier improvements;
- a share of the cost savings resulting from suggestions made during early supplier involvement in the firm's product and process design efforts;

e-Business Connection

Using Reverse Auctions for Transportation Resources

"Over the past two years, there's been an increase in supply chain transportation costs of around 20 percent," notes Pete Ward, a senior manager at Texas-based Hitachi Consulting. But the good news, he adds, is that even with an increase this steep, it is possible to deploy specific supply chain practices to avoid or ameliorate the pain.

The starting point, says Ward, is to leverage the Internet to solicit bids for transportation resources. Just as reverse auctions have revolutionized purchasing of both direct and indirect goods and services, global transportation routes also can be auctioned. Take, for example, The Netherlands-based clinical nutrition manufacturer Royal Numico, which makes use of an Internet-based contract tendering system from Freight Traders, headquartered in Virginia.

Initially, Geoff Norris, Royal Numico's international transport manager, was skeptical about the idea. A tough test was therefore set. "We decided to try the system out on a route that I had personally controlled for six or seven years—road freight being shipped from the U.K. to The Netherlands," he says. "I was fairly sure that the rates we were getting couldn't be bettered."

But bettered they were—by a reduction in price of more than 30 percent. What Norris had not been aware of—but the on-line tendering process revealed—was that a carrier's truck route went almost past the factory gate.

With a centralized view of what needs to be dispatched where, the Freight Traders system can identify the lowest-cost way of getting it there, says Peter Surtees, Kimberly-Clark's European logistics director. First introduced in 2003, the system had until recently driven a reduction in freight costs of some 3 to 5 percent a year in real terms on the company's entire European network, he explains.

At the present time, in the booming economies of Eastern Europe, though, those gains are under pressure. "In freight terms, Eastern Europe is a seller's market right now—it's very tough. We're probably doing no more than beating inflation on our Eastern European routes. There's a shortage of both truck drivers and truck capacity," rues Surtees.

Yet the downward pressure on freight costs is not being achieved at the expense of carriers' profit margins. The best price quote, explains Freight Traders' Managing Director Garry Mansell, often emerges in situations where carriers are offering capacity that might otherwise be wasted—trucks returning empty from delivering a consignment, for example. "What we aim to do," he says, "is put the right freight with the right carrier."

Source: Wheatley, M. "Manufacturers Meet Globalization Challenges with New Supply Chain Practices, Technology." *Manufacturing Business Technology,* 25, no. 3 (2007): 28. Used with permission.

- more business and/or longer contracts;
- access to in-house training seminars and other resources; and
- company and public recognition in the form of awards.

These benefits tend to stimulate further capital investment among suppliers to improve their operating capabilities, leading to even greater levels of quality, cost, and service performance. The U.S. healthcare industry is a good case in point. Purchasing costs for hospitals tend to be escalating rapidly, so hospital managers are beginning to offer incentives to suppliers to keep costs down. The Nebraska Medical Center (NMC) in Omaha, for example, partnered with Cardinal Health, a health system consulting firm in 2003 to explore out-of-the-box options for supply cost reductions. Their agreement with NMC provided an incentive of 30 percent of any savings they generated. They created a JIT inventory system that improved control and reduced inventory carrying costs. They also assigned several of their employees to work at the NMC facility (recall from the earlier chapter discussion that this is known as supplier co-location). These and other supply strategies have saved NMC millions of dollars while allowing them to maintain a 99 percent in-stock performance.[45]

Benchmarking Successful Sourcing Practices

Benchmarking, or the practice of copying what other businesses do best, is a very effective way to quickly improve sourcing practices and supply chain performance. Without benchmarking, firms must learn through experience the methods and tools that work the best.

Successful benchmarking allows firms to potentially leapfrog the experience-gaining stage by trying things that have worked well for other companies. Meaningful benchmarking data regarding sourcing practices can be obtained in any number of ways, both formal and informal—from using evaluation surveys distributed to a firm's customers and suppliers regarding *their* sourcing and supplier management practices, to discussing sourcing strategies with colleagues at business association meetings or conferences, to collecting published trade information on benchmarking studies.

A large number of resources are available for firms seeking to learn about and implement successful sourcing practices. The Center for Advanced Purchasing Studies (CAPS), the Arizona-based, nonprofit, independent research organization, helps firms achieve competitive advantage by providing leading-edge research information regarding strategic purchasing. For instance, CAPS provides research studies, benchmarking reports, and best practices case studies, along with organizing annual purchasing symposiums and roundtable discussions for purchasing professionals and academics.

Another organization, the Supply-Chain Council headquartered in Washington, DC, helps practitioners reduce their supply chain costs and improve customer service by providing their Supply Chain Operations Reference (SCORE) model as a framework for supply chain improvement. They also provide case studies and bring together practitioners to discuss best practices in periodic business conferences around the world.

The Arizona-based Institute for Supply Management (ISM), established in 1915, provides a wide variety of resources to supply management professionals worldwide, including a monthly publication featuring the latest supply management trends and information and the globally recognized Certified Purchasing Manager (C.P.M.), Certified Professional in Supply Management (CPSM), and Accredited Purchasing Practitioner (APP) programs. They also publish the globally recognized *Journal of Supply Chain Management,* organize several global supply management conferences, and support many seminars and Web conferences for supply management professionals.

The issue of best purchasing practices has been the subject of a number of research studies over the years, and these findings have proven very beneficial for firms seeking to benchmark best sourcing practices.[46] Some of the research has found a positive relationship between purchasing benchmarking and firm performance. Some of the successful sourcing practices found to be common among the companies studied were

- use of a central database to access information on parts, suppliers, lead times, and other purchasing information;
- software applications for sharing information with suppliers;
- use of the Internet for supplier searches;
- alliances with key suppliers for specific components;
- supplier certification and the elimination of incoming quality checks for key supplier deliveries;
- involving suppliers in the research and development processes of new products;
- development and use of articulated and coordinated purchasing and supply management strategies;
- rationalizing the firm's supply base;
- continuous measurement of supplier performance, and establishing supplier improvement targets; and
- continuous efforts to drive down purchasing costs.

Finally, Drs. Trent and Monczka have identified three sourcing trends that continue to impact companies today:

1. A focus on core competencies and technologies with outsourcing of noncore requirements.

2. Pressure to innovate and improve continuously in critical performance areas, including quality, delivery, cycle time, and product/process technology.

3. The presence of intense, worldwide competition with constant cost reduction pressure.

Using Third-Party Supply Chain Management Services

The use of **third-party logistics (3PLs)** and supply chain management services is a growing trend, as firms seek to gain quick competitive advantage from the deployment of proven, effective supply chain strategies. The term *3PL* today encompasses both logistics and supply chain management services. With the demands for shipping capabilities, speed, and visibility increasing, the trend in use of 3PLs is growing at about a 20-percent-per-year rate, and in 2006 the U.S. market for 3PLs eclipsed $104 billion.[47] These services assume some or all of a firm's sourcing, materials management, and product distribution responsibilities; charge a fee for their services while saving costs (estimated at 10 to 20 percent of total logistics costs); and improve service, quality, and profits for their clients.

For firms with limited resources and supply chain management experience, these services can be a worthwhile investment. Even large firms use these services, since supply chain cost savings can amount to tens of millions of dollars annually. As a matter of fact, 66 percent of U.S. Fortune 500 companies are using 3PLs, with General Motors, Wal-Mart, Chrysler, and Ford each using thirty or more.[48] For example, Ford uses 3PLs to move products between continents and to coordinate shipments from its North American assembly plants to its North American dealer network. In the first year of this arrangement, Ford saved $125 million in inventory carrying costs while decreasing delivery time to dealers by four days.[49] Emerson Process Management uses third-party transportation management specialist Precision Software to incorporate *country skipping* in their strategy for delivering products to customers. This concept is discussed in the Global Perspective feature.

As supply chain management has grown in strategic importance, some shippers are experimenting with the use of fewer 3PL services, or even one primary 3PL provider, more commonly referred to as a 4PL or **lead logistics provider (LLP)**. Some shippers argue they need at least two or three 3PLs to guard against service disruptions or coverage problems. "While tactically it is better to consolidate the number of providers, recent capacity shortages have shown that shippers need to ensure they have enough coverage," says Dick Armstrong, CEO of logistics consultant Armstrong & Associates, headquartered in Wisconsin. Other managers, though, believe it is better from a control perspective to have only one logistics service provider. Philip Prinzi, logistics director for Colorado-based Ball Corp., believes that having "one throat to choke" provides for better leverage and control. "Leverage was the key for us in choosing one provider," he said.[50]

As with benchmarking, use of 3PLs allows firms to quickly gain competitive advantage without gaining the experience beforehand. It also allows firms not specializing

---

Global Perspective

Country Skipping at Emerson Process Management

Missouri-based Emerson Process Management plays a profitable tune with respect to how their freight reaches its intended carrier. Handing it over at the dock may not be as cost-effective as handing it over part-way along the route. In terms of global logistics, it's a supply chain best practice known as "country skipping," explains Greg Lloyd, president of trade and transportation management specialist Precision Software.

"It's an extension of 'zone skipping,'" Lloyd explains, a concept familiar to U.S. manufacturers as a way of reducing the cost of coast-to-coast shipments. Rather than being shipped individually via a carrier such as FedEx or UPS, multiple packages are consolidated into container loads or truckloads for the long overland portion of the journey. These packages are split apart upon crossing the border of the country that is their final destination. Individual items are then handed over to FedEx or UPS for the cheaper intra-zone journey to their ultimate destination.

Country skipping allows Emerson to consolidate transatlantic shipments in the United States delivering them to Europe as a single consignment. Split apart upon arrival in Europe, the individual packages continue to their final destination—a tactic that has yielded a 7.38 million euro saving in just over two years, with Precision Software providing both the global trade management and the consolidation/deconsolidation application.

Source: Wheatley, M. "Manufacturers Meet Globalization Challenges with New Supply Chain Practices, Technology." *Manufacturing Business Technology,* 25, no. 3 (2007): 28. Used with permission.

in supply chain management to focus more resources on core capabilities while conserving valuable resources. Investments in technology, buildings, people, and equipment for supply chain management purposes can be quite high and subject to change as customers, competition, products, and other requirements change, making the use of these services seem even more appealing. Supply chain management services also provide geographical flexibility.

Firms can enter new regional and global markets quickly with less capital investment and then leave quickly with smaller losses if sales do not materialize. Some key disadvantages when using 3PL providers include loss of control, loss of communication with customers and suppliers, the potential spread of confidential information to customers and suppliers, and the potential damage to the firm's reputation if mistakes are made by the 3PLs. Companies must realize that these service providers are not internal employees and may not be fully aware of company policies and practices.

Also, companies providing logistics and supply chain management services must be evaluated the same way as other suppliers. Care must be taken to identify, screen, and select the appropriate 3PL service provider, and their performance should be periodically monitored. Flexibility may be one of the primary criteria for selection; for instance, can they adjust to new product requirements, can they tailor services to exactly fit the firm's needs, and can they handle last-minute requests? With time, trust can develop between 3PLs and their clients, leading to 4PL alliances, potentially providing long-term benefits for both parties.

Firms may also use a number of specialized supply chain management service companies for transportation management, repair services, inventory management, Web-enabled communications, public warehousing, reverse auction services, or small package delivery services; or they may contract out a wide range of supply chain management services to one company, such as Ryder, UPS, or Federal Express.

Finally, as an extension of VMI, some firms today are experimenting with outsourcing some or all of the supply management function to 3PL services. Arguments in favor of this are that overhead costs are reduced, knowledgeable buyers can be utilized, and purchase costs can be lowered since the centralized buying firm gains huge purchase volume leverage by combining the demand from all of its customers, resulting in quantity pricing discounts. The downside, particularly for firms engaged in proactive supply chain management, should be fairly obvious. Supply management does much more than just purchasing. As more of the supply management function is performed by outside services, it ceases to be viewed as a strategic component of the firm. Additionally, the firm risks the loss of important key suppliers. However, firms have successfully outsourced the purchasing of items with less strategic importance, such as MRO items. Using a 3PL provider for purchasing may also make sense for small firms with limited purchasing staff and knowledge.

Assessing and Improving the Firm's Purchasing Function

As has been stated throughout this segment of the textbook, the purchasing function is one of the most value-enhancing functions in any organization. Today, as supply management staff members are expected more often to generate cost savings and service and quality enhancements for the organization, they must be viewed as strategic internal suppliers of the organization. Bearing this in mind, it may then be preferable to periodically monitor the purchasing function's performance against set standards, goals, and/or industry benchmarks. Thus, as the firm strives to continuously improve its products and processes, supply management can also gauge its success in improving its value-enhancing contributions to the firm and its varied supply chains.

As was stated earlier in this chapter and in Chapter 3 when discussing supplier assessment, criteria can also be utilized here to provide feedback to the supply management staff regarding their contributions to the strategic goals of the firm. Surveys or audits of this nature can be administered as self-assessments among buyers as part of the annual evaluation process, and assessments can also include feedback from internal customers of the supply management or sourcing function, such as engineers and sales, or marketing and finance personnel. Feedback may even be included from supplier representatives. Assessment criteria to evaluate the purchasing department's performance should include some or all of the following:

- participating in and leading of multifunctional teams;
- participating in value engineering/value analysis efforts;
- finding and evaluating suppliers, and optimizing the supply base;
- managing and developing local, regional, and global suppliers;
- creating early supplier involvement initiatives;
- creating strategic supplier alliances;
- furthering the integration and development of existing key suppliers;
- contributing to new product development efforts;
- utilizing e-procurement systems;
- initiating supplier cost reduction programs;
- contributing to the improvement of purchased product and service quality;
- improving time to market; and
- maintaining and improving intrafirm cooperative relationships.

Since these criteria require both qualitative and quantitative assessments, the performance evaluation tool recommended here would be the weighted-factor rating method, covered in Chapter 3. Because of the tremendous potential value of these many activities, supply management staff members should continuously audit their capabilities and successes in these areas.

Thus, the skill set requirements of purchasing professionals have been changing as supply management has evolved from the tactical, clerical function it was about thirty years ago to the highly demanding strategic function it is today. To achieve the type of world-class performance suggested by the preceding assessment criteria, sourcing personnel must today exhibit world-class skills. While quite a bit of research has been conducted on this topic over the years, one study identified just such a world-class skill set for purchasing.[51] The ten skills identified by 136 experienced purchasing professionals were:

1. interpersonal communication,
2. ability to make decisions,
3. ability to work in teams,
4. analytical skills,

5. negotiation skills,

6. ability to manage change,

7. customer focus,

8. influencing and persuasion skills,

9. strategic skills, and

10. understanding business conditions.

We can see that supply management personnel today must develop an impressive set of skills to achieve the type of influence within the organization that leads to long-term success for the department, the firm, and its supply chains.

SUMMARY

Achieving supply chain management success starts with the sourcing activity. We hope we have provided in this chapter, and the previous two, evidence of the strategic role played within the firm by the sourcing function and the impact of sourcing on the management of the supply chain. Firms that fail to recognize this importance will simply not experience the same level of success in the long run. The sourcing process comprises a number of related activities that, when taken together, provide competitive advantage for the firm. Firms can maximize this advantage by developing effective supply chain strategies and then assessing and revising these strategies periodically as markets, competitors, and technologies change. As we head into the internal operations segment of this text, we hope you will continue to consider the sourcing issues discussed in Part 2 and how they interact with other processes as materials, services, and information move down the supply chain toward the immediate customers and, eventually, the end users.

KEY TERMS

acceptance sampling, 111

backsourcing, 115

benchmarking, 126

billback penalty, 124

channel equity, 110

co-managed inventories, 118

co-sourcing, 116

collaborative negotiations, 121

collaborative relationships, 109

distributive negotiations, 122

e-procurement, 123

early supplier involvement, 117

electronic data interchange (EDI), 118

functional products, 106

green sourcing, 111

insourcing, 115

integrative negotiations, 122

key suppliers, 108

lead logistics provider (LLP), 128

outsource, 105

purchasing spend, 106

reorder point (ROP), 118

reverse auctions, 123

scorecards, 109

selective sourcing, 116

sourcing, 105

statistical process control (SPC), 111

strategic alliance development, 119

strategic sourcing, 105

strategic supplier alliances, 110

supplier co-location, 118

supplier evaluation, 109

supplier management, 119

supply base optimization, 108

supply base rationalization, 108

supply base reduction, 108

sustainability, 112

sustainable procurement, 111

third-party logistics (3PLs), 127

value engineering, 117

vendor-managed inventory, 117

DISCUSSION QUESTIONS

1. What is the difference between *purchasing* and *strategic sourcing*?

2. Describe the differences between *functional* and *innovative products,* and provide some examples of each of these from your household possessions.

3. What's wrong with hard-bargaining suppliers, in order to generate a lower annual spend?

4. Using the strategy development framework shown in Figure 4.1, show how an electronics retail store might benefit from its use.

5. What is *supply base rationalization,* and what are its advantages and disadvantages?

6. What do you think the most important evaluation criteria would be for Wal-Mart's suppliers? McDonald's suppliers? Harley-Davidson's suppliers?

7. Define *channel equity* and discuss what it has to do with supply chain management.

8. Why would a firm want to develop *strategic supplier alliances?* When would it be wise not to do this?

9. What advantages do company-designed supplier certification programs have over industry certifications like ISO 9000?

10. Define the term *sustainable procurement,* and describe how this is different from *green sourcing.* Why is green sourcing a good sourcing strategy?

11. What does ISO 14000 have to do with green sourcing?

12. Would a firm ever want to *outsource* a core product or process? Why or why not?

13. When would firms want to *insource* a product or process? How is this different from *co-sourcing?*

14. What is the role of sourcing in *value engineering,* and what benefits does this give to the firm?

15. Why is early supplier involvement a good way to integrate the supply chain?

16. Describe the differences between *vendor managed inventories* and *co-managed inventories,* and when it might be advisable to do either of them.

17. Describe the historical developments of *JIT II* including its advantages and disadvantages.

18. What is the difference between *supplier management* and *alliance development?*

19. What makes supplier alliances fail? How can firms reduce the failure rate?

20. Describe the differences between *integrative* and *distributive negotiations,* and when each should be used.

21. Why are second- and third-tier suppliers important to the focal firm?

22. What is a common method for developing second-tier suppliers?

23. Discussion Problem: If your firm had 500 suppliers and they each had 100 suppliers, how many second-tier suppliers would your firm have? What if your firm reduced its supply base to twenty?

24. When would your firm want to use an *e-procurement system?* A *reverse auction?* Is a reverse auction a type of e-procurement?

25. If you work for a company, describe how it rewards and punishes its suppliers. Do you think appropriate methods are used? Why or why not?

26. What are some different ways you could use benchmarking to improve your performance at school?

27. What is a *3PL provider?* What advantages could a 3PL provider give to a small firm? A large firm?

28. What is a *4PL*? When would you use a 4PL instead of a 3PL?

29. How would you rate your skill-level on the world-class skill set listed at the end of the chapter?

INTERNET QUESTIONS

1. Go to the International Organization for Standardization Web site (http://www.iso.ch) and write a short description and history of the organization, including the various certifications that can be obtained.

2. Go to the CAPS Web site (http://www.capsresearch.org) and find the latest cross-industry benchmarking report and determine the overall purchase dollars as a percent of sales in the United States. What benchmarking research are they doing now?

3. Go to the site for the North American Green Purchasing Initiative (www.NAGPI.net) and describe several best practices listed at the site.

4. Go to the Goldman Environmental Prize Web site (www.goldmanprize.org) and describe the most recent award winners.

5. What is an ASP? Find some on the Internet that are not listed in the chapter, and describe what they do.

INFOTRAC QUESTIONS

Access http://www.infotrac.cengagelearning.com to answer the following questions:

1. Search on the term "bullwhip effect" and write a paper on the impacts of the bullwhip effect and the companies profiled in the papers you find.

2. Search on the term "sustainability laws" and write a report on recent laws that deal with sustainability.

3. Report on some of the companies using reverse auctions today. How popular is the practice?

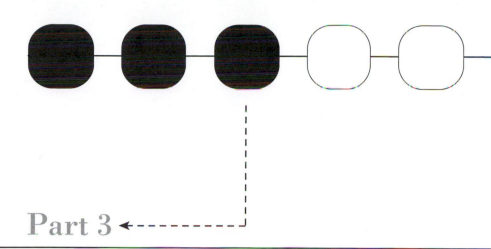

Part 3

Operations Issues in Supply Chain Management

Chapter 5

DEMAND FORECASTING

An organization's ability to control variability in areas such as forecasts and customer demand will be key to effective responsiveness. Massachusetts Institute of Technology (MIT) research of corporate supply chain practices reveals that variability at the end of the supply chain is magnified and distorted as it proceeds up the chain. In the business world, such distortions and miscommunications of supply and demand information can have a negative impact across the supply chain, raising inventory levels, increasing manufacturing and transportation costs, and limiting the optimization of available resources.[1]

Never make forecasts, especially about the future.

–Samuel Goldwyn

Learning Objectives

After completing this chapter, you should be able to

- Explain the role of demand forecasting in a supply chain.
- Identify the components of a forecast.
- Compare and contrast qualitative and quantitative forecasting techniques.
- Assess the accuracy of forecasts.
- Explain collaborative planning, forecasting, and replenishment.

Chapter Outline

Introduction

Forecasting Overview

Forecasting Techniques

Forecast Accuracy

Useful Forecasting Web Sites

Collaborative Planning, Forecasting, and Replenishment

Software Solutions

Summary

Supply Chain Management in Action   *The ISM Report on Business*

The Institute of Supply Management (ISM), formerly known as the National Association of Purchasing Management (NAPM), surveys more than 300 purchasing and supply executives in the United States using a questionnaire seeking information on "changes in production, new orders, new export orders, imports, employment, inventories, prices, leadtimes, and the timeliness of supplier deliveries in their companies comparing the current month to the previous month." The *ISM Report on Business*, available on the first business day of each month, is considered to be an accurate indicator of the overall direction of the economy and the health of the manufacturing and nonmanufacturing sectors. Three quotes regarding the value of the report follow:[2]

> *I find the surveys conducted by the purchasing and supply managers to be an excellent supplement to the data supplied by various departments and agencies of the government.*

Alan Greenspan, Former Chairman of the Federal Reserve Board

> *The ISM Manufacturing Report on Business has one of the shortest reporting lags of any macroeconomic series and gives an important early look at the economy. It also measures some concepts (such as lead times and delivery lags) that can be found nowhere else. It makes an important contribution to the American statistical system and to economic policy.*

Joseph E. Stiglitz, former Chairman of President Clinton's Council of Economic Advisors

> *The ISM Manufacturing Report on Business is extremely useful. The PMI, the Report's composite index, gives the earliest indication each month of the health of the manufacturing sector. It is an essential component for assessing the state of the economy.*

Michael J. Boskin, Hoover Institute Senior Fellow

The ISM report provides several indices for the manufacturing sector: Customers' Inventories, New Orders, Production, Manufacturing Employment, Supplier Deliveries, Inventories, Price, Backlog of Orders, New Export Orders, and Imports. The most important index is the Purchasing Managers Index (PMI) developed by Theodore Torda, Senior Economist of the U.S. Department of Commerce, and introduced in 1982. The PMI is a composite of five weighted seasonally adjusted indices (weights are shown in parentheses): New Orders (0.30), Production (0.25), Employment (0.20), Supplier Deliveries (0.15), and Inventories (0.10). A reading below 50 represents contraction and a reading over 50 indicates expansion. The purchasing surveys provide comprehensive information for tracking the economy and developing business forecasts. ISM has reports on both the manufacturing and the nonmanufacturing sectors.

Purchasing and supply executives use the report in a variety of ways. For example, the Customers' Inventories Index is a strong indicator of future new orders and production, and is used to measure changes in supply chain activity. Norbert J. Ore, Group Director, Strategic Sourcing and Procurement, Georgia-Pacific LLC, in the April 2007 ISM Report on Business noted that "Manufacturing activity increased in April as the PMI reflects accelerating growth for the month. New Orders and Production improved significantly as did Employment. Manufacturers are now in their ninth month of inventory reduction, so supply chains are generally in balance."[3]

Note: Some parts of this feature came from the Institute for Supply Management Manufacturing and Non-Manufacturing Report on Business Web site: http://www.ism.ws/ISMReport/content.cfm?ItemNumber=10743&navItemNumber=12944.

Introduction

Much has been written about demand-driven supply chains. In today's competitive environment organizations are moving toward a more effective demand-driven supply chain to enable them to respond quickly to shifting customer requirements. Marketplaces around the world have consumers who are now more demanding and discriminating than ever before. The market has evolved into a "pull" environment with customers dictating to the supplier what products they desire and when they need them delivered. If a retailer cannot get the product it wants at the right quantity, price, and time from one supplier, the retailer will look for another company that can meet its demands. Any temporary stockout has a tremendous downside on sales, profitability, and customer relationships.

There are several ways to closely match supply and demand. One way is for a supplier to hold plenty of stock available for delivery at any time. Whereas this approach maximizes sales revenues, it is also expensive because of the cost of carrying inventory and the possibility of write-downs at the end of the selling season. Use of flexible pricing is another approach. During heavy demand periods, prices can be raised to reduce peak demand. Price discounts can then be used to increase sales during periods with excess inventory or slow demand. This strategy can still result in lost sales, though, as well as stockouts and thus cannot be considered an ideal or partnership-friendly approach to satisfying demand. In the short term, companies can also use overtime, subcontracting, or temporary workers to increase capacity to meet the demand for their products and services. In the interim, though, firms may lose sales as they train workers and quality may also tend to suffer.

Managing demand is challenging because of the difficulty in forecasting future consumer requirements accurately. For supply chain integration to be successful, suppliers must be able to accurately forecast demand so that they can produce and deliver the right quantities demanded by their customers in a timely and cost-effective fashion. The Aberdeen Group's recent research on benchmarking demand management practices in consumer industries identified several qualities of best-in-class firms:[4]

- They continually enhance their demand management technologies—74 percent of these companies make recommendations to management for improving demand management technologies (versus 63 percent of all companies);
- They are twice as likely to use a commercial solution for demand planning/forecasting than all other companies;
- They are 70 percent more likely to use a single demand forecast with inputs from different sources within the organization than their peers— companies that are performing poorly tend to have multiple nonintegrated demand forecasts.

The study also found that 60 percent of companies forecasted at a frequency of less than one month. This finding indicates that companies may have to reevaluate the frequency of forecasting in response to the dynamic nature of the consumer industry and resort to frequent forecasting. For example, Procter & Gamble performs daily forecasting for the one- to four-week time period, in addition to preparing monthly forecasts. The study concluded that the use of interdisciplinary sales, marketing, and operations team combined with technology and the use of demand-related data were necessary for successful demand management.

Thus, it is imperative that suppliers along the supply chain find ways to better match supply and demand to achieve optimal levels of cost, quality, and customer service to enable them to compete with other supply chains. Any problem that adversely affects the timely delivery of products demanded by consumers has ramifications throughout the entire chain. Sport Obermeyer, a high-end fashion skiwear design and merchandising company headquartered in Aspen, Colorado, sells its products through department stores and ski shops. Sport Obermeyer's selling season is from September to January, with peak sales in December and January. Since the selling season is short and sales of high-end fashion apparel are more profitable than those of traditional apparel, it is critical that Sport Obermeyer supply the demand for high-end fashion apparel without getting stuck with excessive inventories at the end of the season. With improved forecasting capabilities and implementation of a quick response program that keeps its suppliers notified of forecasts, sales patterns, and marketing campaigns, Sport Obermeyer is able to mitigate supply-demand mismatch problems, thus reducing stockouts during the season and heavy markdowns at the end of the season.[5] Sport Obermeyer represents an effective approach to matching supply and demand while minimizing risk and cost.

Forecasting Overview

Forecasting is an important element of demand management. It provides an estimate of future demand and the basis for planning and sound business decisions. Since all organizations deal with an unknown future, some error between a forecast and actual demand is to be expected. Thus, the goal of a good forecasting technique is to minimize the deviation between the actual demand and the forecast. Since a forecast is a prediction of the future, factors that influence demand, the impact of these factors, and whether these factors will continue to influence future demand must be considered in developing an accurate forecast. In addition, buyers and sellers should share all relevant information to generate a single consensus forecast so that correct decisions on supply and demand can be made.

Improved forecasts benefit not only the focal company but also the trading partners in the supply chain. Generating accurate demand forecasts allows the purchasing department to order the right amount of products, the operations department to produce the right amount of products, and the distribution department to deliver the right amount of products. Thus timely and accurate demand information is a critical component of an effective supply chain. Inaccurate forecasts will lead to imbalances in supply and demand. In today's competitive business environment, collaboration (or cooperation and information sharing) between buyers and sellers is the rule rather than the exception. The benefits of better forecasts are lower inventories, reduced stockouts, smoother production plans, reduced costs, and improved customer service.

For more than 60 years, the Institute of Supply Management (ISM) has been publishing monthly indices for the manufacturing sector, such as Customers' Inventories, New Orders, Production, Manufacturing Employment, Supplier Deliveries, Inventories, Price, Backlog of Orders, New Export Orders, and Imports. Many business executives use these indices to forecast the overall direction of the economy and the health of the manufacturing sector. For example, purchasing and supply managers utilize the Customers' Inventories Index to help forecast future new orders, make production decisions and measure changes in supply chain activity. The *Wall*

Street Journal publishes the *ISM Report on Business,* which includes both the manufacturing and nonmanufacturing sectors. The *ISM Report on Business* is profiled in the chapter opening Supply Chain Management in Action feature.

Many have argued that demand forecasting is both an art and a science. Since there are no accurate crystal balls available, it is therefore impossible to expect 100 percent forecast accuracy at all times. The impact of poor communication and inaccurate forecasts resonates throughout the supply chain and results in the bullwhip effect, causing stockouts, lost sales, high costs of inventory and obsolescence, material shortages, poor responsiveness to market dynamics, and poor profitability.

For instance, Sony's PlayStation 1 (PS1) and PlayStation 2 (PS2) were huge successes when these products were first introduced to the public. Even though Sony had prior experience with the launch of the original PlayStation (PS), the company was unable to accurately predict the tremendous response from consumers for the PS2. Initial sales for Sony's PS2 were more than ten times that of the original PS's introduction 5 years earlier.[6] However, the launch of the latest PlayStation 3 (PS3) in November 2006 was not as successful as hoped. Although there was a lot of hype surrounding the launch, the actual sales of Sony's PS3 have been disappointing. According to the NPD Group, sales of game boxes in the U.S. through May 2007 were 5.6 million Xbox 360s, 2.8 million Wiis, and 1.4 million PS3s. Nintendo's Wii, which was introduced at about the same time as the PS3, had exceeded all expectations and outsold Sony by a huge margin. Consequently, Sony had a $1.8 billion annual loss in its game division and announced that it would lay off 3 percent of its workers in California.[7] This time it was not Sony that had to ramp up production quickly, but rather it was Nintendo that had to meet the unexpectedly high demand for Wiis. In response Sony cut the prices of PS3s to $500 to be more competitive with the Xbox Elite.[8] The objective in reducing prices was to get more people to buy the PS3. This scenario exemplifies the challenges faced by companies in forecasting sales and ramping up production quickly to meet the unexpectedly high demand for their products and to defend their market position.

Apple's revolutionary iPhone created a lot of buzz when it was first announced by Steve Jobs, CEO of Apple, during his keynote address at the Macworld Conference and Expo on January 9, 2007. The iPhone is a combination mobile phone, camera, iPod, and Internet communications device. The phone is expected to redefine what a mobile phone really is. The iPhone is considered by many as an evolutionary phone. Before the iPhone was launched on June 30, 2007, there was a prediction of shortages due to the high forecasted demand for the innovative phone. Goldman Sachs estimated initial sales of 700,000 units during the weekend of the launch, double its originally predicted demand of 350,000 units. As a result, Goldman Sachs increased the forecast for iPhones to 5.3 million from 4 million units.[9] The iPhones did not sell out in the first few hours of the launch as predicted and were readily available over the launch weekend. As part of the rollout of the iPhones, Apple had signed an exclusive multiyear agreement with AT&T to provide cellular service for this phone. AT&T reported some activation problems for the iPhones due likely to the high demand for the service. As a result of the lower than expected sales of iPhones, Apple's stock fell 6.1 percent.[10] Subsequently, Apple attempted to stimulate sales by reducing the price of the iPhones by $200 and offered rebates to those who purchased the iPhone earlier. Not only did Apple have to estimate demand accurately, but it also had to deal with complex issues involved in the introduction of new products to the market.

In the airline industry both Airbus and Boeing are the two major competitors. Competition has been fierce with each manufacturer trying to get the upper hand. In 2005, Airbus unveiled the A380, the largest passenger aircraft ever made, which can carry more than 500 passengers. At that time the A380 was heralded as the next big evolution in aviation. To accommodate the A380, airports around the world may have to spend millions to upgrade their infrastructures. For example, Los Angeles International airport is expected to spend $53 million on new runways, loading areas, and airport improvements.[11] Currently, Airbus is behind schedule in delivering the A380s. Production problems pushed delivery of the A380 back several times and cost overruns sent the company into a tailspin. FedEx and UPS subsequently cancelled orders for the cargo version of the A380. This resulted in Noel Forgeard, CEO of Airbus, being fired in the summer of 2006. His successor, Christian Streiff, lasted just 100 days before being replaced by Louis Gallois.

Boeing's new model approach was totally different from that of Airbus. They decided that the future was in mid-sized planes and that fuel efficiency was important. Boeing developed the 787 Dreamliner made for long-haul flights, which could carry between 200 and 300 passengers and was able to serve both small as well as large airports.[12] The Dreamliner was scheduled to be in service by 2008. Demand for fuel-efficient airliners such as the 787 Dreamliner is expected to increase as fuel prices continue to rise. Airbus responded by developing the A350 to compete with the 787. However, by 2007 Airbus had firm orders for just 93 A350s, whereas the Dreamliner had firm orders for more than 600.[13] More important, would the problems surrounding the A380 also delay the A350? The issues afflicting Airbus have resulted in Boeing overtaking Airbus in total plane sales for the first time since 2000. The Boeing 787 has become the fastest-selling airplane in aviation history. However, production problems caused by the shortage of parts delayed the first deliveries of Boeing 787s by 6 months. This unexpected outcome could affect future sales of the plane. Thus we can see that forecasting demand for new products is a difficult proposition.

Forecasting Techniques

Knowing that a forecast is very often inaccurate does not mean that nothing can be done to improve the forecast. Both quantitative and qualitative forecasts can be improved by seeking inputs from trading partners. Qualitative forecasting methods are based on opinions and intuition, whereas quantitative forecasting methods use mathematical models and relevant historical data to generate forecasts. The quantitative methods can be divided into two groups: time series and associative models.

Qualitative Forecasting Methods

Qualitative forecasting methods are approaches to forecasting based on intuition or judgmental evaluation and are generally used when data are limited, unavailable, or not currently relevant. Although this approach can be very inexpensive, the effectiveness depends to a large extent on the skill and experience of the forecaster(s) and the amount of time and relevant information available.

The qualitative techniques are often used to develop long-range projections when current data are no longer very useful, and for new product introductions when current data does not exist. Discussions of four common qualitative forecasting models follow.

Jury of Executive Opinion

A group of senior management executives who are knowledgeable about the market, competitors, and the business environment collectively develop the forecast. This technique has the advantage of several individuals with considerable experience working together, but if one member's views dominate the discussion, then the value and reliability of the outcome can be diminished. The **jury of executive opinion forecast** technique is applicable for long-range planning and new product introductions.

Forecasting high fashion, for instance, is risky since there is often no historical basis to generate the forecast. Sport Obermeyer's buying committee estimates its demand based on a general consensus reached by its committee members. Because a dominant member of the group might carry more weight in the discussion, the resulting forecast could potentially be biased and inaccurate. Consequently, Sport Obermeyer averages the individual forecast of each committee member to provide an overall demand forecast.[14]

Delphi Method

Using the **Delphi method forecast**, a group of internal and external experts are surveyed during several rounds in terms of future events and long-term forecasts of demand. Group members do not physically meet and thus avoid the scenario where one or a few experts could dominate a discussion. The answers from the experts are accumulated after each round of the survey and summarized. The summary of responses is then sent out to all of the experts for the next round, wherein members can modify their responses based on the group's response summary. The iterative process goes on until a consensus is reached. The process can be both time consuming and very expensive. This approach is applicable for high-risk technology forecasting; large, expensive projects; or major, new product introductions. The quality of the forecast depends largely on the knowledge of the experts.

Sales Force Composite

The sales force represents a good source of market information; thus the **sales force composite forecast** is generated based on the sales force's knowledge of the market and estimates of customer needs. Owing to the proximity of the sales personnel to the consumers, the forecast tends to be reliable but individual biases could negatively impact the effectiveness of this approach. For example, if bonuses are paid when actual sales exceed the forecast there is a tendency for the sales force to underforecast.

Consumer Survey

For the **consumer survey forecast**, a questionnaire is developed that seeks input from customers on important issues such as future buying habits, new product ideas, and opinions about existing products. The survey is administered through telephone, mail, Internet, or personal interviews. Data collected from the survey are analyzed using statistical tools and judgments, to derive a set of meaningful results. For example, Wyeth-Ayerst, the ninth-largest pharmaceutical company in the world, uses this type of market research to create forecasts for new products.[15] The challenge is to identify a sample of respondents who are representative of the larger population and to get an acceptable response rate.

Quantitative Forecasting Methods

Quantitative forecasting models use mathematical techniques that are based on historical data and can include causal variables to forecast demand. **Time series forecasting** is based on the assumption that the future is an extension of the past; thus, historical data can be used to predict future demand. **Cause-and-effect forecasting** assumes that one or more factors (independent variables) are related to demand and, therefore, can be used to predict future demand.

Since these forecasts rely solely on past demand data, all quantitative methods become less accurate as the forecast's time horizon increases. Thus, for long time horizon forecasts, it is generally recommended to utilize a combination of both quantitative and qualitative techniques.

Time Series Forecasting Models

A time series forecast typically has four components:

Trend variations represent either increasing or decreasing movements over time and are due to factors such as population growth, population shifts, cultural changes, and income shifts. Common trends are linear, S-curve, exponential, or asymptotic.

Cyclical variations are wavelike movements that last longer than one year and are influenced by macroeconomic and political factors. One example is the **business cycle** (recession or expansion). Recent business cycles in the U.S. have been affected by global events such as the 1973 oil embargo, 1991 Mexican financial crisis, 1997 Asian economic crisis, September 11, 2001 terrorist attacks in the U.S., and hurricanes Katrina and Rita in 2005.

Seasonal variations show peaks and valleys that repeat over a consistent interval such as hours, days, weeks, months, years, or seasons. Owing to seasonality, many companies do well in certain months and not so well in other months. For example, snow blower sales tend to be higher in the fall and winter, but taper off in the spring and summer; a fast-food restaurant will see higher sales during the day around breakfast, lunch, and dinner; and U.S. hotels experience large crowds during traditional holidays such as July 4, Labor Day, Thanksgiving, Christmas, and New Year.

Random variations are due to unexpected or unpredictable events such as natural disasters (hurricanes, tornadoes, fire), strikes, and wars. An example is the 2002 dock worker strike that shut down West Coast ports in California, Oregon, and Washington in the U.S. and caused shipping delays of auto parts that forced automakers such as Honda, NUMMI, and Mitsubishi to stop production briefly.

As discussed earlier, time series forecasts are dependent on the availability of historical data. Forecasts are estimated by extrapolating the past data into the future. A recent survey[16] of forecasting models showed that time series models were the most widely used (72 percent), while judgmental models were used the least (11 percent). The study also found that within the time series models, the ones that were most commonly used were the simpler models (moving averages and simple trends) and exponential smoothing. In general, demand forecasts were used in planning for procurement, supply, replenishment, and corporate revenue.

Some of the more common time series approaches such as the naïve, simple moving average, weighted moving average, simple exponential smoothing, and linear trend forecasts are discussed next.

Naïve Forecast

Using the **naïve forecast**, the forecast for the next period is equal to the actual demand for the immediate past period. This can be expressed as:

$$F_{t+1} = A_t$$

where F_{t+1} = forecast for period $t+1$

A_t = actual demand for period t

For example, if the current period's actual demand is 100 units, then next period's forecast is 100 units. This method is inexpensive to understand, develop, store data, and operate. However, there is no consideration of causal relationships and the method may not generate accurate forecasts. Many economic and business series are considered good candidates for using the naïve forecast because the these series behave randomly.

Simple Moving Average Forecast

The **simple moving average forecast** uses historical data to generate a forecast and works well when the demand is fairly stable over time. The n-period moving average forecast can be expressed as:

$$F_{t+1} = \frac{\sum\limits_{i=t-n+1}^{t} A_i}{n}$$

where F_{t+1} = forecast for period $t+1$

n = number of periods used to calculate moving average

A_i = actual demand in period i

When n equals 1, the simple moving average forecast is the naïve forecast. The average tends to be more responsive if fewer data points are used to compute the average. However, random events can also impact the average adversely. Thus the decision maker must balance the cost of responding slowly to changes versus the cost of responding to random variations. The advantage of this technique is that it is simple to use and easy to understand. A weakness of the weighted moving method is its inability to respond to trend changes quickly. Example 5.1 illustrates the calculation of a simple moving average forecast.

Weighted Moving Average Forecast

The **weighted moving average forecast** allows greater emphasis to be placed on more recent data to reflect changes in demand patterns. The weights used also tend to be based on the experience of the forecaster. Although the forecast is more responsive to underlying changes in demand, the forecast still lags demand because of the averaging effect. As such the weighted moving average method does not do a good job of

Example 5.1   Simple Moving Average Forecasting

PERIOD	DEMAND
1	1600
2	2200
3	2000
4	1600
5	2500
6	3500
7	3300
8	3200
9	3900
10	4700
11	4300
12	4400

Using the actual demand data shown here, calculate the forecast for period 5 using a four-period simple moving average.

SOLUTION

$$F_5 = \frac{1600 + 2200 + 2000 + 1600}{4} = 1850$$

The solution using an Excel spreadsheet is shown in Figure 5.1.

tracking trend changes in the data. The weighted moving average forecast can be expressed as:

$$F_{t+1} = \sum_{i=t-n+1}^{t} w_i A_i$$

where F_{t+1} = forecast for period $t + 1$

n = number of periods used in determining the weighted moving average forecast

A_i = actual demand in period i

w_i = weight assigned to period i; with $\Sigma w_i = 1$

Example 5.2 illustrates the calculation of a weighted moving average forecast.

Simple Exponential Smoothing Forecast

The **simple exponential smoothing forecast** is a sophisticated weighted moving average forecasting technique in which the forecast for the next period's demand is the current period's forecast adjusted by a fraction of the difference between the current period's actual demand and forecast. This approach requires less data than the weighted moving average method because only two data points need to be used. Owing to its simplicity and minimal data requirement, simple exponential smoothing is one of the more widely used forecasting techniques. This model, like the other time series models, is suitable for data that show little trend or seasonal patterns. Other higher order exponential smoothing models can be used for data exhibiting trends and seasonalities. The simple exponential smoothing forecasting formula is:

Figure 5.1	Simple Moving Average Forecasting Using Excel Spreadsheet

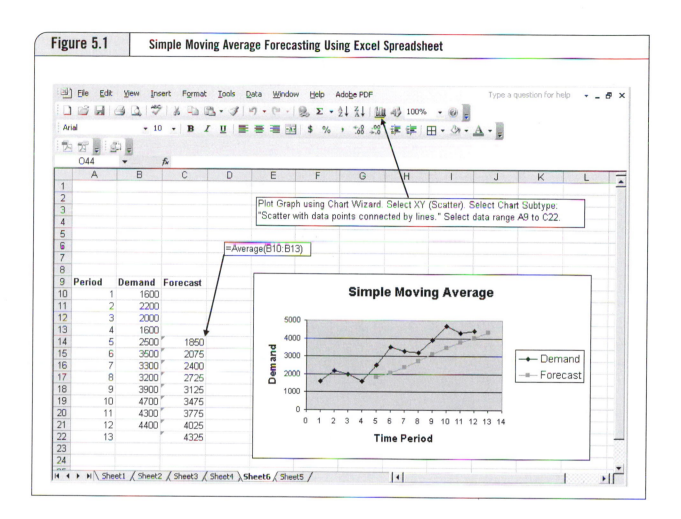

Example 5.2   Weighted Moving Average Forecasting

Using the data provided in Example 5.1, calculate the forecast for periods 5 and 13 using a four-period weighted moving average. The weights of 0.4, 0.3, 0.2, and 0.1 are assigned to the most recent, second most recent, third most recent, and the fourth most recent periods, respectively.

SOLUTION

$$F_5 = 0.1(1600) + 0.2(2200) + 0.3(2000) + 0.4(1600) = 1840$$

Similarly,

$$F_{13} = 0.1(3900) + 0.2(4700) + 0.3(4300) + 0.4(4400) = 4380$$

The solution using Excel spreadsheet is shown in Figure 5.2.

Figure 5.2	Weighted Moving Average Forecasting Using Excel Spreadsheet

Plot Graph using Chart Wizard. Select Line Chart (with markers displayed at each data point)(Chart subtype).

Period	Demand	Weight	Forecast
1	1600	0.1	
2	2200	0.2	
3	2000	0.3	
4	1600	0.4	
5	2500		1840
6	3500		2100
7	3300		2670
8	3200		3030
9	3900		3220
10	4700		3530
11	4300		4020
12	4400		4230
13			4380

Forecast for period 5 = Sumproduct(B10:B13,C$10:C$13)

Weighted Moving Average (chart with Actual and Forecast series; Demand on y-axis, Time Period on x-axis)

$$F_{t+1} = F_t + \alpha(A_t - F_t)$$

or

$$F_{t+1} = \alpha A + (1 - \alpha)F_t$$

where F_{t+1} = forecast for period $t+1$

F_t = forecast for period t

A_t = actual demand for period t

α = smoothing constant $(0 \leq \alpha \leq 1)$

The simple exponential smoothing forecast is equivalent to the naïve forecast when α is equal to 1. As the α value becomes closer to 1, there is a greater emphasis on recent data, resulting in a major adjustment of the error in the last period's forecast. Thus with a high α value, the model is more responsive to changes in the recent demand. When α has a low value, more weight is placed on past demand (which is contained in the previous forecast), and the model responds slower to changes in demand. The impact of using a small or large value of α is similar to the effect of using a large or small number of observations in calculating the moving average. In general, the forecast will lag any trend in the actual data because only partial adjustment to the most recent forecast error can be made. The initial forecast can be estimated using the naïve method, that is, the forecast for the second period is simply assumed to be the actual demand from the first period. Example 5.3 illustrates the simple exponential smoothing forecasting method.

Linear Trend Forecast

In the **linear trend forecast**, the trend can be estimated using simple linear regression to fit a line to a series of historical data. This model is also referred to as the simple trend model. The trend line is determined using the least squares method, which minimizes the sum of squared deviations to determine the characteristics of the linear equation.

$$\hat{Y} = b_0 + b_1 x$$

where $\hat{Y}$ = forecast or dependent variable

$\quad$ x = time variable

$\quad$ b_0 = vertical axis intercept of the line

$\quad$ b_1 = slope of the line

The coefficients b_0 and b_1 are calculated as follows:

$$b_1 = \frac{n \sum (xy) - \sum x \sum y}{n \sum x^2 - \left(\sum x \right)^2}$$

$$b_0 = \frac{\sum y - b_1 \sum x}{n}$$

where b_1 = slope of the line

$\quad$ x = independent variable values

$\quad$ y = dependent variable values

$\quad$ n = number of observations

Example 5.4 illustrates use of the linear trend forecast.

Example 5.3   Simple Exponential Smoothing Forecasting

Using the data provided in Example 5.1, calculate the forecast for period 3 using the simple exponential smoothing method. Assume the forecast for period 2 is 1600. Use a smoothing constant (α) value of 0.3.

SOLUTION

Given: $F_2 = 1600$ and $\alpha = 0.3$

$$F_{t+1} = F_t + \alpha(A_t - F_t)$$

$$F_3 = F_2 + \alpha(A_2 - F_2) = 1600 + 0.3(2200 - 1600) = 1780$$

Thus the forecast for week 3 is 1780.

The solution using an Excel spreadsheet is shown in Figure 5.3.

Figure 5.3	Simple Exponential Smoothing Forecasting Using Excel Spreadsheet

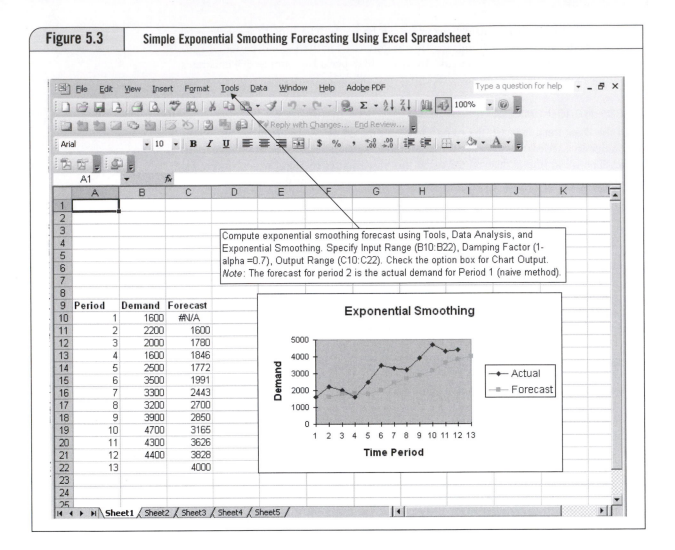

Cause-and-Effect Forecast Models

The cause-and-effect models have a cause (independent variable or variables) and an effect (dependent variable). One of the more common models used is regression analysis. In demand forecasting, the external variables that are related to demand are first identified. Once the relationship between the external variable and demand is determined, it can be used as a forecasting tool. A review of several cause-and-effect models follows.

The Simple Linear Regression Forecast

When there is only one explanatory variable, the **simple linear regression forecast** is equivalent to the trend forecast described earlier. The difference is that the x variable is no longer time but an explanatory variable of demand. For example, demand could be dependent on the size of the advertising budget. The equation is expressed as follows:

$$\hat{Y} = b_0 + b_1 x$$

where $\hat{Y}$ = forecast or dependent variable

$x =$ explanatory or independent variable

$b_0 =$ vertical axis intercept of the line

$b_1 =$ slope of the line

Example 5.5 illustrates the calculation of the simple linear regression forecast.

Example 5.4   Linear Trend Forecasting

The demand for toys produced by the Miki Manufacturing Company is shown in the following table.

PERIOD	DEMAND	PERIOD	DEMAND	PERIOD	DEMAND
1	1600	5	2500	9	3900
2	2200	6	3500	10	4700
3	2000	7	3300	11	4300
4	1600	8	3200	12	4400

(a) What is the trend line?

(b) What is the forecast for period 13?

SOLUTION

PERIOD (x)	DEMAND (y)	x^2	xy
1	1600	1	1600
2	2200	4	4400
3	2000	9	6000
4	1600	16	6400
5	2500	25	12,500
6	3500	36	21,000
7	3300	49	23,100
8	3200	64	25,600
9	3900	81	35,100
10	4700	100	47,000
11	4300	121	47,300
12	4400	144	52,800
$\sum x = 78$	$\sum y = 37{,}200$	$\sum x^2 = 650$	$\sum xy = 282{,}800$

$$b_1 = \frac{n\sum(xy) - \sum x \sum y}{n\sum x^2 - (\sum x)^2} = \frac{12(282,800) - 78(37,200)}{12(650) - 78^2} = 286.71$$

$$b_0 = \frac{\sum y - b_1 \sum x}{n} = \frac{37,200 - 286.71(78)}{12} = 1236.4$$

(a) The trend line is $\hat{Y} = 1236.4 + 286.7x$

(b) To forecast demand for period 13, we substitute $x = 13$ into the trend line equation above.

Forecast for period $13 = 1236.4 + 286.7(13) = 4963.5 \approx 4964$

The solution using Excel spreadsheet is shown in Figure 5.4.

Figure 5.4   Linear Trend Forecasting Using Regression and Excel Spreadsheet

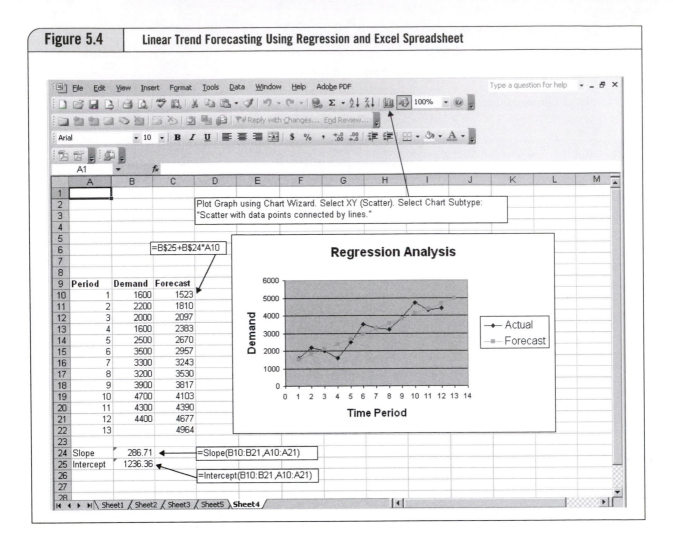

The Multiple Regression Forecast

When several explanatory variables are used to predict the forecast, a **multiple regression forecast** is applicable. Regression analysis works well when the relationships between demand (dependent variable) and other factors (independent or explanatory variables) impacting sales are strong and stable over time. The multiple regression forecast equation is as follows:

$$\hat{Y} = b_0 + b_1 x_1 + b_2 x_2 + \ldots + b_k x_k$$

where $\hat{Y}$ = forecast or dependent variable

x_k = kth explanatory or independent variable

b_0 = constant

b_k = regression coefficient of the independent variable x_k

Although the mathematics involved in determining the parameters of the multiple regression equation are complex, numerous software such as Excel Spreadsheet, SAS,

Example 5.5   Simple Linear Regression Forecasting

Data on sales and advertising dollars for the past 6 months are shown in the following table.

$ SALES (y)	$ ADVERTISING (x)
100,000	2000
150,000	3000
125,000	2500
50,000	1000
170,000	3500
135,000	2750

Determine the linear relationship between sales and advertising dollars.

SOLUTION

$ SALES (y)	$ ADVERTISING (x)	x^2	xy
100,000	2000	4,000,000	1,200,000,000
150,000	3000	9,000,000	450,000,000
125,000	2500	6,250,000	312,500,000
50,000	1000	1,000,000	50,000,000
170,000	3500	12,250,000	595,000,000
135,000	2750	7,562,500	371,250,000
$\sum y = 730{,}000$	$\sum x = 14{,}750$	$\sum x^2 = 40{,}062{,}500$	$\sum xy = 1{,}978{,}750{,}000$

$$\hat{Y} = b_0 + b_1 x$$

$$b_1 = \frac{n\sum(xy) - \sum x \sum y}{n\sum x^2 - (\sum x)^2} = \frac{6(1{,}978{,}750{,}000) - 14{,}750(730{,}000)}{6(40{,}062{,}500) - 14{,}750^2}$$

$$= 48.43836$$

$$b_0 = \frac{\sum y - b_1 \sum x}{n} = \frac{730{,}000 - 48.43836(14{,}750)}{6}$$

$$= 2589.041$$

$$\hat{Y} = 2589.04 + 48.44x$$

The results indicate a linear relationship between sales and advertising dollars and that a $1 increase in advertising will increase sales by $48.44.

and SPSS statistical packages can be used to solve the equation. Any statistics textbook should provide the formula for calculating the regression coefficient values and discussion of the assumptions and challenges of using multiple regression techniques. Multiple regression forecasting requires much more data than any of the other techniques discussed earlier and the additional cost must be balanced against possible improvement in the level of forecast accuracy.

Forecast Accuracy

The ultimate goal of any forecasting endeavor is to provide an accurate and unbiased forecast. The costs associated with prediction error can be substantial and include the cost of lost sales, excess inventories, unsatisfied customers, and loss of goodwill. Companies must strive to do a good job of tracking forecast error and taking the necessary steps to improve their forecasting techniques so as to reduce error. Typically, forecast error at the disaggregated (stock keeping unit) level is higher than at the aggregated level (company as a whole). **Forecast error** is the difference between actual quantity or demand and the forecast. Forecast error can be expressed as:

$$e_t = A_t - F_t$$

where e_t = forecast error for period t

A_t = actual demand for period t

F_t = forecast for period t

Several measures of forecasting accuracy are shown below:

Mean absolute deviation (MAD) $= \dfrac{\sum\limits_{t=1}^{n} |e_t|}{n}$

Mean absolute percentage error (MAPE) $= \dfrac{100}{n} \sum\limits_{t=1}^{n} \left| \dfrac{e_t}{A_t} \right|$

Mean square error (MSE) $= \dfrac{\sum\limits_{t=1}^{n} e_t^2}{n}$

Running Sum of Forecast Errors (RSFE) $= \sum\limits_{t=1}^{n} e_t$

where e_t = forecast error for period t

A_t = actual demand for period t

n = number of periods of evaluation

The RSFE is an indicator of bias in the forecasts. **Forecast bias** measures the tendency of a forecast to be consistently higher or lower than the actual demand. A positive RSFE indicates that the forecasts are generally lower than actual demand, which will lead to stockouts. A negative RSFE shows that the forecasts are generally higher than actual demand, resulting in excess inventory carrying costs.

The **tracking signal** is a tool used to check the forecast bias. It is expressed as:

$$\text{Tracking signal} = \frac{\text{RSFE}}{\text{MAD}}$$

The tracking signal determines if the forecast bias is within acceptable control limits. If the tracking signal falls outside the pre-set control limits, there is a bias problem with the forecasting method and an evaluation of the way forecasts are generated is warranted. A biased forecast will lead to excessive inventories or stockouts. Some inventory experts suggest using ± 4 for high-volume items and ± 8 for lower-volume items while others prefer a lower limit. For example, GE Silicones started off with a control limit for their tracking signal of ± 4. Over time, the quality of forecasts improved and the control limits were reduced to ± 3. As tighter limits are instituted there is a greater probability of finding exceptions that require no action, but it also means catching changes in demand earlier. Eventually, with additional improvements in the forecasting system, the control limits were further reduced to ± 2.2. The greater sensitivity allowed

Example 5.6

The demand and forecast information for the XYZ Company over a 12-month period is shown in the following table.

PERIOD	DEMAND	FORECAST	PERIOD	DEMAND	FORECAST
1	1600	1523	7	3300	3243
2	2200	1810	8	3200	3530
3	2000	2097	9	3900	3817
4	1600	2383	10	4700	4103
5	2500	2627	11	4300	4390
6	3500	2957	12	4400	4677

Calculate the MAD, MSE, MAPE, and tracking signal. Assume that the control limits for the tracking signal are ± 3. What can be concluded about the quality of forecasts?

SOLUTION

PERIOD	DEMAND	FORECAST	ERROR (e)	ABSOLUTE ERROR	e^2	ABSOLUTE % ERROR
1	1600	1523	77	77	5929	4.8
2	2200	1810	390	390	152,100	17.7
3	2000	2097	−97	97	9409	4.9
4	1600	2383	−783	783	613,089	48.9
5	2500	2670	−170	170	28,900	6.8
6	3500	2957	543	543	294,849	15.5
7	3300	3243	57	57	3249	1.7
8	3200	3530	−330	330	108,900	10.3
9	3900	3817	83	83	6889	2.1
10	4700	4103	597	597	356,409	12.7
11	4300	4390	−90	90	8100	2.1
12	4400	4677	−277	277	76,729	6.3
Total			0	3494	1,664,552	133.9
Average				291.17	138,712.7	11.16
				MAD	MSE	MAPE

MAD = 291.2

MSE = 138,712.7

MAPE = 11.2 percent

RSFE = 0

$$\text{Tracking Signal} = \frac{\text{RSFE}}{\text{MAD}} = 0$$

The results indicate no bias in the forecasts and the tracking signal is well within the control limits of ± 3. However, the forecasts are on average 11 percent off from actual demand. This situation might require attention to determine the underlying causes of the variation.

GE Silicones to quickly identify changing trends and resulted in further improvement in their forecasts.[17] Example 5.6 illustrates use of these forecast accuracy measures.

In one study, researchers found that bias in the forecast could be intentional, driven by organizational issues such as motivation of staff and satisfaction of customer demands, influencing the generation of forecasts.[18] For example, sales personnel tend to favor under-forecasting so they can meet or exceed sales quotas, and production people tend to over-forecast because having too much inventory presents less of a problem than the alternative. The key to generating accurate forecasts is collaborative forecasting with different partners inside and outside the company working together to eliminate forecast error. A collaborative planning, forecasting and replenishment system, discussed later in the chapter, provides for free exchange of forecasting data, point-of-sale data, promotions, and other relevant information between trading partners; this collaborative effort, rather than more sophisticated and expensive forecasting algorithms, can account for significant improvements in forecasting accuracy.

Useful Forecasting Web Sites

Several forecasting Web sites that provide a wealth of information on the subject are shown here:

1. Institute for Forecasting Education (http://www.forecastingeducation.com/)

    The Institute for Forecasting Education (IFE) runs on-site customized workshops for companies and organizations worldwide. As a public service, IFE maintains a free database on forecasting software evaluation. The Institute also publishes *Foresight — The International Journal of Applied Forecasting*, which focuses on issues facing the forecasting practitioner.

2. International Institute of Forecasters (http://www.forecasters.org/)

    The International Institute of Forecasters lists the following objectives on their Web site:

    - *Develop and unify forecasting as a multidisciplinary field of research drawing on management, behavioral sciences, social sciences, engineering, and other fields.*
    - *Contribute to the professional development of analysts, managers, and policy makers with responsibilities for making and using forecasts in business and government.*
    - *Bridge the gap between theory and practice, with practice helping to set the research agenda and research providing useful results.*
    - *Bring together decision makers, forecasters, and researchers from all nations to improve the quality and usefulness of forecasting.*

3. Forecasting Principles: Evidence-Based Forecasting (http://www.forecasting principles.com/)

    The *Forecasting Principles* site summarizes all useful knowledge about forecasting so that it can be used by researchers, practitioners, and educators. (Those who might want to challenge this are invited to submit missing information.) This knowledge is provided as principles (guidelines, prescriptions, rules, conditions, action statements, or advice about what to do in given situations).

4. Stata (Data Analysis and Statistical Software): Statistical Software Providers (http://www.stata.com/links/stat_software.html).

Their Web site provides links to statistical software providers.

Collaborative Planning, Forecasting, and Replenishment

According to the New Jerseybased Voluntary Interindustry Commerce Standards (VICS) Association, **"Collaborative planning, forecasting and replenishment** (CPFR®) is a business practice that combines the intelligence of multiple trading partners in the planning and fulfillment of customer demand. CPFR links sales and marketing best practices, such as category management, to supply chain planning and execution processes to increase availability while reducing inventory, transportation and logistics costs." The objective of CPFR is to optimize the supply chain by improving demand forecast accuracy, delivering the right product at the right time to the right location, reducing inventories across the supply chain, avoiding stockouts, and improving customer service. Basically, this can be achieved only if the trading partners work closely together and share information and risk through a common set of processes.

The real value of CPFR comes from an exchange of forecasting information rather than from more sophisticated forecasting algorithms to improve forecasting accuracy. The fact is that forecasts developed solely by the firm tend to be inaccurate. When both the buyer and the seller collaborate to develop a single forecast, incorporating knowledge of base sales, promotions, store openings or closings, and new product introductions, it is possible to synchronize buyer needs with supplier production plans, thus ensuring efficient replenishment. The jointly managed forecasts can be adjusted in the event that demand or promotions have changed, thus avoiding costly corrections after the fact.

On the surface, when decisions are made with incomplete information, it may appear that companies have "optimized" their internal processes when, in reality, inventory has merely shifted along the supply chain. Without trading partners in the supply chain collaborating and exchanging information, the supply chain will always be suboptimal, resulting in less-than-maximum supply chain profits.

CPFR is an approach that addresses the requirements for good demand management. The benefits of CPFR include the following:

- strengthening supply chain partner relationships;
- providing analysis of sales and order forecasts;
- using point-of-sale data, seasonal activity, promotions, new product introductions, and store openings or closings to improve forecast accuracy;
- managing the demand chain and proactively eliminating problems before they appear;
- allowing collaboration on future requirements and plans;
- using joint planning and promotions management;
- integrating planning, forecasting, and logistics activities;
- providing efficient category management and understanding of consumer purchasing patterns; and

- providing an analysis of key performance metrics (e.g., forecast accuracy, forecast exceptions, product lead times, inventory turnover, percentage stockouts) to reduce supply chain inefficiencies, improve customer service, and increase revenues and profitability.

Most companies and their supply chain trading partners implement CPFR using some form of the Voluntary Interindustry Commerce Standards (VICS) Association CPFR Process Model (see Figure 5.5). The Global Commerce Initiative (GCI), created by a global network of 40 of the largest manufacturers and retailers, is a recommended standard for globalizing CPFR by combining portions of VICS CPFR publications and adding new materials. The GCI Executive Board is a voluntary body created in 1999 with a mission to "lead global value chain collaboration through the identification of business needs and the implementation of best practices and standards to serve consumers better, faster and at less cost."[19]

Figure 5.5	VICS's CPFR Model with Retailer and Manufacturer Tasks Aligned with Their Corresponding Collaboration Tasks

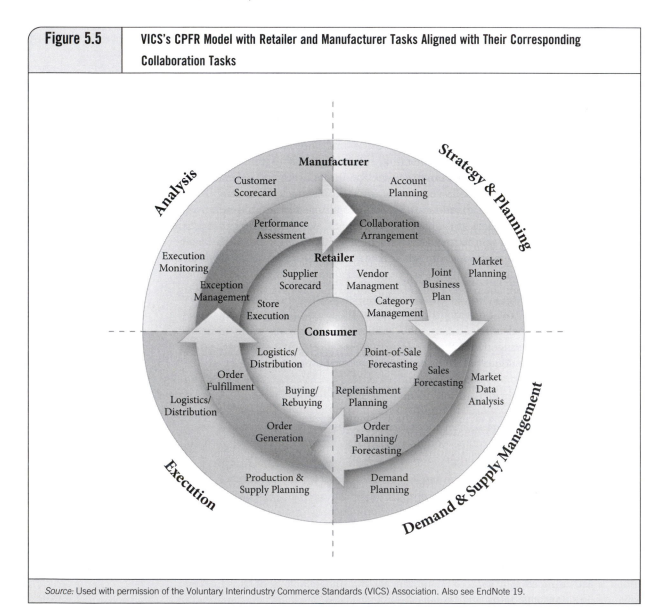

Source: Used with permission of the Voluntary Interindustry Commerce Standards (VICS) Association. Also see EndNote 19.

A new CPFR model was introduced by VICS in 2004. Originally the implementation process involved nine linear business processes but today the revised CPFR model involves an iterative cycle of four key activities (see Figure 5.5) where full implementation of every element is not necessary to achieve value. According to VICS, the manufacturer and retailer participate in four collaborative activities to improve performance[20]:

- *Strategy and Planning*: Establish the ground rules for the collaborative relationship. Determine product mix and placement, and develop event plans for the period.
- *Demand and Supply Management*: Project consumer (point-of-sale) demand, as well as order and shipment requirements over the planning horizon.
- *Execution*: Place orders, prepare and deliver shipments, receive and stock products on retail shelves, record sales transactions and make payments.
- *Analysis*: Monitor planning and execution activities for exception conditions. Aggregate results, and calculate key performance metrics. Share insights and adjust plans for continuously improved results.

In the revised 2004 CPFR model, the consumer is at the center of the collaboration. The model lists eight collaboration tasks instead of the nine steps in the original CPFR model[21]:

- Task 1: Collaboration Arrangement
- Task 2: Joint Business Plan
- Task 3: Sales Forecasting
- Task 4: Order Planning/Forecasting
- Task 5: Order Generation
- Task 6: Order Fulfillment
- Task 7: Exception Management
- Task 8: Performance Assessment

Shown in Figure 5.6 is a VICS self-assessment template for organizations to evaluate their readiness to implement CPFR programs.

West Marine is an example of a company that has benefited greatly from CPFR implementation. The pilot program was started in January 2001. By late 2004, West Marine had CPFR relationships with 200 suppliers, 85 percent forecast accuracy, 80 percent on-time shipments, and 96 percent in-stock delivery during the peak season. West Marine had to address both business processes and cultural issues internally and with their suppliers. The company worked closely with its suppliers to match supply and demand. Whereas collaboration with external constituents is critical for CPFR success, it is equally important that effective collaboration within the company is emphasized. For example, logistics, planning and replenishment personnel must work closely together. West Marine identified the following ten performance improvement steps in their successful implementation of CPFR[22]:

1. *Seek long-term, holistic solutions, not quick or myopic fixes.*
2. *Reconcile conflicting goals and metrics.*
3. *Pursue inclusive problem solving, not dependence on "experts" who have no accountability for the business.*
4. *Instill collaborative processes that encourage idea creation, shared problem solving, and high adoption rates across organizational boundaries.*

Figure 5.6	CPFR® Rollout Readiness Self-Assessment

Place a *check mark next to each statement* that is true for your business, then sum up the marks to determine your total score.

A. Organizational Readiness

- The value proposition for collaboration is well understood in the company.
- There is an agreed company strategy and an adequate budget for collaboration initiatives.
- Collaboration process owners have been assigned and empowered.
- Affected organizations have performance goals and incentives aligned with collaboration objectives.

B. Retailer Process Readiness

(Retailers rate themselves and suppliers rate their customers' readiness in this section.)

- Details of promotions and other retail events are captured and kept up to date so that consumer demand impact can be correlated with them.
- Consumer demand is forecasted based on historical sales and planned promotional activities.
- Ordering processes are driven from forecasted consumer demand.
- Feedback from collaboration can be incorporated in future plans and forecasts.

C. Supplier Readiness

(Suppliers rate themselves and retailers rate their suppliers' readiness in this section.)

- Supplier sales and service/logistics personnel coordinate their response to customer issues and opportunities.
- Collaboration (consumer POS) data can be effectively used in the supplier's sales and operations planning (S&OP) process.
- A unified approach to collaboration allows the supplier's insights to reflect the demands of multiple customers.

D. Technology Readiness

Internet data transport (EDIINT AS2) capabilities are production-ready.

- XML translation capabilities for B2B initiatives are production-ready.
- Enterprise planning applications have supported interfaces for collaboration data (import and export).
- A scalable CPFR solution is available.

Total Score

Evaluating Your Score

If you scored 11–15

- Your strategic trading partners should all be live in collaboration.
- You should be driving CPFR best practices in the industry.

If you scored 6–10

- You are ready to begin rollouts, starting with demand/supply visibility.
- Address key gaps to enhance ROI of collaboration.

If you scored 0–5

- You should act quickly to close gaps, starting with organizational ones.
- Work to sustain momentum in existing collaboration relationships, to gain experience that can be applied to future efforts.

Figure 5.6	**CPFR® Rollout Readiness Self-Assessment (continued)**

Suggestions for Improving Your Score

Enhancing Organizational Readiness

- Conduct a collaboration ROI assessment
- Engage in strategy and program development

Enhancing Retailer Process Readiness

- Invest in event visibility and demand forecasting technology/processes
- Enable continuous replenishment processes

Enhancing Supplier Readiness

- Enhance SOP practices to leverage customer-specific POS forecast data
- Implement supplier scorecards

Enhancing Technology Readiness

- Implement Internet data transport, translation and mapping technologies
- Establish interoperability among installed enterprise solutions and CPFR programs

(*Source:* Used with permission of the Voluntary Interindustry Commerce Standards (VICS) Association. See also EndNote 19.)

---

5. *Use a disciplined and iterative set of methodologies such as CPFR, SCOR, or Six Sigma to help teams define issues, root causes, and solutions.*

6. *Develop a culture of continuous improvement, particularly at the customer-facing associate level, because those employees are most likely to know what's needed.*

7. *Create clear accountabilities and assign authority with a focus on core business processes rather than on traditional organizational "silos" or loyalties.*

8. *Commit to technology enablement for execution, communication, exception management, and root-cause analysis.*

9. *Reduce decision cycle times.*

10. *Implement rapidly.*

ITT's Jabsco division, West Marine's largest customer, also implemented CPFR and in the process they experienced a reduction in cycle time from twenty-five days to three days, an increase in total sales of 11 percent, and an improvement in on-time deliveries from 74 to 94 percent.[23] It must be noted that Jabsco had coupled their existing lean Six-Sigma program with CPFR to achieve the outstanding results.

The success of the relationship can be measured using common performance metrics such as gross margin percent, return on investment, and sales growth. Other metrics include in-stock percent at point of sale, inventory turnover, inventory level, sales forecast accuracy, potential sales lost due to stockout, manufacturing cycle time, order cycle time, shipping cycle time, problem resolution time, rate of emergency or cancelled orders, and percent shipped or delivered on time.

Using CPFR, companies are working together to develop mutually agreeable plans and take responsibility for their actions. The collaborative effort leads to benefits that are greater than if each partner was to go at it independently. According to VICS, the CPFR concept is consumer driven without losing focus on best practices within the supply chain. Setting common goals for organizations pulls individual efforts together into a cohesive plan, supports better execution of the plan, and invites improved planning in the next business planning exercise. The improved planning drives sales gains through to the consumer and lowers costs throughout the supply chain.[17] Examples of companies using CPFR include Eastman Kodak, Federated Department Stores, Hewlett-Packard, JC Penney, Kimberly-Clark, Kmart, Nabisco, Procter & Gamble, Target, Wal-Mart, and Warner-Lambert. A 2006 study found that 38 percent of companies surveyed had initiated CPFR, compared to 26 percent in a 2005 survey, indicating an increasing trend in CPFR adoption.[24] The industries that are most involved with CPFR are consumer products and food and beverage.

Fujitsu Siemens Computers reported savings of over 10 million euros after implementing the i2 Demand Planner software. The i2 Demand Planner application is a "comprehensive management solution that enables enterprises, and ultimately demand planners, to accurately and effectively manage their demand by eliminating and addressing the challenges and pain points."[25] Other results reported by Fujitsu were the improvement in forecasting accuracy from 50 to 70 percent, increase in inventory turns from twenty-five to forty, decrease in planning cycle time from thirty to seven days, and improvement in delivery promise reliability from 85 to 95 percent.[26]

The top three challenges for CPFR implementation are the difficulties of making internal changes, total implementation cost, and trust.[27] As with any major implementation, internal resistance to change must be addressed by top management. Change is always difficult; however, if top management is committed to the project, then the project is much more likely to succeed. Companies will need to educate their employees on the benefits of the process changes and the disadvantages of maintaining the status quo.

There is also the question of reducing the scale of CPFR and, therefore, the cost of implementation for smaller trading partners. Although cost is an important factor, companies with no plans for adopting CPFR should determine whether they are at a competitive disadvantage, as more and more companies implement CPFR.

Trust, a major cultural issue, is considered a big hurdle to widespread implementation of CPFR because many retailers are reluctant to share the type of proprietary information required by CPFR. Whereas the suppliers of Wal-Mart, for instance, may be willing to share sensitive data with Wal-Mart, they do not want other suppliers to obtain this information. However, other experts do not believe that trust is the stumbling block for mass adoption of CPFR. Jim Uchneat, of Benchmarking Partners, Inc., says, "Trust may be a catch-all phrase that covers a host of other problems, but I have never found trust between people to be the issue. CPFR won't shift the power dynamics in a retailer/buyer relationship. If people are hoping that this is the case and refer to this as 'trust,' then they are fooling themselves. Lack of trust is more often related to the unreliable data in systems and the lack of integration internal to retailers and manufacturers."[28]

The real challenge to widespread adoption of CPFR is that it requires a fundamental change in the way buyers and sellers work together. Companies must ensure that their information technology systems, organizational structures, business processes, and internal data are conducive to implementing CPFR. For instance, many organizations are hampered by legacy systems that will have to be replaced, lack of executive management support, and an unwillingness to share sensitive information. The Global Perspective feature presents a discussion of CPFR at Wal-Mart.

Global Perspective

Collaborative Planning, Forecasting, and Replenishment at Wal-Mart

Sam Walton opened the first Wal-Mart in 1962 in Rogers, Arkansas. Today, the company offers four different retail concepts: Wal-Mart discount stores, Supercenters, Neighborhood Markets, and SAM'S Club warehouses. The emphasis on customer satisfaction and "Always Low Prices" for their products has resulted in Wal-Mart becoming the world's largest retailer with annual global revenues exceeding $340 billion in 2007. Years ago, Sam Walton said, "Let's be the most friendly—offer a smile of welcome and assistance to all who do us a favor by entering our stores. Give better service—over and beyond what our customers expect. Why not? You wonderful, caring associates can do it and do it better than any other retailing company in the world ... exceed your customers' expectations. If you do, they'll come back over and over again."[29] The company has more than 3000 non-U.S. retail units with more than 550,000 associates in countries including Argentina, Brazil, Canada, China, Costa Rica, El Salvador, Guatemala, Honduras, Japan, Mexico, Nicaragua, Puerto Rico, and the United Kingdom. In August 2007, Wal-Mart agreed to partner with Bharti Enterprises in India, to establish a joint venture called Bharti Wal-Mart Private Limited for wholesale cash-and-carry in India. The first store in India was expected to begin its operations in late 2008. Wal-Mart is considered one of the world's best supply chain operators, with cost of goods 5 to 10 percent less than its major competitors, thus providing the company with a competitive advantage.

Wal-Mart is one of the early adopters of collaborative planning, forecasting, and replenishment (CPFR), a holistic approach to managing a network of trading partners in the supply chain. CPFR enabled Wal-Mart to develop a single, short-term forecast for each item sold, which is then frozen. This mutually agreed-upon single forecast becomes the driver of improved demand management, resulting in better control over replenishment and inventory levels. The CPFR program implementation enabled Wal-Mart to move to a just-in-time system that resulted in significant savings in inventory carrying costs for Wal-Mart, as well as its suppliers. According to Joseph Eckroth Jr., Chief Information Officer at Mattel, Inc., "My ability to get information about the sales pace of a toy and either ramping up or shutting down manufacturing depends on my having data. Having sales data on a daily or hourly basis is necessary to figure out on a micro level what is selling best where and tailoring manufacturing accordingly. The greatest efficiencies will appear when the kind of trusting, mutually beneficial relationship Mattel has with Wal-Mart is duplicated with the rest of the manufacturer's retail outlets.... Having that data on a global basis from every one of my customers allows me to optimize the sales of my products and the fill rates of my customers."[30]

Wal-Mart initiated a data warehouse program to enable it to accumulate historical data in a central computer, analyze the data, have a better understanding of the business environment, and consequently make better decisions. Initially only point-of-sales and shipment data were collected. Subsequently, the data warehouse was expanded to include sixty-five weeks of data on inventory, forecasts, demographics, markdowns, returns, and market baskets by item, by store, and by day. The warehouse contains data on Wal-Mart's operations as well as its competitors.

These data are not only accessible to Wal-Mart's buyers, merchandisers, and logistics and forecasting associates but also to Wal-Mart's 3500 partners. For example, when a competitor expands its grocery department, Wal-Mart is interested in finding out the effect of this action on its sales performance. The forecasting process begins with the data warehouse. Wal-Mart uses data mining software developed by NeoVista Software (acquired by J&A Software Group, Inc.) to analyze a year's point-of-sale data in Wal-Mart's data warehouse and generates buying patterns and other results for each of its U.S. stores. Wal-Mart's return on investment was better than the cost of the initial data warehouse implementation.[31] The objective is to save millions of dollars of inventory by having a better understanding of seasonal and week-to-week variations in sales and alignment of marketing and business plans with customer demand.

The forecasting process with one of Wal-Mart's supplier partners works in this way: Wal-Mart's buyers generate a preliminary forecast, which appears on the Warner-Lambert CPFR server. (In 2000, Warner-Lambert, a global pharmaceutical company, merged with Pfizer.) The comments and revisions suggested by Warner-Lambert's planning staff are shared with Wal-Mart's planners. A final consensus forecast is generated for each product and used for inventory management at Wal-Mart and production planning at Warner-Lambert. Wal-Mart uses the same system with its other suppliers.

The data mining software has found some interesting surprises. For example, the buying patterns vary significantly from store to store and throughout the year for high-inventory consumer products such as mouthwash and pet food. The findings are used to continuously improve Wal-Mart's automated product ordering and replenishment system. The application allows Wal-Mart to analyze up to 700 million store-item combinations and deliver the right item, at the right store, at the right time, and at the right price to the customers. As a result, Wal-Mart has achieved increased accuracy in its forecasting process and a competitive advantage in the retail industry. Armed with this information, Wal-Mart makes adjustments to its product assortment based on customer requirements by individual stores. Thus Wal-Mart international stores such as in China carry a different assortment of products than Wal-Mart's stores in Mexico or Brazil.

Each year during the hurricane season, retailers such as Home Depot, Publix, and Wal-Mart have to predict what products the stores would need to stock up ahead of the storm's landfall. According to Linda M. Dillman, Wal-Mart's chief information officer, the company could "start predicting what's going to happen, instead of waiting for it to happen."[32] Wal-Mart was able to mine the huge data base of shopper history it had accumulated and determine which products were needed. They found that in addition to the usual flashlights, Pop-Tarts were selling at seven times the normal rate. Wal-Mart also found that beer was the top-selling pre-hurricane product. By stocking the right items, Wal-Mart could increase its sales as well as profit. During the hurricane season, Wal-Mart did not have a standardized approach to product assortment at each store. Instead, each store's need was assessed locally since each store's market needs were different.

Note: Some parts of this feature came from C. Stedman. "Wal-Mart Mines for Forecasts." *Computerworld* (May 26,1997); P. S. Foote and M. Krishnamurthi. "Forecasting Using a Data Warehousing Model: Wal-Mart's Experience." *The Journal of Business Forecasting Methods & Systems* 20, no. 3 (fall 2001): 13–17; Wal-Mart Web site, www.walmart.com; M. Troy. "When Hurricanes Strike … Landfall Could Mean Windfall." *Retailing Today* 46, no. 9 (June 4, 2007): 4–33; C. L. Hays. "What Wal-Mart Knows About Customers' Habits." November 14, 2004, available from: http://www.nytimes.com/2004/11/14/business/yourmoney/14wal.html.

Software Solutions

Forecasting Software

Forecasting is seldom calculated manually. If a forecaster uses a quantitative method, then a software solution can be used to simplify the process and save the time required to generate a forecast. Microsoft Excel and Lotus 1-2-3 are two widely used spreadsheet software programs that have basic forecasting capabilities. In addition, a recent survey[33] found that the top four forecasting software applications were John Galt (23 percent), SAS (16 percent), NewEnergy Associates (13 percent), and Forecast Pro (12 percent). The applications are briefly discussed below.

1. *John Galt (*http://www.johngalt.com/*)*

   John Galt Solutions, a privately owned company headquartered in Illinois, was founded in 1996. The company provides "affordable forecasting and inventory management solutions for the consumer-driven supply chain." The company's basic forecasting software, ForecastX Wizard, is an Excel add-in that can perform statistical forecasting, compute safety stock, develop inventory plans, and plan new product introductions. The ForecastX Wizard Premium software provides additional features such as safety stock and replenishment computation, on-fly forecast adjustment, and customer user interface. Premium ice cream maker Wells Dairy, headquartered in Iowa, used the software to reduce forecast percentage error from 13.9 to 9.5 percent.

2. *SAS (*http://www.sas.com/*)*

   The North Carolina-based company's software, SAS Forecast Server, provides large-scale, automated forecasting as well as time series mining to uncover time-related patterns and trends. SAS's customers include Alcon, Inc. (the world's leading eye-care company), AmBev (Latin America's largest beverage company, America West Airlines (now US Airways), CartaSí (Italy's most commonly used credit card), and Kirin Brewery Company. The SAS Forecast Server was awarded the "Trend-Setting Products of the Year" for 2005 by KMWorld magazine.

3. *NewEnergy Associates (*http://www.newenergyassoc.com/*)*

   Georgia-based NewEnergy, which was founded in 1975, was acquired by Ventyx, the world's largest private software provider to the utility industry in 2007. Their forecasting software, NOSTRADAMUS®, is a "neural network-based, short-term demand and price forecasting system, utilized by electric and gas utilities, system operators and power pools, electric cooperatives, energy marketers, and gas pipelines." NewEnergy's customers are in all sectors of the energy industry: power and gas utilities, marketers and traders, energy retailers, power generators, and transmission.

4. *Business Forecast Systems, Inc. (*www.forecastpro.com/*)*

   The Massachusetts-based company was founded in 1986. Today, their Forecast Pro software package is used by over 55,000 companies worldwide. The company offers three editions of Forecast Pro to address the different needs of their customers: Forecast Pro Basic, Forecast Pro XE, and Forecast Pro Unlimited. Several of the forecasting approaches discussed in this chapter such as moving average, trend, and exponential smoothing models are included in the software. One of the company's customers, Brooks Sports, an athletic shoe manufacturer based in Washington, used Forecast Pro to improve forecast accuracy by 40 percent, lower unfulfilled demand from 20 percent to less than 5 percent, and reduce closeouts by more than 60 percent.

CPFR Software

A CPFR software solution typically includes a forecasting module and other modules for planning procurement, supply, replenishment, and so on. The supply chain software industry has experienced consolidation over the years with numerous mergers and acquisitions, reducing the number of key players in the industry. Examples of three leading suppliers of CPFR solutions are provided here:

1. *JDA Software Group, Inc. (http://www.jda.com/)*

   Canada-based JDA Software Group's clients have won the VICS Collaborative Commerce Achievement Award for "Best in VICS CPFR(R) Implementation." JDA acquired Manugistics in July 2006, which included their CPFR solution. The CPFR software enables organizations to collaborate and share critical information with partners on forecasts, inventory, replenishment plans, point-of-sale data, promotional activities, and transportation requirements.

2. *i2 Technologies (http://www.i2.com)*

   i2, headquartered in Texas, has their Demand Collaboration application which supports the CPFR process as defined by VICS and "enables trading partners to collaborate on both demand forecasts and capacity availability, to synchronize supply chain planning, and execute for multiple customers. Through Demand Collaboration, companies get better visibility into long-term, medium-term, and short-term customer demand so demand/supply mismatch problems can be resolved before they adversely affect the planning processes or customer satisfaction. Planners can reach forecast consensus with customers, provide supply commitments, and resolve exceptions, resulting in better supply chain plans for the enterprise and its customers."[34]

3. *Oracle (http://www.oracle.com/index.html)*

   Retek purchased Syncra Systems, a leader in CPFR technology in 2004. Software giant Oracle then outbid SAP for Retek in 2005. In addition, Oracle has acquired Demantra, Hyperion, and PeopleSoft (which had earlier acquired JD Edwards). Oracle's Advanced Supply Chain Planning application is an Internet-based planning solution that allows a company to "perform simultaneous material and capacity planning across multiple distribution and manufacturing facilities and time horizons in a single planning run, while at the same time accounting for the latest consensus forecast, sales orders, production status, purchase orders, and inventory policy recommendations." The Oracle solution enables the company to "increase forecast accuracy, implement vendor managed and consigned inventory processes, increase global supply visibility, reduce supply shortages, and lower expediting cost."

The e-Business Connection feature profiles two major online exchanges and their use of CPFR.

e-Business Connection

Online Exchanges and CPFR

Mega online exchanges such as Transora and Agentrics understand the importance and benefits of CPFR and have incorporated this solution into their product offerings. A description of the two exchanges are provided here.

- **1SYNC** (http://www.transora.com/home.html)
  In mid-2000, members of the Grocery Manufacturers of America established Transora, a business-to-business exchange for the consumer packaged goods industry. UCCnet and Transora later merged to form a single organization — 1SYNC in August, 2005. 1SYNC is a not-for-profit subsidiary of GS1 US™. 1SYNC's vision statement is "To be the leader in synchronizing data across the global supply and demand chains." It operates in the United States, Europe, Mexico, and South America. Its members include Ace Hardware, Coca-Cola, Colgate Palmolive, E J Gallo, Gillette, Hormel Foods, Johnson & Johnson, Kraft, Kroger, Lowe's, Nestle, Office Depot, Paramount, Pep Boys, PepsiCo, Procter & Gamble, Sara Lee, SUPERVALU, Unilever, Wal-Mart, and Wegmans Food Markets. Its CPFR provider is Oracle.

- **Agentrics** LLC (http://www.agentrics.com/en/index.html)
  In 2006, GlobalNetXchange (GNX) and WorldWide Retail Exchange merged to form Agentrics LLC, the retail industry Internet-based trading exchange. GNX is a retail industry exchange with equity partners such as Carrefour SA; Coles Myer Ltd.; Karstadt Quelle AG; The Kroger Co.; Metro AG; Pinault-Printemps-Redoute SA; J Sainsbury Plc; and Sears, Roebuck and Co. WorldWide Retail Exchange (WWRE), founded in March 2000, is an industry-sponsored marketplace for retailers and suppliers in the food, general merchandise, textile/home, and drugstore sectors. Its membership consists of leading retailers from Africa, Asia, Europe, South America, and the United States and include Aeon, Ahold, Albertson's, Auchan, Best Buy, Groupe Casino, CVS, Delhaize Group, El Corte Ingles, J.C. Penney, Kingfisher, Lotte, Marks & Spencer, Makro (SHV), REWE, Safeway, SCA, SCA Hygiene, Target, Tesco, and Walgreens. Its CPFR provider is Oracle. Agentrics recently received 2007 *VICS Most Innovative Third Party Technology Provider (Tie) Award*. The VICS Collaborative Commerce Achievement Awards are "designed to identify and reward excellence in supply chain collaboration."

The major retail exchanges such as Transora and Agentrics argue that CPFR is best included in an e-marketplace. Carrefour, a founding member of GNX (now Agentrics), is an example of a company committed to the exchange-based CPFR.

SUMMARY

Forecasting is an integral part of demand management, since it provides an estimate of future demand and the basis for planning and making sound business decisions. A mismatch in supply and demand could result in excessive inventories and stockouts, and loss of profits and goodwill. Proper demand forecasting enables better planning and utilization of resources for businesses to be competitive. Both qualitative and quantitative methods are available to help companies forecast demand better. The qualitative methods are based on judgment and intuition, whereas the quantitative methods use mathematical techniques and historical data to predict future demand. The quantitative forecasting methods can be divided into time series and cause-and-effect models. Since forecasts are seldom completely accurate, management must monitor forecast errors and make the necessary improvements to the forecasting process to reduce error.

Forecasts made in isolation tend to be inaccurate. Collaborative planning, forecasting, and replenishment (CPFR) is an approach in which companies work together to develop mutually agreeable plans and take responsibility for their actions. The objective of CPFR is to optimize the supply chain by generating a consensus demand forecast, delivering the right product at the right time to the right location, reducing inventories, avoiding stockouts, and improving customer service. The Global Commerce Initiative and Voluntary Interindustry Commerce Standards have been instrumental in standardizing and promoting CPFR worldwide. Major corporations such as Wal-Mart, Warner-Lambert, and Proctor & Gamble were early adopters of CPFR.

The computation involved in generating a forecast is seldom done manually. Forecasting software packages such as Forecast Pro, SAS, SPSS, and Microsoft Excel are readily available. Major CPFR solutions providers include JDA Software, i2, and Oracle. Online exchanges such as Transora and Agentrics are incorporating CPFR solutions into their product offerings for their partnering companies.

KEY TERMS

business cycle, 144

cause-and-effect forecasting, 144

collaborative planning, forecasting and replenishment, 157

consumer survey forecast, 143

cyclical variations, 144

delphi method forecast, 143

forecast bias, 154

forecast error, 154

jury of executive opinion forecast, 143

linear trend forecast, 149

mean absolute deviation (MAD), 154

mean absolute percentage error (MAPE), 154

mean square error (MSE), 154

multiple regression forecast, 152

naïve forecast, 145

random variations, 144

running sum of forecast errors (RSFE), 154

sales force composite forecast, 143

seasonal variations, 144

simple exponential smoothing forecast, 146

simple linear regression forecast, 150

simple moving average forecast, 145

time series forecasting, 144

tracking signal, 154

trend variations, 144

weighted moving average forecast, 145

DISCUSSION QUESTIONS

1. What is demand management?

2. What is demand forecasting?

3. Why is demand forecasting important for effective supply chain management?

4. Explain the impact of a mismatch in supply and demand. What strategies can companies adopt to influence demand?

5. What are qualitative forecasting techniques? When are these methods more suitable?

6. What are the main components of a time series?

7. Explain the difference between a time series model and an associative model. Under what conditions would one model be preferred to the other?

8. What is the impact of the smoothing constant value on the simple exponential forecast?

9. Compare and contrast the jury of executive opinion and the Delphi techniques.

10. Explain the key differences between the weighted moving average and the simple exponential smoothing forecasting methods.

11. What are three measures of forecasting accuracy?

12. What is a tracking signal? What information does the tacking signal provide that managers can use to improve the quality of forecasts?

13. What are the key features of CPFR? Why would a company consider adopting CPFR?

14. What are the eight tasks associated with the CPFR model? Why is sharing data important in CPFR implementation? What are the benefits of sharing information?

15. West Marine identified ten performance improvement steps in their successful implementation of CPFR. Is West Marine's approach unique or can their experience be duplicated at another company? What are the key challenges that other companies might face in implementing CPFR?

16. Why is widespread adoption of CPFR below expectations?

INTERNET QUESTIONS

1. Go to the Web sites of i2 (http://www.i2.com) and JDA Software (http://www.jda.com) and write a report comparing the capabilities of these two CPFR solutions.

2. The VICS Web site at http://www.cpfr.org shows the road map for CPFR implementation. What are the key success elements and roadblocks to the implementation of CPFR?

3. Business Forecasts System (http://hwww.forecastpro.com) is considered one of the leading providers of forecasting software, with their product Forecast Pro. Compare their three versions of forecasting software: Forecast Pro, Forecast Pro XE, and Forecast Pro Unlimited.

INFOTRAC QUESTIONS

Access http://academic.cengage.com/infotrac to answer the following questions:

1. Search for the term "demand management" and write a report on demand management in the retail or healthcare industry.

2. Search for the term "forecasting software" and write a report on the more popular forecasting software used by companies. What are the key features of the software that make them highly desirable?

3. Search for the term "capacity planning, forecasting, and replenishment" and write a report on the state of implementation of CPFR in the retail industry. Is the rate of implementation as expected? Please explain.

4. Search for the term "CPFR software" and write a report on the state of the supply chain software industry with respect to the mergers and acquisitions (M&As). Are the M&As beneficial in general for supply chains?

SPREADSHEET PROBLEMS

1. Ms. Winnie Lin's company sells computers. Monthly sales for a six-month period are as follows:

MONTH	SALES
Jan	18,000
Feb	22,000
Mar	16,000
Apr	18,000
May	20,000
Jun	24,000

(a) Plot the monthly data on a sheet of graph paper.

(b) Compute the sales forecast for July using the following approaches: (1) A four-month moving average; (2) A weighted three-month moving average using .50 for June, .30 for May, and .20 for April; (3) A linear trend equation; (4) Simple exponential smoothing with α (smoothing constant) equal to .40 and assuming a February forecast of 18,000.

(c) Which method do you think is the least appropriate? Why?

2. The owner of a Chocolate Outlet Store wants to forecast chocolate demand.

Demand for the preceding 4 years is shown in the following table:

YEAR	DEMAND (POUNDS)
1	68,800
2	71,000
3	75,500
4	71,200

Forecast demand for Year 5 using the following approaches:

(a) A three-year simple moving average

(b) A three-year weighted moving average using .40 for Year 4, .20 for Year 3, and .40 for Year 2

(c) Simple exponential smoothing with $\alpha = .30$ and assuming the forecast for Period 1 = 68,800

3. The forecasts generated by two forecasting methods and actual sales are as follows:

MONTH	SALES	FORECAST 1	FORECAST 2
1	269	275	268
2	289	266	287
3	294	290	292
4	278	284	298
5	268	270	274
6	269	268	270
7	260	261	259
8	275	271	275

Compute the MSE, the MAD, the MAPE, and the tracking signal for each forecasting method. Which method is better? Why?

Chapter 6

RESOURCE PLANNING SYSTEMS

The advantage of having a single ERP vendor is that there are fewer throats to choke when things go bad... As companies become increasingly more global, senior management is also attracted to the notion of using a single vendor of ERP, rather than mixing and matching tools from various niche, or so-called best-of-breed vendors.[1]

When ERP is discussed today, it is rarely in the context of planning how resources are to be expended. Rather, it refers to an enterprise view of business—in other words, a view of a company and all its parts as a connected whole, rather than small silos of activity.[2]

Learning Objectives

After completing this chapter, you should be able to

- Describe the hierarchical operations planning process in terms of materials planning (APP, MPS, MRP) and capacity planning (RRP, RCCP, CRP).
- Describe MRP, closed-loop MRP, MRP-II, DRP, and ERP, and their relationships.
- Understand the terms used in MRP computation.
- Know how to compute available-to-promise quantities, MRP explosion, and DRP implosion.
- Understand the limitations of legacy MRP systems.
- Describe an ERP system, and understand its advantages and disadvantages.
- Understand why manufacturers and service firms are migrating from legacy MRP systems to integrated ERP systems.
- Describe the various modules of an integrated ERP system, and have a general knowledge of the ERP market.
- Understand best-of-breed versus single integrator ERP implementations.
- Understand why many ERP implementations fail.
- Understand how an integrated ERP system works.

Chapter Outline

Supply Chain Management in Action

Manufacturing Planning at General Nutrition Centers, Inc.

General Nutrition Centers, Inc. (GNC), the world's largest nutritional supplements retailer, began as a single humble store in Pittsburgh, Pennsylvania. Then it became a health food store called Lackzoom, where profits were initially modest. With the advent of the health-conscious 1960s, however, founder David Shakarian was able to expand his business outside of Pennsylvania and into other states. A name change ensued, and GNC soon began producing not only supplements, but food, drinks, and cosmetics as well. Today, the company has more than 5,000 locations inside the United States and more than 830 locations in 46 international markets.[3] As implied by the company's motto, "Live Well," GNC focuses on making quality products that encourage consumers to pursue healthier lifestyles. GNC ensures product integrity in various fashions, from engaging in scientific research and product discovery to requiring transparency about ingredient safety.

Nutra Manufacturing, the manufacturing division of GNC, produces these nutritional supplements in a plant with an annual capacity of 13 billion units in Greenville, South Carolina. The bulk products are shipped to a 300,000 square-foot facility about 30 miles away in Anderson, South Carolina, for packaging. Nutra Manufacturing faces multiple production challenges. First, the production process is extremely intricate, with multiple changeable parts. There are roughly eight primary manufacturing operations per product, and each of these operations may be individually associated with alternative operations. Second, production planning proves difficult with the sheer number of products Nutra Manufacturing produces. Third, the dietary supplement market has a very short product life cycle and new supplements come in vogue quickly due to shifting demographics.

Nutra Manufacturing needed new planning and information technology to combat these production challenges. A project team within Nutra Manufacturing was formed to improve manufacturing planning. After the evaluation of a range of solutions, the team settled on Voyager Manufacturing Planning software from Logility, an Atlanta-based supplier of collaborative solutions to optimize supply chains.[4] Selected for its affordability and user-friendliness, the new solution enables Nutra Manufacturing to collaborate and synchronize planning, sourcing, production, and logistics activities with its supply chain members. Internally, the solution enables the manufacturing division to quickly create constraint-based capacity plans and master production schedules. Moreover, the new solution also indicates excess capacity available that can be sold to third-party customers.

The solution quickly proved its worth by providing greater confidence that production plans can become executable schedules. In addition to standardizing packaging across the various nutritional supplements, the solution also allowed analysts to review things such as backlog levels, trends in demand, and production plan performance compared to the budget, among other capabilities. This was a marked improvement where previously Nutra Manufacturing utilized Microsoft Excel for operations planning and scheduling. The former system had numerous acute limitations, such as no constraint visibility, suboptimal production schedules, no graphical analysis of planning, and most importantly, the creation of production plans that were not always executable. Another notable benefit of the new implementation at Nutra Manufacturing is the ability of the new solution to integrate with GNC's enterprise resource planning (ERP) system. This improved synchronization has improved workflows, inventory turnovers, and information-sharing across functional divisions within the firm, and unlocked valuable ERP data for strategic business planning and decision making.

Note: Some information in this feature also came from Anonymous. "Taking Manufacturing Planning to the Next Level." *APICS Magazine,* 17, no. 7 (July/August 2007): 52–53.

Introduction

Resource planning is the process of determining the production capacity required to meet demand. In the context of resource planning, **capacity** refers to the maximum work load that an organization is capable of completing in a given period of time. A discrepancy between an organization's capacity and demand results in an inefficiency, either in underutilized resources or unfulfilled orders. The goal of resource planning is to minimize this discrepancy.

One of the most critical activities of an organization is to efficiently balance the production plan with capacity; it directly influences how effectively the organization deploys its resources in producing goods and services. Developing feasible operations schedules and capacity plans to meet delivery due dates and minimize waste in manufacturing or service organizations is a complex problem. The need for better operations scheduling continues to challenge operations managers, especially in today's intensely competitive global marketplace. In an environment fostering collaborative buyer–supplier relationships, the challenge of scheduling operations to meet delivery due dates and eliminate waste is becoming a more complex problem. The problem is compounded in an integrated supply chain, where a missed due date or stockout cascades downstream, magnifying the **bullwhip effect** and adversely affecting the entire supply chain.

Operations managers are continuously involved in resource and operations planning to balance capacity and output. Capacity may be stated in terms of labor, materials, or equipment. With too much excess capacity, production cost per unit is high due to idle workers and machinery. However, if workers and machinery are overutilized, quality and customer service levels are likely to deteriorate. Firms generally run their operations at about 85 percent capacity to allow time for scheduled repairs and maintenance and to meet unexpected demand.

This chapter describes the hierarchical operations planning process in terms of materials and **capacity planning**. A hypothetical industrial example is used to demonstrate the hierarchical planning process. This chapter also discusses the evolution of the manufacturing planning and control system from the material requirements planning (MRP) system to the **enterprise resource planning (ERP)** system.

Operations Planning

Operations planning is usually hierarchical and can be divided into three broad categories: (1) *long-range*, (2) *intermediate or medium-range*, and (3) *short-range planning horizons*. While the distinctions among the three planning horizons can be vague, long-range plans usually cover a year or more, tend to be more general, and specify resources and outputs in terms of aggregate hours and units. Medium-range plans normally span 6 to 18 months, whereas short-range plans usually cover a few days to a few weeks depending on the type and size of the firm. Long-range plans are established first and are then used to guide the medium-range plans, which are subsequently used to guide the short-range plans. Long-range plans usually involve major, strategic decisions in capacity, such as the construction of new facilities and purchase of capital equipment, whereas medium-range plans involve more minor changes in capacity such as changes in employment levels. Short-range plans are the most detailed and specify the exact end items and quantities to make on a daily or hourly basis.

Figure 6.1 shows the planning horizons and how a business plan cascades into the various hierarchical materials and capacity plans. The **aggregate production plan (APP)** is a long-range materials plan. Since capacity expansion involves the construction of a new facility and major equipment purchases, the aggregate production plan's capacity is usually considered fixed during the planning horizon. The aggregate production plan sets the aggregate output rate, workforce size, utilization and inventory, and/or backlog levels for an entire facility. The **master production schedule (MPS)** is a medium-range plan and is more detailed than the aggregate production plan. It shows the quantity and timing of the end items or services that will be produced. The **materials requirement planning (MRP)** is a short-range materials plan. The MRP, also known as little mrp or MRP-I, is the detailed planning process for components and parts to support the master production schedule. It is a system of converting the end items from the master production schedule into a set of time-phased component and part requirements.

A **closed-loop MRP** is an MRP-based manufacturing planning and control system that incorporates the aggregate production plan, the master production schedule, the material requirements plan, and the capacity requirements plan. It is an extension of MRP. **Manufacturing resource planning (MRP-II)** is an outgrowth and extension of the

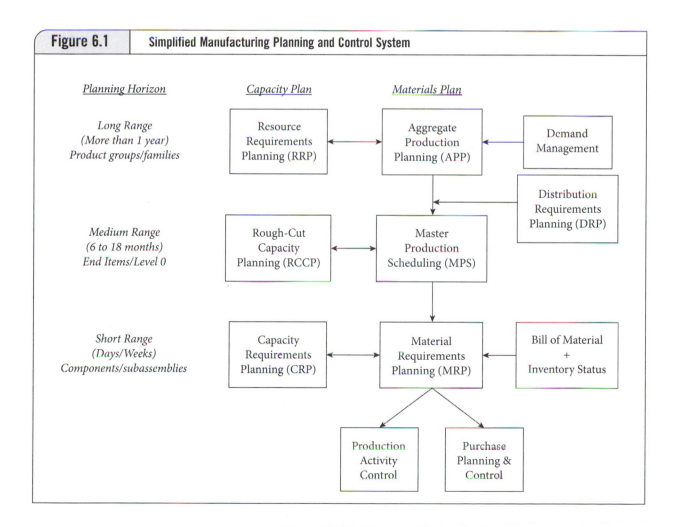

| Figure 6.1 | Simplified Manufacturing Planning and Control System |

closed-loop MRP system. It incorporates the business and sales plans with the closed-loop MRP system and has simulation capabilities to answer "what-if" types of planning questions. A further extension of the MRP-II system is ERP.

Distribution requirements planning (DRP) describes the time-phased net requirements from central supply warehouses and distribution centers. It is equal to the customer demand minus any on-hand and in-transit inventories. Distribution requirements planning links production with distribution planning by providing aggregate time-phased net requirements information to the master production schedule.

The Aggregate Production Plan

Aggregate production planning is a hierarchical planning process that translates annual business and marketing plans and demand forecasts into a production plan for all products in a plant or facility. As shown in Figure 6.1, *demand management* includes determining the aggregate demand based on forecasts of future demand, orders received from internal and external customers, special promotions, and safety stock requirements. This forecast of demand then sets the aggregate utilization, production rate, workforce levels, and inventory balances or backlogs. Aggregate production plans are typically stated in terms of product families or groups. A **product family** consists of different products that share similar characteristics, components, or manufacturing processes. For example, an all-terrain-vehicle (ATV) manufacturer that produces both automatic and manual drive options may group the two different types of ATVs together, since the only difference between them is the drive option. Production processes and material requirements for the two ATVs can be expected to be very similar and, thus, can be grouped into a family.

The planning horizon covered by the APP is usually at least one year and is usually extended or rolled forward by 3 months every quarter. This allows the firm to see its capacity requirements at least one year ahead on a continuous basis. The APP *disaggregates* the annual demand forecast information it receives and links the long-range business and marketing plans to the medium-range master production schedule. The objective is to provide sufficient finished goods in each period to meet the sales plan while meeting financial and production constraints.

Costs relevant to the aggregate planning decision include inventory cost, setup cost, machine operating cost, hiring cost, firing cost, training cost, overtime cost, and costs incurred for hiring part-time and temporary workers to meet peak demand. There are three basic production strategies for addressing the aggregate planning problem: (1) the *chase strategy*, (2) the *level strategy*, and (3) the *mixed strategy*. Example 6.1 provides a detailed illustration of an APP.

The Chase Production Strategy

The pure **chase production strategy** adjusts capacity to match the demand pattern. Using this strategy, the firm will hire and layoff workers to match its production rate to demand. The workforce fluctuates from month to month, but finished goods inventory remains constant. Using Example 6.1, the ATV Corporation will use six workers to make 120 units in January, and then lay off a worker in February to produce 100 units, as shown in Table 6.2. In March, the firm must hire ten additional workers so that it has enough labor to produce 300 units. An additional eight workers must be hired in April. The firm continues its hiring and layoff policy to ensure its

Example 6.1   An Aggregate Production Plan for the ATV Corporation

The ATV Corporation makes three models of all-terrain vehicles—Model A, Model B, and Model C. Model A uses a 0.4-liter engine, Model B uses a 0.5-liter engine, and Model C uses a 0.6-liter engine. The aggregate production plan is the 12-month plan that lumps all three models together in total monthly production. The planning horizon is 12 months. The aggregate production plan sets the size of the workforce, which is the constrained resource. Table 6.1 shows the annual aggregate production plan from January to December, assuming the beginning inventory for January is 100 units (30 units each of Model A and Model B, and 40 units of Model C), and the firm desires to have an ending inventory of 140 units at the end of the year. On average, one unit of ATV requires eight labor hours to produce, and a worker contributes 160 (8 hours × 5 days × 4 weeks) hours per month. The 1,120 labor hours needed in December as shown in Table 6.1 excludes the labor required to produce the additional 40 units (8 hours × 40 units = 320 hours) of ending inventory.

Table 6.1   ATV Corporation's Aggregate Production Plan

PERIOD	FORECAST DEMAND (UNITS)	CAPACITY (LABOR HOURS) NEEDED (HOURS)	PLANNED
January	120	960	10 workers
February	100	800	10 workers
March	300	2400	12 workers + overtime
April	460	3680	18 workers + overtime
May	600	4800	25 workers + overtime
June	700	5600	25 workers + overtime + subcontracting
July	760	6080	25 workers + overtime + subcontracting
August	640	5120	25 workers + overtime
September	580	4640	25 workers + overtime
October	400	3200	20 workers
November	200	1600	10 workers
December	140	1120	10 workers
Total	5000	40,000	

workforce and production capacity matches demand. In December, 180 units will be produced (although the demand is 140) because of the firm's desire to increase its ending inventory by 40 units in December. This strategy obviously has a negative motivational impact on the workers, and it assumes that workers can be hired and trained easily to perform the job. In a chase strategy, the finished goods inventories always remain constant but the workforce fluctuates in response to the demand pattern. Figure 6.2 shows that the chase production is a perfect overlap of the demand while the inventory level remains constant at 100 units until December when it

Table 6.2	An Example of Chase Production Strategy				
PERIOD	FORECAST DEMAND (UNITS)	CAPACITY (LABOR)		PRODUCTION (UNITS)	ENDING INVENTORY (UNITS)
		HOURS	WORKERS		
January	120	960	6	120	100
February	100	800	5	100	100
March	300	2400	15	300	100
April	460	3680	23	460	100
May	600	4800	30	600	100
June	700	5600	35	700	100
July	760	6080	38	760	100
August	640	5120	32	640	100
September	580	4640	29	580	100
October	400	3200	20	400	100
November	200	1600	10	200	100
December	140 + 40	1120 + 320	9	180	140
Total	5040	40,320	252	5040	

Figure 6.2	Constant Inventory Level Under the Chase Production Strategy

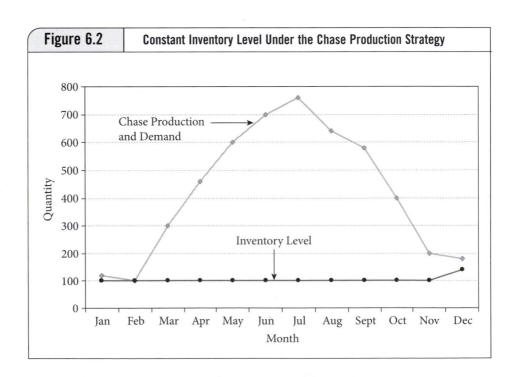

increases by 40 units. Hiring, training, and layoff costs are significant cost components in the chase production strategy.

This strategy works well for **make-to-order manufacturing firms** since they cannot rely on finished goods inventory to satisfy the fluctuating demand pattern. Make-to-order firms generally produce one-of-a-kind, specialty products based on customer specifications. Make-to-order firms cannot build ahead of orders since they do not know the actual specifications of the finished goods. However, make-to-order products generally require highly skilled labor that is capable of producing unique products using general purpose equipment. Although the chase production strategy works well when low-cost, unskilled labor is hired and abandoned, the strategy can be problematic when highly skilled workers are needed, especially in a tight labor market.

The Level Production Strategy

A pure **level production strategy** relies on a constant output rate and capacity while varying inventory and backlog levels to handle the fluctuating demand pattern. Using this strategy, the firm keeps its workforce levels constant and relies on fluctuating finished goods inventories and backlogs to meet demand. Since the level production strategy maintains a constant output rate and capacity, it is better suited for firms requiring highly skilled labor. The workforce can be expected to be more effective and morale is likely to be better when compared to the chase strategy. Again using Example 6.1, a level production strategy calls for a monthly production rate of 420 units [(5,000 units yearly demand + 40 units additional ending inventory) ÷ 12 months]. Thus, this strategy requires a constant workforce of 21 workers, as shown in Table 6.3.

The firm allows finished goods inventories to accrue while cumulative demand remains less than cumulative production and then relies on a series of backlogs to handle the demand from August through November. Figure 6.3 shows that level production is characterized by the fluctuating inventory/backlog level while the workforce and production capacity remain constant. Inventory carrying costs and stockout costs are major cost components in the level production strategy. This strategy works well for **make-to-stock manufacturing firms**, which typically emphasize immediate delivery of off-the-shelf, standard goods at relatively low prices compared to the chase strategy. Thus, firms whose trading partners seek the lowest prices of stock items might select this type of production strategy. The level production strategy works well in a situation where highly skilled workers are needed in a tight labor market.

The Mixed Production Strategy

Instead of using either the pure chase or level production strategy, many firms use a mixed production strategy that strives to maintain a stable core workforce while using other short-term means such as overtime, an additional shift, subcontracting, or the hiring of part-time and temporary workers to manage short-term high demand. Usually, these firms will then schedule preventive maintenance, engage in producing complementary products that require similar resources but different demand cycles, or continue to produce the end items, holding these as finished goods inventory during the off-peak demand periods.

For example, an all-terrain-vehicle manufacturer can produce snowmobiles to smooth out the seasonal effects of the two products. Table 6.1 shows a mixed strategy in which the firm strives to maintain a minimum core workforce of ten workers

Table 6.3		An Example of Level Production Strategy			
		CAPACITY (LABOR)			ENDING
PERIOD	FORECAST DEMAND (UNITS)	HOURS	WORKERS	PRODUCTION (UNITS)	INVENTORY/ (BACKLOG)
January	120	960	21	420	400
February	100	800	21	420	720
March	300	2400	21	420	840
April	460	3680	21	420	800
May	600	4800	21	420	620
June	700	5600	21	420	340
July	760	6080	21	420	0
August	640	5120	21	420	(220)
September	580	4640	21	420	(380)
October	400	3200	21	420	(360)
November	200	1600	21	420	(140)
December	140 + 40	1120 + 320	21	420	140
Total	5040	40,320	252	5040	

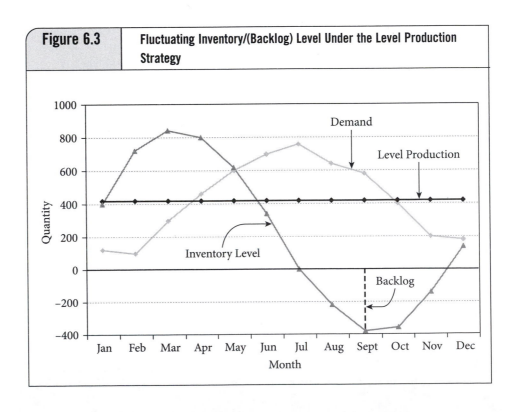

Figure 6.3   Fluctuating Inventory/(Backlog) Level Under the Level Production Strategy

while avoiding hiring above 25 workers during peak season. Hiring above 25 workers may strain other capacities, such as machine capacity and the availability of component parts. Instead, the mixed strategy uses overtime and subcontracting to cope with excessively high demand. If labor is the only constrained capacity, it may hire enough workers to run an additional shift to cope with exceptionally high demand. We can see here that firms with multiple products and with customers seeking both low-cost and make-to-order items may opt for this type of production strategy to minimize stockouts and cycle time.

Master Production Scheduling

The master production schedule is a detailed disaggregation of the aggregate production plan, listing the exact end items to be produced by a specific period. It is more detailed than the aggregate production plan and is easier to plan when demand is stable. Its planning horizon is shorter than the aggregate production plan but longer than the lead time to produce the item. Otherwise, the end item cannot be completed within its MPS planning horizon.

For example, disaggregating ATV Corporation's January and February aggregate production plans may yield the master production schedule shown in Table 6.4. The plan results in time-phased production requirements of the specific model of ATV to produce for every week in January and February. The sum of the master production schedule is equal to the total of the monthly production plan. For example, the master production schedule for January and February in Table 6.4 equals 120 and 100 units, respectively. The master production schedule also provides more detail by breaking down the aggregate production plan into the specific weekly output of Model A, Model B, and Model C.

For the service industry, the master production schedule may just be the appointment log or book, which is created to ensure that capacity in the form of skilled labor or professional service is balanced with demand. Appointments (or the MPS) are

Table 6.4	ATV's Master Production Schedule for January and February		
PERIOD	MODEL A	MODEL B	MODEL C
January—week 1	10	10	10
January—week 2	10	10	10
January—week 3	20	0	10
January—week 4	0	20	10
February—week 1	20	0	0
February—week 2	0	20	0
February—week 3	0	0	20
February—week 4	20	20	0
Total	80	80	60

not overbooked to ensure capacity is not strained, but operations continue to revise and add appointments to the MPS until it obtains a schedule that is optimal. An example of an MPS in the service sector is the appointment book of a clinic for scheduling patients' appointments for the next 3 months.

Master Production Schedule Time Fence

The master production schedule is the production quantity required to meet demand from all sources and is the basis for computing the requirements of all time-phased end items. The material requirements plan uses the MPS to compute component part and subassembly requirements. Frequent updates or changes to the MPS can be costly and may create *system nervousness*.

System nervousness is defined as a situation where a small change in the upper-level production plan causes a major change in the lower-level production plan. For example, in the case of the clinic booking new appointments, it would be very difficult for the clinic to book additional appointments for the current period if it is very likely that the appointment book is already completely filled. If a patient insists that she must see the doctor immediately, it is likely that another patient's appointment may have to be delayed or the clinic would need to work overtime to see an additional patient. However, it would be much easier for the clinic to book new appointments farther into the future, when the appointment book is not full.

System nervousness can also create serious problems for manufacturing firms. For example, if the January master production schedule for the ATV Corporation is suddenly doubled during the second week of January, the firm would be forced to quickly revise purchase orders, component assembly orders, and end-item production orders, causing a ripple effect of change within the firm and up its supply chain to its suppliers. The change would also likely cause missed delivery due dates. The firm needs sufficient lead time to purchase items and manufacture the end items, especially if manufacturing lead times and lot sizes are large.

Many firms use a *time fence system* to deal with this problem. The time fence system separates the planning horizon into two segments—a *firmed* and a *tentative segment*. A *firmed segment* is also known as the **demand time fence**, and it usually stretches from the current period to a period several weeks into the future. A firmed segment stipulates that the production plan or master production schedule cannot be altered except with the authorization of senior management. The *tentative segment* is also known as the **planning time fence**, and it typically stretches from the end of the firmed segment to several weeks farther into the future. It usually covers a longer period than the firmed segment, giving the master scheduler time to change production to meet changing conditions. Beyond the planning time fence, the computer can schedule the MPS quantities automatically, based on existing ordering and scheduling policies.

Available-to-Promise Quantities

In addition to providing time-phased production quantities of specific end items, the MPS also provides vital information on whether additional orders can be accepted for delivery in specific periods. This information is particularly important when customers are relying on the firm to deliver the right quantity of products purchased on the desired delivery date. This information is the **available-to-promise (ATP) quantity** or the uncommitted portion of the firm's planned production (or scheduled MPS). It is the difference between confirmed customer orders and the quantity the firm planned to produce, based on the MPS. The available-to-promise quantity provides a mechanism to allow the master scheduler or sales personnel to quickly negotiate new orders and delivery due dates with customers or to quickly respond to a trading partner's changing demands. The three basic methods of calculating the available-to-promise quantities are (1) *discrete available-to-promise*, (2) *cumulative available-to-promise without look ahead*, and (3) *cumulative available-to-promise with look ahead*. The discrete available-to-promise (ATP:D) computation is discussed next. Readers who are interested in the other two methods are referred to Fogarty, Blackstone, and Hoffmann (1991).[5]

The ATV Corporation's January and February master production schedule for Model A, Model B, and Model C is used in Table 6.5 to demonstrate the ATP:D method for computing the ATP quantities. Let us assume that there are four weeks each in January and February, which are shown in the first row and labeled Week 1 to Week 8. The MPS row indicates the time-phased production quantities derived from the master production schedule in Table 6.4. These are the quantities to be produced by manufacturing as planned. The number labeled "BI" is the beginning inventory for the first week in January. Committed customer orders are orders that have already been booked for specific customers. Finally, the ATP:D quantities are the remaining unbooked or unpromised units.

Calculating Discrete Available-to-Promise Quantities

The discrete available-to-promise (ATP:D) is computed as follows:

1. The ATP for Period 1 is the sum of the BI and the MPS, minus the sum of all the committed customer orders (CCOs) from Period 1 up to but not including the period of the next scheduled MPS.

Table 6.5	Discrete ATP Calculation for January and February							
				WEEK				
		1	2	3	4	5	6	7	8
Model A—0.4-liter engine									
MPS	BI = 30	10	10	20	0	20	0	0	20
Committed customer orders		10	0	28	0	0	20	0	10
ATP:D		30	2	0	0	0	0	0	10
Model B—0.5-liter engine									
MPS	BI = 30	10	10	0	20	0	20	0	20
Committed customer orders		20	10	7	0	0	20	18	0
ATP:D		13	0	0	2	0	0	0	20
Model C—0.6-liter engine									
MPS	BI = 40	10	10	10	10	0	0	20	0
Committed customer orders		20	10	0	0	0	10	0	15
ATP:D		30	0	10	0	0	0	5	0

2. For all subsequent periods, there are two possibilities:
   a. If no MPS has been scheduled for the period, the ATP is zero.
   b. If an MPS has been scheduled for the period, the ATP is the MPS quantity minus the sum of all the CCOs from that period up to the period of the next scheduled MPS.
3. If an ATP for any period is negative, the deficit must be subtracted from the most recent positive ATP, and the ATP quantities must then be revised to reflect these changes.

As a check, the sum of the BI and the MPS quantities for all periods in the calculation must equal the sum of all CCOs and ATPs. Using these guidelines, the ATP:D quantities in Table 6.5 are computed as follows:

Model A

1. $ATP_1 = BI + MPS_1 - CCO_1 = 30 + 10 - 10 = 30$.
2. $ATP_2 = MPS_2 - CCO_2 = 10 - 0 = 10$.
3. $ATP_3 = MPS_3 - CCO_3 - CCO_4 = 20 - 28 - 0 = -8$ (need to use 8 units from ATP_2).

   Revising, $ATP_2 = 10 - 8 = 2$ and $ATP_3 = -8 + 8 = 0$.
4. $ATP_4 = 0$ (no scheduled MPS).
5. $ATP_5 = MPS_5 - CCO_5 - CCO_6 - CCO_7 = 20 - 0 - 20 - 0 = 0$.
6. $ATP_6 = 0$ (no scheduled MPS).
7. $ATP_7 = 0$ (no scheduled MPS).
8. $ATP_8 = MPS_8 - CCO_8 = 20 - 10 = 10$.

Checking the calculations, the sum of the BI and the MPS quantities for the eight periods equals 110 units, and the sum of the CCOs and the ATPs for the eight periods also equals 110 units. Further, the calculation shows that 30 units of the Model A ATV can be promised for delivery in the first week of January or later, 2 units can be promised in the second week or later, and another 10 units can be promised for delivery in the eighth week or later. The eight-period total ATP of 42 units is the difference between the sum of the BI and MPS quantities (110), and the sum of the CCOs (68) for the eight-week time frame. Also note that although no MPS has been scheduled for the sixth week, the committed customer orders of 20 units in that same week is still possible, since the units can come from the scheduled and uncommitted MPS of the fifth week.

Model B

1. $ATP_1 = BI + MPS_1 - CCO_1 = 30 + 10 - 20 = 20$.
2. $ATP_2 = MPS_2 - CCO_2 - CCO_3 = 10 - 10 - 7 = -7$ (need to use 7 units from ATP_1).

   Revising, $ATP_1 = 20 - 7 = 13$ and $ATP_2 = -7 + 7 = 0$.
3. $ATP_3 = 0$ (no scheduled MPS).
4. $ATP_4 = MPS_4 - CCO_4 - CCO_5 = 20 - 0 - 0 = 20$.
5. $ATP_5 = 0$ (no scheduled MPS).
6. $ATP_6 = MPS_6 - CCO_6 - CCO_7 = 20 - 20 - 18 = -18$ (need to use 18 units from ATP_4 since $ATP_5 = 0$).

   Revising, $ATP_4 = 20 - 18 = 2$ and $ATP_6 = -18 + 18 = 0$.

7. $ATP_7 = 0$ (no scheduled MPS).

8. $ATP_8 = MPS_8 - CCO_8 = 20 - 0 = 20.$

Checking, the BI plus the eight MPS quantities equals 110, and the CCOs plus the ATPs for the eight periods also equals 110. The calculation shows that 13 units of the Model B ATV can be promised for delivery in the first week or later, 2 units can be promised for delivery in the fourth week or later, and another 20 units can be promised for delivery in the eighth week or later. The eight-period total ATP quantity of 35 is the difference between the sum of the BI and MPS (110), and the sum of the committed orders (75) for the 8-week period. Note that although no MPS has been scheduled for the seventh week, the CCO of 18 units in that same week is still possible, since the units can come from the scheduled and uncommitted units from the MPS of the fourth week.

Model C

1. $ATP_1 = BI + MPS_1 - CCO_1 = 40 + 10 - 20 = 30.$

2. $ATP_2 = MPS_2 - CCO_2 = 10 - 10 = 0.$

3. $ATP_3 = MPS_3 - CCO_3 = 10 - 0 = 10.$

4. $ATP_4 = MPS_4 - CCO_4 - CCO_5 - CCO_6 = 10 - 0 - 0 - 10 = 0.$

5. $ATP_5 = 0$ (no scheduled MPS).

6. $ATP_6 = 0$ (no scheduled MPS).

7. $ATP_7 = MPS_7 - CCO_7 - CCO_8 = 20 - 0 - 15 = 5.$

8. $ATP_8 = 0$ (no scheduled MPS).

Checking, the total BI and eight-period MPS is 100 units. The total CCOs and ATPs for the eight periods is also 100 units. The calculation shows that 30 units of Model C ATV can be promised for delivery in the first week of January or later, 10 units can be promised in the third week or later, and another 5 units can be promised for delivery in the seventh week or later. The total eight-period ATP quantity of 45 units is the difference between the sum of the BI and MPS (100), and the sum of the committed orders (55) for the 8-week period.

Note that while the total uncommitted production quantity can easily be computed by subtracting all CCOs from the scheduled MPS, it lacks time-phased information. For this reason, the ATP quantities must be determined as shown here. This enables the master scheduler or salesperson to quickly book or confirm new sales to be delivered on specific due dates. Reacting quickly to demand changes and delivering orders on time are necessities in high-performing supply chains, and the tools discussed here enable firms to effectively meet customer needs. In supply chain relationships, using the MPS and ATP information effectively is essential to maintaining speed and flexibility (which impacts customer service) throughout the supply chain as products make their way to end users.

The Bill of Materials

The **bill of materials (BOM)** is an engineering document that shows an inclusive listing of all component parts and assemblies making up the final product. Figure 6.4 is an example of a *multilevel bill of materials* for the ATV Corporation's all-terrain vehicles. It shows the parent–component relationships and the specific units of components,

Figure 6.4 | **Bill of Materials for the ATV**

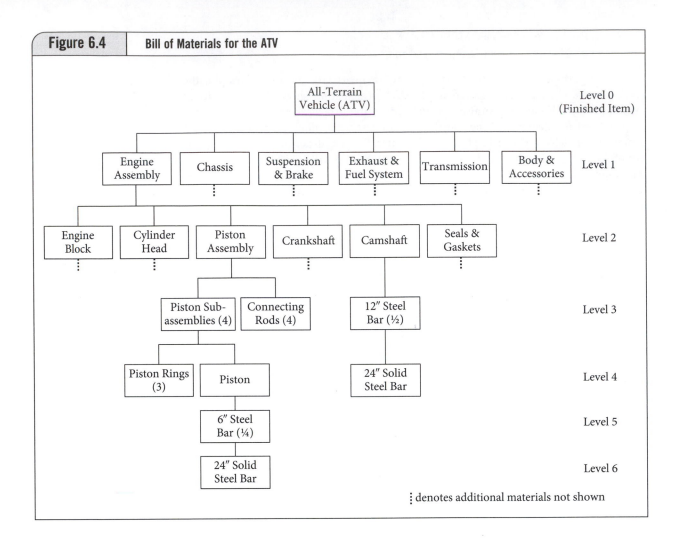

known as the **planning factor**, required for making a higher-level part or assembly. For example, "engine assembly" is an immediate *parent* of "engine block," and conversely "engine block" is an immediate *component* of "engine assembly." The "24-inch solid steel bar" is a *common component part*, because it is a component of the "6-inch steel bar" and the "12-inch steel bar." The *planning factor* of "connecting rods" shows that four connecting rods are needed to make one "piston assembly." Twelve "piston rings" (3 × 4) are needed to assemble one unit of ATV since there are three "piston rings" in each "piston subassembly," and there are four "piston subassemblies" in each "piston assembly."

The BOM is shown in various levels, starting from Level 0. The level numbers increase as one moves down the BOM. Level 0 is the final product, which is the **independent demand** item. In this case, it is an ATV. It has a demand pattern that is subject to trends and seasonal variations, and general market conditions. Gross requirements of Level 0 items come from the master production schedule (i.e., Table 6.4 in the ATV Corporation example). The next level in the BOM is Level 1, which consists of all components and subassemblies required for the final assembly of one unit of the ATV. The gross requirements of Level 1 components and subassemblies are computed based on the demand for ATVs as specified in Level 0. Therefore, the requirements for all the items in Level 1 and below are called **dependent demand** items. For example, the engine assembly, chassis, suspension and brake, and transmission used to assemble the ATV are dependent demand items. However, if the components or subassemblies are sold as *service parts* to customers for repairing the ATV, then they are independent demand items.

Correspondingly, the multilevel bill of materials can also be presented as an **indented bill of materials** as shown in Table 6.6. At each level of indentation, the level number increases by one. The indented bill of materials in Table 6.6 can be seen as a representation of the multilevel bill of materials (Figure 6.4) rotated 90 degrees counterclockwise.

Another type of bill of materials is the **super bill of materials**, which is useful for planning purposes. It is also referred to as a *planning bill of materials, pseudo bill of materials, phantom bill of materials,* or *family bill of materials*. Using the ATV Corporation's BOM in Figure 6.4 as an example, a simplified product structure diagram

Table 6.6	**Indented Bill of Materials—All-Terrain Vehicles**	
PART DESCRIPTION	**LEVEL**	**PLANNING FACTOR**
Engine assembly	1	1
Engine block (components not shown)	2	1
Cylinder head (components not shown)	2	1
Piston assembly	2	1
Piston subassembly	3	4
Piston rings	4	3
Pistons	4	1
6-inch steel bar	5	1/4
24-inch solid steel bar	6	1
Connecting rods	3	4
Crankshaft (components not shown)	2	1
Camshaft	2	1
12-inch steel bar	3	1/2
24-inch solid steel bar	4	1
Seals and gaskets (components not shown)	2	1
Chassis (components not shown)	1	1
Suspension and brake (components not shown)	1	1
Exhaust and fuel system (components not shown)	1	1
Transmission (components not shown)	1	1
Body and accessories (components not shown)	1	1

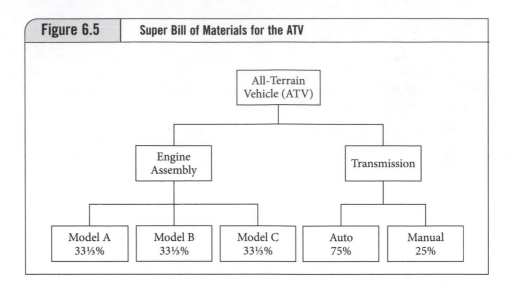

Figure 6.5 | Super Bill of Materials for the ATV

can be created for the family of ATVs that consists of different engine sizes (i.e., models) and transmission options. Instead of stating the planning factor, the percentage of each option is used. Figure 6.5 shows that 33⅓ percent of the ATVs are Model A, Model B, and Model C, respectively. Similarly, 75 percent of the ATVs use automatic transmissions and the remaining 25 percent use manual transmissions. Therefore, ATV Corporation's January planned production (120 units) consists of 40 units each of Model A, Model B, and Model C (see Table 6.4). Similarly, 90 (75 percent × 120) units of the ATVs will be manufactured with automatic transmissions and the remaining 30 (25 percent × 120) units will be manufactured with manual transmissions.

The super bill of materials enables the firm to forecast the total demand of ATVs and then break down the forecast into different models and transmission options using the proper percentage, instead of forecasting the demand of each option individually. It provides quick information on the quantity of components for each option needed for the scheduled production. In addition, it also reduces the number of master production schedules. For the ATV Corporation example, the number of master production schedules was reduced from six (3 models × 2 transmission options) to one.

When the exact proportion of each option is uncertain, the percentage can be increased slightly to cover the uncertainty. For example, the ATV Corporation may increase its automatic transmission option to 78 percent and manual option to 27 percent, for a total of 105 percent. The firm raises its total planned production by 5 percent to cover demand uncertainty. This is known as **option overplanning**.

Material Requirements Planning

As illustrated in the ATV example, dependent demand is a term used to describe the internal demand for parts based on the independent demand of the final product in which the parts are used. Subassemblies, components, and raw materials are examples of dependent demand items. Dependent demand may have a pattern of abrupt and dramatic changes because of its dependency on the demand of the final product, particularly if the final product is produced in large lot sizes. Dependent demand can be calculated once the demand of the final product is known. Material requirements planning (MRP) software can be used to compute these exact dependent material requirements, along with when they should be ordered or assembled.

For example, the ATV Corporation's MPS (Table 6.4) shows that 120 ATVs will be produced in January. The firm thus knows that 120 handlebars and 480 wheel rims will be needed. This demand for handlebars, wheel rims, and all of the other dependent demand items can be calculated using the MRP, based on the bill of materials information and the demand of the final product as stated on the MPS.

Material requirements planning systems have been used widely by manufacturing firms for computing dependent demand, along with timing requirements. MRP is a computer-based materials management system. With the advent of computer and information technologies, the span of MRP evolved to include aggregate production planning, master production scheduling, and capacity requirements planning to become closed-loop MRP. It further evolved into manufacturing resource planning (MRP-II) by including other aspects of materials and resource planning, demand management, and the ability to perform "what-if" analyses. A complete MRP-II system consists of many modules that enable the firm to book orders, schedule production, control inventory, and perform accounting and financial analyses.

While there are hundreds of suppliers still selling and supporting their original MRP systems, some suppliers have expanded their systems to enable the users to perform more sophisticated analyses and integrate organization-wide activities, including operations and facilities that are located in different countries from the head office. This new generation of MRP system is known as the *enterprise resource planning (ERP)* system.

The material requirements plan is used to calculate the exact quantities, need dates, and planned order releases for subassemblies and materials required to manufacture the final products listed on the MPS. MRP begins the computation process by first obtaining the requirements of the final product (the Level 0 item on the BOM) from the MPS to calculate the requirements of Level 1 components and materials, and then works its way down to the lowest level components, taking into account existing inventories and the time required for each processing step. While these manufacturing and delivery lead times are ignored in the MPS, they are considered in the MRP computation process. For example, if a parent item requires an immediate component with a three-week lead time, the component must be ordered three weeks ahead of the need date.

For MRP, a dependent demand management system, to work effectively, it requires (1) the independent demand information (the demand for the final product or service part) from the master production schedule; (2) parent–component relationships from the bill of materials, including the planning factor and lead-time information; and (3) the inventory status of the final product and all of the components. MRP takes this information to compute the *net requirements* of the final product and components, and then offsets the net requirements with appropriate lead times to ensure orders are released on time for fabricating higher-level components. This information is one of the most important outputs of the MRP system, known as **planned order releases**. For items manufactured in-house, planned order releases are transmitted to the shop floor, but for purchased items, planned order releases are transmitted to the suppliers directly or via the purchasing department.

A major advantage of the MRP system is that it provides planning information. Production information—such as scheduled receipts, on-hand inventories, net requirements, and planned order releases—is available for the entire planning horizon, enabling schedulers and operators to plan ahead. However, a major disadvantage of the MRP system is its *loss of visibility* due to the requirement of offsetting net requirements by the appropriate lead time to obtain planned order releases. This problem is especially acute for products with a deep bill of materials. Another drawback of MRP systems is that they ignore capacity and shop floor conditions.

Terms Used in Material Requirements Planning

Prior to examining how the MRP logic works, let us look at some terms as they apply to the MRP:

1. *Parent* The item generating the demand for lower-level components. Level 0 is the final product. It is the parent of all Level 1 components. Similarly, each Level 1 item becomes the parent of the Level 2 components used to make the item. For example, Figure 6.4 shows that "piston assembly" is a parent of "piston subassemblies" and "connecting rods."

2. *Components* The parts demanded by a parent. For example, Figure 6.4 shows that "piston assembly" is a component of "engine assembly."

3. *Gross requirement* A time-phased requirement prior to netting out on-hand inventory and the lead-time consideration. The gross requirement is satisfied from inventory and/or production.

4. *Net requirement* The unsatisfied item requirement for a specific time period. It equals the gross requirement for that period minus the current on-hand inventory and any scheduled receipts in that period.

5. *Scheduled receipt* A committed order awaiting delivery for a specific period. It is an order released in a past period and due to be received in a specific later period. This information is updated automatically by the MRP computer logic system once an order has been placed. For example, an item with a 2-week delivery lead time ordered on the first week of the month automatically becomes a scheduled receipt for the third week.

6. *Projected on-hand inventory* The projected closing inventory at the end of the period. It equals the beginning inventory minus the gross requirement, plus any scheduled receipts and planned receipts from earlier planned order releases.

7. *Planned order release* A specific order to be released to the shop (if the component is made in-house) or to the supplier (if the component is purchased) to ensure that it is available on the need date. Planned order releases of the parent are translated into gross requirements of the components.

8. *Time bucket* The time period used on the MRP. It is usually expressed in days or weeks. The current period is the *action time bucket*.

9. *Explosion* The common term used to describe the process of converting a parent item's planned order releases into component gross requirements.

10. *Planning factor* The number of components needed to produce a unit of the parent item. For example, Figure 6.4 shows that four units of "connecting rods" are needed to produce a unit of "piston assembly."

11. *Firmed planned order* A planned order that the MRP computer logic system does not automatically change when conditions change. The primary purpose of a firmed planned order is to prevent system nervousness, similar to the time fence system discussed earlier in the MPS segment.

12. *Pegging* Relates gross requirements for a component part to the planned order releases that created the requirements. It is essentially the reverse of the explosion process.

13. *Low-level coding* Assigns the lowest level on the bill of materials to all common components to avoid duplicate MRP computations. For example, Figure 6.4 shows that "24-inch solid steel bar" is a common component that appears in Level 4 and Level 6. Instead of computing its planned order releases at Level 4 and Level 6 separately, a low-level code of 6 is assigned to the item. Its net requirements at Level 4 are added to those at Level 6, and the MRP explosion logic is performed at Level 6 only.

14. *Lot size* The order size for MRP logic. Lot size may be determined by various lot-sizing techniques, such as the FOQ (a fixed order quantity) or lot-for-lot (LFL—order whatever amount is needed in each period). A lot size of 50 calls for orders to be placed in multiples of 50. For example, with a net requirement of 85 units, using LFL order sizing will result in an order of 85 units; however, an order of 100 units would be placed when using a fixed order quantity of 50.

15. *Safety stock* Protects against uncertainties in demand, supply, quality, and lead time. Its implication in MRP logic is that the minimum projected on-hand inventory should not fall below the safety stock level.

A material requirements planning example is provided in Example 6.2.

Level 0 MRP Computation—Model A ATV

The first row is the planning horizon for the eight weeks in January and February. The gross requirements are derived directly from the MPS. The scheduled receipt of 10 units in Week 2 is due to an order placed last week (or earlier but rescheduled to be delivered on Week 2), which automatically becomes a scheduled receipt two weeks later (note that scheduled receipts are only shown for orders that were placed in periods previous to the current period). The order size for the Model A ATV is in multiples of 10 units, the lead time is two weeks, and the desired safety stock is 15 units. The projected on-hand inventory of 20 units for the first week is computed by taking the beginning inventory of 30 units and subtracting the gross requirement of 10 units in that week. The projected on-hand inventory of 20 units in Week 2 is computed by taking the previous balance of 20 units, adding the scheduled receipt of 10 units, and subtracting the gross requirement of 10 units.

During the third week, additional Model A ATVs must be received to ensure the on-hand balance is above the safety stock level of 15 units. The net requirement here is 15 units (since all of the incoming inventory is consumed to satisfy the gross requirement of 20 units). Since orders must be in multiples of 10, then 20 units must be ordered in the first week to satisfy both the lead time and the safety stock requirements. Simply stated, if 20 units are needed in the third week, the 2-week lead time requires the order to be placed two weeks ahead, which explains why there is a planned order release of 20 units in the first week. The on-hand inventory balance of 20 units at the end of the third week is computed by taking the previous balance of 20 units, adding the planned order receipt of 20 units (due to the planned order release in the first week), and subtracting the gross requirement of 20 units.

Similarly, the gross requirements of 20 units each in the fifth and eighth weeks consumed the beginning of period inventory, triggering a net requirement of 15

Example 6.2   An MRP Example at the ATV Corporation

Model A's production schedule for the ATV Corporation is used to illustrate the MRP logic. Its gross requirements are first obtained from the master production schedule in Table 6.4, and the inventory status shows that thirty units of Model A are available at the beginning of the year. The parent–component relationships and planning factors are available from the BOM in Figure 6.4. Assuming that lot sizes (Q), lead times (LT), and safety stocks (SS) are used as shown under each record, the MRP computations of the Model A ATV and some of its components are as follows:

Model A ATV–Level 0		1	2	3	4	5	6	7	8
Gross Requirements		10	10	20	0	20	0	0	20
Scheduled Receipts			10						
Projected On-hand Inventory	30	20	20	20	20	20	20	20	20
Planned Order Releases		20		20			20		

Q = 10; LT = 2; SS = 15

Engine Assembly–Level 1		1	2	3	4	5	6	7	8
Gross Requirements		20		20			20		
Scheduled Receipts		20							
Projected On-hand Inventory	2	2	2	0	0	0	0	0	0
Planned Order Releases		18			20				

Q = LFL; LT = 2; SS = 0

Piston Assembly–Level 2		1	2	3	4	5	6	7	8
Gross Requirements		18			20				
Scheduled Receipts		20							
Projected On-hand Inventory	10	12	12	12	22	22	22	22	22
Planned Order Releases				30					

Q = 30; LT = 1; SS = 10

Connecting Rods–Level 3		1	2	3	4	5	6	7	8
Gross Requirements				120					
Scheduled Receipts									
Projected On-hand Inventory	22	22	22	52	52	52	52	52	52
Planned Order Releases			150						

Q = 50; LT = 1; SS = 20

units for those periods and a planned order release of 20 units each during the third and sixth weeks, respectively.

Level 1 MRP Computation—Engine Assembly

The BOM in Figure 6.4 indicates that the gross requirements for the Engine Assembly are derived from the planned order releases of the Model A ATV. Since the planning factor is 1 unit (meaning that 1 Engine Assembly is required for each Model A ATV), then Model A ATV's planned order releases translate directly into the gross requirements for Engine Assembly in the first, third, and sixth weeks. The scheduled receipt of 20 units in the first week is due to an order placed two weeks earlier (although it could also be a rescheduled delivery from some earlier week). The gross requirements of 20 units each for the third and sixth week triggered net requirements in the same weeks and planned order releases of 18 and 20 units, respectively, for the first and fourth weeks (note here that since no safety stock is required and the lot size is LFL, the planned order releases equal the net requirements, and the inventory balances are allowed to stay at a projected level of zero once the on-hand inventory is consumed).

Level 2 MRP Computation—Piston Assembly

The gross requirements for the Piston Assembly are derived directly from the planned order releases of Engine Assembly. Therefore, the gross requirements for Piston Assembly are 18 and 20 units, respectively, for the first and fourth weeks. Computations of its projected on-hand balances and planned order releases are similar to earlier examples (note again here that inventories must not drop below the safety stock requirement of 10 and that order quantities must be made in multiples of 30).

Level 3 MRP Computation—Connecting Rods

The BOM in Figure 6.4 indicates that 4 Connecting Rods are required for each Piston Assembly. Therefore, the gross requirement for Connecting Rods in the third week is obtained by multiplying the planned order releases for Piston Assemblies by 4. Note that due to the requirement to offset the lead times in each MRP computation, the planned order release for Connecting Rods can be determined only up to the second period, although the gross requirements of the Model A ATV are known for the first eight weeks. This is referred to as *loss of visibility*, as discussed earlier.

Since there are no lower-level components shown for the Connecting Rods, we can assume that the ATV Corporation purchases this component. Thus, the planned order releases would be used by the purchasing department (as shown by the purchase planning and control function in Figure 6.1) to communicate order quantities and delivery dates to its Connecting Rod supplier. Production activity control involves all aspects of shop floor scheduling, dispatching, routing, and other control activities. In supply chain settings, manufacturing firms share their planned order release information with their strategic suppliers either through **electronic data interchange (EDI)** communications, FAX transmissions, or their ERP system. Since the firm manufactures its own Piston Assemblies, the planned order release information for this part is communicated to shop floor manufacturing personnel and used to trigger production. We can see, then, that planned order releases for purchased items eventually become the independent demand gross requirements for the firm's suppliers. Communicating this information accurately and quickly to strategic suppliers is a necessary element in an effective supply chain information system.

Capacity Planning

The material plans (the aggregate production plan, the master production schedule, and the material requirements plan) discussed so far have focused exclusively on production and materials management but organizations must also address capacity constraints. Excess or insufficient capacity prevents a firm from fully taking advantage of the efficiency and effectiveness of the manufacturing planning and control system. Thus, a set of capacity plans is used in conjunction with the materials plan to ensure capacity is not over- or underutilized.

In the context of capacity planning, capacity refers to a firm's labor and machine resources. It is the maximum amount of work that an organization is capable of completing in a given period of time. Capacity planning follows the basic hierarchy of the materials planning system as shown in Figure 6.1. At the aggregate level, **resource requirements planning (RRP)**, a long-range capacity planning module, is used to check whether aggregate resources are capable of satisfying the aggregate production plan. Typical resources considered at this stage include gross labor hours and machine hours. Generally, capacity expansion decisions at this level involve a long-range commitment, such as new facilities or additional capital equipment. If existing resources are unable to meet the aggregate production plan, then the plan must be revised. The revised aggregate production plan is reevaluated by the resource requirements plan until a feasible production plan is obtained.

Once the aggregate production plan is determined to be feasible, the aggregate production information is disaggregated into a more detailed medium-range production plan, the master production schedule. Although RRP has already determined that aggregate capacity is sufficient to satisfy the aggregate production plan, medium-range capacity may not be able to satisfy the master production schedule. For example, the master production schedule may call for normal production quantities when much of the workforce typically takes vacation. Therefore, the medium-range capacity plan, or **rough-cut capacity plan (RCCP)**, is used to check the feasibility of the master production schedule.

The RCCP takes the master production schedule and converts it from production to capacity required, then compares it to capacity available during each production period. If the medium-range capacity and production plans are feasible, the master production plan is firmed up. Otherwise, it is revised or the capacity is adjusted accordingly. Options for increasing medium-range capacity include overtime, subcontracting, adding resources, and an alternate routing of the production sequence.

Capacity requirements planning (CRP) is a short-range capacity planning technique that is used to check the feasibility of the material requirements plan. The time-phased material requirements plan is used to compute the detailed capacity requirements required at each workstation during specific periods to manufacture the items specified in the material requirements plan. Although the RCCP may show that sufficient capacity exists to execute the master production schedule, the CRP may indicate that production capacity is inadequate during specific periods.

Capacity Strategy

Capacity expansion or contraction is an integral part of an organization's manufacturing strategy. Effectively balancing capacity with demand is an intricate management decision as it directly affects a firm's competitiveness. Short- to medium-term capacity can be increased through the use of overtime, additional shifts, and subcontracting, whereas long-term capacity can be increased by introducing new manufacturing techniques, hiring additional workers, and adding new machines and facilities. Conversely, capacity contraction can be attained by reducing the workforce, and disposing of idle machines and facilities.

The three commonly recognized capacity strategies are lead, lag, and match capacity strategies. A **lead capacity strategy** is a proactive approach that adds or subtracts capacity in anticipation of future market condition and demand, whereas a **lag capacity strategy** is a reactive approach that adjusts capacity in response to demand. In a favorable market condition, the lag strategy generally does not add capacity until the firm is operating at full capacity. The lag capacity strategy is a conservative approach that may result in lost opportunity when demand increases rapidly, whereas the lead strategy is more aggressive and can result in excess inventory or idle capacity. Industry leaders in the electronic industry usually favor the lead capacity strategy because of the short product life cycles. A **match or tracking capacity strategy** is a moderate strategy that adjusts capacity in small amounts in response to demand and changing market conditions.

Distribution Requirements Planning

Distribution requirements planning (DRP) is a time-phased finished goods inventory replenishment plan in a distribution network. DRP is a logical extension of the MRP system and its logic is analogous to MRP. DRP ties the physical distribution system to the manufacturing planning and control system by determining the aggregate time-phased net requirements of the finished goods, and provides demand information for adjusting the MPS. A major difference between MRP and DRP is that while MRP is driven by the production schedule specified in the MPS to compute the time-phased requirements of components, DRP is driven by customer demand of the finished goods. Hence, MRP operates in a dependent demand situation, whereas DRP operates in an independent demand setting. The result of MRP execution is the production of finished goods inventory at the manufacturing site, whereas DRP time-phases the movements of finished goods inventory from the manufacturing site to the central supply warehouse and distribution centers.

An obvious advantage of the DRP system is that it extends manufacturing planning and control visibility into the distribution system, thus allowing the firm to adjust its production plans and to avoid stocking excessive finished goods inventory. By now it should be evident that excessive inventory is a major cause of the bullwhip effect. Distribution requirements planning provides time-phased demand information needed for the manufacturing and distribution systems to effectively allocate finished goods inventory and production capacity to improve customer service and inventory investment. A distribution requirements planning example is provided in Example 6.3.

The Legacy Material Requirements Planning Systems

For over four decades, a material requirements planning (MRP) system was the first choice among manufacturing firms in the U.S. for planning and managing their purchasing, production, and inventories. To improve the efficiency and effectiveness of the manufacturing planning and control system, many manufacturers utilized EDI to relay planned order releases to their suppliers. This information system worked well for coordinating internal production as well as purchasing.

By the end of the twentieth century, however, the global business environment was rapidly changing. Many savvy manufacturers and service providers were building multi-plant international sites, either to take advantage of cheaper raw materials and labor or to expand their market. Business executives found themselves spending more time

Example 6.3   A DRP Example at the ATV Corporation

ATV Corporation's January and February distribution schedule for its Model A ATV is used to illustrate the DRP replenishment schedules from the firm's central supply warehouse to its two distribution centers. The time buckets used in the DRP are the same weekly time buckets used in the MRP system. DRP uses the order quantity, delivery lead time, on-hand balance, and safety stock information to determine the planned order releases necessary to meet anticipated market demand.

Gross requirements from the two distribution centers in Las Vegas and East Lansing are first obtained from the demand management system. The same MRP logic is used to compute the planned order releases of the two distribution centers. The gross requirements of the central supply warehouse reflect the cascading demand of Las Vegas and East Lansing distribution centers. The gross requirements of fourteen units in the first week for the central supply warehouse are the sum of the planned order releases of the two distribution centers. The planned order releases of the central supply warehouse are then passed on to the manufacturing facility where they become part of the MPS. This process is commonly referred to as **implosion** where demand information is gathered from a number of field distribution centers and aggregated in the central warehouse, and eventually passed onto the manufacturing facility. While both the processes are similar, the DRP logic is different from the *explosion* notion in MRP where a Level 0 finished good is broken into its component requirements.

Scheduled Receipts and Projected On-hand Inventory

Las Vegas Distribution Center (Q = 2; LT = 2; SS = 0)

Model A ATV		1	2	3	4	5	6	7	8
Gross Requirements		0	1	1	0	1	0	6	0
Scheduled Receipts									
Projected On-hand	1	1	0	1	1	0	0	0	0
Planned Order Releases		2	0	0	0	6	0	0	0

East Lansing Distribution Center (Q = 2; LT = 1; SS = 0)

Model A ATV		1	2	3	4	5	6	7	8
Gross Requirements		3	11	0	1	0	2	0	15
Scheduled Receipts									
Projected On-hand	3	1	1	1	0	0	0	0	1
Planned Order Releases		12	0	0	0	2	0	16	0

2 + 12 = 14

6 + 2 = 8

Central Supply Warehouse		1	2	3	4	5	6	7	8
Gross Requirements		14	0	0	0	8	16	0	0
Scheduled Receipts									
Projected On-hand Inventory	16	2	2	2	2	4	3	3	3
Planned Order Releases		0	0	10	15	0	0	0	0

Q = 5; LT = 2; SS = 2

dealing with international subcontractors using different currencies and languages among varying political environments. The need to access real-time information on foreign customers' requirements, production levels and available capacities, system-wide inventory levels, and plants capable of meeting current order requirements increased. The existing MRP systems simply could not handle these added tasks.

To fully coordinate the information requirements for purchasing, planning, scheduling, and distribution of an organization operating multiple facilities in a complex global environment, an enterprise-wide information system was needed. Thus, enterprise resource planning (ERP) systems that operated from a single database were engineered to replace the older legacy MRP systems.

The term **legacy MRP system** is a broad label used to describe an older information system that usually works at an operational level to schedule production within a single facility. Many legacy systems were implemented in the 1960s, 1970s, and 1980s and subjected to extensive modifications as requirements changed over the years. Today, these systems have lasted beyond their originally intended life span. The continuous modifications of these systems made them complex and cumbersome to work with, especially when considering they were not designed to be user friendly in the first place. Legacy systems were designed to perform a very specific operational function and were programmed as independent entities with little regard for meeting system requirements or coordinating with other functional areas. Communication between legacy MRP systems is often limited, and visibility across functional areas is severely restricted. Legacy systems were implemented to gather data for transactional purposes and thus lacked any analytical capabilities required for today's complex global environment.

Manufacturing Resource Planning

The development of the legacy system can be traced back to the evolution of the MRP system, the closed-loop MRP system, and the manufacturing resource planning (MRP-II) system. The development of closed-loop MRP was a natural extension of the MRP system. It was an attempt to further develop the MRP into a formal and explicit manufacturing planning and control system by adding capacity requirements planning and feedback to describe the progress of orders being manufactured. The originally developed MRP is a part of the closed-loop MRP system.

Manufacturing resource planning was an outgrowth of the closed-loop MRP system. Business and sales plans were incorporated, and a financial function was added to link financial management to operations, marketing, and other functional areas. The concept of manufacturing resource planning was that the information system should link internal operations to the financial function to provide management with up-to-date data, including sales, purchasing, production, inventory, and cash flow. It should also be able to perform "what-if" analyses as internal and external conditions change. For example, MRP-II enables the firm to determine the impact on profit and cash flow if the firm is only able to fill 85 percent of its orders due to late deliveries of raw materials. MRP-II is an explicit and formal manufacturing information system that integrates the internal functions of an organization, enabling it to coordinate manufacturing plans with sales, while providing management with essential accounting and financial information.

Today, manufacturing resource planning has further evolved to include other functional areas of the organization. Although it synchronizes an organization's information systems and provides insight into the implications of aggregate production plans, master production schedules, capacities, materials plans, and sales, it primarily focuses on one unit's internal operations. It lacks the capability to link the many operations of an organization's foreign branches with its headquarters. It also lacks the capability to directly interface with external supply chain members, such as suppliers and customers. Thus, enterprise-wide information systems began to be developed for this reason.

The Development of Enterprise Resource Planning Systems

While traditional or legacy MRP systems continue to be used and modified to include other functional areas of an organization, the emergence and growth of supply chain management, e-commerce, and global operations have created the need to exchange information directly with suppliers, customers, and foreign branches of organizations. The concept of the manufacturing information system thus evolved to directly connect all functional areas and operations of an organization and, in some cases, its suppliers and customers via a common software infrastructure and database. This type of manufacturing information system is referred to as an ERP system.

The typical ERP system is an umbrella system that ties together a variety of specialized software applications, such as production and inventory planning, purchasing, logistics, human resources, finance, accounting, customer relationship, and supplier relationship management using a common, shared centralized database. However, exactly what is tied together varies on a case-by-case basis, based on the ERP vendor and the needs of the organization. Figure 6.6 illustrates a generic ERP system, where a common centralized database and software infrastructure are used to drive a firm's information systems and to link the operations of its branches with the firm's headquarters.

Enterprise resource planning is a broadly used industrial term to describe the multimodule application software for managing an enterprise's functional activities, suppliers, and customers. Initially, ERP software focused on integrating the internal business activities of a multifacility organization, or enterprise, to ensure that it was operating under the same information system, with the same data. With the onset of supply chain management, ERP vendors today are designing their products to include the capabilities of managing suppliers and customers. For example, ERP enables an organization to deal directly with suppliers to assess the availability of their

| Figure 6.6 | Generic ERP System |

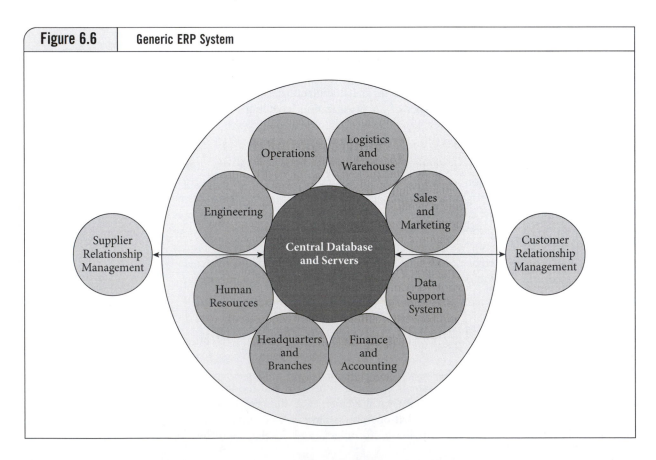

resources, as if they are an external process of the firm. Similarly, ERP also allows business customers to access the firm's inventory information and manufacturing and delivery schedules directly.

ERP utilizes the idea of a centralized and shared database system to tie the entire organization together, as opposed to the traditional legacy MRP system that uses multiple databases and interfaces that frequently result in duplicate and inconsistent information across different branches or even departments within an organization. With ERP, information is entered once at the source and made available to all users. It eliminates the inconsistency and incompatibility created when different functional areas use different systems with overlapping data.

The legacy MRP system typically utilizes multiple software packages and databases for different functional areas. Usually, each functional area implements its information system based on its unique needs, with very little input or coordination from the other functional areas. The different packages within an organization often are incompatible with each other and prevent transactions from taking place directly between systems. The multiple databases also cause the same information to be stored in multiple locations; thus, multiple entries of the same data are required. This need to enter the same data repeatedly is a major cause of inconsistency in database management. For example, an industrial customer's name, ATV Inc., may be entered as ATV Inc. in one database and ATV Incorporated in another database. From an information system's perspective, ATV Inc. and ATV Incorporated are two distinct customers.

With a shared centralized database system, the ERP is capable of automating business processes rapidly and accurately. For example, when taking a sales order, a sales agent has all the necessary information of the customer (the credit history, rating, and limit from the finance and accounting module, for instance), the company's production and inventory levels (from the operations module), and the delivery schedule (from the sales and marketing module) to complete the sale. After the sale is confirmed and entered into the centralized database, other supply chain partners affected by the transaction can directly utilize the same information system to take appropriate proactive steps. For example, suppliers can find out the production schedules planned by upstream supply chain members so that appropriate raw materials and components can be produced accordingly to support sales. Similarly, downstream companies can also utilize the same information system and database to access delivery schedules of raw materials and components ordered from their upstream supply chain members.

Thus, ERP integrates the internal operations of an enterprise with a common software platform and centralized database system. It also ties together supply chain members through the same information system. ERP provides the mechanism for supply chain members to efficiently share information so that scarce resources can be fully utilized to meet demand, while minimizing supply chain inventories. Production changes and other modifications can also be executed efficiently and quickly to minimize delivery lead times. Example 6.4 illustrates a typical ERP transaction.

The Rapid Growth of Enterprise Resource Planning Systems

The use of ERP systems has gradually spread from manufacturing to the service sector and has become commonly used in many university classrooms. Many universities in the U.S., for instance, have cooperated with major ERP software providers to integrate ERP training into their business curricula. There are many reasons, some of

Example 6.4   A Hypothetical ERP Transaction

The following example demonstrates a hypothetical ERP transaction for the ATV Corporation. The ATV Corporation makes three models of all-terrain vehicles—Model A, Model B, and Model C. The corporation is headquartered in the United States with manufacturing facilities in the United States and Mexico. ATV sells its products in the United States, Canada, and Mexico. Its sales representatives make quarterly visits to customers to take sales orders and provide necessary customer services. The following steps describe a sales transaction by a sales representative during a typical visit to a retail customer in Canada.

We assume here that the retailer ordered 100 units of Model A and 150 units of Model B, to be delivered within thirty days.

1. *Ordering:* The field sales representative takes the order of 100 units of Model A and 150 units of Model B. Using the Internet, the sales representative accesses the sales and marketing module of the ERP system at the U.S. headquarters to check the price and other related information, such as quantity discounts, guarantees, and rebates. The sales representative also accesses the customer's credit history and rating from the finance and accounting module.

2. *Availability:* Simultaneously, the ERP system checks the inventory status and the available-to-promise quantities of its manufacturing facilities in the United States and Mexico and notifies the sales representative whether the order can be filled on time. The sales representative finds that the Mexico factory has sufficient inventory to fill the Model A order immediately, while the Model B order can be manufactured in ten days from the U.S. factory. Logistics information shows that shipping from Mexico to Canada takes two weeks, and delivery time from the U.S. factory takes 1 week. Thus, the entire order is accepted and the factory in Mexico receives instructions to ship 100 units of Model A to the Canadian retailer immediately.

   Its inventory status is updated accordingly. An invoice in English will be printed, and the finance and accounting module will be updated to reflect the partial delivery upon shipment of the goods from Mexico.

3. *Manufacturing:* The operations module immediately schedules the production of 150 units of Model B at the U.S. factory. All dependent demand items and labor necessary to produce 150 units of Model B are scheduled, to meet the due date. For items and components manufactured in-house, planned order releases are transmitted to the shop floor. For purchased items, the information is sent to the purchasing department and then on to key suppliers.

   The human resource module checks to ensure that there are sufficient workers scheduled in the U.S. factory to complete the order. If not, the personnel manager will be notified and additional workers may be scheduled or employed.

4. *Order tracking:* The customer relationship management module allows the customer to access certain parts of ATV Corporation's ERP system to track the status of its order. Thus, the customer knows the exact status of the order and its shipping schedule.

which are discussed in the following paragraph, for the rapid growth of ERP since the early 1990s.

At the turn of the century, many firms were uncertain as to how the Year 2000 Millennium Bug or Y2K bug (conversion of the year from 1999 to 2000) would affect their information systems. Most information systems installed were programmed to use the last two digits of the year (the year 1998 would be shown as 98). Using the same logic, the year 2000 would be recorded as 00 and would be interpreted as 1900, or 98 years prior to 1998. This could adversely affect time-sensitive programming logic (interest calculations for instance). In addition, the legacy MRP systems had been modified so extensively over the years that the many layers of program codes made it too complex and redundant to correctly assess the true impact of Y2K. The extensive modifications to the legacy systems had also made them too expensive to maintain. Thus, many savvy business managers took a proactive approach to set aside sufficient budgetary funds to replace their legacy MRP systems with the more efficient ERP systems to reduce costs and deal with the Y2K problem.

The rapid development of computer and information technology over the last two decades has also contributed positively to the growth of ERP. Tasks that were previously limited to mainframe computers are today easily implemented on servers and desktop computers that cost only a fraction of the capital investment previously

Global Perspectives

ERP Adoption for Shianco Furniture, China

The Chinese economy has undergone a radical transformation in the past 30 years, since the economic reforms of Premier Deng Xiaoping. Paralleling the enormous growth of the Chinese economy is the growth of ERP expenditures. From 2000 to 2005, ERP annual expenditures in China increased from $71 to $380 million. However, only about 10 percent of firms implementing ERP judge their efforts to be successful. This figure stands in stark contrast to the 30–50 percent of North American firms who judged their ERP implementations to be successful. In China, the development of ERP has been much different from its development in the Western economies.

Shianco Company, based in Guangdong, China, produces outdoor furniture for export to the United States, Canada, Australia, and Europe. The company was established by a Taiwanese investor in 1989 and expanded rapidly from a single 250,000 square-foot factory to four manufacturing facilities in Shunde, Shanghai, Qingdao, and Tianjin in China. In addition to its offices throughout China, Shianco also has sales offices in the United States, Europe, Australia, and Taiwan.

As the enterprise expanded, its original information technology (IT) systems no longer sufficed and in 2003, Shianco began to explore ERP solutions. The company chose SAP and with the help of IBM, introduced the ERP solution first in Shunde and Guangdong, then in Hong Kong and Taiwan. Shianco is immensely committed to training its staff for the new system. Since its adoption of the new ERP solution, the company has expanded its IT project implementation team from one to thirty people.

However, the commitment to change in Shianco is not without its own unique problems. Overshadowing this commitment are other factors that take precedence, like opening new offices or finding new markets. Also, few ERP-trained employees are available on the open market. Thus, it is crucial for Shianco to train employees and retain ERP-trained staff. The new ERP systems were met initially with resistance; the previous system was so basic that in order to be proficient with the current systems, staff had to be trained in computing and keyboard basics. An unprecedented level of support was given to devising these training regimens. Users were not given identification cards until they passed the examinations, underscoring the importance of employees achieving competence on these systems during this change.

Note: Some information in this feature also came from Brown, D. H. and S. He. "Patterns of ERP Adoption and Implementation in China and Some Implications." *Electronic Markets*, 17, no. 2 (2007): 132–41.

needed. Information systems that were previously off limits are now accessible to many smaller organizations. Today, ERP is expected to remain the key building block of global business management information systems. As the global business environment continues to change, ERP is expected to evolve to become more flexible to adapt to mergers and acquisitions and to provide more real-time monitoring and response. The Global Perspectives feature illustrates the adoption of an ERP system by a furniture firm in China to handle its global business.

Implementing Enterprise Resource Planning Systems

ERP systems have continued to evolve, and integration of e-commerce, customer relationship management (CRM), and supplier relationship management (SRM) applications are now considered ERP requirements by most organizations. While many firms believe a well-designed and implemented ERP system can translate into a substantial competitive advantage, research analysts and industrial practitioners are still debating the usefulness of ERP, and the advantages and disadvantages of using a **best-of-breed solution** versus a **single integrator solution**. It is important to understand that ERP is not a panacea for poor business decisions, but a valuable tool that can be used to enhance competitiveness.

The *best-of-breed* solution picks the best application or module for each individual function in the supply chain (thus, best-of-breed), from potentially different software vendors. The resulting system includes several different applications that must be integrated to work as a single coordinated system to achieve the global scope required of the ERP. A major criticism of the best-of-breed solution is that multiple software infrastructures and databases may have to be used to link the multiple applications obtained from different vendors. This may severely affect the ability of the system to update the databases rapidly and efficiently—a similar problem of the legacy MRP systems.

The *single integrator* approach picks all the desired applications from a single vendor for the ERP system. Obvious advantages are that all of the applications should work well together and getting the system up and running should be easier. As companies become more global, the notion of using a single integrator solution becomes more attractive. On the other hand, as information technology continues to evolve and as competition increases in the ERP software market, ERP vendors are designing their products to be more compatible with each other. Therefore, implementing an ERP system using the best-of-breed solution approach is becoming easier. Best-of-breed vendors will continue to serve an important void in the ERP market with specialized applications that mainstream ERP vendors typically do not provide. A few examples are provided here:

Bookham Technology,[6] an integrated optical component firm based in the United Kingdom with sales offices in the U.S., the United Kingdom, France, Italy, Japan, and China, recently started a £2 million project to improve its information systems to better link its customers, partners, and employees together. The new project was designed to replace its seven legacy business systems with a single global enterprise solution. Bookham Technology used the single integrator approach to ERP implementation by selecting an SAP-packaged solution.

General Motors Corp. (GM)[7] was confronted with the issue of how to implement ERP applications while utilizing several software providers they felt had the best capabilities for the automobile industry. So, GM utilized the best-of-breed ERP implementation approach by selecting the financials and indirect materials modules from SAP and a human resources module from PeopleSoft. GM then linked their SAP and PeopleSoft applications using integration software from TSI International Software Ltd.

A further discussion of the single integrator and best-of-breed ERP implementations is discussed in the e-Business Connection feature.

Implementing an ERP system has proved to be a real challenge for many companies. Most ERP systems are written based on the best practices of selected firms. Thus, a condition required for implementation of the system is that the user's business processes must conform to the approaches used in the software logic. These processes can be significantly different from those currently used within the company. Adapting a company's business processes to conform to a software program is a radical departure from the conventional business practice of requiring the software to be designed around the business processes.

Two primary requirements of successful implementation of ERP are computer support and accurate, realistic inputs. Instead of implementing the entire system at once, some organizations choose to implement only those applications or modules that are absolutely critical to operations at that time. New modules are then added in later phases. This ensures that the system can be implemented as quickly as possible while minimizing interruption of the existing system. However, many implementations have failed due to a variety of reasons. Some of the more common reasons for failed ERP implementations follow:

- *Lack of top management commitment.* While management may be willing to set aside sufficient funds to implement a new ERP system, it may not take an active role in providing ongoing encouragement during the implementation process. Often, this leads users to revert to the old processes or systems because of their lack of knowledge and interest to learn the capabilities of the new ERP system.

- *Lack of adequate resources.* Implementing a new ERP system is a long-term commitment requiring substantial capital investment. Although the cost has become more affordable due to the rapid advent of computer technology, full implementation may still be out of reach for many small organizations. In addition, small firms may not have the necessary workforce and expertise to implement the complex system.

- *Lack of proper training.* Many employees may already be familiar with their legacy MRP systems. Thus, when a new ERP system is implemented, top management may assume that users are already adequately prepared and underestimate the training required to get the new system up and running. Lack of financial resources can also reduce the amount of training available for its workforce.

- *Lack of communication.* Lack of communication within an organization and/or between the firm and its ERP software provider can also be a major hindrance for successful implementation. Lack of communication usually results in the wrong specifications and requirements being implemented.

- *Incompatible system environment.* In certain cases, the firm's environment does not give ERP a distinct advantage over other systems. For example, there is no distinct advantage for a small family-owned used car dealer in a small town to implement an expensive new ERP system.

e-Business Connection

Single Integrator ERP Solution or Best-of-Breed ERP Implementation?

Choosing whether to utilize a single integrator ERP solution, or to combine niche software, is a challenge facing many companies today. If the IT department of a company has its way, the company will usually choose a single integrator solution to ERP implementation; if people who oversee business procedures have their way, the company is more likely to choose best-of-breed solutions.

The past decade saw a surge in growth of ERP, especially right before the Y2K scramble. Called "the system of record for midsize manufacturers today," ERP offers many benefits to companies that employ it. With broader, better integrated, and more user-friendly software, ERP now has more functions, like service-oriented architecture, than its predecessors. Today, implementation of ERP promises, among other things, to centralize planning and control tasks to one group and to standardize systems across different sectors of a company, such as human resources and payroll.[8]

However, the emergence of single integrator ERP solutions does not signal the extinction of best-of-breed software vendors. While it is more difficult for a best-of-breed company like Texas-based i2 Technologies to emerge as a major company, best-of-breed vendors will continue to fill the niches left by large ERP vendors. Some businesses require the unique best-of-breed software to do advanced analytical decision making, allowing companies such as i2 Technologies to become profitable once again. Businesses are often interested in tasks that extend beyond the core ERP functions, into areas like sales and operations planning or analysis using ERP data. Many best-of-breed supply chain management vendors have thrived by creating early software innovations around the "edges of ERP," exploiting gaps left by ERP product suites. Many of these surviving vendors are in inventory management systems.[9] Finally, businesses often turn to best-of-breeds when the cost savings expected from ERP implementations fail to materialize. In general, these solutions are better suited to more intricate workplaces, while single integrator ERP solutions fit the less complex environment.[10]

Supply chain management software application revenue as a portion of total ERP revenue is growing, in part from ERP vendors establishing their own application structures and in part from acquisitions. For instance, ERP giant Oracle has acquired demand-planning vendor Demantra, retail logistics vendor Retek, and transportation management vendor G-LOG. In 2005, SAP and Oracle were the two largest vendors in the supply chain management software application market, with best-of-breeds such as i2, Manhattan Associates, RedPrairie Corp., and Swisslog rounding out the top ten. While ERP vendors are most commonly used for supply chain management applications, best-of-breed vendors are most commonly used for transportation management.[11]

While it is easier to couple specific business needs to niche solutions, it is not so easy to integrate these separate modules. To combat this pitfall, niche software vendors are broadening their offerings to be more ERP-like. At the same time, ERP vendors are broadening their software suites as well to include, among others, Web and direct marketing channels. Thus the line between single integrator ERP and best-of-breeds solutions is becoming blurred, as both expand their functionality to appeal to potential clients.

Note: Some information in this feature also came from Field, A.M. "Stretching the Limits of ERP." Journal of Commerce, 8 (January 2007): 76–78.

Advantages and Disadvantages of Enterprise Resource Planning Systems

When properly installed and operating, an ERP system can provide a firm and its supply chain partners with a significant competitive advantage, which can fully justify the investments of time and money in ERP. A fully functional ERP system is capable of enhancing the firm's capability to fully utilize capacity, accurately schedule production, reduce inventory, meet delivery due dates, and enhance the efficiency and effectiveness of the supply chain. Some specific advantages and disadvantages are discussed here.

Enterprise Resource Planning System Advantages

As mentioned earlier, the primary advantage of ERP over the legacy MRP systems is that ERP uses a single database and a common software infrastructure to provide a broader scope and up-to-date information, enabling management to make better decisions that can benefit the entire supply chain. ERP is also fairly robust in providing real-time information and, thus, is able to communicate information about operational changes to supply chain members with little delay. ERP systems are also designed to take advantage of Internet technology. Thus, users are able to share information and communicate via the Internet.

ERP helps organizations reduce supply chain inventories due to the added visibility throughout the entire supply chain. It enables the supply, manufacturing, and logistics processes to flow smoothly by providing visibility of the order fulfillment process throughout the supply chain. Supply chain visibility leads to reductions of the bullwhip effect (the buildup of supply chain safety stock inventories) and helps supply chain members to better plan production and end-product deliveries to customers.

ERP systems also help organizations to standardize manufacturing processes. Manufacturing firms often find that multiple business units across the company make the same product using different processes and information systems. ERP systems enable the firm to automate some of the steps of a manufacturing process. Process standardization eliminates redundant resources and increases productivity.

ERP enables an organization, especially one with multiple business units, to efficiently track employees' time and performance and to communicate with them via a standardized method. Performance can be monitored across the entire organization using the same measurements and standards. The use of a single software platform and database also allows the ERP system to integrate financial, production, supply, and customer order information. By having this information in one software system rather than scattered among many different systems that cannot communicate with one another, companies can keep track of materials, orders, and financial status efficiently and coordinate manufacturing, inventory, and shipping among many different locations and business units at the same time.

Enterprise Resource Planning System Disadvantages

While the benefits of ERP systems can be impressive, ERP is not without shortcomings. For example, a substantial capital investment is needed to purchase and then implement the system. Considerable time and money must be set aside to evaluate ERP software applications and their suppliers, to purchase the necessary hardware and software, and then to train employees to operate the new system. Total cost of ERP ownership includes hardware, software, professional services, and internal staff costs. ERP is also very complex and has proved difficult to implement.

However, the primary criticism of ERP is that the software is designed around a specific business model based on specific business processes. Although business processes are usually adopted based on best practices in the industry, the adopting firm must change its business model and associated processes to fit the built-in business model designed into the ERP system. Thus, the adopting firm must restructure its processes to be compatible with the new ERP system. This has resulted in a very unusual situation where a software system determines the business practices and processes a firm should implement, instead of designing the software to support existing business practices and processes.

Despite the widespread adoption of costly ERP systems by large firms since the Y2K scramble, many implementation challenges remain unsolved and scores of ERP systems are grossly underutilized.[12] Intricate business process reengineering challenges arise when business processes are adapted to the software. Consequently, firms struggle to justify their investment and find ways to better utilize their ERP systems. This raises the question of whether large firms can effectively manage their operations and supply chain activities without sophisticated information technology.

Enterprise Resource Planning Software Modules

ERP systems typically consist of many modules that are linked together to access and share the same database. Each module performs different functions within the organization and is designed so that it can be installed on its own or with a combination of other modules. Most ERP software providers design their products to be compatible with their competitors' products, so that modules from different providers can be combined. Integration of customer relationship management, supplier relationship management, and e-procurement modules into the ERP system is now becoming relatively commonplace. Although each ERP software provider configures its products differently from its competitors, some common modules of ERP systems are described here:

- *Accounting and finance.* This module assists an organization in maintaining financial control and accountability. It tracks accounting and financial information such as revenues, costs, assets, liabilities, and other accounting and financial information of the company. It is also capable of generating routine and advanced accounting and financial reports, product costing, budgeting, and analysis.

- *Customer relationship management.* This module provides the capability to manage customers. It enables collaboration between the organization and its customers by providing relevant, personalized, and up-to-date information. It also enables customers to track sales orders. The customer relationship management module allows the user to communicate effectively with existing customers and acquire new customers through sales automation and partner relationship management. Finally, it allows the firm to segment its customers and design customized promotions appealing to each customer segment.

- *Human resource management.* It assists an organization to plan, develop, manage, and control its human resources. It allows the firm to deploy the right people to support its overall strategic goals and to plan the optimal workforce levels based on production levels.

- *Manufacturing.* It schedules materials and tracks production, capacity, and the flow of goods through the manufacturing process. It may even include the capability for quality planning, inspection, and certifications.

- *Supplier relationship management.* This module provides the capability to manage all types of suppliers. It automates processes and enables the firm to more effectively collaborate with all its suppliers corporate-wide. It also monitors supplier performance and tracks delivery of goods purchased. It enables the user to effectively manage business processes through real-time collaboration during design, production, and distribution planning with suppliers. Supplier relationship management adds value to the supply chain by reducing supply chain inventory, decreasing delivery lead times, and improving inventory turns while increasing customer satisfaction.

- *Supply chain management.* This module handles the planning, execution, and control of activities involved in a supply chain. It assists the firm in strengthening its supply chain networks to improve delivery performance. It may cover various logistics functions, including transportation, warehousing, and inventory management. In this context, supply chain management refers to a firm's logistics management in which the focus is the distribution and storage of finished goods. The supply chain management module creates value by allowing the user to optimize its internal and external supply chains. Effective supply chain management requires the organization to have comprehensive management information systems to synchronize plans with customers and suppliers, collaborate in real time, execute plans, handle changes, and measure supply chain performance.

ERP systems have continued to evolve in the twenty-first century. One of the latest developments is the integration of e-business capabilities to use the Internet to conduct business transactions, such as sales, purchasing, inventory management, and customer service. Customers and suppliers are demanding access to certain information, such as order status, inventory levels, and invoice reconciliation through the ERP system. As information technology continues to become more complex and sophisticated, ERP software providers continue to add new functions and capabilities to their systems.

Enterprise Resource Planning Software Providers

There are hundreds of ERP software providers, each targeting a specific market segment and industry type. Thus, choosing an appropriate ERP software package can be a very challenging task. At one time, SAP, Oracle, PeopleSoft, JD Edwards, and Baan were among the most popular ERP providers. However, there was a series of mergers and acquisitions in the maturing ERP industry in the early 2000s. JD Edwards was acquired by PeopleSoft in 2003, which was subsequently purchased by the database giant Oracle in 2005. Baan was sold to Invensys in 2000, but was later acquired by SSA Global Technologies in 2003 and renamed to SSA ERP Ln. In 2006, Atlanta-based Infor Global Solutions bought SSA Global Technologies to become the world's third largest ERP provider. SSA ERP is still one of the most popular ERP products for the discrete manufacturing industry, especially for the make-to-order market. However, SAP remains the world's largest ERP provider followed by Oracle.

While Oracle has focused on aggressively acquiring other ERP vendors to broaden its product line, the German-based SAP has adopted an internal software development strategy to expand the functionality of its products. Microsoft has also gained a foothold in the ERP market with its recent purchase of Great Plains in 2001 and Navision in 2002. In addition to the mainstream ERP software systems, there are also many specialized software companies in the business of producing add-on software to provide specific functions or interact with preexisting legacy systems.

A new development in the ERP market appears to be the ability to provide "*appli-structure*"[13]—a term used to describe the merger of enterprise application and infrastructure technology. SAP, Oracle, and Microsoft are the three dominant vendors who provide ERP applications on their own infrastructure. Those vendors without their own infrastructure technology must build their applications on others' architectures. Another large IT firm, IBM, offers **applistructure** but it does not have its own ERP software. If the new concept is realized, dominant applistructure vendors will thrive in the future, but smaller vendors will continue to be acquired by the large, dominant applistructure vendors.

SUMMARY

While both manufacturing and service organizations rely on effective production and capacity planning to balance demand and capacity, manufacturers have the added advantage of being able to build up inventory as stored capacity. Service firms are unable to inventory their services, so they rely upon backlogs or reservations, cross-training, or queues to match supply with demand. However, excess capacity results in underutilized equipment and workforce and eventually leads to unnecessary cost, adversely impacting all firms along the supply chain.

This chapter covered material requirements planning, capacity planning, and ERP applications that are widely used for balancing demand with supply. An example was used to demonstrate how the aggregate production plan, master production schedule, material requirements plan, and distribution requirements plan are related to each other. This chapter also briefly discusses how the various materials plans are related to the capacity plans. A central piece of the materials plan is the material requirements plan, which takes information from the master production schedule, the bill of materials, and inventory status to compute planned order releases. For items that are produced in-house, planned order releases are released to the shop floor to trigger production. For purchased items, planned order releases are released to the purchasing department or directly to suppliers.

Finally, this chapter discussed the ERP system, including its relationships with the traditional MRP and MRP-II systems, its advantages and disadvantages, implementation issues, ERP modules, and major ERP software providers. The goal of ERP development was to build a single software application that runs off a common shared database to serve the needs of an entire organization, regardless of its units' geographical location and the currency used. Despite its complexity and considerable implementation costs, ERP provides a way to integrate different business functions of different businesses, on different continents. The integrated approach can have a tremendous payback if companies select the right applications and implement the software correctly. Unfortunately, many companies that have installed these systems have failed to realize all of the initial benefits expected.

Implementing ERP should be viewed as a long-term, ongoing project. No matter what resources a firm has initially committed to replacing legacy systems, selecting and implementing ERP applications, and training users, ERP requires ongoing management commitment and resources. As needs and technologies change and new applications are designed, new functionality and business processes will need to be continuously revisited and improved.

KEY TERMS

aggregate production plan (APP), 175

applistructure, 208

available-to-promise (ATP) quantity, 182

best-of-breed solution, 202

bill of materials (BOM), 185

bullwhip effect, 174

capacity, 174

capacity planning, 174

capacity requirements planning (CRP), 194

chase production strategy, 176

closed-loop MRP, 175

demand time fence, 182

dependent demand, 187

distribution requirements planning (DRP), 176

electronic data interchange (EDI), 193

enterprise resource planning (ERP) system, 174

implosion, 196

indented bill of materials, 187

DISCUSSION QUESTIONS

1. Why is it important to balance production with capacity?

2. Describe long-range, medium-range, and short-range planning in the context of the materials plan and capacity plan. How are they related?

3. Describe aggregate production planning, master production scheduling, material requirements planning, and distribution requirements planning. How are these plans related?

4. Describe the relationships among MRP, closed-loop MRP, MRP-II, and ERP.

5. Compare and contrast chase versus level production strategies. Which is more appropriate for an industry where highly skilled laborers are needed? Why?

6. Is a level production strategy suitable for a pure service industry, such as professional accounting and tax services or law firms? Can these firms inventory their outputs?

7. What is the purpose of low-level coding?

8. What is the purpose of the available-to-promise quantity, and how is it different from on-hand inventory?

9. What is system nervousness? Discuss how it can be minimized or avoided.

10. What are the crucial inputs for material requirements planning?

11. What is a BOM, and how is it different from the super BOM?

12. How are manufacturing and purchasing lead times considered in the MPS and the MRP?

13. What is the difference between scheduled receipts and planned order releases?

14. What is the difference between an MRP explosion and a DRP implosion?

15. Briefly describe resource requirements planning, rough-cut capacity planning, and capacity requirements planning. How are these plans related?

16. How are the various capacity plans (ERP, RCCP, CRP) related to the material plans (APP, MPS, MRP)?

17. Why are production planning and capacity planning important to SCM?

18. Why have so many firms rushed to implement ERP over the past 10 years?

19. Describe the limitations of a legacy MRP system.

20. Why is it important to learn the fundamentals of the traditional MRP system even if it is considered an outdated, legacy system?

21. What are the advantages of an ERP system over the legacy MRP system?

22. Explain best-of-breed and single integrator ERP implementations. What are the advantages and disadvantages of the best-of-breed implementation?

23. Explain why many ERP implementations have failed to yield the expected benefits over the last 10 years.

24. Briefly describe how an integrated ERP system works.

INTERNET QUESTIONS

1. Visit the Web sites of SAP, Oracle, and Microsoft, and use the information to write a write a brief report of the companies and their ERP software. Do their products offer the same configurations or functionalities?

2. Use the Internet to search for relevant information to prepare a brief report on how SAP and Oracle have expanded their product lines. Which of the two firms is known for its aggressive strategy to acquire smaller best-of-breed providers, and what are the latest firms to be acquired?

3. Use information on the Internet to prepare a report on acquisition and consolidation of ERP providers over the last 5 years in the ERP industry. Do you notice any obvious trends?

4. Use the Internet to search for information to write a report on whether the trend is toward single integrator or best-of-breed ERP implementations.

5. Utilize information on the Internet to prepare a report that describes "appli-structure." How is it going to affect the maturing ERP industry?

6. Use resources available on the Internet to write a report on the status of ERP adoption in China and compare that to the U.S.

7. Use resources available on the Internet to prepare a report on the current and projected ERP market total revenue and the rate of growth over the next 5 years.

8. Use resources available on the Internet to prepare a success story of a firm that has successfully implemented an ERP system.

9. Use resources available on the Internet to prepare a report that describes a failed ERP implementation. What can be learned from this company?

10. Explore the Web sites of SAP and Oracle, and use the information to write a report to discuss their (a) supply chain management, (b) supplier relationship management, and (c) customer relationship management software.

11. Use resources on the Internet to write a report to describe Microsoft's strategy and competitive position in the ERP market.

INFOTRAC QUESTIONS

Access http://academic.cengage.com/infotrac to answer the following questions:

1. Search on the term "enterprise resource planning" and write a paper on the current stage of ERP implementation in the U.S., Europe, and China.

2. Search on the terms "single integrator ERP" and "best-of-breed ERP," and write a report to describe which implementation strategy is preferred today.

3. Search on the terms "materials planning" and "capacity planning" and write a report on how these two strategies can be used to enhance a firm's competitiveness.

4. Search on the term "applistructure" and write a paper on how this concept is shaping the future ERP market.

5. Report on some of the companies that have successfully used single integrator ERP implementations.

6. Report on some of the companies that have successfully used best-of-breed ERP implementations.

SPREADSHEET PROBLEMS

1. Given the following production plan, use (a) chase production strategy and (b) level production strategy to compute the monthly production, ending inventory/(backlog), and workforce levels. A worker is capable of producing 100 units per month. Assume the beginning inventory at January is zero, and the firm desires to have zero inventory at the end of June.

MONTH	JAN	FEB	MAR	APR	MAY	JUN
Demand	2000	3000	5000	6000	6000	2000
Production						
Ending inventory						
Workforce						

2. Given the following production schedule, compute the available-to-promise quantities.

WEEK		1	2	3	4	5	6	7	8
Model A									
MPS	BI = 60	20	30	20	20	20	50	0	20
Committed customer orders		50	10	30	10	20	20	10	0
ATP:D									

3. Given the following production schedule, compute the available-to-promise quantities.

WEEK		1	2	3	4	5	6	7	8
Model B									
MPS	BI = 20	20	0	20	20	0	20	20	20
Committed customer orders		10	10	10	10	10	0	0	10
ATP:D									

4. The bills of materials for two finished products (D and E), inventory status, and other relevant information are given below. Compute the planned order releases and projected on-hand inventory balances for parts D, E, and F.

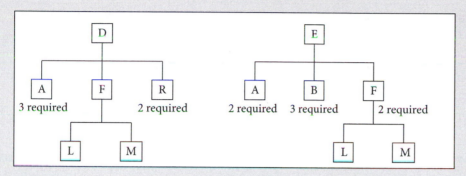

PART D		1	2	3	4	5	6
Gross requirements		7	11	9	5	8	6
Scheduled receipts							
Projected on-hand inventory	10						
Planned order releases							

$Q = 30$; $LT = 1$; $SS = 0$

PART E		1	2	3	4	5	6
Gross requirements		10	12	15	11	6	8
Scheduled receipts			11				
Projected on-hand inventory	15						
Planned order releases							

$Q = LFL$; $LT = 2$; $SS = 3$

PART F		1	2	3	4	5	6
Gross requirements							
Scheduled receipts		60					
Projected on-hand inventory	20						
Planned order releases							

$Q = 60$; $LT = 1$; $SS = 0$

5. Crop-Quick Inc. replenishes its three distribution centers in Boston, Denver, and Houston from its Las Vegas central supply warehouse. The distribution schedule for one of its products for the next six weeks is shown below. Use proper distribution requirements planning logic to complete the replenishment schedules of the three distribution centers and the central supply warehouse.

BOSTON DISTRIBUTION CENTER		1	2	3	4	5	6
Gross requirements		0	20	0	55	0	0
Scheduled receipts							
Projected on-hand inventory	10						
Planned order releases							

$Q = 30$; $LT = 1$; $SS = 5$

DENVER DISTRIBUTION CENTER		1	2	3	4	5	6
Gross requirements		0	20	10	0	0	20
Scheduled receipts			11				
Projected on-hand inventory	15						
Planned order releases							

Q = LFL; LT = 2; SS = 2

HOUSTON DISTRIBUTION CENTER		1	2	3	4	5	6
Gross requirements		10	0	0	45	0	0
Scheduled receipts							
Projected on-hand inventory	20						
Planned order releases							

Q = 60; LT = 1; SS = 0

LAS VEGAS CENTRAL WAREHOUSE		1	2	3	4	5	6
Gross Requirements							
Scheduled Receipts							
Projected On-hand Inventory	50						
Planned Order Releases							

Q = 20; LT = 1; SS = 0

Chapter 7

INVENTORY MANAGEMENT

Inventory, and how to manage it, is a source of headaches: there is never enough inventory available for a company's customer-service managers, but there's usually too much of it for top management's liking. It's said that there is a fine line between managing company inventory and letting inventory manage the company. Too little of it can sink a company; too much of it creates a host of other problems, including the cost of storing unsold goods. Excess inventory can also mask underlying flaws in a company, including its supply chain, less-than-reliable vendors, bad forecasting and poor communications.[1]

Learning Objectives

After completing this chapter, you should be able to

- Distinguish dependent from independent demand inventories.
- Describe the four basic types of inventories and their functions.
- Understand the costs of inventory and inventory turnovers.
- Understand ABC classification, the ABC inventory matrix, and cycle counting.
- Further understand RFID and how it can be used in inventory management.
- Understand the EOQ model and its underlying assumptions.
- Understand the quantity discount and the EMQ models and their relationships with the basic EOQ model.
- Understand and distinguish the various statistical ROP models.
- Describe the continuous review and periodic review systems.

Chapter Outline

Introduction

Dependent Demand and Independent Demand

Concepts and Tools of Inventory Management

Inventory Models

Summary

Supply Chain Management in Action

Improving Return on Investment by Restricting Inventory Growth

Sam and Bud Walton opened the first Wal-Mart store in Rogers, Arkansas, in 1962. By 1967, the company owned twenty-four stores, with $12.6 million in sales. The company was incorporated as Wal-Mart Stores, Inc. in late 1969 and was traded as a publicly held company in 1970. By 1987, Wal-Mart's twenty-fifth anniversary, the company owned 1198 stores, with sales of $15.9 billion, and it employed 200,000 associates. By its fortieth anniversary in 2002, Wal-Mart was the world's largest retailer, with $218 billion in sales. By 2007, Wal-Mart employed about 1.9 million associates worldwide and operated around 6500 stores and wholesale clubs in 13 countries including China, Korea, Mexico, Puerto Rico, Canada, Argentina, Brazil, Germany, and the United Kingdom. The company generated nearly $348.7 billion in total revenue and a gross profit of $84.50 billion in the fiscal year ending January 31, 2007.

Wal-Mart owes much of its success and expectation for future growth to its advanced information technology and sophisticated supply chain management system, including a vast global network of 240 strategically located distribution centers and a very efficient private trucking fleet with 8000 drivers who travel more than 900 million miles a year to supply its stores worldwide. Sales increased 10.45 percent from $315.7 billion in 2006 to $348.7 billion in 2007, but the value of its inventory increased by just 4.64 percent from $32.2 billion to $33.7 billion.[2] In the same fiscal year ending 2007, Target Corporation's[3] sales and inventory increased by 13.06 and 7.13 percent, respectively, whereas Sears Holdings Corporation's[4] (which operates Kmart) sales and inventory increased by 7.91 and 9.25 percent, respectively. While Wal-Mart continues to improve its in-stock performance, the company is pursuing an aggressive goal to improve its return on investment (ROI) by limiting the growth of inventories to less than half of that of sales. Wal-Mart essentially replaced the need to hold huge amounts of inventory to support its vast distribution system with its complex information system. This unique capability enabled Wal-Mart to restrict inventory growth while maintaining a strong in-stock position.

In 2005, Wal-Mart launched its Remix initiative to reduce inventory by changing from a traditional category-based to a velocity-based distribution network. The 5000 fastest-turning products are shipped to each store on the same truck and are expedited directly to the shelves. Radio frequency identification (RFID) is used to track inventory, and suppliers are able to view that information via the Retail Link information system when goods are unloaded from the Remix trailer to the floor. This reduces replenishment lead time significantly. Moreover, less-than-truckload (LTL) shipments from smaller vendors are consolidated into full truckloads (TLs) to take advantage of cheaper unit shipping cost and to reduce congestion at the receiving stores. The program changes the way in which goods are processed and shipped at the distribution centers.

Wal-Mart's Remix initiative also embraces some in-store measures to further reduce inventory levels. Merchandise stored on the higher shelves in the stores create safety hazards and are not accessible to the customers, thus are not value adding. The retailer removes the clutter in the stores and risers from atop the gondolas, except in the toy department where additional storage is needed. To further improve inventory turnover, a small aluminum trolley called Rocket Cart, which is narrow enough so as not to block the aisles the way a pallet would, is used by associates to restock high-velocity products throughout the day.

Note: Some parts of this feature came from Troy, M. "Wal-Mart's Inventory Equation." *Retailing Today,* 45 (September 11, 2006): 9–11.

Introduction

Inventory can be one of the most expensive assets of an organization. It may account for more than 10 percent of total revenue or 20 percent of total assets for some organizations. Although companies in the manufacturing sector usually carry more inventory than service firms, effective inventory management is nonetheless important to both manufacturers and service organizations. Table 7.1 shows the amount of inventory, and the ratio of inventory to total revenue and total assets of a few large corporations in the U.S. While the inventory to total assets ratio for service organizations such as casino hotels is relatively low compared to most manufacturers, inventory management for service firms poses a different challenge. Casino hotels carry a wide range of perishable food items to stock the diverse restaurants operating in these resorts. Managing this perishable inventory poses a unique challenge to operations managers.

Inventory management policy affects how efficiently a firm deploys its assets in producing goods and services. Developing effective inventory control systems to reduce waste and stockouts in manufacturing or service organizations is a complex problem. The right amount of inventory supports manufacturing, logistics, and other functions, but excessive inventory is a sign of poor inventory management that creates unnecessary waste of scarce resource. Besides, excessive inventory adversely affects financial performance. The need for better inventory management systems continues to challenge operations managers.

This chapter first explains the difference between **dependent demand** and **lindependent demand** items. Then, the chapter focuses on the independent demand items to

Table 7.1	Inventory Investment Compared to Total Revenue and Total Assets					
COMPANY	FINANCIAL YEAR END	TOTAL REVENUE	TOTAL ASSETS	YEAR END INVENTORY	INVENTORY/ TOTAL REVENUE (%)	INVENTORY/ TOTAL ASSETS (%)
Harrah's Entertainment Inc.	Dec. 31, 2006	9674	22,285	63	0.65	0.28
MGM Mirage	Dec. 31, 2006	7176	22,146	488	6.80	2.20
Microsoft Corp.	Jun. 30, 2007	51,122	63,171	1127	2.20	1.78
Ford Motor Co.	Dec. 31, 2006	160,123	278,554	11,578	7.23	4.16
Toyota Motor Corp.	Mar. 31, 2007	202,864	275,941	15,281	7.53	5.54
General Motors Corp.	Dec. 31, 2006	207,349	186,192	20,046	9.67	10.77
Wal-Mart Stores, Inc.	Jan. 31, 2007	348,650	151,193	33,685	9.66	22.28
Target Corp.	Feb. 3, 2007	59,490	37,349	6254	10.51	16.74
Pfizer Inc.	Dec. 31, 2006	48,371	114,837	6111	12.63	5.32
Intel Corp.	Dec. 30, 2006	35,382	48,368	4314	12.19	8.92
Advanced Micro Devices Inc.	Dec. 31, 2006	5649	13,147	814	14.41	6.19

Note: All numbers in millions, except ratios.
Source: Annual reports on Form 10-K.

describe the basic concepts and tools of inventory management, including the **ABC inventory control system**, **inventory costs**, radio frequency identification, and cross-docking. This chapter also discusses the three fundamental deterministic inventory models and the two major types of stochastic inventory models.

Dependent Demand and Independent Demand

Inventory management models are generally separated by the nature and types of the inventory being considered and can be classified as *dependent demand* and *independent demand models.*

Dependent demand is the internal demand for parts based on the demand of the final product in which the parts are used. Subassemblies, components, and raw materials are examples of dependent demand items. Dependent demand may have a pattern of abrupt and dramatic changes because of its dependency on the demand of the final product, particularly if the final product is produced in large lot sizes. Dependent demand can be calculated once the demand of the final product is known. Hence, material requirements planning (MRP) software is often used to compute exact material requirements.

The dependent demand inventory system was discussed in Chapter 6. For example, the ATV Corporation's master production schedule discussed in Table 6.4 of Chapter 6 shows that 120 all-terrain vehicles will be produced in January. The firm thus knows that 120 handlebars and 480 wheel rims will be needed. The demand for handlebars, wheel rims, and other dependent demand items can be calculated based on the bill of materials and the demand of the final product as stated on the master production schedule. Recall that a bill of materials is an engineering record showing all the component parts and assemblies needed for making a unit of the final product.

Independent demand is the demand for final products and has a demand pattern affected by trends, seasonal patterns, and general market conditions. For example, the customer demand for all-terrain vehicles is independent demand. Batteries, headlights, seals, and gaskets originally used in assembling the all-terrain vehicles at the ATV Corporation are dependent demands; however, the same batteries, headlights, seals, and gaskets sold as *service parts* to the repair shops or end users would be classified as independent demand items. Similarly, the original battery used in assembling your new car is a dependent demand item to the automobile manufacturer, but the replacement battery (a service part sold by the automobile manufacturer through a dealer) that you bought to replace the original battery is an independent demand item. Independent demand items cannot be derived using the material requirements planning logic from the demand for other items and, thus, must be forecasted based on market conditions.

Concepts and Tools of Inventory Management

Savvy operations managers are concerned with controlling inventories not only within their organizations, but also throughout their supply chains. An effective independent demand inventory system ensures smooth operations and allows manufacturing firms to store up production capacity in the form of work-in-process and finished goods inventories. While some service firms are unable to inventory their output, such organizations may rely on appointment backlogs, labor scheduling, and cross-training to balance supply and demand.

All manufacturing and service organizations are concerned with effective inventory planning and control. Inventory requires capital investment, handling and storage space, and it is also subject to deterioration and shrinkage. Although a firm's operating costs and financial performance can be improved by reducing inventory, the increased risk of stockouts can be devastating to customer service. Therefore, companies must strike a delicate balance between inventory investment and customer service. This section discusses some important concepts and tools of inventory management. The concepts of vendor-managed inventory and co-managed inventory were discussed in Chapter 4 and thus, will not be repeated here.

The Functions and Basic Types of Inventory

Inventory includes all the materials and goods that are purchased, partially completed materials and component parts, and the finished goods produced. The primary functions of inventory are to *buffer* uncertainty in the marketplace and to "*decouple*" or break the dependencies between stages in the supply chain. For example, appropriate amounts of inventory, usually known as *safety stock* or *buffer stock*, can be used to cushion uncertainties due to fluctuations in supply, demand, and/or delivery lead time. Similarly, the right amount of inventory enables a work center to operate without interruption when other work centers in the same production process are off-line for maintenance or repair. Keeping the correct amount of inventory at each work center also allows a faster work center to operate smoothly when it is constrained by slower upstream work centers.

In this increasingly global environment, it is not unusual that organizations use the concept of *geographical specialization* to manufacture their products in the developing countries where labor and raw materials are cheaper and readily available. In this scenario, the developing countries specialize in cheap labor and abundant raw materials, whereas the manufacturing firms provide the technology and capital to produce the goods. The ability to geographically separate the consumption of the finished goods from production is a key function of inventory. For manufacturers, inventory also acts as *stored capacity*. For instance, snowmobile manufacturers can build up inventory by producing snowmobiles year-round in anticipation of peak demand during the busy winter season.

There are four broad categories of inventories—raw materials, work-in-process, finished goods, and maintenance, repair, and operating (MRO) supplies.

- *Raw materials* are defined as unprocessed purchased inputs or materials for manufacturing the finished goods. Raw materials become part of finished goods after the manufacturing process is completed. There are many reasons for keeping raw material inventories, including volume purchases due to quantity discounts, stockpiling in anticipation of future price increases, safety stock to guard against supplier delivery or quality problems, volume purchases to create transportation economies, and stockpiling to avoid a possible short supply in the future.
- *Work-in-process (WIP)* describes materials that are partially processed but not yet ready for sales. One reason to keep excess WIP inventories is to decouple processing stages or to break the dependencies between work centers.

- *Finished goods* are completed products ready for shipment. Excess finished goods inventories are often kept as a buffer against unexpected demand changes and in anticipation of production process downtime; to ensure production economies when the setup cost is very high; and/or to stabilize production rates, especially for seasonal products.
- *Maintenance, repair, and operating (MRO) supplies* are materials and supplies used when producing the products but are not parts of the products. Solvents, cutting tools, and lubricants for machines are examples of MRO supplies. The two main reasons for storing MRO supplies are to gain purchase economies and to avoid material shortages that may shut down production.

Inventory Costs

The bottom line of effective inventory management is to control inventory costs and minimize stockouts. Inventory costs can be categorized in many ways—direct and indirect costs, fixed and variable costs, and order and carrying costs.

Direct costs are those that are directly traceable to the unit produced, such as the amount of materials and labor used to produce a unit of the finished good. **Indirect costs** are those that cannot be traced directly to the unit produced, and they are synonymous with manufacturing overhead. Maintenance, repair, and operating supplies, heating, lighting, buildings, equipment, and plant security are examples of indirect costs. **Fixed costs** are independent of the output quantity, but **variable costs** vary as a function of the output level. Buildings, equipment, plant security, heating, and lighting are examples of fixed costs, whereas direct materials and labor costs are variable costs. A key focus of inventory management is to control variable costs since fixed costs are generally considered *sunk costs*.

Order costs are the direct variable costs associated with placing an order with the supplier, whereas **holding** or **carrying costs** are the costs incurred for holding inventory in storage. Order costs include managerial and clerical costs for preparing the purchase, as well as other incidental expenses that can be traced directly to the purchase. Examples of holding costs include handling charges, warehousing expenses, insurance, pilferage, shrinkage, taxes, and the cost of capital. In a manufacturing context, **setup costs** are used in place of order costs to describe the costs associated with setting up machines and equipment to produce a batch of product. However, in inventory management discussions, order costs and setup costs are often used interchangeably.

Inventory Investment

Inventory serves many important functions for manufacturing and service firms; however, excessive inventory is detrimental to a firm's financial health and competitive edge. Whether inventory is an asset that contributes to organizational objective or a liability depends on its management. The chapter opening feature, Supply Chain Management in Action, demonstrates that even a huge retailer with sophisticated information technology such as Wal-Mart must diligently monitor its inventory investment to ensure that it is not adversely affecting the firm's competitiveness.

Inventory is expensive and it ties up working capital. Moreover, inventory requires storage space and incurs other carrying costs. Some products such as perishable food items and hazardous materials (hazmat) require special handling and storage that add to the cost of holding inventory. Inventory can also deteriorate quickly while it is in storage. In addition, inventory can become obsolete very quickly as new materials and technologies are being introduced. Most important, large piles of inventory delay a firm's ability to respond swiftly to production problems and changes in technologies and market conditions.

Inventory investment can be measured in various ways. The typical annual physical stock counts to determine the total dollars invested in inventory provides an absolute measure of inventory investment. The inventory value is then reported on a firm's balance sheet. This value can be used to compare the budget and past inventory investment. However, the absolute dollars invested in inventory does not provide a sufficient clue regarding whether the company is using its inventory wisely. A widely used measure to analyze how efficiently a firm uses its inventory to generate revenue is the **inventory turnover ratio** or **inventory turnovers**. This ratio shows how many times a company turns over its inventory in an accounting period. Faster turnovers are generally viewed as a positive trend because it indicates that the company is able to generate more revenue per dollar in inventory investment. Moreover, faster turnovers allow the company to increase cash flow and reduce warehousing and carrying costs. Conversely, a low inventory turnover may point to overstocking or deficiencies in the product line or marketing effort.

The formula for inventory turnover ratio is:

$$\text{Inventory turnovers} = \frac{\text{cost of revenue}}{\text{average inventory}}$$

where

cost of revenue = cost of goods sold from a firm's income statement

average inventory = mean of the beginning and ending inventory

Table 7.2	**Inventory Turnover Ratios**				
COMPANY	**FINANCIAL YEAR END**	**TOTAL REVENUE**	**COST OF REVENUE**	**YEAR END INVENTORY**	**INVENTORY TURNOVER RATIO**
Harrah's Entertainment Inc.	Dec. 31, 2006	9674	4857	63	77.10
MGM Mirage	Dec. 31, 2006	7176	3813	488	7.81
Microsoft Corporation	Jun. 30, 2007	51,122	10,693	1127	9.49
Ford Motor Co.	Dec. 31, 2006	160,123	148,869	11,578	12.86
Toyota Motor Corporation	Mar. 31, 2007	202,864	162,883	15,281	10.66
General Motors Corporation	Dec. 31, 2006	207,349	164,682	20,046	8.22
Wal-Mart Stores, Inc.	Jan. 31, 2007	348,650	264,152	33,685	7.84
Target Corporation	Feb. 3, 2007	59,490	39,399	6254	6.30
Pfizer Inc.	Dec. 31, 2006	48,371	7640	6111	1.25
Intel Corporation	Dec. 30, 2006	35,382	17,164	4314	3.98
Advanced Micro Devices Inc.	Dec. 31, 2006	5649	2856	814	3.51

Note: All numbers in millions, except ratios.
Source: Annual Reports on Form 10-K.

The inventory turnover ratio can be computed for any accounting period, such as monthly, quarterly, or annually. However, a firm's inventory may fluctuate widely in a financial year; thus, the average of the beginning and ending inventory may be a poor indicator of the firm's average inventory for the year. In this case, the average of the twelve-month ending inventories can be used as the average inventory when computing the annual inventory turnover ratio. Table 7.2 shows the annual inventory turnovers for a few large manufacturing and service firms in the U.S. In 2006, Harrah's Entertainment Inc. turned over its inventory a staggering 77.1 times. However, the nature of Harrah's business may suggest that a major portion of its revenue came from hotel room and gaming sales, but the inventory consisted of mostly goods for the restaurants. Therefore, the revenue generated by hotel room and gaming sales could be excluded from the calculation of the ratio.

The e-Business Connection feature shows how inventory turnovers and return on assets are used to gauge a firm's competitiveness in the supply chain.

e-Business Connection — *The Top 25 Supply Chains of 2007*

For the past two decades, companies have increasingly turned to supply chain management, resulting in remarkable gains in productivity. For industry leaders such as Apple, Microsoft, and Nike, supply chain management yields multiple benefits: increased efficiency, competitive differentiation, and rapid new product launches, among others. The *Top 25 Supply Chains of 2007* chosen by the AMR Research have excelled in performance metrics such as return on assets (ROA) and revenue growth. These companies hail from diverse industries and include ranked industrial leaders, such as Paccar, Lockheed-Martin, and Toyota. Technology giants IBM, Cisco Systems, and Hewlett-Packard also make an appearance, and have learned what "solution-selling" really means—"that supply chain processes need to serve the consumer, not the technology itself." Not surprisingly, common amongst the three pharmaceutical firms, Johnson & Johnson, GlaxoSmithKline, and AstraZeneca, all in the *Top 25*, are very high ROAs. Five of the *Top 25* are retailers—Wal-Mart, Tesco, Lowe's, Best Buy, and Publix—and are especially adept at creating unique shopping experiences and collaborating with strategic suppliers to improve inventory management along their supply chains.

The *Top 25* of 2007 demonstrate many significant trends in supply chain management. For example, creative and logical functions are gaining prominence. Eager consumers spent more than $2 billion on Apple's iTunes, a *zero-inventory* product. Apple's spectacular inventory turnover of 50.8 helped to propel the company to nearly the top of the ranking. Also, Hewlett-Packard and Nike show that companies do not have to rely solely on low cost to win business. The 2007 *Top 25* list also reveals the intense competition in the mobile phone industry. The *Top 25* include cell-phone makers Nokia, Samsung, and Motorola. The low prices put out by these companies allow universal access to their products. In the future, however, they will be expected not only to make mobile phones but to enable wireless content creation as well, which will force design partnerships with other telecommunications and entertainment corporations. This obviously creates additional inventory management challenges along the supply chain.

AMR's *Top 25* ranking was based on two main criteria: a financial and a qualitative component of a company's performance. The financial component was based on ROA, inventory turnovers, and revenue growth. The qualitative component was based on equally weighted opinions from a peer panel of supply chain professionals and the AMR Research Panel.

Note: Some parts of this feature came from O'Marah, K. "The Top 25 Supply Chains of 2007." *Supply Chain Management Review*, 11, no. 6 (September 2007): 16–22.

The ABC Inventory Control System

A common problem with many inventory management systems is the inability to maintain accurate inventory records. **Cycle counting** is a commonly used technique in which physical inventory is counted on a periodic basis to ensure that physical inventory matches current inventory records. Cycle counting helps identify obsolete stocks and inventory problems so that remedial action can be taken in a reasonable amount of time. However, cycle counting can be costly and time consuming and can disrupt operations. The ABC inventory control system is a useful technique for determining which inventories should be counted more frequently and managed more closely and which others should not. ABC analysis is often combined with the **80/20 rule** or **Pareto analysis**. Applied to inventories, the 80/20 rule suggests that 80 percent of a firm's total annual inventory expenditures are accounted for by 20 percent of its inventory part or product items. This also means that the remaining 20 percent of the inventory expenditures are taken up by 80 percent of the inventory items. The Pareto analysis recommends that inventories falling into the first category be assigned the highest priority and be managed closely.

The ABC inventory control system prioritizes inventory items into three groups— A, B, and C. However, it is not uncommon that some firms choose to use more than three categories. A items are given the highest priority, while C items have the lowest priority and are typically the most numerous. Greater attention, safety stocks, and resources are devoted to the high-priority or A items. The priority is most often determined by annual dollar usage. However, priority may also be determined by product shelf life, sales volume, whether the materials are critical components, or other criteria.

When prioritizing inventories by annual dollar usage, the ABC system suggests that approximately 20 percent of the items make up about 80 percent of the total annual dollar usage and these items are classified as the A items. The B items make up roughly 40 percent of the inventory items and account for about 15 percent of the total annual dollar usage, while the C items are the remaining 40 percent of the items making up about 5 percent of the total annual dollar usage of inventory. A summary of the classification is provided in Table 7.3. Since the A items are the highest annual dollar usage items, these items should then be monitored more frequently and may have higher safety stock levels to guard against stockouts, particularly if these items are used in products sold to supply chain trading partners. The C items would then be counted less frequently, and stockouts may be allowed to save inventory space and carrying costs.

Table 7.3	ABC Inventory Classification	
CLASSIFICATIONS	PERCENT OF TOTAL ANNUAL DOLLAR USAGE	PERCENT OF TOTAL INVENTORY ITEMS
A Items	80	20
B Items	15	40
C Items	5	40

An ABC inventory classification can be done monthly, quarterly, annually, or at any fixed period. For the fast-moving consumer market, an *A item* may become a *C item* within months or even weeks; thus, an ABC inventory classification based on annual dollar usage may not be useful to management in this environment. An illustration of an ABC inventory classification using annual dollar usage is shown in Example 7.1.

The ABC Inventory Matrix

ABC inventory analysis can be expanded to assist in identifying obsolete stocks and to analyze whether a company is stocking the correct inventory by comparing two ABC analyses. First, an ABC analysis is done on current inventory based on the inventory value (quantity on-hand × price) to classify physical inventory into A, B, and C groups. Next, a second ABC analysis is done on inventory usage (quantity used × price) to classify inventory usage into A, B, and C groups. The two ABC analyses can be combined to form an **ABC inventory matrix** as shown in Figure 7.1. *A items* based on physical inventory classification should match the *A items* based on inventory usage. Similarly, the *B* and *C items* should also match between the two ABC analyses. Otherwise, the company is stocking the wrong items. The ABC inventory matrix also suggests that some overlaps are expected between two borderline classifications. For instance, some marginal *B items* based on inventory usage may appear as *C items* based on physical inventory classification and vice versa.

The upper left triangle of the ABC inventory matrix indicates that the *C* and *B items* based on physical inventory classification correspond to the *A items* based on inventory usage classification, suggesting that the company has understocked its

---

Example 7.1   ABC Inventory Classification

Note that in this example, the *A items* only account for about 67 percent of the total annual dollar volume, while the *B items* account for about 28 percent. This illustrates that judgment must also be applied when using the ABC method and the 80/20 rule should only be used as a general guideline.

AN ABC INVENTORY CLASSIFICATION BASED ON ANNUAL DOLLAR USAGE

INVENTORY ITEM NUMBER	ITEM COST ($)	ANNUAL USAGE (UNITS)	ANNUAL DOLLAR USAGE ($)	PERCENT OF TOTAL ANNUAL USAGE (%)	CLASSIFICATION BASED ON ANNUAL DOLLAR USAGE
A246	1.00	22,000	22,000	35.2	A
N376	0.50	40,000	20,000	32.0	A
C024	4.25	1468	6239	10.0	B
R221	12.00	410	4920	7.8	B
P112	2.25	1600	3600	5.8	B
R116	0.12	25,000	3000	4.8	B
T049	8.50	124	1054	1.7	C
B615	0.25	3500	875	1.4	C
L227	1.25	440	550	0.9	C
T519	26.00	10	260	0.4	C
Total Annual Dollar Usage:			$62,498	100%	

Figure 7.1 | ABC Inventory Matrix

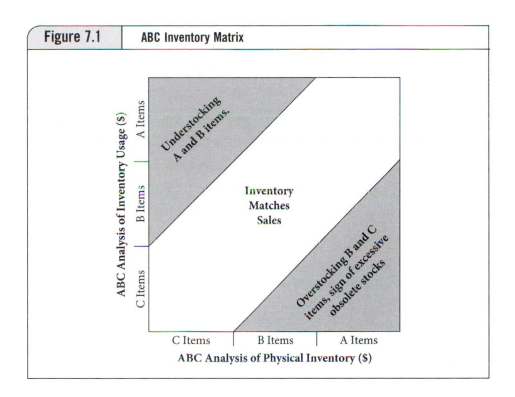

A and B items. Conversely, the lower right triangle shows that the A items based on physical inventory classification correspond to the C and B items based on inventory usage, thus indicating that the company has overstocked noncrucial inventory. This may point to the presence of excessive *obsolete stock* if the inventory turnover ratio is very low. Obsolete stocks should be disposed of so that valuable inventory investment and warehouse space can be used for productive inventory. When used in conjunction with inventory turnovers, the ABC inventory matrix is a powerful tool for managing inventory investment.

Using the ABC inventory usage dollar classification from Example 7.1, let us assume that the physical inventory and its ABC classifications are as shown in Example 7.2. The two ABC analyses can be combined to form the ABC inventory matrix as shown in Figure 7.2. Each inventory item can be plotted on the matrix by using the "percent of total physical inventory" on the horizontal axis and the "percent of total annual usage" on the vertical axis. For instance, the coordinate of the item "T519" is (40.5, 0.4). The analysis in Figure 7.2 shows that the six items along the diagonal matched, although it is not necessary that the appropriate levels are stocked. The company has probably overstocked items "T519" and "L227," but understocked "N376." It is important that the inventory turnover ratio be used in conjunction with the ABC inventory matrix to get a sense of how fast or slow inventories are turning over.

Radio Frequency Identification

For decades, barcodes have been used to identify the manufacturer and content of a carton. However, barcodes cannot store enough information to differentiate goods at the item level. Also, a direct line of sight is required for the reader to read a barcode; moreover, the information stored on the barcode is static and not updatable.

Example 7.2   ABC Inventory Matrix

INVENTORY ITEM NUMBER	ITEM COST ($)	PHYSICAL INVENTORY (UNITS)	PHYSICAL INVENTORY ($)	PERCENT OF TOTAL PHYSICAL INVENTORY (%)	CLASSIFICATION BASED ON PHYSICAL INVENTORY DOLLAR
T519	26.00	300	7800	40.5	A
A246	1.00	5600	5600	29.1	A
L227	1.25	1200	1500	7.8	B
C024	4.25	348	1479	7.7	B
R221	12.00	80	960	5.0	B
P112	2.25	352	792	4.1	B
T049	8.50	50	425	2.2	C
N376	0.50	800	400	2.1	C
R116	0.12	2100	252	1.3	C
B615	0.25	120	30	0.2	C

Total Physical Inventory ($): $19,238   100%

Figure 7.2   ABC Inventory Matrix for Example 7.2

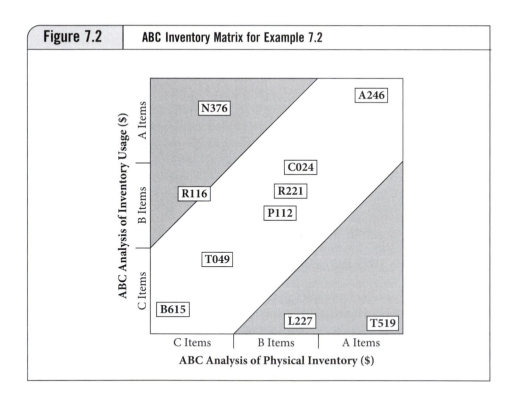

Radio frequency identification (RFID) is an eventual successor to the barcode for tracking individual units of goods. RFID does not require a direct line of sight for the reader to read a tag, and the information on the tag is updatable. RFID technology is also used in libraries, passport recognition, animal tracking, the medical industry, toll payments, and many other fields.

There are two major RFID standards—the **electronic product code (EPC)** standard managed by EPCglobal, Inc.,[5] a subsidiary of GS1 that created the UPC barcode, and the 18000 standard of the International Organization for Standardization (ISO). Wal-Mart and the U.S. Department of Defense (DOD) are the two largest adopters of RFID. By 2005, both organizations had issued mandates for their top suppliers to use RFID technology to identify their products.[6] Wal-Mart has adopted the EPC standard, whereas the Department of Defense has chosen the EPC standard for general purpose application but has decided to use the ISO standard for air interface communication between the RFID readers and the tags. The EPC standard is more widely adopted, especially in the commercial sector.

Similar to barcode technology, an RFID reader reads the information stored in RFID tags. However, the reader does not have to be placed directly in line of sight of the tag to read the radio signal—a significant advantage of RFID over barcode. The EPC standards call for five classes of tags over time (Table 7.4). Class 0 tags are read only, but class 1 tags can be programmed once to update the information stored on the tags. Similar to a rewritable CD media, class 2 tags can be read and re-written several times. Classes 0, 1, and 2 are passive tags that do not store power on the tags, but Classes 3 and 4 are active tags that contain a power source to boost their range. The current thrust of the EPC standard is the 96-bit UHF Class 1, General 2 Write Once Read Many (WORM) tag. This generation of tags is expected to pave the way for the Class 2 high-memory full Read/Write tags. A 256-bit version of the tag is being defined but full details were not yet available as of the end of 2007.

The current 96-bit EPC is a number made up of a header and three sets of data as shown in Figure 7.3. The 8-bit *header* identifies the version of the EPC being used; the 28-bit *EPC manager* identifies the manufacturer (and even plant) of the product; the 24-bit *object class* identifies the unique product family; and the 36-bit *serial number* uniquely identifies the individual physical item being read. The 8-bit header can identify 256 (2^8) versions of EPC; the 28-bit EPC manager can classify 268,435,456 (2^{28}) companies; the 24-bit object class can identify 16,777,216 (2^{24}) product families per company; and the 36-bit serial number can differentiate 68,719,476,736 (2^{36}) specific items per product family. Using this mammoth combination that is unmatched by any barcode, it is not difficult to envisage that RFID will revolutionize inventory management along the supply chain.

Table 7.4	EPCglobal's Tag Classes	
EPC CLASS TYPE	**FEATURES**	**TAG TYPE**
Class 0	Read Only	Passive (64 bits only)
Class 1	Write Once, Read Many	Passive (minimum 96 bits)
Class 2	Read/Write	Passive (minimum 96 bits)
Class 3	Read/Write with battery power to enhance range	Semiactive
Class 4	Read/Write active transmitter	Active

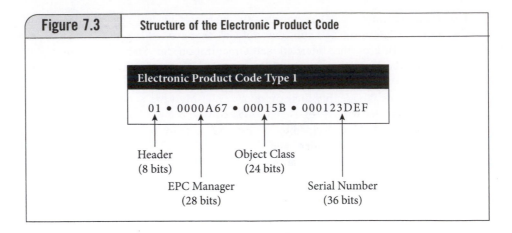

Figure 7.3 | **Structure of the Electronic Product Code**

Electronic Product Code Type 1

01 • 0000A67 • 00015B • 000123DEF

Header
(8 bits)

EPC Manager
(28 bits)

Object Class
(24 bits)

Serial Number
(36 bits)

Components of a Radio Frequency Identification System

An RFID system consists of four parts—the tag, reader, communication network, and RFID software. The tag consists of a computer chip and an antenna for wireless communication with the handheld or fixed-position RFID reader and the communication network connects the readers to transmit inventory information to the enterprise information system. The RFID software manages the collection, synchronization, and communication of the data with warehouse management, ERP, and supply chain planning systems, and stores the information in a database. Figure 7.4 shows an RFID system.

Though RFID was designed for use at the item level to identify individual items, current implementation focuses at the aggregate level where tags are placed on cases, crates, pallets, or containers due to the high cost of the tags. A passive RFID tag costs approximately 10 cents today, compared to $2 in 1999,[7] but it is still not financially

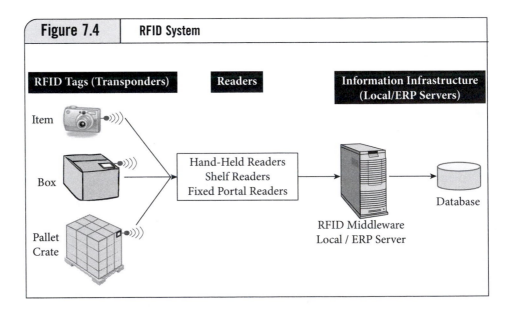

Figure 7.4 | **RFID System**

RFID Tags (Transponders)   Readers   Information Infrastructure
(Local/ERP Servers)

Item

Box

Pallet
Crate

Hand-Held Readers
Shelf Readers
Fixed Portal Readers

RFID Middleware
Local / ERP Server

Database

feasible to tag individual low-ticket items. Thus, the existing focus is at the aggregate level focusing on cases or pallets of items, although some retailers have started to place passive RFID tags on individual high-ticket items such as cameras and electronic products to prevent theft and closely manage the expensive inventory.

How Radio Frequency Identification Automates the Supply Chain

RFID is a valuable technology for tracking inventory in the supply chain. It can synchronize information and physical flow of goods across the supply chain from manufacturers to retail outlets and to the consumers at the right place at the right time. Likewise, RFID can track returned goods through the supply chain and prevent counterfeit. It also helps to reduce out-of-stock items. There is no doubt that RFID is invaluable for improving inventory management and supply chain efficiency. Next, we describe how RFID can automate the supply chain.

Materials management: As the supply vehicle enters the warehouse, the fixed-portal RFID reader positioned at the entrance reads the tags on the pallets or individual items to provide handling, routing, and storage information of the incoming goods, and the inventory status can be updated automatically.

Manufacturing: An RFID tag can be placed on the unit being produced so that specific customer configurations can be incorporated automatically during the production process. This is invaluable in a make-to-order environment.

Distribution center: As the logistics vehicle arrives at the loading dock, the fixed-portal RFID tag reader communicates with the tag on the vehicle to confirm that it is approved to pickup goods. When the loaded vehicle leaves the dock and crosses the portal, the reader picks up the signals from the tags to alert the RFID software and ERP system to update the inventory automatically and initiate an advanced shipping notice (ASN), proof of pickup, and invoices.

Retail store: As the delivery vehicle enters the unloading dock, the fixed-portal reader picks up the signals from the tags, and the RFID software application processes the signals to provide specific handling instructions and initiates automatic routing of the goods. An RFID tag reader can also be placed on the store shelf to trigger automatic replenishments when an item reaches its reorder point. Moreover, inventory status can be updated automatically in real time at any stage of the supply chain, and hand-held tag readers can be used to assist in cycle counting. Item-level tagging can be used to recommend complementary products. For instance, a computer screen and a tag reader can be placed in the changing room, so when a consumer tests a tagged suit in the changing room, the reader picks up the signal to suggest matching shirts and shoes on the LCD screen. When RFID is fully implemented at the item level, it is not difficult to envisage that instead of waiting for a cashier, a consumer should be able to simply walk out of the door of a store, automating the purchase. A tag reader built into the retailer's door should be able to recognize the items in the cart and charge the customer accordingly. The customer would not have to stop to pay for the purchase if a prearranged credit facility or account has been established with the store.

The Global Perspective feature provides an overview of the challenges and status of current RFID implementation in North America, Europe, and China.

Global Perspective

A Status Report and the Challenges of Current RFID Implementations

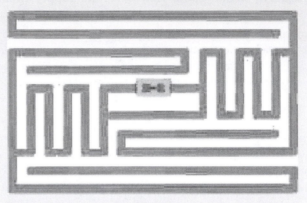

An RFID Tag[8]

Radio frequency identification (RFID) is one of the latest developments in inventory management, especially for the retail sector. A couple of years after the RFID mandate issued by Wal-Mart, more than 100 top suppliers began to ship RFID tagged pallets and cases to the giant retailer by early 2005. The company has since expanded the requirement to 500 additional large suppliers, and was set to include its top 1000 suppliers by the end of 2007. Not surprisingly, RFID technology has also been adopted by other major retailers worldwide, including Marks & Spencer and Tesco in the United Kingdom and Metro Group in Germany. However, tagging strategies differ considerably by region. In the United States, the focus is on case or pallet-level tagging whereas European retailers focus on item-level tagging.

Retailers in the United States focus on case and pallet-level tagging for inventory management to help reduce inventory and stockouts while simultaneously improving customer service. Consumer-privacy issues and high implementation costs for hardware and tags deter American retailers from moving into item-level tagging. In Europe, the cultural climate has made it easier to deploy RFID, and retailers are using the technology at the item level for category management and garment sorting, and are looking at RFID on smart shelves for use with automatic replenishment. While most retailers in Asia expect to gain from integrating RFID technology across the supply chain, China is skeptical about sharing potentially confidential information with foreign businesses. In Japan, the RFID market focuses on government applications, logistics usage, and asset tagging.

RFID tag and system costs are among the major impediments to a faster adoption of the technology. Currently, each passive-type tag costs about 7¢ in the United States, 10¢ in Europe, and 30¢ in Asia. Differences between radio frequencies in different parts of the world are another major hurdle to broader adoption. While businesses in the United States favor the 915 MHz UHF, the Europeans prefer the 868 MHz UHF. The Chinese favor frequencies below 860 or above 960 MHz because the 860–960 MHz UHF is used for telecommunications. In Japan, the standard is 950–956 MHz UHF.

While considerable progress has been made on code standardization over the last few years, much work remains to be done. The United States and Europe have jointly worked on a common standard based on the modified EPCglobal UHF Gen-2 standard, but China and Japan have decided to develop their own. China supports its own EPC-classification system for domestic product labeling whereas Japan uses its Ubiquitous ID standard. Using competing RFID standards is likely to eventually lead to the need for costly multiprotocol readers that can handle tags that comply with the different standards. Despite all the challenges, RFID is likely to replace barcode technology in inventory management.

Note: Some parts of this feature came from Fish, L. A. and W. C. Forrest. "A Worldwide Look at RFID." *Supply Chain Management Review*, 11, no. 3 (April 1, 2007): 48–55.

Inventory Models

A variety of inventory models for independent demand items are examined in this section by classifying the models into two broad categories. First, the deterministic inventory models are discussed that assume demand, delivery lead time, and other parameters are deterministic. These models use fixed parameters to derive the optimum *order quantity* to minimize *total inventory costs*. Thus, these models are also known as **fixed order quantity models**. The economic order quantity model, quantity discount model, and economic manufacturing quantity model are the three most widely used fixed order quantity models. Thereafter, the statistical reorder point is discussed, where demand and/or lead time are not constant but can be estimated by means of a normal distribution. Finally, the continuous review and periodic review systems are briefly discussed.

The Economic Order Quantity Model

The **economic order quantity (EOQ) model** is a classic independent demand inventory system that provides many useful ordering decisions. The basic order decision is "What is the correct order size to minimize total annual inventory costs?" The issue revolves around the trade-off between annual inventory holding costs and annual order costs. When order sizes for an item are small, orders have to be placed on a frequent basis, causing high annual ordering costs. However, the firm has a low average inventory level for this item, resulting in low annual inventory holding costs. When order sizes for an item are large, orders are placed less frequently, causing lower annual order costs. Unfortunately, this also causes the average inventory level for this item to be high, resulting in higher expenses to hold the inventory. The EOQ model seeks to determine an optimal order quantity, where the sum of the annual order cost and the annual inventory holding cost is minimized. In EOQ computations, *carrying cost* is often used in place of holding cost and *setup cost* is used in place of order cost.

Assumptions of the Economic Order Quantity Model

Users must carefully consider several assumptions when determining the economic order quantity:

1. *The demand must be known and constant.* For example, if there are 365 days per year and the annual demand is known to be 730 units, then daily usage must be exactly two units throughout the entire year.

2. *Order lead time is known and constant.* For example, if the order lead time is known to be ten days, each and every delivery will arrive exactly ten days after the order is placed.

3. *Replenishment is instantaneous.* The entire order is delivered at one time, and partial shipments are not allowed.

4. *Price is constant.* Quantity or price discounts are not allowed.

5. *The holding cost is known and constant.* The cost or rate to hold inventory must be known and constant.

6. *Ordering cost is known and constant.* The cost of placing an order must be known and remains constant for all orders.

7. *Stockouts are not allowed.* Inventory must be available at all times.

Deriving the Economic Order Quantity

The economic order quantity can be derived easily from the total annual inventory cost formula using simple calculus. The total annual inventory cost is the sum of the annual purchase cost, the annual holding cost, and the annual order cost. The formula can be shown as:

$$\text{TAIC} = \text{annual purchase cost} + \text{annual holding cost} + \text{annual ordering cost}$$

$$\text{TAIC} = \text{APC} + \text{AHC} + \text{AOC} = (R \times C) + (Q/2 \times k \times C) + (R/Q \times S)$$

where

TAIC = total annual inventory cost;

APC = annual purchase cost;

AHC = annual holding cost;

AOC = annual ordering cost;

R = annual requirement or demand;

C = purchase cost per unit;

S = cost of placing one order;

k = holding rate, where annual holding cost per unit = $k \times C$;

Q = order quantity.

Since R, C, k, and S are deterministic (i.e., assumed to be constant terms), Q is the only unknown variable in the TAIC equation. The optimum Q (the EOQ) can be obtained by taking the first derivative of TAIC with respect to Q and then setting it equal to zero. A second derivative of TAIC can also be taken with respect to Q to prove that the TAIC is a concave cost curve, and thus $\frac{d\text{TAIC}}{dQ} = 0$ is at the lowest point (i.e., minimum) of the cost curve.

$$\Rightarrow \frac{d\text{TAIC}}{dQ} = 0 + (1/2 \times k \times C) + (-1 \times R \times S \times 1/Q^2)$$

$$= \frac{kC}{2} - \frac{RS}{Q^2}.$$

Setting the above equation equal to zero,

$$\frac{kC}{2} - \frac{RS}{Q^2} = 0$$

or

$$\frac{kC}{2} = \frac{RS}{Q^2}$$

or

$$Q^2 = \frac{2RS}{kC}$$

then

$$EOQ = \sqrt{\frac{2RS}{kC}}.$$

The second derivative of TAIC is

$$\Rightarrow \frac{d^2 TAIC}{dQ^2} = 0 - \left(-2 \times \frac{RS}{Q^3} \right) = \left(\frac{2RS}{Q^3} \right) \geq 0,$$

implying that the TAIC is at its minimum when

$$\frac{dTAIC}{dQ} = 0.$$

In the calculations above, the annual purchase cost drops off after the first derivative is taken. The managerial implication here is that the purchase cost does not affect the order decision if there is no quantity discount (the annual purchase cost remains constant regardless of the order size, as long as the same annual quantity is purchased). Thus, the annual purchase cost is ignored in the classic EOQ model. Example 7.3 provides an illustration of calculating the EOQ.

Example 7.3   Calculating the EOQ at the Las Vegas Corporation

The Las Vegas Corporation purchases a critical component from one of its key suppliers. The operations manager wants to determine the economic order quantity, along with when to reorder, to ensure that the annual inventory cost is minimized. The following information was obtained from historical data:

Annual requirements (R)	=	7200 units;
Setup cost (S)	=	$100 per order;
Holding rate (k)	=	20 percent;
Unit cost (C)	=	$20 per unit;
Order lead time (LT)	=	6 days;
Number of days per year	=	360 days.

Thus,

$$EOQ = \sqrt{\frac{2RS}{kC}} = \sqrt{\frac{2 \times 7200 \text{ units} \times \$100}{0.20 \times \$20}} = 600 \text{ units}.$$

1. The annual purchase cost $= R \times C = 7200$ units $\times \$20 = \$144{,}000$.
2. The annual holding cost $= (Q/2) \times k \times C = (600/2) \times 0.20 \times \$20 = \$1200$.
3. The annual ordering cost $= (R/Q) \times S = (7200/600) \times \$100 = \$1200$.
   (Note that at the EOQ, the annual holding cost equals the annual order cost.)
4. The total annual inventory cost $= \$144{,}000 + \$1200 + \$1200 = \$146{,}400$.
5. For an order lead time of six days, the **reorder point (ROP)** would be

$$ROP = (\text{daily demand}) \times LT = (7200/360) \times 6 = 120 \text{ units}.$$

Example 7.3   Calculating the EOQ at the Las Vegas Corporation (continued)

Thus, the purchasing manager should reorder the component from the supplier whenever the physical stock is down to 120 units, and 600 units should be ordered each time.

The order cycle can also be computed as follows:

6. Number of orders placed per year $= R/Q = 7200/600 = 12$ orders.

7. Time between orders $=$ (days per year)/(number of orders per year) $= 360/12 = 30$ days.

Figure 7.5 shows the relationships between annual holding cost, annual ordering cost, and the total annual holding plus order cost. At the EOQ (600 units), annual holding cost ($1200) equals annual ordering cost ($1200). At or close to the EOQ, the total cost curve is rather flat, indicating that it is not very sensitive to small variations in the economic order quantity. Therefore, the classic EOQ model is said to be very *robust* to minor errors in estimating cost parameters, such as holding rate, order cost, or annual usage. Table 7.5 compares the annual total costs at an EOQ of 600 units, and at quantities 10 percent below and above the EOQ. The analysis shows that the cost variations range from only 0.01 percent to 0.56 percent above the minimum cost.

Figure 7.5 and Table 7.5 show that if the order size is smaller than the EOQ, the annual holding cost is slightly lower, whereas the annual ordering cost is slightly higher. The net effect is a slightly higher annual total cost. Similarly, if the order quantity is slightly larger than the EOQ, the annual holding cost is slightly higher, whereas the annual ordering cost is slightly lower. The net effect is also a slightly higher annual total cost.

Figure 7.6 shows the movement of physical inventory and the relationships of the EOQ, average inventory, lead time, reorder point, and order cycle. At time 0, the firm is assumed to start with a complete order of 600 units. The inventory is consumed at a steady rate of twenty units per day. On the twenty-fourth day, the firm places its first order of 600 units, and it arrives six days later (on the thirtieth day). On the twenty-fourth day, 120 units of inventory are left, which will be totally consumed immediately prior to the arrival of the first order. The vertical line on the thirtieth day shows that all 600 units are received (this is the instantaneous replenishment assumption of the EOQ model). A total of twelve orders (including the initial 600 units) will be placed during the year to satisfy the annual requirements of 7200 units.

The Quantity Discount Model

The **quantity discount model** or **price break model** is one variation of the classic EOQ model. It relaxes the constant price assumption by allowing purchase quantity discounts. In this case, the unit price of an item can vary with the order size. For example, a supplier may offer a price of $5 per unit for orders up to 200 units, a price of $4.50 per unit for orders between 201 and 500, and a price of $4 per unit for orders of more than 500 units. This creates an incentive for the buyer to purchase in large quantities to take advantage of the quantity discount, but with the added cost of holding more inventory.

Unlike the EOQ model, the purchase cost now becomes an important criterion in determining the optimal order size and the corresponding total annual inventory cost. The quantity discount model must consider the trade-off between purchasing a large quantity to take advantage of the price discount and the lower annual order cost against holding higher average inventory levels along with the corresponding higher annual holding cost. With the quantity discount model, there are two unknowns in the TAIC equation (the purchase price C and the order quantity Q). Hence a new approach is needed to find the optimal order quantity.

Figure 7.5	The Economic Order Quality and Total Costs

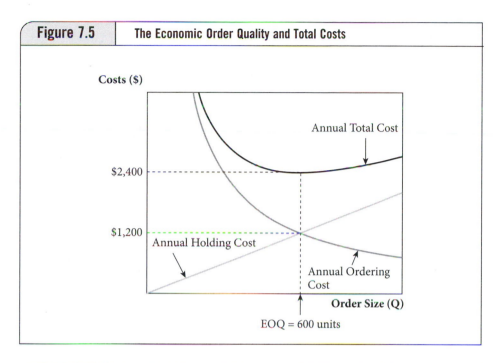

Table 7.5	Percent Variation in Total Annual Cost

Q (UNITS)	AHC ($)	AOC ($)	ATC ($)	VARIATION (%)
540	1080.00	1333.33	2413.33	0.56
550	1100.00	1309.09	2409.09	0.38
560	1120.00	1285.71	2405.71	0.24
570	1140.00	1263.16	2403.16	0.13
580	1160.00	1241.38	2401.38	0.06
590	1180.00	1220.34	2400.34	0.01
EOQ = 600	1200.00	1200.00	2400.00*	0.00
610	1220.00	1180.33	2400.33	0.01
620	1240.00	1161.29	2401.29	0.05
630	1260.00	1142.86	2402.86	0.12
640	1280.00	1125.00	2405.00	0.21
650	1300.00	1107.69	2407.69	0.32
660	1320.00	1090.91	2410.91	0.45

*Indicates minimum total cost at EOQ.

The unit purchase price, C, is no longer fixed, as assumed in the EOQ derivations. The total annual inventory cost now must include an annual purchase cost which varies depending on the order quantity. The TAIC formula shown here is the same as shown above, except the first term, APC, is now considered variable, since C varies:

$$TAIC = APC + AHC + AOC = (R \times C) + (Q/2 \times k \times C) + (R/Q \times S)$$

Figure 7.6	Physical Inventory with the EOQ Model

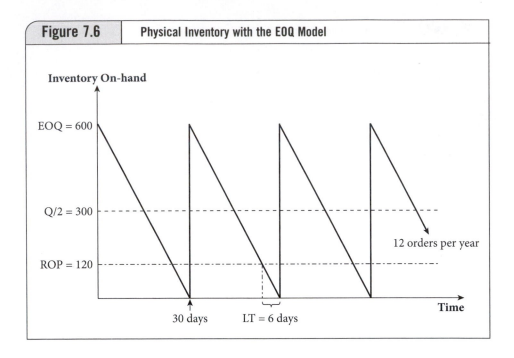

The quantity discount model yields a different total annual inventory cost for each purchase price level. The relevant total annual inventory cost curve for all purchase quantities is a combination of portions of several cost curves, starting with the curve associated with the highest purchase price, and then dropping down to a lower cost at each **price break point**. A price break point is the minimum quantity required to get a price discount. There is an EOQ associated with each price level, but the EOQ may not be *feasible* at that particular price level because the order quantity may not lie in the range corresponding to its unit price. Owing to the stepwise shape of the total annual inventory cost curve, the optimal order quantity is either one of the *feasible EOQs* or one of the *price break point* quantities. Figures 7.7 and 7.8 both illustrate the quantity discount total annual inventory cost curve, and are used in the examples that follow.

A fairly straightforward two-step procedure can be used to solve the quantity discount problem. Briefly, the two steps can be stated as follows:

1. Starting with the lowest purchase price, compute the EOQ for each purchase price level until a feasible EOQ is found. If the feasible EOQ found is for the lowest purchase price, this is the optimal order quantity (the quantity resulting in the lowest total annual inventory cost). The reason is that the EOQ for the lowest price level is the lowest point on the total annual inventory cost curve (see Figure 7.7). If the feasible EOQ is not associated with the lowest purchase price, proceed to step 2.

2. Compute the total annual inventory cost for the feasible EOQ found in step 1, and for all the price break points at each *lower* price level. Price break points *above* the feasible EOQ will result in higher total annual inventory costs, thus need not be evaluated. The quantity that yields the lowest total annual inventory cost is then the optimal order quantity.

Examples 7.4 and 7.5 illustrate the quantity discount model.

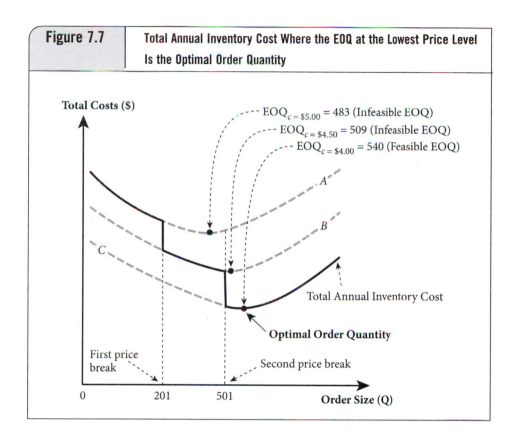

Figure 7.7 — Total Annual Inventory Cost Where the EOQ at the Lowest Price Level Is the Optimal Order Quantity

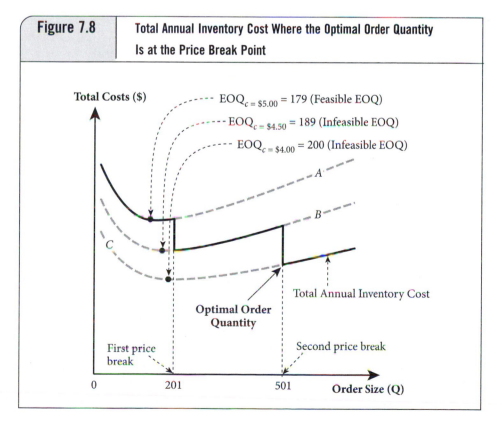

Figure 7.8 — Total Annual Inventory Cost Where the Optimal Order Quantity Is at the Price Break Point

---

Example 7.4   Finding the Optimal Order Quantity with Quantity Discounts at the Kuantan Corporation

The Kuantan Corporation purchases a component from a supplier that offers quantity discounts to encourage larger order quantities. The operations manager of the company wants to determine the optimal order quantity to ensure that their total annual inventory cost is minimized. The manager estimates that the company's annual demand for the item is 7290 units, the order cost is $20 per order, and the annual holding rate is 25 percent. The price schedule for the item is given in the following table:

ORDER QUANTITY	PRICE PER UNIT ($)
1–200	5.00
201–500	4.50
501 and above	4.00

The two questions to consider are: 1) what is the optimal order quantity that will minimize the total annual inventory cost for this component? And 2) what is the total annual inventory cost?

SOLUTION

Step 1: Find the first feasible EOQ starting with the lowest price level:

$$EOQ_{C=\$4.00} = \sqrt{\frac{2 \times 7290 \text{ units} \times \$20}{0.25 \times \$4}} = 540 \text{ units.}$$

This is a *feasible* EOQ because order size of 540 units corresponds to the price level of $4.00 per unit (see table above). Thus, 540 units is the optimal order quantity. In this case, the optimal order size falls on an EOQ. The total annual inventory cost is

$$
\begin{aligned}
TAIC = APC = AHC = AOC &= (R \times C) + (Q/2 \times k \times C) + (R/Q \times S) \\
&= (7290 \times \$4) + (540/2 \times 0.25 \times \$4) + (7290/540 \times \$20) \\
&= \$29{,}160 + \$270 + \$270 = \$29{,}700.00.
\end{aligned}
$$

Note that the annual holding cost equals the annual ordering cost because the optimal order quantity is an economic order quantity.

Cost curves A, B, and C in Figure 7.7 are the annual inventory costs at price levels of $5, $4.50, and $4, respectively. Since each cost curve is only applicable for its price range, the relevant total annual inventory cost is the combination of these three cost curves where the total cost drops vertically at each price break point, curve by curve, to the next lower cost curve. Figure 7.7 shows that the feasible EOQ for the lowest price level is the lowest point on the total annual inventory cost curve; hence, it is the optimal order quantity. The two infeasible EOQs for the price levels of $4.50 and $5 are also shown in Figure 7.7 to reiterate that if an EOQ falls outside its price range, it is not a feasible order quantity and thus is irrelevant to the total annual inventory cost calculation.

The Economic Manufacturing Quantity Model

The **economic manufacturing quantity (EMQ)** or **production order quantity (POQ)** model is another variation of the classic EOQ model. It relaxes the *instantaneous replenishment* assumption by allowing usage or partial delivery during production. The EMQ model is especially appropriate for a manufacturing environment where items are being manufactured and consumed or delivered simultaneously; hence the name

Example 7.5   Finding the Optimal Order Quantity with Quantity Discounts at the Soon Corporation

The Soon Corporation is a multinational company that purchases one of its crucial components from a supplier who offers quantity discounts to encourage larger-order quantities. The operations manager wants to determine the optimal order quantity to minimize their total annual inventory cost. The manager estimates that its annual demand for the item is 1000 units, its ordering cost is $20 per order, and its annual holding rate is 25 percent. The price schedule is given in the following table:

ORDER QUANTITY	PRICE PER UNIT ($)
1–200	5.00
201–500	4.50
501 and above	4.00

The first price break point is at 201 units and the second price break point is at 501 units. The operations manager desires to determine the optimal order quantity that will minimize the total annual inventory cost for this component, and the corresponding total annual inventory cost.

SOLUTION

Step 1: Find the first feasible EOQ starting with the lowest price level:

$$\text{(A) } EOQ_{C=\$4.00} = \sqrt{\frac{2 \times 1000 \text{ units} \times \$20}{0.25 \times \$4}} = 200 \text{ units.}$$

This quantity is infeasible because an order quantity of 200 units does not qualify for the $4 price level. Instead, the unit price for an order quantity of 200 units is $5. Next, we evaluate the EOQ at the next higher price level of $4.50:

$$\text{(B) } EOQ_{C=\$4.50} = \sqrt{\frac{2 \times 1000 \text{ units} \times \$20}{0.25 \times \$4.50}} = 189 \text{ units.}$$

This quantity is also infeasible because it fails to qualify for the $4.50 price level. We move on to the next higher price level of $5:

$$\text{(C) } EOQ_{C=\$5.00} = \sqrt{\frac{2 \times 1000 \text{ units} \times \$20}{0.25 \times \$5}} = 179 \text{ units.}$$

This order quantity is the *first feasible EOQ* because a 179-unit order quantity corresponds to the correct price level of $5 per unit.

Step 2: Find the total annual inventory costs for the first feasible EOQ found in step 1, and for all the (minimum) price break points at each lower price level. There are two price break points larger than the first feasible EOQ of 179 units at 201 and 501 units, respectively (these are the minimum purchase quantities to qualify for each of the discounted prices of $4.50 and $4.00).

$$TAIC = APC + AHC + AOC = (R \times C) + (Q/2 \times k \times C) + (R/Q \times S).$$

$$\text{(A) } TAIC_{EOQ=179} = (1000 \times \$5) + (179/2 \times 0.25 \times \$5) + (1000/179 \times \$20)$$
$$= \$5000 + \$111.88 + \$111.73 = \$5223.61.$$

$$\text{(B) } TAIC_{Q=201, \ C=\$4.50} = (1000 \times \$4.50) + (201/2 \times 0.25 \times \$4.50) + (1000/201 \times \$20)$$
$$= \$4500 + \$113.06 + \$99.50 = \$4712.56.$$

> **Example 7.5   Finding the Optimal Order Quantity with Quantity Discounts
> at the Soon Corporation (continued)**
>
> (C) $\text{TAIC}_{Q=501,\ C=\$4.00} = (1000 \times \$4) + (501/2 \times 0.25 \times \$4) + (1000/501 \times \$20)$
> $$= \$4000 + \$250.50 + \$39.92 = \$4290.42.$$
>
> Comparing the total annual inventory costs in A, B, and C, the optimal order quantity is 501 units, which qualifies for the deepest discount. In this case, the optimal order size falls on a *price break point*; hence, the annual holding cost ($250.50) is not equal to the annual ordering cost ($39.92). When the purchase cost savings due to the quantity discount is large compared to the holding cost, it makes sense to purchase a large quantity and hold more inventory. However, this ignores the fact that excessive inventory can hide production problems and can result in obsolete inventories. Thus, in the attempt to find the optimal order quantity to minimize inventory cost, a manager should also consider the impacts of excessive inventory on longer-term firm performance. Figure 7.8 demonstrates the characteristics of the cost curves for this example. Cost curves A, B, and C are the annual inventory costs at price levels of $5, $4.50, and $4, respectively. The relevant total annual inventory cost is derived from these three cost curves by joining the relevant portion of each cost curve vertically at the price break point. Figure 7.8 also shows that the EOQ of 200 units for the lowest price level is the lowest point on cost curve C, but it is infeasible.

economic manufacturing quantity. Inventory builds up gradually during the production period rather than at once as in the EOQ model.

For instance, assuming that the production lot size of a manufacturer is 600 units, its production rate is 100 units per day, and its demand is 40 units per day, then the manufacturer will need 6 days (600/100) to produce a batch of 600 units. While being produced, the items are also consumed simultaneously; hence inventory builds up at the rate of 60 units (100 − 40) per day for 6 days. The maximum inventory is then 360 units (60 × 6 days), which is less than the lot size of 600 units as would have been the case for the classic EOQ model. The lower inventory level implies that the holding cost of the EMQ model is less than the EOQ model given the same cost parameters. It is also clear that the production rate must be greater than the demand rate, otherwise, there would not be any inventory buildup. On the seventh day, the production of the first batch stops and the inventory starts to deplete at the demand rate of 40 units for the next 9 days (360/40). The first production lot and the subsequent usage of the inventory take 15 days (6 + 9) to complete and then the cycle repeats.

Figure 7.9 depicts the inventory versus time scenario for the EMQ model. The item is produced in a lot size of Q, at the production rate of P and consumed at the demand rate of D. Hence, inventory builds up at the rate of $(P − D)$ during the production period, T_P. At the end of the production period (T_P), inventory begins to deplete at the demand rate of D until it is exhausted at the end of the inventory cycle, T_C. The production rate, P, which can be expressed as Q/T_P, is the production lot size divided by the time required to produce the lot. The maximum inventory, Q_M, can be obtained by multiplying the inventory build-up rate with the production period, and can be expressed as $(P − D) \times T_P$. These relationships can be stated as:

$$P = \frac{Q}{T_P} \text{ and } Q_M = (P − D) \times T_P.$$

| **Figure 7.9** | **Physical Inventory with the Economic Manufacturing Quantity Model** |

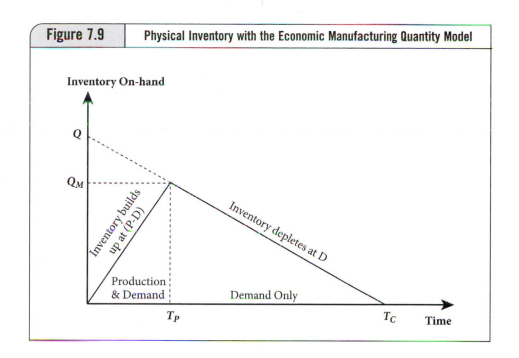

Therefore, $T_P = Q/P$ and substituting Q/P for T_P in Q_M gives:

$$Q_M = (P - D) \times \frac{Q}{P}$$

$$= \frac{PQ}{P} - \frac{DQ}{P}$$

$$= Q\left(1 - \frac{D}{P}\right).$$

Hence, the average inventory, $\dfrac{Q_M}{2} = \dfrac{Q}{2}\left(1 - \dfrac{D}{P}\right).$

Now,

Total annual
inventory cost = annual product cost + annual holding cost + annual setup cost,

or

$$\text{TAIC} = \text{APC} + \text{AHC} + \text{ASC} = [R \times C] + \left[\left(\frac{Q}{2}\left(1 - \frac{D}{P}\right)\right) \times k \times C\right] + [R/Q \times S],$$

where

TAIC = total annual inventory cost;

APC = annual product cost;

AHC = annual holding cost;

ASC = annual setup cost;

R = annual requirement or demand;

C = total cost of one unit of the finished product;

S = cost of setting up the equipment to process one batch of the product;

k = holding rate, where annual holding cost per unit = $k \times C$;

Q = order quantity.

Like the EOQ model where Q is the only unknown variable in the TAIC equation, the optimum Q (the EMQ) can be obtained by taking the first derivative of TAIC with respect to Q and then setting it equal to zero. A second derivative of TAIC can also be taken with respect to Q to prove that the TAIC is a concave cost curve, and thus $\frac{dTAIC}{dQ} = 0$ is at the lowest point or minimum of the cost curve.

$$\Rightarrow \frac{dTAIC}{dQ} = 0 + \left[\frac{1}{2}\left(1 - \frac{D}{P}\right) \times k \times C\right] + [-1 \times R \times S \times 1/Q^2]$$
$$= \left[\frac{kC}{2}\left(1 - \frac{D}{P}\right)\right] - \frac{RS}{Q^2}.$$

Then setting equal to zero,

$$\left[\frac{kC}{2}\left(1 - \frac{D}{P}\right)\right] - \frac{RS}{Q^2} = 0$$

or

$$\left[\frac{kC}{2}\left(1 - \frac{D}{P}\right)\right] = \frac{RS}{Q^2}$$

or

$$Q^2 = \frac{2RS}{kC\left(1 - \frac{D}{P}\right)} = \frac{2RS}{kC\left(\frac{P-D}{P}\right)} = \frac{2RS}{kC}\left(\frac{P}{P - D}\right).$$

Then the

$$EMQ = \sqrt{\left(\frac{2RS}{kC}\right)\left(\frac{P}{P - D}\right)}.$$

The second derivative of the TAIC is:

$$\Rightarrow \frac{d^2TAIC}{dQ^2} = 0 - \left(-2 \times \frac{RS}{Q^3}\right) = \left(\frac{2RS}{Q^3}\right) \geq 0,$$

implying that the TAIC is at its minimum when $\frac{dTAIC}{dQ} = 0$.

Similar to the EOQ model, the annual product cost drops out after the first derivative is taken indicating that product cost does not affect the order decision if the unit cost of each product produced is constant; thus, the annual product cost is also ignored in the EMQ model. Example 7.6 provides an illustration of calculating the EMQ for a fictitious manufacturing company.

The Statistical Reorder Point

The two major inventory management decisions are to determine the right order quantity or lot size and when to release a purchase order. Three basic independent demand lot-sizing techniques have been presented to discuss the optimal order quantity or lot size, and now the question regarding when to order can be discussed. The **reorder point (ROP)** is the lowest inventory level at which a new order must be placed to avoid a stockout. In a deterministic setting where both the demand and delivery lead time are known and constant, Example 7.3 shows that the reorder point is simply equal to the

Example 7.6   Calculating the EMQ at the Lone Wild Boar Corporation

The Lone Wild Boar Corporation manufactures a crucial component internally using the most advanced technology. The operations manager wants to determine the economic manufacturing quantity to ensure that the total annual inventory cost is minimized. The daily production rate (P) for the component is 200 units, annual demand (R) is 18,000 units, setup cost (S) is \$100 per setup, and the annual holding rate (k) is 25 percent. The manager estimates that the total cost (C) of a finished component is \$120. It is assumed that the plant operates year-round, and there are 360 days per year.

SOLUTION

1. The daily demand rate, $D = 18,000/360 = 50$ units per day.

2. $\text{EMQ} = \sqrt{\left(\frac{2RS}{kC}\right)\left(\frac{P}{P-D}\right)} = \sqrt{\left(\frac{2 \times 18,000 \times 100}{0.25 \times 20}\right)\left(\frac{200}{200-50}\right)} = 400$ units.

3. The highest inventory level, $Q_M = Q\left(1 - \frac{D}{P}\right) = 400\left(1 - \frac{50}{200}\right) = 300$ units.

4. The annual product cost $= R \times C = 18,000$ units $\times \$120 = \$2160,000.$

5. The annual holding cost $= \frac{Q_M}{2} \times k \times C = \frac{300}{2} \times 0.25 \times \$120 = \$4500.$

6. The annual setup cost $= R/Q \times S = (18,000/400) \times \$100 = \$4500.$

   (Note that when using the EMQ, the annual holding cost equals the annual setup cost.)

7. The total annual inventory cost, TAIC $= \$2,160,000 + \$4500 + \$4500 = \$2,169,000.$

8. The length of a production period, $T_P = \frac{\text{EMQ}}{P} = 400/200 = 2$ days.

9. The length of each inventory cycle, $T_C = \frac{\text{EMQ}}{D} = 400/50 = 8$ days.

10. The rate of inventory buildup during production, $(P - D) = 200 - 50 = 150$ units per day.

11. The number of inventory cycles per year $= 360$ days/8 days $= 45$ times.

Figure 7.10 illustrates the EMQ model for Lone Wild Boar Corporation.

A unique observation regarding the classical EOQ, quantity discount and EMQ models is that when ordering the EOQ or producing the EMQ, the annual setup cost equals the annual holding cost (recall this is not the case in the quantity discount model when the optimal order quantity falls on a price break point).

demand during the order lead time. However, in reality, the demand and delivery lead time are rarely ever constant. Since variable demand or lead time raises the possibility of stockouts, *safety stock* must be held to safeguard against these variations. Next, we discuss how the probabilistic demand pattern and lead time affect the reorder point.

The Statistical Reorder Point with Probabilistic Demand and Constant Order Lead Time

This model assumes the order lead time of a product is constant and the demand during the order lead time is unknown, but can be specified by means of a normal distribution. Since the statistical reorder point specifies that an order is to be placed when the remaining inventory is reduced to some specific level, stockouts can occur only during the delivery lead time. Figure 7.11 illustrates the relationship of safety stock and the probability of a stockout. If the average demand during the order lead time is represented by μ and the reorder point is represented by x, then the safety stock is $(x - \mu)$, which can be derived from the standard deviation formula, $Z = (x - \mu)/\sigma$. Then, if the probability of stockout is represented by α, the probability that inventory is sufficient to cover demand (the *in-stock probability*) is $(1 - \alpha)$. The in-stock probability is commonly referred to as **service level** (actually, calculation of the true service level requires use of a loss function, which is beyond the scope of

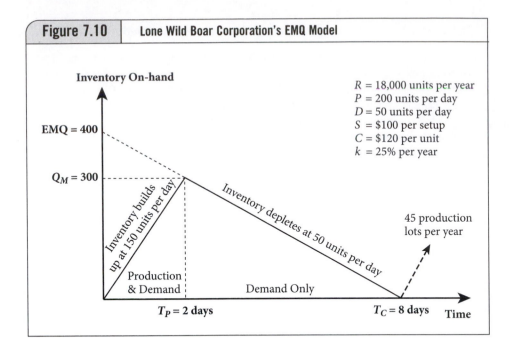

Figure 7.10 | **Lone Wild Boar Corporation's EMQ Model**

$R = 18{,}000$ units per year
$P = 200$ units per day
$D = 50$ units per day
$S = \$100$ per setup
$C = \$120$ per unit
$k = 25\%$ per year

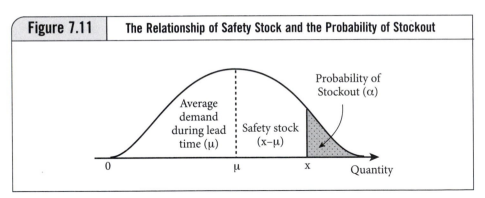

Figure 7.11 | **The Relationship of Safety Stock and the Probability of Stockout**

this text). Next, the Z-value can be determined from the standardized normal curve and the desire for a specific in-stock probability (see Z-Table in Appendix). For example, a 97.5 percent in-stock probability or 2.5 percent stockouts ($\alpha = 2.5$ percent) corresponds to a Z-value of 1.96. At the middle of the normal curve where the reorder point equals the average lead time demand, the safety stock is zero and the probability of stockout is 50 percent. Thus, if no safety stock was incorporated into the ROP and the firm ordered when the existing inventory level was equal to the average lead time demand, then the firm would expect to stockout 50 percent of the time prior to receiving the order.

The statistical reorder point (x) can be calculated as the average demand during the order lead time plus safety stock, or:

$$\text{ROP} = \bar{d}_{LT} + Z\sigma_{dLT}$$

Here, the safety stock is $Z\sigma_{dLT}$ or ($x - \mu$) and is derived from the standard deviation formula of the normal curve as described above. Example 7.7 illustrates the calculation of the ROP.

> ## Example 7.7   Calculating the Statistical Reorder Point at Company London Inc.
>
> London Inc. stocks a crucial part that has a normal distribution demand pattern during the order lead time period. Past demand shows that the average demand during lead time (μ) for the part is 550 units and the standard deviation of demand during the order lead time period (σ_{dLT}) is 40 units. The manager wants to determine the safety stock required and the statistical reorder point that would result in 5 percent stockouts, or an in-stock probability of 95 percent. What would the ROP and required safety stock be if the manager decided to attain a 99 percent in-stock probability?
>
> ### SOLUTION
>
> 1. The normal table or Z-Table in the Appendix shows that a 95 percent in-stock probability corresponds to a Z-value of 1.65 standard deviations above the mean.
>
> 2. The required safety stock is then $Z\sigma_{dLT} = 1.65 \times 40 = 66$ units.
>
> 3. The ROP $= \bar{d}_{LT} + Z\sigma_{dLT} = 550 + 66$ units $= 616$ units.
>
> 4. The required safety stock at a 99 percent in-stock probability $= Z\sigma_{dLT} = 2.33 \times 40 = 93$ units, and the ROP $= 550 + 93 = 643$ units.

The safety stock computation as shown in Example 7.7 must be modified if the standard deviation is expressed for daily demand instead of lead time demand. In this situation, if the order lead time is greater than one day, the standard deviation of daily demand (σ_d) must be converted to the standard deviation of demand during the order lead time period (σ_{dLT}). If the daily demand is identically distributed, we can use the statistical premise that the variance of a series of independent occurrences is equal to the sum of the variances. That is, the variance of demand during the lead time equals the sum of the variances of all the identical daily demands for the lead time period. This can be expressed as:

$$\sigma^2_{dLT} = \sigma^2_d + \sigma^2_d + \sigma^2_d + \ldots = \sigma^2_d LT,$$

where

σ^2_{dLT} = variance of demand during the order lead time period,

σ^2_d = variance of the identically and independently distributed daily demands,

LT = order lead time in days.

Thus, the standard deviation of demand during lead time, $\sigma_{dLT} = \sigma_d \sqrt{LT}$. Hence the safety stock and statistical reorder point can also be stated as:

$$\text{Safety stock, } (x - \mu) = Z\sigma_d \sqrt{LT},$$

and then

$$\text{ROP} = \bar{d}_{LT} + Z\sigma_d \sqrt{LT}$$

Example 7.8 demonstrates this calculation.

The Statistical Reorder Point with Constant Demand and Probabilistic Order Lead Time

When the demand of a product is constant and the lead time is unknown but can be specified by means of a normal distribution, then safety stock is used to buffer

Example 7.8   Calculating the Statistical Reorder Point at Brussels Inc.

Brussels Inc. is a local retail store that specializes in selling beer to college students at discount prices. Historical data shows that the demand for beer has a normal distribution. The average daily demand for beer at Brussels is 150 cases, and the standard deviation for daily demand is 30 cases. Brussels' supplier maintains a very reliable and constant lead time of 6 days. What is the standard deviation of demand during lead time, and what is the safety stock and statistical reorder point that results in an in-stock probability of 97.5 percent? What is the required safety stock if the manager decides to ensure a 90 percent in-stock probability?

SOLUTION

Average daily demand, $\bar{d} = 150$ cases.

Standard deviation of daily demand, $\sigma_d = 30$ cases.

Lead time, $LT = 6$ days.

The standard deviation of demand during the lead time, $\sigma_{dLT} = \sigma_d\sqrt{LT}$
$$= 30\sqrt{6} \text{ cases} = 73.48 \text{ cases.}$$

The Z-Table shows that a 97.5 percent in-stock probability (allowing 2.5 percent stockouts) corresponds to a Z-value of 1.96 standard deviations from the mean.

The corresponding safety stock $Z\sigma_d\sqrt{LT} = 1.96 \times 30\sqrt{6} = 144$ cases.

The ROP = average demand during lead time + safety stock = $\bar{d} \times LT + 144$
$$= 150 \times 6 + 144 = 1044 \text{ cases.}$$

The required safety stock at a 90 percent in-stock probability = $Z\sigma_d\sqrt{LT}$
$$= 1.28 \times 30\sqrt{6} = 94 \text{ cases.}$$

against variations in the lead time instead of variations in demand. The safety stock is then (daily demand $\times Z\sigma_{LT}$), and the reorder point is:

ROP = (daily demand × average lead time in days) + (daily demand × $Z\sigma_{LT}$),

where

σ_{LT} = the standard deviation of order lead time in days.

This calculation is demonstrated in Example 7.9.

The Statistical Reorder Point When Both Demand and Order Lead Time Are Probabilistic

When both the demand and the order lead time of a product are unknown but can be specified by means of a normal distribution, safety stock must be held to cover the variations in both demand and lead time; thus the safety stock would be higher than if there was variation in the demand or lead time only. The reorder point can be computed as follows:[9]

Reorder point = (average daily demand × average lead time) + $Z\sigma_{dLT}$,

---

Example 7.9   Calculating the Statistical Reorder Point at the Harpert Store

The Harpert Store has an exclusive contract with Brussums Electronics to sell their most popular mp3 player. The demand of this mp3 player is very stable at 120 units per day. However, its order lead time varies and can be specified by a normal distribution with a mean lead time of 8 days and standard deviation of 2 days. What is the safety stock and reorder point for a 95 percent in-stock probability?

SOLUTION

Daily demand (d) = 120 units.

Mean lead time ($\overline{LT}$) = 8 days.

Standard deviation of lead time (σ_{LT}) = 2 days.

An in-stock probability of 95 percent yields a $Z = 1.65$ from the Z-Table.

Required safety stock = $d \times Z\sigma_{LT}$ = 120 units $\times$ 1.65 $\times$ 2 = 396 units.

ROP = $(d \times \overline{LT})$ + safety stock = (120 units $\times$ 8) + 396 units = 1356 units.

---

where

$$\sigma_{dLT} = \text{Standard deviation of demand during lead time}$$

$$= \sqrt{\sigma_{LT}^2(\text{average daily demand})^2 + \sigma_d^2(\text{average lead time})},$$

and

σ_d = Standard deviation of daily demand,

σ_{LT} = Standard deviation of lead time in days.

Note that the standard deviation formula (σ_{dLT}) can be applied to all the previous reorder point examples by observing the following fact—"constant" or "no variation" means zero standard deviation. Therefore,

1. When the demand and lead time are constant, then σ_d and σ_{LT} are zero, and the average daily demand and average order lead time would be the deterministic demand and lead time. Thus, the reorder point is the demand during the order lead time period.

2. When the daily demand is probabilistic and order lead time is constant, then σ_{LT} is zero and the average lead time would be the deterministic lead time. Using this guideline, the reorder point in Example 7.8 can also be computed as:

$$\text{ROP} = (150 \times 6) + 1.96\sqrt{0^2(150)^2 + 30^2(6)} = 900 + 1.96 \times 30\sqrt{6} = 1044 \text{ cases.}$$

3. When the daily demand is constant and the order lead time is probabilistic, then σ_d is zero and the average daily demand would be the deterministic daily demand. Using this guideline, the reorder point in Example 7.9 can also be computed as:

$$\text{ROP} = (120 \times 8) + 1.65\sqrt{2^2(120)^2 + 0^2(8)} = 960 + 1.65 \times 2(120) = 1356 \text{ units.}$$

Example 7.10 demonstrates the safety stock and reorder point computation when both the daily demand and lead time are probabilistic.

Example 7.10 Calculating the Statistical Reorder Point at the Dosseldorf Store

The Dosseldorf Store is the sole distributor of a popular cell phone. The demand of this cell phone is normally distributed with an average daily demand of 120 units and a standard deviation of 18 units per day. The cell phones are ordered and shipped directly from the manufacturer. Past delivery records of the manufacturer show that lead time is normally distributed with an average of 8 days and a standard deviation of 2 days. What is the required safety stock and reorder point for a 95 percent in-stock probability?

SOLUTION

Average daily demand $(\bar{d}) = 120$ units.

Standard deviation of daily demand $(\sigma_d) = 18$ units.

Average lead time $(\overline{LT}) = 8$ days.

Standard deviation of lead time $(\sigma_{LT}) = 2$ days.

For in-stock probability of 95 percent, $Z = 1.65$ from the Z-Table.

Required safety stock $= Z\sigma_{dLT}$

$$= 1.65 \times \sqrt{\sigma_{LT}^2(\text{average daily demand})^2 + \sigma_d^2(\text{average lead time})}$$

$$= 1.65 \times \sqrt{2^2(120)^2 + 18^2(8)} = 1.65 \times 245.34 = 405 \text{ units.}$$

$$ROP = (\bar{d} \times \overline{LT}) + \text{Safety stock}$$

$$= (120 \times 8) + 405 = 1365 \text{ units.}$$

The Continuous Review and the Periodic Review Inventory Systems

The order quantity and reorder point inventory models discussed thus far assume that the physical inventory levels are precisely known at every point in time.. This implies that stock movements must be updated in real time and there is no discrepancy between physical inventory and the stock record. However, this is not always possible in practice. Thus, a *continuous review* of the physical inventory can be used to make sure that orders are initiated when the actual physical inventory reaches the reorder point. Reviewing inventory levels continuously, though, can be very expensive to implement. Inventory review costs can be reduced by using a **periodic review system**, where physical inventory is reviewed at regular intervals, such as weekly or monthly. However, more safety stock is required in the periodic review system to buffer the added demand variation due to the longer review period.

For analysis of the continuous review and periodic review systems, the following symbols are used:

s = reorder point,

S = maximum inventory level,

Q = order quantity,

R = review period,

n = 1, 2, 3,....

The Continuous Review System

The **continuous review system** implies that the physical inventory level must be known at all times, so it is more expensive to administer. In this case, the only uncertainty is the magnitude of demand during the order lead time period; thus safety stock is required only for potential stockouts during this period. There are two continuous review systems, and these are described below.

1. *(s, Q) continuous review policy*: This policy orders the same quantity Q when physical inventory reaches the reorder point s. The quantity Q can be determined by one of the fixed order quantity methods (such as the EOQ). This policy works properly only if the quantity demanded is one unit at a time. Otherwise, the inventory level may fall below the reorder point s.

2. *(s, S) continuous review policy*: When multiple-unit demand causes the physical inventory level to fall below the reorder point s, a sufficient quantity is ordered to bring the inventory up to a pre-determined level S. If the quantity demanded is one unit at a time, this system is the same as the (s, Q) policy. However, if the quantity demanded causes the physical inventory level to fall below the reorder point, then the order quantity must be larger than Q. For instance, if $s = 10$, $S = 120$ and current inventory is 11 units, and if the next quantity demanded is 3 units, then on-hand inventory will be reduced to 8 units, which is less than s. Consequently, an order size of 112 units would be released.

The Periodic Review System

The periodic review system reviews physical inventory at specific points in time. Although this system is cheaper to administer, a higher level of safety stock is needed to buffer against the uncertainty in demand over a longer planning horizon. There are three periodic review systems, as described below.

1. *(nQ, s, R) periodic review policy*: If at the time of the inventory review period R, the physical inventory is less than or equal to the reorder point s, the quantity nQ is ordered to bring the inventory up to a level between s and $(s + Q)$. Recall that $n = 1, 2, 3, \ldots$, and the order size is then a multiple of Q. No order is placed if physical inventory is higher than the reorder point. For example, let $s = 100$ and $Q = 50$. If the physical inventory is 20 units at the time of review, then a quantity of $2Q$ or $(2 \times 50 = 100)$ is ordered to bring the inventory level up to 120 units.

2. *(S, R) periodic review policy*: At each review period R, a sufficient quantity is ordered to bring the inventory up to a pre-determined inventory level S. This policy places an order as long as the physical inventory is less than the maximum inventory level S. If the cost of each order is high, this is obviously not a preferred system. However, this policy may work well if a large variety of items are ordered each time from the same supplier.

3. *(s, S, R) periodic review policy*: If at the time of inventory review the physical inventory is less than or equal to the reorder point s, then a sufficient quantity is ordered to bring the inventory level up to the pre-determined inventory level S. However, if the physical inventory level is higher than the reorder point s, no order is placed. This policy addresses the major deficiency of the (S, R) policy.

SUMMARY

Organizations rely on inventory to balance supply and demand, and to buffer uncertainty in the supply chain. However, inventory can be one of the most expensive assets of an organization; hence it must be managed effectively. The right amount of inventory supports business operations, but too little of it can adversely affect customer service. Conversely, excess inventory not only leads to unnecessary holding cost but can hide production problems and other flaws in a company.

This chapter covers the crucial roles of inventory and various inventory management techniques that are widely used for balancing demand with supply. The standard ABC inventory classification method was discussed, and an ABC inventory matrix was proposed as a means to monitor if a firm is stocking the right inventory. Ample examples were used to demonstrate the order size and order period inventory models. This chapter also covered one of the latest developments in inventory management—RFID. Radio frequency identification certainly has the potential to drastically change the way inventory will be managed in the future.

KEY TERMS

80/20 rule, 223

ABC inventory control system, 218

ABC inventory matrix, 224

continuous review system, 249

cycle counting, 223

dependent demand, 217

direct costs, 220

economic manufacturing quantity (EMQ) or production order quantity (POQ), 238

economic order quantity (EOQ) model, 231

electronic product code (EPC), 227

fixed costs, 220

fixed order quantity models, 231

holding or carrying costs, 220

independent demand, 217

Indirect costs, 220

inventory costs, 218

inventory turnover ratio or inventory turnovers, 221

order costs, 220

Pareto analysis, 223

periodic review system, 248

price break point, 236

quantity discount model or price break model, 234

radio frequency identification (RFID), 226

reorder point (ROP), 242

service level, 243

setup costs, 220

variable costs, 220

DISCUSSION QUESTIONS

1. Compare and contrast dependent versus independent demand. Give at least two examples of each.

2. Describe the four basic types of inventory.

3. What is the ABC inventory system, and how is it used to manage inventory?

4. What is the ABC inventory matrix, and how is it used to manage inventory?

5. Describe inventory turnover and how is it used to manage inventory.

6. Why is it important to conduct cycle counting?

7. What is the electronic product code (EPC)?

8. Briefly describe how RFID can be used to manage inventory.

9. Explain why "item-level" tagging is more expensive than "case-level" tagging in RFID.

10. What are the two basic types of RFID tag? When would you want to use each of these?

11. What is the purpose of the economic order quantity and the reorder point?

12. What are the assumptions of the EOQ model?

13. What are the two major costs considered in the EOQ model? Why is the total annual purchase cost not a factor affecting the EOQ?

14. How is the quantity discount model related to the EOQ model?

15. How is the EMQ model related to the EOQ model?

16. Discuss whether the EOQ model is still useful if a small error was made while estimating one of the cost parameters used in the EOQ computation.

17. Assume you have used the EOQ model to compute the order quantity for an item, and the answer was 20 units. Unfortunately, the minimum lot size for the item is 24 units. Discuss how this is going to impact your annual holding cost, annual ordering cost, and total annual inventory cost.

18. Why is inventory management important to supply chain management?

19. Explain when you would want to use a continuous review or periodic review inventory system.

INTERNET QUESTIONS

1. Visit the Web site of EPCglobal, Inc. and use the information to write a brief report on RFID technology and the current state of RFID implementation.

2. Use the Internet to search for relevant information to prepare a brief report comparing the state of RFID implementation in North America, Europe, and Asia.

3. Use resources available on the Internet to prepare a report on the RFID implementation at Wal-Mart Stores, Inc.

4. Use resources available on the Internet (e.g., http://finance.yahoo.com/) to access the annual reports (Financial Statements and Balance Sheets) of three of your favorite listed companies to (a) extract their latest total revenue, total assets, and year-end inventory, and then use these numbers to (b) prepare their inventory/total revenue ratio, inventory/total assets ratio, and the inventory turnover ratio. Comment on how they perform based on these ratios. (Hint: see Tables 7.1 and 7.2.)

INFOTRAC QUESTIONS

Access http://academic.cengage.com/infotrac to answer the following questions:

1. Search on the terms "active RFID tags" and "passive RFID tags" and write a paper comparing the two types of tags—their cost, their usages, and their implementation concerns.

2. Search on the term "inventory turnover" and write a report discussing the normal inventory turnover for the following industries: (a) automobile manufacturers, (b) hotels, and (c) retailers.

3. Report on some of the companies in the U.S. that are very advanced in their RFID implementations.

4. Report on some of the companies in Europe that are very advanced in their RFID implementations.

PROBLEMS SETS

1. The annual revenue for a firm is $2,500,000. Its cost of revenue is $850,000 and its average inventory value for the year is $62,000. What is the inventory turnover?

2. Given the following information, compute the economic order quantity, annual holding cost, annual ordering cost, and total annual inventory cost.

Annual requirements (R)	= 50,000 units;
Setup cost (S)	= $150 per order;
Holding rate (k)	= 15 percent;
Unit cost (C)	= $100 per unit.

3. Icy Snowmobile Inc. has an annual demand of 1200 snowmobiles. Their purchase cost for each snowmobile is $2500. It costs about $250 to place an order, and the holding rate is 35 percent of the unit cost. Compute the EOQ, annual holding cost, annual order cost, and total annual inventory cost.

4. Steamy Speedboats has an annual demand of 1500 speedboats. Its supplier offers quantity discounts to promote larger-order quantities. The cost to place an order is $300, and the holding rate is 32 percent of the purchase cost. The purchase cost for each speedboat is based on the price schedule given below. Compute the optimal order quantity, annual purchase cost, annual holding cost, annual order cost, and total annual inventory cost.

ORDER QUANTITY	PRICE PER UNIT ($)
1–50	18,500
51–100	18,000
101–150	17,400
151 and above	16,800

5. Use the Steamy Speedboats problem above and assume that the order cost has dropped from $300 to $50. What is the optimal order quantity, annual purchase cost, annual holding cost, annual order cost, and total annual inventory cost?

6. Frankfurt Electronics produces a component internally using state of the art technology. The operations manager wants to determine the optimal lot size to ensure that the total annual inventory cost is minimized. The daily production rate for the component is 500 units, annual demand is 36,000 units, setup cost is $150 per setup, and the annual holding rate is 30 percent. The manager estimates that the total cost of a finished component is $80. Assuming that the plant operates year-round and there are 360 days per year, what is the (a) daily demand, (b) optimal lot size, (c) highest inventory, (d) annual product cost, (e) annual holding cost, (f) annual setup cost, (g) total annual inventory cost, (h) length of a production period, (i) length of each inventory cycle, (j) rate of inventory buildup during the production cycle, and (k) the number of inventory cycles per year? Finally, (l) plot the movement of the inventory during one production cycle using time on the horizontal axis and on-hand inventory on the vertical axis (see Figure 7.10).

7. Paris Store stocks a part that has a normal distribution demand pattern during the order lead time period. Its average demand during the order lead time is 650 units and the standard deviation of demand during the order lead time is 60 units. What is the safety stock and statistical reorder point that result in 2.5 percent stockouts?

8. Lindner Congress Bookstore sells a unique calculator to college students. The demand for this calculator has a normal distribution with an average daily demand of 15 units and a standard deviation of 4 units per day. The order lead time for this calculator is very stable at 5 days. Compute the standard deviation of demand during the order lead time period and determine the safety stock and statistical reorder point that result in a 95 percent in-stock probability.

9. The daily demand of a product is very stable at 250 units per day. However, the order lead time varies and can be specified by a normal distribution with a mean lead time of 12 days and standard deviation of 3 days. What is the safety stock and reorder point for a 97.5 percent in-stock probability?

10. The daily demand of a product can be specified by a normal distribution. The average daily demand is 250 units with a standard deviation of 40 units. The order lead time for this product is also normally distributed with an average of 10 days and a standard deviation of 3 days. What is the safety stock and reorder point for a 95 percent in-stock probability?

SPREADSHEET PROBLEMS

1. Given the following inventory information, perform an ABC analysis.

ITEM NUMBER	UNIT COST ($)	ANNUAL USAGE
B8867	6.00	100
J1252	5.25	6500
K9667	0.25	4000
L2425	1.00	1500
M4554	5.50	2000
T6334	70.00	500
W9856	0.75	800
X2215	1.50	8000
Y3214	32.00	1000
Y6339	4.00	3500

2. Given the following inventory information, construct the ABC inventory matrix and comment on whether the firm is stocking the correct inventory.

ITEM NUMBER	UNIT COST ($)	ANNUAL USAGE	PHYSICAL INVENTORY
B8867	6.00	100	8000
J1252	5.25	6500	120
K9667	0.25	4000	1000
L2425	1.00	1500	375
M4554	5.50	2000	500
T6334	70.00	500	800
W9856	0.75	800	20,000
X2215	1.50	8000	2000
Y3214	32.00	1000	500
Y6339	4.00	3500	125

3. Given the following information for an important purchased part, compute the (a) economic order quantity, (b) total purchase cost, (c) annual holding cost, (d) annual ordering cost, (e) annual total cost, (f) reorder point, (g) number of orders placed per year, and (h) time between orders. Use Microsoft Excel to plot the cost curves (annual holding cost, annual ordering cost, and annual total cost) on the vertical axis, and the order quantity on the horizontal axis.

Annual requirements (R)	=	5000 units;
Setup cost (S)	=	$100 per order;
Holding rate (k)	=	20 percent;
Unit cost (C)	=	$20 per unit;
Lead time (LT)	=	6 days;
Number of days per year	=	360 days.

Chapter 8

PROCESS MANAGEMENT: LEAN PRODUCTION AND SIX SIGMA QUALITY ISSUES IN SUPPLY CHAIN MANAGEMENT

In concept, lean is brilliant. In execution, it is more theory than reality. We all know what we need to do. It's doing it that's hard.[1]

Six Sigma provides robust processes for continuous improvement. Anything can be measured, but you must understand what really matters and focus on that.[2]

Learning Objectives

After completing this chapter, you should be able to

- List and discuss the major elements of lean production and Six Sigma quality.
- Describe why lean production and Six Sigma quality are integral parts of SCM.
- Discuss the Toyota Production System and its association with lean production.
- Discuss the linkage between lean production and environmental protection.
- Describe the historical developments of lean production and Six Sigma.
- Describe and use the various tools of Six Sigma.
- Understand the importance of statistical process control for improving quality.

Chapter Outline

Introduction

Lean Production and the Toyota Production System

Lean Production and Supply Chain Management

The Elements of Lean Production

Lean Production and the Environment

The Origins of Six Sigma Quality

Six Sigma and Lean Production

Six Sigma and Supply Chain Management

The Elements of Six Sigma

The Statistical Tools of Six Sigma

Summary

Supply Chain Management in Action   *Running Lean at Exide*

Robert Weiner ran lean manufacturing programs for 20 years at companies including General Electric and Pratt & Whitney. When he joined battery manufacturer Exide Technologies of Georgia as senior vice president of product delivery, he knew that without process improvements, the company was headed for trouble. In fact, Exide had filed for Chapter 11 bankruptcy protection several months earlier. "From a lean perspective, it was like walking into the dark ages," says Weiner.

Consequently, the company initiated EXCELL, an extensive program involving lean production, kaizen, and Six Sigma processes, says Weiner. The company trained lean leaders at each location to implement the system and maintain continuous improvements.

"We are still in the beginning phases, but the results have been incredible," he says. "In just nine months, we have seen cost reductions of nearly 20 percent."

The company reduced internal inefficiencies using Six Sigma processes to find root causes of waste. For example, Exide produces its own lead. The amount of lead kept on hand in plants went from 25–30 days to 24 days, says Weiner.

"Our largest customers require confidence in our ability to supply the right product to them on time," says Weiner. "Anything below 100 percent fulfillment means that there are dissatisfied customers and lost sales." Exide's fill rates for on-time delivery have markedly improved. Consequently, sales have increased, adds Weiner. "We have exceeded our planned improvements and expect to come out of Chapter 11 stronger than ever," says Weiner. "Without adopting lean programs, we wouldn't be here now."

Exide's Vice President of Supply Chain Management Heidi Skillman said the company is implementing a strategic sourcing initiative to assess and consolidate the suppliers to those that could support a lean manufacturing environment. The first wave looked at purchases from 736 suppliers and consolidated these to 75 suppliers. "We have already seen significant savings in administrative costs," she says. "Going forward, as we improve our quality and reduce costs, we want to see our suppliers doing the same."

One of the distributors that has worked with Exide throughout its lean implementation is Illinois-based Bearing Distributors, Inc. (BDI). "We are customer driven, so when they make changes, it impacts us," says branch manager Bill Holland. "In this case, the changes were positive."

The demand for improved quality required increased documentation and rationalization of part numbers and other changes on the part of BDI, says Holland. It has resulted in better communication and both Exide and BDI have a better understanding of each other's business. "We have the infrastructure they require," says Holland. "We also have a relatively flat organization, so each of our branches is able to be flexible to meet our customer's needs."

He says he has served Exide's local plant for five years and the account has doubled in size while the activity base associated with the account has dropped. "It is amazing the improvements they have made," he says. "I used to be called out there at night continually to deal with emergencies."

Exide and BDI surveyed the machines and are better aware of the plant's requirements, says Holland. Now both companies are better prepared to keep the machines running and deal with problems as they arise. "As a result, they have realized our strengths and have been bringing more business to us," he says. "Our product width has grown and they have asked us to increase our capabilities as they reduce their supplier base."

Source: Trombly, R. "Running Lean, Running Strong." *Industrial Distribution,* 91, no. 8 (2002): 53–55. Used with permission.

Introduction

As already discussed in earlier chapters, supply chain management is all about achieving low cost along with high levels of quality and responsiveness throughout the supply chain. Customers today expect these things, making it necessary for firms to adopt strategic initiatives emphasizing speed, innovation, cooperation, quality, and cost-effectiveness.

Lean production and **Six Sigma** quality, two important operating philosophies that are central to the success of supply chain management, seek to achieve these strategic initiatives, while at the same time resolve the trade-offs that can exist when simultaneously pursuing the goals of high quality, fast response, and low cost.

In the 1990s, supply chain management emerged as the paradigm that combined several strategies already in use, including **quick response (QR)**, **efficient consumer response (ECR)**, just-in-time (JIT), and Japanese **keiretsu relationships**. The first two are concerned with speed and flexibility, while keiretsu involves partnership arrangements. The QR program had been developed by the textile industry in the mid-1980s as an offshoot of JIT and is based on merchandisers and suppliers working together to respond more quickly to consumer needs by sharing information, resulting in better customer service and less inventory and waste. In the early 1990s, ECR was developed by a grocery industry task force charged with making grocery supply chains more competitive. In this case, point-of-purchase transactions at grocery stores are forwarded via computer to distributors and manufacturers, allowing the stores to keep stocks replenished while minimizing the need for safety stock inventories. Keiretsu networks are cooperative coalitions between Japanese manufacturing firms and their suppliers. In many cases, keiretsus are formed as the result of financial support given to suppliers by a manufacturing firm.

Supply chain management is thus closely associated with JIT. While many may argue that Henry Ford and his company essentially invented JIT practices, the term just-in-time was originally associated with Toyota managers like Mr. Taiichi Ohno along with his kanban system, encompassing continuous problem solving to eliminate waste. Use of the term *lean* has begun to replace use of the term JIT, and is associated with the **Toyota Production System**. Lean is broader, although closely related to JIT, and describes a philosophy incorporating tools that seek to economically optimize time, human resources, assets, and productivity, while improving product and service quality. In the early 1980s, these practices started making their way to the Western world, first as JIT and then today, as lean production or **lean manufacturing**. Lean production has evolved into a way of doing business for many organizations.

Quality assessment and improvement is a necessary element of lean production. First, as the process of waste elimination begins to shrink inventories, problems with human resource requirements, queues, lead times, quality, and timing are typically uncovered both in production and with inbound and outbound materials. Eventually, these problems are remedied, resulting in higher levels of quality and customer service. Second, as the drive to continuously reduce throughput times continues, the need for a continuing emphasis on improving quality throughout the productive system results in the need for an overall quality improvement or Six Sigma program. Six Sigma stresses a commitment by the firm's top management to enable the firm to identify customer expectations and excel in meeting and exceeding those expectations. Since environmental changes and changes in technology and competition cause customer expectations to change, firms must then commit to a program of continual reassessment and improvement; this, too, is an integral part of Six Sigma quality. Thus, to achieve the primary objectives of low cost, high quality, and reduced lead times, supply chain management requires the use of lean and Six Sigma thinking throughout the supply chain.

Lean Production and the Toyota Production System

The term *lean production* essentially refers to the Toyota Production System in its entirety, which was created by several of Toyota's key executives over a number of decades. Several of the important events in the creation of the Toyota Production System are described next.

Mr. Sakichi Toyoda invented the power loom in 1902 and in 1926 founded the Toyoda Automatic Loom Works. In 1937, he sold his loom patents to finance an automobile manufacturing plant to compete with Ford and General Motors, which accounted for over 90 percent of the vehicles manufactured in Japan at the time. Sakichi's son Kiichiro Toyoda was named managing director of the new facility.[3]

Kiichiro spent a year in Detroit studying Ford's manufacturing system and others, and then returned to Japan, where he adapted what he learned to the production of small quantities of automobiles, using smaller, more frequently delivered batches of materials. This later was referred to as the just-in-time system within Toyoda. At Ford, their system was designed such that parts were fabricated, delivered directly to the assembly line, and then assembled onto a vehicle within just a few minutes. Henry Ford had called this *flow production*, the precursor to JIT.[4]

Mr. Eiji Toyoda, nephew of Sakichi, began working at Toyoda in 1936 and was named managing director of the renamed and reorganized Toyoda Automotive Works in 1950. Eiji, too, traveled to Detroit to study Ford's automobile manufacturing system and was particularly impressed with their quality improvement activities, most notably their employee suggestion system. He was also impressed with Ford's daily automobile output of 7000 cars, compared to Toyoda's cumulative 13-year output of just 2700 cars. Back in Japan, he implemented the concepts he had seen in the U.S. and this became the foundation of what was later referred to as the Toyota Production System. In 1957, the company was again renamed, and became the Toyota Company. In 1982, Eiji established Toyota Motor Sales USA, and finally in 1983, Eiji renamed the firm the Toyota Motor Corporation.

Taiichi Ohno began his career at the Toyoda Automatic Loom Works in 1932. He expanded on the concepts established by Kiichiro and Eiji, by developing and refining methods to produce items only as needed for final assembly. He visited Detroit several times to observe auto manufacturing techniques. After World War II, the Toyoda production facilities were rebuilt, with Taiichi playing a major role in establishing the low-batch production principles developed earlier. These principles proved very valuable at the time, since postwar Japan was experiencing severe materials shortages. What Taiichi and Eiji had both realized during their trips to the U.S. was the tremendous waste everywhere (referred to as **muda** in Japan). These wastes of labor, inventories, space, time, and processing were certainly things Toyoda could not afford. From this realization came the idea that parts should be produced only as needed by the next step in an entire production process. When a type of signal or card (called a **kanban**) was used, the system became much more efficient. This began to be called the kanban or JIT system within Toyoda.

Refinements to the JIT concepts continued under Taiichi's tutelage, and he later attributed the system to two things—Henry Ford's autobiography wherein he explained the Ford manufacturing system which was the forerunner of modern JIT systems, and U.S. supermarket operations characterized by daily supply deliveries, which he observed during a visit to the U.S. in 1956. The final two notables in the development of the Toyota Production System were Shigeo Shingo, a quality consultant hired by Toyota, and W. Edwards Deming, who happened to be in Japan after the war helping to conduct the census, and who began attending professional meetings to discuss statistical quality control techniques. In the 1950s in Japan, Deming created and discussed his 14-point quality management guideline, and his ideas for continuous improvement with many Japanese manufacturing engineers and managers.

Shingo developed the concept of **Poka-Yoke** in 1961, when he was employed at Toyota. Poka-Yoke means error- or mistake-proofing. The idea is to design processes such that mistakes or defects are prevented from occurring in the first place, and if they do occur, further errors are also prevented. Poka-Yoke mechanisms can be electrical, mechanical, visual, procedural, or any other method that prevents problems, errors, or defects, and they can be implemented anywhere in the organization. Error-proofing thus leads to higher levels of quality and customer service.[5]

By 1959, Toyota was making 100,000 cars per year. In the latter part of the 1950s, though, they were experiencing quality problems which were impacting sales in the U.S. To remedy this, Toyota implemented what they referred to as total quality control (TQC) in concert with their JIT system. This then became the final piece of the Toyota Production System, and was later refined and renamed total quality management (TQM). Interestingly, in the first quarter of 2007, Toyota sold more vehicles worldwide than General Motors, ending GM's 76-year reign as the world's largest auto maker. This fact underscores the importance car buyers today are placing on fuel-efficient, high-quality, reasonably priced vehicles, and Toyota's lean production system appears to be serving them well.[6]

Actually, the term *lean production* did not originate at Toyota. It was first used in a benchmarking study conducted by the International Motor Vehicle Program (IMVP) at the Massachusetts Institute of Technology. The IMVP conducted a global automobile quality and productivity benchmarking study which culminated in the book, *The Machine that Changed the World* wherein the elements of lean production and the benchmarking results were presented.[7] The word "lean" was suggested because the Japanese plants in the benchmarking study when compared to their U.S. counterparts, used half the manufacturing labor, half the space, and half the engineering hours to produce a new automobile model in half the time. They also used much less than half the average inventory levels to produce the same number of vehicles, with far fewer defects.

Finally, it should be emphasized that lean production is suited for services, small businesses, and nonprofits as well as manufacturing facilities. Many hospitals have implemented lean programs to improve employee productivity, improve patient flow (and thus reduce patient time at the hospital), and reduce materials cost, among other improvements. The Flinders Medical Centre in Australia used lean thinking to map patient flow in their emergency care area and was able to reduce emergency room congestion and reduce by 50 percent the number of people leaving without completing their care.[8] Small businesses, too, can use lean thinking to streamline product flow, reduce inventories, improve customer service, and improve employee productivity. Mike Shanahan, co-owner of Connecticut-based small manufacturer Cadco Ltd., used lean thinking to speed up the production of warming trays and revise the layout of their facility. According to Mr. Shanahan, "The concept of lean is nothing like we thought it would be. It doesn't have to be complicated, unruly or expensive. In my eyes, it's all about finding the simplest way to accomplish a task or an operation. And its success can be measured in small increments, astounding results, or something in between. Either way, it can be applied to almost any operation or any size."[9] The Global Perspective feature profiles Schmitz Cargobull's implementation of a kanban and lean production system.

Global Perspective

The Supplier Kanban System at Schmitz Cargobull

One manufacturer that is reaping the benefits of an efficient supplier kanban system is trailer producer Schmitz Cargobull U.K. The County Durham-based manufacturer is a subsidiary of a German parent of the same name, and the U.K. firm has completely transformed its business over the past five years. Back in 2000, the U.K. business faced declining profits as market prices dropped for its vehicles. It embarked on a lean program, which began with identifying and eliminating waste from the production processes, but which also aimed to make the business more responsive to customer demand. The North East Productivity Alliance, a government funded initiative to help industrial firms in the area, put up funding and support to kick off the program. Dave Sidlow, Schmitz Cargobull's operations director, explains: "The whole company went on a 'back to school' initiative, with 80 percent of our workforce gaining vocational qualifications in areas such as business improvement, and we have established dedicated improvement teams. New principles of efficiency and profitability have been instilled throughout the company."

As part of the lean journey, the company found it had a number of problems with its existing component procurement network, which centered on a basic bin top-up system. Regular stockouts were a problem. The size of the trailers being produced, more than 13 meters long in some cases, means that a lack of even a basic part causes severe disruption and expense. A typical temperature-controlled trailer, for example, requires thousands of piece parts per trailer ranging from bearings and rivets to electrical components and thermometers. Schmitz was losing six-figure sums each year just in the cost of moving trailers to and from assembly lines because of lack of parts.

Insufficient data was also a problem: with too much of the stock located in a storage area rather than on the factory floor, managers were unable to determine usage by area of the factory, leading to inaccurate reporting and forecasting.

Using a large number of suppliers also resulted in extra paperwork and administration. Almost an entire team, including management, was involved in purchasing stock and dealing with multiple invoices.

This was pinpointed as a real opportunity to streamline resources. The company wanted a supply partner that had the capacity to source additional and new products, a service its existing supply network was struggling to provide. Schmitz invited a number of companies to tender for the supply of 200 parts and consumables and, after evaluation, chose Henry Halstead.

The supplier conducted qualitative and quantitative research on-site among team leaders before presenting its recommendations. In the meantime, a Schmitz Cargobull team was given a tour of Henry Halstead's live kanban system at another large end user. The Henry Halstead guarantee is a total component management system that supplies parts to exact usage requirements, not to stock. For Schmitz Cargobull, this meant it would

- supply all components via 22 new two-bin kanban stations located on the factory floor, giving quicker and easier access to stock;
- vastly reduce the stock held in the stores area;
- provide more sophisticated data including usage by area of factory;
- provide daily delivery and service visits; and
- implement a comprehensive training program for team leaders on kanban principles.

The installation of the new kanban system was carried out over three weeks, while Schmitz gradually ran down its commitments with existing suppliers. Workshops were held for team leaders and factory operatives, delivered by Halstead representatives along with Operations Director Dave Sidlow, a move engineered to gain support from the workers. As Sidlow explains, "I have experienced the benefits of well-run kanban systems at some of Europe's biggest manufacturers, so it was important to share this knowledge. A successful kanban system is down to the service of the supplier and the discipline of the user and this was a vital chapter of the workshops."

Henry Halstead supplies over 400 parts to Schmitz Cargobull, including cables, fuses, switches, traditional fasteners, electrical components, copper tubes, belts, goggles, tape, screwdriver bits, and bulbs. This number is expected to double by the end of 2006.

Schmitz Cargobull is now a company on the up. During the past three years there has been a 55 percent increase in turnover with only a 5 percent increase in staff, resulting in record profits for 2004/05 and even higher profits forecast for 2005/06.

"The impact of the kanban system has been instant and significant," says Sidlow. "The acid test was always going to be the Christmas run in. It is the busiest period of the year in this industry and the demand for consumables and parts creates a bottleneck for many suppliers. We've experienced substantial stockouts and shortages in past years, but Henry Halstead has ensured the peak period is smooth and problem free. Rather than worry about the next stockout crisis looming just around the corner, the production team has the confidence to concentrate on getting the job done and increasing value." What is more, the reduction in invoices means admin resources have been redeployed elsewhere.

Sidlow readily admits that the transition to lean is not an overnight process and it has been something that the company worked hard to sustain for the first couple of years before it saw real bottom-line improvements. Now, however, "we've seen astonishing improvements in performance that competitors will find nearly impossible to achieve," he says.

Source: Cork, L. "A Sign of Things to Come." *Works Management,* 59, no. 2 (2006): 26–28. Used with permission.

Lean Production and Supply Chain Management

Simply put, the objective of supply chain management is to balance the flow of materials with customer requirements throughout the supply chain, such that costs, quality, and customer service are at optimal levels. Lean production emphasizes reduction of waste, continuous improvement, and the synchronization of material flows from within the organization and eventually including the organization's immediate suppliers and customers. In many respects, then, supply chain management seeks to incorporate lean elements across the entire supply chain. Supply chain management encourages cross-training, satisfying internal customer demand, moving products through the production system quickly, and communicating end-customer demand forecasts and production schedules up the supply chain. In addition, it seeks to optimize inventory levels across the entire supply chain.

These elements of supply chain management are all supported by lean production. For example, as we saw in the opening feature, Supply Chain Management in Action, firms practicing lean production will seek to improve the quality and delivery characteristics of their suppliers through supply base rationalization and the formation of strategic alliances. When this same firm begins to practice supply chain management with other members of a supply chain, the focus will be on **channel integration,** or extending these strategic alliances to suppliers' suppliers and to customers' customers.

Lean production is an overall operating philosophy of waste reduction and value enhancement that can include a number of activities or elements, which are reviewed in subsequent sections. A number of firms are already practicing lean very well. The U.K.-based grocery chain Tesco refills its shelves with small but very frequent deliveries. Photographic material company Eastman Kodak, headquartered in New York, now has materials pulled for production only when needed, and their inbound inventory has dropped from one week's supply to a one day supply. The Top-Flite Golf Co. of Massachusetts is putting the lean philosophy to work in its distribution center. "Once people see the benefits and impact of the changes, they are more open to the process," says Jude Prych, Top-Flite distribution chief.[10]

Many firms do not implement all of the lean activities but, rather, select elements based on resources, product characteristics, customer needs, and supplier capabilities. Still, companies that have begun to implement lean activities find it easier to expand these efforts into a proactive supply chain management program. In a recent survey of manufacturing, distribution, and warehousing managers, respondents said the most important practices in manufacturing were continuous improvement and lean manufacturing, while the most important practices in warehousing were continuous improvement, value-added services, and lean inventories.[11]

Organizations that are successfully managing their supply chains evolve through four stages, as shown in Table 8.1. In Stage 1, the firm is internally focused, organizational functions are managed separately, and performance is monitored based on achieving departmental goals. This **silo effect** causes the firm to be reactive and short-term-goal oriented. At this stage, no internal functional integration is occurring.

In Stage 2, the firm has begun integrating efforts and resources among internal functions. In this stage, the focus of the firm has started to shift toward an emphasis on the flow of goods and information through the firm to achieve production efficiencies and reduce throughput times.

Table 8.1	Supply Chain Management Evolution			
STAGE 1: **INTERNALLY FOCUSED**	**STAGE 2:** **FUNCTIONAL INTEGRATION**	**STAGE 3:** **INTERNAL INTEGRATION**	**STAGE 4:** **EXTERNAL INTEGRATION**
• Functional silos • Top-down management • Internal measures used to monitor performance • Reactive, short-term planning • No internal integration	• Focus on internal flow of goods • Emphasis on cost reduction • Realization of efficiencies gained by internal integration	• Realization of integration of goods flow throughout firm • Focus on logistics and lean production activities to manage flow of goods and information • Measurement of supplier performance and customer service performance	• Extending integration efforts to suppliers and customers • Realization of need to control goods and information to second- and third-tier suppliers and customers • Emphasis on alliance development and communication capabilities

Source: Adapted from Stevens, G. C. "Integrating the Supply Chain." *International Journal of Physical Distribution and Logistics Management,* 19, no. 8 (1989): 3–8.

In Stage 3, internal integration of goods and information has been achieved, and the focus begins to shift toward linking suppliers and customers to the firm's processes. Thus, at this stage, there is an emphasis on using logistics capabilities to manage the movement and storage of goods from suppliers' deliveries to distribution to customers. Lean production activities begin to be used as the firm realizes the impact of reduced throughput times on customer service and inventory cost. As inventory levels are reduced, the need for improved quality from suppliers is magnified and firms begin to take a more proactive approach to managing and developing their suppliers. Successful use of lean production activities also impacts the firm's customers in terms of better quality products, more flexibility, and faster delivery times; and firms begin to realize the need to proactively manage their customer relationships as well.

Stage 4 is characterized by efforts to broaden the firm's supply chain influence beyond immediate or first-tier suppliers and customers, as well as strengthening relationships with existing key suppliers and customers. Firms have become comfortable with lean production processes and are seeking ways to further improve the flow of information, as well as waste reduction, quality, flexibility, and processing efficiencies. They begin to work with their most important suppliers and customers to aid in their respective lean implementation efforts. Supply chain management and external integration have become legitimate concerns at this stage.

Thus, throughout Stage 3 and Stage 4, we see an emphasis on lean production methods to integrate the firm's processes with its trading partners. The following section is a discussion of the lean production elements.

The Elements of Lean Production

Table 8.2 shows the major lean production elements that are discussed in this section of the chapter, along with a short description of each element. Readers should note that lean programs can vary significantly, based on the firm's resource capabilities, product and process orientation, and past failures or successes with other

Table 8.2	Lean Production Elements

ELEMENTS	DESCRIPTION
Waste reduction	Eliminating waste is the overriding concern within the lean philosophy. Includes reducing excess Inventories, material movements, production steps, scrap losses, rejects, and rework.
Lean supply chain relationships	Firm works with buyers and customers with the mutual goal of eliminating waste, improving speed, and improving quality. Key suppliers are considered partners and close customer relationships are also sought.
Lean layouts	WIP inventories are positioned close to each process, and layouts are designed where possible to reduce movement of people and materials. Processes are positioned to allow smooth flow of work through the facility.
Inventory and setup time reduction	Inventories are reduced by reducing production batch sizes, setup times, and safety stocks. Tends to create or uncover processing problems which are then managed and controlled.
Small batch scheduling	Firm produces frequent small batches of product, with frequent product changes to produce a level production schedule. Smaller, more frequent purchase orders are communicated to suppliers, and more frequent deliveries are offered to customers. Kanbans are used to pull WIP through the system.
Continuous improvement	As queues and lead times are reduced, problems surface more quickly causing the need for continual attention to problem solving and process improvement. With lower safety stocks, quality levels must be high to avoid process shut downs. Attention to supplier quality levels is high.
Workforce empowerment	Employees are cross-trained to add processing flexibility and to increase the workforce's ability to solve problems. Employees are trained to provide quality inspections as parts enter a process area. Employee roles are expanded and they are given top management support and resources to identify and fix problems.

improvement projects. Firms with a mature lean production implementation status will most likely be practicing a significant number of these elements.

Waste Reduction

One of the initial and long-term goals of all lean endeavors is waste reduction. The flip-side of waste reduction is value enhancement. Firms can thus reduce costs and add value to their products and services by eliminating waste from their productive system. Robert Martichenko, president of LeanCor LLC, a lean logistics consultancy based in Kentucky, points out that the best way to reduce waste is to "lower the water level" or to slowly reduce inventory, including work-in-process inventory, until only what is crucial to a smooth production flow is left. Anything else is not necessary, and therefore a waste that can be eliminated.[12]

Waste is a term that encompasses things such as excess wait times, inventories, material and people movements, processing steps, variabilities, and *any other non-value-adding activity*. Taiichi Ohno of Toyota, described what he called the **seven wastes**, which have since been applied across many industries around the world, to identify and reduce waste. The seven wastes are shown and described in Table 8.3. The common term across the seven wastes is *excess*. Obviously, firms require inventory, production, material and worker movements, and processing steps, but the idea is to determine the *right* levels of these things and then decide how best to achieve them.

Table 8.3	The Seven Wastes

WASTES	DESCRIPTION
Overproducing	Production of unnecessary items to maintain high utilizations.
Waiting	Excess idle machine and operator time; materials experiencing excess wait time for processing.
Transportation	Excess movement of materials between processing steps; transporting items long distances using multiple handling steps.
Overprocessing	Non-value-adding manufacturing, handling, packaging, or inspection activities.
Excess inventory	Storage of excess raw materials, work-in-process, and finished goods.
Excess movement	Unnecessary movements of employees to complete a task.
Scrap and rework	Scrap materials and product rework activities due to poor-quality materials or processing.

Source: Based in part on Avni, T. "Simulation Modeling Primer." *IIE Solutions,* 31, no. 9 (1999): 38–41.

Virginia-based multinational manufacturing company Honeywell International was able to realize a $1.2 billion productivity improvement gain in 2002, when they implemented their lean enterprise and Six Sigma programs. Their lean enterprise program included cycle time and waste reduction in all manufacturing and business processes.[13]

Unfortunately, many companies view these excesses as simply a cost of doing business. To identify and eliminate waste, workers and managers must therefore be continually assessing processes, methods, and materials for their value contributions to the firm's salable products and services. This is accomplished through worker–management interactions and commitment to the continued elimination of waste, and frequent solicitation of feedback from customers. Significant waste reduction results in a number of positive outcomes including lower costs, shorter lead times, better quality, and greater competitiveness. The waste reduction theme runs through all of the lean production elements.

Implementing the Five-Ss

Another method used for waste reduction has been termed the **Five-Ss**. The original five-Ss came naturally, from Toyota, and were Japanese words relating to industrial housekeeping. The idea is that by implementing the five-Ss, the workplace will be cleaner, more organized, and safer, thereby reducing processing waste and improving productivity. Table 8.4 lists and describes each of these terms, and presents the equivalent S-terms used in the English version of the five-S system.

The goals of the first two (sorting and simplifying) are to eliminate searching for parts and tools, avoid unnecessary movements, and avoid using the wrong tools or parts. Work area tools and materials are evaluated for their appropriateness, and approved items are arranged and stored near their place of use. Seiso/sweep refers to proper workplace cleaning and maintenance, while seiketsu/standardize seeks to reduce processing variabilities by eliminating nonstandard activities and resources. Shitsuke/self-discipline deals with forming and refining effective work habits. Global

Table 8.4	The Five-Ss	
JAPANESE S-TERM	**ENGLISH TRANSLATION**	**ENGLISH S-TERM IN USE**
1. Seiri	Organization	Sort
2. Seiton	Tidiness	Set in order
3. Seiso	Purity	Sweep
4. Seiketsu	Cleanliness	Standardize
5. Shitsuke	Discipline	Self-discipline

Source: Becker, J. "Implementing 5S: To Promote Safety & Housekeeping." *Professional Safety,* 46, no. 8 (2001): 29–31.

drive, control, and motion product manufacturer Bosch Rexroth, headquartered in Illinois, has developed their Bosch Production System, which essentially incorporates the five-S system. "We're going through to make sure that everything is identifiable, that there's a place for everything," says Kurt Greissinger, product marketing manager for Bosch Rexroth. "Everything has been standardized so that it makes finding parts and tools more efficient. We're putting pedometers on employees to measure how far they need to walk to fulfill an order or to get parts needed to assemble a system. Then we're going through and studying all those processes and putting together a new plant layout to eliminate the transportation and motion wastes inherent with that," he adds.[14]

The five-S system can be employed in any service or manufacturing environment. Many lean efforts begin with the implementation of the five-Ss. Firms conduct a "waste hunt" using the five-Ss, then follow up with a "red-tag event" to remove or further evaluate all nonrequired, red-tagged items. Some companies have also added a sixth-S, for safety, to assess the safety of work conditions and reduce the risk profile of the work area.[15]

Lean Supply Chain Relationships

Quite commonly, firms must hold safety stocks of purchased products because their suppliers' delivery times are inconsistent or the quality of purchased goods does not always meet specifications. On the distribution side, firms hold stocks of finished goods in warehouses prior to shipment to customers, in some cases for months at a time, to avoid stockouts and maintain customer service levels. Holding these inbound and outbound inventories costs the firm money while not adding value to the products; thus, it is considered a waste.

When the focal firm, its suppliers, and its customers begin to work together to identify customer requirements, remove waste, reduce cost, and improve quality and customer service, it marks the beginning of **lean supply chain relationships**. Wal-Mart sources directly from manufacturers for many of its products, to get the greatest cost reductions. In 2006, Wal-Mart was doing business with about 4400 manufacturers worldwide, with another 40,000 second- and third-tier manufacturers indirectly producing for Wal-Mart, via its supply base. In the future, Wal-Mart expects to establish closer ties to these indirect companies to further reduce supply chain costs.[16] At MeadWestvaco's paper mill in Alabama, they use their customers to influence plant investments that ultimately result in better product quality and acceptability. "Without question, customers are driving our business model," says Jack Golclfrank, coated board division president. They conduct a survey every 18 months to assess product, service, reputation, practices, price, and value. The surveys allow them to determine where customers want improvement, and if a problematic trend exists.[17]

Using lean thinking with suppliers includes having them deliver smaller quantities, more frequently, to the point of use in the focal firm. This serves to reduce average inventory levels. More frequent deliveries, though, mean higher inbound transportation costs; to reduce these costs, suppliers are often required to distribute products from warehouses or production facilities located in close proximity to the buyer. Many distribution centers today transform and repackage products for customers as they are needed. For example, PetsMart's busiest day of the week is Saturday. During the week, warehouses serving PetsMart receive truckloads of supplies; by Thursday, they are assembling store load quantities in anticipation of that Saturday's business.[18]

Making small, frequent purchases from just a few suppliers puts the focal firm in a position of greater dependence on these suppliers. It is therefore extremely important that deliveries always be on time, delivered to the right location, in the right quantities, and be of high quality, since existing inventories will be lower. Ford, for instance, partnered with Ryder Logistics, making them responsible for the total product inflow and outflow at a number of their assembly plants to maximize logistics efficiencies.[19]

Firms can also use lean thinking with their key customers. As these relationships develop, firms begin to reserve greater levels of capacity for a small number of large, steady customers. They locate production or warehousing facilities close to these customers and make frequent small deliveries of finished product to their points of use within the facility, thus reducing transportation time and average inventory levels. Lean thinking with customers means determining how to give them exactly what they want while minimizing waste as much as possible. When consumer product giant Procter & Gamble saw its profit decline a few years ago, it reduced its distribution centers worldwide to reduce costs, while reorganizing its logistics processes to increase product velocity to its key customers—it boosted the shipping frequency of its higher-demand products, while achieving a better balance in its management of truckload and less-than-truckload shipments, effectively reducing transportation cost while improving many of their customer relationships.[20]

It can be seen, then, that mutual dependencies and mutual benefits occur among all of these lean supply chain relationships, resulting in increased product value and competitiveness for all of the partners.

Lean Layouts

The primary design objective with **lean layouts** is to reduce wasted movements of workers, customers, and/or work-in-process (WIP), and achieve smooth product flow through the facility. Moving parts and people around the production floor does not add value. Lean layouts allow people and materials to move when and where they are needed, as quickly as possible. Whenever possible, processing centers, offices, or departments that transfer parts, customers, or workers between them should be located close together, to minimize this type of waste.

Lean layouts are very visual, meaning that lines of visibility are unobstructed, making it easy for operators at one processing center to monitor work occurring at other centers. In manufacturing facilities, all purchased and WIP inventories are located on the production floor at their point of use, and the good visibility makes it easy to spot inventory buildups as bottlenecks occur. When these and other production problems occur, they are spotted and rectified quickly. The relative closeness of the processing centers facilitates teamwork and joint problem solving and requires less floor space than conventional production layouts.

Lean layouts allow problems to be tracked to their source more quickly as well. Since material and parts flow directly from one processing center to the next, a quality problem, when found, can generally be traced to the previous work center, provided inspections are performed at each processing stage. In the United Kingdom, the British Aerospace Military Aircraft facility at Yorkshire was redesigned using lean concepts. One of the goals was to eliminate the non-value-added days where components sat between processing stages. After rearranging the layout, some parts that had traveled 3 kilometers during processing, moved only one-tenth of that distance. In addition, it was projected that productivity would increase by 20 percent and inventory levels would fall by 55 percent.[21]

Manufacturing Cells

Manufacturing cells are designed to process similar parts or components, saving duplication of equipment and labor, as well as centralizing the area where units of the same purchased part are delivered. In many cases these manufacturing cells are U-shaped to facilitate easier operator and material movements within the cell. In assembly line facilities, manufacturing cells are positioned close to the line, feeding finished components directly to the line instead of delivering them to a stock area where they would be brought back out when needed. Manufacturing cells are themselves small assembly lines and are designed to be flexible, allowing machine configurations to change as processing requirements dictate.

Inventory and Setup Time Reduction

In lean parlance, excess inventories are considered a waste, since they tend to hide a number of purchasing, production, and quality problems within the organization. Just as water hides boat-damaging rocks beneath its surface, so inventory hides value-damaging problems along the supply chain. And, just as reducing water levels causes rocks to become detectable, so too the reduction of inventory levels causes problems to surface in the organization and among its trading partners. Once these problems are detected, they can be solved, improving product value and allowing the system to run more efficiently.

For example, reducing safety stocks of purchased materials will cause stockouts and potential manufacturing disruptions when late deliveries occur. Firms must then either find a way to resolve the delivery problem with the supplier or find a more reliable supplier. Either way, the end result is a smoother running organization with less inventory investment. The same story can be applied to production machinery. Properly maintained equipment breaks down less often, so less safety stock is needed to keep downstream processing areas fed with parts to be further processed.

Another way to reduce inventory levels is to reduce purchase order quantities and production lot sizes. Figure 8.1 illustrates this point. When order quantities and lot sizes are cut in half, average inventories are also cut in half, assuming usage remains

Figure 8.1	Relationship between Order Quality, Lot Size, and Average Inventory

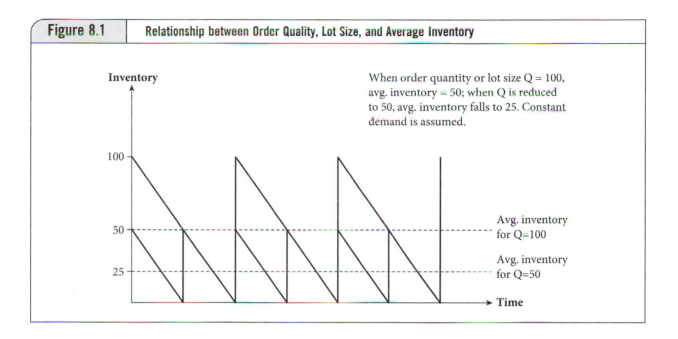

When order quantity or lot size Q = 100, avg. inventory = 50; when Q is reduced to 50, avg. inventory falls to 25. Constant demand is assumed.

constant. Unfortunately, this means that the firm must make more purchase orders and perform more production **setups**. Thus, ordering costs must be reduced and this can be accomplished by automating or simplifying the purchasing process. Companies today are developing **virtual inventory** systems so that distributors can feed their inventory information into one shared database, allowing small buyers to order in a lean environment from distributors offering the quickest response times.[22]

Since setting up production equipment for the next production run takes valuable time, increasing the number of setups means the firm must find ways to reduce setup times. Setup times can be reduced in a number of ways including doing setup preparation work while the previous production lot is still being processed, moving machine tools closer to the machines, improving tooling or die couplings, standardizing setup procedures, practicing various methods to reduce setup times, and purchasing machines that require less setup time.

Finally, once inventories have been reduced and the flow problems uncovered and solved, the firm can reduce inventories still further, uncovering yet another set of problems to be solved. With each inventory reduction iteration, the firm runs leaner, cheaper, faster, and with higher levels of product quality.

Small Batch Scheduling

Saying that a firm should purchase small quantities, more frequently, from good suppliers and produce small lot sizes and have more setups is one thing, but actually accomplishing this feat is something else. Many firms have tried these two things and failed, eventually returning to carrying higher levels of inventory and producing large batches to sell product, rather than dealing with the many problems accompanying lean production. Level schedules of small batches though, communicated throughout the production process and to outside suppliers, is what is needed to support lean production.

Small batch scheduling drives down costs by reducing purchased, WIP, and finished goods inventories, and it also makes the firm more flexible to meet customer

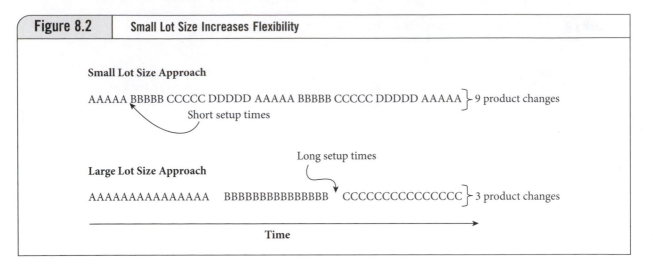

| Figure 8.2 | Small Lot Size Increases Flexibility |

Small Lot Size Approach

AAAAA BBBBB CCCCC DDDDD AAAAA BBBBB CCCCC DDDDD AAAAA ⎱ 9 product changes
Short setup times

Large Lot Size Approach

Long setup times

AAAAAAAAAAAAAAAA   BBBBBBBBBBBBBBBB   CCCCCCCCCCCCCCCC ⎱ 3 product changes

Time

demand. Figure 8.2 illustrates this point. In the same period of time, the firm with small lot sizes changes products nine times, while the firm with large lot sizes has only changed production three times, and has yet to produce product D. Maintaining a set, level, small batch production schedule will allow suppliers to anticipate and schedule deliveries also, resulting in fewer late deliveries.

Moving these small production batches through a lean production facility is accomplished with the use of kanbans. Kanban is a Japanese word for card, and in lean facilities it has come to mean a signal. When manufacturing cells need parts or materials, they use a kanban to signal their need for these things from the upstream manufacturing cell, processing unit, or external supplier providing the needed material. In this way, nothing is provided until a downstream demand occurs. That is why a lean system is known as a **pull system**. Ideally, parts are placed in standardized containers, and kanbans exist for each container. Figure 8.3 illustrates how a kanban pull system works. When finished components are moved from Cell B to the assembly line, the following things happen:

1. The container holding finished parts in Cell B's output area is emptied and a **production kanban** (a light, flag, or sign) is used to tell Cell B to begin processing more components to restock the empty container in its output area.

2. During this stage, when parts are moved from Cell B's input area for processing, the container holding these parts is emptied and a **withdrawal kanban** (a light, flag, or sign) is used to indicate to Cell A that more parts are needed. This allows a full container of parts to move from Cell A's output area to Cell B's input area, and the empty container is moved to Cell A's output area.

3. As this movement occurs, a production kanban is now used to allow Cell A to begin processing parts to restock its empty container in the output area.

4. Finally, as full containers of parts are emptied and used in Cell A's processing area, these empty containers in Cell A's input area create a withdrawal kanban seen by the external supplier who then restocks Cell A's empty containers in the input area.

Thus, it can be seen that kanbans are used to control the flow of inventory through the facility. Inventories are not allowed to accumulate beyond the size of each container and the number of containers in the system. When containers are full, production

Figure 8.3	A Kanban Pull System

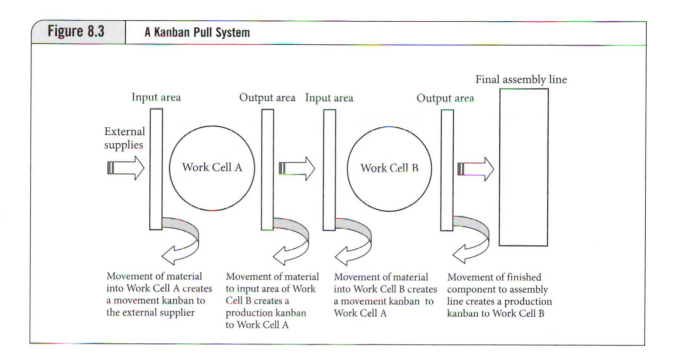

Movement of material into Work Cell A creates a movement kanban to the external supplier

Movement of material to input area of Work Cell B creates a production kanban to Work Cell A

Movement of material into Work Cell B creates a movement kanban to Work Cell A

Movement of finished component to assembly line creates a production kanban to Work Cell B

stops until another production kanban is encountered. The U.K.-based cutting tool manufacturer Dormer Tools implemented lean production to better compete with Chinese manufacturers. Machines were prioritized using kanban cards, which helped to reduce WIP inventories by 25 percent and reduce lead times from twelve weeks to four.[23]

A simple relationship can be used to determine the number of containers or kanban card sets for a lean production system:

$$\text{No. of containers} = \frac{DT(1+S)}{C},$$

where

$D =$ the demand rate of the assembly line;

$T =$ the time for a container to make an entire circuit through the system, from being filled, moved, being emptied, and returned to be filled again;

$C =$ the container size, in number of parts; and

$S =$ the safety stock factor, from 0 to 100 percent.

For example, suppose the assembly line demand is twenty of Part A per hour for Work Cell B, and the standard container size used for this part holds five Part A's. If it takes 2 hours for a container to make a circuit from Work Cell B to the assembly line and back again, and if it is desired to carry 10 percent excess of Part A in the system, then the number of containers needed in the system is 8.8 or 9, when rounding up. The maximum inventory for this system would then be the total number of containers times the container size, or 45 units. Finally, reducing inventory in the system (one of the objectives of lean production) occurs by reducing the number of containers. Consequently, when the number of containers is reduced, the circuit time for each container would also have to be reduced to enable the demand to be met. This can be done by reducing setup time, processing time, wait time, and/or move time.

Continuous Improvement

As alluded to already, lean systems are never-ending works in progress. Compact layouts are designed to allow work to logically flow through the facility. Inventory is moved from supplier delivery vehicles to the shop floor and placed in containers in designated manufacturing cell storage areas.

Purchase orders and production batches are small. In this system, problems often will surface, at least initially, as suppliers struggle to deliver more frequently and on time, and as workers strive to maintain output levels while spending more time during the day, setting up machines for small production runs. To make the lean system work better, employees continuously seek ways to reduce supplier delivery and quality problems, and in the production area they improve movement problems, visibility problems, machine breakdown problems, machine setup problems, and internal quality problems. In Japanese manufacturing facilities, this is known as **kaizen.**

Once the problems created by the small batch sizes are solved, removal of an inventory container from one of the manufacturing cells starts the problem-solving cycle all over again—thus, the need for continuous improvement in all lean systems. Until things are always where they need to be, at the expected time and in the right quality and quantity, improvements must be sought out.

Quality improvement is certainly part of the ongoing continuous improvement efforts in lean systems. For example, receiving a batch of goods from an external supplier or an internal manufacturing cell that does not satisfy design specifications is like not getting a shipment at all. Because of low safety stock levels, processing areas needing these supplies will be out of stock and unable to work in short order. High-quality levels are then necessary throughout the production system to meet demand. Further discussion of quality and continuous improvement can be found in the next section of this chapter.

Workforce Commitment

Since lean systems depend so much on waste reduction and continuous improvement for their success, dedicated employees must play a significant role in this process. Managers must show strong support for lean production efforts by providing subordinates with the skills, tools, time, and other necessary resources to identify process problems and implement solutions. Managers must create a culture in which workers are encouraged to speak out when problems exist. To improve productivity at Chrysler's distribution centers, management personnel rely on warehouse workers for suggestions. By working closely with workers to develop ideas, the company has been able to improve throughput, efficiency, and morale.[24] And, as W. Edwards Deming so eloquently pointed out in his theory of management, eliminating fear in the workplace is one of the primary requirements for creating a successful company.[25]

In lean production systems, employees are cross-trained in many of the various production processes to enable capacities to be adjusted at different manufacturing cells as needed when machines break down or workers are absent. Employees are given time during their day to work on reducing machine setup times as well as solve other production problems as they occur. They are also expected to perform a number of quality checks on processed items coming into the manufacturing cell. When quality problems are found, workers are empowered to shut down the production process until the source of the problem can be found and corrected. Most employees who work for lean companies enjoy their jobs; they are given a number of responsibilities and are considered one of the most important parts of a successful lean organization.

Lean Production and the Environment

In Chapter 4, the topics of green sourcing, sustainable procurement and sustainability were introduced and their importance to supply chain management was discussed. Since lean production is ultimately concerned with waste reduction throughout the firm and its supply chains, the linkage between lean production and environmental sustainability should seem clear.

Many organizations have realized the positive impact lean production can have on their environmental performance—adopting lean practices reduces the cost of environmental management and then leads to improved environmental performance. Further, lean production increases the possibility that firms will adopt more advanced environmental management systems, leading to yet further improvements in environmental performance. Professors King and Lennox analyzed thousands of companies in the early 1990s and found ample evidence of this linkage between the concept of lean and environmental sustainability. They found that firms that minimized inventory and adopted quality standards were more likely to practice pollution prevention and had lower toxic chemical emissions.[26]

Toyota, the world's leading lean producer as well as the most profitable automobile manufacturer, produces the (U.S.) Prius, a very successful hybrid vehicle combining lean and green. In 1997, when the Prius first appeared on the U.S. market, gasoline was comparatively low priced and plentiful in the U.S., and consumer priorities were not focused on vehicle emissions. Now, the world marketplace has changed dramatically, U.S. gasoline prices are much higher, the Prius is considered visionary, and the market for green vehicles in the U.S. is exploding.[27]

Other examples abound. Illinois-based Hospira, maker of pharmaceutical products, is not only dedicated to eliminating waste in all areas of production, but is also making headway on reducing the 2.4 billion pounds of waste that hospitals produce every year in the U.S. As an example, Hospira developed and launched a new IV (intravenous) bag that produces 40–70 percent less waste than other flexible IV bags.[28]

At New Jersey-based printing company Pictorial Offset Corp., managements' desire to reduce waste led them to remove 300 chemical products from the plant and begin recycling corrugated and steel strapping waste. The firm has achieved a number of industry environmental firsts, including obtaining the ISO 9000 and ISO 14000 certifications simultaneously. They are also recognized as being **carbon-neutral** in part by planting 5000 trees in New Jersey to offset the carbon footprint of its operations. These practices have also helped Pictorial Offset's sales—they have gained a number of new clients who sought out the printing firm because of their environmental reputation.[29]

As we have illuminated in this first portion of the chapter, achieving lean production is a necessary element in successful supply chain management. A second, equally necessary, element is the practice of continuous quality improvement. And, one of the best examples of this is Six Sigma quality. While we introduced the concept of Six Sigma quality and its relationship to lean production earlier in the chapter, we would like to now more fully explore Six Sigma quality and its relationship to supply chain management.

The Origins of Six Sigma Quality

Six Sigma quality, many times simply referred to as Six Sigma, was pioneered by global communications leader Motorola in 1987, and is a statistics-based decision-making framework designed to make significant quality improvements in value-adding processes. Six Sigma (with capital S's) is a registered trademark of Motorola. At the time, a senior staff engineer at Motorola named Mikel Harry formed a team of engineers to experiment with problem solving using statistical analyses, and this became the foundation for Six Sigma. Richard Schroeder, vice president of customer service at Motorola, heard about Harry's work, and applied the methodology to his work at Motorola. Soon, both groups were announcing large reductions in errors and various costs. Ultimately, both men left Motorola and formed the Six Sigma Academy in Arizona.[30]

Quality perfection is represented by the term Six Sigma, which refers to the statistical likelihood that 99.99966 percent of the time, a process sample average will fall below a control limit placed 4.5 standard deviations (or sigmas) above the true process mean, assuming the process is in control. This represents the goal of having a defect occur in a process only 0.00034 percent of the time, or 3.4 times out of every million measurement opportunities. This description makes it sound like the methodology should be called 4½ sigma. The 1½ sigma difference is the subject of much debate, and refers to a somewhat confusing term called **sigma drift**.[31] Sigma drift posits that process variations will grow over time, as process measurements drift off target. In truth, any process exhibiting a change in process variation of 1.5 sigma would be detected using quality **control charts**, instigating an improvement effort to get the process back on target. Table 8.5 shows the **defects per million opportunities (DPMO)** to be expected for various sigmas, using the Six Sigma methodology.

But the Six Sigma concept is not only about statistics. It is a broad improvement strategy that includes the concepts or ideas of total quality management (TQM), a focus on the customer, performance measurement, and formal training in quality control methods. Six Sigma embodies more of an organizational culture wherein everyone from CEO, to production worker, to frontline service employee is involved in quality assessment and improvement. Six Sigma is proactive in nature and seeks to permanently

Table 8.5	Six Sigma Metrics	
NUMBER OF STANDARD DEVIATIONS ABOVE THE MEAN	**PERCENT OF OUTPUT THAT IS DEFECT-FREE**	**DEFECTS PER MILLION OPPORTUNITIES (DPMO)**
2	69.15	308,537
2.5	84.13	158,686
3	93.32	66,807
3.5	97.73	22,750
4	99.38	6210
4.5	99.865	1350
5	99.977	233
5.5	99.9968	32
6	99.99966	3.4

Note: Standard deviations include 1.5 sigma "drift."

fix the root causes of problems, instead of repeatedly spending time and money tinkering with and patching-up processes as problems occur in the business. In Six Sigma, sources of process variation are sought out and remedied prior to the time these variations can cause production and customer satisfaction problems.

Today, many organizations practice Six Sigma, including early adopters Honeywell, General Electric, and Dow Chemical. In 1999, Ford Motor Company became the first U.S. automaker to adopt the Six Sigma strategy. Automobile manufacturing provides a great example of the need for Six Sigma quality thinking. Since automobiles have approximately 20,000 **opportunities for a defect to occur (OFD)**, and assuming an automobile company operates at the $5\frac{1}{2}$ sigma level, this would equate to about one defect for every two cars produced. Improving to the Six Sigma quality level would mean about one defect for every 15 automobiles produced.[32] Calculating the DPMO can be accomplished using the following formula:

$$DPMO = \frac{\text{number of defects}}{(\text{OFD per unit})(\text{number of units})} \times 1,000,000$$

Example 8.1 illustrates the calculation of DPMO and the use of Table 8.5.

Today, these and other types of firms focus on generating cost savings or increased sales as a result of process improvements. In fact, Motorola at one time stated that their savings to date from use of Six Sigma had exceeded $17 billion.[33] This type of outcome is possible as firms identify customer requirements, uncover all of the opportunities for errors or defects to occur, review performance against Six Sigma performance standards, and then take the actions necessary to achieve those standards. The most successful projects meet strategic business objectives, reduce product and service variations to optimal levels, and produce a product or service that satisfies the customer. The e-Business Connection feature profiles a hospital's use of Six Sigma and a software application to solve a room scheduling problem.

Like all improvement programs, however, Six Sigma cannot guarantee continued or even initial business success. Poor management decisions and investments, and a company culture not conducive to change can undermine even the best Six Sigma program. Six Sigma originator Motorola has struggled financially for a number of years and has laid off tens of thousands of workers since 2000.[34] Camera and film

---

Example 8.1   Calculating DPMO for Blakester's Speedy Pizza

Blake, owner of Blakester's Speedy Pizza, a home delivery pizza operation, keeps track of customer complaints. For each pizza delivery, there are three possible causes of complaints: a late delivery, a cold pizza, or an incorrect pizza. Each week, Blake calculates the rate of delivery "defects" per total pizza deliveries, and then uses this information to determine his company's Six Sigma quality level. During the past week, his company delivered 620 pizzas. His drivers received 16 late delivery complaints, 19 cold pizza complaints, and 5 incorrect pizza complaints.

Blake's defects per million opportunities is:

$$DPMO = \frac{\text{number of defects}}{(\text{OFD per unit})(\text{number of units})} \times 1,000,000$$

$$= \frac{40}{(3)(620)} \times 1,000,000 = 21,505 \text{ defective pizza deliveries per million.}$$

From Table 8.5, it can be concluded that Blakester's is operating at slightly better than 3.5 sigma.

e-Business Connection

Blending Technology with Six Sigma at OSF Saint Francis

In Peoria, Illinois, Order of Saint Francis (OSF) Saint Francis is a 710-bed tertiary referral center and teaching hospital. Like in many other hospitals, patient backlogs due to inpatient bed availability forced medical staff to divert emergency patients to other emergency rooms. On the best of days, getting a patient into the right room at the right time in a way that maximized all existing resources—beds, rooms, emergency facilities, nursing staff, transport staff and specialized intensive care units, to name a handful—was a challenge.

In 2002, the organization adopted a Six Sigma approach. The group decided to pursue an IT-based solution for managing patient flow and bed availability. The Six Sigma group knew that OSF Saint Francis needed redesigned internal processes to support the technology, and also that adding software to the equation could not put any more work on anyone's plate.

The group researched products from several vendors and favored most the Bed Management Suite from Tele-Tracking Technologies Inc. Implementation began in January 2005 and took three months. Essentially, implementation went very smoothly.

New software and new internal processes worked together like hand-in-glove.

As part of its redesigned processes, OSF Saint Francis established a new patient logistics department to consolidate bed management and patient placement. The entire logistics process is monitored in real-time on strategically located flat screen video displays, so staff in intensive care and other units are constantly updated on bed availability. At any point in the day, a patient logistics coordinator knows the exact status of each hospital bed and can anticipate when beds will become available.

Technology provides a seamless flow of communication among many disparate departments so that each step in the process is addressed. This data stream makes the information transparent to each individual who is involved, allowing individuals to be more accountable for their separate roles and simultaneously allowing all the players in the process to perform their roles in sequence without delay or disruption.

"We trained our staff on the new processes first," says Hoa Cooper, operations manager, adult hospitalist service, "before introducing them to the software." After everyone understood the new process, Tele-Tracking sent in training experts to work with staff and stay on-site during the go-live week.

OSF Saint Francis has saved more than $300,000 in personnel costs by reducing (through redeployment) the number of staff needed to identify available rooms and manage their readiness. The hospital has improved its discharge-by-noon rates by nearly 30 percent, vacating more rooms earlier in the day for reoccupation by afternoon. Intrahospital phone calls related to patient flow have just about stopped, since everyone who needs patient-flow data uses the electronic bed board. The average turnover time for a patient room is now less than 1 hour.

Source: OSF Saint Francis Medical Center. "Sustain the Gain." *Health Management Technology,* 27, no. 11 (2006): 28–31. Used with permission of Nelson Publishing, Inc., www.healthmgttech.com.

maker Polaroid, another early user of Six Sigma, filed for Chapter 11 bankruptcy protection in 2001, and the following year, they sold their name and all assets to a subsidiary of Illinois-based Bank One Corp.[35]

Six Sigma and Lean Production

Six Sigma and lean production actually have many similarities. For lean production to be successful, purchased parts and assemblies, work-in-process, and finished goods must all meet or exceed quality requirements. Also, recall that one of the elements of lean production is continuous improvement, and these are the areas where the practice of Six Sigma can be put to good use in a lean system. Evidence points to the idea that firms are now pursuing both of these initiatives simultaneously. The Avery Point Group, an executive search firm headquartered in Connecticut, did a sampling recently of Internet job board postings, and found that about half of the companies seeking candidates with one of the two skill sets, wanted the other skill set as well. Tim Noble, managing principal of Avery Point Group explains, "Core to both methodologies is the idea that challenges need to be approached with an open mind, because solutions can sometimes come from the most unlikely of sources. True Six Sigma and lean practitioners will view this marriage with an open mind and realize that these are truly complementary tool sets, not competing philosophies."[36]

Competitive companies must ultimately offer high-quality goods at reasonable prices, while providing a high level of customer service. Rearranging factory floor layouts and reducing batch sizes and setup times will reduce manufacturing lead times and inventory levels, providing better delivery performance and lower cost. These are lean production activities. Use of statistical quality control charts for production processes, creating long-term relationships with high-quality suppliers, and reducing distribution problems falls under the purview of Six Sigma. This short explanation describes how the two concepts can work together to achieve better overall firm performance. Lean production is all about reducing waste, while Six Sigma is all about improving quality.

Lean Six Sigma

A new term is now being used to describe the melding of lean production and Six Sigma quality practices—**Lean Six Sigma**, or simply **Lean Six**. Maryland-based aeronautics firm Lockheed Martin's Missiles and Fire Control Operations in Arkansas combines lean and Six Sigma to improve production processes, reduce lead times, and reduce costs. Their Lean Six Sigma program was responsible for reducing the lead time for Patriot missiles from 18 down to 12 months, and over a 5-year period, 91 Lean Six Sigma projects saved more than $23 million.[37]

After the dot-com bust of 2001, many companies began considering implementing some form of lean, Six Sigma, or combination approach. Four companies in particular that had implemented Lean Six after 2001 were studied by *Electronic Business* magazine in 2006—Canada-based Celestica, ON Semiconductor headquartered in Arizona, California-based Solectron, and Xerox, headquartered in Connecticut. All four firms were healthier in 2006 than in 2001, and three claimed their business turnaround was a direct result of Lean Six. "Three years ago, we had 16 quarters of losses, but now we have nine quarters of gain behind us," says Marc Onetto, Solectron's executive vice president. "There are many other factors, but Lean Six Sigma is a big contributor," he adds. Onetto described a typical Lean Six technique—the Lean Six team would follow a worker around, tracing the exact steps the worker walked, leading to what Onetto called a spaghetti chart. From there, the team and other workers would rearrange things such as storage bins for components to straighten out the spaghetti, creating a better path for the worker. "People start seeing the results and want to apply it to their own processes," says Robert Hemmant, lean architect at Celestica. The company has Lean Six projects in human resources, finance, and purchasing. Xerox applied Lean Six across its entire organization starting in 2003. They appointed 33 Lean Six Sigma "champions" at the time, each responsible for project deployments in their respective areas. Now, about two-thirds of their 55,000 employees have received some level of Lean Six training. Xerox is even helping their customers develop their own Lean Six programs.[38]

Recently, members of IBM's Institute for Business Value analyzed a number of leading companies that had implemented a Lean Six Sigma program. These companies used Lean Six to pursue an innovation agenda. The programs enabled them to produce breakthrough innovations that caused profound improvements in their business performance. In short, these firms had created an organizational climate where innovation was expected. One of these firms was global construction equipment manufacturer Caterpillar. They undertook a massive Lean Six Sigma program in 2001 (although they just referred to it at the time as Six Sigma) which led to product innovations and redesigned processes, including a streamlined supply chain. By 2005, revenues had grown by a whopping 80 percent. Their initial effort spawned over 1100 projects. Some generated subtle operational improvements while others resulted in innovative new products and radically different ways of doing things. One of the first changes involved more interaction between design personnel and customers. Employees and clients began working collaboratively to identify problems and develop solutions. According to Vice President and CFO Dave Burritt, "The machine, the engine, and financial products businesses have all benefited from the rigor of Six Sigma. Without question, we are in the best of times at Caterpillar and the improvements would have been much less without Six Sigma."[39]

Six Sigma and Supply Chain Management

By now, the supply chain management outcomes of better customer service, lower costs, and higher quality should be starting to sound familiar. To sustain and improve competitiveness, firms must perform better in these areas than their competitors. Through better process integration and communication, trading partners along the supply chain realize how poor-quality products and services can cause negative chain reactions to take place, such as greater levels of safety stock throughout the supply chain, lost time and productivity due to product and component repairs, the increased costs of customer returns and warranty repairs, and, finally, loss of customers and damage to reputations.

The impact of poor quality on the supply chain and potential damage to a firm's reputation can be illustrated by the problems toy-maker Mattel had to deal with regarding the Chinese-made toys it was selling in many of its global markets. In August 2007, Mattel announced it was pulling 9 million Chinese-made Barbies, Polly Pockets, and other toys off store shelves, only two weeks after it had already pulled 1.5 million Fisher-Price infant toys off shelves. The quality problems with their toys included use of lead paint and tiny magnets that could be swallowed. At the time of this writing, one U.S. child had died and 19 others had needed surgery after swallowing magnets. Mattel took out full-page ads in the *New York Times*, *Wall Street Journal*, and *USA Today* to announce it was working to address safety concerns. It also began offering replacement products. Obviously, the cost to Mattel in terms of dollars and loss of reputation was very high.[40] Thus, the impact of better quality can be felt throughout the supply chain and ultimately by end customers.

Six Sigma is an enterprise-wide philosophy, encompassing suppliers, employees, and customers. It emphasizes a commitment by the organization to strive toward excellence in the production of services and products that customers want. Firms implementing a Six Sigma program have made a proactive decision to understand, meet, and then strive to exceed customer expectations; and this is the overriding objective in all Six Sigma programs. Since Six Sigma is all about pleasing the customer, a very straightforward customer-oriented definition of quality can be employed here: "The ability to satisfy customer expectations." This definition is echoed by the American Society for Quality when it states: "Quality is defined by the customer through his/her satisfaction." In this sense, both a fast-food hamburger and a steakhouse chopped sirloin sandwich can be considered to possess equally high quality, if they meet or exceed the expectations of their customers.

In a supply chain setting, quality is exemplified by a machine tool manufacturer identifying its industrial customers, determining their tooling needs and requirements, and then setting out to design, modify, or improve processes to meet those requirements and make the sale. With worldwide competition expanding, the desire to practice Six Sigma can be seen in all industries and all sizes of organizations.

In countries such as China and India, where competitive advantage has largely been due to their low cost of labor, many firms are beginning to pay more attention to quality management when preparing to compete in global markets. The Automotive Industry Action Group (a group of U.S. auto-manufacturing-firm representatives who meet to discuss business problems) has recently joined with Michigan-based

© 1999 Ted Goff

"Courtesy, up 25%. Effort, up 25%. Quality, up 25%. Customer retention, up 250%."

quality consulting firm Omnex to offer Six Sigma and lean training to auto manufacturing suppliers in China, India, and Thailand.[41]

Six Sigma programs aim to assure that the firm is capable of satisfying customers now and into the future. Good supply chain trading partners use Six Sigma methods to assure that their own suppliers are performing well, and that their customers' needs are being met. Ultimately, this translates into end consumers getting what they want, when they want it, for a price they are willing to pay. While Six Sigma programs tend to vary somewhat in the details from one organization to another, all tend to employ a mix of qualitative and quantitative elements aimed at achieving customer satisfaction. The most common elements addressed in most Six Sigma programs are discussed in the following section.

The Elements of Six Sigma

The philosophy and tools of Six Sigma are borrowed from a number of resources including quality professionals, such as W. Edwards Deming, Philip Crosby, and Joseph Juran; the Malcolm Baldrige National Quality Award and the International Organization for Standardization's ISO 9000 and 14000 families of standards; Motorola and General Electric practices; and TQM, along with **statistical process control (SPC)** techniques originally developed by Walter Shewhart. From these resources, a number of commonly used elements emerge that are collectively known today as Six Sigma quality. A few of the quality resources are discussed next, followed by a brief look at the qualitative and quantitative elements of Six Sigma.

Deming's Contributions

W. Edwards Deming's Theory of Management essentially holds that since managers are responsible for creating the systems that make organizations work, they must also be held responsible for the organization's problems. Thus, only management can fix problems, through application of the right tools, resources, encouragement, commitment, and cultural change. Deming's Theory of Management was the centerpiece of his teachings around the world (Deming died in 1993) and includes his Fourteen Points for Management, shown in Table 8.6.

Deming's Fourteen Points are all related to Six Sigma principles, covering qualitative as well as quantitative aspects of quality. He was convinced that quality was the outcome of an all-encompassing philosophy geared toward personal and organizational growth. He argued that growth occurs through top management vision, support, and value placed on all employees and suppliers. Value is demonstrated through investments in training, equipment, continuing education, support for finding and fixing problems, and teamwork both within the firm and with suppliers. Use of statistical methods, elimination of inspected-in quality, and elimination of cost-based decisions are also required to improve quality. Today, Deming's work lives on through the Deming Institute, and companies all over the world have adopted Deming's Fourteen Points as an integral part of their firm's operating philosophy.

Crosby's Contributions

Philip Crosby, a former vice president of quality at New York-based manufacturer ITT Corporation, was a highly sought-after quality consultant during the latter part of his life and wrote several books concerning quality and striving for zero defects,

Table 8.6	Deming's Fourteen Points for Management
1. **Create constancy of purpose toward improvement of product and service.**	Define values, mission, and vision to provide long-term direction for management and employees. Invest in innovation, training, and research.
2. **Adopt the new philosophy.**	Adversarial management–worker relationships and quota work systems no longer work in today's work environment. Management must work toward cooperative relationships aimed at increasing quality and customer satisfaction.
3. **Cease dependence on inspection to improve quality.**	Inspecting products does not create value or prevent poor quality. Workers must use statistical process control to improve quality.
4. **End the practice of awarding business on the basis of price.**	Purchases should not be based on low cost; buyers should develop long-term relationships with a few good suppliers.
5. **Constantly improve the production and service system.**	Significant quality improvement comes from continual incremental improvements that reduce variation and eliminate common causes.
6. **Institute training on the job.**	Employees should receive adequate job training and statistical process control training.
7. **Institute leadership.**	Managers are leaders, not supervisors. They help, coach, encourage, and provide guidance to employees.
8. **Drive out fear, so that everyone may work effectively.**	A supportive organization will drive out fear of reprisal, failure, change, the unknown, and loss of control. Fear causes short-term thinking.
9. **Break down barriers between departments.**	Teamwork focuses workers, breaks down departmental barriers, and allows workers to see the big picture.
10. **Eliminate slogans, exhortations, and targets for the workforce.**	Slogans and motivational programs are directed toward workers and they are not the cause of poor quality. These cause worker frustration when slogans do not work.
11. **Eliminate quotas and MBO and substitute leadership.**	Quotas are short-term thinking and cause fear. Numerical goals have no value unless methods are in place that will allow them to be achieved.
12. **Remove barriers to pride of workmanship.**	Too often, workers are given boring tasks with no proper tools, and performance is appraised by supervisors who know nothing about the job.
13. **Institute a vigorous program of education and self-improvement.**	All employees should be encouraged to further broaden their skills through continuing education.
14. **Put everyone to work to accomplish the transformation.**	Management must have the courage to break with tradition and explain to a critical mass of people that the changes will involve everyone. Management must speak with one voice.

most notably *Quality Is Free* and *Quality Without Tears* (he died in 2001). His findings about quality improvement programs as discussed in *Quality Is Free* were that these programs invariably more than paid for themselves. In *Quality Without Tears*, Crosby discussed his four Absolutes of Quality, shown in Table 8.7. Industrial giants such as IBM and General Motors have benefited greatly from implementing Crosby's ideas. Crosby emphasized commitment to quality improvement by top management, development of a prevention system, employee education and training, and continuous assessment—all very similar to the teachings of Deming.

Juran's Contributions

Joseph Juran, founder of The Juran Institute, helped to write and develop the *Quality Control Handbook* in 1951, now in its fifth edition, and wrote a number of other books on quality. Born in 1904, Juran was actively writing and overseeing his Juran

Table 8.7	Crosby's Four Absolutes of Quality	
1. **The definition of quality is conformance to requirements.**	Adopt a do-it-right-the-first-time attitude. Never sell a faulty product to a customer.	
2. **The system of quality is prevention.**	Use SPC as part of the prevention system. Make corrective changes when problems occur. Take preventive action.	
3. **The performance standard is zero defects.**	Insist on zero defects from suppliers and workers. Education, training, and commitment will eliminate defects.	
4. **The measure of quality is the price of nonconformance.**	The price of nonconformance is the cost of poor quality. Implementing a prevention program will eliminate this.	

Foundation in New York right up until his death in February 2008. "My job of contributing to the welfare of my fellow man," Juran wrote, "is the great unfinished business."[42]

Like Deming, Juran helped to engineer the Japanese quality revolution starting in the 1950s. Juran, similar to both Crosby and Deming, strived to introduce new types of thinking about quality to business managers and employees, but Juran's recommendations varied somewhat from those of Crosby and Deming. He is recognized as the person who brought the human element to the practice of quality improvement. Juran did not seek cultural change but sought to work within the system to instigate change. He felt that to get managers to listen, your message had to be spoken in dollars. To get workers to listen, you had to speak the language of things. So, he advocated the determination of the costs of poor quality to get the attention of managers, and the use of statistical control methods for workers.

Juran's recommendations are focused on his Quality Trilogy, as shown in Table 8.8. He found in his dealings with companies that most have given priority to quality control but paid little attention to quality planning and improvement. Thus, while both Japan and the U.S. were using quality control techniques since the 1950s, Japan's overall quality levels grew faster than those of the U.S. because Japan's quality planning and improvement efforts were much greater.

Many characteristics though, of the Deming, Crosby, and Juran philosophies are quite similar. All three focus on top management commitment, the need for continuous improvement efforts, training, and the use of statistical methods for quality control purposes.

Table 8.8	Juran's Quality Trilogy	
1. **Quality planning.**	The process of preparing to meet quality goals. Identify internal and external customers, determine their needs, and develop products that satisfy those needs. Managers set short- and long-term goals, establish priorities, compare results to previous plans.	
2. **Quality control.**	The process of meeting quality goals during operations. Determine what to control, establish measurements and standards of performance, measure performance, interpret the difference between the actual measure and the standard, and take action if necessary.	
3. **Quality improvement.**	The process of breaking through to unprecedented levels of performance. Show the need for improvement, identify projects for improvement, organize support for the projects, diagnose causes, implement remedies for the causes, provide control to maintain improvements.	

The Malcolm Baldrige National Quality Award

The **U.S. Baldrige Quality Award** was signed into law on August 20, 1987, and is named in honor of then U.S. President Reagan's Secretary of Commerce, who helped draft an early version of the award, and who was tragically killed in a rodeo accident shortly before the award was enacted. The objectives of the award, given only to U.S. firms, are to stimulate American firms to improve quality and productivity, to recognize firms for their quality achievements, to establish criteria and guidelines so that organizations can independently evaluate their quality improvement efforts, and to provide examples and guidance to those companies wanting to learn how to manage and improve quality and productivity.

The Baldrige Award is administered by the National Institute of Standards and Technology (NIST) and is presented by the President of the U.S. each year, to U.S. small businesses, service and manufacturing firms, and education, healthcare, and nonprofit organizations that are judged to be outstanding in seven areas—leadership; strategic planning; customer and market focus; measurement, analysis, and knowledge management; human resource focus; process management; and results. Up to three awards can be given annually in each of the categories. Table 8.9 shows the Baldrige Award winners from 1988 through 2006. At the time of this writing, there were no Nonprofit category winners, so this category is not shown in the table.[43]

All Baldrige Award applications are reviewed by quality professional volunteers and scored in the seven categorical areas listed above. Finalists are visited wherein performance is reassessed and final scores tabulated, with the winners selected from this group. Organizations are encouraged by NIST to obtain a copy of the Baldrige Award criteria and perform self-assessments using the form and its point scoring guidelines. Completing a self-assessment process using the Baldrige Award criteria identifies a firm's strengths and weaknesses and aids the firm in implementing various quality and productivity improvement initiatives. Reviewing the criteria reveals a number of areas consistent with the Six Sigma philosophy and, to date, thousands of firms have requested copies of the application criteria.

The ISO 9000 and 14000 Families of Management Standards

In 1946, delegates from 25 countries met in London and decided to create a new international organization, with the objective "to facilitate the international coordination and unification of industrial standards." The new organization, called the International Organization for Standardization or ISO, officially began operations on February 23, 1947. Now located in Geneva Switzerland, the ISO today has over 155 member countries.[44]

ISO standards are voluntary, are developed in response to market demand, and are based on consensus among the member countries. This ensures widespread applicability of the standards. ISO considers evolving technology and member interests by requiring a review of its standards at least every 5 years to decide whether they should be maintained, updated, or withdrawn. In this way, ISO standards retain their position as state of the art.

ISO standards are technical agreements which provide the framework for compatible technology worldwide. Developing consensus on this international scale is a major operation. In all, there are some 3000 ISO technical groups with approximately 50,000

| Table 8.9 | Malcolm Baldrige National Quality Award Recipients, 1988–2006 | | | | |

YEAR	SMALL BUSINESS	MANUFACTURING	SERVICE	EDUCATION	HEALTHCARE
1988	Globe Metallurgical	Motorola Westinghouse – Comm. Nuclear Fuel Div.			
1989		Xerox – Bus. Products and Sys. Milliken & Co.			
1990	Wallace Co.	Cadillac Motor Car Co. IBM – Rochester	FedEx Corp.		
1991	Marlow Industries	Solectron Corp. Zytec Corp.			
1992	Granite Rock Co.	AT&T – Network Sys. Texas Instruments – Def. Sys. & Elec. Grp.	AT&T – Univ. Card Svcs. The Ritz-Carlton Hotel Co.		
1993	Ames Rubber Corp.	Eastman Chemical Co.			
1994	Wainwright Indus.		AT&T – Consumer Comm. Svcs.		
1995		Armstrong World Ind. – Bldg. Prod. Ops. Corning – Telecomm. Prod. Div.			
1996	Custom Research Trident Precis. Mfg.	ADAC Laboratories	Dana Comm. Cred.		
1997		3M – Dental Prod. Div. Solectron	Merrill Lynch Cred. Corp. Xerox – Bus. Svcs.		
1998	Texas Nameplate	Boeing – Airlift and Tanker Programs Solar Turbines			
1999	Sunny Fresh Foods	ST Microelectronics–Region Americas	BI The Ritz-Carlton Hotel Co.		
2000	Los Alamos Nat'l. Bank	Dana Corp. – Spicer Driveshaft Div. KARLEE Co.	Operations Mgt. Int'l.		
2001	Pal's Sudden Svc.	Clarke American Checks		Chugach Sch. Dist. Pearl River Sch. Dist. Univ. of Wisc.-Stout	
2002	Branch-Smith – Printing Div.	Motorola – Comm., Gov't., and Indus. Sol. Sector			SSM HealthCare
2003	Stoner, Inc.	Medrad, Inc.	Boeing Aero. Support Caterpillar Fin. Svcs. Corp.	Comm. Consol. Sch. Dist. 15	Baptist Hosp., Inc. St. Luke's Hosp. of Kan. City
2004	Texas Nameplate	The Bama Cos., Inc.		K. W. Monfort Coll. of Bus.	R. W. Johnson Univ. Hosp.
2005	Park Place Lexus	Sunny Fresh Foods	DynMcDermott Petroleum Ops. Co.	Jenks Public Schools Richland College	Bronson Meth. Hosp.
2006	MESA Products		Premier, Inc.		N. Miss. Medical Ctr.

experts participating annually to develop ISO standards. To date, ISO has published over 16,000 international standards. Examples include standards for agriculture and construction, mechanical engineering, medical devices, and information technology developments, such as the digital coding of audio–visual signals for multimedia applications.

In 1987, ISO adopted the ISO 9000 series of five international quality standards, revised them in 1994, and again in 2000. The standards have been adopted in the U.S. by the American National Standards Institute (ANSI) and the American Society for Quality (ASQ) and also by Japan. To date, over 500,000 organizations worldwide have received ISO 9000 certifications. The standards apply to all types of businesses. In many cases worldwide, companies will not buy from suppliers who do not possess an ISO 9000 certification.

After the rapid acceptance of ISO 9000, and the increase of environmental standards around the world, ISO assessed the need for international environmental management standards. They formed an advisory group on the environment in 1991, which eventually led to the adoption of the ISO 14000 family of international environmental management standards in 1997. To date, more than 300,000 organizations have become ISO 14000 certified. The most recently adopted 14000 standards are the ISO 14064 standard for greenhouse gas accounting and verification and the ISO 14065 standard, which provides the requirements for the accreditation of bodies that carry out these activities. These standards will help organizations address climate change and support emissions trading schemes.

Together, the ISO 9000 and 14000 families of certifications are the most widely used standards of ISO, with organizations in over 160 countries holding one or both types of certifications. The standards that have earned the ISO 9000 and ISO 14000 families a worldwide reputation are known as "generic management system standards," meaning that the same standards can be applied to any type of organization. Generic also means that no matter what the organization's scope of activity, if it wants to establish a quality management system or an environmental management system, then relevant standards of the ISO 9000 or ISO 14000 families provide the requirements.

The DMAIC Improvement Cycle

Figure 8.4 shows the five-step DMAIC improvement cycle, an important element of Six Sigma outlining the steps necessary to drive process improvement. The cycle can be applied to any process or project, both in services and manufacturing firms. The improvement cycle begins with customer requirements and then seeks to analyze and modify processes or projects so they meet those requirements. Each of the steps is described here:

1. *Define.* Identify customers and their service or product requirements critical to achieving customer satisfaction (also known as **critical-to-quality (CTQ) characteristics**). Identify any gaps between the CTQ characteristics and process outputs. Where gaps exist, create Six Sigma projects to alleviate the gaps.

2. *Measure.* Prepare a data-collection plan to quantify process performance. Determine what to measure for each process gap and how to measure it. Use **check sheets** to organize measurements.

3. *Analyze.* Perform a process analysis using the performance data collected. Use **Pareto charts** and **fishbone diagrams** to identify the root causes of the process variations or defects.

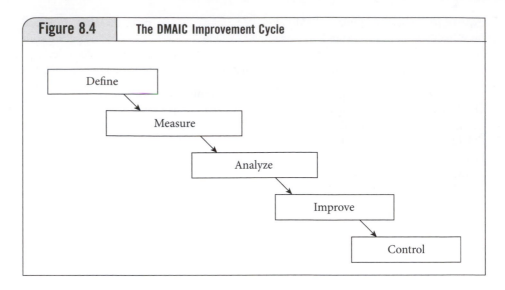

| Figure 8.4 | The DMAIC Improvement Cycle |

4. *Improve.* Design an improvement plan, then remove the causes of process variation by implementing the improvement plan. This will require modifying, redesigning, or reengineering the process. Document the improvement and confirm that process gaps have been significantly reduced or eliminated.

5. *Control.* Monitor the process to assure that performance levels are maintained. Design and use statistical process control charts to continuously monitor and control the process. When performance gaps are once again identified, repeat Steps 1–5.

Using the DMAIC improvement cycle allows the firm to continuously monitor and improve processes that are keys to customer satisfaction. By concentrating on these key processes and the CTQ characteristics, firms can make large and radical improvements in processes, products, and customer satisfaction.

Six Sigma Training Levels

In order to develop and successfully complete Six Sigma improvement projects, specific training in quality improvement methods is required. A number of organizations offer various training courses and certifications in Six Sigma methods, and the somewhat standardized training levels are summarized in Table 8.10. Global manufacturing giant GE began using Six Sigma in the 1980s, and today, all GE employees are trained in the strategy, statistical tools, and techniques of Six Sigma. Eventually, all employees earn their Six Sigma Green Belt designations. Training courses are offered at various levels including basic Six Sigma awareness seminars, team training, Master Black Belt, Black Belt, and Green Belt training.[45] Several of the quantitative tools of Six Sigma are discussed next.

The Statistical Tools of Six Sigma

Flow Diagrams

Also called **process diagrams** or **process maps**, this tool is the necessary first step to evaluating any manufacturing or service process. **Flow diagrams** use annotated boxes representing process action elements and ovals representing wait periods, connected

Table 8.10	General Description of Six Sigma Training Levels[46]
TRAINING LEVELS	**DESCRIPTION**
Yellow Belt	Basic understanding of the Six Sigma Methodology and the tools within the DMAIC problem-solving process, including process mapping, cause-and-effect tools, simple data analysis, and process improvement and control methods. Role is to be an effective team member on process improvement project teams.
Green Belt	A specially trained team member allowed to work on small, carefully defined Six Sigma projects, requiring less than a Black Belt's full-time commitment. Has enhanced problem-solving skills, and can gather data and execute experiments in support of a Black Belt project. They spend approximately 25% of their time on Six Sigma projects of their own or in support of Black Belt projects.
Black Belt	Has a thorough knowledge of Six Sigma philosophies and principles. Exhibits team leadership, understands team dynamics, and assigns team members with roles and responsibilities. Has a complete understanding of the DMAIC model in accordance with the Six Sigma principles, a basic knowledge of lean concepts, and can quickly identify "non-value-added" activities. Knowledge and use of advanced statistics, coaches successful project teams, and provides group assessments. Identifies projects and selects project team members, acts as an internal consultant, mentors Green Belts and project teams, provides feedback to management.
Master Black Belt	A proven mastery of process variability reduction, waste reduction, and growth principles. and can effectively present training at all levels. Challenges conventional wisdom through the demonstration of the application of the Six Sigma methodology, and provides guidance and knowledge to lead and change organizations. Directs Black and Green Belts on the performance of their Six Sigma projects and also provides guidance and direction to management teams regarding the technical proficiency of Black Belt candidates, the selection of projects, and the overall health of a Six Sigma program.

by arrows to show the flow of products or customers through the process. Once a process or series of processes is mapped out, potential problem areas can be identified and further evaluated for excess inventories, wait times, and capacity problems. An example of a customer flow diagram is shown in Figure 8.5. Using the diagram, managers can then be observing and analyzing each process action and wait period element for potential problems.

Check Sheets

Check sheets allow users to determine frequencies for specific problems. For the restaurant example shown in Figure 8.5, managers could make a list of potential problem areas based on experience and observation, and then direct employees to keep count of each problem on check sheets for a given period of time (long enough to allow for problem discrimination). At the end of the data-collection period, problem areas can be reviewed and compared. Figure 8.6 shows a typical check sheet that might be used in a restaurant.

Pareto Charts

Pareto charts, useful for many applications, are based on the work of Vilfredo Pareto, a nineteenth-century economist. For our purposes here, the charts are useful for presenting data in an organized fashion, indicating process problems from most to least severe. It only makes sense when utilizing a firm's resources, to work on solving the most severe problems first (Pareto theory applied here suggests that most of a firm's problem "events" are accounted for by just a few of the problems). As shown in Figure 8.6, the top two problems account for about 40 percent of the instances where problems were observed. Figure 8.7 shows two Pareto charts for the problems counted in

Figure 8.5	Process Map for Customer Flow at a Restaurant

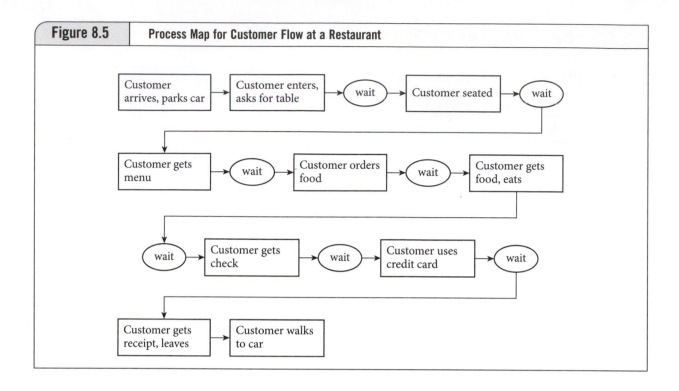

Figure 8.6	Problem Check Sheet for a Restaurant

Problem	Mon.	Tues.	Wed.	Thurs.	Fri.	Sat.	Sun.	Totals	% of Total
Long wait	//////	/////	////////	//////	/////////	//////////	////	48	26.5
Cold food		//	/	/	///	//		9	5.0
Bad food	//	/	///		/	////		11	6.1
Wrong food	/////	//	/	//	/////	///	/	19	10.5
Bad server	//////	///	/////	/	//////	//	/	24	13.3
Bad table		/	//		/	///	/	8	4.4
Room temp.			//	///	/////	/////		15	8.3
Too expensive	/	//	/	/	///	///		11	6.1
No parking			//		/////	///////		14	7.7
Wrong change	//////	/	////		////	///		18	9.9
Other		/	//			/		4	2.2
Totals	26	18	31	14	42	43	7	181	100

Figure 8.6. Note that we could look at the total problem events either from a problem-type or day-of-the-week perspective and see that *long wait* and *bad server* are the two most troublesome problems, while Saturdays and Fridays are when the most problem events occur. Finding and implementing solutions for these two problems would significantly decrease the number of problem events at the restaurant.

| Figure 8.7 | Pareto Charts for Restaurant Problems |

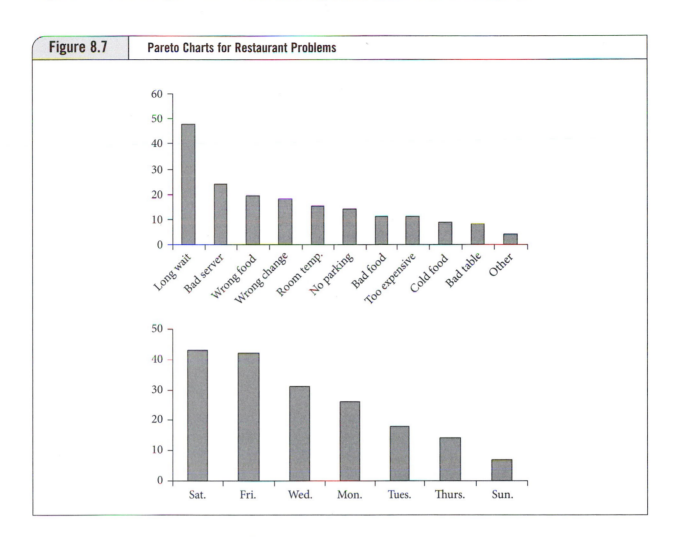

Cause-and-Effect Diagrams

Once a problem has been identified, **cause-and-effect diagrams** (also called fishbone diagrams or **Ishikawa diagrams**) can be used to aid in brainstorming and isolating the causes of a problem. Figure 8.8 illustrates a cause-and-effect diagram for the most troublesome *long wait* problem of Figure 8.7. The problem is shown at the front end of the diagram. Each of the four diagonals of the diagram represents potential groups of causes. The four groups of causes shown, Material, Machine, Methods, and Man-power, or the 4 Ms, are the standard classifications of problem causes and represent a very thorough list for problem–cause analyses. In almost all cases, problem causes will be in one or more of these four areas.

Typically, Six Sigma team members will gather and brainstorm causes for a problem in these four areas. Each branch on the four diagonals represents one potential cause. Subcauses are also part of the brainstorming process and are shown as smaller branches attached to each of the primary causes. Breaking a problem down like this into its causes and subcauses allows workers to then go back to the process and determine the relative significance of each cause and subcause using more specific checklists and Pareto charts once again. Eventually, the firm begins working to eliminate

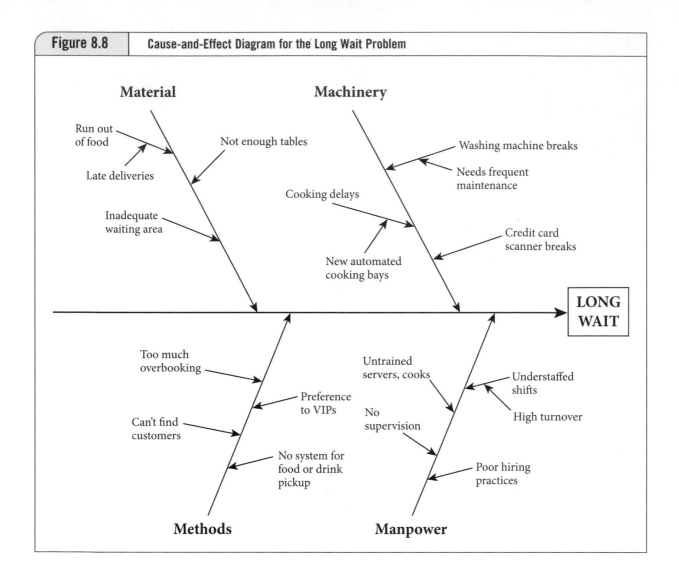

Figure 8.8 | **Cause-and-Effect Diagram for the Long Wait Problem**

the causes of the problem, starting with the most significant causes and subcauses, until most of the problem's impact disappears.

A properly thought-out cause-and-effect diagram can be a very powerful tool for use in Six Sigma efforts. Without its use, workers and management risk trying to eliminate causes that have very little to do with the problem at hand or working on problems that are quite minor compared to other, more significant problems. Once most of the problems' causes are identified and solved, the process should be back under control and meeting customer requirements. At this point, firms can design and begin using statistical process control charts, discussed next.

Statistical Process Control

A necessary part of any quality improvement effort, statistical process control (SPC) allows firms to visually monitor process performance, compare the performance to desired levels or standards, and take corrective steps quickly before process variabilities get out of control and damage products, services, and customer relationships. Once a process is working correctly, firms gather process performance data, create control charts to monitor process variabilities, and then collect and plot sample measurements of the process over time. The means of these sample measures are plotted on the control charts. If the sample means fall within acceptable limits and appear *normally distributed* around the desired measurement, we say the process is in *statistical control* and the process is permitted to continue; sample measurements and control chart plots also continue. When a sample plot falls out of the acceptable limits or when the plots no longer appear normally distributed around the desired measurement, the process is deemed to be *out of control.* The process is then stopped, problems and their causes are identified, and the causes are eliminated as described earlier. Control chart plots can then resume.

Control charts are graphic representations of process performance over time, showing the desired measurement (the center line of the control chart) and the process's upper and lower control limits. This visual aid makes it very easy for operators or other workers to plot data and compare performance over time.

Variations

Variations in process measurements can be either **natural variations** or **assignable variations.** All processes are affected by these variations, and environmental noise or natural variations are to be expected. When only natural variations are present, the process is in statistical control. Assignable variations are those that can be traced to a specific cause (such as the causes shown in Figure 8.8). These assignable variations are created by causes that can be identified and eliminated and thus become the objective of statistical process control efforts.

Samples

Because of the presence of variations in process measures, samples of data are collected and their means are then plotted onto control charts. Sample measures can be either **variable data** or **attribute data,** and each requires a different type of control chart. Variable data are continuous, such as weight, time, and length (as in the weight of a box of cereal, the time to serve a customer, or the length of a steel girder). Attribute data indicate the presence of some attribute such as color, satisfaction, workability, or beauty (for instance, determining whether or not a car was painted the right color, if a customer liked the meal, if the light bulb worked, or if the dress was pretty).

Variable data samples are shown as an average of the sample's measures (for instance, an average of 12.04 ounces in five boxes of cereal), whereas attribute data are shown as the percent defectives within a sample (for instance, 10 percent, or 0.10 of the light bulb sample that did not work). Let us look at the two types of control charts next.

Variable Data Control Charts

When measuring and plotting variable process data, two types of control charts are needed: the $\bar{x}$-**chart** and the **R-chart.** The $\bar{x}$-chart is used to track the central tendency of the sample means, while the R-chart is used to track sample ranges, or the variation of the measurements within each sample. A perfect process would have sample means equal to the desired measure and sample ranges equal to zero. It is necessary to view *both of these charts* in unison, since a sample mean might look fine, even though two of the sample measures might be far from the desirable measure, making the sample range very high. It could also be the case that the sample range looks fine (all measures are quite close to one another), even though all sample measures are far from the desirable measure, making the sample mean look bad. For variable data then, both the x̄-chart and the R-chart must show that the samples are in control before the process itself is considered in control.

Constructing the $\bar{x}$-Chart and the R-Chart

The first step in constructing any control chart is to gather data (provided the process is already in control and working well). Typically about twenty-five or thirty samples of size five to ten are collected, spaced out over a period of time. Then for each sample, the mean ($\bar{x}$) and the range (R) are calculated. Next, the *overall mean* ($\bar{\bar{x}}$) and the *average range* ($\bar{R}$) of all the samples are calculated. The $\bar{\bar{x}}$ and $\bar{R}$ measures become the center lines (the desired measures) of their respective control charts. Example 8.2 provides the data used to illustrate the calculation of the center lines of the $\bar{x}$-chart and the R-chart. The formulas used to calculate the center lines $\bar{\bar{x}}$ and $\bar{R}$ are

Example 8.2   Variable Control Chart Data for Soup Cans at Hayley Girl Soup Co.

The Hayley Girl Soup Co., a soup manufacturer, has collected process data in order to construct control charts to use in their canning facility. They collected 24 samples of 4 12 oz. cans each hour over a 24-hour period, and the data is shown below for each sample:

HOUR	1	2	3	4	$\bar{x}$	R
1	12	12.2	11.7	11.6	11.88	0.6
2	11.5	11.7	11.6	12.3	11.78	0.8
3	11.9	12.2	12.1	12	12.05	0.3
4	12.1	11.8	12.1	11.7	11.93	0.4
5	12.2	12.3	11.7	11.9	12.03	0.6
6	12.1	11.9	12.3	12.2	12.13	0.4
7	12	11.7	11.6	12.1	11.85	0.5
8	12	12.1	12.2	12.3	12.15	0.3
9	11.8	11.9	12	12	11.93	0.2
10	12.1	11.9	11.8	11.7	11.88	0.3
11	12.1	12	12.1	11.9	12.03	0.2
12	11.9	11.9	11.7	11.8	11.83	0.2
13	12	12	11.8	12.1	11.98	0.3
14	12.1	11.9	12	11.7	11.93	0.4
15	12	12	11.7	11.2	11.73	0.8
16	12.1	12	12	11.9	12.00	0.2
17	12.1	12.2	12	11.9	12.05	0.3
18	12.2	12	11.7	11.8	11.93	0.5
19	12	12.1	12.3	12	12.10	0.3
20	12	12.2	11.9	12	12.03	0.3
21	11.9	11.8	12.1	12	11.95	0.3
22	12.1	11.8	11.9	12	11.95	0.3
23	12.1	12	11.9	11.9	11.98	0.2
24	12	12.3	11.7	12	12.00	0.6
MEANS					**11.96**	**0.39**

$$\bar{\bar{x}} = \frac{\sum_{i=1}^{k} \bar{x}_i}{k} \text{ and } \bar{R} = \frac{\sum_{i=1}^{k} R_i}{k},$$

where k indicates the number of samples and i indicates the specific sample.

For the data shown in Example 8.2 for the Hayley Girl Soup Co., we see that $\bar{\bar{x}} = 11.96$ and $\bar{R} = 0.39$. If these measures are seen as acceptable by Hayley Girl Soup Co., then they can use these to construct their control charts. These means are also used to calculate the upper and lower control limits for the two control charts. The formulas are

$$\text{UCL}_{\bar{x}} = \bar{\bar{x}} + A_2\bar{R} \text{ and } \text{LCL}_{\bar{x}} = \bar{\bar{x}} - A_2\bar{R}$$

$$\text{UCL}_R = D_4\bar{R} \text{ and } \text{LCL}_R = D_3\bar{R},$$

where the A_2, D_3, and D_4 are constants based on the size of each sample, and are shown in Table 8.11 (the constants used are based on an assumption that the sampling distribution is normal, and that the control limits are ± 3.0 standard deviations from the population mean, which contains 99.73 percent of the sampling distribution). The constants for various sample sizes are shown in Table 8.11.

Using the data in Example 8.2 and Table 8.11 for a sample size of four, we can determine the upper and lower control limits for both the $\bar{x}$-chart and the R-chart for the Hayley Girl Soup Co. variable data:

$$\text{UCL}_{\bar{x}} = \bar{\bar{x}} + A_2\bar{R} = 11.96 + 0.729(0.39) = 12.24 \text{ ounces}$$

$$\text{LCL}_{\bar{x}} = \bar{\bar{x}} - A_2\bar{R} = 11.96 - 0.729(0.39) = 11.68 \text{ ounces}$$

and

$$\text{UCL}_R = D_4\bar{R} = 2.282(0.39) = 0.89 \text{ ounces}$$

$$\text{LCL}_R = D_3\bar{R} = 0(0.39) = 0 \text{ ounces}$$

Next, we can use the means and control limits to construct our two control charts. In Figure 8.9, we have plotted the original data sample means and ranges onto the two variable data control charts, showing the center lines and the control limits. From these plots, it appears that the process is indeed in statistical control, and the Hayley Girl Soup Co. can begin using these charts to monitor the canning process. If the process appears out of control on either chart, the control charts

Table 8.11	Constants for Computing Control Chart Limits $(\pm 3\sigma)$[47]		
SAMPLE SIZE, n	MEAN FACTOR, A_2	UCL, D_4	LCL, D_3
2	1.88	3.268	0
3	1.023	2.574	0
4	0.729	2.282	0
5	0.577	2.115	0
6	0.483	2.004	0
7	0.419	1.924	0.076
8	0.373	1.864	0.136
9	0.337	1.816	0.184
10	0.308	1.777	0.223

Figure 8.9	$\bar{x}$- and R-Charts for the Hayley Girl Soup Co.

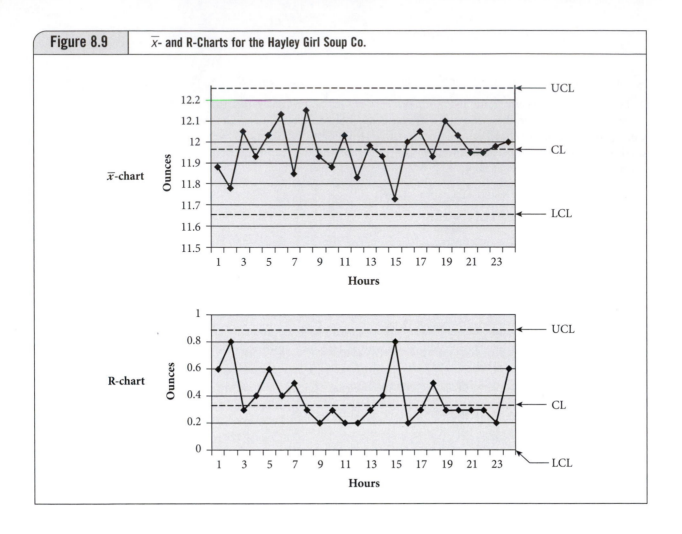

would not be useful and should be discarded until problems are identified and eliminated and the process is once again in statistical control.

Once a good set of control charts have been created and samples from the process are being statistically monitored, the following steps should be followed:

1. Collect samples of size 4–5 periodically (depending on the type of process and ease of data collection).
2. Plot the sample means on both control charts, monitoring whether or not the process is in control.
3. When the process appears out of control, use check sheets, Pareto charts, and fishbone diagrams to investigate causes and eliminate process variations.
4. Repeat Steps 1–3.

Attribute Data Control Charts

When collecting attribute data regarding whether or not a process is producing good or bad (nondefective or defective) output, use of $\bar{x}$- and R-charts no longer apply. In these cases, we use either **P-charts**, which monitor the *percent defective* in each sample, or **C-charts**, which count the *number of defects* per unit of output. Let us discuss each of these next.

Using and Constructing P-Charts

This is the most commonly used attribute control chart. If we use large sample sizes when collecting data samples, we can assume they are normally distributed and use the following formulas to calculate the center line ($\bar{P}$) and the upper and lower control limits for the P-chart:

$$\bar{P} = \frac{\Sigma_{i=1}^{k} P_i}{k},$$

where $\bar{P}$ is the mean fraction defective for all samples collected, k represents the number of samples, P is the fraction defective in one sample, and i represents the specific sample; and

$$\text{UCL}_P = \bar{P} + z\sigma_p$$
$$\text{LCL}_P = \bar{P} - z\sigma_p,$$

where z is the number of standard deviations from the mean (recall when $z = 3$, the control limits will contain 99.73 percent of all the sample data plots) and σ_P is the standard deviation of the sampling distribution. The sample standard deviation is calculated using

$$\sigma_P = \sqrt{\frac{(\bar{P})(1 - \bar{P})}{n}},$$

where n is the size of each sample. Example 8.3 provides the data used to determine $\bar{P}$, σ_P, and the control limits for the P-chart.

As shown in Example 8.3, $\bar{P} = 0.014$. Calculating σ_P, we get

$$\sigma_P = \sqrt{\frac{(0.014)(0.986)}{100}} = 0.012.$$

Now the control limits can be calculated (assuming we want limits containing 99.73 percent of the data points, or $z = 3$):

$$\text{UCL}_P = 0.014 + 3(0.012) = 0.05,$$

and

$$\text{LCL}_P = 0.014 - 3(0.012) = 0.$$

Note that the lower control limit is truncated at zero, as is the case in most P-charts. Figure 8.10 shows the P-chart for the CeeJay Lightbulb Co. with the fraction defectives from Example 8.3 Viewing the chart, we see that the process appears to be in control, since the data points are randomly dispersed around the centerline and about half the data points are on each side of the centerline. Thus, the CeeJay Lightbulb Co. can begin using this control chart to monitor their lightbulb quality.

Using C-Charts

When multiple errors can occur in a process resulting in a defective unit, then we can use C-charts to control the *number* of defects per unit of output. C-charts are useful when a number of mistakes or errors can occur per unit of output, but they

Example 8.3   Attribute Control Chart Data for the CeeJay Lightbulb Co.

The CeeJay Lightbulb Co. makes 100-watt light bulbs, and they have decided to begin monitoring their quality using a P-chart. So, over the past 30 days, they have collected and tested 100 bulbs each day. The chart below shows the fraction defectives for each sample and the overall average fraction defective, or $\bar{P}$.

DAY	FRACTION DEFECTIVE	DAY	FRACTION DEFECTIVE
1	0.01	16	0.04
2	0.02	17	0
3	0	18	0
4	0.03	19	0.01
5	0	20	0.03
6	0.01	21	0.02
7	0.04	22	0
8	0	23	0.01
9	0	24	0.02
10	0.02	25	0.01
11	0.02	26	0.03
12	0.03	27	0
13	0	28	0.02
14	0.04	29	0.01
15	0.01	30	0

$\bar{P} = 0.014$

occur infrequently. Examples can include a hotel stay, a printed textbook, or a construction project. The control limits for C-charts are based on the assumption of a Poisson probability distribution of the item of interest (commonly used when defects are infrequent). In this case, the distribution variance is equal to its mean. For C-charts then,

Figure 8.10   P-Chart for the CeeJay Lightbulb Co.

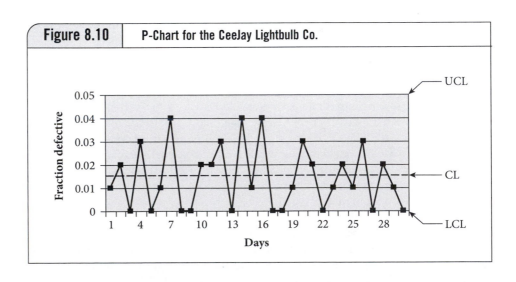

Example 8.4   Monitoring Editorial Defects at Klooster Publishing, Inc.

Eight editorial assistants are monitored for defects in the firm's printed work on a monthly basis. Over the past 30 days, a total number of 872 editorial mistakes were found. Computing the centerline and control limits, we find:

$$\bar{c} = \frac{872}{30} = 29.1 \text{ mistakes per day, and the}$$

$$UCL_c = 29.1 + 3\sqrt{29.1} = 45.3 \text{ and } LCL_c = 29.1 - 3\sqrt{29.1} = 12.9.$$

$\bar{c}$ = mean errors per unit of measure (and also the sample variance),

$\sqrt{\bar{c}}$ = sample standard deviation, and

$\bar{c} \pm 3\sqrt{\bar{c}}$ = control limits.

Example 8.4 can be used to illustrate the calculation of the C-chart's control limits. In the example, the units of measure are days, thus the average daily defects are 29.1 (the centerline and also the variance). The upper and lower control limits are 45.3 and 12.9, respectively. The Klooster Publishing Co. can now use the C-chart centerline and control limits based on the 30-day error data to monitor their daily editorial error rate.

Acceptance Sampling

When shipments of a product are received from suppliers, or before they are shipped to customers, samples can be taken from the batch of units and measured against some quality acceptance standard. The quality of the sample is then assumed to represent the quality of the entire shipment (particularly when shipments contain many units of product, sampling is far less time consuming than testing every unit to determine the overall quality of an incoming or outgoing shipment). Ideally, if strategic alliance members within a supply chain are using Six Sigma quality improvement tools to build quality into the products they provide, **acceptance sampling** can be eliminated and used only when new or nonalliance suppliers furnish products or materials to the firm. In these situations, acceptance sampling can be used to determine whether or not a shipment will be accepted, returned to the supplier, or used for billback purposes when defects are fixed or units are eliminated by the buyer.

One topic that arises is how big to make the test sample. One way to assure that the quality of the sample is identical to the quality of the entire shipment is to make the sample size equal to the size of the shipment (in other words, examine every unit). Since this is usually impractical, firms must assume the risk of incorrectly judging the quality of the shipment based on the size of the sample: the smaller the sample size, the greater the risk of incorrectly judging shipment quality.

There is a cost to both the supplier and buyer when incorrect quality assessments are made. When a buyer rejects a shipment of good-quality units because the sample quality level *did not* meet the acceptance standard, this is termed **producer's risk.** When this happens, it is called a **type-I error.** Conversely, when a buyer accepts a shipment of poor-quality units because the sample *did* meet the acceptance standard, this is termed **consumer's risk** and results in a **type-II error.** Obviously, trading partners wish to avoid or minimize the occurrence of both of these outcomes. To minimize type-I and type-II errors, buyers and sellers must derive an acceptable sampling plan by agreeing on unacceptable defect levels and a sample size big enough to result in minimal levels of type-I and type-II errors.

Statistical Process Control and Supply Chain Management

Ideally, long-standing strategic supply chain partners would not need to monitor their inbound and outbound product quality—quality would already be extremely high, and employees could spend their time in more productive pursuits. However, most processes and suppliers are not yet perfect, and the level of competition is so fierce in most industries that firms find they must continually be assessing and re-assessing process and product quality levels. Managers should identify processes that are critical to achieving the firm's objectives, decide how to monitor process performance, gather data and create the appropriate control charts, and create policies for collecting process samples and monitoring process and product quality over time. Managers must also work to create a culture where quality improvements are encouraged and employees are empowered to make the changes that will result in improved product and service quality.

SUMMARY

Supply chain management, lean production, and Six Sigma quality management make up a hierarchy for breakthrough competitive advantage. In order for supply chain management to reach its full potential and provide benefits to its members, trading partners must adopt a lean production philosophy. Similarly, the primary ingredient in the success of a lean production program is the use of Six Sigma thinking and improvement tools. There are a number of practices mentioned within each of these topics that overlap or are very similar such as top management support, workforce involvement, and continuous improvement. This is not surprising given the close ties between supply chain management, lean production, and Six Sigma. We have spent considerable time here, covering lean production and Six Sigma because of their critical importance in achieving successful supply chain management, and we hope you have gained an appreciation for the topics presented here.

KEY TERMS

acceptance sampling, 297

assignable variations, 291

attribute data, 291

C-charts, 295

carbon-neutral, 273

cause-and-effect diagrams, 289

channel integration, 262

check sheets, 285

consumer's risk, 297

control charts, 274

critical-to-quality (CTQ) characteristics, 285

defects per million opportunities (DPMO), 274

efficient consumer response (ECR), 257

fishbone diagrams, 285

five-Ss, 265

flow diagrams, 286

Ishikawa diagrams, 289

kaizen, 272

kanban, 259

keiretsu relationships, 257

lean layouts, 267

lean manufacturing, 257

lean production, 257

lean Six/lean Six Sigma, 277

lean supply chain relationships, 266

manufacturing cells, 268

muda, 259

natural variations, 291

opportunities for a defect to occur (OFD), 275

P-charts, 295

Pareto charts, 285

Poka-Yoke, 259

process diagrams, 286

process maps, 286

producer's risk, 297

production kanban, 270

pull system, 270

quick response (QR), 257

R-chart, 291

setups, 269

seven wastes, 264

sigma drift, 274

silo effect, 262

Six Sigma, 257

statistical process control (SPC), 280

Toyota Production System, 257

Type-I error, 297

Type-II error, 297

U.S. Baldrige Quality Award, 283

variable data, 291

virtual inventory, 269

withdrawal kanban, 270

$\overline{x}$-chart, 291

DISCUSSION QUESTIONS

1. Explain why lean production and Six Sigma are so important to successful supply chain management.

2. Briefly explain the primary concerns and objectives of lean production.

3. How is lean production associated with JIT?

4. What does the Toyota Production System have to do with JIT and lean production?

5. Looking at Table 8.1, which stage of supply chain management would you say Wal-Mart is in? How about a locally owned sandwich shop and the university you are attending?

6. What are the *seven wastes*, and can you discuss these in terms of a business you are familiar with?

7. Apply the five-Ss to improve how you should be completing your daily homework or study assignments.

8. What are the advantages and disadvantages of making small, frequent purchases from just a few suppliers? How do we overcome the disadvantages?

9. What are *work cells*, and why are they important in lean production?

10. Why should lean layouts be "visual"?

11. Reducing lot sizes and increasing setups are common practices in most lean production settings. Why?

12. What are *kanbans* and why are they used in lean production systems?

13. What is *kaizen*, and why is it so important for successful lean production?

14. Discuss the linkage between lean production and environmental sustainability.

15. Describe Six Sigma's origins and the main parties involved.

16. Describe the Lean Six Sigma approach.

17. Describe three ways by which your university could improve quality.

18. What does Deming's Theory of Management have to do with quality?

19. In looking at the list of Baldrige Award winners (Table 8.9), do you think these firms have high-quality products? How successful are they now?

20. In viewing the Baldrige Award's seven performance categories, how would your firm stack up in these areas (use the university or your most recent job if you are not currently employed).

21. What are the two most widely used ISO standards, and why are they so popular?

22. What are *critical-to-quality characteristics*, and how are they used in Six Sigma?

23. Construct a flow diagram of the registration process at your university.

24. Construct a cause-and-effect diagram for the following problem: The university course registration process is too long. Brainstorm some potential causes.

25. What are the two types of *process variation*, and which one does statistical process control seek to eliminate?

26. Describe *variable data* and explain why two control charts are needed to assure that the process is under control.

27. Can a process exhibit sample measurements that are all within the control limits and still be considered out of control? Explain.

28. What are some variable data and attribute data that could be collected to track the quality of education at your university?

29. How could P-charts be used in a manufacturing facility?

30. Can a process be considered in control but incapable of meeting design requirements? Explain.

31. If a goal of a supplier partnership is to eliminate acceptance sampling, then who does it?

INTERNET QUESTIONS

1. Go to the Baldrige Award Web site (http://www.quality.nist.gov) and find out what organizations have won the award since this book was published. Report on any new developments with respect to the Baldrige Award.

2. Why is not the International Organization for Standardization called the IOS? (*Hint:* There is a discussion of this topic at the ISO Web site, http://www.iso.ch.)

INFOTRAC QUESTIONS
Access http://academic.cengage.com/infotrac to answer the following questions:

1. Write a report on the Toyota Production System, concentrating particularly on the most recent developments at Toyota with regard to lean production.

2. Search on the terms "sustainability" and "supply chain management" and write a report on the importance of sustainability in the practice of supply chain management, using company examples.

3. Search on the term Lean Six and write a report on the latest uses of this method.

PROBLEMS

1. Jenkins Compressors uses a lean production assembly line to make its compressors. In one assembly area, the demand is 100 parts per 8-hour day. It uses a container that holds eight parts. It typically takes about 6 hours to round-trip a container from one work center to the next and back again. Jenkins also desires to hold 15 percent excess of this part in the system. How many containers should Jenkins Compressors be using?

2. Eakins Enterprises makes model boats, and it is switching to a lean manufacturing process. At one assembly area, Eakins is using one part container that holds 250 parts, and it wants the output to be approximately 100 finished parts per hour; they also desire a 10 percent safety stock for this part. How fast will the container have to make it through the system to accomplish this?

3. Darryl Seale, owner of Darryl's Bike Rentals, wants to start analyzing his company's quality. For each bike rental, there are four types of customer complaints: bike not working properly, bike wrong size, bike uncomfortable, and bike broken during operation. During the past week, his company rented 280 bikes. He received 26 total complaints.

   a. What is his company's DPMO for the past week?

   b. What is their Six Sigma operating level?

4. The following sample information was obtained by taking four doughnuts per hour for 12 hours from the Casey Bakery doughnut process and weighing them:

HOUR	WEIGHT (GRAMS)	HOUR	WEIGHT (GRAMS)
1	110, 105, 98, 100	7	89, 102, 101, 99
2	79, 102, 100, 104	8	100, 101, 98, 96
3	100, 102, 100, 96	9	98, 95, 101, 100
4	94, 98, 99, 101	10	99, 100, 97, 102
5	98, 104, 97, 100	11	102, 97, 100, 101
6	104, 97, 99, 100	12	98, 100, 100, 97

For the data shown above,

a. Find the $\bar{x}$ and R for each sample.

b. Find the $\bar{\bar{x}}$ and $\bar{R}$ for the 12 samples.

c. Find the 3-sigma UCL and LCL for the mean and range charts.

d. Does the process look to be in statistical control? Why?

5. Through process sampling of cooking and delivery times, Mary Jane's Pizzeria finds the mean of all samples to be 27.4 minutes, with an average sample range of 5.2 minutes. They tracked four deliveries per hour for 18 hours to obtain their samples.

a. Is this an example of variable or attribute sampling data?

b. Find the UCL and LCL for both the $\bar{x}$ and R charts.

6. Ten customers per hour were asked by the cashier at Stanley's Deli if they liked their meal, and the fraction that said "no" are shown below, for a 12-hour period.

HOUR	FRACTION DEFECTIVE	HOUR	FRACTION DEFECTIVE
1	0	7	0.1
2	0.2	8	0
3	0.4	9	0
4	0.1	10	0.2
5	0.1	11	0
6	0.2	12	0.1

For the data shown above, find

a. $\bar{P}$

b. σ_P.

c. The 3-sigma UCL and LCL.

d. Does customer satisfaction at Stanley's appear to be in statistical control? How could we improve the analysis?

7. Le Robert's Steakhouse tracks customer complaints every day and then follows up with their customers to resolve problems. For the past 30 days, they received a total of 22 complaints from unhappy customers. Using this information, calculate.

a. $\bar{c}$

b. The 3-sigma control limits.

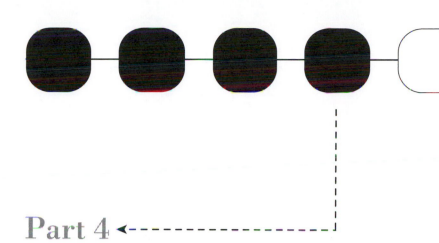

Part 4

Distribution Issues in Supply Chain Management

Chapter 9

DOMESTIC U.S. AND INTERNATIONAL LOGISTICS

Next-day service used to be a premium service, but now it's pretty much a minimal requirement of being in business. It's going to be more prevalent than it ever has been because shipper expectations are increasing.[1]

It used to be that you gave the freight to trucker A and waited to hear if it got there. But today, logistics providers will advise the shipper on how to best move the freight given the list of expected constraints and maybe they only move some of it but not all of it for the shipper.[2]

Learning Objectives

After completing this chapter, you should be able to

- Understand the strategic importance of logistics.
- Identify the various modes of transportation.
- Discuss the international aspects of logistics.
- Describe how logistics affects supply chain management.
- Examine and understand the interrelatedness of transportation, warehousing, and material handling.
- Identify a number of third-party logistics service providers.
- Summarize the important aspects of transportation regulation and deregulation.
- Describe the various reverse logistics activities.
- Discuss some of the e-commerce issues in logistics management.

Chapter Outline

Introduction

The Fundamentals of Transportation

Warehousing and Distribution

The Impacts of Logistics on Supply Chain Management

Logistics Management Issues

International Logistics

Reverse Logistics

Summary

Supply Chain Management in Action   *Logistics in China*

China's logistics landscape is a patchwork of astonishing progress and infuriating road-blocks. Just before Christmas, somewhere in Tianjin or Chongqing or almost any other major city in China for that matter, a truck was being loaded with parts destined for a factory else-where in the country. The factory managers worried about when the goods would arrive. They knew how much red tape they would have to wade through to get the parts they needed.

If anything is likely to crimp China's growth, it will be logistics bottlenecks. Freight transporta-tion can be downright primitive by global standards; there's a fair chance that the truck in Tian-jin was loaded by hand, that its driver had to pay off a low-level government official somewhere along the road, and that the condition of the road itself made for unpredictable delivery.

If China's economy is to maintain its momentum, its logistics costs—currently up to three times the level of those in developed countries—must come down. Nobody who has seen first-hand the pace of road-building and port construction around a coastal metropolis such as Shanghai doubts that enormous effort is being applied to bring logistics operations in line with those of the developed world. But it simply isn't enough, particularly as growth corri-dors begin to extend westward up the Yangtze River and toward inland manufacturing hubs such as Chongqing.

Much of China's logistics landscape remains oversubscribed and clogged with inefficiencies. On top of that come cultural hurdles; corruption remains endemic, and red tape is as thick as ever. Here's a closer look:

Rail was the main form of transportation under the old communist model, but it has not adapted to the new Chinese economy. It is primarily geared to moving bulk commodities long distances. In theory, it should also have strong capability to move containers from ports to in-land cities. But it is a gross understatement to say that China's railroads have a chronic lack of capacity; they would need to double capacity just to cope with current demand.

Roads—think "pothole." Until the late '90s, much of China was served by the most rudimen-tary road system. The best network was concentrated around coastal cities, and even here roads were variable in quality. From 2004, there has been vast investment in road-building, but if anything, the bias toward the eastern coastal cities has increased. The development of pan-China road services is also limited by the many internal barriers to movement im-posed by local governments, a situation that magnifies the economic isolation of one region from another. Since 1996, about two-thirds of government expenditure on infrastructure has been invested in the development of road networks. The program is scheduled to last until 2015, when the network should reach about 35,000 km of toll highways. But the needs will continue to outpace the road network's capacity for years.

The Chinese transportation and logistics market is one of the most highly regulated in the world. However, it is slowly opening up to outside competition, and this process has been fa-cilitated by China's 2001 accession to the World Trade Organization. By acceding, China com-mitted to a timetable of liberalization for various industry sectors. For example, the limits on foreign equity in road haulage, warehousing, and similar services were abolished at the end of 2005.

In addition to the regulations that control foreign access to the Chinese market, there are other controls that constrain both foreign and domestic operators. For example, the number of freight trucks is controlled through a permit system. Permits are awarded by local or regional authorities, and restrictions are imposed on carriers from outside of the region. In addition, there are myriad regulatory bodies, including China's Ministry of Communications, the Ministry of Foreign Trade, and the China State Post Bureau. Thus, getting the green light for any logistics project in China still relies heavily on the strength of contacts within China's bureaucracy.

But for all its challenges, the China story is one that more and more U.S. and European managers are finding that they simply cannot ignore. As long as there is a Yuan to be made, the trucks will keep rolling, however slowly and inefficiently, all across China.

Source: Kerr, J. "A Roadmap to China's Logistics Landscape." *Logistics Management,* 46, no. 1 (2007): 1S. Used with permission.

Introduction

Logistics is necessary for moving purchased goods from the supplier to the buying organization, moving finished goods to the customer, and storing these items along the way. An effective logistics system is needed for commerce to flourish in any industrialized society. Products have little value to the customer until they are moved to the customer's point of consumption, at a point in time when they are needed. Logistics thus provides what is termed **time utility** and **place utility**. Time utility is created when customers get products delivered at precisely the right time, not earlier and not later. The logistics function creates time utility by determining when items are delivered and how long they are held in storage before delivery. Place utility is created when customers get things delivered to the desired location.

The official definition of logistics from the Council of Logistics Management (now called the Council of Supply Chain Management Professionals) is:

> *...the process of planning, implementing, and controlling the efficient, effective flow and storage of goods, services, and related information from point of origin to point of consumption for the purpose of conforming to customer requirements.*[3]

So, it can be seen that transportation, warehousing, and information systems play very significant roles in the logistics function. For supply chains in particular, logistics is what creates the efficient flow of goods between supply chain partners, allowing profits and competitive advantage to be maximized.

When moving around a city, between cities, or between countries, it is impossible to ignore the business of logistics, whether it be large trucks ambling along the roadways, trains pulling boxcars, cattle-cars, and tankers next to the highway, warehouses storing goods in a city's industrial section, airplanes taking off at the airport, container ships unloading cargo, or barges floating slowly down the river. In the United States and other highly industrialized nations, the movement of goods is ever-pervasive. Without it, we as consumers would never have the opportunity to find whatever we want, when we want it, at the many retail outlets we routinely visit each day.

At the end of 2004, the total annual U.S. for-hire logistics services contribution to the U.S. gross domestic product (GDP) was approximately 3 percent, or $330 billion. Table 9.1 shows the growth of for-hire logistics expenditures in the U.S., which has

Table 9.1	Total U.S. For-Hire Logistics Services Contribution to GDP (Current $ billions)						
	1980	1985	1990	1995	2000	2002	2004
Total U.S. GDP	2796	4220	5803	7398	9817	10,470	11,713
For-Hire Logistics Services GDP (% U.S. GDP)	102.3 (3.7)	136.3 (3.2)	169.4 (2.9)	226.3 (3.1)	301.6 (3.1)	304.6 (2.9)	330.1 (2.8)
Truck GDP (% For-Hire GDP)	28.1 (27.5)	39.0 (28.6)	52.6 (31.1)	70.1 (31.0)	92.8 (30.8)	95.7 (31.4)	108.0 (32.7)
Rail GDP (% For-Hire GDP)	22.4 (21.9)	23.1 (16.9)	20.6 (12.2)	25.0 (11.0)	25.5 (8.5)	26.2 (8.6)	30.2 (9.1)
Water GDP (% For-Hire GDP)	3.3 (3.2)	3.7 (2.7)	4.6 (2.7)	5.8 (2.6)	7.2 (2.4)	7.0 (2.3)	9.0 (2.7)
Air GDP (% For-Hire GDP)	12.8 (12.5)	19.0 (13.9)	26.8 (15.8)	41.0 (18.1)	57.7 (19.1)	48.3 (15.9)	44.9 (13.6)
Pipeline GDP (% For-Hire GDP)	6.1 (6.0)	8.7 (6.4)	7.2 (4.3)	8.1 (3.6)	8.7 (2.9)	11.5 (3.8)	9.6 (2.9)
Warehouse GDP (% For-Hire GDP)	5.6 (5.5)	8.4 (6.2)	11.8 (7.0)	16.8 (7.4)	25.0 (8.3)	26.8 (8.8)	30.1 (9.1)
Other GDP[a] (% For-Hire GDP)	24.1 (23.6)	34.3 (25.2)	45.7 (27.0)	59.5 (26.3)	84.7 (28.1)	89.1 (29.3)	98.3 (29.8)

Source: U.S. Dept. of Commerce, Bureau of Economic Analysis—www.bea.gov.
[a] Includes transit, ground passenger, and other transportation and support activities.

more than tripled in 24 years. Notice that for the past 20 years or so, for-hire logistics expenditures have stayed close to 3 percent of GDP, which roughly coincides with the post-transportation deregulation time period in the U.S. Also note the fairly steady rise in the use of truck and air transportation and warehousing since 1980 and the steady decrease in the use of rail and water transportation prior to the most recent time periods. This may be due in part to the need for faster and more flexible transportation coming from customers, and from the increased security placed on air and water transportation entering the U.S. since 2001.

In this chapter the many logistics activities are discussed, along with logistics nomenclature and events that affect businesses each day. Included in this chapter are discussions of the modes of transportation, transportation regulation and deregulation, warehousing and distribution, a number of logistics decisions firms must make, the impact of logistics on supply chain management, the international issues affecting logistics, the impact of e-commerce on logistics activities, and management of product returns, also called **reverse logistics**. Some transportation basics are reviewed next.

The Fundamentals of Transportation

This section reviews a number of important transportation elements within the logistics function including the objective of transportation, legal forms of transportation, the modes of transportation, **intermodal transportation**, transportation pricing, **transportation security**, and transportation regulation and deregulation in the U.S. This provides a good foundation for discussion of the remaining topics in the chapter, and also provides an appreciation for the complex nature of transportation issues in logistics.

The Objective of Transportation

Though you may think the overriding objective of transportation is obvious, that is, moving things from point A to point B, for-hire transportation services can go broke doing this inefficiently. For example, over the past ten years a number of U.S. passenger airlines have sought bankruptcy protection and asked for concessions from labor unions to keep operating. Some of these airlines include United Airlines,

Continental Airlines, America West, US Airways, Delta Air Lines, Northwest Airlines, Hawaiian Airlines, and Aloha Airlines.[4]

Logistics managers seek to maximize value for their employers by correctly communicating their service needs and negotiating prices with transportation service providers such that the suppliers' delivery costs are covered and they have generated an acceptable profit contribution, and then making sure the desired services are performed as effectively as possible. In the airline industry, competitive prices may not be high enough to cover the firm's fixed and variable costs, and this has created a tremendous problem for a number of carriers as mentioned above. In the most general terms, transportation objectives should be centered on satisfying customer requirements while minimizing costs and making a reasonable profit. For logistics managers, this also means deciding which forms of transportation, material handling, and storage, along with the most appropriate vehicle scheduling and routing to use.

© 1997 Ted Goff

"Unfortunately, we need a delivery service that operates on more than one day a year."

Legal Forms of Transportation

For-hire transportation service companies are classified legally as common, contract, exempt, or **private carriers**. The distinguishing characteristics of each of these classifications are discussed below.

Common Carriers

Common carriers offer transportation services to all shippers at published rates, between designated locations. Common carriers must offer their transportation services to the general public without discrimination, meaning they must charge the same rates for the same service to all customers. Because common carriers are given the authority to serve the general public, they are the most heavily regulated of all carrier classifications. Some U.S. examples of common carriers are Southwest Air, Amtrak, Greyhound, and Carnival Cruise Lines.

Contract Carriers

Contract carriers are also for-hire carriers like common carriers; however, they are not bound to serve the general public. Instead, contract carriers serve specific customers under contractual agreements. Typical contracts are for movement of a specified cargo for a negotiated and agreed-upon price. Some contract carriers have specific capabilities that allow them to offer lower prices than common carriers might charge for the same service, although common carriers can also be contract carriers. For instance, Southwest Air might enter into a contractual agreement with the Dallas Cowboys professional football team to provide transportation for their team's out-of-town games. Shippers and carriers are free to negotiate contractual agreements for price, the commodity carried, liability, delivery timing, and types of service.

Exempt Carriers

Exempt carriers are also for-hire carriers, but they are exempt from regulation of services and rates. Carriers are classified as exempt if they transport certain exempt products such as produce, livestock, coal, or newspapers. The exempt status was originally established to allow farmers to transport agricultural products on public roads, but today the status has been broadened to include a number of commodities. **Rail carriers** hauling coal between specific locations are exempt from economic regulation, for instance. All carriers can also act as exempt carriers for these specific commodities.

Private Carriers

A private carrier is not subject to economic regulation and typically transports goods for the company owning the carrier. Firms transporting their own products typically own and operate fleets large enough to make the costs of transportation less than what it would be if the firm hired the service. Flexibility and control of product movements may also play a role in the ownership of a private carrier. Wal-Mart, for instance, owns a fleet of trucks to transport products from their regional distribution centers to their retail outlets.

The Modes of Transportation

There are five modes of transportation: motor, rail, air, water, and **pipeline carriers**. These modes and the amount of freight they hauled were shown in Table 9.1. Each of these modes offers distinct advantages to their customers, and their choice depends on the goods transported, how quickly goods are needed, and the locations of the origination and destination.

Motor Carriers

Motor carriers (or trucks) are the most flexible mode of transportation and, as shown on Table 9.1, account for more than one-third of all U.S. for-hire transportation expenditures. Motor carriage offers door-to-door service, local pick-up and delivery, and small as well as large shipment hauling. They have very low fixed and variable costs and can thus compete favorably with rail and **air carriers** for short to medium hauls (distances shorter than 1000 miles), and are still competitive with other forms of transportation for cross-country shipments, particularly if there are multiple delivery destinations. Motor carriers can also offer a variety of specialized services from refrigerated, to livestock, to automobile hauling.

The primary disadvantages for motor carriers are weather and traffic problems. The tragic collapse of the eight-lane Minneapolis Interstate 35 West bridge over the Mississippi River in August 2007 provided a painful reminder of the importance of a nation's transportation infrastructure. Per day, more than 140,000 vehicles, including approximately 5700 commercial vehicles, used Minnesota's busiest bridge. In 2005, the bridge was inspected and received a low rating, indicating that it needed to be either repaired or replaced.[5]

Motor carriers are most often classified as **less-than-truckload (LTL) carriers** or **truckload (TL) carriers**. LTL carriers move small packages or shipments that take up less than one truckload, and the shipping fees are higher per hundred weight (cwt) than TL fees, since the carrier must consolidate many small shipments into one truckload, then break the truckload back down into individual shipments at the destination for individual deliveries. However, for small item shippers, using LTL carriers is still a much less expensive alternative than using an entire TL carrier. The LTL industry in the U.S. is made up of many national LTL carriers such as Transway Transportation, US Freightways, and ABF Freight System, and regional LTL carriers (specializing in shipments of fewer than 500 miles). Most of the regionals are small, privately owned companies that specialize in overnight and second-day deliveries. Today, they must contend with increased competition from the national carriers, since regional carriage represents the fastest growing segment of the trucking industry. In fact, the majority of tonnage hauled by motor carriers today travels fewer than 500 miles.[6]

Motor carriers can also be classified based on the types of goods they haul. **General freight carriers** carry the majority of goods shipped in the U.S. and include common carriers, whereas **specialized carriers** transport liquid petroleum, household goods, agricultural commodities, building materials, and other specialized items.

Motor carriers offer fast, reliable, relatively inexpensive service with low levels of shipment damage. Their geographic coverage is very good, and for short trips, no other mode can compete. Wages have been declining, though, in the U.S. trucking industry since deregulation (discussed later in the chapter) and with the current trend in de-unionization.[7]

Rail Carriers

Rail carriers compete most favorably when the distance is long and the shipments are heavy or bulky. At one time in the U.S., rail carriers transported the majority of goods shipped; however, since World War II, their share of the transportation market has steadily fallen. Today, U.S. railroads account for only approximately 9 percent of total for-hire transportation expenditures.

Rail service is relatively slow and inflexible; however rail carriers are less expensive than air and motor carriers and can compete fairly well on long-hauls. To better compete, railroads have begun purchasing motor carrier companies and can thus offer point-to-point pick-up and delivery service using motor carriers and rail flatcars that carry truck trailers (known as **trailer-on-flatcar [TOFC] service**). Railroads are also at somewhat of a disadvantage compared with motor carriers with respect to shipment damage, equipment availability, and service frequency.

Since rail companies use each other's rail cars, keeping track of rail cars and getting them where they are needed can be problematic. However, with advances in railroad routing and scheduling software and rail car identification systems, this has become less of a problem for rail carriers. In the U.S., railroad infrastructure and aging equipment have also been problems for the railroads; however, there has been a spending resurgence since the mid-1980s to replace worn track segments and rail cars, to upgrade terminals, and to consolidate through mergers and acquisitions.

One of the trends in rail transportation is the use of **high-speed trains**. Today, they are operated by Amtrak along the U.S. northeast corridor (Boston–New York–Washington, D.C.). Bombardier Inc., a Montreal-based transportation and aerospace company, designed and manufactured Amtrak's Acela Express, an electric high-speed train operating along the U.S. northeast corridor. These trains can make the Washington, D.C. to Boston trip in about 6.5 hours, averaging approximately 70 miles per hour, although top speeds can reach 120 miles per hour (other slower trains and lack of straight-line track has tended to reduce the average speeds).[8] While the Acela Express is the only high-speed railroad operating in the U.S., other states such as California, Illinois, and Florida are considering its use.

Countries such as France and Japan have much more developed high-speed rail lines compared to the U.S.. The inaugural high-speed French rail service between Paris and Lyon was in 1981, and has since expanded to connect cities across France and in neighboring countries. France holds the record for the fastest wheeled train (357 miles per hour on April 3, 2007) and also for the world's highest average speed for regular passenger service. The Japanese shinkansen (high-speed) rail began operations in 1964 between Tokyo and Osaka. Today, the shinkansen rail network has expanded to many cities in Japan, with average speeds in the 170 miles per hour range. A number of other European countries also use high-speed rail. High-speed rail can provide an attractive alternative to air and other forms of ground transportation, depending on the cost and location of terminals.[9]

Air Carriers

Transporting goods by air is very expensive relative to other modes, but also very fast, particularly for long distances. Air carriers account for approximately 14 percent of the U.S. for-hire transportation expenditures. The amount of freight hauled, though, is quite small, since airlines cannot carry extremely heavy or bulky cargo. For light, high-value goods that need to travel long distances quickly, air transportation is the best of the modal alternatives. For movements over water, the only other modal alternative is water carriage, where the transportation decision is based on timing, cost, and shipment weight. Though the incidence of shipment damage is quite low and schedule frequency is good, air transportation is limited in terms of geographic coverage. Most small cities in the U.S., for example, do not have airports and regularly scheduled air service; therefore, motor carrier service must be combined with regional air transportation for these locations.

Today, about half of the goods transported by air are carried by freight-only airlines like FedEx, the world's largest air cargo airline. This represents a significant change since the late 1960s when most air cargo was hauled by passenger airlines. Most passenger air carriers are opting to use smaller, more fuel efficient aircraft, which has reduced their ability to haul cargo. However, growth in markets such as China have fueled large increases in international air cargo, and airlines are scrambling to catch up with demand. The demand for wide-body air freighters such as the Boeing 747-400 has been very high and is expected to double over the next 15 years.[10]

A number of these freight-only airlines have also added motor carrier fleets to enable point-to-point pick-up and delivery service. As shown in Table 9.1, the growth in air transportation expenditures was very strong during the 1980s and 1990s because of deregulation and the increased desire for quick deliveries, but it has slowed down, partly owing to security concerns, since 2001. Transportation security is discussed later in this section.

Water Carriers

Shipping goods by **water carrier** is very inexpensive but also very slow and inflexible. There are several types of water transportation including inland waterway, lakes, coastal and intercoastal ocean, and international deep-sea transportation. Most of the inland waterway transportation is used to haul heavy, bulky, low value materials such as coal, grain, and sand, and competes primarily with rail and pipeline carriers. Inland water transport is obviously limited to areas accessible by water, and hence growth in this area of transportation is also limited. There has actually been a slight decline in water transportation as a percentage of total for-hire transportation costs over the past 20 years. Like rail and air transportation, water carriers are typically paired with motor carriers to enable door-to-door pick-up and delivery service.

In the U.K., efforts are underway to increase inland waterway usage, as this has less environmental impact when compared to motor freight carriers. British Waterways, the organization responsible for managing U.K. waterways, is investing heavily to reduce highway congestion and pollution by increasing trade along their inland waterways. For example, a single river barge can carry the equivalent of 24 truck loads. Freight on inland waterways also produces lower emissions, less noise, and is visually unobtrusive. At present, 3.5 million tons of nontime-sensitive freight per year are moved via 2000 miles of U.K. inland waterways.[11]

There have also been developments in **deep-sea transportation** that have made water transportation cheaper and more desirable, even with the slow transportation times. The development and use of supertankers and containerships have added a new dimension to water transportation. Many of today's oil supertankers are more than 1200 feet long (that's four U.S. football fields) and carry over 2 million barrels of oil. The largest oil supertanker is the *Jahre Viking*, measuring 1500 feet in length and able to carry more than 560,000 tons or 4 million barrels of oil (the *Jahre Viking* has now been renamed the *Knock Nevis* and is permanently moored as a floating oil storage unit in Qatar).[12] Oil-producing nations can now cheaply ship large quantities of oil to anywhere around the globe where demand exists, and even small shippers can ship items overseas cheaply, because of the ability to consolidate small shipments in containers that are placed on board containerships.

Containers allow most any packaged product to be shipped overseas and add an element of protection to the cargo. Containerships carry the majority of the world's water-transported manufactured goods, and they can carry more than 10,000 twenty-foot containers, with total value sometimes as high as $300 million. At any given time, there are approximately 5 to 6 million containers being shipped between countries using containerships.[13]

Pipeline Carriers

Pipeline carriers are very specialized with respect to the products they can carry; however, once the initial investment of the pipeline is recovered, there is very little additional maintenance cost, so long-term pipeline transportation tends to be very inexpensive. Pipelines can haul materials that are only in a liquid or gaseous state, and so the growth potential for pipelines is quite limited. One of the items pipelines haul is coal, and they do this by first pulverizing coal into small particles, then suspending it in water to form **coal slurry**. When the coal slurry reaches its destination, the coal and water are separated. Other items transported include water, oil, gasoline, and natural gas. The continuous nature of pipeline flow is what makes it unique. Once the product reaches its destination, it is continuously available. So long as the world remains dependent on energy products such as coal, oil, and natural gas, there will be a need for pipeline transportation.

Intermodal Transportation

Intermodal transportation, or the use of combinations of the various transportation modes, is becoming an extremely popular transportation arrangement, and makes the movement of goods much more convenient and efficient. Most large logistics service companies today offer one-stop, door-to-door shipping capabilities—they transport goods for one price, then determine the best intermodal transportation and warehousing arrangements to meet customer requirements as cheaply as possible.

Here is a shipping example using a number of intermodal combinations:

> A manufacturing company packs a standard 8' by 8' by 20' container for shipment to an overseas customer. The container is sealed and connected to a motor carrier trailer for transport to a nearby rail terminal. The container is then loaded onto a flatcar and double-stacked with another container where it is then transported to a seaport on the U.S. west coast. Upon arrival, the container is placed aboard a container ship and transported to Japan. In Japan, the container moves through customs and then is loaded onto another motor carrier trailer for transport to its final destination, where it is unpacked. In this example, goods were only packed and unpacked one time. The container was used in three modes of transportation, and remained sealed until the final destination when customs authorities unsealed, examined, and accepted the goods.

The above example highlighted a number of intermodal transportation combinations. The most common are truck trailer-on-flatcar (TOFC) and **container-on-flatcar (COFC)**, also called **piggyback service**. The same containers can be placed on board containerships and airliners. These combinations attempt to combine the flexibility of motor carriers with the economy of rail and/or water carriers. The Burlington Northern Santa Fe Corporation (BNSF), headquartered in Texas, operates one of the largest railroad networks in North America, with about 50,000 track miles covering 27 states and two Canadian provinces. BNSF moves more intermodal traffic than any other rail system in the world today, and intermodal combinations account for about half of the number of units transported by BNSF. In 2005, BNSF had 40,000 employees, 5790 locomotives, and approximately 82,000 freight cars.[14]

Another example of intermodal transportation are **RO-ROs** or *roll-on-roll-off* containerships. These allow truck trailers and containers to be directly driven on and off the ship, without use of cranes. The Atlantic Container Line operates some of the largest and most versatile RORO containerships in the world, capable of carrying a wide variety of oversized cargo. Their RORO fleet allows all vehicles and oversized cargo to be securely parked under deck in RORO garages, providing protection. Their RORO vessels are some of the most flexible ships operating today; their G-3 vessel is 958 feet long, with a capacity of 3100 containers.[15]

Transportation Pricing

There are two pricing strategies used by logistics service providers: **cost-of-service pricing** and **value-of-service pricing**. These strategies are discussed below, along with some related pricing issues.

Cost-of-Service Pricing

Cost-of-service pricing is used when carriers desire to establish prices that vary based on their fixed and variable costs. To accomplish this, firms must be able to identify the relevant costs and then accurately allocate these to each shipment. Cost-of-service pricing varies based on volume and distance. As shipping volume increases, the portion of fixed costs that are allocated to each shipment goes down, allowing the carrier to reduce prices. Large volume shipments also allow carriers to charge carload or truckload rates instead of less-than-carload or less-than-truckload rates. As the shipping distance increases, prices will tend to rise, but not proportionally with distance, because fixed costs are essentially constant regardless of distance.

Value of Service Pricing

In this case, carriers price their services at competitive levels the market will bear. Prices are thus based on the level of competition and the current volume of demand for each service. This is a profit-maximizing pricing approach. If a carrier has a service that is in high demand with little competition, prices will tend to be quite high. As other carriers notice the high profit potential of this service, competition will eventually increase and prices will fall. As the level of competition increases, carriers will seek ways to reduce their costs to maintain profitability. In the highly competitive passenger airline industry, Southwest Airlines has been able to keep their costs low by using only one type of airplane, flying relatively short distances between stops, keeping their planes in the air, and using fuel price hedging strategies, which has enabled them to remain profitable as of 2007, their 34th consecutive year of profit.[16]

Terms of Sale

In many cases, suppliers' terms of sale affect transportation costs. When products are purchased from a supplier, they may quote a price that includes transportation to the buyer's location. This is known as **FOB destination pricing**, or free-on-board to the shipment's destination. This also means that the supplier will be the legal owner of the product until it safely reaches its destination. For high-value shipments, small shipments, or when the buyer has little transportation expertise, FOB destination is typically preferred. Otherwise, the buyer may decide to purchase goods and provide its own transportation to the shipping destination; in this case, the supplier quotes lower **FOB origination prices**. The goods then become the legal responsibility of the buyer at the shipment pick-up location.

Pricing Negotiation

Since the deregulation of transportation in the U.S., negotiating transportation prices has become much more common. In addition, shippers today are inclined to develop alliances with logistics companies because of the key role they play in making supply chains responsive to changing demand. This has also tended to increase the use of pricing negotiations. Negotiations tend to be based on the carrier's fixed and variable costs. To maintain an equitable partnership, prices are negotiated that allow carriers to cover their fixed and variable costs and make a reasonable profit.

Rate Categories

Carrier prices or rates can be classified in a number of different ways. **Line haul rates** are the charges for moving goods to a nonlocal destination, and these can be further classified as *class rates*, *exception rates*, *commodity rates*, and *miscellaneous rates*. **Class rates** are based on the particular class of the product transported—some products have higher published class rates than others. **Exception rates** are published rates that are lower than class rates for specific origin-destination locations or volumes. **Commodity rates** apply to minimum quantities of products that are shipped between two specified locations. **Miscellaneous rates** apply to contract rates that are negotiated between two parties and to shipments containing a variety of products (in this case, the rate is based on the overall weight of the shipment). Today, many of the rates carriers charge are classified as miscellaneous, since negotiated rates tend to be used primarily for large shipments.

Transportation Security

Transportation security in the U.S., particularly **airline security**, has become a very important issue since September 11, 2001. Congress passed the Aviation and Transportation Security Act on Nov. 19, 2001, creating a large bureaucracy (the Transportation Security Administration or TSA) to oversee transportation security as well as creating high hopes among the many government contractors. Today, the TSA oversees 429 U.S. airports. In addition, the Department of Homeland Security (DHS) was created in 2003 with a first-year budget of more than $41 billion to provide overall U.S. security leadership.

A number of problems and actions have resulted from this heightened emphasis on security in the U.S. The TSA has had four agency chiefs since 9/11 and has spent more than $12 billion to improve security on airplanes and in airports. Despite these expenditures, a number of reports from U.S. agencies such as the DHS, the FBI, and the Coalition of Airline Pilots have concluded the U.S. air system is still at risk to terrorist attacks and warned that there were serious gaps in aviation security at airports as of 2005.[17]

Other forms of transportation have taken a backseat to airline security concerns, although an executive order from President Bush on December 5, 2006, sought to strengthen surface transportation security. These surface security issues are troublesome—for example, no "safe" rail corridors exist in the northeastern U.S. and the 24 million trucks on U.S. roads makes tight security regulation difficult. Added to this is the issue of Mexican truckers being allowed to operate in the U.S., a promise made to Mexico as part of the **North American Free Trade Agreement (NAFTA)** (although as of the time of this writing, U.S. trucks are still not allowed in Mexico and Mexican trucks are not allowed further than 25 miles into the U.S.).

Some of the agency funding is beginning to bear fruit—in January 2007, the DHS began its Secure Freight Initiative to test nuclear detection portals at six foreign ports that process cargo bound for the U.S. A number of other research efforts funded by the DHS began to surface in 2007 including better nuclear detectors for all cargo, including motor carriers, and BioWatch, a system to detect airborne pathogens.

At the present, the challenge is to create transportation security regulations without crippling the transportation industry. James Calderwood, an attorney with Washington, D.C.–based Zuckert, Scoutt & Rasenberg, and an authority on transportation law explains, "We have to move along in a responsible way, so that those in transportation and supply chain management will not be encumbered with rules that are difficult to follow." Examples of regulations that are in the works include the Transportation Worker Identification credential system, inspection of all air cargo moving within the U.S., railroad hazardous material and freight security measures, new inspection requirements for ocean-going containers entering the U.S., new railroad safety measures, the Port Security Improvement Act, and improved security awareness training for pipeline employees.[18]

Transportation Regulation and Deregulation in the U.S.

The U.S. has gone through periods of regulation and deregulation with respect to the transportation industry. On the one hand, government regulation of transportation is argued by many to be good in that it tends to assure adequate transportation service throughout the country while protecting consumers in terms of monopoly pricing, safety, and liability. On the other hand, **transportation deregulation** is argued to be good because it encourages competition and allows prices to adjust as demand and negotiations dictate. In addition, antitrust laws already in place tend to protect transportation consumers. This debate was the subject of a study in 1994 to determine the impact deregulation had on the U.S. motor carrier industry. The study concluded that transportation deregulation has resulted in greater use of cost-of-service pricing, rising freight rates for LTL shipments, and more safety problems as operators have tended to let fleets age and to reduce maintenance.[19] Today, the U.S. transportation industry remains essentially deregulated; however, carriers must adhere to a number of regulations (primarily safety regulations). Some of the history of transportation regulation and deregulation in the U.S. is reviewed next.

Transportation Regulation

Table 9.2 summarizes the transportation regulations in the U.S., starting with the **granger laws** of the 1870s, which led to the Interstate Commerce Act of 1887. Before this time, the railroads in the U.S. were charging high rates and discriminating against small shippers. So, a number of midwestern states passed laws to broadly regulate the railroads to establish maximum rates, prohibit local discrimination, forbid rail mergers (to encourage competition), and prohibit free passes to public officials. Though the U.S. Supreme Court later struck down these laws, the granger movement made Congress realize the impact of railroad monopolies. This led to the passage of the **Interstate Commerce Act of 1887**.

The 1887 act created the Interstate Commerce Commission (ICC) that required rail carriers to charge reasonable rates; to publish rates, file them with the ICC, and make these available to the public; and prohibited discriminatory practices (charging some shippers less than others for the same service). The act also prohibited agreements between railroads to pool traffic or revenues. Between 1887 and 1910, a number of amendments made to the 1887 act increased the ICC's control and enforcement power. These amendments restricted railroads from providing rates and services that were not in the public's best interest, created penalties for failure to follow published rates or for offering and accepting rebates, set maximum rates, and prevented railroads from owning pipelines or water carriers, unless approved by the ICC.

By 1917, increased competition combined with the rate restrictions had created a rail system unable to offer the efficient service the U.S. government needed in its war efforts, and thus the federal government seized the railroads. Railroad companies were guaranteed a profit while the government poured large sums of money into upgrading the rail system. By the end of World War I, Congress had come to realize that all of the negative controls placed on railroads were unhealthy for the industry. They wanted to return the railroads to private ownership. This brought about the first of a number of regulations aimed at positive control, the **Transportation Act of 1920**.

Table 9.2	U.S. Transportation Regulations	
DATE	**REGULATION**	**SUMMARY**
1870s	Granger Laws	Midwestern states passed laws to establish maximum rates, prohibit discrimination, and forbid mergers for railroads.
1887	Interstate Commerce Act	States cannot regulate transportation; established Interstate Commerce Commission; regulated and published rates, outlawed discriminatory pricing, prohibited pooling agreements, to encourage competition.
1920	Transportation Act	Instructed the ICC to establish rates that allowed RRs to earn a fair return; established minimum rates; gave control to ICC to set intrastate rates; allowed pooling agreements if they were in the public's best interest.
1935	Motor Carrier Act	Extended the ICA of 1887 to include motor carriers and brought them under ICC control; established five classes of operators: common, contract, private, exempt, and broker; mergers must be approved by ICC.
1938	Civil Aeronautics Act	Established the Civil Aeronautics Board to regulate air carriers; new entrants had to get CAB approval; CAB controlled rates; Civil Aeronautics Administration controlled air safety.
1940	Transportation Act	Extended the ICA of 1887 to include ICC control over domestic water transportation; ICC controlled entry, rates, and services.
1942	Freight Forwarders Act	Extended the ICA of 1887 to include ICC control over freight forwarders; ICC controlled entry, rates, and services.
1948	Reed-Bulwinkle Act	Amendment to the ICA of 1887 legalizing rate bureaus or conferences.
1958	Transportation Act	Amended the rule of rate making by stating that rates couldn't be held up to protect the traffic of any other mode.
1958	Federal Aviation Act	Created the Federal Aviation Agency to assume the mission of the CAA; FAA empowered to manage and develop U.S. airspace, and plan the U.S. airport system.
1966	Department of Transportation Act	Assumed mission of FAA and a number of other agencies for research, promotion, safety, and administration of transportation; organized into nine operating and six administrative divisions; also established the National Transportation Safety Board.
1970	Railway Passenger Service Act	Created the National Railroad Passenger Corp. to preserve and upgrade intercity rail passenger service; resulted in the creation of Amtrak.

The 1920 act instructed the ICC to ensure that rates were high enough to provide a fair return for the railroads each year (Congress initially set this at 6 percent return per year). When companies made more than the prescribed 6 percent, half of the excess was taken and used to fund low interest loans to the weaker operators for updating their systems and increasing efficiency. The act also allowed the ICC to set minimum rates, allowed joint use of terminal facilities, allowed railroads to enter into pooling agreements, and allowed rail company acquisitions and consolidations. Finally, to keep the railroads from becoming overcapitalized, the act prohibited railroads from issuing securities without ICC approval. The rail system thus became a regulated monopoly.

From 1935 to 1942, regulations were passed that applied to other modes of transportation, and these were similar in nature to the 1920 act. A great deal of money was spent during the 1920s and during the depression building the U.S. highway system. The time was ripe then for the emergence of for-hire motor carriers. The number of small trucking companies grew tremendously during this period, thus creating competition for the railroads, as shippers opted to use the cheaper for-hire motor carriers. The **Motor Carrier Act of 1935** brought motor carriers under ICC control, thus controlling entry into the market, establishing motor carrier classes of operation, setting reasonable rates, mandating ICC approval for any mergers or acquisitions, and controlling the issuance of securities.

In 1938, the federal government enacted another extension of the Interstate Commerce Act by including regulation of air carriers in the **Civil Aeronautics Act of 1938**. This act promoted the development of the air transportation system and promoted air safety and airline efficiency by establishing the Civil Aeronautics Board to oversee market entry, establish routes with appropriate levels of competition, develop regional feeder airlines, and establish reasonable rates. The Civil Aeronautics Administration was also established to regulate air safety.

The **Transportation Act of 1940** further extended the Interstate Commerce Act of 1887, establishing ICC control over domestic water transportation. The provisions for domestic water carriers were similar to those imposed on rail and motor carriers. In 1942, the 1887 act was once again extended to cover **freight forwarders**, with the usual entry, rate, and service controls of the ICC. Freight forwarders were also prohibited from owning any carriers.

A number of other congressional enactments occurred up through 1970, further strengthening and refining the control of the transportation market. In 1948, the **Reed-Bulwinkle Act** gave groups of carriers the ability to form rate bureaus or conferences wherein they could propose rate changes to the ICC. The **Transportation Act of 1958** established temporary loan guarantees to railroads, liberalized control over intrastate rail rates, amended the rule of rate making to ensure more intermodal competition, and clarified the differences between private and for-hire motor carriers. The **Federal Aviation Act of 1958** replaced the Civil Aeronautics Administration with the Federal Aviation Administration (FAA) and gave the FAA authority to prescribe air traffic rules, make safety regulations, and plan the national airport system. In 1966, the **Department of Transportation Act** created the Department of Transportation (DOT) to coordinate the executive functions of all government entities dealing with transportation-related matters. It was hoped that centralized coordination of all the transportation agencies would lead to more effective transportation promotion and planning. Finally, to preserve and improve the rail system's ability to service passengers, the **Railway Passenger Service Act** was passed in 1970, thus creating Amtrak.

Transportation Deregulation

Commencing in 1976, Congress enacted a number of laws to reduce transportation regulation. These are summarized in Table 9.3. This began the movement toward less regulation by allowing market forces to determine prices, entry, and services. At this point in transportation history, consumers and politicians had the opinion that transportation regulation was administered more for the benefit of the carriers than the public. In addition, with the bankruptcy filings of a number of railroads in the mid-1970s combined with the Arab oil embargo of the same period, regulation was receiving much of the blame for an inefficient transportation system.

The **Railroad Revitalization and Regulatory Reform Act**, commonly known as the 4-R Act, was passed in 1976 and made several regulatory changes to help the railroads. First, railroads were allowed to change rates without ICC approval, limited by **threshold costs** on

Table 9.3	U.S. Transportation Deregulation	
DATE	**DEREGULATION**	**SUMMARY**
1976	Railroad Revitalization and Regulatory Reform Act	The "4-R Act." Railroads were allowed to change rates without ICC approval, within limits; ICC procedures were sped up.
1977	Air Cargo Deregulation Act	Freed all air cargo carriers from CAB regulations
1978	Air Passenger Deregulation Act	Airlines freed to expand routes, change fares within limits; small community routes were subsidized; CAB ceases to exist in 1985.
1980	Motor Carrier Act	Fewer restrictions on entry, routes, rates, and private carriers.
1980	Staggers Rail Act	Freed railroads to establish rates within limits; legalized contract rates; shortened ICC procedure turnaround.
1982	Bus Regulatory Reform Act	Amended the 1980 MCA to include buses.
1984	Shipping Act	Partial deregulation of ocean transportation.
1994	Trucking Industry Regulatory Reform Act	Motor carriers freed from filing rates with the ICC.
1994	FAA Authorization Act	Freed intermodal air carriers from economic regulation by the states.
1995	ICC Termination Act	Eliminated the ICC and moved regulatory duties to Department of Transportation.
1998	Ocean Shipping Reform Act	Deregulated ocean liner shipping; allowed contract shipping; rate filing not required.

one end and **market dominance** on the other. Threshold costs were defined as the firm's variable costs, and the ICC determined whether the firm was in a market dominant position (absence of market competition). A number of ICC procedures were also sped up to aid transportation manager decision making. These same ideas appeared again in later deregulation efforts.

Air freight was deregulated in 1977. No longer were there any barriers to entry provided the firms were deemed fit by the Civil Aeronautics Board. Size restrictions were also lifted, and carriers were free to charge any rate provided there was no discrimination. Finally, carriers did not have to file freight rates with the CAB. This was followed soon after by deregulation of air passenger service in 1978. This was a phased-in approach, wherein carriers could slowly add routes to their systems, while protecting other routes from competition. Fares could be adjusted within limits without CAB approval. To protect small communities from losing service, all cities with service in 1977 were guaranteed service for ten additional years. In 1981, all route restrictions were to be released, allowing any carrier to operate any route. Airline rates and mergers were to be released from regulation in 1983. Finally, the CAB was to shut down in 1985. The impact of these changes on the airline industry was significant—there were 34 air passenger carriers in 1977 and by 1982 the number had increased to 90. Some fares dropped substantially, while other fares went up, and routes to low-demand areas decreased.

Motor carriers were deregulated in 1980. The objectives of this act were to promote competitive as well as safe and efficient motor transportation. Entry regulations were eased to make it easier to enter the market—firms had only to show a "useful public purpose" would be served. Route restrictions were removed, and restrictions deemed to be wasteful of fuel, inefficient, or contrary to public interest were also removed. As with the 4-R Act, a **zone of rate freedom** was also used. And, as with air passenger deregulation, a large number of new motor carriers began service. By 1981, more than 2400 new motor carriers had started up in the U.S.

Railroads were further deregulated with the **Staggers Rail Act of 1980**. The financial condition of railroads was worsening, and this act was aimed at improving finances for the rail industry. With this act, rail carriers were free to change rates within a zone of rate freedom, but the ceiling or market dominance rate was established more definitively as 160 percent of variable costs and varied up to 180 percent depending on ICC cost formulas. After 1984, rate increases were to be tied to the rate of inflation. Contract rates were also allowed between railroads and shippers.

The **Shipping Act of 1984** marked the end of the initial push by Congress to deregulate transportation. This act allowed ocean carriers to pool or share shipments, assign ports, publish rates, and enter into contracts with shippers. More recently, with the passage of the **ICC Termination Act of 1995** and the **Ocean Shipping Reform Act of 1998**, the Interstate Commerce Commission was eliminated and the requirement for ocean carriers to file rates with the Federal Maritime Commission also came to an end.

Thus, we have seen a number of changes in the U.S. transportation industry over the past century. Economic regulation of transportation occurred for several reasons. Initial transportation regulations were instituted to establish the ground rules as new forms of transportation developed, and to control prices, services, and routes when monopoly power existed in the industry. Later, regulations were eased to encourage competition and increase efficiency and safety. In the future, as economic conditions change, and as technology, political, and social changes occur, transportation regulations will also continue to change, as we have seen with transportation security regulations.

Warehousing and Distribution

Warehousing provides a very strategic service, in that it enables firms to store purchases, work-in-progress, and finished goods, and perform **breakbulk** and assembly activities, while providing faster and more frequent deliveries of finished products to customers, resulting in better customer service when the system is designed and managed correctly. Right now, readers may be questioning the need for warehouses, particularly as this textbook has been singing the praises of low inventories, JIT deliveries, efficient supply chains, and the like. But just the opposite is true today. As disposable income in the U.S. increases, consumers buy more goods that must move through various distribution systems. Even though U.S. freight distribution systems move goods from manufacturers to end users in an increasingly efficient manner, the growth in demand for warehouse space has overcome this improved efficiency. Between 1980 and 2005, the amount of occupied warehouse space grew by 49 percent in the 50 largest markets in the U.S. for a total growth in warehouse stock of more than 2.5 billion square feet.[20]

In many cases today, warehouses aren't used to store things, but rather to receive bulk shipments, break them down, repackage various items into outgoing orders, and then distribute these orders to a manufacturing location or retail center. These activities are collectively referred to as **cross-docking**. In this case, the warehouse is more accurately described as a **distribution center**. In other cases, firms are moving warehouses closer to suppliers, closer to customers, or to more centralized locations, depending on the storage objectives and customer service requirements. So, warehouses are still very much in use—some just to store things and others to provide efficient throughput of goods. This section discusses a number of warehousing issues including their importance and the types of warehouses, **risk pooling** and warehouse location, and **JIT warehousing**.

The Importance and Types of Warehouses

Firms hold inventories for a number of reasons, as explained in Chapter 6, wherein warehouses are used to support purchasing, production, and distribution activities. Firms order raw materials, parts, and assemblies, which are typically shipped to a warehouse location close to the buyer's facility, and then eventually transferred to the buyer's facilities as needed. In a retail setting, the warehouse might be regionally located, with the retailer receiving bulk orders from many suppliers, breaking these down and reassembling outgoing orders for delivery to each retail location, then using a private fleet of trucks or for-hire transportation provider to move the orders to the retail locations. Similar distribution centers are used when manufacturers deliver bulk shipments to regional market areas, then break these down and ship LTL outgoing order quantities to customers.

Conversely, firms may operate **consolidation warehouses** to collect large numbers of LTL shipments from nearby regional sources of supply, where these are then transported in TL or CL quantities to a manufacturing or user-facility located at some distance from the consolidation center. The use of consolidation warehouses and distribution warehouses allows firms to realize both purchase economies and transportation economies. Firms can buy goods in bulk at lower unit costs, and then ship these goods at TL or CL rates either to a distribution center or directly to a manufacturing center. They can also purchase and move small quantity purchases at LTL rates to nearby consolidation warehouses.

Private Warehouses

Just as with the private forms of transportation, **private warehouses** refer to warehouses that are *owned by the firm storing the goods*. For firms with large volumes of goods to store or transfer, private warehouses represent an opportunity to reduce the costs of warehousing. Besides the potential cost benefit private warehouses provide, another consideration is the *level of control* provided by private warehouses. Firms can decide what to store, what to process, what types of security to provide, and the types of equipment to use, among other operational aspects of warehouses. Private warehousing can also enable the firm to better utilize its workforce and their expertise in terms of transportation, warehousing, and distribution center activities. Also, as supply chains become more global to take advantage of cheaper sources of supply or labor, the use of private warehouses tends to increase. Finally, private warehouses can generate income and tax advantages through leasing of excess capacity and/or asset depreciation. For these reasons, private warehousing accounts for the vast majority of warehouse space in the U.S.[21]

Owning warehouses, though, can also represent a financial risk and loss of flexibility to the firm. The costs to build, equip, and then operate a warehouse can be very high, and most small to moderate-sized firms simply cannot afford private warehouses. Private warehouses also bind firms to locations that may not prove optimal as time passes. Warehouse size or capacity is also somewhat inflexible, at least in the short term.

Public Warehouses

As the name implies, **public warehouses** are for-profit organizations that contract or lease various warehousing and distribution services to other companies. Public warehouses provide a number of specialized services that firms can use to create customized services for various shipments and goods. These services include the following:

- Breakbulk—large quantity shipments are broken down so that items can be combined into specific customer orders, and then shipped out.
- Repackaging—after breakbulk, items are repackaged for specific customer orders. Warehouses can also do individual product packaging and labeling.
- Assembly—some public warehouses provide final assembly operations to satisfy customer requests and create customized final products.
- Quality inspections—warehouse personnel can perform incoming and outgoing quality inspections.
- Material handling, equipment maintenance, and documentation services.
- Short- and long-term storage.

Besides the services shown here, public warehouses provide the flexibility and investment cost savings that private warehouses cannot offer. If demand changes or products change, the short-term commitments to public warehouses allow firms to quickly change warehouse locations. Public warehouses also allow firms to test market areas and withdraw quickly if demand does not materialize. The cost of a public warehouse can also be very small, particularly if the capacity requirements are minimal. Nabisco spends several million dollars per year to outsource to 10 major public warehouse providers and about 200 carriers for its warehousing and delivery business, which delivers to large food chains, mass merchants, drugstores, retailers, and grocery wholesalers.[22]

One of the main disadvantages associated with public warehouses is the lack of control provided to the goods owner. Other problems include communication problems with warehouse personnel, lack of specialized services or capacity at the desired locations, and the lack of care and security that might be given to products.

Firms might also find it advantageous to use public warehouses in some locations and private warehouses in others. For large established markets and relatively mature products, large firms may decide that owning and operating a warehouse makes the most sense, whereas the same firm may lease space and pay for services at public warehouses in developing markets or low-demand areas.

Today, many public warehouses are finding new ways to add value for their clients, including the offering of specialized services such as refrigerated warehouses, customs clearance, reverse logistics, freight consolidation, claims processing, real-time information control, and direct-store deliveries.

Risk Pooling and Warehouse Location

One of the more important decisions regarding warehouses is where to locate them. This decision will affect the number of warehouses needed, their required size or capacity, the warehousing system inventory level, customer service levels, and the warehousing system cost. For a given market area, as the number of warehouses used increases, the system becomes more *decentralized*. Responsiveness and delivery service levels will increase since goods can be delivered more quickly to customers; however, warehousing system operating and inventory costs will also increase. Other costs that come into play here are outgoing transportation costs to customers, and the transportation costs associated with the incoming deliveries of goods to each warehouse. Thus, the tradeoff between costs and customer service must be carefully considered as the firm makes its warehousing location decisions. This brings up the very important topic of risk pooling, which is discussed below.

Risk Pooling

Risk pooling describes the relationship between the number of warehouses, inventory, and customer service, and it can be explained intuitively as follows: when market demand is random, it is very likely that higher-than-average demand from some customers will be offset by lower-than-average demand from other customers. As the number of customers served by a single warehouse increases, these demand variabilities will offset each other more often, thus reducing overall demand variance and the likelihood of stockouts and, consequently, the amount of safety stock required to guard against stockouts. Thus, the more *centralized* a warehousing system is, the lower the safety stock required to achieve a given system-wide customer service level (recall that in inventory parlance the customer service level is inversely proportional to the number of stockouts per period).

Risk pooling assumes that the demand at the markets served by the warehouses is negatively correlated (when demand at one market is greater than average, then demand at another market will be less than average). Thus, the greater the positive correlation between demands, the smaller the benefit because of risk pooling.

The effect of risk pooling can be estimated by the **square root rule**, which suggests that the system average inventory (impacted by adding warehouses to the system) is equal to the old system inventory times the ratio of the square root of the new number of warehouses to the square root of the old number of warehouses.[23] A simple example to illustrate risk pooling is shown in Example 9.1. In the example, reducing the

---

Example 9.1   Risk Pooling

Perkins Western Boot Emporium currently owns two warehouses in Houston and Seattle to store its boots before shipping them out to various retail customers across the western U.S. Greg Perkins, the owner, is considering using a centralized warehouse in Denver to service all their retail customers, and is curious to know the impact this will have on their inventory requirements. Their current average inventory level is approximately 6000 boots *at each* warehouse. He has found that this level of stock will result in warehouse stockouts approximately 1 percent of the time. Using the square root rule, he calculates the new average inventory level needed at the central warehouse to maintain the 99 percent customer service level:

$$S_2 = \frac{\sqrt{N_2}}{\sqrt{N_1}}(S_1) = \frac{1.0}{1.41}(12,000) = 8511 \text{ boots}$$

where

$S_1 = $ total system stock of boots for the N_1 warehouses;

$S_2 = $ total system stock of boots for the N_2 warehouses;

$N_1 = $ number of warehouses in the existing system; and

$N_2 = $ number of warehouses in the proposed system.

number of warehouses from two to one causes a reduction in average inventory of approximately 29 percent.

The differences between centralized and decentralized warehousing systems can be expressed as follows:

- Safety stock and average system inventory—as the firm moves toward fewer warehouses and a more centralized warehousing system, safety stocks and thus average inventory levels across the system are decreased. The magnitude of the reduction depends on the demand correlations in the various market areas.

- Responsiveness—as warehouse centralization increases, delivery lead times increase, increasing the risk of late deliveries to customers and reducing the ability of the organization to respond quickly to changes in demand. Customer service levels may thus decrease, because of issues such as traffic problems and weather delays.

- Customer service to the warehouse—as centralization increases, customer service levels provided by suppliers is likely to increase, reducing the likelihood of stockouts for a given level of average system warehouse inventory.

- Transportation costs—as centralization increases, outbound transportation costs increase, as LTL shipments must travel farther to reach customers. Inbound transportation costs decrease, since manufacturers and other suppliers are able to ship larger quantities at TL rates to fewer warehouse locations. The overall impact on transportation costs thus depends on the specific warehouse locations, the goods stored, the locations of suppliers, and the modes of transportation used.

- Warehouse system operating costs—as centralization increases, total operating costs decrease because there are fewer warehouses, fewer employees, less equipment, and less maintenance costs.

Today, some companies are moving toward the use of a **hybrid centralized distribution system**, using IT systems to combine a more decentralized warehousing system with a central control of stocks. One example is the integrated logistics contract between DHL Worldwide Express and Roche Diagnostics to operate Roche's distributed warehousing operation. The system consists of a DHL parts center in Hoofddorp, Netherlands, to handle Roche's routine deliveries and storage of spare parts. Deliveries are handled by DHL's air express carriers. Emergency stocks are held at DHL strategic parts centers and delivered using DHL's door-to-door couriers. The combination of storage and delivery centers allows Roche to offer reliable response to customer requests while avoiding stockpiling of spare parts inventories.[24]

Warehouse Location

A number of location models and theories have been proposed over the years to optimally locate factories, services, and warehouses. In Chapter 11 a number of location analysis tools are discussed and these can certainly be useful for locating warehouses. Early in the development of modern transportation and warehousing networks, several well-known economists posited theories regarding warehouse locations which are discussed in this section.

In the 1920s, Edgar Hoover recommended three types of location strategies: the market positioned, product positioned, and **intermediately positioned strategies.**[25] The **market positioned strategy** locates warehouses close to customers, to maximize distribution service and to allow the firm to generate transportation economies by using TL and CL deliveries to each warehouse location. This strategy is recommended when high levels of distribution flexibility and service are required and when there are few sources of supply. The **product positioned strategy** locates warehouses close to the sources of supply, to enable the firm to collect various goods and then consolidate these into TL or CL quantities for shipment to customers. This strategy works well when there are many sources of supply, multi-product factories, and assortments of goods ordered by customers. The intermediately positioned strategy places warehouses midway between the sources of supply and the customers. This strategy is recommended when distribution service requirements are high and customers order product assortments from various locations.

Later, Johan Heinrich von Thunen argued that transportation costs alone should be minimized when considering facility location.[26] His model assumed that market prices and production costs would be identical regardless of the location of the warehouse, so the optimum location would be the one that resulted in the minimum transportation costs. Weber's location theory was very similar to von Thunen's, in that he argued that the optimum location would be found when the sum of the inbound and outbound transportation costs was minimized.[27]

Greenhut's theory was based on profit instead of transportation costs.[28] He argued that the optimum location would be the one that maximized profits, which may not coincide with the minimum cost location, because demand and prices can potentially vary based on location.

Several location methods have been developed based on transportation costs, one of which is the center-of-gravity approach, discussed in Chapter 11. The weakness of this approach as well as some of those discussed here is that they fail to consider a number of other factors such as labor availability, labor rates, land cost, building codes, tax structure, construction costs, utility costs, and the local environment. If the firm is using a public warehouse, the location selection criteria would need to include warehouse services, lease costs, communication capabilities, reporting frequency, and reputation. These factors may best be addressed using the weighted factor location analysis, also discussed in Chapter 11.

JIT Warehousing

As firms develop their supply chain management capabilities, items will be moving more quickly through inbound and outbound warehouses and distribution centers. These warehouses and distribution centers will thus have to develop more JIT capabilities. Some examples of these capabilities include the following:

- A commitment to customers and service quality—warehouse employees must perform warehouse activities so as to meet the requirements of their inbound and outbound suppliers and customers.
- Reduced lot sizes and shipping quantities—inbound and/or outbound shipping quantities are likely to be smaller and more frequent, containing mixed quantities of goods, and thus requiring more handling.
- Greater emphasis on crossdocking—warehouse employees must receive shipments and mix these quickly into outgoing shipments. Far fewer goods will be stored for any appreciable time, and average warehouse inventory levels will decrease, while the number of stockkeeping units will increase.
- Increased automation—to improve handling speed and reliability, more warehouse activities will become automated, from scanner/barcode computer tracking systems, to automated storage and retrieval systems.

- Increased assembly operations—as more firms implement JIT combined with mass customization, warehouses will be called upon to perform final assembly operations to meet specific customer requirements. This will change the skill requirements of warehouse employees, along with equipment requirements.

Most hospitals have adopted JIT warehousing concepts. "Transportation plays a key role in our ability to serve our customers," says Mr. Craig Smith, of Owens & Minor, a national distributor of medical supplies based in Virginia. "We have 89 different stockless programs, each with different delivery requirements," says Smith. In California at UCLA's hospital, Owens & Minor delivers supplies directly to 123 different locations within the facility from their distribution center.[29]

The Impacts of Logistics on Supply Chain Management

As mentioned earlier in this chapter, logistics refers to the movement and storage of products from point of origin to point of consumption within the firm and throughout the supply chain and is thus responsible for creating time utility and place utility. In a managed supply chain setting, these logistics elements are extremely important in that products must be routinely delivered to each supply chain customer on-time, to the correct location, and at a reasonable cost. As mistakes occur in deliveries along the supply chain, more safety stocks must be held, impacting both customer service levels and costs. To make up for lost time, overnight deliveries might also have be used, adding yet more costs to the transportation bill.

For international supply chains, the logistics function is even more critical. Providing adequate transportation and storage, getting items through customs, delivering to foreign locations in a timely fashion, and logistics pricing can all impact the ability of a supply chain to serve a foreign market competitively. In many cases, firms are forced to use outside agents or **third-party logistics services (3PLs)** to move items into foreign locations effectively.

International purchases are also similarly affected by logistics considerations. When firms begin evaluating and using foreign suppliers, logistics costs and timing become critical factors in the sourcing decision. For instance, Chinese suppliers delivering goods to buyers along the U.S. east coast are in many cases favoring an all-water route through the Panama Canal, rather than dealing with port and traffic congestion on the U.S. west coast. Buyers get cheaper freight rates and can plan on shipments arriving at a specific time when using an all-water route, whereas the chances of domestic U.S. shipments being held up because port and traffic congestion and missed rail connections can be significant. All-water shipments have risen about 65 percent since the early 1990s.[30] These issues become part of the negotiating process between buyer and foreign supplier, and in many cases, buyers with limited foreign purchasing experience must use a knowledgeable 3PL service to purchase from foreign suppliers and make logistics decisions effectively and efficiently.

Thus, we can see the value created for supply chains by logistics. It is what effectively links each supply chain partner. Poor logistics management can literally bring a supply chain to its knees, regardless of the production cost or quality of the products. Alternatively, good logistics management can be one of the elements creating a competitive advantage for supply chains. A number of these topics are explored further in this section.

Third-Party Logistics Services

Most logistics companies offer both transportation and warehousing services, allowing firms to make better use of the distribution alternatives, such as transportation mode, storage location, and customs clearance. Some 3PLs even provide complete end-to-end supply chain management services. For small firms with no internal logistics expertise and large firms with many sizeable and varied logistics needs, outsourcing logistics requirements to these third-party logistics services can help firms get what they want at reasonable prices. Many firms outsource some or all of their logistics needs to allow more attention to be placed on core competencies. Whatever the reason, demand for 3PL services is growing rapidly.

According to an annual survey conducted by the Georgia Institute of Technology, the most widely outsourced logistics functions are transportation, warehousing, customs clearance, and brokerage, with the 3PL selection decision based on cost, service quality, and global reach. Of the companies surveyed, 92 percent saw information technology as a key 3PL requirement, and only 35 percent were satisfied with their provider in this respect. Rolls-Royce Corporation, a global aerospace and defense manufacturer, was one respondent to the survey. They chose CEVA Logistics (formerly TNT Logistics), based in the UK, for their North American logistics needs based on quality, cost, delivery, and responsiveness considerations. "All our 3PLs are critical to our success. There are some things that are not core, but regardless, are critical to our success," says Mark Linville, Director, Production Planning and Control at Rolls-Royce. When asked about their partnership with Rolls-Royce, CEVA CEO Dave Kulik replied, "We have an open relationship. We let them know up front what the costs are, and what changes we feel they need to make in order to facilitate our solution."[31]

Outsourcing All Supply Chain Management Activities

In some cases, firms may opt to partner with a 3PL for the provision of most or all supply chain management activities. For small firms, it may be a question of lack of expertise. The sheer scale of supply chain activities and cost may also attract very large firms that prefer to free up valuable resources for other activities. For example, global automaker General Motors formed a joint venture with CNF, Inc. (now renamed Con-way Inc. and based in California) to manage the automaker's entire supply chain, specifically all of GM's existing third-party logistics providers for both inbound and outbound movements over a 3-year transition period. The joint venture company, Vector SCM, termed a **lead logistics provider (LLP)** or **fourth-party logistics provider (4PL)** managed all of GM's worldwide 3PL providers.[32] Vector also assumed responsibility for managing some 180 million pounds of materials from GM's 12,000 worldwide suppliers every day. Over the years, Vector became valuable enough that GM decided to buy out Con-way's stake in the company in 2006.[33]

Ocean Flavor, a small low-sodium salt company, found its demand growing so rapidly that it needed to find a 3PL company quickly to handle all of the details of their global supply chain. The Global Perspective profiles Ocean Flavor's use of a total supply chain management service provider.

Logistics Management Issues

Logistics provides a vital strategic link between organizations in a supply chain and must therefore be managed effectively to meet customer due dates and other shipping requirements at a reasonable cost. Thus, suppliers, customers, end users, and 3PLs all

Global Perspective

Ocean Flavor's Use of a Supply Chain Management Provider

Ocean Flavor Sea Salt would not be able to distribute its products without outside assistance. It began as what Alan Fisher, its president, describes as a hobby. With his partner Al Kirchner the two had a method of producing a naturally low-sodium sea salt, something Fisher says is unique in the world.

A worldwide search for a production facility led them to Mexico's Baja California, which has the largest solar salt-producing plant in the world. The fledgling company had its salt and patent—everything but customers. At the urging of the company that was packaging the salt for Ocean Flavor, the partners attended the major Institute of Food Technologists show in Las Vegas, using a small space in the packager's booth. "For the first hour after the show opened, nothing happened," Fisher recalls. "Within an hour and a half after the show started, it was like a tidal wave. And from that point on, until the end of the show, we actually needed help to answer people."

In February 2005, Campbell's began using Ocean Flavor's salt to lower the sodium content of their products. Fisher claims that from February 20 to December 31, 2005, gross revenues climbed to $2.5 million.

The company outsources all of its supply chain activities to Weber Distribution. Ocean Flavor salt is trucked by Mexican companies to a warehouse in Tijuana, and then taken across the border. It is then housed in the U.S. in Weber's 103,000 sq. ft. facility in San Diego. The Mexican plant handles all documentation that accompanies the salt. Since the plant has been moving salt across the border for more than 40 years, it is well aware of necessary documentation to verify that the product meets all U.S. requirements.

From the San Diego storage facility, the salt is sent directly to Ocean Flavor customers by truck or shipped via BNSF rail to Tekpak, in Marion, Alabama. Tekpak is the company's master distributor. It reformulates and repackages the salt, then ships it on to final customers who include Tyson Foods, Fairfield Farms, and Unilever among others.

The company has now started selling its own branded salt. It is expanding its retail market in other ways and will continue to rely on Weber. "We outsource everything," explains Fisher. "Weber will be handling exports to Asia and now, imports, because we just signed an exclusive contract for Dead Sea Salt out of Israel. We're bringing it into Mobile, AL. It's the highest trace mineral salt in the world. It will be Ocean Flavor Dead Sea Salt."

Source: Morton, R. "Outsourced Services Add Spice to the Business." *Logistics Today,* 48, no. 6 (2007): 24–25. Used with permission.

have a stake in good logistics management. Effective logistics management can also be a source of profitability for the firm, as logistics managers find ways to package, store, and move products more efficiently along the supply chain. Because of the important role of logistics, the job of managing logistics issues for an organization has been elevated and enlarged to include a number of issues such as environmental sustainability in logistics, 3PL supply base reduction, mode and 3PL selection, logistics management software applications, measuring logistics performance, creating strategic 3PL alliances, performing **logistics audits**, and use of e-commerce technologies in logistics. These logistics management issues are discussed next.

Environmental Sustainability in Logistics

Today, firms are facing increasing pressure to improve their environmental reputation from customers as well as local, state, and federal governing bodies. With regard to **green logistics**, California is attempting to limit rail idling, Wal-Mart is demanding more environmentally sensitive packaging, and the U.S. government has passed tougher truck engine emissions standards. Becoming more "green" also has some positive financial implications, as described in earlier chapters. A lot of energy is used in the supply chain, and shippers and 3PLs alike are finding quite a bit of low-hanging fruit in the areas of transportation and warehousing where energy costs can be reduced. For example, Mr. Brice Russell, senior vice president for supply chain at Masterfoods, an internal division that handles the Mars global candy supply chain, told the Council of Supply Chain Management Professionals at their 2006 annual meeting that Mars had saved approximately $7 million and cut fuel use by about 1.2 million gallons so far, with a route-by-route analysis of its transportation network. "We have to train our suppliers to think about energy costs," says Russell. "The transportation and energy cost component is making us think differently."[34]

Massachusetts-based Staples, one of the world's largest office supply retailers, is headed toward its goal of reducing carbon emissions by 7 percent by 2010 from its 2001 levels, even as they have expanded with new stores and warehouses. They have installed governors on their trucking fleet to cap truck speeds at 60 miles per hour, saving 500,000 to 750,000 gallons of fuel per year. Global chemical manufacturer Dow reformulated its stretch wrap materials, reducing the weight of its annual shipments by approximately 1 billion pounds. Less packaging weight means fewer truck and rail trips, which has saved transportation costs for Dow.

When building distribution centers, firms are now focusing on more efficient designs to save money. Staples' warehouses, lit by skylights and solar power, enable the company to pay less for energy. Colorado-based ProLogis, the world's largest owner, manager, and builder of distribution centers, uses advanced building materials, energy sources, and architecture to make its facilities airtight and environmentally controlled for less waste heat and cooling. "People don't ask how cheap you can build a building, but how efficiently and what is the energy configuration," says Kenneth Hall, managing director for European development at ProLogis.[35]

3PL Supply Base Reduction

As discussed in Chapter 4, reducing the supply base can provide a number of advantages for the organization. With 3PL suppliers, the discussion is very similar—using fewer 3PLs enables the firm to select and use only the best performing 3PLs as well as to give these 3PLs a bigger share of their logistics needs. This in turn results in better levels of service and potentially cheaper prices. The larger share of business given to each 3PL can be used as leverage when negotiating prices, shipping schedules, and services. By the end of 2005, for instance, Hewlett-Packard had halved the number of 3PLs it was using and expected to halve it again by the end of 2007. Other companies are similarly seeking an "irreducible minimum" number of 3PL suppliers.[36] Thus, 3PL supply base reduction should become an integral part of an effective logistics management strategy particularly in markets characterized by numerous supplier choices.

Mode and 3PL Selection

When attempting to minimize logistics costs and/or improve customer service along the supply chain, firms must identify the most desirable transportation modes and 3PL services available for the various markets they serve as well as for their inbound purchased materials. Also, other costs will be affected by this decision including inventory-in-transit carrying costs, packaging costs, warehousing costs, and shipment damage costs. Chapters 2 and 3 both discussed the topic of evaluating and selecting suppliers, and again, the topic here is very similar. Firms use a mix of quantitative and qualitative factors to evaluate and select 3PLs and there are a number of comparative methods available to aid in the decision process, the most common of which is the weighted factor analysis. In a number of surveys conducted, important selection factors were found to be transit-time reliability, transportation rates, total transit time, willingness to negotiate rates and services, damage-free delivery frequency, financial stability, use of electronic data interchange, and willingness to expedite deliveries.[37] In their most recent logistics survey at the Georgia Institute of Technology, global capabilities and security processes were also seen as important factors.[38]

In some cases, companies enlist the help of **transportation intermediaries** to find the most appropriate transportation mode or 3PL service. For many small companies where logistics expertise may be limited and in some cases for large companies where the scale of logistics needs are great, use of an intermediary can make good economic sense. A few of these intermediaries are discussed here.

Freight Forwarders

Freight forwarders consolidate a large number of small shipments to fill entire truck trailers or rail cars that transport items at truckload or carload prices. They can also provide air transportation consolidation services. These companies pass some of the savings on to the small shippers and keep the rest of it as revenue. Thus, freight forwarders provide valuable services to both the shipper (lower prices) and the carrier (consolidation). Freight forwarders can specialize in either domestic or international shipments, as well as air or ground shipments. These companies also provide documentation services, special freight handling, and customs clearance.

Several changes are occurring in the freight forwarding arena today, as some customers opt to save money by using slower, second-day and economy shipping options. Doug Brittin, vice president of marketing and business development at Emery, says even JIT shipments can be shipped using slower, cheaper transportation alternatives if they are secure and reliable. Better software also helps shippers make better shipping decisions and obtain more shipment visibility from carriers. "Information and visibility are almost as important as transportation itself," says Brittin.[39]

Transportation Brokers

Also referred to as **load brokers, transportation brokers** bring shippers and transportation companies (mainly truckers) together. The transportation broker is legally authorized to act on the shipper's or carrier's behalf and typically these companies are hired because of their extensive knowledge of the many transportation alternatives available or the many shippers needing transportation. Many transportation brokers use a Web site to bring parties together. The transportation posting service Getloaded.com is profiled in the e-Business Connection feature.

e-Business Connection

Load Brokering and Getloaded.com

There's more than one way to catch a quality carrier. For 30 years Virginia-based VHI Transport has been a certified transportation broker serving shipper's needs by reaching out to get capacity. VHI matches loads to carriers that call in, beginning at 7:00 am, and those that are called in the day before. It also uses several posting services to help with locating trucks. One of them is Getloaded.com. "As soon as we add the load into our computer system, it spiders out to Getloaded.com and we get assistance from them," VHI's director of operations, Connie Alexander says, "We also get postings from trucking companies and drivers at truck stops. They are all watching load-matching boards. So we could get a call from a truck stop, a driver, or a dispatcher who is monitoring our board, or the dot coms themselves."

For its part, Getloaded.com handles 140,000 loads each day. More than 23,000 trucking companies are registered with the Internet load board, representing more than 500,000 trucks. VHI does all of the qualification of trucking companies and shippers itself. The company also uses Getloaded.com to check carrier insurance for safety ratings.

Source: Morton, R. "Modern Day Load Brokering." *Logistics Today,* v. 48, no. 3 (2007): 20. Used with permission.

Typical arrangements might find small businesses using a transportation broker to handle many of their shipping needs, or trucking companies using brokers to find a back-haul job after a delivery is completed. A number of transportation broker directories exist, enabling shippers and carriers to find one meeting their needs. For instance, the Red Book Transportation Brokers Rating Service is an online directory of transportation brokers in the U.S. and Canada. The Web site provides user ratings of the various transportation brokers as well as information about each of the brokers and their services.[40]

Shippers' Associations

The American Institute for Shippers' Associations (AISA) defines **shippers' associations** as "non-profit membership cooperatives which make domestic or international arrangements for the movement of members' cargo." Thus, their job is to consolidate their members' shipments into full carloads, truckloads, or container loads to achieve volume discounts for the members, and to negotiate for improved terms of service. These associations also benefit the transportation companies, in that they help to better utilize their equipment. Because shippers' associations do not identify themselves as 3PLs or transportation providers, they are not required to publish or adhere to tariff rates and can keep service contracts confidential. Some of the disadvantages of membership include required minimum shipment volumes to receive the benefits of reduced rates, and some ocean carriers refusing to do business with shippers' associations. A number of shippers' associations exist for different industries. For example, the U.S. Department of Agriculture lists thirteen shippers' associations for agricultural shippers.[41]

Intermodal Marketing Companies

Intermodal marketing companies (IMCs) are companies that act as intermediaries between intermodal railroad companies and shippers. They typically purchase large blocks of flatcars for piggyback service, then find shippers to fill containers, or motor carriers with truckloads, to load the flatcars. They get volume discounts from the railroads and pass some of this on to the shippers. These companies facilitate intermodal shipping and have become an important intermediary. Many IMCs utilize Internet, cell phone, and satellite transmissions to allow real-time communications between themselves, the carriers, and the shippers. This also enables accurate delivery predictions for customers.[42]

Logistics Management Software Applications

As mentioned briefly in Chapter 6, logistics management software applications can be added to ERP software suites of applications, as the firm's needs and the users' level of experience dictates. Some of the more popular logistics management applications include **transportation management systems**, **warehouse management systems**, and **returns management systems**. Companies are finding significant benefits with these logistics execution systems. Purchases in this area are growing rapidly—worldwide expenditures on logistics software applications were nearly $3 billion in 2006.[43] These systems are briefly discussed next.

Transportation Management Systems

Transportation management system (TMS) applications allow firms to select the best mix of transportation services and pricing to determine the best use of containers or truck trailers, to better manage transportation contracts, to rank transportation options, to clear customs, to track fuel usage and product movements, and to track carrier performance. Regulatory bodies, shippers, and customers want to know where goods are in-transit, thus real-time information about shipment location while it is being transported to the final destination is required. Consequently, information may need to be provided by the manufacturer, third-party logistics providers, agents, freight forwarders and others as products move through global supply chains. Technologies employed to provide this visibility include barcode scanners, RFID tags, the Internet, and GPS devices.

The desire to secure national borders against unwanted shipments has increased recently due to terrorist concerns, causing a number of governments to more closely regulate the flow of goods across its borders. This has potentially added transportation delay problems to shipments as companies deal with an added layer of bureaucracy and reporting at various border entry sites. To help mitigate delay problems, many TMS software applications have capabilities for customs declaration, calculation and payment of **tariffs**, duties and duty drawbacks, and advanced filing of shipment manifests.

These features are catching the attention of company executives, and TMS purchases are expected to grow by approximately 7 percent over the next decade. "Transportation management is moving out of the shadows and into a strategic role in driving supply chain excellence," says Beth Enslow, vice president of enterprise research at Massachusetts-based Aberdeen Group, a business research company. Greg Ami, director of supply chain research at another business research firm, Massachusetts-based AMR Research, expects demand for TMS applications to continue to rise. "We'll see continued growth in TMS because there is no end in sight for the problems that transportation managers are facing today," he says.[44]

Warehouse Management Systems

When ERP systems include a TMS coupled with a warehouse management system (WMS), supply chain management effectiveness is even further enhanced. For example, a company might use their TMS to forecast shipping volumes based on data provided by their WMS and then recommend the most efficient modes of shipping. The WMS could then pick and schedule warehouse usage based on TMS shipping requirements. Warehouse management systems track and control the flow of goods from the receiving dock of a warehouse or distribution center until the item is loaded for outbound shipment to the customer. RFID tags placed on products and pallets within the distribution center are used to control the flow of goods. The goals of a WMS include reducing distribution center labor costs, streamlining the flow of goods, reducing the time products spend in the distribution center, managing distribution center capacity, reducing paperwork, and managing the cross-docking process.

Frozen Gourmet, a California-based wholesale food distributor, has seen demand for space at their warehouse grow by 80 percent over the past ten years. According to David McDaniel, warehouse manager at Frozen Gourmet, "Ten years ago, when I started with the company we were small. Our inventory management system consisted of poking our head into the freezer, counting the products, and that was it." Because of their expanded warehouse and greater number of products stored, they installed SmartTurn's Web-hosted WMS in 2006 and found that it increased shipment accuracy; provided real-time inventory visibility; and allowed them to automate purchasing, receiving, ordering, picking, and shipping.[45]

WMSs are also being used in manufacturing shop floor applications. For example, Hewlett-Packard uses a WMS to route incoming materials from the receiving docks to the assembly lines at some of its computer assembly facilities. H-P then uses the system to manage finished goods from the production lines to the shipping docks for delivery to customers.[46]

As mentioned above, use of TMSs and WMSs has increased the use of RFID tags and technologies. Joe Dunlap, supply chain solutions head at Michigan-based Siemens-Dematic, thinks that RFID has the potential to completely change the supply chain. "In a WMS that directs order pick-up or delivery by scanning bar codes, there's the possibility of the operator putting the load in the wrong place, but scanning the correct location barcode label, thus producing an out-of-stock situation." The use of RFID would eliminate that potential for error as readers automatically collect the information.[47] In 2006, Wal-Mart began using hand-held RFID scanners in storage areas to identify products needed to restock shelves. Wal-Mart has since found that stockouts have been reduced by 16 percent.[48]

Returns Management Systems

Reverse logistics, discussed later in this chapter, refers to the processes involved in returning products for replacement, repair, or refund. Returns management systems (RMS) are thus being created to provide global visibility, standardization, and documentation of product returns, while minimizing reverse logistics costs. In addition to managing returns, the RMS can also be designed to handle returnable transportation items such as pallets, platforms, and containers.

In many cases, RMS capabilities are built into WMS applications. Some companies use their WMS to facilitate the returns process before the original product is even shipped. "Many direct-to-consumer companies will have the WMS create a return label when they are printing out the initial paper work," says Noah Dixon, industry strategy leader at RedPrairie, a Wisconsin-based logistics system provider. "A residential customer can then go to a shipper like FedEx, UPS, or the post office and use that label to process the return."[49] Product recalls can also be handled using an RMS in combination with the WMS. A WMS with lot and serial number tracking capability, for example, allows a company to bring back only units of product that have been identified with a particular defect.

Measuring Logistics Performance

Rising fuel costs, carrier capacity constraints, and increasing customer service demands from customers have increased the importance of measuring both the performance of 3PLs and the firm's internal logistics department. Measuring logistics performance allows the firm to identify problem areas and then make changes, resulting in improved logistics services and improved management of logistics. Measures of performance can be compared with predetermined standards, competitive benchmarks, or previous period performance to identify problems. For 3PLs, the measures themselves are very similar to those used initially to select 3PL providers: transportation cost, percent on-time deliveries, average transit time, service flexibility, billing accuracy, and damage-free delivery frequency, to name a few.

Several years ago, global diversified manufacturer Eaton Corp. began increasing its ability to manage global logistics activities to better control its costs. The company's key to achieving its desired goal of end-to-end visibility of their supply chain by 2010 is the use of lead logistics providers, or 4PLs. They now employ 4PLs in several important regions of the world and measure their performance using four metrics—speed to implementation, cost of implementation, speed to savings, and speed to efficiency. Eaton shares performance information with its 4PLs on a monthly basis and conducts regular quarterly reviews with them. "We have been able to see a relatively rapid increase, within six months, increase in logistics efficiencies within our own different businesses," says Mario Hegewald, director of global logistics at Eaton.[50]

California-based headwear and handbag retailer Dorfman Pacific measures logistics provider performance using their warehouse management software application. The system creates a performance scorecard for each of its 3PLs, which are communicated to each firm periodically, to help improve performance. By tracking and analyzing on-time performance, service consistency, billing accuracy, and price competitiveness, companies such as Dorfman Pacific are finding improvements in services provided, transportation rates, and 3PL capacity availabilities.[51]

Creating Strategic 3PL Alliances

Building and managing an effective supply chain network very often includes the creation of strategic alliances with providers of logistics services. In fact, in several surveys of various businesses and industries, transportation and warehousing companies were included as supply chain partners in more than 50 percent of the survey respondents who were actively managing their supply chains.[52] These partnerships underscore the importance and role played by logistics in supply chain management. A few examples are given here.

Partnerships between railroads and automakers in the U.S. have resulted in seven out of every ten vehicles produced being moved by rail to the dealerships, along with a large percentage of the vehicle parts moving to assembly plants. Railroads have invested billions of dollars fabricating special boxcars designed to the automakers' specifications, autorack rail cars with premium cushioning, auto-carrier trucks, a network of vehicle distribution centers, and for information systems to make railroad companies function as an integral part of automakers' organizations. In 2000, Wal-Mart piloted a **collaborative transportation management** project with partners Proctor & Gamble and motor carrier J.B. Hunt. By working together and sharing forecasting, planning, and replenishment information, J.B. Hunt has been able to act on information sooner and keep trucks full and moving, resulting in a 16 percent decrease in unloading time, and a 3 percent drop in empty miles, while Wal-Mart significantly reduced the number of steps to process goods for its promotions.[53] In the past 12 years, Auto-Zone, an automobile parts retailer based in Tennessee, grew from 1000 stores to over 3800 stores in the U.S. and Mexico. AutoZone uses a unique combination of their private trucking fleet and strategic partner 3PLs, to make sure as many loads as possible are consolidated into TL shipments using crossdocking at AutoZone's distribution centers and to allow their private fleet to maximize backhaul utilization. AutoZone partners with Texas-based 3PL Transplace for domestic shipments and Connecticut-based 3PL Kuehne & Nagel for international shipments.

Performing Logistics Audits

Each organization has a unique set of inbound and outbound logistics requirements based on customer and supplier locations, requirements for specific services, products purchased and sold, distribution center locations, manufacturing site locations, and the 3PLs available. With the passage of time, these characteristics all tend to change, requiring firms to periodically audit their logistics system with the objective of finding an optimal mix of both cost and service. Since the logistics system affects a number of functional areas within the firm as well as supply chain partners, it is wise to include personnel from various areas of the firm to participate in an audit and to develop recommendations for changes to the logistics system. This audit team might include personnel from customer service, traffic, warehousing, purchasing, production, and quality, as well as representatives from supply chain partners.

When conducting a logistics audit, firms must consider system constraints such as facility locations, customer locations, and the existing domestic and international logistics infrastructures. Given these constraints, an audit seeks to determine the most effective way to move products to the firm from suppliers, between firm locations, and then from the firm to its customers. Complicating factors include JIT or lean system requirements that the firm or its customers may have, special services, quantities, packaging needs, and any legal aspects of transporting and storing goods. Given these factors, there are typically a large number of logistics options available, and the firm must evaluate each of these options to determine the most optimal system configuration.

Apart from auditing the logistics system, internal logistics departments may also need to be audited to assure executive management that the logistics department is functioning as effectively as possible. Logistics managers should consider the appropriateness of technologies, use of outsourcing, types of 3PL contracts used, internal resources, and reports generated when performing a departmental audit.

Use of e-Commerce Technologies in Logistics

For many logistics service providers, the growth in e-commerce has opened up a new distribution channel for their services. For shippers, the Internet has reduced the time to find transportation providers, enabled quicker price comparisons, and allowed companies to further automate their logistics systems. For 3PLs, e-commerce capabilities are quickly becoming a requirement. Customers are demanding Web-enabled shipment execution capabilities, online payment capabilities, and real-time shipment status information. Some of the specific e-commerce issues that are affecting logistics today include electronic invoice presentment and payment, supply chain visibility technologies, and third-party electronic transaction platforms. These topics are briefly discussed below.

Electronic Invoice Presentment and Payment

Electronic invoice presentment and payment (EIPP) technology, or sending and receiving invoices and payments online, represents one of the most commonly used B2B transactions, and it is designed to create greater efficiencies among the companies using the technology. Companies such as AT&T Wireless, Con-way Transportation Services, and General Electric have been able to lower their invoice processing costs, reduce billing errors, improve cash flow, and provide better customer service using EIPP. Today, software suppliers of EIPP applications are generating even more value for their customers by enabling their EIPP software to be integrated with existing ERP, purchasing, accounts payable, and call center systems. In 2004, the annual report on e-commerce and development by the United Nations Conference on Trade and Development (UNCTAD) quantified the enormous growth in the use of the Internet for B2B purposes. As of June 2004 there were more than 51,500,000 Web sites worldwide, which was 26 percent more than the year before. In addition, the number of Web sites supporting secure transactions grew by more than 50 percent for the same period.[54]

Con-way Transportation Services hopes to cut invoicing costs by 90 percent, using electronic billing. Con-way's customers, however, see the benefits of EIPP from the ability to get copies of their shipping manifests online, being able to check the status of their shipments, and reconcile invoices with purchase orders and delivery records without having to pick up the phone. The reductions in phone calls have also reduced the need for call center representatives.[55]

Supply Chain Visibility Technologies

For supply chains to be successful, time is definitely a factor that must be managed, and e-commerce technologies are helping companies to achieve tremendous time-related benefits by providing **supply chain visibility** for customers, shippers, and 3PLs. The BNSF Railway Web page, for instance, allows shippers to plan the movement of their freight; get immediate rates and special service fees; make orders; trace their shipments; manage other elements of their shipments such as demurrage, storage, and diversion needs; and pay invoices online.[56] BNSF has taken the lead in Internet-based rail transportation management systems. Maine-based Fairchild Semiconductor conducts trade in more than 45 countries and uses a transportation software application to track its inbound and outbound shipments across country borders. Their online system also allows Fairchild to obtain advance customs approvals and compliance for work-in-progress shipments as they move around the world for completion.[57] Finally, Japanese-based NNR Aircargo Service, a global freight forwarder, uses Web-based applications to connect its 85 locations in eleven countries, supporting international air and ocean freight transactions, including the creation of airway bills and bills of lading, cargo order tracking, and the creation of online reports.[58]

Third-Party Electronic Transaction Platforms

A number of software application providers are developing specialty Web platforms to allow shippers and carriers to perform various transactions over the Web. Currently, there are literally thousands of third-party Web portals and exchanges dealing with logistics. These sites provide freight-matching services, auctions, and on-line communities or marketplaces. A number of these examples have been provided in this chapter already. Most online logistics sites offer a mixture of portal, exchange, and catalog offerings.[59] One example is a Web site designed to help shippers, freight forwarders, and ocean carriers comply with the U.S. Customs Service's Advance Manifest Regulation, more commonly known as the "24-hour rule." GTN, operated by GT Nexus, Inc. helps companies achieve compliance with U.S. Customs rules by allowing shippers to prepare and transmit key shipping documents to their 3PLs, thereby reducing system delays.[60] In the U.S. since 1995, NTE, formerly the National Transportation Exchange, offers a number of logistics management applications, including an online marketplace for buyers and sellers of ground transportation. Buyer and seller members interactively trade ground transportation capacity, at market-driven prices in a neutral exchange, somewhat like the stock market. The exchange offers complete execution processing, shipment tracking, and guaranteed payment.[61]

International Logistics

For international goods movements, logistics managers must be aware of the availability, services, costs, and limitations of the various modes of transportation. In the U.S., freight movement to Europe or Asia involves either air or water transportation, and then most likely motor and/or rail transportation to the final destination. Between most contiguous countries, rail and motor shipments tend to be the most common modes of transportation.

There are many logistics problems and infrastructure differences found as goods are moved from one country to the next. In Europe, rail transportation tends to be much more prevalent and reliable than rail transportation in the U.S., because European track, facilities, and equipment are newer and better maintained. This is partly because most transportation modes are government owned and maintained in Europe. Water carriers may be the dominant mode of transportation in countries with a great deal of coastline and developed inland waterways. In under- and undeveloped countries, ports may be very poorly maintained and equipped, and the highway system may be almost nonexistent. A number of international logistics topics are discussed next.

International Freight Security

One of the most troublesome and debated issues facing international freight logistics today is the issue of security. In 2003, U.S. Customs introduced the idea of mandatory electronic prenotification for all air and land cargo coming into the U.S., similar to the already implemented 24-hour rule for ocean freight. The rule requires Customs to be notified 24 hours before shipment of the cargo. This rule, combined with additional restrictions and inspections put in place after September 11, 2001, further slows down shipment times from overseas, making air transportation a less attractive option. For instance, an international shipment that used to take two days to get through customs at JFK Airport in New York now typically takes four days. Perhaps the hardest hit sector of this industry is the custom shipment or air charter market. A number of operators have already gone out of business because their former customers no longer had the money to pay for these types of shipments.[62]

In 2006, there were more than 22 million truck crossings into the U.S. from Canada and Mexico. In the past few years, the trucking industry has worked with U.S. Customs to develop the **Customs-Trade Partnership Against Terrorism program (C-TPAT)** and its security program called the **Free and Secure Trade program (FAST)**. The overall goal is to ensure the security of international supply chains in general and international trucking in particular. To participate in FAST, motor carriers must become C-TPAT certified and their commercial drivers must complete an application and undergo a background check. FAST participants receive expedited cargo clearance provided their customers are also C-TPAT certified, and they receive access to a dedicated FAST lane at border crossings.[63]

International Logistics Intermediaries

International logistics intermediaries provide international shipping, consolidation, and import/export services for firms and offer expertise that can prove very useful for most organizations involved in global commerce. A number of these intermediaries that have not already been discussed are briefly discussed in this section.

Customs Brokers

Customs brokers move international shipments through customs for companies as well as handle the necessary documentation required to accompany the shipments. These specialists are often used by companies requiring expertise in exporting goods to foreign countries; their knowledge of the many import requirements of various countries can significantly reduce the time required to move goods internationally and clear them through customs.

International or Foreign Freight Forwarders

These services move goods for companies from domestic production facilities to foreign customer destinations using surface and air transportation and warehouses. They consolidate small shipments into larger TL, CL, or container shipments, decide what transportation modes and methods to use, handle all of the documentation requirements, and then disperse the shipments at their destination. They also determine the best routing to use, oversee storage, breakbulk, and repackaging requirements and provide for any other logistics requirements of the seller. Use of **foreign freight forwarders** can reduce logistics costs, increase customer service, and allow shippers to focus resources on other activities. Most companies exporting their goods use the services of foreign freight forwarders because of their expertise and presence in the sellers' foreign markets. Some of the top-rated companies providing these services include: USF Worldwide, EGL Global logistics, UPS Sonic Air, and Kintetsu World Express.[64]

Trading Companies

Trading companies put buyers and sellers from different countries together and handle all of the export/import arrangements, documentation, and transportation for both goods and services. Most trading companies are involved in exporting, and they usually take title to the goods until sold to foreign buyers. They enjoy economies of scale when exporting goods as they ship large quantities of consolidated shipments, using established transportation and warehousing services. In the U.S., the Export Trading Company Act was signed into law in 1982 to promote U.S. exports and to help U.S. exporters improve their competitiveness. Within the U.S. Department of Commerce, the Export Trading Company Affairs (ETCA) office helps promote the development of joint ventures between U.S. and foreign companies and the use of export trade intermediaries. The ETCA office was created by the Export Trading Company Act of 1982.[65]

Non-Vessel Operating Common Carriers

Also referred to as NVOCCs, **non-vessel operating common carriers** operate very similarly to international freight forwarders, but normally use scheduled ocean liners. They consolidate small international shipments from a number of shippers into full container loads and then handle all of the documentation and transportation arrangements from the shippers' dock area. NVOCCs also handle distribution to consignees at the destination dock area.

Foreign Trade Zones

Foreign trade zones (FTZs) are secure sites within the U.S. under the supervision of the U.S. Customs Service. These sites are authorized by the Foreign Trade Zones Board, chaired by the U.S. Secretary of Commerce, and are comparable to the so-called *free trade zones* that exist in many other countries today. FTZs are considered to be outside U.S. Customs territory, where foreign or domestic merchandise can enter without formal customs entry or payment of duties or excise taxes. FTZs bring goods and materials into the site and offer storage, exporting, manufacturing, assembly, repacking, testing, and repairing services. No retail activities are allowed however. If the final product is exported out of the U.S., no domestic duties or excise taxes are levied. If the final product is imported into the U.S., duties and taxes are paid at the time of formal entry to U.S. Customs.

Congress established the Foreign Trade Zones Board in 1934 to encourage U.S. firms to participate in international trade. As of 2006, there were approximately 250 active FTZs in the U.S., with more than $400 billion in merchandise coming into these areas per year. Petroleum, pharmaceutical, automotive, and electronics companies are the largest users of U.S. FTZs.[66]

The North American Free Trade Agreement

Implementation of the North American Free Trade Agreement (NAFTA) began on January 1, 1994, and will eventually remove most barriers to trade and investment among the U.S., Canada, and Mexico.[67] Many tariffs (published import fees) and quotas were eliminated immediately, and most others will be eliminated by 2008. NAFTA forms the world's second largest open market, somewhat smaller in size than the European Union. The objectives of NAFTA are to facilitate cross-border trade between the three countries, increase investment opportunities, and promote fair trade.

NAFTA has not been without its detractors. U.S. labor groups have argued that jobs are being lost as companies move to Mexico to take advantage of cheap foreign labor, undermining labor union negotiating power. Environmental groups have been concerned that pollution and food safety laws have become more difficult to enforce. Others argue that because of subsidized agricultural exports to Mexico, the small Mexican farmer is being run out of business. In response to these concerns, supplementary agreements have been added to NAFTA that address these and other issues. Gary Hufbauer, a fellow with the Peter G. Peterson Institute for International Economics, says that economic integration between the three countries was well underway before NAFTA and progress would have continued without it, albeit at a slower pace. "I think everyone who has looked at it concludes that trade with Mexico, in particular, had had a big boost in two-way traffic due to NAFTA. Before the agreement, trade barriers between Canada and the United States were much lower than they were with Mexico prior to NAFTA," he says.[68]

Reverse Logistics

Reverse logistics refers to the backward flow of goods *from* customers in the supply chain occurring when goods are returned, either by the end-product consumer or by an organization within the supply chain. In other words, reverse logistics refers to the movement and storage of returned goods. Returns are increasing today because, in part, of the growth of online shopping, direct-to-store shipments, and direct-to-home shipments. Recently, the use of cheap and untested foreign suppliers has also caused a relatively high number of product recalls in the U.S. On August 1, 2007, California-based Mattel, the world's biggest toymaker, recalled almost 1 million Chinese-made toys because they were covered with paint containing lead. The very next week, Mattel again was forced to announce a toy recall for lead-based paint, and for toys containing small magnets which posed a choking hazard. In fact, eight of Mattel's nine toy recalls from 2004 to 2007 were for Chinese-made products.[69]

Retail customer returns account for approximately 6 percent of sales and can sometimes be as high as 40 percent. And the logistical costs to process these returns can also be very high—now running approximately $100 billion each year in the U.S. for transportation, handling, processing, disposal, and lost sales. Besides the significant impact on costs, returns also can have a direct negative impact on customer service, the firm's reputation, and profitability if not managed properly. New Jersey–based shoe manufacturer Aerosoles positions returns as a customer benefit. Much of their sales is through Internet and catalog sales, and they typically receive 35,000 to 40,000 return packages each year. Aerosoles uses Texas-based Newgistics to manage its reverse logistics process. Each shipment to its customers contains a prepaid return label to make customer returns as convenient as possible. Merchandise is returned to a Newgistics distribution center where it is sorted, and either disposed of or reprocessed before being returned to the Aerosoles warehouse.[70]

The Impact of Reverse Logistics on the Supply Chain

Returns can represent significant challenges to a supply chain. In many cases, reverse logistics is viewed as an unwanted activity of supply chain management. In these cases, reverse logistics is seen simply as a cost of doing business or a regulatory compliance issue. Problems include the inability of information systems to handle returns or monitor reverse product flow, lack of worker training in reverse logistics procedures, little or no identification on returned packages, the need for adequate inspection and testing of returns, and the placing of potentially damaged returned products into sales stocks. A poor reverse logistics system can affect the entire supply chain financially and can have a large impact on how a consumer views a product brand, potentially impacting future sales. A recent report by the Aberdeen Group, which studies the use of technology in business, found that 60 percent of the 175 leading manufacturing company executives it questioned were dissatisfied with their firms' approach to product returns.

Today, though, many successful supply chain participants view reverse logistics as a strategic activity that can ultimately enhance customer service, repeat sales, and competitiveness. From a marketing perspective, an effective returns process can create goodwill and enhance customers' perceptions of product quality and purchase risk. From a logistics perspective, returned products can still create value as original products, refurbished products, or repair parts. This also tends to reduce disposal costs.

Reverse Logistics and the Environment

Reverse logistics can have a positive impact on the environment through activities such as recycling, reusing materials and products, or refurbishing used products. **Green reverse logistics programs** include reducing the environmental impact of certain modes of transportation used for returns, reducing the amount of disposed packaging and product materials by redesigning products and processes, and making use of reusable totes and pallets.

Traditionally, organizations have used landfills for routine product and material disposal, but today, landfills have become much more expensive to use. Local, state, and federal governments are also imposing stricter rules regarding use of landfills. These changes have led to innovative ways of dealing with used products or product waste. New Jersey–based Campbell Soup Company now uses a system that tears soup cans into small strips and then washes and separates the metal. It also crushes and washes glass containers. The remaining vegetable matter is dried and sold as feed to local farmers.[71] Advanced Micro Devices, based in Texas, works with its suppliers to find ways to decrease packaging waste and handling activities. In one instance, the company had traditionally used 55-gallon drums to store some of their bulk chemicals, but changed to 300-gallon totes and eventually to bulk tankers to reduce packaging waste that would eventually be delivered to a landfill.[72]

SUMMARY

This chapter has discussed the important role of logistics in any industrialized society in general and to supply chains in particular. Though this is a very broad topic, we have attempted to review the elements within U.S. domestic and international logistics to give the reader an adequate understanding of the entire field of logistics. These elements include the basics of transportation, third-party transportation providers, warehousing, international logistics, logistics management, and reverse logistics. It is hoped that readers have gained an understanding of the many elements within the broad topic of logistics and why these are so important to the management of supply chains.

KEY TERMS

air carriers, 310

airline security, 316

breakbulk, 321

Civil Aeronautics Act of 1938, 319

class rates, 315

coal slurry, 313

collaborative transportation management, 336

commodity rates, 316

common carriers, 309

consolidation warehouses, 322

container-on-flatcar (COFC), 314

contract carriers, 310

cost-of-service pricing, 314

cross-docking, 321

customs brokers, 339

Customs-Trade Partnership Against Terrorism program (C-TPAT), 339

deep-sea transportation, 313

Department of Transportation Act, 319

distribution center, 321

electronic invoice presentment and payment (EIPP), 337

exception rates, 316

exempt carriers, 310

Federal Aviation Act of 1958, 319

FOB destination pricing, 315

FOB origination prices, 315

foreign freight forwarders, 339

foreign trade zones (FTZs), 340

fourth-party logistics provider (4PL), 328

Free and Secure Trade program (FAST), 339

freight forwarders, 319

general freight carriers, 311

granger laws, 317

green logistics, 330

green reverse logistics programs, 342

high-speed trains, 312

hybrid centralized distribution system, 325

ICC Termination Act of 1995, 321

intermediately positioned strategies, 325

intermodal marketing companies (IMCs), 332

intermodal transportation, 308

Interstate Commerce Act of 1887, 317

JIT warehousing, 322

lead logistics provider (LLP), 328

less-than-truckload (LTL) carriers, 311

line haul rates, 315

load brokers, 331

logistics audits, 329

market dominance, 320

market positioned strategy, 325

miscellaneous rates, 316

Motor Carrier Act of 1935, 319

motor carriers, 310

non-vessel operating common carriers, 340

North American Free Trade Agreement (NAFTA), 316

Ocean Shipping Reform Act of 1998, 321

piggyback service, 314

pipeline carriers, 310

place utility, 307

private carriers, 309

private warehouses, 322

product positioned strategy, 326

public warehouses, 323

rail carriers, 310

Railroad Revitalization and Regulatory Reform Act, 319

DISCUSSION QUESTIONS

1. Why are transportation and warehousing important issues in supply chain management?

2. What are the important activities or elements in logistics?

3. List the legal forms and modes of transportation. Which mode is the least expensive? Which mode carries the most freight? Which mode is growing the fastest? Shrinking the fastest?

4. What are some intermodal transportation alternatives?

5. What does "piggyback service" refer to?

6. When would you want to use value-of-service pricing instead of cost-of-service pricing?

7. What does transportation security refer to, and which mode of transportation is most affected by security concerns?

8. In the U.S., which has been best for all concerned, transportation regulation or deregulation? Why?

9. Is transportation in the U.S. regulated today, or deregulated? Why?

10. Describe three different types of warehouses and the advantages of each.

11. What is the difference between a distribution center and a warehouse?

12. Define risk pooling and the advantages and disadvantages of centralized warehousing. What assumption does risk pooling make?

13. **Discussion Problem:** For the following warehouse system information, determine the average inventory levels for three warehouses, and then one warehouse, using the square root rule: Current warehouse system—six warehouses, with 3000 units at each warehouse.

14. What is a JIT warehouse? When are they used?

15. What are 3PLs and why are they used? What are 4PLs?

16. What role does logistics play in supply chain management?

17. How can logistics affect environmental sustainability?

18. What does a logistics audit seek to accomplish?

19. Describe several international logistics intermediaries. Could they also be considered 3PLs?

20. What are the three logistics management system applications, and how do they benefit users?

21. How has NAFTA affected trade between the U.S., Canada, and Mexico?

22. What is reverse logistics? How does it impact supply chain management?

23. How can reverse logistics have a positive impact on the environment? On profits?

INTERNET QUESTIONS

1. Go to the BNSF Web site (http://www.bnsf.com) and describe the types of intermodal services offered.

2. Go to the NTE Web site (http://www.nte.com) and find two highly rated carriers and two poorly rated carriers.

INFOTRAC QUESTIONS

Access http://academic.cengage.com/infotrac to answer the following questions:

1. Write a report on cross-border trucking traffic between the U.S. and Mexico, and how security concerns have affected these cross-border movements.

2. Search on the term "green logistics" and write a report on logistics strategies that are used to reduce carbon emissions.

3. Search on the term "logistics management software" and describe how these software applications help to assure port security and international cargo security.

Chapter 10

CUSTOMER RELATIONSHIP MANAGEMENT

When I look at CRM applications I see high-performance race cars, with all the horse-power necessary to tear down a track, if they have the right fuel in them. That is the problem: CRM often lacks the right fuel.[1]

Want to know the easiest way to find out what customers think about your company? Ask them.[2]

Learning Objectives

After completing this chapter, you should be able to

- Discuss the strategic importance of CRM.
- Describe the components of a CRM initiative.
- Calculate customer lifetime value.
- Discuss the implementation procedures used for CRM programs.
- Describe how information is used to create customer satisfaction and greater profits for the firm.
- Describe some of the popular CRM applications and their suppliers.

Chapter Outline

Introduction

Customer Relationship Management Defined

CRM's Role in Supply Chain Management

Key Tools and Components of CRM

Designing and Implementing a Successful
  CRM Program

CRM Software Applications

Trends in CRM

Summary

Supply Chain Management in Action   *CRM at StemCell Technologies*

StemCell Technologies helps medical research happen—the firm sells specialized media and cell separation products, antibodies, and tissue culture reagents, plus services that include contract assays, proficiency testing, and training. StemCell has been trying to get straight with CRM since 2002, when the launch of global satellite offices and sales teams required changes to its business process framework. "The challenge," says Cam Büschel, sales and marketing analyst for StemCell, "was to synchronize all of that information and make it available in a meaningful format to the technical support and research departments at our head office."

As the company's client base grew and its sales team expanded globally, StemCell's salespeople became increasingly independent. This posed a challenge to the managers to be accessible to customers and prospects in remote sales regions. StemCell needed to centralize all of the information its sales teams were collecting and share it with its growing field sales force. Today, the company is using Maximizer Enterprise 8, to set up global marketing campaigns and track responses. Before purchasing the product StemCell's sales and marketing managers met with the sales team and support staff to discuss their requirements and to gain insight into what information each department needed, how they wanted to work, and how their working styles affected each other. "We wanted to get as much user buy-in as possible," says Andrew Knowles, assistant sales manager. "We knew our CRM investment would only provide value if those it was meant for actually used it."

After evaluating various CRM software products, StemCell selected Maximizer Enterprise 8 and has deployed it to sales reps in France, North America, and the United Kingdom, and to technical support staff in the corporate head office. Users keep copies of the Maximizer Enterprise database on their computers and they can log into the corporate database whenever it's convenient. "We wouldn't have been able to develop our field force without Maximizer Enterprise," Knowles says. "In order to have functional field reps, we needed a way for them to report in, provide updates, and get information from us. Maximizer Enterprise gave us a way to work live remotely." Now the firm's sales reps have access to part and order numbers, purchase dates, shipment notes, and more. Knowles says the company is flourishing with the new CRM: "Maximizer Enterprise has become a one-stop shop for our sales reps to see all of the critical information they need to intelligently and successfully service an account."

Maximizer Enterprise has enabled StemCell Technologies to track activity on more than 60,000 customers and prospects, have its sales force self-generate reports, reduce staff training times, provide updates to remote sites monthly, and achieve a 500 percent ROI on its $20,000 CRM investment.

Source: Lager, M. "Test-Tube Implementation." *Customer Relationship Management,* 11, no. 7 (2007): 50–51. Used with permission.

Introduction

Customer relationship management becomes necessary once a company finds a market and customers for its products and services. To keep these customers satisfied and coming back, firms must continually find ways to add value to these products and services provided to customers. The often-told story that "finding a new customer costs five times as much as keeping an old customer" is the motivation behind customer relationship management. Over time, value continues to be demonstrated to customers through reliable on-time delivery, high quality products and services, competitive pricing, innovative new products and services, attention to various customer needs, and the flexibility to respond to those needs adequately. First and foremost, managing customer relationships starts with building core competencies that focus on customer requirements, and then delivering products and services in a manner resulting in high levels of customer satisfaction.

Today, customer relationship management, or CRM, has come to be associated with automated transaction and communication applications—a suite of software modules or a portion of a larger enterprise resource planning (ERP) system as described in Chapter 6. Most large firms have made very sizeable investments in CRM software applications and Web sites in an effort to automate the customer relationship process, and in some respects, this has provided significant benefits to these firms and their customers. In many cases though, the expected monetary benefits from these automated applications have proved to be elusive. In fact, studies indicate that the vast majority of CRM software implementations in recent years has failed to meet the original objectives of the adopting firms. According to a 2007 survey of more than 1000 firms worldwide, the percentage of firms using a CRM application has risen to 67 percent in 2007 from 45 percent in 2001, although the number reporting revenue improvements following their CRM software investments is only about one in five.[3]

Customers today may like the convenience of communicating or transacting over the Internet; however, individualized contact between a company and its customers is also needed to ultimately keep customers satisfied and coming back. American Airlines, a heavy user of CRM applications, knows who their profitable customers are, and they use this information to create mutually beneficial relationships. If, for example, the flight of a valued customer is going to be delayed, a personalized text message is sent to the client so his or her departure for the airport can be delayed.[4] The Cincinnati, Ohio daily newspaper, *The Cincinnati Enquirer*, uses its Web site, Cincinnati.com, to survey its readers, to gauge their opinions about certain topics, and then write articles based on the survey results. It also uses Web site surveys to receive feedback from its business accounts.[5]

Other businesses are rediscovering the need to provide personalized services to their customers. Many have come full-circle starting with the Internet B2B and B2C transactions; today we see that a firm's Internet presence, though desirable for many types of information or product transactions, is not sufficient to satisfy most customers in a wide range of industries. Touching products and talking face-to-face with company representatives remain integral parts of the supplier/customer interface. Thus CRM must still include talking to customers, understanding their behavior and their requirements, and then building a system to satisfy those requirements.

With technological changes occurring as rapidly as they are today, many new and exciting ways to obtain and utilize customer information have been developed and many of these will be highlighted in this chapter. Though supplier/customer interactions become more automated and more e-services are created, organizations will find they must continue to identify and develop new ways to add value to customer relationships in order to maintain a competitive advantage. Cultivating the human element in customer relationships will always remain a necessary factor in creating that value. Ultimately, CRM, if used effectively, allows both sides to win—customers get what they want from businesses, and businesses continue to get customers.

Customer Relationship Management Defined

CRM can actually be a confusing term, because in many circles CRM stands for *customer relationship marketing*, though in others it is customer relationship management. Many other terms have also popped up in recent years, and they all ultimately refer to the same thing. These days it appears that customer relationship management is winning out as the term of choice to describe building and maintaining profitable long-term customer relationships. The elements comprising CRM vary based on the industry and the definition used. As mentioned in the Introduction, the advent of CRM software and modules within ERP systems has made the water even muddier. In the final analysis though, all forms of CRM seek to keep the firm's customers satisfied, creating profits or other benefits for the firm. A few specific definitions of CRM are provided here:

- "The infrastructure that enables the delineation of and increase in customer value, and the correct means by which to motivate valuable customers to remain loyal—indeed to buy again."[6]
- "...managing the relationships among people within an organization and between customers and the company's customer service representatives in order to improve the bottom line."[7]
- "...a core business strategy for managing and optimizing all customer interactions across an organization's traditional and electronic interfaces."[8]
- "... to keep track of customers, learning about each one's likes and dislikes from various sources like transaction records, call-center logs, web site clicks, and search engine queries."[9]

Because of the intense competitive environment in most markets today, CRM has become one of the leading business strategies of the new millennium—and potentially one of the most costly. Most executives who haven't already implemented CRM applications, are planning on investing in them soon. Currently, worldwide CRM revenues reported by software development firms are in the range of $12 billion per year, and growing at a rate of 9 percent per year.[10] Unfortunately, it appears that much of this investment is not fundamentally improving customer relationships or resulting in positive returns for many of the companies implementing CRM.

So, why are so many CRM programs failing? Perhaps it is because some companies simply don't understand or care about what their customers want. Though corporations may collect customers' purchase, credit, and personal information, place it on a database, use it to initiate some type of direct marketing opportunity, and then sell the database information to other companies, no efforts are put forth to engender a customer's trust and loyalty—*to build customer relationships*. If building and maintaining relationships were truly what companies were seeking, they would for instance, return phone messages, make it easy to return or service products, and make it easy for customers to get accurate information and to contact the right people inside the organization. Consider this—how often, in your dealings with organizations, have you, the customer, been made to feel valued?

Too often, companies today have delegated customer relationship management, certainly one of the most important activities of the firm, to third-party CRM services, software developers, and internal IT departments whose goal is to design databases and use models to predict buying patterns. Though it is a potentially valuable support element in CRM programs, data mining alone does not build the customer relationship.

A number of years ago, Ms. Jessica Keyes, a well-known information system author and consultant, stated in an interview in the magazine *Infotrends*, "Technology does not beget a competitive advantage, any more than paint and canvas beget a Van Gogh."[11] These kinds of activities should be used in tandem with individual attention to build genuine long-term customer relationships. Successful CRM programs require cultural change in many organizations, leading to strategies that are focused on cultivating long-term relationships with customers, aided by the software capabilities found in CRM applications.

Simply put, firms need to *treat customer's right*. Not only does this mean providing the products and services customers want at competitive prices, but it also means providing support services and other offerings that add value and create real satisfaction for customers. Because customers are not all the same, firms must identify and segment their customers, then provide different sets of desired products and services to each segment. Thus, a successful CRM program is both simple and complex—it is simple in that it involves treating customers right and making them feel they are valued. It is complex in that it also means finding affordable ways to identify (potentially millions of) customers and their needs, and then designing customer contact strategies geared toward creating customer satisfaction and loyalty. The services of e-tailer Amazon.com are very simple for the consumer for example, though actually some very complicated CRM tasks take place behind the scenes. "I think what ensured that Amazon was a dotcom winner was being dedicated to the initial principle of focusing on the customer," says Ms. Rakhi Parekh, group product manager at Amazon.co.uk. "We started off by passing on the cost advantage of the model to consumers, with low prices, then extended that to clever use of their data so that we could work out what else they might enjoy."[12]

CRM's Role in Supply Chain Management

In Chapters 2, 3, and 4, the importance of building and maintaining strong relationships with good suppliers was discussed, in order to enhance value along the supply chain and create profits for supply chain participants. In those chapters, the firm was the customer and saw the value that could be created when high quality suppliers, and their suppliers, were found that were willing to design their services and products around the firm's, and the firm's customers' needs. The buying firm had requirements that needed to be met. The distribution side of the supply chain, though, is equally important. Here, our buying firm is now the supplier, seeking to be a key and value-enhancing supplier to its customers. To be successful, the firm must find ways to meet its customers' needs; otherwise, just as any firm would react with a nonperforming supplier, the customer goes elsewhere and takes years of future purchases with him. Regardless of a firm's place in the supply chain—retailer, wholesaler, distributor, manufacturer, or service provider—the importance of meeting and exceeding the needs and expectations of customers cannot be understated.

In an integrated supply chain setting, the need to be a good supplier, to adequately meet the needs of supply chain customers, is paramount to the success of supply chains. As products make their way along the supply chain to the end-user, close, trusting, and high-performance relationships must be created among all of the key supplier-customer pairs along the way. Thus, just as firms must create methods for finding and developing good suppliers, they must also create methods for becoming and staying good suppliers themselves.

Because many firms do not sell directly to the consumer, CRM in supply chain settings should also include first-tier customer training and education to ensure proper use of purchased products and consequently, maximum end-customer benefit. In many cases, care should also be used when establishing B2B relationships. These business customers represent suppliers' products to their customers. In these situations, businesses have a significant influence on the brand and reputation of their suppliers' products. Just as with suppliers, it may be necessary for a firm to certify its business customers as to their ability to adequately represent the firm's products. Automakers, for example, go to great lengths to establish and maintain strong end-customer-focused relationships with dealers to make sure their products are represented adequately. General Motors (GM) Canada is building CRM capabilities across all of their marketing channels including direct mail, telemarketing, the Internet, e-mail, and its 765 dealers across Canada. Harry Kuntz, director of corporate marketing for GM, says "As important as a marketing program is, ongoing communication is extremely important because what we're trying to do in the end is to be able to identify different customers, their different needs, and be able to talk to them differently."[13] Chrysler uses a VoIP (voice-over-Internet protocol)-enabled click-to-call feature on their Web site to allow users to connect immediately with company representatives who can assist them with making a purchasing decision or applying for finance. Users are also given an option to enter their telephone number for a call-back immediately or in one, three, or five minutes.[14]

Key Tools and Components of CRM

A number of elements are required for the development of effective CRM initiatives and these include segmenting customers, predicting customer behaviors, determining **customer value**, personalizing customer communications, automating the sales force, and managing **customer service** capabilities. Each of these elements is discussed in detail below.

Segmenting Customers

One of the most basic activities in CRM is to **segment customers**. Companies group customers in varieties of ways so that specialized communications about their products can be directed to specific customer groups. Customer segmentation can occur based on sales territory or region, preferred sales channel, profitability, products purchased, sales history, demographic information, desired product features, and service preferences, just to name a few. Analyzing this type of customer information can tell companies something about customer preferences and the likelihood of their responding to various types of **target marketing** efforts. By targeting specific customer segments, firms can save labor and postage costs with respect to these efforts, as well as avoid becoming a nuisance to some customers. The global insurance and financial services company, Hartford Financial Services Group for example, has provided auto and homeowner insurance to people above the age of 60 for more than 20 years. Their call center's automated voice answering system features a low-pitched male voice to allow words to be heard very clearly; speech recognition has been incorporated into their touch tone system; and the company has nine gerontologists on staff to advise the firm on everything from service to product design to marketing.[15] Customer segmentation at direct food marketer Harry & David is discussed in the e-Business Connection feature.

e-Business Connection

Segmenting Customers at Harry & David

Oregon-based Harry & David, a gourmet fruit and food marketer with annual sales of approximately $600 million, got its start as a B2B supplier but cultivated its business over the years through a consumer-oriented gift catalog. Recently, it has taken steps to target its most profitable customer segment: corporate clients. The company created a new division with an emphasis on customer relationship management. "The strategy was to identify and recognize valuable customers and integrate cross-channel strategies," said David Giacomini, director of the customer value management group at Harry & David.

Taking its existing marketing database, the company divided customers into segments. It found that its B2B clientele, which represented 10 percent of its database, generated much higher sales and profits at a much lower advertising-as-a-percent-of-sales ratio than consumers. Since recognizing that fact, the company has increased B2B spending by approximately 15 percent, including hiring additional salespeople. The marketer uses information derived from segmentation analysis and applies it to marketing tactics such as trade shows, telemarketing, e-mail, and direct mail efforts. "Instead of going to broad-based trade shows, we identify vertical industries that respond well," Giacomini said.

One challenge Harry & David encountered was retaining and up-selling current customers; so the company created a specific group to focus on retention. A change in compensation packages for sales employees was deemed necessary, as commissions had been based almost exclusively on generating new sales. "The sales team was more skewed to acquisition rather than retention," Giacomini said. "There was little incentive to retain or grow an account." After the company increased commissions for retained and reactivated sales, the effect was significant and immediate. "Two months ago, we were below plan for the year. Right now, we're at plan, and we're optimistic that we'll exceed sales goals for the year," Giacomini said. "I didn't think changing compensation would have an effect that quickly."

Harry & David, a category leader that mails 40 million catalogs yearly, continues to market to business customers through its folksy consumer catalog. About 10 years ago, it created a dedicated B2B catalog but later decided to scrap it. "We found the consumer catalog worked just as well for business," Giacomini said. Its corporate direct mail package contains the consumer catalog, along with a personalized letter and a 16-page brochure containing gift ideas.

Source: Krol, C. "Harry & David Returns to Roots." *B to B,* 87, no. 13 (2002): 15. Used with permission.

Permission Marketing

An extension of target marketing is **relationship marketing** or **permission marketing**. The idea here is to let customers select the type and time of communication with organizations. These days, consumers are bombarded with thousands of commercial messages each day, and the general consensus is that this is far too many, and that no one is doing anything about it. The ad industry seems forever on the lookout for new ways to introduce commercial messages—one of the latest is mobile marketing, or placing advertising messages on mobile phones. For advertisers today, permission marketing may be the best bet for gaining customer acceptance. "Anytime there's a new destination for people, like YouTube or mobile phones, the assumption is we've got to find a way to put some ads there," says Bob Barocci, president of the

Advertising Research Foundation. "That's just going to make things worse because there's no social contract. If mobile phone companies would say, 'We'll reduce your bill if you accept ads,' then that's a contract and that's smart."[16]

In permission marketing, customers can choose to be placed on and then taken off specific e-mail or traditional mailing lists for information about new products, or they can be reminded of upcoming sales or other events. It is becoming possible on Web sites for consumers to specify exactly what they are interested in, when they want information, what type of information they want, and how they want it communicated. This kind of customer contact requires sophisticated software capabilities to track individual customers and their interaction preferences as well as the capability to update these preferences over time. With this capability, firms can better design multiple, parallel marketing campaigns around small, specific segments of their customer base, automate portions of the marketing process, and simultaneously free up time previously spent manually managing the marketing process.

U.K.-based Silverpop combines both permission marketing and target marketing. They offer e-mail marketing services to companies using a permission-based database of potential customers. If a firm wanted to reach men in London who had recently purchased a tie, Silverpop would use this portion of their database to execute an e-mail campaign and then analyze the results afterward. On MySpace.com, advertisers are creating their own customized pages. Because visitors to these pages are self-selecting, this essentially amounts to permission marketing. This enables companies to identify interested consumers and engage in dialogue with them. As of 2007, the Toyota Yaris MySpace site, for example, had more than 60,000 "friends."[17]

Cross-Selling

Cross-selling occurs when customers are sold additional products as the result of an initial purchase. E-mails from Amazon.com describing other books bought by people who have also purchased a book the customer just bought is an attempt at cross-selling. If the additional products or services purchased are more profitable than the original purchase, this can provide significant additional profit for the firm. In addition, if firms are successful at cross-selling the right products at the right time to the right customers, then customers perceive this as individualized attention, and it results in satisfied loyal customers. The Belgian bank KBC Group, for instance, has been quite successful at cross-selling insurance, investment products, and banking services to its clients. In a 2002 study of cross-selling, KBC Group was placed at the top of the 34 banks reviewed. Clients are segmented based on the type of customer and their current and potential profitability. Clients with the highest levels of current and potential profitability will be proactively marketed by a relationship manager, while those in the lowest profitability segment will be left alone and serviced when the client makes a request.[18] The Haddad Group uses loyalty cards at its four Kansas City-area restaurants. User cards are scanned and updated at each location and the front of the card displays each user's loyalty point total after each transaction, along with regularly changing marketing or promotional messages geared to cross-sell products or services to users.[19]

Predicting Customer Behaviors

By understanding customers' purchasing behaviors, future behaviors can be predicted. These predictions allow firms to forecast which products customers are likely to purchase next and how much they are willing to pay. In this way, companies can revise pricing policies, offer discounts, and design promotions to specific customer segments. Hilton Hotels' CRM software analyzes demographic information from its Hilton Honors program, and behavioral patterns are used to help create direct mail campaigns and to help hotel managers plan for upcoming seasonal activity by business travelers.[20] One of the more desirable CRM attributes falling under this category is **customer defection analysis**.

Customer Defection Analysis

Reducing customer defections or **customer churn** is a necessary component of managing long-term profitable customer relationships. And it pays handsomely as well. According to Harvard Business School research, a 5 percent improvement in customer retention can result in a 75 percent increase in profits.[21] Today, competition in almost every product category is very high, and along with it, customer savvy. "The average consumer has more information at his fingertips with which to make informed decisions about a relationship with companies than he has had in the past," says Jonathan Trichel, principal of customer and market strategy at Deloitte Consulting. Knowing which customers have quit purchasing and why can be very valuable information for organizations. Not only can these customers be approached to encourage additional purchases, but the knowledge gained can be used to reduce future defections. "If I've got an 80 percent satisfaction rate, the focus needs to be on the 20 percent of dissatisfied customers," says Bob Furniss, president of CRM consultancy Touchpoint Associates of Tennessee. "If I can understand what's occurring in the 20 percent, then my impact is much more profound than being satisfied with the satisfaction rate."[22]

Offers of money or free minutes from telephone service companies are examples of efforts to regain customers who have defected to another phone service. In some cases, organizations may actually want some customers (unprofitable ones) to defect. By determining the value or profitability of each of the defecting customers, firms can design appropriate policies for retaining or regaining customers as well as policies to discourage additional purchases. In some department stores, for instance, customers who repeatedly return merchandise are at some point given only store credit instead of cash. By monitoring purchase histories, these firms can see if this type of discouragement makes customers quit returning merchandise.

Customer Value Determination

Until recently, determining customer value or customer profitability, as mentioned above, was difficult for most CRM systems. Today though, by integrating with ERP systems, capturing customer profitability information is possible for many businesses. However, use of this information can potentially cause poor decisions to be made regarding some customers. For instance, customers that are unprofitable now, may be profitable later. A health club for instance, may have some unmarried members who rarely make other purchases at the club but frequently visit and use the facility. Though this type of member may be seen as unprofitable, it is likely that if they are satisfied with the club, they will tell others; and at some point they may marry and upgrade to a family membership. Thus, it is necessary to determine **customer lifetime value** or profitability such that appropriate benefits, communications, services, or policies can be directed toward (or withheld from) customers or customer segments.

Unless a firm has knowledge of customer profitability, they may be directing sizeable resources catering to customers who are actually unprofitable. For instance in a study published by consultant and database marketing author Arthur Middleton

Hughes, he described how Boston-based Fleet Bank's marketing staff was working hard trying to retain customers who were in fact unprofitable. In fact, half of Fleet's customers were deemed unprofitable, and the bottom 28 percent were offsetting 22 percent of the bank's annual profits.[23] Calculating customer lifetime value is based on a customer's current purchases, the average profit margin on the items they purchase, and the present value of their projected lifetime purchases. Example 10.1 illustrates this calculation.

Example 10.1   Calculating Customer Lifetime Value

Miller's Kentucky Bluegrass Seed Company sells grass seed and other Kentucky-area plant seeds to area plant nurseries. They have decided to begin calculating the expected lifetime profitability of each of their nursery customers in order to design more cost-effective marketing efforts for their existing customers. Their top two customers have the following characteristics:

	AVG. SEED SALES/YR.	AVG. PROFIT MARGIN	EXPECTED LIFETIME
Nursery A:	$22,000	20%	5 years
Nursery B:	$16,000	15%	15 years

Using a discount rate of 8 percent, and treating the average sales figures as annuities, the present value of the two nursery lifetime values is:

$$NPV_A = a\left[\frac{(1+i)^n - 1}{i(1+i)^n}\right] = \$22,000(.2)\left[\frac{(1+.08)^5 - 1}{.08(1+.08)^5}\right] = \$4400\left[\frac{0.469}{0.118}\right] = \$17,488$$

$$NPV_B = a\left[\frac{(1+i)^n - 1}{i(1+i)^n}\right] = \$16,000(0.15)\left[\frac{(1+.08)^{15} - 1}{.08(1+.08)^{15}}\right] = \$2400\left[\frac{2.172}{0.254}\right] = \$20,522$$

where

a = average annual profit, or the (annual sales) × (profit margin)

i = annual discount rate

n = expected lifetime in years

Based on these calculations, Nursery B is the more important customer because of the higher expected lifetime value.

Determining the firm's share of their customers' total purchases can also help to focus resources on managing the right customers. Take two industrial customers for example, one whose purchases are worth $2 million per year and the other whose purchases amount to $1 million per year. At first glance, the first customer might seem more valuable; however, if that customer's total purchases from all suppliers for similar products is $3 million whereas the second firm has total purchases of similar products worth $20 million, then the second firm suddenly has much more potential for additional sales and should be managed more carefully.

Personalizing Customer Communications

Knowledge of customers, their behaviors, and their preferences allows firms to customize communications aimed at specific groups of customers. Referring to customers by their first name, or suggesting services used in the past communicates value to the customer and is likely to result in greater levels of sales. The Ritz-Carlton Hotel for instance, profiles its customers in order to provide the accommodations each person prefers on subsequent visits. Web sites of online retailers can remember a customer's credit card number, name, **clickstreams**, and items purchased in order to personalize future site visits by offering products, ads, and shipping preferences that fit each customer's profile.

CRM software that can analyze a customer's clickstream, or how they navigate a Web site, can tailor a Web site's images, ads, or discounts based on past usage of the site. Web site businesses may also send personalized e-mails for instance with incentives to lure customers back, if it has been a while since their last purchase. A quick-change oil and lube shop might send a postcard to a customer's address every 90 days, reminding them it's time for an oil change and to offer a discount on the next visit. On the same card, they may also offer discounts on other services that customer has used in the past, such as a radiator flush, a tune-up, or a tire-rotation. With time, this customization capability improves, as the firm learns of additional services, products, and purchasing behaviors exhibited by various customers.

Event-Based Marketing

Another form of personalized communication comes with the ability to offer individual promotions tied to specific events. Banks, for example, may try to market automated mortgage payment services to all of their customers who have recently applied for and received a home mortgage loan. The same bank might offer home improvement loans to customers once their mortgages reach an age of 5 years. The idea with **event-based marketing** is to offer the right products and services to customers at the right time. When entertainment venues ask for the birth dates of their customers as they buy season passes or day passes, for instance, they can direct future discounts to occur on days they are likely to be celebrating. With large volumes of customers, event-based promotion strategies are impossible without computer automation, so event-based marketing capabilities tend to be popular among firms seeking to purchase CRM systems.

Automated Sales Force Tools

Sales force automation (SFA) products are used for documenting field activities, communicating with the home office, and retrieval of sales history and other company-specific documents in the field. Today, salespeople need better ways to manage their accounts, their business opportunities, and communications while away from the office. To supply these capabilities, firms have been using CRM tools since the early 1990s to help management and sales force personnel keep up with the ever-more complicated layers of information that are required as customers and prospects increase. When field sales personnel have access to the latest forecasts, sales, inventory, marketing plans, and account information it allows more accurate and timely decisions to be made in the field, ultimately increasing sales force productivity and improving customer service capabilities.

Global pharmaceutical manufacturer Merck is turning to the latest SFA technologies to help field sales reps achieve their goals. Merck's sales people will be able to access all of their materials and customer information through a lightweight tablet PC, allowing for better presentations and more information packed into each sales call. "The advantage is that we can cover a lot more information with the customer in a shorter amount of time," says Gary Pond, executive director of multichannel communications at Merck. "Physicians that have a positive experience with the rep will be more likely to ask questions. If you're asked a question and you can't find the answer quick enough, you lose their confidence and they'll walk away."[24] Some of the desired CRM capabilities in the area of sales force automation are discussed next.

Sales Activity Management

These tools are customized to each firm's sales policies and procedures and offer sales personnel a sequence of sales activities that guide them through the sales process with each customer. These standardized sales process steps assure that the proper sales activities are performed and put forth a uniform sales process across the entire organization. The use of a **sales activity management** tool reduces errors and improves customer satisfaction and productivity. Along with these prescribed sales steps, field sales reps can be reminded of key customer activities as they are needed, generate mailings for inactive customers, be assigned tasks by management, and generate to-do lists. Pharmaceutical distributor AmerisourceBergen, headquartered in Pennsylvania, needed an easy way to reach customers with a consistent message. With the help of a consultant and an automated message management software application, they created an interactive portal on their intranet for their sales reps. This allowed salespeople to customize presentation slides, brochures, proposals, e-mail, follow-up letters, and other forms of client communication. "It's true situational selling," says Scan Markey, VP of business operations at AmerisourceBergen. "And it's cool how it saves time, not having to mill through a myriad of collateral or making your own sales pieces."[25]

Sales Territory Management

Sales territory management tools allow sales managers to obtain current information and reporting capabilities regarding each salesperson's activities on each customer's account, total sales in general for each sales rep, their sales territories, and any ongoing sales initiatives. Using these tools, sales managers can create sales teams specifically suited to a customer's needs, generate profiles of sales personnel, track performance, and keep up with new leads generated in the field.

Lead Management

Using a **lead management** tool allows sales reps to follow prescribed sales tactics when dealing with sales prospects or opportunities, to aid in closing the deal with a client. These products can generate additional steps as needed to help refine the deal closing and negotiation process. During this process, sales reps can generate product configurations and price quotes directly, using laptops or hand held devices remotely linked to the firm's server. In addition, leads can be assigned to field sales personnel as they are generated, based on the requirements of the prospect and the skill sets of the sales reps. Thus, lead management capabilities should result in higher deal closing success rates in less time. Another common characteristic allows managers to track the closing success of sales personnel and the future orders generated by each lead.

Knowledge Management

Sales personnel require access to a variety of information before, during, and after a sale including information on contracts, client and competitor profiles, client sales histories, corporate policies, expense reimbursement forms, regulatory issues and laws, sales presentations, promotional materials, and previous client correspondence. Easy access to this information enables quick decision making, better customer service, and a better-equipped and more productive sales staff.

Managing Customer Service Capabilities

The key element of any successful CRM initiative is the ability to provide good customer service. In fact, with any process that deals with the customer, one of the primary objectives is always to provide adequate levels of customer service. But what does customer service actually mean? In Chapter 7, customer service was discussed in terms of safety stock and filling customer orders. In Chapter 9, customer service was tied to delivering goods on time. And as mentioned earlier in this chapter, customer service can also mean answering customers' questions and having disputes or product and service problems fixed appropriately and quickly. Thus, many definitions of customer service can be found. Today, complaints about shoddy customer service abound in many organizations and this represents one area where organizations can create real competitive advantage, if customer service processes are designed and operated correctly. The next segment defines customer service and discusses several elements of customer service.

Customer Service Defined

One customer service definition covers most of the elements mentioned above, and that is the "**Seven Rs Rule**."[26] The seven Rs stand for having the *right* product, in the *right* quantity, in the *right* condition, at the *right* place, at the *right* time, for the *right* customer, at the *right* cost. A perfect order occurs when all seven Rs are satisfied. This customer service definition can be applied to any service or manufacturer, and to any customer. A misstep in any of the seven areas results in lower customer service. Consequently, competitive advantage can be engendered by creating an organization which routinely satisfies the seven Rs.

Organizational performance measures are often designed around satisfying the seven Rs. For example, reducing stockouts to 1 percent means that customers get the right product or service 99 percent of the time; and having an on-time delivery performance of 97 percent means that customers get their orders at the right time 97 percent of the time. Other customer service measures are typically designed to measure *flexibility* (responding to changes in customer orders), *information system response* (responding to requests for information), *recovery* (the ability to solve customer problems), and *post-sales support* (providing operating information, parts, equipment, and repairs). In the airline industry, customer service is measured using frequencies of lost or damaged baggage, bumped passengers, canceled flights, on-time flights, and customer complaints. In the U.S., Southwest Air, JetBlue, and AirTran tend to be the top air carriers in terms of customer service, and the other airlines state that customer service improvements are major objectives for upcoming years. United Airlines even created a new division to focus on customer issues as it emerged from bankruptcy in 2006.[27]

Providing these kinds of services to customers keeps customers returning, but comes at a cost. Firms must consider the costs of improving customer service (such as faster transport, greater safety stock levels, and better communication systems) as well as the benefits (keeping customers and their future profit streams). In organized supply chain relationships, firms often work together in determining (and paying for) adequate customer service, because the costs of poor customer service can be substantial.

Customer service elements can be classified as **pretransaction**, transaction, and **posttransaction** elements. Each of these is briefly discussed next.

"This month's customer service award
goes to Bob for giving up double
onion garlic burgers."

- Pretransaction elements: these customer service elements precede the actual product or service and examples are customer service policies, the mission statement, organizational structure, and system flexibility.
- Transaction elements: these elements occur during the sale of the product or service and include the order lead time, the order processing capabilities, and the distribution system accuracy.
- Posttransaction elements: these elements refer to the after-sale services and include warranty repair capabilities, complaint resolution, product returns, and operating information.

Thus, to provide high levels of service and value to customers, firms seek to continually satisfy the seven Rs and develop adequate customer service capabilities before, during, and after the sale of products and services. Call centers have been used in many organizations to improve customer service and supply chain performance and this topic is discussed next.

Call Centers

Call centers or **customer contact centers** have existed for many years, and some organizations have used these effectively to satisfy and keep customers loyal, although others have seen them as a necessary cost of doing business and viewed them as a drain on profits. As call centers became automated, customer service representatives were then able to quickly see how similar questions were answered in the past, and resolve problems more quickly, resulting in greater call center effectiveness. Call center systems can now categorize all calls, determine average resolution time, and forecast future call volume. These automated systems can reduce call center labor costs and training time, and improve the overall productivity of the staff, while increasing customer satisfaction levels. Lately, call centers have implemented virtual queuing systems as well, as callers see this as a very convenient call center characteristic. Automated tools allow callers to request a callback from an agent without losing their place in the phone queue, which frees up callers' time and also reduces call center toll charges for keeping callers on hold. Atmos Energy, a natural gas distributor in the U.S., implemented a virtual queuing system and actually found that most callers preferred the virtual queue, average call time was reduced by 10 percent, and caller complaints decreased.[28]

Unfortunately, the call center process can get bogged-down when agents are not hired or trained effectively. Critics and many consumers have also argued that automated answering programs and hard-to-understand call center agents in outsourced foreign call centers are reducing customer satisfaction. In a study of 1000 North American consumers in 2007 conducted by Massachusetts-based Aspect Software, automated call center systems were given an overall grade of "D" for efficiency, ease of use, speed, quality, wait time, transfers, and caller empathy. The report also found however, that a consumer who is satisfied with an automated experience is 2.5 times as likely to conduct business with the firm in the future.[29] "The good news is that there are more people open to trying automation," says Paul Stockford, chief analyst at Arizona-based contact center research firm Saddletree Research. "The bad news is the automation is still not delivering the way it should."

Contrary to popular belief, most call center work today is done in-house. In the U.K., fully 80 percent of all call centers are housed within the firm. Much of the emphasis in call center management is on product training and information software usage. "There's nothing worse than phoning your service provider and finding you know more than the person on the other end of the line," says Neil Armstrong, marketing director at U.K. broadband service provider PlusNet.[30] But low labor costs still make call center outsourcing an attractive option for some companies. In the U.S., nearshore locations such as the Dominican Republic, Jamaica, and Nicaragua offer lower labor cost, good English- and Spanish-speaking capabilities, and proximity such that management has better control over training and tools used by offshore call centers. The Global Perspective feature describes the growth of nearshore call centers in Jamaica.

Today, organizations are realizing how important call centers can be in managing customer relationships. In many firms, call centers have a dedicated, well-trained staff providing 24/7 call support. And they have implemented technologies to better customize the help and information customers receive. For example, calls can be routed to various call center geographic locations based on the time of day, specialization required, or the current wait time at each of the call center locations. NICE Systems Ltd. of Israel, for example, sells an automated system that digitally records customer-agent conversations and scans for words such as "cancel"; these conversations are flagged and then managers are sent reports with the customers' names so they can potentially resolve customers' problems.[31]

Web Site Self-Service

Web sites act as support mechanisms for call centers by making commonly requested information available to visitors of the site. Customers can, among other things, access their account information, and get flight schedules, operating hours, contact information, locations, directions, and product information or return policies. On most sites, organizations provide space for e-mailing questions or complaints; some sites even offer online chat capabilities with company personnel or with other customers who are currently visiting the site. Well-designed **Web site self-service** capabilities can further reduce the need for call center staffers while adequately handling most customer queries.

Global Perspective

Call Center Nearshoring in Jamaica

Jamaica, known throughout the world for its reggae, rum, and Rastafarianism, now has a new claim to fame as the Caribbean's top choice for investors looking to establish near-shore call center operations. The island's government has made vigorous efforts to promote it as a sensible, low-cost outsourcing alternative to Asia. Christopher McNair, an IT adviser at the government investment promotion agency Jampro, says 19 companies now operate call centers in Jamaica.

In May 2006, e-SGI, whose 1500 workers annually process more than 30 million transactions for a variety of U.S. and foreign clients, announced it had landed a contract to provide customer care and reservation services for Delta Air Lines. The megadeal, whose value wasn't disclosed, is expected to double the company's Jamaica workforce to 3000 and fuel an expansion to St. Lucia. "We selected e-SGI based on its proven ability to deliver high-quality customer service at a significant cost savings, as well as its proximity to the United States," says Steve Scheper, vice president of reservations at Delta.

Patrick Casserly, who founded e-SGI in 2002 with back-office processing for one client and a staff of 35, says his company grew 55 percent in the first three years. "We anticipate that with the success of the [Delta] program, our partnership will redefine the outsource sector in Jamaica, and we are putting all resources in place to ensure a successful agreement."

Tour and holiday company Apple Vacations has 110 employees in Montego Bay, and Unique Vacations, which handles reservations for the Sandals resort chain, recently moved its call center operation from Florida to Jamaica. "Our biggest advantage is proximity," McNair says. "People are no longer looking to travel two days to get to Mumbai or Bangalore. We're just 90 minutes by air from the U.S. coastline."

McNair says Jamaican wages are one third of the U.S.—approximately $2.75 per hour compared to the $8 an hour earned by the average U.S. call center employee. He says the industry generates more than $100 million in revenue annually for Jamaica.

Accent Marketing Services officially opened its first wholly owned non-U.S. call center, in New Kingston, in November. The center provides outsourced customer-care support to more than 2.5 million customers. Accent has already hired and trained 280 agents, support staff, and managers. "Jamaica has a good infrastructure, good educational levels, and high unemployment, so you can get a lot of people who are qualified and waiting for work," says Ryan Carey, general manager of Accent Marketing Jamaica.

Indeed, though critics claim call center operations lure jobs away from American shores, in poor countries such as the Dominican Republic, Jamaica, and Nicaragua, they often mean the difference between poverty and prosperity. "The United States still has the largest population of agent positions in the world," McNair says. Besides, he adds, if transferring jobs to the Caribbean helps a company remain in business and stay competitive, then it's a no-brainer. "According to the experts, for every dollar the United States actually outsources [in call center jobs], it gets $1.50 back," he says. "So from my point of view, the United States benefits."

Source: Luxner, L. "Jamaica's In." *Customer Relationship Management,* 11, no. 2 (2007): 15–16. Used with permission.

Field Service Management

Those who have worked for a firm with an older copying machine may have wished that the field service process for maintaining and fixing the machine was automated. In many cases still, the field servicing process consists of calling a customer service number, having someone diagnose the problem, and then waiting for a repair technician to be sent for the repair. Even then, a repair may take days or weeks if parts must be ordered or if the original diagnosis was incorrect. When this process is automated, customers can communicate directly with product specialists using wireless communication devices and the right diagnosis can be made more quickly. The correct specialist can be sent for more effective action, and when at the scene, the repair person can access repair manuals, instructions, specifications, part order forms, and other information via wireless connection to the organization's server.

Measuring Customer Satisfaction

Measuring customer satisfaction remains somewhat of a tricky proposition. Customers are frequently given opportunities to provide feedback about a product, service, or organization through customer feedback cards placed at cash registers or on tables, mailed customer surveys or surveys provided with purchased products, or surveys shown on firm Web sites. In most cases, the only time these forms are filled out is when customers are experiencing a problem. Given this, companies still can find valuable uses for this information. Responses can be analyzed and used to solve the most commonly occurring problems. In CRM programs, customer satisfaction surveys can be personalized to fit specific customer segments, and responses can be matched to the respondent's profile to provide the company direction on how to improve its communication and service capabilities for various groups of customers.

The design of the surveys themselves can be a particular problem for companies. In many cases, surveys don't ask the questions customers want to answer. On many Web site surveys, customers are more often asked about the design of the Web site instead of how the firm is performing or what the customer may be happy or unhappy about. In a study of both brick-and-mortar and Internet banks, for instance, less than half of all the banks studied even used customer comment cards or surveys, and only two banks in the study (both were Internet banks) offered service quality surveys.[32]

Customer Privacy Considerations

One important issue from the customer's perspective, is the ability to assure privacy when information is given to businesses, and the ability to minimize customer harassment resulting from unwanted solicitations. In fact, by late 2005, the U.S. Congress and 28 states were working on anti-spyware legislation. In addition, the U.S. Secret Service has more than 3300 agents worldwide pursuing hackers, identity thieves, and other Internet defrauders. Companies such as Earthlink and Microsoft have also been very aggressive in prosecuting spammers.[33] CRM applications today are trying to determine not only the preferred channel and message, but also each customer's preferred frequency of solicitation. Other features such as "opt-in" and "opt-out" policies and posted privacy policies have become very common on most Internet-oriented marketing messages.

In this section, the common elements necessary for successful CRM programs were reviewed. Many of these involve the use of technology and software. But having all the software applications does not necessarily guarantee success. A number of other factors come into play before, during, and after programs are implemented that must be adhered to, in order to give the firm and its CRM program a good chance of finding and keeping profitable customers. The next section will discuss this very important aspect of CRM.

Designing and Implementing a Successful CRM Program

Designing and then implementing a CRM program can be a real challenge, because it requires an understanding of and commitment to the firm's customers, adherence to CRM goals, knowledge of the tools available to aid in CRM, support from the firm's top executives and the various departments that will be using the CRM tools, and a continuous awareness of customers' changing requirements. Poor planning is typically the cause for most unsuccessful CRM initiatives, because of the temptation to start working on a solution or to hire a CRM application provider before understanding the problems that CRM is meant to solve. The firm must first answer this question: *What are the problems CRM is going to solve?* This must involve employees from all functional groupings across the firm, as well as input from the firm's key customers. Putting together a sound CRM plan will force the organization to think about CRM needs, technology alternatives, and the providers that sell them. Selecting the right tools and providers is an important step, but should not occur until a CRM plan is completed.

Aside from creating a CRM plan and getting the firm's employees to buy-in to the idea and uses of CRM, firms must also consider the existing CRM initiatives implemented in piecemeal fashion across the firm. Integrating existing applications into one enterprise-wide initiative should be part one of the primary objectives of the CRM implementation process. In addition, the firm must decide on specific performance outcomes and assessments for the program and provide adequate training to the CRM application users.

Creating the CRM Plan

Putting together a solid plan for a CRM project is crucial as an aid to purchasing and implementing CRM applications, and to obtain executive management approval and funding for the project. The plan should include the objectives of the CRM program, its fit with corporate strategy, new applications to be purchased or used, the integration or replacement of existing methods or legacy systems, the requirements for personnel, training, policies, upgrades and maintenance, and the costs and time frame for implementation. Once this document is completed, the firm will have a roadmap for guiding the purchase and implementation process, as well as the organizational performance measures to be used once the program is in place.

The objectives of any CRM initiative should be customer-focused. Examples might include increasing sales per customer, improving overall customer satisfaction, more closely integrating the firm's key customers with internal processes, or increasing supply chain responsiveness. These will vary somewhat based on the overall strategic focus of the firm. Once these objectives are in place, tactical goals and plans can be instituted at the functional level, consistent with the CRM objectives. Finally, tactical performance measures can be used to track the ongoing performance of the CRM program. This performance will serve to justify the initial and ongoing costs of the program.

Involving CRM Users from the Outset

In order to get acceptance of this or any other new initiative, employee involvement and support are required. This comes about by enlisting the help of everyone affected by the initiative from the very beginning. Employees need to understand how the CRM initiative will affect their jobs before they will buy-in to the program. Creating a project team with members from sales, customer service, marketing, finance, and production, for instance, will tremendously aid in the selection, training, use, and acceptance of the initiative. The team can contact CRM application providers and collect information regarding capabilities and costs, and they can also collect baseline customer service, sales, complaint, and other meaningful performance information. The team should also be heavily involved in evaluating and selecting the applications, and then implementing and integrating the applications in each department. As the implementation or "burn-in" continues, closely monitoring system performance will keep users convinced of the value of the initiative, and keep everyone committed to its success.

Selecting the Right Application and Provider

Once the organization has completed its plan for CRM, it should have a fairly good idea of what they are going to do, and which activities will require automation or technology. The job then becomes one of finding an appropriate application, and deciding how much customization will be required to get the job done.

Finding the best application and supplier can be accomplished a number of ways including:

- visiting a CRM-oriented trade show;
- using a CRM consulting firm;
- searching CRM or business publications such as *Call Center Magazine*, *Call Center News*, and *Inside Supply Management*[34];
- using the knowledge of internal IT personnel, who already know the market; and
- searching the many CRM supplier directories and Web sites.

Firms should seek help from a number of these alternatives, and internal IT personnel should be viewed as internal consultants in the application and supplier identification and selection process. Firms must analyze and compare the various products available. In her CRM handbook, Dychè recommends comparing the following characteristics[35]:

- integration and connection requirements (look at hardware, software and networking requirements and capabilities);
- processing and performance requirements (what volume of data and number of users it can support);
- security requirements;
- reporting requirements (preformatted and customized reporting capabilities);
- usability requirements (ability for users to customize the software, display graphics, print information, etc.);
- function enabling features (workflow management, e-mail response engine, predictive modeling);
- performance requirements (quick response times for various queries); and
- system availability requirements (ability to accommodate various time zones).

Comparing these CRM capabilities should narrow the list of qualified vendors substantially. When finally selecting a supplier for the application, one of the primary criteria for firms to consider is the support available from the application provider. Vendors offering implementation and after-sale user support that meets the needs of the firm (e.g., 24/7 phone support) should be valued more highly than other vendors. Suppliers that offer free trial usage so the firm can verify the product's capabilities is another element the firm needs to consider. Finally, cost and contract negotiations should be carefully considered.

Integrating Existing CRM Applications

In most firms, CRM is not one single product, but rather a suite of various applications that have been implemented over time. One of the biggest mistakes made is that departments across the firm implement various forms of CRM without communicating these actions to other departments. Eventually, these systems will interfere with each other, as they communicate with the same customer, sending confusing and irritating signals that can chase customers away quickly.

Customer contact mechanisms need to be coordinated so that every CRM application user in the firm knows about all the activity associated with each customer. Today, this lack of integration is leading to real problems as call centers and sales offices seek to please and retain customers by adopting customer loyalty programs, frequent user cards, and other types of customer satisfaction programs without making this information available firm-wide. In addition, multiple individual applications throughout the company result in duplication of effort, incompatible formats, and wasted money. What is needed are compatible modules for each department's use, linked to one centralized database or **data warehouse** containing all customer information. Thus, from one database, users in the organization can retrieve information on a customer's profile, purchase history, promotion responses, payment history, Web visitations, merchandise returns, warranty repairs, and call center contacts.

By integrating CRM information obtained throughout the firm, decision makers in the firm can analyze the information and make much more customer-focused decisions. Using predictive models and statistical analyses, firms can identify customers most likely to purchase certain products, respond to a new promotion, or churn. This ability to track and segment a single view of each customer at the enterprise level allows firms to truly personalize and focus their efforts and products where they will do the most good, resulting in maximum benefit for the firm *and* its customers.

Establishing Performance Measures

Performance measures that are linked to what the firm hopes to accomplish with CRM allows users and managers to witness the progression of a CRM project in meeting its original objectives. It also serves to keep everyone excited and informed about the benefits of a well-designed program, and will identify any implementation or usage problems as they occur, allowing causes to be found and solutions to be implemented quickly.

At the organizational level, performance measures should concentrate on areas deemed strategically important, such as CRM productivity or sales generated from the CRM program. Some examples of these measures are listed in Table 10.1. At the user level, other more tactical performance measures should be developed and tracked, supporting the firm-wide strategic measures. Linking performance measures in this way

Table 10.1	CRM Performance Measures		
PERFORMANCE MEASUREMENT TYPE	**DEPARTMENT OR USER-LEVEL PERFORMANCE MEASURES**		
	FIELD SALES	**CALL CENTER**	**MARKETING**
Customer/Strategic Partner Loyalty	1. % customer repurchases 2. avg. # repurchases 3. # customer referrals	1. # customer product information requests 2. # customer praises	1. % customers responding to solicitations or promotions 2. avg. # of campaign responses
Customer/Partner Satisfaction	1. # customer visits to resolve problems 2. # field service visits per customer	1. # logged complaints per customer 2. customer satisfaction survey results	1. % customers who have responded more than once to promotions
Average Sales Revenue per Customer/Partner	1. # sales quotas met 2. % repeat visits resulting in sales	1. # customer calls for catalogs 2. # customer phone orders	1. # Web site visits per customer 2. Web site purchases per customer
CRM Productivity	1. % sales quotas met among FS reps 2. # new leads generated 3. % new leads closed	1. avg. caller time 2. # complaints successfully resolved 3. sales generated from customer calls	1. # segment catalogs produced 2. # promotional e-mails sent 3. # marketing campaigns
CRM User Satisfaction	1. annual internal user satisfaction survey	1. annual internal user satisfaction survey	1. annual internal user satisfaction survey
CRM User Training	1. hrs. training per year per rep 2. # CRM applications trained per rep	1. hrs. training per year per rep 2. # CRM applications trained per rep	1. hrs. training per year per user 2. # CRM applications trained per user

Note: CRM = customer relationship management; FS reps = facility support representatives.

will give the firm the best chance of a successful program implementation and continued revision and use of the program into the future.

Providing Training for CRM Users

Another important step in the implementation process is to provide and require training for all of the initial users, and then provide training on an ongoing basis as applications are added or as other personnel begin to see the benefits of CRM and its use spreads through the organization. Training can also help convince key users such as sales, call center, and marketing personnel of the benefits and uses of CRM applications. Training managers and users in the key customer contact areas can also help the firm decide what customizations to the CRM applications are required before the system is put into use. This is particularly important for larger firms where supply chains and the sales and marketing processes are complex. In many cases, CRM implementation means that other systems already in place will be phased out or merged with the CRM system. Training can help personnel decide how best to phase out old systems and phase in the new ones. CRM consultant Barton Goldenberg suggests that firms should create a training profile for each of its CRM system users to provide training before, during, and after the implementation process in one or more of these areas: computer literacy training, business process training, CRM application training, remedial training, and new user training.[36]

CRM Software Applications

A very large number of CRM software providers can be found quickly by searching the Web. Today while there is significant consolidation occurring in the industry, new application providers are also continually entering the market with new products. Even very small companies are now purchasing CRM software—by the end of 2007, it is projected that more than one third of the CRM market will be companies with fewer than 100 employees. Many of these small businesses will use what is termed **on-demand CRM** or **Web-based CRM**, which allows firms to use a provider's Web site CRM applications, and even customize them for specific industries such as retailing or maintenance.[37]

NetSuite's On-Demand CRM

One example of on-demand CRM is the provider NetSuite. This company provides tools for small businesses to manage their customers and prospects. Applications within CRM include *sales force automation* which includes team selling, territory tracking and assignment, prospect management and forecasting; *marketing automation,* which lets companies build, execute, and measure the success of their marketing campaigns; and *customer support and service,* which focuses on improving online customer support and service, attracting new customers, keeping existing customers, and lowering customer service costs.[38] The price in 2007 for the NetSuite service was $499 per month and $99 per user per month.

A number of other on-demand providers including Salesforce.com, RightNow, and Oracle's Siebel CRM On Demand compete with NetSuite. SugarExchange even provides a library of more than 100 **open-source CRM products,** where users can download free CRM applications and participate in user forums.

Oracle's CRM Application

Oracle CRM applications are for marketing, sales, and service and integrate with many other applications in their E-Business Suite. Apart from their on-demand solutions, Oracle CRM software applications are installed on firms' servers and allow users to manage customers across their entire organization while increasing data and information quality, and customer satisfaction and loyalty. The Oracle CRM applications include Oracle Marketing, which enables firms to plan, execute, and analyze marketing campaigns and trade promotions; Oracle Sales for identifying prospects, executing upsell/cross-sell opportunities, creating proposals, handling complex quotes and contracts, and fulfilling orders; and Oracle Service, which allows for management of Web self-service, agent-assisted service via the customer contact center, and field service.[39]

Microsoft Dynamics CRM Application

Microsoft Dynamics CRM uses the Microsoft Office system and gives users direct access to customer information through Office Outlook, allowing the creation, saving, and reuse of favorite views of customer data without the distraction of unneeded information. The software provides a Service Calendar allowing service schedulers and dispatchers to schedule activities by resource, time, or service; a Marketing Automation Module that makes it easy to build customer or lead lists, create marketing campaigns, and then track campaign progress; and a Campaign Wizard that sends out "e-mail blasts" to targeted lists and then tracks responses. Microsoft's CRM application allows users to easily customize views and business logic, to automate repetitive tasks, and transfer data to Microsoft Excel for analysis.[40]

Trends in CRM

A number of trends are affecting the way CRM programs are designed today, and these trends will likely continue to influence CRM programs, application providers, the companies that use them, and finally the customers themselves. One of these is *privacy*. As the use of the Internet grows, more and more customers are becoming concerned about their personal information becoming compromised or being shared with other companies to find new ways to generate income. New privacy regulations are springing up as consumer protection groups continue to push for stronger Internet regulatory measures. As consumer fears mount, companies must take a proactive stand at reassuring their customers that their information will be protected, as well as convincing them to allow information to be used in the first place. Unfortunately, customer data is sometimes compromised, and this news frequently hits the media. For example TD Ameritrade of Nebraska in 2006 reported a loss of $4 million as the result of customer account breaches. Hackers captured customer account information and passwords, then used these accounts in a market manipulation scheme, according to TD Ameritrade. Even more alarming was the U.S. Department of Veterans Affairs' loss of a laptop computer containing personal information of 28.6 million American veterans discharged since 1975. And, according to a 2006 data breach study from Michigan-based Ponemon Institute, the average total cost of lost customer records now stands at $182 per record.[41]

Some of the measures firms can take to reduce information security and wrongful use fears is to develop a privacy policy and post it on the company Web site, as well as on surveys and other information-gathering forms; allow customers to opt-in and opt-out of mailing lists and promotional campaigns; allow customers to access their accounts online so they can view the information collected about them; require customers to state their privacy preferences, build this into their profiles, and use these preferences when developing one-to-one promotions; make someone in the firm (a customer privacy manager, for instance) responsible for enforcing privacy policies and communicating these to employees and customers; and periodically perform a privacy audit to assure that privacy policies are being communicated and enforced properly.

Another trend is in the use of **application service providers** or ASPs. This is also referred to as the **software-as-a-service model (SaaS model)**. Perhaps as many as 50 percent of all CRM programs are now designed and maintained for clients by ASPs. In many cases, firms do not have the time, knowledge, or infrastructure to buy and build an effective CRM program, so they use Internet on-demand CRM services provided by an ASP. These providers also offer high levels of data security, which many firms find very attractive. Some firms may prefer instead to concentrate their resources on core competencies. Besides, as technologies and Web site capabilities have become more sophisticated, customers today have no way of knowing who is answering their questions, who is maintaining their data, and who is designing marketing campaigns aimed at them. ASP clients have access to a wide array of CRM services, as well as the expertise to train internal users of the systems. Perhaps most important is the speed of implementation an ASP can offer. Clients who are in a hurry to increase their customer management capabilities most often turn to an ASP. As shown earlier, these services can also be quite reasonably priced, particularly for small users.

Adapting CRM for global uses is also increasing. Foreign locations of a firm need access to centralized customer databases, particularly when dealing with multinational business customers. Today, suppliers must cater to customer needs in a similar manner regardless of where those customers are located. Companies such as H-P, GE, and many of Wal-Mart's major suppliers have setup global account management systems to cater to these demands. Field sales and service personnel also need access to centralized customer information when dealing with issues that may have been encountered before at other locations for the same customer. Products may be purchased for instance in one country, only to end up being used in yet another country. Call centers that service an array of international customers will also need to offer support in a number of languages. Privacy laws and issues will also vary from one country to the next, so firms must be cognizant of this when collecting customer information or designing marketing initiatives.

Integration issues also continue to be a significant issue for CRM. Salesforce.com's latest version of its hosted software includes a built-in link to SAP's ERP software application, in response to integration requests by users. Sage Software has also begun providing integrated business processes so workflow components in their CRM software systems can be linked to accounting transactions and other back office systems.[42]

Finally, as briefly mentioned in the previous section, *open source CRM* is becoming more commonly available, allowing firms to obtain the source code for their own use and modification. Typically the "free" applies only to the basic software, not the support, documentation, or advanced CRM applications. For these reasons, open source CRM applications tend to be the most time-consuming and expensive option. Firms offering open source solutions also typically host an open source community, where users can interact and share innovations.

SUMMARY

In this chapter we discussed the elements of CRM, its place within the field of supply chain management, the requirements for successful CRM program implementation, the trends in CRM, and then finally, we described several CRM application providers. As we learned in this chapter, customer relationship management is really all about just treating customers right, and for as long as there have been businesses, some firms have been very successful at keeping customers satisfied and coming back, while others have not. For the past 10 or 15 years, though, both the level of competition in the market place as well as available computer technology and software capabilities have been increasing quite dramatically. Thus, we have seen a shift in CRM toward use of technology and software to better analyze, segment, and serve customers with the objective being to maximize long-term customer profitability.

Firms today are learning how to combine many channels of customer contact to better serve customers, resulting in better service and more sales. Though many of the CRM applications are expensive, firms can use a structured approach to design an appropriate plan, and then analyze and select the right applications and vendors to implement a successful CRM program.

KEY TERMS

application service providers, 368

call centers or customer contact centers, 359

clickstreams, 356

cross-selling, 353

customer churn, 354

customer defection analysis, 354

customer lifetime value, 354

customer service, 351

customer value, 351

data warehouse, 365

event-based marketing, 356

lead management, 357

on-demand CRM, 367

open-source CRM products, 367

posttransaction, 358

pretransaction, 358

relationship marketing or permission marketing, 352

sales activity management, 357

sales force automation (SFA), 356

sales territory management, 357

segment customers, 351

seven Rs Rule, 358

software-as-a-service model (SaaS model), 368

target marketing, 351

Web site self-service, 360

Web-based CRM, 367

DISCUSSION QUESTIONS

1. Define the term *customer relationship management* and how this definition has changed during the past 20 years.

2. How does the actual practice of CRM differ from the use of CRM software?

3. Why have so many CRM efforts failed? Can you cite a personal example of a CRM effort?

4. Describe why CRM is so important in managing supply chains. Use an example in your discussion.

5. What is *segmenting customers* and why is it perhaps the most important activity in CRM?

6. Define these terms: *permission marketing, cross-selling,* and *churn reduction.*

7. How would an analysis of customer defections help the firm become more competitive?

8. Why is the determination of customer lifetime value important?

9. **Discussion Problem:** From the information given, rank these customers in terms of customer lifetime value.

	AVG. ANNUAL SALES	AVG. PROFIT MARGIN	EXPECTED LIFETIME
Customer A:	$2500	17%	8 years
Customer B:	$4000	12%	6 years
Customer C:	$1200	30%	12 years

Use a discount rate of 6 percent and treat the average sales figures as annuities.

10. How can CRM applications increase the effectiveness and productivity of a firm's sales force?

11. How does *your definition* of customer service compare to the *Seven Rs Rule*?

12. What are the three elements of customer service, and how are they important to CRM?

13. Are call centers good for CRM? Explain.

14. Do you think call center outsourcing negatively affects customer service? Explain.

15. How can customer satisfaction be measured?

16. Do you think CRM applications unnecessarily invade customers' privacy? Explain.

17. Describe the steps necessary for designing and implementing a successful CRM program.

18. What is *on-demand CRM* and what are its advantages?

19. How does *open-source CRM* differ from *on-demand CRM*?

INTERNET QUESTIONS

1. Go to the Web site www.callcentermagazine.com and look at several new issues of the magazine. Describe a new development in call center usage or technology.

2. Identify an open-source CRM provider and see if you can determine what is "free" and what is not.

INFOTRAC QUESTIONS

Access http://academic.cengage.com/infotrac to answer the following questions:

1. Search on the term "call center technology" and describe a few of the latest uses of technology in call centers.

2. Find an example of a firm that segments customers and report on how it is done.

3. What are some of the latest developments in Internet privacy laws?

Chapter 11

GLOBAL LOCATION DECISIONS

Companies are queuing up to invest in China, lured by the prospect of competitive labor costs and vast market potential. No fewer than 400 of the Fortune 500 companies have already invested in China, and surveys of senior executives of multinationals consistently show China to be the global location of choice for investment.[1]

No two countries that both had McDonald's had fought a war against each other since each got its McDonald's.

–Thomas Friedman in *The Lexus and the Olive Tree*

Learning Objectives

After completing this chapter, you should be able to

- Explain the impact of global location decisions on a supply chain.
- Identify the factors influencing location decisions.
- Understand the impact of the regional trade agreements on location decisions.
- Use several location evaluation models.
- Understand the advantages of business clusters.
- Understand the importance of sustainable development.

Chapter Outline

Supply Chain Management in Action

The Growing Presence of Foreign Auto Plants in the United States

When Honda opened the first Japanese transplant in Marysville, Ohio, in 1982, it was to avoid political pressure and import quotas. Honda currently has eight production facilities and 13,000 employees in the U.S.[2] Nissan followed shortly thereafter when they opened a plant in Smyrna, Tennessee, in 1983 to produce Sentra cars. Over the years, the Smyrna facility has been expanded to include Frontier trucks and Xterra sport utility vehicles (SUVs). In 1988, Toyota built a factory in Kentucky, which has been expanded to assemble the Avalon and Camry cars and Sienna minivans. The landscape of the auto industry has changed as local and international auto manufacturers continue to move away from the Midwest. Toyota Motor Corp. is expected to add two more assembly plants in North America by the end of the decade as part of the company's overall strategy to capture a bigger portion of the U.S. auto market and to supplant General Motors as the world's number one auto manufacturer. Toyota will have manufacturing facilities in several U.S. states: Mississippi, West Virginia, Texas, Indiana, California, and Kentucky. Toyota has announced that it will build a $1.3 billion assembly plant in Mississippi (which beat out Tennessee and Alabama in the location selection process). The manufacturing plant will be up and running by 2010 and is scheduled to assemble Highlanders. Toyota has recently begun production of its full-sized pickup trucks in their manufacturing facility in San Antonio, Texas.[3]

The southern U.S. has witnessed a transformation of its agrarian economy to an industrial economy. In 1994, BMW opened a manufacturing facility in South Carolina to produce Z3 roadsters. Today, the BMW plant has been expanded to build the Z4 roadsters as well as X5 SUVs. BMW chose South Carolina because of tax and training incentives, good access to highways and ports, and a strong work ethic in the state.[4]

In the mid-1990s, Alabama pulled off a major coup by attracting Mercedes-Benz to build a sport utility factory in Vance, Alabama, with incentives amounting to $325 million. Alabama then offered Honda $158 million in economic incentives to open a $500 million auto and engine plant near Lincoln in 2001. The major incentive categories included the $16 million site, a $30 million training program, about $45 million in road improvements around the site, and $56 million in tax abatements over a 20-year period. Honda chose Alabama because of the "outstanding community of people, excellent transportation systems, and the necessary infrastructure to support industry."[5] The Honda Odyssey minivans and Pilot SUVs are assembled at the Alabama facility.

In 2000, the state legislature in Mississippi introduced the "Advantage Mississippi" program to offer tax and job training incentives to attract industrial recruits to the state. State leaders were rewarded for their hard lobbying work when Nissan announced that it would open a $930 million plant in Mississippi by summer 2003 employing 4000 workers. According to Emil Hassan, Nissan's senior vice president, the company had decided at the onset to locate in the South because "it is the best location for having a good, reliable, trainable workforce."[6]

The Hyundai Motor Company had previously considered sites in Kentucky, Ohio, and Mississippi but eventually decided on Montgomery, Alabama. The $1 billion plant, which opened in 2005, built cars and SUVs and employed about 2000 workers initially. Hyundai received incentives valued at $118 million for worker training from the state.[7] The other reasons cited by Hyundai for its decision include the "high-quality workforce, its strategic location in proximity to American population centers, the superb automotive parts supply chain available in the region, and the commitment shown by the state of Alabama and the city of Montgomery, which provided the best environment for the new plant."[8]

The money spent on incentives by state and local governments was expected to show a positive return on investment in additional employment and industry spin-offs. According to a study carried out by Michigan's Center for Automotive Research, one additional job at a new automotive plant created 5.5 additional jobs in supplier factories or related businesses in the community.[9] Foreign-owned factories in the south had so far been able to stave off efforts at unionization by the UAW. Alabama, Mississippi, South Carolina, and Tennessee are all right-to-work states. In 2001, the UAW was unsuccessful in organizing a union at Nissan's plant in Tennessee by a two-to-one vote.[10] In summary, the south offered a supportive business environment, training and tax incentives, and a mostly nonunion workforce.

Introduction

Locating a facility is an important decision affecting the cost of managing the supply chain, the level of service provided to customers, and the firm's overall competitive advantage. A supply chain is a network of facilities, and the location of production facilities, warehouses, distribution centers, and suppliers determines the efficient flow of goods to and from these facilities. Once a decision on locating a facility is made, it is costly to move or shut down the facility. Thus, facility location has a long-term impact on the supply chain and must be an integral part of the firm's supply chain strategy. With increased globalization and investments in technology infrastructure, faster transportation, improved communications, and open markets, companies are able to locate anywhere in the world – something previously thought to be impossible. According to Gene DePerez, National Director of Business Location Strategies for PricewaterhouseCoopers, "Site selection must always be done to meet the corporate objectives and to integrate the factors, opportunities, and the risks that are important to a company at a particular time. Every industry out there is going through major transformations, changing the way they all do business. We are seeing higher levels of automation, changes in how companies deal with customers, and, often, manufacturing done in various parts of the world, then all brought together just-in-time."[11]

However, it would appear that easy access to global markets and corporate networks makes the role of location less important as a source of competitive advantage. Nonetheless, successful business clusters such as those in Silicon Valley, Wall Street, the California wine region, and the Italian leather fashion industry show that location still matters. The existence of business clusters in many industries provides clear evidence that innovation and successful competition are concentrated geographically. Dr. Michael Porter suggests that the immediate business environment is just as important as those issues that impact companies internally in affecting location decisions.[12] Business clusters are discussed in detail later in this chapter.

Global location decisions involve determining the location of the facility, defining the strategic role of the facility, and identifying markets served by the facility. For example, Honda's global location strategy is to "put cost-effective plants in areas that best meet the needs of local customers."[13] The result is the establishment of more than 100 factories in 33 countries. Honda's "Small Born" manufacturing strategy is to start small and expand production as local demand increases. This approach allows Honda to be efficient and profitable, even when production volumes are low. In 1982, Honda built its first U.S. auto plant to assemble Accords in Marysville, Ohio. Then Honda added a second factory to produce Civics. As the demand for Honda automobiles continued to increase, Honda opened another facility to assemble the Odyssey minivans in Alabama (as discussed in the Supply Chain Management in Action feature at the beginning of the chapter).

The early prediction regarding the Internet was that Web-based business-to-business and business-to-consumer sales would transcend borders and boundaries, thus making the facility location decision somewhat irrelevant. However, the outcome has been exactly the opposite of what was predicted. Although it is true that anyone can access the Internet from anywhere in the world, it is equally true that geography still affects the speed of delivery and cost in serving the customer. Dell Computers, the leader in the customized, direct-to-customer computer industry, realized that manufacturing in one location in Texas was costing the company more to transport the computers than to assemble them.[14] Consequently, Dell built a second facility in Tennessee to be closer to customers in the eastern U.S. markets.

When e-commerce first emerged, the initial thought was that companies could serve customers without requiring the heavy investments in infrastructure of a Wal-Mart or a Sears. The reasoning was that e-commerce companies could use subcontractors to manage inventory, replenish orders, and resolve customer service issues. The truth is that e-retailers have to control their own distribution centers and deliveries to reliably satisfy customer orders. As described in the e-Business Connection feature, Illinois-based online grocery delivery service Peapod experienced difficulties when its vendors were unable to ship some of the grocery items ordered by its online customers. Because of these difficulties, Peapod likely lost many early users of its online grocery service.[15]

e-Business Connection

Amazon.com's Facility Network

Jeff Bezos founded Amazon.com in 1995. Amazon's business strategy is to "offer Earth's biggest selection and to be Earth's most customer-centric company, where customers can find and discover anything they may want to buy on-line."[16] The company's global retail Web sites include www.amazon.com, www.amazon.ca, www.amazon.de, www.amazon.fr, www.amazon.co.jp, www.amazon.co.uk, www.joyo.com (the Chinese Web site was acquired in 2004), www.shopbop.com, and www.endless.com. In 2006, international sales represented 45 percent of total sales.[17]

The early belief in electronic commerce was that millions of customers could be served without requiring the type of infrastructure of a Sears or a Wal-Mart. However, online retailers are finding out that without their own warehouses and shipping capabilities, customer service could suffer. For example, Peapod Inc., an online grocery retailer, discovered that 8 to 10 percent of its online orders were not shipped to customers because its contracted supplier was out of stock.[18] In the late 1990s, Amazon.com went on a warehouse-building spree, adding new facilities in

Nevada, Kentucky, and Kansas to its existing distribution system. The objective was to improve logistics and cut shipping times to customers by one day.[19]

Whereas recognizing that distribution systems will help the company manage the delivery process better and improve customer service, there is still a need to manage costs and turn a profit. With the heavy investments in distribution centers in the United States and worldwide, companies are finding that the flow of goods through their distribution system must be improved to reduce distribution costs. Amazon.com uses the NetWorks Strategy module from the Manugistics e-Business suite to organize the movement of products through its transportation and facility network in the United States and Europe. The software determines which of Amazon.com's distribution centers to retain or expand and the quantity of each product to keep in stock. The resulting distribution system organization and configuration have saved Amazon.com $50 million.[20] As part of its ongoing restructuring process toward profitability, the distribution center in McDonough, Georgia, was closed. In addition, the company will operate its Seattle, Washington, distribution center only during the busy Christmas holiday season.[21] The company currently has U.S. distribution facilities in New Castle, Delaware; Coffeyville, Kansas; Campbellsville and Lexington, Kentucky; Fernley, Nevada; and Grand Forks, North Dakota. There are three European distribution centers in the United Kingdom, France, and Germany. The arrangement in Japan is a little different, with Nippon Express serving as the distribution services provider for orders from www.amazon.co.jp. These fulfillment centers account for a total of 12 million square feet of warehouse space.[22]

Amazon.com uses the NetWorks Transport software to schedule trucks, trains, and planes and track shipments, including expedited loads. The software also computes the shipping cost for an item from the country of origin to the Amazon.com storage location, plans the shipping of products between a supplier and an Amazon.com facility or between two company facilities, and decides which items can be delivered in the same container. Inventory turnover for 2006, 2005, and 2004 was 13, 14, and 16, respectively. The primary reason inventory turnover has declined in the past few years can be attributed to the changes in product mix and the continuing focus on availability of in-stock inventory.[23]

According to Bezos, "Customers are now shopping at Amazon as much for our lower prices as for our selection and convenience."[24] By strategically locating its distribution centers and improving operations, Amazon.com is able to enhance its supply chain by reducing its inventory, minimizing logistics cost, and improving the speed and reliability of delivery of orders to its customers.

Global Location Strategies

Global location decisions are made to optimize the performance of the supply chain and be consistent with the firm's competitive strategy. According to Gene DePerez of PricewaterhouseCoopers, the location strategist needs to ask, "How will this location affect our performance by cost, access to talent, and access to customers?"[25] A firm competing on cost is more likely to select a location that provides a cost advantage. Amazon.com has located warehouses in areas that minimize logistics and inventory costs. Many toy manufacturers have moved their factories to Singapore, Thailand, or China because of cost advantages provided by these countries.

A firm that competes on speed of delivery such as the FedEx Corporation uses the hub-and-spoke approach to location determination. FedEx's first and largest hub in the U.S. is in Memphis, Tennessee. This site covers 300 acres and is the heart of the company's sorting operations. More than 160,000 packages and 325,000 letters an hour can be sorted at this facility. FedEx has instituted procedures to ensure that packages are moved as efficiently as possible. According to Reggie Owens, FedEx's vice president of national hub operations for day and weekend business, "Before, a package from New York going to New York left New York and went to Memphis and then went back. Now, if we have a package from the East Coast that's going to be delivered to an East Coast location, it never leaves the East Coast."[26] To accomplish this, FedEx has smaller U.S. hubs in Anchorage, Chicago, Fort Worth, Indianapolis, Los Angeles, Newark, and Oakland, and foreign hubs in Germany, France, Japan, Philippines, China, the United Arab Emirates, and the United Kingdom. Each of the hubs has been picked for its central location and easy access to customers.

To get the most out of foreign-based facilities, managers must treat these locations as a source of competitive advantage. These foreign facilities have a strategic role to perform. Dr. Kasra Ferdows suggests a framework consisting of six strategic roles depending on the strategic reason for the facility's location and the scope of its activities:[27]

- *Offshore factory.* An **offshore factory** manufactures products at low cost with minimum investment in technical and managerial resources. These products tend to be exported. An offshore factory imports or locally acquires parts and then exports all of the finished products. The primary objective is simply to take advantage of low labor costs. Little engineering or development work is done at the factory, and local management is not involved in making decisions regarding key suppliers and outbound logistics providers. For example, in the early 1970s, Intel built a labor-intensive offshore factory to produce simple, low-cost components in Penang, Malaysia.

- *Source factory.* A **source factory** has a broader strategic role than an offshore factory, with plant management heavily involved in supplier selection and production planning. The source factory's location is dictated by low production cost, fairly developed infrastructure, and availability of skilled workers. For example, Hewlett-Packard's plant in Singapore started as an offshore plant in 1970 but with significant investments over a 10-year period was able to become a source factory for calculators and keyboards.[28]

- *Server factory.* A **server factory** is setup primarily to take advantage of government incentives, minimize exchange risk, avoid tariff barriers, and reduce taxes and logistics costs to supply the regional market where the factory is located. The factory is involved in making minor improvements in products and processes. An example would be Coca-Cola's international bottling plants, each serving a small geographic region.

- *Contributor factory.* The **contributor factory** plays a greater strategic role than a server factory by getting involved in product development and engineering, production planning, making critical procurement decisions, and developing suppliers. For example, in 1973, Sony built a new server factory in Bridgend, Wales. By 1988, the factory was involved in the design and development of many of the products it produced, and it now serves as a contributor plant in Sony's global manufacturing network.[29]

- *Outpost factory.* The **outpost factory** is setup in a location with an abundance of advanced suppliers, competitors, research facilities, and knowledge centers to get access to the latest information on materials, components, technologies, and products. Since the facility normally produces something, its secondary role can be that of a server or an offshore factory. For example, Lego still produces molds and toys in Denmark, Germany, Switzerland, and the U.S.

in spite of the higher manufacturing cost.[30] Lego's factories serve as outpost facilities with access to research facilities, institutions of higher learning, and sophisticated suppliers of plastic materials.

- *Lead factory.* A **lead factory** is a source of product and process innovation and competitive advantage for the entire organization. It translates its knowledge of the market, competitors, and customers into new products. The Intel factory in Penang, Malaysia, and the Hewlett-Packard factory in Singapore are examples of lead factories. In the early 1970s, both Intel and Hewlett-Packard established offshore factories in Southeast Asia. Over time, the strategic roles of these factories were upgraded to that of lead factories.

Global Perspective   *China—The Location of Choice*

Many industry experts have often referred to the 21st Century as "China's century." Several reasons for that observation are shown below:[31]

- China is one of the largest recipients of foreign direct investment in the world.
- China has the world's largest population with nearly 1.3 billion inhabitants (about 22 percent of the world's population).
- China is the world's most dynamic economy, with economic growth rates over the past ten years averaging about 8 percent per year.
- China is the third largest trading nation in the world.
- China is the second largest exporter to the United States.
- China is the world's largest consumer of coal, grain, and meat.
- Children in China (1–18) represent 7 percent of the world's population (382 million), greater than the total population of the U.S.
- China has surpassed Germany as the world's third largest maker of automobiles (VW sells more cars in China than in Germany).

China is also the world's largest manufacturer of coal, steel, cement, color TVs, and mobile phones. In 2006, China had an overall FDI of 69.5 billion, with Hong Kong, British Virgin Islands, Japan, and South Korea as the top investors.[32] In the past few years, commodity prices have increased by more than 50 percent mainly due to China's industrial sectors' huge appetite for raw materials. China now consumes nearly 14 percent of the world's energy.[33]

Its huge population means the country has a tremendous labor pool to draw from. Owing to the abundant labor in China, labor cost has been relatively low and this represents an important factor in drawing foreign businesses to locate there. In a recent study by Accenture,[34] China is the clear choice for low-cost sourcing for European and U.S. organizations. Brazil and Mexico are excellent nearshore locations for the U.S. Likewise, Eastern European countries such as the Czech Republic, Poland, and Hungary are attractive nearshore choices for EU companies. More than 450 of the Fortune 500 companies are already investing in China. Foreign-invested enterprises hire more than 24 million Chinese citizens.[35] Whereas low cost is a criterion for many organizations looking for global sourcing, quality is becoming a key consideration. China now has the capability to produce at quality levels demanded by many global organizations. No wonder many organizations consider China to be the location of choice for manufacturing facilities.

To be successful in China requires an understanding of the country's unique cultural environment. According to Hofstede, "Culture is more often a source of conflict than of synergy.

Cultural differences are a nuisance at best and often a disaster."[36] Hofstede's international cultural issues study points to the following analysis on China[37]:

1. Long-term orientation has the highest ranking, indicating "a society's time perspective and an attitude of persevering."

2. China has a low individualism score compared with other Asian countries meaning that China is more of a collectivist society with an emphasis on family.

3. China has a higher Power Distance ranking compared with the world average, indicating "a high level of inequality of power and wealth within the society."

In addition, there is great respect for elders and hierarchy in Chinese society. The concept of *face* is another important cultural aspect—in personal or business dealings one must avoid any action that would cause a friend or an acquaintance to lose face. Cultivating *guanxi* (relationships) is critical in doing business in China because of the underdeveloped legal system.

As China's economy continues to develop at a fast pace, there is a shift from labor-intensive industries to higher-value areas such as marketing, product design, and the production of high technology products. Consequently, there is a looming shortage of world-class graduates in key areas such as business and engineering. This shortage is a major problem for multinationals, for local companies, and for China's policy makers. Thus the challenge is one of attracting and retaining highly skilled management talent. Companies such as Microsoft and Google have been quick at snapping up top graduates from local institutions of higher learning such as Peking University and Tsinghua University and paying them top salaries. To compete, other companies have to invest in training and developing the talent needed to manage world-class organizations. The abundance of jobs in China means that trained employees can hop around and "cherry pick" the organizations that can afford to pay them best for their capabilities; executive compensation has risen faster than inflation owing to the strong demand for such skills. Currently, a relatively high proportion of Chinese students who study abroad do not return home.[38] These graduates have the skills needed to work for multinationals but are currently lost to the Chinese labor market. South Korea, India, and Taiwan had similar experiences in the past but have seen a reversal with an increasing number of graduates and citizens who have many years of international experience going home. The implication for making location decisions is affected heavily by wage differentials in different regions in China and access to technical skills for the high technology industries.

An emerging labor issue in China is the review of the Employment Contract law by the National People's Congress, which is in its final stages as of the end of 2007. The revised law includes issues that affect foreign investors such as "noncompete agreements, termination provisions, and the creation of company rules and regulations."[39] Another development is that the All-China Federation of Trade Unions (ACFTU) is aggressively targeting some of the bigger foreign companies for unionization. Wal-Mart has strongly resisted unionization of its stores worldwide. However, the ACFTU has been pressuring Wal-Mart to establish union branches in its stores in China. Today, 16 of Wal-Mart's 60 Chinese stores are unionized with more stores being organized.[40] The success of the ACFTU has major implications for other foreign companies.

According to the editor's note of the People's Daily Online, "China's fast economic development over the past years has been remarkable and aroused worldwide attention. But it is based on high input, high energy consumption and low output. Thus the central government has decided to pursue a new mode of economic growth mainly relying on innovation and developing a circular economy and establish resource-efficient society. To balance economic and social development, scientifically deal with relations between development and environment protection, especially in air, water and soil will remain a long-term task for every Chinese from government, business to non-governmental organizations."[41] This indicates a significant shift in policy by the government and addresses the issue about sustainable development in China. The government has strengthened environmental legislation and invested heavily in environmental protection. Beijing, Qingdao, and Nanjing will be transformed as China is looking forward to achieving a green Olympics in 2008, following in the footsteps of the Sydney 2000 Olympics.

Critical Location Factors

One of the most challenging tasks as a company grows, relocates, or starts up is where to position assets strategically to create a long-term competitive advantage. Some of the questions that need to be addressed for each potential location are set out as follows:

- What will be the reaction of shareholders, customers, competitors, and employees?
- Will the location provide a sustainable competitive advantage?
- What will be the impact on product or service quality?
- Can the right people be hired?
- What will be the effect on the supply chain?
- What is the projected cost?
- What will be the impact on delivery performance?
- How will the market react?
- Is the transfer of people necessary, and, if so, are employees willing to move?

There are basically three levels of location decisions: the global market or country selection, the subregion or state selection, and the community and site selection. The process starts with an analysis of the market region of the world that bears a strategic interest to the organization; and, eventually, a country is targeted. Once the country is selected, the focus shifts to finding a subregion or state within the country that best meets the company's location requirements. Finally, the community and site for the facility are selected. The weighted-factor rating model, which is discussed later in this chapter, can be used to make a location decision at each of the levels mentioned here.

Table 11.1 lists a number of factors and issues affecting facility location, and a discussion of each of these follows.

Regional Trade Agreements and the World Trade Organization

An understanding of **regional trade agreements** and the **World Trade Organization (WTO)** is critical to the facility location decision process because of their impact on tariffs, costs, and the free flow of goods and services. As initially discussed in Chapter 2, the WTO[42] is the successor to the General Agreement on Tariffs and Trade (GATT), which was responsible for setting up the multilateral trading system after the Second World War. Today, the WTO is the only international organization dealing with the

Table 11.1	Important Factors in the Location Decision Process		
LOCATION FACTOR	**COUNTRY**	**REGION/STATE**	**COMMUNITY**
Regional trade agreements—trade barriers, tariff, import duties	X		
Competitiveness of nation â economic performance, government efficiency, business efficiency, and infrastructure	X		
Federal taxes and incentives	X		
Currency stability	X		
Environmental issues	X	X	X
Access and proximity to market	X	X	X
Labor issues	X	X	X
Access to supplies and cost	X	X	X
Transportation issues	X	X	X
Utility availability and cost	X	X	X
Quality-of-life issues	X	X	X
State taxes and incentives		X	X
Right-to-work state		X	X
Local taxes and incentives			X
Land availability and cost			X

rules of trade between nations. Its functions include administering the WTO agreements, providing a forum for trade negotiations, handling trade disputes, monitoring national trade policies, providing technical assistance and training programs for developing countries, and cooperating with other international organizations.

On December 11, 2001, China became a member of the WTO. China's entry has resulted in faster economic, legal, and environmental reforms, a further relaxation of tariffs, and increasing economic growth. In 2006, China was one of the world's top recipients of foreign direct investment. To date, more than 190 countries have invested in China. In 2006, the U.S. was the fifth largest source of foreign direct investment in China.[43]

There are 162 regional trade agreements under GATT and the WTO that are in force today.[44] Examples of the better-known regional trade agreements are the **European Union (EU)**, the **North American Free Trade Agreement (NAFTA)**, the **Southern Common Market (MERCOSUR)**, the **Association of Southeast Asian Nations (ASEAN)**, and the **Common Market of Eastern and Southern Africa (COMESA)**. Several of these are discussed here:

- *The European Union.* Setup after the Second World War, the European Union was officially launched on May 9, 1950, with France's proposal to create a European federation consisting of six countries: Belgium, Germany, France, Italy, Luxembourg, and the Netherlands. A series of accessions in 1973 (Denmark, Ireland, and the United Kingdom), 1981 (Greece), 1986 (Spain and Portugal), 1995 (Austria, Finland, and Sweden), 2004 (Czech Republic, Estonia, Cyprus, Latvia, Lithuania, Hungary, Malta, Poland, Slovenia, and Slovakia), and 2007

(Bulgaria and Romania) resulted in a total of 27 member states in 2007. Currently, the EU has three candidate countries—Croatia, Former Yugoslav Republic of Macedonia, and Turkey.[45] Two highlights of the EU are the establishment of the Single Market in 1993 and the introduction of the Euro notes and coins on January 1, 2002. The EU has a population of 500 million people (7 percent of world's population), a GDP of 10,816.9 billion Euros (more than the GDP of the U.S.), and accounts for 20 percent of the world's exports and imports.[46]

- *The North American Free Trade Agreement (NAFTA).* This trade agreement among the U.S., Canada, and Mexico was implemented on January 1, 1994. NAFTA created the world's largest free trade area with 406 million people and producing more than $11 trillion of goods and services annually. Many tariffs were eliminated with immediate effect, while others are being phased out over periods ranging from 5 to 15 years. From 1993 to 2005, trading among partners grew 173 percent from $297 billion to $810 billion. For the same period, real GDP growth was 48 percent for the U.S., 40 percent for Mexico, and 49 percent for Canada.[47]

- *The Southern Common Market (MERCOSUR).* This agreement among Argentina, Brazil, Paraguay, and Uruguay was fashioned in March 1991 with the signing of the Treaty of Asuncion. The agreement was created with the goal of forming a common market/customs union between the participating countries and was based on economic cooperation between Argentina and Brazil that had been in place since 1986.[48]

- *The Association of Southeast Asian Nations (ASEAN).* This association was created in 1967 and today comprises the following countries in the Southeast Asian region: Brunei, Cambodia, Indonesia, Laos, Malaysia, Myanmar, the Philippines, Singapore, Thailand, and Vietnam.[49] The primary objective of ASEAN is to promote economic, social, and cultural development of the region through cooperative programs.

- *The Common Market of Eastern and Southern Africa (COMESA).* This treaty involves the establishment of a customs union to foster economic growth among the member countries. The member countries are Angola, Burundi, Comoros, Entrea, Ethiopia, Kenya, Lesotho, Malawi, Mauritius, Rwanda, Sudan, Swaziland, Tanzania, Uganda, Zaire, Zambia, and Zimbabwe.

Competitiveness of Nations

A nation's competitiveness is defined by the Organization of Economic Cooperation and Development (OECD) as "the degree to which a country can, under free and fair market conditions, produce goods and services which meet the rest of international markets, while simultaneously maintaining and expanding the real incomes of its people over the long term."[50] There are two competing sources for a world competitiveness ranking. One is the *World Competitiveness Yearbook*[51] published annually by IMD and the other is the *Global Competitiveness Report*[52] prepared by the World Economic Forum. Since the two organizations use different criteria for their rankings, the listings are typically different.

The *World Competitiveness Yearbook* features 55 industrialized and emerging economies and provides businesses with basic information on location decisions. There are 323 criteria, which are broadly grouped into four competitiveness factors:[53]

- *Economic Performance* (79 criteria). "Macro-economic evaluation of the domestic economy: Domestic Economy, International Trade, International Investment, Employment and Prices."

- *Government Efficiency* (72 criteria). "Extent to which government policies are conducive to competitiveness: Public Finance, Fiscal Policy, Institutional Framework, Business Legislation and Societal Framework."
- *Business Efficiency* (71 criteria). "Extent to which the national environment encourages enterprises to perform in an innovative, profitable and responsible manner: Productivity and Efficiency, Labor Market, Finance, Management Practices and Attitudes and Values."
- *Infrastructure* (101 criteria). "Extent to which basic, technological, scientific and human resources meet the needs of business: Basic Infrastructure, Technological Infrastructure, Scientific Infrastructure, Health and Environment and Education."

The publication provides an analysis of the data collected and ranks nations according to their ability to create and maintain their organizations' competitiveness. Data from the report can be used to compare countries globally, to see 5-year trends, to understand strengths and weaknesses, and to examine factors and subfactors. In addition, businesses can use the publication to determine investment plans and assess locations for new operations.[54] Rankings for the *World Competitiveness Yearbook* appear in Table 11.2. As shown in the table, the top three countries in terms of competitiveness in 2006/2007 were the U.S., Hong Kong, and Singapore.

The rankings of the top 16 countries in the *Global Competitiveness Report 2006–2007* are also shown in Table 11.2. This ranking is based on a comprehensive annual survey conducted by the World Economic Forum together with leading research institutes and business organizations. For the latest report, over 11,000 business leaders were polled in a record 131 countries. At the top of the list of the world's most competitive economies are Switzerland, Finland, and Sweden according to this publication. One surprising finding is that Finland, ranked number two on the *Global Competitiveness Report*, does not even appear on the *World Competitiveness Yearbook* list. This illustrates the differences between the two publications.

Each of the 321 criteria covered in the *World Competitiveness Report* are issues that a company would like to know about the country before making a location decision. All things being equal, a country that has a higher competitiveness ranking would potentially be a better candidate for a facility location than one that is not as competitive. According to Augusto Lopez-Claros, chief economist and director, Global Competitiveness Network, "The top rankings of Switzerland and the Nordic countries show that good institutions and competent macroeconomic management, coupled with world-class educational attainment and a focus on technology and innovation, are a successful strategy for boosting competitiveness in an increasingly complex global economy."[55]

Government Taxes and Incentives

Government incentives, business attitude, economic stability, and taxes are important location factors. Several levels of government must be considered when evaluating potential locations. At the federal level, a **tariff** is a tax imposed by the government on imported goods to protect local industries, support the country's balance of payments, or raise revenue. Thus, countries with high tariffs would discourage companies from importing goods into the country. At the same time, high tariffs encourage multinational corporations to setup factories to produce locally. However, membership in the WTO requires countries to open up their markets and to reduce their tariffs imposed on imported goods. Regional trade agreements such as NAFTA, MERCOSUR, and the EU

Table 11.2	2006–2007 World Competitiveness Rankings	
RANKING	**GLOBAL COMPETITIVENESS REPORT (WORLD ECONOMIC FORUM)[a]**	**WORLD COMPETITIVENESS YEARBOOK (IMD)[b]**
1	Switzerland	United States
2	Finland	Singapore
3	Sweden	Hong Kong
4	Denmark	Luxembourg
5	Singapore	Denmark
6	United States	Switzerland
7	Japan	Iceland
8	Germany	Netherlands
9	Netherlands	Sweden
10	United Kingdom	Canada
11	Hong Kong	Austria
12	Norway	Australia
13	Taiwan	Norway
14	Iceland	Ireland
15	Israel	China
16	Canada	Germany

Sources: [a] www.weforum.org/en/initiatives/gcp/Global%20Competitiveness%20Report/index.htm.
[b] www.imd.ch/research/publications/wcy/index.cfm.

also serve to reduce tariffs among member nations to promote the free movement of goods. Many countries have setup **foreign trade zones (FTZs)** where materials can be imported duty-free as long as the imports are used as inputs to production of goods that are eventually exported. If the goods are sold domestically, no duty is paid until they leave the FTZ.

In the U.S., 43 states have a personal income tax and 46 states have a corporate income tax. For example, Nevada is a business-friendly state that does not have a corporate income tax, state personal income tax, corporate franchise tax, or inventory tax. Companies such as Amazon.com have taken advantage of this by setting up warehouses in Nevada. The other states that do not have an individual income tax are Alaska, Florida, South Dakota, Texas, Washington, and Wyoming.[56]

Currency Stability

One factor that impacts business costs and consequently location decisions is any instability in currency exchange rates. Since its introduction in 1999, for instance, the Euro depreciated in value against the U.S. dollar, but since 2002 it has been on an upward trend. The strengthening of the Euro has increased the business cost for

Euro countries competing against businesses in the U.S. Several countries such as China, Hong Kong, and Malaysia currently have fixed exchange rates and, therefore, provide for a more stable environment for investment. Any organization involved with international business is subjected to the risk of currency exchange rate fluctuation. For example, Amazon.com is exposed to foreign exchange rate fluctuations and risks associated with their international Web site operations.[57]

Access and Proximity to Markets/Customers

According to Daniel Malachuk, partner and worldwide director of business location at Arthur Andersen in New York, "The trend in manufacturing is to be within delivery proximity of your customers. Logistics timeliness and costs are the concerns, so that reinforces a clustering effect of suppliers and producers to places that offer lower cost labor and real estate."[58] As pointed out earlier in this chapter, Honda is a global company that aims to build plants in locations that best satisfy the needs of local customers. Honda has assembly plants in the U.S., Japan, Malaysia, China, and Indonesia, to name a few markets where Honda sells its vehicles.

Recently, Eli Lilly made a strategic decision to move its Asian headquarters from Singapore to Hong Kong. According to Richard Smith, president of Lilly's Asian operations, "The critical mass, the center of gravity is moving north, and the real growth industries are in China. Taiwan and the countries in Southeast Asia are becoming less important in terms of critical mass in customers. Hong Kong is a springboard for us to expand into China, one of the fastest growing pharmaceutical markets in the world."[59] For a long time, Singapore had been a good location for Eli Lilly, but the shifting business environment meant that the company had to rethink its long-term strategy for the Asian market; now it is closer to its rapidly growing Chinese customer base. Halliburton, the Texas-based energy services company, announced recently that it will open a corporate headquarters in Dubai, emerging quickly as the business hub in the Middle East. The move is considered strategic as the company is looking to concentrate its business in the Middle East and surrounding areas. Halliburton's business has over the past several years shifted its customer base to locations such as Kuwait, Russia, Libya, Australia, Vietnam, and Africa. This follows the trend in the energy business where the customer base is changing from traditional Western oil companies to oil companies in developing countries.[60]

For services, proximity to customers is even more critical, when compared to manufacturing firms. Few customers will frequent a remotely located gas station or a supermarket if another more accessible alternative is available. Similarly, fast-food restaurants are well situated next to busy intersections to take advantage of heavy traffic areas. An earlier study notes that an effective location strategy is "... an integral part of corporate strategy for retail firms. Whether selling goods or services, the choice of outlet location is perhaps the most important decision a retailer has to make."[61]

Wal-Mart's early supercenters were located in predominantly rural markets to avoid direct competition with major discount stores in large metropolitan areas. Many regional U.S. chains, such as Jamesway, Bradlees, Caldor, Venture, Hills, McCrory's, and Rose's, went out of business because they could not compete with the larger and smarter competitors such as Wal-Mart and Target.[62] More recently, Wal-Mart has changed its location strategy to include urban locations in the western and northeastern regions of the U.S.

Environmental Issues

How the environment is managed has a significant impact on human health. The inability to dispose of solid and hazardous waste, plus the presence of illegal waste, contributes to high incidences of diseases such as hepatitis A and amebiasis. Global warming, air pollution, and acid rain are issues that are increasingly being debated as the price to pay for industrialization. Millions of people live in cities with unsafe air, with asthma cases at an all-time high. The U.S. has the world's biggest ecological footprint. For example, the U.S. is unfortunately ranked number one in the world in the following areas: emission of carbon dioxide (the green house gas that impacts climate change); consumption of forest products; and municipal waste per person.[63] In the U.S., the Environmental Protection Agency (EPA) is the federal agency responsible for the enforcement of environmental laws and regulations.

In the U.S., the Clinton Administration negotiated the North American Agreement on Environmental Cooperation (NAAEC) to "promote sustainable development through mutually supportive environmental and economic policies" as a supplementary environmental agreement to NAFTA.[64] The agreement provides a framework for the three countries to conserve, protect, and enhance the North American environment and to effectively enforce the environmental laws.

With trade liberalization, there is a need for environmental cooperation. The WTO understands the need for sound national and international environmental policies. A WTO report on trade and the environment was prepared in 1999 to address three key questions: (1) Is economic integration through trade and investment a threat to the environment? (2) Does trade undermine the regulatory efforts of governments to control pollution and resource degradation? and (3) Will economic growth driven by trade help the move toward sustainable use of the world's environmental resources?[65] Several environmental trends were identified in the report:

- The increasing use of global energy resources has raised the level of greenhouse gas emissions.
- Consumption of ozone depletion substances (contributing to global warming) has gone down, but it will take another 50 years to get back to normal levels.
- Sulfur dioxide emissions (a cause of acid rain) continue to increase in developing countries.
- Excessive generation of nitrogen continues from fertilizers, human sewage, and burning of fossil fuel.
- Continued deforestation occurs in developing countries.
- The increasing global water consumption will result in water shortages in many countries unless serious water conservation efforts are begun.

The report finds that neither trade nor economic growth is the real issue. The challenge is "to strengthen the mechanisms and institutions for multilateral environmental cooperation, just like countries 50 years ago decided that it was to their benefit to cooperate on trade matters."[66] The issues raised in that report are still valid today. Thus we can see that environmental problems are taking a long time to resolve.

Labor Issues

Issues such as labor availability, productivity, and skill; unemployment and underemployment rates; wage rates; turnover rates; labor force competitors; and employment trends are key factors in making facility location decisions. Mexico has for years competed on cheap labor but cannot continue to depend on this source of competitive advantage because of the emergence of lower labor cost in countries like China. For example, China's manufacturing labor cost averages $0.88 for every $2.50 paid to workers in Mexico.[67] Singapore-based Flextronics, one of the world's largest contract manufacturers, is moving its plants in Malaysia and Singapore to China because of the large number of engineering students graduating from Chinese universities each year and because of the lower labor costs. One report indicated that China and India had 600,000 and 350,000 engineers graduating each year, respectively, compared with 70,000 engineers graduating in the U.S.[68]

Owing to a shortage of skilled workers, companies are likely to seek help from the community in offsetting the cost of training new employees. BMW in South Carolina and Nissan in Tennessee and Mississippi all have joint training programs with these states as part of the incentive package offered to the auto manufacturers. For example, the South Carolina state government setup the South Carolina Technical College System in 1992 to provide training programs and since its inception has reimbursed BMW for training costs in excess of $25 million.[69]

Although it is true that low labor cost is an important factor in making location decisions, sustainable competitive advantage depends on productive use of inputs and continual product and process innovations. When Ely Lilly moved its Asian headquarters to Hong Kong, an important factor was the availability of a highly educated workforce with outstanding administrative and professional people.[70] An empirical study recently found that human capital is one of the most important determinants of foreign direct investment, and its importance has increased significantly over time.[71] The study suggests that developing countries would have to increase the level of worker skills and develop human resource capabilities if they want to be attractive as locations for foreign direct investment.

Right-to-Work Laws

In the U.S. today, there are 22 states with **right-to-work laws**. These states are Alabama, Arizona, Arkansas, Florida, Georgia, Idaho, Iowa, Kansas, Louisiana, Mississippi, Nebraska, Nevada, North Carolina, North Dakota, Oklahoma, South Carolina, South Dakota, Tennessee, Texas, Utah, Virginia, and Wyoming. A right-to-work law "secures the right of employees to decide for themselves whether or not to join or financially support a union."[72] As discussed in the Supply Chain Management in Action feature at the beginning of this chapter, there has been a shift in the U.S. auto industry to the southern states, with assembly plants built in Tennessee, South Carolina, and Alabama, all of which are right-to-work states.

Access to Suppliers and Cost

Many firms prefer locations close to suppliers because of material availability and transportation cost reasons. The proximity of suppliers has an impact on the delivery of materials and, consequently, the effectiveness of supply chains. Royal Philips Electronics, headquartered in the Netherlands, moved its computer monitor plant in Juarez, Mexico, to an existing plant in Suzhou, China, because of a more competitive supplier base.[73] Japanese electronics makers are finding that China is a better place to setup manufacturing facilities even though it means that the cost of transporting finished products to the U.S. market is higher. Japanese companies reason that a high proportion of components needed to make finished electronic products have to be imported from outside NAFTA because U.S., Mexican, and Canadian manu-facturers are not cost competitive.[74]

Utility Availability and Cost

The availability and cost of electricity, water, and gas are also important location considerations. In economically emerging countries, it is not unusual that the supply of electricity has not kept pace with the high speed of development, resulting in work stoppages from electrical outages. Even developed countries such as the U.S. are not immune from energy problems, although for different reasons. For example, California experienced rolling blackouts in the early 2000s causing an electrical crisis. The rolling blackout was repeated in 2005 in southern California when a key trans-mission line went out. In April 2006, Texas had a rolling blackout due to excessive use of air conditioners in response to the high temperatures.[75]

In heavy industries such as steel and aluminum mills, the availability and cost of energy are critical considerations. The concern for companies is to have the power available when needed and at an affordable price. Consequently, areas such as up-state New York, the Tennessee Valley, and parts of Canada, which provide low-cost power, are gaining in facility location popularity because of their plentiful energy sup-ply. With the explosive growth in energy-intensive industries such as machinery, auto, and steel, demand for electricity has outpaced the generation capacity in China, and the country has experienced power shortages since 2002. However, China has seen a surge in their power generation capabilities, with double-digit growth in re-cent years, and these new plants will help ease their energy shortage.[76]

Telecommunication costs have dropped dramatically in the past decade, resulting in many organizations setting up back-office operations and call centers internationally to serve the U.S. market. For example, Sheraton Hotels offloads some of its work from its North American operations to its call center in Ireland. Outsourcing International LLC services companies in the airlines, banking, insurance, computer hardware and soft-ware, and tourism industries. The customer dials a toll-free number in the U.S., and the call is routed to India where the call centers are located. Labor costs in India are less than 20 percent of those in many developed countries. In addition, the working hours are off-peak hours in India, resulting in a complete synergy.[77]

Quality-of-Life Issues

Quality of life can be defined as "a feeling of well-being, fulfillment, or satisfac-tion resulting from factors in the external environments."[78] So what exactly are the is-sues affecting quality of life? Although there is no definitive agreement on a set of **quality-of-life factors**, the Chamber of Commerce in Jacksonville, Florida, has annually prepared a report on the quality of life in the Jacksonville metropolitan area based on a comprehensive set of factors, which include the following:[79]

- *Education.* This includes the public education system that comprises prekin-dergarten through twelfth grade and higher education. Performance in terms of high-school graduation rates, college entrance test scores, teacher salaries, student-teacher ratios, and number of degrees awarded at universities and higher-education institutions provides an indicator of the quality of the edu-cation system. For example, a high student graduation rate and highly paid teachers are indicators of a high-quality education system.
- *Economy.* This includes the standard of living and community economic health. Performance indicators such as net employment growth, new housing

starts, and the unemployment rate show the economic health of the community. The economy must also be sufficiently diverse to allow for long-term careers for both spouses. Thus, a low unemployment rate and an increase in the number of jobs show a vibrant local economy.

- *Natural Environment.* This category includes the quality and availability of clean water and air. Today, cities are monitoring the air-quality index and the amount of recycled waste diverted from landfills. A viable recycling program and clean air indicate a community's commitment to a green environment and the future health of the community.

- *Social environment.* Issues in this category include equal opportunity, racial harmony, emphasis on family, human services, and charitable contributions. A community where people and organizations contribute time and money to helping others in need shows a happy, affluent, and caring environment. The net result is a community that is a better place in which to live.

- *Culture/recreation.* A community that offers choice in terms of cultural, entertainment, recreational, and sporting activities is a more attractive location than one that offers fewer of these options. Measures of this aspect of quality of life include the number of organized sporting activities at city parks and pools, performing and visual arts events, and public parks. People feel better knowing they can go to a Swan Lake ballet, Britney Spears concert, or Lion King show, even if they are not fans of these types of activities.

- *Healthcare.* The medical and healthcare system is another critical element affecting the wellness of residents in the community. Measures such as infant deaths per thousand live births, number of physicians per thousand residents, and use of tobacco among residents are used to determine the health and fitness of the community. Recently, the U.S. medical profession has been facing a dramatic increase in malpractice insurance premiums in many states, with the result that many medical doctors are moving to areas with lower insurance costs. The ability to access good, affordable medical care provides residents with peace of mind and determines whether the community is a desirable place to reside.

- *Government/politics.* This category examines how well the local government is performing and how involved the residents are in public affairs. Issues in this category are the percentage of registered voters, how many actually vote, approval ratings of the mayor, and how well the city government meets the needs of the residents. Recently, many state and local governments in the United States have been struggling to balance their budgets due to a weak economy and are considering cutting services and increasing taxes. This is likely to impact both workers' and firms' location decisions.

- *Mobility.* The ability to travel easily within the area and to other locations affects the quality of life of the residents. Issues such as the average commuting time to work, the number of direct flights from the local airport, and the availability and efficiency of the public transport system provide measures of mobility. If the roads are constantly jammed with traffic, there is a huge loss of productive time. With respect to logistics, the quality of highways, railways, waterways, and airways has a significant impact on the performance of the supply chain in such areas as transportation cost, speed of delivery, and customer satisfaction.

- *Public safety.* Crime and accidents are two of the biggest public safety factors. The quality of law enforcement affects the crime rate. Better road systems and law enforcement are likely to lead to lower accident rates. In addition, fire protection and rescue services are issues of concern to the local residents. In the U.S., there has been a trend toward suburban living because of the perception of safer neighborhoods and, therefore, a better place to locate. In Mexico, especially in towns close to the U.S. border, many foreign businesses are concerned about the crime rate and the safety of expatriates working in maquiladora industries. The kidnapping of a high-level U.S. executive in Tijuana in 2006 shocked the maquiladora companies. Considered a highly organized form of crime, kidnapping is second only to large-scale drug trafficking in Mexico. Executives in Tijuana's 580 maquiladora factories had avoided any kidnapping incidences since 1996 when a Sanyo Video Components vice president was kidnapped.[80] Thus, the recent incidence of this crime in Tijuana could frighten off firms considering a move to that area.

Land Availability and Cost

As land and construction costs in big cities continue to escalate, the trend is to locate in the suburbs and rural areas. Suburban locations can be attractive because of the cost and wide choice of land, available workforce, and developed transportation network. As mentioned earlier, when automaker Honda first decided to setup a factory in the U.S., they located it in Marysville, a small town about 40 miles from Columbus, Ohio. Affordable land near the highway was readily available, and Honda could draw its workforce from several communities around Marysville. Similarly, when Honda built its assembly plant in Alabama to meet the increased demand for its Odyssey minivans and SUVs, the site was located in Lincoln, 40 miles east of Birmingham. When New Jersey-based diversified manufacturer Honeywell decided to move a manufacturing facility in Phoenix, Arizona, to China, the decision was to go to Suzhou, a city about 30 miles from Shanghai. Although the Pudong industrial zone in Shanghai was an attractive site, Suzhou had lower land and labor costs, which were deemed to be important decision factors.

Facility Location Techniques

Two techniques that are commonly used by organizations to assist in making global location decisions are described here: the weighted-factor rating model and the break-even model. For discussion of more complex location models readers should consult textbooks focused specifically on facility location. The two techniques are discussed below.

The Weighted-Factor Rating Model

The **weighted-factor rating model** is a method commonly used to compare the attractiveness of several locations along a number of quantitative and qualitative dimensions. Selecting a facility location using this approach involves the following steps:

1. Identifying the critical factors that are considered important to the facility location decision.

2. Assigning weights to each factor in terms of their relative importance. Typically, the weights sum to 1.

3. Determining a relative performance score for each factor considered. Typically, the score varies from 1 to 100, although other scoring schemes can be used.

4. Multiplying the factor score by the weight associated with each factor and summing the weighted scores for all factors.

5. The location with the highest total weighted score is the recommended location.

Since the factors, the individual weights, and the scores are subject to interpretation and bias by the analyst, it is highly recommended that a team approach be used when performing this type of analysis. Ideally, the team should include representatives from marketing, purchasing, production, finance, and transportation and possibly a key supplier and customer impacted by the location.

Determining the scores for each factor can include several intermediate steps. Comparing a labor cost score, for instance, would include determining the acceptable wage scale, along with insurance, taxes, and training costs and any other associated labor costs for each potential location. Then the total labor costs can be compared and translated into the final labor cost scores for each location by assigning the maximum score to the lowest labor cost location and then assigning the other locations a score based on their respective labor costs. Example 11.1 illustrates the use of the weighted-factor location model.

Example 11.1   Using the Weighted-Factor Location Model

The following factors have been identified as critical to making a location decision among the three countries of China, Singapore, and Indonesia. A group of functional managers has determined the factors, weights, and relative performance scores to be used in the analysis.

CRITICAL LOCATION FACTORS	FACTOR WEIGHTS (SUM TO 1)	CHINA SCORES (1–100)	SINGAPORE SCORES (1–100)	INDONESIA SCORES (1–100)
Labor cost	0.20	100	40	90
Proximity to market	0.15	100	60	80
Supply chain compatibility	0.25	80	80	60
Quality of life	0.30	70	90	60
Stability of government	0.10	80	100	50

In which country should the new facility be located?

SOLUTION

The weighted scores for the three countries are calculated as follows:

$$\text{China} = 0.20(100) + 0.15(100) + 0.25(80) + 0.30(70) + 0.10(80)$$
$$= 20 + 15 + 20 + 21 + 8 = 84$$
$$\text{Singapore} = 0.20(40) + 0.15(60) + 0.25(80) + 0.30(90) + 0.10(100)$$
$$= 8 + 9 + 20 + 27 + 10 = 74$$
$$\text{Indonesia} = 0.20(90) + 0.15(80) + 0.25(60) + 0.30(60) + 0.10(50)$$
$$= 18 + 12 + 15 + 18 + 5 = 68$$

Based on the total weighted score, China would be the recommended country in which to locate the new facility.

The Break-Even Model

The **break-even model**, originally discussed in Chapter 2, can also be used as a location analysis technique when fixed and variable costs can be determined for each potential location. This method involves the following steps:

1. Identifying the locations to be considered.

2. Determining the fixed cost for each facility. The components of fixed cost are the costs of land, property taxes, insurance, equipment, and buildings.

3. Determining the unit variable cost for each facility. The components of variable cost are the costs of labor, materials, utilities, and transportation.

4. Constructing the total cost lines for each location on a graph.

5. Determining the break-even points on the graph. Alternatively, the break-even points can be solved algebraically, however if there are more than two locations, then a graph is recommended to visualize the alternatives.

6. Identifying the range over which each location has the lowest cost.

Example 11.2 illustrates the use of the break-even model.

Helpful Online Information for Location Analysis

Several Web sites are available that provide useful information for use in location analysis:

1. www.FacilityCity.com—This Web site "is the search engine for top-level facility executives who make significant decisions involving the long- and short-term needs of their company and facilities. FacilityCity.com is a powerful, searchable platform that covers issues such as choosing a new location, managing major renovations and modernization projects, initiating facility improvements and selecting products and services." The Web site also provides direct links to *Business Facilities: The Location Advisor* and *Today's Facility Manager*, and *The TFM Show. The TFM Show* (sponsored by *Today's Facility Manager* magazine) is "… the nation's premier forum for senior facility management executives, drawing attendees from every corner of the world."

2. www.developmentalliance.com—The Development Alliance Web site is developed by the International Economic Development Council and Conway Data, Inc., publishers of *Site Selection* magazine (the *Site Selection* online Web site is located at http://siteselection.com). The Development Alliance Web site is a portal for community information that includes the following features:

   • Community Demographics—detailed state, county, micropolitan, and metropolitan statistical data for companies seeking new business locations.

   • IEDN Criteria-based Search—use up to 19 criteria to find and compare counties throughout the U.S.

   • U.S. Legislative Climates—from Alabama through Wyoming. Includes state contact information.

   • Doing Business Database—World Bank's tool for evaluating the impacts on business and property rights protection of regulatory schemes in 175 countries.

   • FDI.net—MIGA's unique Web portal that offers free, on-demand country analysis and information on all things related to foreign direct investment in 175 countries.

   • International Guide—maps, government and economic information, and contacts for area development agencies from Afghanistan to Zimbabwe.

   • Business Parks Directory—listings of business parks with prepared sites for sale or lease in the U.S., Canada, and Mexico.

Example 11.2   Using the Break-Even Model

Three locations have been identified as suitable candidates for building a new factory. The fixed and unit variable costs for each of three potential locations have been estimated and are shown in the following table.

LOCATION	ANNUAL FIXED COST	VARIABLE COST PER UNIT
A	$500,000	$300
B	$750,000	$200
C	$900,000	$100

The forecasted demand is 3000 units per year. Which is the best location?

SOLUTION

First, plot the three total cost curves, represented by

$$TC_A = 500,000 + 300Q$$
$$TC_B = 750,000 + 200Q$$
$$TC_C = 900,000 + 100Q$$

The three curves are shown in Figure 11.1.

Determine the break-even points between Location A and Location B as follows:

$$TC_A = TC_B$$
$$500,000 + 300Q = 750,000 + 200Q$$
$$100Q = 250,000 \text{ and then } Q = 2500 \text{ units.}$$

This indicates that producing less than 2500 units per year would be cheaper at Location A (when the lower fixed cost predominates), while producing more than 2500 units per year would be cheaper at Location B (when the lower variable cost predominates).

Next, determine the break-even points between Location B and Location C as follows:

$$TC_B = TC_C$$
$$750,000 + 200Q = 900,000 + 100Q$$
$$100Q = 150,000 \text{ and then } Q = 1500 \text{ units.}$$

This indicates that producing less than 1500 units per year would be cheaper at Location B, while producing more than 1500 units per year would be cheaper at Location C.

Finally, determine the break-even points between Location A and Location C as follows:

$$TC_A = TC_C$$
$$500,000 + 300Q = 900,000 + 100Q$$
$$200Q = 400,000 \text{ and then } Q = 2000 \text{ units.}$$

This indicates that producing less than 2000 units per year would be cheaper at Location A, while producing more than 2000 units per year would be cheaper at Location C.

Based on the cost curves shown in Figure 11.1, Location C has the lowest total cost when producing the forecasted quantity of 3000 units per year. If, however, the annual demand forecast was 1000 units, then Location A would be preferred. From Figure 11.1, it can be seen that Location B would never be the preferred location when comparing the costs of all three sites simultaneously.

Figure 11.1 | Break-Even Graph

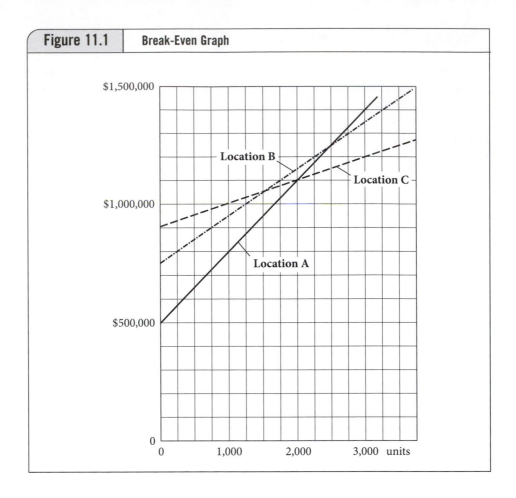

- Property Marketplace—listings of properties for sale or lease in the U.S, Canada, and Mexico.
- Economic Developers—*Site Selection* magazine's guide to area economic development agencies.
- Service Provider Directory—*Site Selection* magazine's first annual directory of Web-based real estate services.

3. www.mappinganalytics.com/consulting/site-selection.html—Since 1989, Mapping Analytics has helped their clients "... determine where their customers are; how they can be best served; and the best places to locate salespeople, stores, or branches."[81] The company applies location-based business intelligence, providing their customers with a competitive advantage, and enabling their customers to better identify opportunities, allocate resources, and manage key assets. Several key services provided by the company are shown below:[82]

- Site Selection—"... the process of determining optimal locations for new retail stores, franchise locations, restaurants, financial institutions, and other types of businesses where location is important."
- Customer Profiling—"A customer profile is a description of the customers who buy your product compared to all consumers. It tells you who is most likely to buy the product profiled."

- Sales Territory Design—involves sales territory alignment, design, optimization, and mapping to balance sales potential and minimize sales expense while maximizing sales.
- Market Analysis—"… to analyze, communicate, take action, and measure marketing and sales related activities."

Business Clusters

Over the past decade, a number of trends have dramatically impacted the facility location process. Markets are increasingly globalized due to the liberalization of trade, technological advances, and increased demand from many regions of the world. Countries compete against one another for foreign direct investment. Having the necessary information to compare countries across a multitude of factors helps managers make better location decisions. Today, we are seeing more **business clusters** being created globally. Research parks and special economic/industrial zones serve as magnets for business clusters.

The concept of business clusters represents a new way of thinking about location decisions, challenges conventional logic on how companies should be configured, and provides a different approach to organizing a supply chain. So, what exactly are business clusters? According to Dr. Michael Porter, "Clusters are geographic concentrations of interconnected companies and institutions in a particular field. Clusters encompass an array of linked industries and other entities important to competition."[83] Locating research and development, component manufacturing, assembly operations, marketing, and other associated businesses in one area can improve the supply chain, technology sharing, and information sharing.

Silicon Valley and Hollywood in California are probably the two most well-known and successful business clusters. Another high-tech cluster fashioned after Silicon Valley is Massachusetts' Route 128. In the competitiveness study, "Our Competitive Future: Building the Knowledge Driven Economy," conducted by the U.K. government, they find that "business development is often strongest when firms cluster together, creating a critical mass of growth, collaboration, and competition and opportunities for investment and knowledge sharing."[84] Small business clusters can also be found in neighborhoods—hospitals, for instance, are usually accompanied by physician's offices, pharmacies, and other medical-related businesses nearby. These businesses share parking facilities, buildings, and support services such as office supply retailers and restaurants.

Governments today recognize the need to develop existing clusters of similar businesses into world-class units. Although clusters are more prevalent in advanced economies, several emerging or newly developed economies such as Mexico, Singapore, India, and Taiwan have created high-tech clusters with the participation of foreign companies.[85] A discussion of each of these follows:

- *Mexico.* There are approximately 900 electronics firms in Mexico, with more than 40 percent located in the northwestern cities of Tijuana, Mexicali, San Luis R.C., and Tecate; 25 percent in the northern cities such as Chihuahua; 22 percent in the northeast in Monterrey, Saltillo, Reynosa, and Tampico; and 8 percent in the west, mostly in Guadalajara. Examples of major global companies operating in Mexico are IBM, Motorola, Hewlett-Packard, Siemens, Ericsson, Sony, and Panasonic. With NAFTA, goods can be exported duty-free to North America, allowing Mexico to become an electronics manufacturing center for the Americas. Mexico produces 24 percent of the world's television receivers.

- *Singapore.* Singapore has recently replaced Japan as the most attractive country for U.S. high-tech manufacturing investment in the Asia Pacific region. Singapore has the greatest technology penetration rates in Asia, the highest per capita GDP in Asia, and a highly skilled workforce. Approximately half of the world's computer disk drives are produced in Singapore.

- *Taiwan.* Taiwan, dubbed the "Silicon Island" by Forbes in 1998, is a leading manufacturer of computer hardware and has the largest global market share for motherboards, modems, and scanners. Intel and Compaq are two major investors in Taiwan, due partly to its large pool of engineers: 6.4 percent of 24-year-olds possess technical degrees.

- *India.* India is an emerging player in the software industry. India has the world's third largest pool of scientific and technical personnel. Half of India's population are less than 25 years old, giving the country a very young demographic profile. India provides a significant cost advantage with reported savings of 25 to 50 percent. Telecommunication penetration has increased from 3.1 percent in 2001 to 12.6 percent in 2006 and is expected to reach 29.6 percent by 2009.[86] Companies such as IBM, Microsoft, Oracle, and Motorola have built facilities in India's silicon valleys: Bangalore, Hyderabad, and Mumbai (formerly Bombay). India could well be the country of choice for customized software development.

There are many reasons why business clusters are successful.[87] One is the close cooperation, coordination, and trust among clustered companies in related industries. Another reason is the fierce competition for customers among rival companies located in the cluster. Companies are more productive in their operations because of easy access to the local supplier base, information, and technologies. Companies can also recruit from the local pool of skilled and experienced workers, thus reducing the recruiting transaction costs. Owing to the intensity of competition, peer pressure, and constant comparison among rivals, companies respond much more quickly to customer needs and trends than do companies located outside a business cluster. Clusters thus provide the competitive environment that promotes an increasing pace of innovation, which will eventually lead to further productivity growth.

Business clusters are not without their problems, though. For example, Michigan suffered through plant closings and employee layoffs in the auto industry due to the industry's overreliance on gas-guzzling auto designs and the oil shock in the 1970s. The groupthink mentality among the cluster participants of General Motors, Ford, and Chrysler in Detroit made it more difficult for individual companies to try new ideas and see the need for radical innovation in fuel economy automobile designs. A business cluster will decline unless companies continue to build capabilities using emerging technologies while attracting supporting firms and research institutions.[88]

Sustainable Development

The United Nations Division for Sustainable Development defines **sustainable development** as "development that meets the needs of the present without compromising the ability of future generations to meet their own needs."[89] Sustainable development is important because what we do today will affect future generations. The critical issues in sustainable development are energy consumption/production, air pollution, and climate change. These issues are strongly related to one another and need to be considered in an integrated manner and linked to economic, social, and environmental policies. At the 15th Session of the Commission on Sustainable Development (United Nations) held in the spring of 2007, many countries have stressed the continuing need for "integrating economic development, social development, and environmental protection as interdependent and mutually reinforcing pillars of sustainable development and that poverty eradication, changing sustainable patterns of production and consumption and protecting and managing the natural resource base of economic and social development are (overarching[sic]) objectives of, and essential requirements for sustainable development."[90] The increased global consumption of fossil fuels has increased global warming. In addition, prices of crude oil have continued to rise as demand has increased. More expensive oil translates to increased cost of production of goods and delivery of services. Ultimately this will affect total supply chain costs. This calls for the development of cleaner, more fuel-efficient, and affordable energy technologies as well as renewable energy technologies.

It is clear that industrial development is the engine for economic growth and eradicating poverty in emerging countries. However, resource efficiency and technology innovation are opportunities for reducing cost and increasing competitiveness and employment, issues that are central to managing effective supply chains. Air pollution has serious impacts on human health, environment, and the economy. A related issue is climate change and preserving the world's ecosystem.

Owing to the importance of climate change, the United Nations has initiated the Framework Convention on Climate Change which "sets an overall framework for intergovernmental efforts to tackle the challenge posed by climate change. It recognizes that the climate system is a shared resource whose stability can be affected by industrial and other emissions of carbon dioxide and other greenhouse gases."[91] The Convention took effect on March 21, 1994. The Kyoto Protocol to the Framework Convention on Climate Change was adopted in Kyoto, Japan, in December 1997 and took effect on December 16, 2005. The Kyoto Protocol "shares the ultimate objective of the United Nations Framework Convention on Climate Change to stabilize atmospheric concentration of greenhouse gases at a level that will prevent dangerous interference with the climate system."[92] The Kyoto Protocol has been ratified by 173 parties thus far. Thirty-five of these countries and the European Economic Community are required to reduce greenhouse emissions specified for each country in the treaty. The U.S. has not yet ratified the agreement, which required it to reduce emissions by 7 percent from 1990 to 2008/2012.[93]

A similar term, **green development**, has been used to describe environmentally friendly development. The difference between green development and sustainable development is that green development "prioritizes what its proponents consider to be **environmental sustainability** over economic and cultural considerations."[94] An example would be the installation of a state-of-the-art waste treatment plant with a very high maintenance cost in a poor country. Owing to the high maintenance cost, the ideal plant from a green standpoint may not be sustainable, and could be shut down due to bankruptcy. From a sustainable development perspective, it would be acceptable to have a less effective environmental technology, but one that can be economically maintained by the users of the equipment. When decision makers consider both economic and social issues in addition to environmental concerns, then sustainable development might be considered more appropriate.

SUMMARY

Facility location decisions can provide organizations with a competitive advantage and, therefore, must be an integral part of their overall strategic plans. The effectiveness of a supply chain is influenced greatly by the location of facilities. Increased globalization and improved technologies have resulted in a variety of options for companies to locate their facilities. Today, companies must consider a number of factors when analyzing potential locations; several comparison methods are available when considering the country, region, and community for a facility location. Business clusters often provide for strong business development, collaboration, growth opportunities, and improved supply chain management. The existence of successful business clusters suggests that innovation and competition are concentrated geographically. China and India today represent attractive locations for many of the world's top companies due to their inexpensive and technically skilled labor forces and their huge markets. Finally, sustainable development and its impact on supply chains was discussed.

KEY TERMS

Association of Southeast Asian Nations (ASEAN), 381

break-even model, 391

business clusters, 395

Common Market of Eastern and Southern Africa (COMESA), 381

contributor factory, 377

environmental sustainability, 397

European Union (EU), 381

foreign trade zones (FTZs), 384

green development, 397

lead factory, 378

North American Free Trade Agreement (NAFTA), 381

offshore factory, 377

outpost factory, 377

quality-of-life factors, 388

regional trade agreements, 380

right-to-work laws, 387

server factory, 377

source factory, 377

Southern Common Market (MERCOSUR), 381

sustainable development, 396

tariff, 383

weighted-factor rating model, 390

World Trade Organization (WTO), 380

DISCUSSION QUESTIONS

1. What is the impact of facility decisions on a supply chain?

2. Why is demand management important for effective supply chain management?

3. What are *business clusters*? Provide several examples of business clusters in a variety of countries. What are the advantages of clustering?

4. What are the critical factors influencing global facility location?

5. Discuss the major regional trade agreements in Asia, Africa, Europe, Latin America, and North America.

6. What is the *WTO* and what is its role in world trade?

7. What are the critical factors in making community and site decisions?

8. Discuss Wal-Mart's location strategy.

9. Define *quality of life*. Why is quality of life an important factor in facility location? Is the set of quality-of-life factors used by the Chamber of Commerce in Jacksonville, Florida, a good one? Please explain.

10. What is a *right-to-work state*? What are the advantages or disadvantages of doing business in a right-to-work state?

11. Why is China an attractive location for many businesses?

12. What are the challenges of doing business in China?

13. Discuss the six strategic roles of a foreign facility.

14. What is *sustainable development* and why is this policy important to a country and the world at large?

15. What is the difference between *green development* and *sustainable development*?

INTERNET QUESTIONS

1. What are the key factors used in the World Competitiveness Ranking? Go to the Web site of the IMD *World Competitiveness Yearbook* at http://www02.imd.ch/wcy. Select any three countries in the Asia Pacific region. Prepare a report discussing the pros and cons for locating a business in each of these countries.

2. What are the factors used in the Global Competitiveness Report? Go to the Web site of the World Economic Forum at www.weforum.org/en/initiatives/gcp/Global%20Competitivenss%20Report/index.htm. Select any three countries in South America. Prepare a report discussing the pros and cons for locating a business in each of these countries.

3. Go to the Web site of the WTO at http://www.wto.org. Outline the development that led to China's entry into the WTO. What is the impact of China's accession into WTO on U.S. companies?

4. Go to the Web site of STAT-US/Internet (a service of the U.S. Department of Commerce) at www.stat-usa.org. First, select a country and an industry in which you are interested. Then, based on the country report, prepare an assessment of the suitability of the country for doing business in the particular industry you selected earlier.

INFOTRAC QUESTIONS

Access http://academic.cengage.com/infotrac to answer the following questions:

1. Search for the term "business cluster" and write a report on a business cluster in India.

2. Search for the term "global competitiveness" and write a report on how companies can use these rankings to help them make location decisions.

3. Search for the term "right-to-work" and write a report on why right-to-work states in the U.S. have a competitive advantage in attracting businesses.

4. Report on how companies use global location strategies to enhance competitiveness.

5. Write a report to show the current state of sustainable development in China.

SPREADSHEET PROBLEMS

1. The Soft Toys Company has collected information on fixed and variable costs for four potential plant locations.

LOCATION	ANNUAL FIXED COST	VARIABLE COST PER UNIT
A	$200,000	$50
B	$300,000	$45
C	$400,000	$25
D	$600,000	$20

   a. Plot the total cost curves for the four plant locations on a single graph.

   b. Compute the range of demand for which each location has a cost advantage.

   c. Which plant location is best if annual demand is 30,000 units?

2. The Bruhaha Brewery is planning to expand internationally. The company has identified six critical location factors and their relative weights. The relative performance scores for each of the three potential sites are shown in the following table. Which site should be selected?

CRITICAL LOCATION FACTORS	FACTOR WEIGHTS (SUM TO 1)	COLUMBUS SCORES (1–100)	LAS VEGAS SCORES (1–100)	SPOKANE SCORES (1–100)
Labor cost	0.15	70	90	50
Proximity to market	0.25	100	90	80
Supplier base	0.20	80	100	70
Quality of life	0.30	90	60	60
Taxes	0.10	60	80	90

Chapter 12

SERVICE RESPONSE LOGISTICS

With all the exciting new trends and technologies in retail supply chains, it's easy to forget that the supply chain exists for the purpose of providing excellent customer service.[1]

There are many variations within the services industry and that is what makes it unique. What works in the hotel industry may not work in the financial services industry.[2]

Learning Objectives

After completing this chapter, you should be able to

- Understand how supply chain management in services differs from supply chain management in manufacturing.
- Define service response logistics and describe all of its elements.
- Understand the importance of service layouts and perform a layout analysis using several techniques.
- Describe the strategies for managing capacity, wait times, distribution, and quality in services.
- Understand queuing system design issues and calculate queue characteristics.
- Use various techniques for managing customers' perceived waiting times.
- Understand the different distribution channels available for services.
- Define service quality and describe how to measure it and improve it.

Chapter Outline

Introduction

An Overview of Service Operations

Supply Chain Management in Services

The Primary Concerns of Service Response Logistics

Summary

Supply Chain Management in Action   *Spinning a Good Yarn*

In 2001, a mother and daughter founded Arizona-based South West Trading Co. (SWTC), a company dedicated to offering innovative, luxurious, and environmentally friendly textile products in the daughter's garage. The family-owned company exports its products to Canada, the United Kingdom, Australia, New Zealand, Mexico, Sweden, and several other countries.

By 2004, the company needed to deal with some growing supply chain issues. SWTC's operations were slowed because the company's package shipments were processed and labeled manually. In addition, its shipments were often delayed while clearing customs at the border. "We had a huge problem with shipping. It was slow, and we had no efficient tracking capabilities. For our import work, we had been booking shipping ourselves and were struggling with customs clearance delays constantly," said Jonelle Raffino, president of SWTC. "Our entire supply line was in chaos."

In addition, the company's distribution center operation was not as efficient or effective as it should have been for SWTC to continue to maintain customer satisfaction while growing so quickly. In just 5 years, SWTC changed locations four times. When the company moved to its current distribution center, its owners thought there was more space than they could ever need, but they quickly found space to be in short supply.

To help streamline its shipping operation and maximize its distribution center space, the company turned to United Parcel Service (UPS), a major global shipping and logistics supplier. As a result of a more efficient shipping operation, SWTC was able to triple the number of packages it could ship per day, "but more important, our customers were immediately notified that a package was en route and provided tracking information," Raffino said.

In order to maximize SWTC's distribution center space, UPS redesigned the layout and provided a new plan for managing the company's inventory. Subsequently, SWTC reduced its inventory by enacting a just-in-time distribution model. These changes resulted in a 25-percent increase in SWTC's capacity and a large increase in efficiency gains.

Currently, SWTC uses one shipping and logistics provider for both its domestic and international needs, including air- and ocean-freight import, customs brokerage, consolidation of multiple less-than-truckload shipments, domestic and international small package delivery, and other services. "We knew all these types of services existed, but didn't think we could afford it as a young company," Raffino said. "It was important that as a small company we be taken seriously and receive the same attention to detail and service as a big company gets. [Our shipping and logistics provider] helped us to understand importing and solidified our supply chain foundation."

Source: Anonymous, "Spinning a Good Yarn … And Supply Chain." *Textile World,* 156, no. 6 (2006): 34–35. Used with permission.

Introduction

While most of the concepts of supply chain management that have been discussed up to this point can be applied to service organizations, this chapter specifically introduces and discusses supply chain concepts suited particularly to services and the service activities of manufacturers. Service firms differ from manufacturers in a number of ways including the tangibility of the end product, the involvement of the customer in the production process, the assessment of product quality, the labor content contained in the end products, and the facility location. For instance, many services are considered **pure services**, offering little or no tangible products to customers. Examples are consultants, legal advisors, entertainers, and stock brokers. Other services may have end products containing a larger tangible component such as restaurants, repair facilities, transportation providers, and public warehouses. Most manufacturers, however, have a relatively small service component associated with their end products including maintenance, warranty repair, delivery, and customer call centers.

In all of these services, customers are either directly or indirectly involved in the production of the service itself. In this sense, services are said to provide **state utility**, meaning that services do something to things that are owned by the customer (such as transport and store supplies, repair machines, cut hair, and provide healthcare). Managing the interactions between service firms and their customers while the service is being performed is the topic of this chapter and is of paramount importance to the ultimate success of service organizations.

To generate customer visits, service firms must be located (or transported to) where the customers are, they must know what their customers want, and they must be able to satisfy these needs quickly, and in a cost-effective manner. This requires service firms to adequately hire, train, and schedule service representatives; to acquire technologies and equipment to aid in the provision of services; and to provide the right facility network and procedures to continually satisfy customers. Problems or mistakes that occur during the delivery of services most likely mean an increase in service delivery time, a reduction in customer satisfaction, lower perceived service quality, and maybe even lost current and future sales.

The important role that services play in the global economy is becoming more evident today as developed countries become increasingly service-oriented. In the U.S. for instance, services account for more than 80 percent of all employment and approximately the same percentage of gross domestic product (GDP).[3] Thus, firms are attempting to identify the customer-desired service elements in their product offerings and provide better value through attention to these elements. These efforts are at the heart of service operations and the topic of service response logistics. Let's first review service operations in general and then move on to discuss service response logistics in particular.

An Overview of Service Operations

Services are by far the largest sector of any post-industrialized nation and include organizations such as retailers, wholesalers, transportation and storage companies, financial institutions, schools, real estate companies, government agencies, hotels, and consulting companies. Since the 1950s, the ratio of services to manufacturing and agriculture in terms of its percentage of the U.S. workforce has been increasing quite dramatically, and it is extremely likely that new entrants to the job market will be employed in some service role. In the U.S., as productivity increased through use of technology and mass-production techniques in the manufacturing sector, fewer employees were needed to maintain the same output level. In addition, as the nation as a whole became wealthier, people began demanding more services. Today, a much smaller workforce in the U.S. produces far more agricultural and manufactured products than were produced in 1950.

India's economic rise in the past 15 years, similar to other emerging economies, has been the result of a shift from an agrarian to a services economy, which has improved the standard of living in India and boosted domestic consumption. This has helped to bolster overall productivity and competitiveness of India's firms, creating higher-value jobs. India, for example, had 120 million mobile telephone users as of the end of 2006—the fifth largest worldwide market for telecom services.[4]

Some of the differences between goods and services are listed below:

- Services *cannot be inventoried*. Typically services are produced and consumed simultaneously—once the mail is delivered, surgical operations are performed, and advice is given, customers have "consumed" the service. For this reason, services often struggle to find ways to utilize their service workers during slow periods and, conversely, manage demand or increase the ability to serve customers during busy periods.

- Services are often *unique*. Good service providers with well-trained and motivated employees have the capability of customizing services to satisfy each customer—insurance policies, legal services, and even fast-food services can be uniquely designed and then delivered to customers. Thus, hiring and training become important issues for satisfying individual customer needs.

- Services have *high customer-server interactions*. Service uniqueness demands more server attention, whether it is delivering purchased products to a specific location on the manufacturing shop floor, analyzing data, answering customer questions, resolving complaints, or repairing machinery. Many services today are finding ways to automate or standardize services, or utilize customers to provide some of their own service, to reduce costs and improve productivity. For instance, the past few years have seen a rapid growth in standardized, self-serve services such as purchasing books, getting cash, and completing one's tax forms.

- Services are *decentralized*. Service facilities must be decentralized because of their inability to inventory their services. Therefore, finding good, high-customer-traffic locations is extremely important (even Web-based services must locate their signs or advertisements where they will be easily seen by people browsing the Web).

Thus, services, whether they are stand-alone organizations or departments in goods-producing firms, must be managed in ways that will take into account these various service characteristics. A number of service elements are discussed next.

Service Productivity

The basic measure of productivity is shown by the following formula:

$$\text{Productivity} = \frac{\text{Outputs produced}}{\text{Inputs used}},$$

where *outputs produced* are typically shown as customers served, services produced, or sales dollars, and *inputs used* can be shown as labor hours or labor dollars (for a **single-factor productivity** measure). Alternately, inputs used can be represented by the sum of labor, material, energy, and capital costs (for a **multiple-factor productivity** measure).

Productivity and its growth over time are commonly used indicators of a firm's (and a country's) economic success. For most services, automation can be a troublesome issue, and the labor content per unit of output can be quite high relative to manufactured goods. These two things can lead to a declining productivity growth rate as a nation's economy becomes less manufacturing-oriented and more service-oriented (as discussed above in reference to the U.S. and other strong economies). This productivity growth problem has been termed **Baumol's disease**, named after noted U.S. economist William Baumol in the 1960s when he and his colleague, William Bowen, argued that productivity growth tends to sag in service-oriented economies. And, in fact, this effect was realized in the U.S. from the mid-1970s through the mid-1990s as productivity growth averaged a relatively low 1.5 percent per year. Since the mid-1990s, however, productivity growth in the U.S. has been up and down, leading to other theories such as the **Wal-Mart effect**, which postulates that the booming growth in information technology has allowed many big-box retailers such as Wal-Mart to realize large productivity growth rates. Today, some economists are even saying that Baumol's disease has been cured.[5]

In services and other high labor cost companies, there is often a desire to reduce labor costs to improve productivity (see the formula for productivity shown above). This can lead companies to relocate to lower labor cost countries or to lay off workers. These can be risky strategies, since relocating to foreign countries can create cultural and training problems, and reducing the workforce can adversely affect service quality and service availability. Other strategies for increasing service productivity include the use of technology (the Wal-Mart effect) and better education and training (such as cross-training service providers to perform multiple services) to increase outputs produced for a given level of inputs. Wisconsin-based Winterthur US Holdings, a property and casualty insurer owned by QBE Insurance Group, uses a real-time quoting application to streamline how their independent agents work with clients. The quoting application gathers information and uses predictive analytics to deliver rating and risk management services to agents, which reduces costs and improves productivity through the reuse of these services across many business units and applications.[6]

Improving service productivity can also be quite challenging because of the desire in many cases for customized services and the corresponding assessment of service quality: Was the car fixed properly? Was the client properly defended? Was the comedian funny? A complete discussion of service quality is discussed later in the chapter. Today, service productivity constitutes the largest segment of overall U.S. productivity; thus finding ways to improve service productivity is directly related to the growth of the U.S. economy.

Global Service Issues

The growth and exportation of services is occurring everywhere, as world economies improve and the demand for services increases. Just a few examples of global service growth as of the middle of 2007 include FedEx (with its network of 20 distribution hubs serving more than 220 countries and territories), Deutsche Bank (serving more than 12 million customers with 1700 branches and 68,000 employees in 75 countries), Wal-Mart International (operating 2900 units and employing 550,000 associates in 13 countries other than the U.S.), and Microsoft (with 345 subsidiary offices and 31,000 employees outside the U.S.). Today, more than one-quarter of all international trade is derived from the provision of services.

Successfully managing global services involves a number of issues including the following:

- Labor, facilities and infrastructure support—cultural differences, education, and expertise levels can prove to be problematic for firms unfamiliar with local human resources. Firms must also do a good job of locating existing support facilities, suppliers, transportation providers, communication systems, and housing.

- Legal and political issues—local laws may restrict foreign competitors, limit available resources, attach tariffs to prices, or otherwise impose barriers to global service expansion. Some foreign countries require the formation of joint ventures with local business partners.
- Domestic competitors and the economic climate—managers must be aware of the local competitors, the services they offer, their pricing structures, and the current state of the local economy. Firms can devise competitive strategies by modifying their services to gain competitive advantage.
- Identifying global customers—perhaps most importantly, firms must find out where their potential global customers are, through use of the Internet, foreign government agencies, a trading partner, or a foreign trade intermediary. Once potential customers are identified, services can begin to decide how their service products can be modified to meet the needs of these customers.

The British firm Vodafone has used company takeovers on their way to becoming the world's largest wireless operator. In early 2007, for example, Vodafone purchased Indian mobile operator Hutchison Essar for about $13 billion in hopes of better competing for a share of the projected 500 million mobile phone subscribers in that country.[7] Wiener Staedtische Versicherung, a big Austrian life insurer, has recently shifted some of its focus from their domestic market to one that generates 30 percent of its premiums from central and eastern European countries, where many households are purchasing financial services such as life insurance for the first time.[8] The Global Perspective feature describes some of the problems with global growth of and demand for banking services.

Service Strategy Development

Manufacturing and service organizations use three generic competitive strategies: cost leadership, differentiation, and focus.[9] Each of these is briefly discussed below, in relation to services.

Cost Leadership Strategy

Using a **cost leadership strategy** requires a large capital investment in automated, state-of-the-art equipment, significant efforts in the areas of controlling and reducing costs, doing things right the first time, standardizing services, and aiming marketing efforts at cost-conscious consumers. Examples of firms employing this strategy are Southwest Airlines, McDonald's, and income tax return preparer H&R Block. In each of these cases, there are efforts to offer routine, no-frills services at a low price. Marketing efforts are geared toward attracting cost-conscious customers with little or no service customization needs. There are also continued efforts to keep costs low among these firms. For example, Southwest Airlines primarily uses one type of aircraft (Boeing 737 jets) to reduce maintenance, pilot training, and purchasing costs. In addition, until 2006 they used a jet fuel hedging strategy to lock in low prices for fuel, while other airlines were caught paying much higher rates for fuel.[10] At McDonald's, their latest cost-savings initiative deals with reducing their "carbon footprint" by introducing energy-saving measures. In 2006, a switch to more efficient lighting at all of its 30,000 restaurants was mandated, and the company also saved 1.65 million pounds of paper through a napkin and packaging redesign and recycling effort.[11]

Global Perspective

The Soaring Demand for Trained Professionals in Global Banking Markets

As more global banks enter the fast-growing Persian Gulf region and set up offices in its gleaming new financial centers, they are competing for a limited pool of trained professionals. Existing banks as well as newcomers are being forced to offer higher salaries and more attractive compensation packages to attract and retain the best employees.

"It is not only the global banks or the newly created banks that are competing for staff," explains Ghazi Abdul-Jawad, president and chief executive of Bahrain-based Arab Banking Corporation (ABC). "There is a severe war for talent, a very vicious war for talent, across the industry, and this will not abate."

The growing demand for financial services in the region means that top bankers are spending more and more of their time on human-resources issues. "In Bahrain in the next three years, the industry will need to double its workforce at the rate of growth in demand for services we are seeing," Abdul-Jawad says from his office in ABC Tower in downtown Manama overlooking the Gulf. "This is driving cost/income ratios higher. We are introducing compensation packages on a par with what is being offered in London and New York," he notes.

Adel El-Labban, group chief executive and managing director of Bahrain-based Ahli United Bank (AUB), says he spends at least 20% of his time on human-resources issues, including attracting, training, and motivating employees. AUB's goal is to create a branch network in all eight countries bordering the Gulf, as well as in Egypt, Lebanon and Yemen, and to add a second European hub in Switzerland to complement its operations in the United Kingdom. "We will expand our network through friendly acquisitions as the right opportunities arise," El-Labban says. "We would like to have a presence in all 13 of these countries."

Saudi Arabia's banking sector has been progressively liberalized since the late 1990s, when foreign-owned branches of Gulf Cooperation Council (GCC) banks were allowed to enter the market. In 2003, the Saudi Arabian Monetary Agency (SAMA) granted Deutsche Bank the first foreign banking license to a non-GCC bank in 20 years. BNP Paribas and JPMorgan Chase received licenses in 2004.

The opening of the Saudi banking market to foreign competition is happening at a time when the domestic economy is enjoying strong growth and the capital markets are becoming deeper and more developed, economists say. This will lessen the impact from the entrance of new participants, many of which were already competing with the local banks by offering services to Saudi Arabian customers from offshore centers in neighboring countries such as Bahrain.

Source: Platt, G. "The Power of People." *Global Finance*, 21, no. 7 (2007): 34–35. © *Global Finance*. Used with permission.

Differentiation Strategy

Implementing a **differentiation strategy** is based on creating a service that is considered unique. The uniqueness can take many forms including customer service excellence (Ritz-Carlton hotels), brand image (McDonald's arches), variety (Wal-Mart merchandise), and use of technology (Southwest Airline's Web site "ding" notification). Differentiation strategies are often created as the result of companies listening to their customers. Retailers are beginning to engage customers more effectively through various touch-points such as the phone, store locations, catalogs, online stores, and chat sites. Jo-Ann Stores, a U.S. decorating and sewing products retailer, created a Web site with more than 50,000 products that enables customers to easily find, preview, and buy products, along with presenting customers offers paralleling their interests. As a result, more than 90 percent of online visitors purchase something.[12] Differentiation does not necessarily mean higher costs; it merely refers to the ability of the service to offer unique elements in their services. In many cases, though, it may mean the customer is willing to pay more for the service. Advertisements, logos, awards, and company reputations all play a part in creating the perception of uniqueness among the service's customers.

Focus Strategy

A **focus strategy** incorporates the idea that a service can serve a narrow target market or niche better than other firms that are trying to serve a broad market. Services that specialize in these market niches can provide customized services and expertise to suit the needs of these customers. For instance, a neighborhood hobby shop is more likely to serve the needs of hobby enthusiasts than a large retailer like Target, even though they might sell some of the same merchandise. Within each market segment, firms can exhibit characteristics of differentiation or cost leadership. Illinois-based Dawson Logistics has found success providing reverse logistics services to pharmaceutical distributors and assembly and delivery services to escalator and elevator companies.[13]

The Service Delivery System

Customers actually purchase a bundle of attributes when purchasing services, including the *explicit service* itself (storage and use of your money) along with the *supporting facility* (the bank building with drive-up tellers and the online Web site), *facilitating goods* (the deposit forms, monthly statements, and the extra services provided), and *implicit services* (the security provided, the atmosphere in the bank, the privacy, and the convenience). Successful services are designed to deliver this bundle of attributes in the most efficient way, while still satisfying customer requirements. Services must therefore define their **service bundle** and then design an effective delivery system with this bundle in mind.

Service delivery systems fall along a continuum with mass-produced, low-customer-contact systems at one extreme (such as ATMs) and highly customized, high-customer-contact systems at the other (such as an expensive beauty salon). Intermediate approaches seek to physically separate high-contact (front-of-the-house) operations from low-contact (back-of-the-house) operations to use various management techniques that will maximize the performance of each area (such as a restaurant). Back-of-the-house operations tend to be managed as a manufacturing center, where the emphasis is on maximizing output and achieving economies of scale. Technical people are hired for specific well-defined tasks, and technology is employed to increase productivity. Front-of-the-house operations are characterized by taking care of customers, hiring front-line service providers with good public relations skills, and giving employees the power and resources to solve customers' problems quickly and effectively.

Hospitals provide a good example of a business characterized by a clear separation of services requiring customer contact and services not requiring customer contact. Administrative offices, labs, storage, laundry, and food preparation, for instance, are services typically never seen by patients in a hospital, although managing these elements of the service bundle can make a tremendous difference in the profitability of a hospital. However, nursing and physician patient care, prescription services, and emergency room services directly involve patients in their delivery of services. In each instance, the customer-server interaction must be managed so that customers get what they came for in a quick and effective way.

Auditing the Service Delivery System

The service system should be audited periodically to assess the system's ability to meet customer expectations in a cost-effective way. Monitoring customer complaints, talking to and observing customers, and tracking customer feedback using customer comment cards and comment forms on the company's Web site are ways to continually monitor customer satisfaction. **Walk-through service audits** should also be performed by management, covering service system attributes from the time customers initially encounter the service until they leave. Several tools have been developed and used for this purpose including service system surveys to be completed by managers, employees, and/or customers, and service process maps (as discussed in Chapter 8). The objective of the service audit is to identify service system problems or areas in need of improvement.

Service Location and Layout Strategies

Good location strategies provide barriers to entry and competitive positioning for services as well as generate additional demand. Once a location has been secured, firms can begin to consider layout strategies to maximize customer service, server productivity, and overall efficiency. Since location strategies and analysis models were discussed in Chapter 11, only a brief discussion of location considerations is included here, followed by the design of service layouts.

Location Strategies

Location decisions are extremely important for almost all services because they have a significant impact on customer visits and, consequently, the long-term profits of the company (how likely is it that customers would visit a clothing store, for instance, in an otherwise abandoned shopping center?). Location decisions are viewed as long-term decisions because of the typical high cost of construction, remodeling, and relocation. (Note: Here, it is assumed that service locations are permanent structures, although some services actually are not bound by this assumption, as with a music teacher who visits customers.) Global market opportunities, global competitors, and technological and demographic changes contribute to the importance of using a good location strategy. In all location evaluations, it is desirable to consider a number of relevant factors to reduce the reliance on intuition. Although intuition can certainly be a valuable location analysis tool, many disastrous location decisions have been made solely on the basis of intuition. A number of location analysis models can be used as an aid in the location decision, and these include the weighted factor location model and the location break-even model. (Refer to Chapter 11 for use of these models.)

Layout Strategies

Service layout strategies work in combination with location decisions to further support the overall business strategies of differentiation, low cost, or market focus. Office layouts tend to be departmentalized to allow specialists to share resources; many retailers like Wal-Mart also tend to be departmentalized to assist customers in finding items to purchase, whereas others may have centers throughout the store to entice customers to try things out and buy on impulse; commercial airliner layouts segment customers, reduce the time to restock and service the galleys and lavatories, and allow for fast passenger boarding and exit (at least in theory!); casino layouts are designed to get customers in quickly and then keep them there by spacing out the attractions; and self-serve restaurant buffet layouts are designed to process customers quickly. These are just a few examples, and many service layouts use multiple layout strategies. As customer preferences, products, technologies, and service strategies change, layouts also tend to change. Several specific service layout design tools are illustrated below.

Departmental Layouts to Reduce Distance Traveled

Service layouts can be designed to reduce the travel times of customers or service workers when moving from one area to another. An example of a layout where this might be a primary consideration would be a health clinic. The waiting area is located in front where customers enter, and the examination rooms are located nearby. The doctors' offices might be centrally located whereas the lab, storage, and x-ray rooms might be located farther to the back of the clinic away from most of the patients. A primary consideration is how far nurses, doctors, and patients have to walk to reach the various areas within the clinic. The objective would be to place high volume traffic departments close to each other to minimize the total distance traveled. Example 12.1 illustrates a design tool useful for this type of layout.

Departmental Layouts to Maximize Closeness Desirability

Designing service layouts to place certain desirable pairs of departments closer to one another is another useful type of layout analysis tool and is often used for retail or office layouts. Here, the importance is placed on the relationship between various departments. In a convenience store, for instance, it would be extremely important to have the cashier close to the entrance and the cold food items in the back, close to the cold storage areas and the rear loading doors of the store. In an office setting, it might be desirable to have the receptionist close to the office entrance and the file room, with the managers close to the conference room. For each department pair, then, a **closeness desirability rating** must be determined, with the objective being to design a layout that maximizes a desirability rating for the entire office. Example 12.2 illustrates this concept. It should also be noted that it might be advisable to use both of the analysis techniques illustrated in Examples 12.1 and 12.2 for a given layout problem; in this way, the evaluation team could consider the best layout from both a distance traveled and closeness desirability perspective.

Supply Chain Management in Services

In many respects, service-producing organizations are like goods-producing organizations: both types make purchases and therefore deal with suppliers and incur order costs and inventory carrying costs; and in both cases the purchased inventories must be transported, counted, assessed for quality, and stored somewhere. For some services, purchased items are part of the service provided and are extremely important sources of competitive advantage (e.g., at a retailer or restaurant), whereas for others, this may be a very minor concern (e.g., law offices and barber shops). In many cases, service firms also purchase **facilitating products** such as computers,

Example 12.1   Layout of Bryson Health Clinic

The Bryson Health Clinic wants to see whether there is a better layout that will reduce the time doctors and nurses spend walking throughout the clinic. The existing layout is shown below, along with the number of trips and the distances between each department.

Existing Layout

Storage (F)	Doctor's offices (C)	Exam rooms (B)	Lobby & waiting area (A)
Nurses (E)	Lab & x-ray (D)		

Interdepartmental Doctors' and Nurses' Trips/Day

	B	C	D	E	F
A	55	0	0	50	0
B		40	15	40	0
C			15	60	10
D				30	0
E					18

Distances Between Departments (Meters)

	B	C	D	E	F
A	20	40	40	60	60
B		20	20	40	40
C			10	20	20
D				20	20
E					10

To analyze the existing layout, the distance traveled must be calculated as follows:

$$\text{Total distance traveled} = \sum_{i=1}^{n} \sum_{j=1}^{n} T_{ij} D_{ij}$$

Where n = number of departments

i, j = individual departments

Example 12.1   Layout of Bryson Health Clinic (continued)

T_{ij} = number of trips between departments i and j

D_{ij} = distance from department i to department j

The objective is to find the layout resulting in the lowest total distance traveled. For the layout of the Bryson Health Clinic above, we find:

$$\text{Total distance traveled} = 55(20) + 50(60) + 40(20) + 15(20) + 40(40) + 15(10)$$
$$+ 60(20) + 10(20) + 30(20) + 18(10) = 9130 \text{ meters}$$

From the layout and distances shown, it can be seen that the nursing station needs to be closer to the lobby and waiting area, closer to the exam rooms, and closer to the doctors' offices. This can be accomplished by switching departments E and D (nurses and lab/x-ray). This also creates a trade-off, since now departments C, B, and A will all be farther from department D. To calculate the new total distance traveled, the distance table must be modified as shown below. The asterisks denote changes made to the table.

Distances Between Departments

	B	C	D	E	F
A	20	40	60*	40*	60
B		20	40*	20*	40
C			20*	10*	20
D				20	10*
E					20*

The new total distance can then be calculated as follows:

$$\text{Total distance traveled} = 55(20) + 50(40) + 40(20) + 15(40) + 40(20) + 15(20)$$
$$+ 60(10) + 10(20) + 30(20) + 18(20) = 7360 \text{ meters}$$

This is a better layout (not necessarily the best), and only one of a large number of potential layouts. Typically a number of layouts are evaluated as shown here, until either the lowest-total-distance layout or some reasonable alternative layout is found.

furniture, and office supplies that are not part of the services sold, but rather consumed inside the firm, and these materials must also be managed. Massachusetts-based facility maintenance service UNICCO, for example, considers their purchasing group to be strategic contributors for the firm. They expended considerable effort consolidating their supply base, identified key suppliers, formed a cross-functional team to select an e-procurement system, and issued employee purchasing cards to be used for orders of less than $1000.[14] Table 12.1 shows some typical transportation, warehousing, and inventory activities at several different types of services.

In other respects though, service firms are unlike goods-producing organizations, in that services typically deal with the end customer in their supply chains, whereas most goods-producing firms deal with wholesalers, distributors, other manufacturers, or retailers. In other words, service products are typically not passed on to customers further down a distribution channel. Thus, any goods that are delivered as part of the service are typically consumed or used by immediate customers.

Example 12.2   Closeness Desirability Rating for an Office Layout

Existing Office Layout

File room (F)	Engineering offices (C)	Marketing offices (B)	Secretary & waiting area (A)
Purchasing (E)	President's office (D)	Conference room (H)	Copy room (G)

Desirability Ratings

	B	C	D	E	F	G	H
A	2	0	−1	2	2	3	−1
B		0	2	1	1	0	3
C			2	2	0	0	1
D				1	−1	−1	3
E					3	1	2
F						3	1
G							0

The desirability ratings are based on a (−1 to 3) scale, where −1 = undesirable, 0 = unimportant, 1 = slightly important, 2 = moderately important, and 3 = very important. To calculate the score for the above layout, we count the closeness desirability score only when departments are adjacent to each other. For this layout, the total score is

$$\text{Closeness desirability score} = (A/B{:}2) + (A/H{:}{-}1) + (A/G{:}3) + (B/C{:}0) + (B/H{:}3)$$
$$+(C/F{:}0) + (C/D{:}2) + (D/E{:}1) + (D/H{:}3)$$
$$+(E/F{:}3) + (G/H{:}0) = 16 \text{ points}$$

Note that department pairs are not counted twice, and are also not counted if only the corners are touching. To find a better layout, we could place the department pairs with a rating of 3 adjacent to each other, and place adjacent pairs with a rating of −1 such that they are not adjacent. For instance, the file room (F) could be moved adjacent to the copy room (G), and the conference room (H) could be moved farther away from the secretary and waiting area (A). The new layout might look like this:

Example 12.2   *Closeness Desirability Rating for an Office Layout (continued)*

New Office Layout

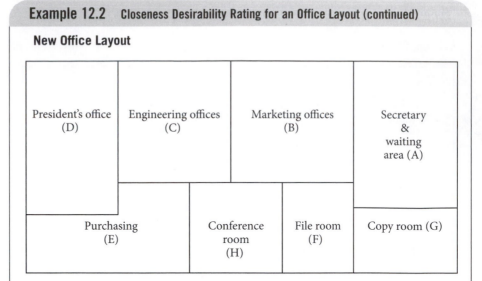

The closeness desirability score for the new layout shown above would then be

Closeness desirability score = (A/B:2) + (A/F:2) + (A/G:3) + (B/C:0) + (B/H:3)
                               + (B/F:1) + (C/D:2) + (C/E:2) + (C/H:1) + (D/E:1)
                               + (E/H:2) + (H/F:1) + (F/G:3) = 23 points

On the basis of this analysis, it can be concluded that the second layout is better; like the previous example, though, there are many potential layouts, so a number of potential new layouts should be evaluated when selecting the most appropriate one.

Service firms deal very closely with their customers, and the services performed in many cases contain higher labor content than manufactured products. Customers may have no idea what resources or facilitating goods were used to deliver the services they purchase; rather, customers' primary concerns are with the service itself and the way it is delivered. For this reason, the distribution elements of interest to services revolve around customers and how they are being served. A good example of this is the transportation industry. When shippers want things moved, they want the move performed at a specific time, delivered to a specific place, delivered on-time, and performed as economically as possible. Most large transportation companies today have sophisticated information systems to allow customers to track deliveries as well as determine the best combination of warehousing, transportation method, port-of-entry, routing, pricing, and consolidation. Toyota, for example, recognized Ryder System, Inc., a global provider of transportation and supply chain management services, as one of their top North American suppliers of logistics services for 2006. Ryder provides logistics services for Toyota at many locations around the U.S. as well as in Argentina, Brazil, Canada, and Mexico.[15]

Service Quality and Customers

The satisfaction or perceived level of quality a customer experiences with regard to the service is of paramount concern to most services. The concept of **service quality** includes many elements—for example, because of health and safety concerns, pharmacies are under intense pressure to provide high quality services to customers. In 2006,

Table 12.1	Transportation and Warehousing Activities in Services	
SERVICES	**TRANSPORTATION ACTIVITIES**	**WAREHOUSING & INVENTORY ACTIVITIES**
Banks	• Movements of checks, coins/cash among branches and operations centers • Movement of checks to cities with Federal Reserve processing centers	• Office supplies and coins/cash • Furniture and computers • Records
Hospitals	• Movement of medical supplies to stockrooms • Transfers of patients • Movement of medical records, test results, and films among units	• Surgical/medical supplies • Pharmaceutical supplies • Office furniture • Medical equipment
Telephone Cos.	• Inbound transportation of switches, parts, and equipment to warehouses • Transportation of construction equipment and supplies to job sites • Routing of consumer products to retail outlets	• Parts, equipment, consumer products • Repair truck parts and equipment • Construction supplies

Source: Adapted from Drazen, E. L., R. E. Moll, and M. F. Roetter. *Logistics in Service Industries*. Oak Brook, IL : Council of Logistics Management, 1991, pp. 24–26.

global pharmaceutical distributor McKesson Corp. announced a high performance pharmacy study with a companion Web site to identify best practices that define high performance pharmacies. Their goal is to allow pharmacies to benchmark these practices to improve their performance. High performance pharmacies are described across eight dimensions—leadership, medication preparation and delivery, patient care services, medication safety, medication use policy, financial performance, human resource management, and education.[16]

Service quality assessments vary based on both the tangible and intangible elements of the services supplied and the satisfaction of the customers receiving the services. As shown above, pharmacy service quality has much to do with patient health and safety issues. With a business such as copy machine servicing, service quality issues are completely different. For WJS Enterprises, a Louisiana-based copier dealer and service provider, it all comes down to response time and the capabilities of their service technicians. Associated Business Systems, based in Oregon, also believes having a local live dispatcher answering the phone when service calls come in assures that a service visit is needed, and that a technician will arrive with the appropriate parts and supplies. Finally, WJS vice president Russ Jacketti notes that technician longevity and field equipment are also indicators of high quality service. "All of our technicians have laptop computers, which serve as diagnostic tools, a source for manuals, and a troubleshooting database that was developed and is maintained by our service trainer," says Jacketti.[17] More about service quality can be found later in this chapter.

All the elements of supply chain management including supplier selection, transportation, warehousing, process management, quality assessment, distribution, and customer service hold strategic importance for the long-term success of service organizations. While the previous chapters and sections above have presented and discussed many of these elements, the remainder of this chapter is devoted to the portion of supply chain management of greatest concern to service organizations and the service arms of good-producing companies—namely, the activities associated with the production and delivery of the actual service.

The Primary Concerns of Service Response Logistics

Service response logistics is the management and coordination of the organization's activities that occur while the service is being performed.[18] Managing these activities often means the difference between a successful service experience and a failure. The four primary activities of concern in service response logistics are the management of **service capacity**, **waiting times**, **distribution channels**, and service quality. Since services cannot be inventoried, managing service capacity enables the firm to meet variable demand—perhaps the most important concern of all services. When demand variability cannot be adequately met, the firm must resort to managing queues or waiting times sufficiently to satisfy customers. **Demand management** tactics also play a role in the service firm's ability to satisfy varying demand. Customer waiting times are closely related to the customer's view of service quality and, ultimately, customer satisfaction. Since services usually must be decentralized to attract customers and provide adequate service delivery times, use of various distribution channels also becomes important to the delivery of service products. Each of these service elements is discussed in detail in the following sections.

Managing Service Capacity

Let's first start by defining the term "service capacity." Service capacity is most often defined as the number of customers per day the firm's service delivery systems *are designed to serve*, although it could also be some other period of time such as customers per hour or customers per shift. Capacity measures can be stated somewhat differently too, depending on the service—for instance, airline companies define capacity in terms of available seat miles per day. Most services desire to operate at some optimal capacity level (less than maximum capacity) to reduce the likelihood of having queues develop and to more effectively serve customers. For services dealing directly with customers, service capacity is largely dependent on the number of employees providing the services and the equipment they use in providing the services.

Since service output can't be inventoried, firms are forced to either turn away customers when demand exceeds capacity, make them wait in line longer, or hire additional personnel. Since hiring, training, supervising, and equipping service personnel is quite costly (in many cases 75 percent of total operating costs), the decision of how many service personnel to hire greatly affects costs, productivity, and ultimately sales and profits. Ideally, firms want enough service capacity (or service personnel) to satisfy demand, without having significant excess (and costly) capacity. This can be a tricky proposition if demand varies throughout the day, week, or month, as is typical in a great many services. So, an important part of a service manager's job is to forecast demand for various segments of time and customer service processes, and then provide (or withhold) capacity to meet the forecasted demand.

When things work out right, services operate at an optimal **capacity utilization**. Capacity utilization is defined below:

$$\text{Capacity utilization} = \frac{\text{Actual customers served per period}}{\text{Capacity}}$$

As utilization approaches (and sometimes even exceeds) 1.0, services become more congested, service times increase, wait times increase, and the perceived quality of service deteriorates. With utilization close to 1.0, even a slightly greater than average service time for several customers can cause queues to become very long (some readers may recall, for instance, waiting 1 or 2 hours beyond an appointment time to see a busy doctor). Thus, an optimal utilization would leave some level of capacity unutilized (perhaps 15 to 25 percent depending on the volatility of demand), so that variations in service times won't severely affect waiting times.

The two most basic strategies for managing capacity are to use a level demand strategy (when the firm utilizes a constant amount of capacity regardless of demand variations) or a **chase demand strategy** (when the amount of capacity varies with demand). (These strategies might also be referred to as the level production and the chase production strategies as mentioned in Chapter 6 or simply level and chase strategies). When a level demand strategy is used, the firm is left to using demand management or **queue management** tactics to deal with excess customers. When a chase demand strategy is used, effective plans must be in place to utilize, transfer, or reduce service capacity when there is excess available and to develop or borrow capacity quickly when demand exceeds capacity. Capacity management techniques that are useful when demand exceeds available service capacity are discussed next, followed by a discussion of capacity management when service capacity exceeds demand.

Capacity Management When Demand Exceeds Available Service Capacity

An initial observation might be to hire workers when demand exceeds existing capacity (or simply let queues develop), and then lay workers off when capacity exceeds demand. Most likely though, we would like to avoid these options because of the expenses of finding, hiring, training, and supervising new workers; the loss of current and future business when letting people wait too long in queues; as well as the expense and damage to the firm's reputation when laying-off workers. Instead, a number of efficient methods can be employed to minimize the costs of hiring workers and then letting them go, and the cost of letting customers wait in line. These include cross-training and sharing employees, using part-time employees, using customers, using technology, using employee scheduling strategies, and, finally, using demand management techniques to smooth or shift demand. Each of these methods is discussed next.

Cross-Training and Sharing Employees

Have you ever been waiting in line to pay for items at a retail store and thought to yourself, "Why don't they use some of these other workers standing around to ring-up customers' purchases?" Many service firms, though, do make wide use of this sharing strategy. Quite often in many service firms, some processes are temporarily overutilized while other processes remain under- or unutilized. Rather than hiring someone to add capacity to the overutilized processes, progressive firms have adequately hired and cross-trained workers to be proficient in a number of different processes. Thus, when demand temporarily exceeds service capacity in one area creating a customer queue, idle workers can quickly move to that process to help serve customers and reduce the time customers spend waiting in a queue.

By sharing employees among a number of processes, firms create the capability to quickly expand capacity as demand dictates while simultaneously minimizing the costs of poor customer service or hiring and laying-off workers. This type of resource sharing arrangement can occur in most any type of organization, from retailers to banks, hospitals, or universities.

Using Part-Time Employees

Part-time employees can also be used as a low cost way to vary capacity. Their hourly wages and the costs of fringe benefits are typically lower than those of full-time employees. Firms use full-time employees to serve that stable portion of daily demand, while scheduling part-timers for those historically busy periods (such as lunch and dinner times, holidays, weekends, or busy seasons). Part-time employees can also be used to fill in during the vacation periods, off-days, and sick-days of full-time employees. Laying-off part-time employees during slower periods is also more acceptable to the permanent full-time workforce and is somewhat expected by the part-time employees.

Using Customers

As the need to contain costs and improve productivity and competitiveness continues, firms are finding that customers themselves can be used to provide certain services, provided it is seen by customers as value-enhancing. The benefits for self-service customers include faster service, more customized service, and lower prices. The benefits for the companies include lower labor costs and extra service capacity. In this sense, customers are "hidden" employees, allowing the firm to hire fewer workers and to vary capacity to some extent as needed. The trade-off for customers is that they expect to pay less for the service, since they are doing some of the work. This might include pumping gas, filling soda cups, filing taxes, or filing legal forms. In other cases, though, customers might actually pay the same or more for the service as when using self-checkout at hotels or using 24-hour automated teller machines, if they perceive the work they do as saving time or providing some other benefit. Thus, if firms can identify service process jobs that customers can perform, if they can provide process directions that are easy to understand and learn, and if they can adequately satisfy customers who are being asked to perform the work, then using customers as employees can provide yet another method for managing capacity. JetBlue has done a very good job of using self-service to improve customer satisfaction and reduce their labor costs. More about JetBlue can be found in the e-Business Connection feature.

Using Technology

Providing technological assistance in the form of computers or other equipment to service company personnel can improve the ability of servers to process customers, resulting in more service capacity, faster service completion times, more or better services, and the need for fewer employees. Voice-activated telephone response systems, online banking, purchasing, selling, and comment systems, and field sales software applications are just a few examples of technology helping to provide services. Some forms of technology may completely replace the need for sales or other types of customer service personnel as in the case of Amazon.com and other online retailers.

Technology can also enable service standardization—providing the service exactly the same way every time, as in automated teller machines or ticketing machines. In many cases, service standardization is viewed as a high quality characteristic by customers seeking specific, periodic services. Standardization allows services to be accessed anywhere at anytime without the need for relearning the service process.

e-Business Connection

JetBlue's Self-Service Initiative Pays Off

Through deployment of a customer communication Web self-service initiative, JetBlue is soaring with a customer satisfaction plan that is planted firmly on the ground. On its Web site, JetBlue promotes the message that the company "exists to provide superior service in every aspect of its customers' air travel experience." However, as the company continued to expand their customer base, the number of inquiries the airline received grew exponentially as well. JetBlue's standard of service became more and more difficult to maintain. As employing thousands of additional contact center agents was not a viable option, JetBlue decided that it needed to help its customers help themselves.

JetBlue dubbed the new Web service "AskBlue" and infused the formatting with the airline's brand. The service went live in June 2006. The results were a great relief for the company's service agents and increased customer satisfaction. With any Web self-service initiative, there is always the concern that customers will continue to opt for live, personal assistance. To combat this issue, says Michelle Hansen, manger of customer feedback at the airline, when the Web site was implemented, "We removed some of the help-me links. It forced our customers to try and experiment with it first."

JetBlue soon found that its customers were not only willing to help themselves, but many preferred it. With 80 percent of JetBlue customers already using their Web site to book flights, most felt comfortable maneuvering around the site to get their questions answered. Almost immediately after implementation, JetBlue saw a 40 percent decrease in e-mail volume. In addition, customer inquiries that could not be answered through AskBlue would be immediately forwarded to an agent. The implementation and integration decreased customer response time from up to 5 days to same-day response.

JetBlue's customer service program has led to agent relief, customer satisfaction, and garnered the company the top ranking spot in the J.D. Power and Associates Airline Customer Satisfaction Study in both 2005 and 2006. Hansen says, "We can give our customers what they've wanted: easy access to the easy questions. Because we are able to manage our e-mail volume, we can allow [our agents] to do what humans do best, to answer questions and offer some emotion."

Source: Sebor, J. "Gaining Altitude." *CRM Magazine,* 11, no. 5, (2007): 44. Used with permission.

Using Employee Scheduling Policies

By properly scheduling workers during the day, service capacity can be varied to accommodate varying demand. Businesses must first forecast demand in half-hour or one-hour increments during the day and then convert the demand to staffing requirements for each period, given the average service capabilities for workers. The problem of assigning workers to shifts is complicated by the number of hours each day and the number of days each week the business is open, the timing of days-off and consecutive days-off, and employee shift preferences. The objective of worker scheduling is to service demand with the minimum number of employees, while also assigning equitable work shifts to employees. Employee scheduling software is available to provide managers with multiple scheduling solutions to this problem.

Use of part-time workers, as stated earlier, makes scheduling easier and is illustrated in Example 12.3. In the example, the manager finds a need for two full-time workers, one 3-day worker, one 2-day worker, and two 1-day workers.

Example 12.3   Use of Part-Time Counter-Help at Don's Plumbing Supply

The manager of Don's Plumbing Supply has determined her counter-help requirements as shown below for the 5-day workweek. Given these requirements, she sees that she needs two full-time employees working all 5 days, resulting in the part-time requirements as shown (found by subtracting 2 from each workday requirement). To satisfy these requirements with the fewest number of part-time employees, she begins by assigning Part-timer No. 1 to the maximum number of workdays (Monday, Thursday, and Friday). Part-timer No. 2 is assigned to the maximum number of workdays remaining (Monday and Friday). Then Part-timers 3 and 4 are assigned to the remaining workday (Friday).

	MONDAY	TUESDAY	WEDNESDAY	THURSDAY	FRIDAY
Workers Required	4	2	2	3	6
Full-time Workers	2	2	2	2	2
Part-time Workers	2	0	0	1	4
Part-timer No. 1	1			1	1
Part-timer No. 2	1				1
Part-timer No. 3					1
Part-timer No. 4					1

Using Demand Management Techniques

Even when accurate forecasting and good capacity management techniques are used, there are many occasions when demand exceeds available capacity. As stated earlier, forcing customers to wait in line for a long period of time may result in lost current and future business and damage to the firm's reputation. Organizations can try to reduce demand during busy periods using several short-term demand management techniques. These include raising prices during busy periods to reduce demand and shift it to less busy periods, taking reservations or appointments to schedule demand for less busy periods, discouraging undesirable demand through use of screening procedures and marketing ads, and segmenting demand to facilitate better service (examples include use of first class and economy class seating, and use of express and regular checkout stations). These tactics are combined with the capacity management techniques discussed earlier to provide the firm with the ability to better serve customers. Let's look now at capacity management techniques when service capacity exceeds demand.

Capacity Management When Available Service Capacity Exceeds Demand

When capacity exceeds demand, the firm is faced with the problem of how to utilize excess capacity. Too much excess capacity means higher fixed costs, resulting in higher prices for the service provided, and may also affect customers' perceptions of quality (readers may recall their own quality perceptions when walking into a deserted restaurant at peak dinner hours). Besides the obvious long-term solution of laying workers off and selling facilities, firms may be able to find other uses for service capacity and use demand management techniques to stimulate demand.

Finding Other Uses for Service Capacity

One way to utilize excess capacity is to develop additional service products. Periodic lack of demand might be particularly troublesome for services with seasonal demand, such as hotels, airlines, and ski resorts. For these services, management may try to develop service products that the firm can provide during their characteristically slow periods. This might include airlines partnering with resorts to provide vacation packages during off-peak seasonal periods, hotels booking business conferences during slow periods, or ski resorts designing mountain bike trails or building cement luge runs for summer use. Firms can also make use of cross-training to shift or transfer employees to other areas needing more capacity. For instance, swimming pool builders might train and then use their construction workers to build pool enclosures during the winter months.

Using Demand Management Techniques

When capacity exceeds demand, demand management techniques are used to stimulate additional demand. These include lowering prices during off-peak periods, as in early-bird dinner specials or mid-week hotel rates, as well as designing aggressive marketing campaigns for use during slow business periods.

Managing capacity in services thus involves techniques to adjust capacity and either stimulate or shift demand to match capacity to demand. When an oversupply or undersupply of capacity exists, service times, waiting times, cost, and service quality all suffer, all of which ultimately impact the competitiveness of the firm. The second concern in service response logistics is discussed next—managing waiting times.

Managing Waiting Times

Waiting times are frequently encountered every day including waiting in line at traffic lights, waiting for a table at a restaurant, and waiting on hold on the telephone. Ideally, service managers would like to design **queuing systems** such that customers never have to wait in line; however, the cost of maintaining enough service capacity to handle demand when it is significantly greater than normal is simply too expensive. Thus, managers use information they have about their customers as well as their service employees to design adequate queuing systems and then couple this with the management of customers' perceived waiting times to minimize the negative impact of waiting in line. Thus, good waiting line management consists of the management of *actual waiting time* and *perceived waiting time*. To accomplish this, managers must consider a number of issues:

- What is the average arrival rate of the customers?
- In what order will customers be serviced?
- What is the average service rate of the service providers?
- How are customer arrival and service times distributed?
- How long will customers actually wait in line before they either leave or lower their perceptions of service quality?
- How can customers be kept in line even longer without lowering their perceptions of service quality?

Answers to these questions will allow the firm to adequately design a queuing system that will provide acceptable service to customers while minimizing service system cost and the cost of lost and disgruntled customers. Properly thought out and designed queuing systems decrease waiting times and subsequently the need for further managing waiting times; however, occasionally, waiting time management tactics must be utilized to decrease perceived waiting times. The design of queuing systems is discussed first, followed by a discussion of managing perceived waiting times.

© 2003 Ted Goff

"Did I keep you waiting long?"

Queuing System Design

The four types of queuing system configurations are shown in Figure 12.1. The choice of queuing system depends on the volume of customers to be served, the willingness of customers to wait in line, the physical constraints imposed by the service structure, and the number and sequence of services to be performed. The outputs from various queuing systems that managers wish to compare are the average number of customers in line and in the system, the average waiting time in line and in the system, and the average server utilization. As alluded to earlier, the primary elements of all queuing systems are the input process, the queue characteristics, and the service characteristics. These elements are discussed next, along with several applications.

The Input Process

The customer arrivals are referred to here as the **demand source**. The size of the demand source can be considered either infinite or finite. Many situations (along with the examples covered later) assume an unlimited demand source such as customers arriving at a retail outlet, whereas other situations have a finite-sized demand source, such as customers showing up for a concert at an arena.

Customers also arrive at a service according to some **arrival pattern**. When students show up for scheduled class, this is an example of a known or deterministic interarrival time. In many cases as in a retail establishment, customers show up in a random pattern, and the *Poisson distribution* is commonly used to describe customer arrivals. Using the Poisson distribution, the probability of x customers arriving within some time period T is expressed as:

$$P_{x(T)} = \frac{e^{-\lambda T}(\lambda T)^x}{x!}$$

where λ = average customer arrivals in time period T

   e = 2.71828 (natural log base), and

   $x!$ = x factorial = $x(x\text{-}1)(x\text{-}2)\dots(1)$.

Example 12.4 illustrates the use of this formula.

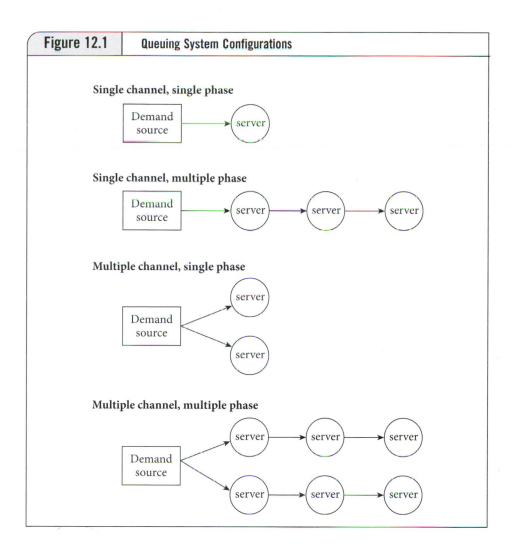

| Figure 12.1 | Queuing System Configurations |

If we assume the number of arrivals per time period is Poisson distributed with a mean arrival rate of λ, then the interarrival time (time between arrivals) is described by the negative exponential distribution, with a mean interarrival time of $1/\lambda$ (so if the mean arrival rate is 10 per hour, then the mean interarrival time is 60 minutes/ 10 arrivals = 6 minutes/arrival).

Most queuing models assume that customers stay in the line once they join it. In other words, customers do not exhibit **balking** (refusing to join the queue once they see how long it is) or **reneging** (leaving the line before completing the service). Though most people have done this at one time or another, queuing analysis becomes much more complex when these arrival characteristics are allowed.

The Queue Characteristics

Queuing models generally assume the length of a queue can grow to an infinite length, although for some situations this is not appropriate (for instance, people with tickets waiting to enter a concert). Queuing configurations can contain single or multiple lines (e.g., the single winding line at Wendy's versus the multiple lines at

Example 12.4   Arrivals per Hour at Jay's Quick Lube Shop

Jay's Quick Lube Shop can service an average of four cars per hour with a partial crew of three employees, and the owner Jay is interested in calculating the probability they can handle all the customers on Saturdays with a partial crew, instead of his usual full crew of five. Given an average arrival rate of three customers per hour on Saturdays, he uses the Poisson distribution to calculate the probabilities for various customer arrivals, shown below.

NUMBER OF ARRIVALS, x	$P_X \text{ (for } T = 1 \text{ hour)} = \dfrac{e^{-3}3^x}{x!}$	CUMULATIVE PROBABILITY
0	0.0498	0.0498
1	0.1494	0.1992
2	0.2240	0.4232
3	0.2240	0.6472
4	0.1680	0.8152

By summing the probabilities for each of the arrival levels, Jay figures that he can handle the demand per hour approximately 82 percent of the time. Conversely, he figures that approximately 18 percent of the time, demand per hour will be greater than four customers, causing queues to develop.

McDonald's). Another queue characteristic is the **queue discipline**. The discipline describes the order in which customers are served. The most common queue discipline is first-come-first-served, although other examples include most-needy-first-served (in emergency rooms) and most-important-first-served (in a VIP line at a nightclub).

The Service Characteristics

The service can be provided either by a single server, or by multiple servers that act in series or in parallel. Multiple servers acting in parallel is referred to as a **multiple channel queuing system**. Multiple servers acting in series is referred to as a **multiple phase queuing system**. Figure 12.1 shows these queuing configurations.

The *single channel, single phase* configuration is the most basic. For standard distribution patterns of customer arrival and service times, the formulas to evaluate this type of system are very straightforward. An example is the one-person retailer. The *single channel, multiple phase* queuing system is the next configuration shown. For this system, customers all contact the same servers, but receive more than one service, and encounter a queue at each service. An example of this type of service is a dentist's office where customers are checked-in by a receptionist, get their teeth cleaned by a dental hygienist, get their teeth x-rayed by a dental assistant, and then get a dental exam by a dentist. For each service, longer than average service times by the preceding customer can mean waiting line build-ups within the system. The third configuration shown is the *multiple channel, single phase* system. Customers enter the system, receive one service from any one of a number of servers, and then exit. Examples of this are retailers' checkout stands, or banks' teller windows. These systems can have queues at each channel or one winding line where all channels receive customers from one line. The final configuration shown is the *multiple channel, multiple phase* queuing system. In this example, customers all receive more than one service in sequence from more than one set or channel of servers. An example here might be a large medical clinic where patients are checked-in by one of several assistants, have their vital signs recorded by one of several nurses, and receive a medical consultation by one of several doctors.

Another characteristic of the service are the times required to complete each of the services provided. For each phase in the system, service times are described by a mean time and probability distribution. Frequently, the *negative exponential distribution* is used to describe the randomness of service time distributions. To determine the probability that the service time *t*, will be less than or equal to some specified time *T*, the following formula can be used:

$$P(t \leq T) = 1 - e^{-\mu T}$$

where $e = 2.71828$ (natural log base), and

$\mu = $ the average service rate.

Example 12.5 illustrates the use of this formula for calculating the probability of completing service within a specified time period.

For single channel systems, we can use the average arrival and service rates to calculate average capacity utilization, by dividing the customer arrival rate by the customer service rate. For example, if the arrival rate is three per hour and the service rate is four per hour, then the average capacity utilization is 75 percent. Although as can be seen in Example 12.4, there will likely be times when utilization for periods during the day approaches or exceeds 100 percent. Now that we've reviewed all of the important elements of queuing systems, let's look at several applications of the models.

Queuing System Applications

When using queuing models, managers collect arrival rate and service rate data by observing, over time, how many customers actually arrive for service, and how many customers are served. Depending on the service, it may take a number of days or weeks to compile meaningful information. Presented below are applications of the single channel, single phase queuing model and the multiple channel, single phase

---

Example 12.5   Service Times at Jay's Quick Lube Shop

Jay's Quick Lube Shop can service an average of four customers per hour, or one customer every 15 minutes, with a crew of three service personnel. The average customer arrival rate on Saturdays is three customers per hour, or one customer every 20 minutes. Jay is interested in calculating the probability that actual service time, *t*, will be within a specific time period, *T*, and he develops a chart showing these probabilities below.

ACTUAL SERVICE TIME	$P(t \leq T \text{ hr.}) = 1 - e^{-4T}$
15 min. (.25 hr.)	$1 - e^{-4(.25)} = 0.6321$
20 min. (.33 hr.)	$1 - e^{-4(.33)} = 0.7329$
30 min. (.5 hr.)	$1 - e^{-4(.5)} = 0.8647$
40 min. (.67 hr.)	$1 - e^{-4(.67)} = 0.9314$
45 min. (.75 hr.)	$1 - e^{-4(.75)} = 0.9502$

Thus, Jay thinks that almost 75 percent of the time, they will service a customer in less than or equal to 20 minutes.

queuing model. These are meant only to be introductory applications. Examples for the other queuing systems and applications can be quite complicated and are beyond the scope of this text. Interested readers are encouraged to examine management science or operations research texts for more advanced treatments of this topic. Several references are provided at the end of this chapter for this purpose.

The Single Channel, Single Phase Queuing Model Application

This is the most widely used and simplest of all queuing models. The assumptions in using the model are as follows:

- Customers come from an infinite population, and are Poisson distributed over time.
- Customers are served in first-come-first-served sequence.
- No balking or reneging occurs.
- Service times are distributed according to the negative exponential distribution.
- The average service rate is greater than the average arrival rate.

The symbols and equations used to determine the operating characteristics for the single channel, single phase queuing model are as follows:

λ = average arrival rate

μ = average service rate

ρ = average server utilization = λ/μ

L_s = expected number of customers in the system = $\lambda/(\mu - \lambda)$

L_q = expected number of customers in the queue
   = $\lambda^2/[\mu(\mu - \lambda)] = L_s - \lambda/\mu$

W_s = expected waiting time in the system = $1/(\mu - \lambda) = L_s/\lambda$

W_q = expected waiting time in the queue = $\lambda/[\mu(\mu - \lambda)] = L_q/\lambda$

P_n = probability that there are n units in the queuing system
   = $(\lambda/\mu)^n(1 - \lambda/\mu)$

The example below illustrates the calculation of operating characteristics for a service.

Kathy's Sewing Shop is a small neighborhood shop that can serve five customers per hour. For the past 2 weeks she has kept track of the customer arrival rate, and the average has been four customers per hour. Kathy is interested in calculating a number of operating characteristics for her store. So she asks one of her customers, a business student at the local university, to help her. The student provides the following information:

λ = 4 customers per hour

μ = 5 customers per hour

ρ = 4/5 = 0.8 or 80% utilization

L_s = $\lambda(\mu - \lambda) = 4/(5 - 4) = 4$ customers

L_q = $L_s - \lambda/\mu = 4 - 4/5 = 3.2$ customers

W_s = $L_s/\lambda = 4/4 = 1$ hour = 60 minutes

W_q = $L_q/\lambda = 3.2/4 = 0.8$ hours = 48 minutes

Kathy also wants to know how likely it will be that more than four customers will be in her shop at one time. So, her student-customer thinks about this and decides that the best way to calculate this is to determine the probabilities of zero, one, two, three, and four customers in the shop, and then add these and subtract the sum from 1.0. So, she provides the following information:

$$
\begin{aligned}
\text{For } n = 0 \quad & P_0 = (4/5)^0(1 - 4/5) = 0.200 \\
n = 1 \quad & P_1 = (4/5)^1(1 - 4/5) = 0.160 \\
n = 2 \quad & P_2 = (4/5)^2(1 - 4/5) = 0.128 \\
n = 3 \quad & P_3 = (4/5)^3(1 - 4/5) = 0.102 \\
n = 4 \quad & P_4 = (4/5)^4(1 - 4/5) = 0.082 \\
\text{For } n > 4 \quad & P_{n>4} = 1 - (P_0 + P_1 + P_2 + P_3 + P_4) \\
& = 1 - (.2 + .16 + .128 + .102 + .082) = 1 - .672 = 0.328
\end{aligned}
$$

So Kathy can expect that there will be more than four people in her shop about 33 percent of the time.

Kathy can purchase a barcode scanner with an automated cash register that will increase her service rate to ten customers per hour. She wants to know how this will change the average wait time in the queue and in the system. Her student-customer then shows her the very significant change this will make:

$$
L_s = \lambda/(\mu - \lambda) = 4/(10 - 4) = 0.67 \text{ customers}
$$
$$
W_q = \lambda/[\mu(\mu - \lambda)] = 4/[10(6)] = 0.067 \text{ hours} = 4 \text{ minutes}
$$
$$
W_s = 1/(\mu - \lambda) = 1/6 \text{ hour} = 10 \text{ minutes}
$$

The Multiple Channel, Single Phase Queuing Model Application

All of the assumptions shown above still apply for the multiple channel, single phase model, except that the number of servers is now greater than 1, and the queuing system consists of multiple servers serving customers from multiple queues. The operating characteristics of this queuing system are as follows:

λ = average arrival rate

$s\mu$ = average service rate, where s = number of service channels

ρ = average server utilization = $\lambda/s\mu$

P_0 = probability of zero customers in the system

$$
= \frac{1}{\sum_{n=0}^{s-1} \frac{(\lambda/\mu)^n}{n!} + \frac{(\lambda/\mu)^s}{s!}\left[\frac{1}{1 - (\lambda/s\mu)}\right]}, \text{ for } s\mu > \lambda
$$

P_n = probability of n customers in the system

$$
= P_0 \frac{(\lambda/\mu)^n}{n!}, \text{ for } n \le s
$$
$$
= P_0 \frac{(\lambda/\mu)^n}{s! \, s^{n-s}}, \text{ for } n > s
$$

L_q = expected number of customers in the queue

$$
= P_0 \frac{(\lambda/\mu)^s(\lambda/s\mu)}{s!(1 - \lambda/s\mu)^2}
$$

$$L_s = \text{expected number of customers in the system}$$
$$= L_q + \lambda/\mu$$

$$W_q = \text{expected waiting time in the queue}$$
$$= L_q/\lambda$$

$$W_s = \text{expected waiting time in the system}$$
$$= W_q + 1/\mu$$

The example for the single channel, single phase shop is extended below, for the two channel, single phase shop, for comparison purposes:

Kathy's Sewing Shop has decided to hire a second worker and buy a second check-out stand with cash register for the shop. Both Kathy and the second worker can serve five customers per hour, and the average arrival rate is four customers per hour. Kathy again wants to know all of the operating characteristics of the new configuration. Once again, her student-customer helps her out:

$$\rho = 4/10 = 0.4, \text{ or 40 percent utilization}$$

$$P_0 = \cfrac{1}{\cfrac{(4/5)^0}{0!} + \cfrac{(4/5)^1}{1!} + \cfrac{(4/5)^2}{2!}\left(\cfrac{1}{1-(4/10)}\right)}$$

$$= \frac{1}{1 + 0.8 + 0.32(1.67)} = \frac{1}{2.33} = 0.428$$

$$L_q = \frac{(4/5)^2(4/10)}{2(1-4/10)^2}(0.428) = 0.152 \text{ customer}$$

$$L_s = 0.152 + 4/5 = 0.952 \text{ customer}$$

$$W_q = 0.152/4 = 0.038 \text{ hours, or 2.28 minute}$$

$$W_s = 0.038 + 0.2 = 0.238 \text{ hours, or 14.28 minute}$$

Note that because of the mean service time and distribution differences, having a two channel, two queue system serving customers with an average service rate of five customers per hour per channel is not the same as having a one channel, one queue system that serves at a rate of ten customers per hour.

Managing Perceived Waiting Times

The final topic of discussion in waiting line management is the management of **perceived waiting times** (sometimes, customers perceive the wait time to be much longer or shorter than it really is). Even though an admirable job may be done designing a queuing system, there are still times when the demand exceeds the queuing capacity (recall the mention earlier of the 2-hour wait in a doctor's office). For these time periods, service firms must have other tools at their disposal to influence customers' perceived waiting times. In a well-known paper written on the topic of waiting lines, David Maister presented some very interesting observations starting with his **First and Second Laws of Service:**[19]

Law #1: Satisfaction = perception − expectation

When customers expect a certain level of service, and then perceive the service they actually receive to be higher, then they will be satisfied. Conversely, when customers' service expectations are higher than their perceptions once the service has been received, they are unsatisfied.

Law #2: It is hard to play catch-up ball

If customers start out happy when the service is first encountered, it is easy to keep them happy. If they start out disgruntled, it is almost impossible to turn things around.

Service Law #1 is interesting in that expectations and perceptions are not necessarily based on reality. For example, customer expectations are formed based on previous experiences, marketing campaigns, signs, information from other people, and the location, while customer perceptions can be affected during the service encounter by a friendly server, mood music, visually pleasant surroundings, and a host of other things. A common practice coming out of Law #1 is to "underpromise and over-deliver." Service Law #2 is good for firms to remember when they are trying to improve service. Investments in service improvements might best be placed at the initial contact or early stages of the service to make sure the service encounter gets off to a good start.

Firms can manage both customer expectations and perceptions by observing and understanding how they are affected when customers wait for service. Waiting time management techniques resulting from this understanding include keeping customers occupied, starting the service quickly, relieving customer anxiety, keeping customers informed, grouping customers together, and designing a fair waiting system.[20] Each of these is briefly discussed next.

Keep Customers Occupied

Firms must try to keep customers occupied while waiting in line. This is why magazines, televisions, and toys for children to play with are often seen in office waiting areas. Other attention-keepers such as music, windows, mirrors, or menus to look at keep customers' minds off the passage of time. In amusement parks such as Disneyland where long lines can be a big problem, customers waiting in line might get entertained by Mickey Mouse, a mime, or a juggler, for instance. All these techniques try to lessen the perceived passage of time and influence customer satisfaction with the waiting experience. The Which Wich sandwich shops in Dallas Texas, for example, use three "news pod" kiosks to both provide line traffic flow and occupy customers while waiting for their orders. Each of the kiosks' four faces contains clipped newspaper articles that are changed daily.[21]

Start the Service Quickly

Giving waiting customers menus, forms to complete, drinks from the bar, or seating them at a lounge, all act to give customers the impression the service has started. When firms acknowledge receipt of an order via telephone, mail, or e-mail, this is another example of extending of beginning the service. If organizations can design pre-process services that begin quickly once a customer encounters a queue, this will act to keep customers occupied and make long waits seem much shorter.

Relieve Customer Anxiety

Customer anxiety is created in many waiting situations, for example, when customers are afraid they've been forgotten, when they don't know how much longer it's going to take, when they don't know what to do, and when they fear they have entered the wrong line. Managers need to observe customers and learn what is likely to cause anxiety, then develop plans to relieve these concerns. These plans might include simply having employees reassure customers, announce how much longer a caller on hold is likely to wait, announcing the lateness of a plane yet to arrive, or using signs to direct customers to the correct line.

Keep Customers Informed

Managers can derail customer anxieties before they even begin by giving customers information as their pre-process and in-process waits progress. When receptionists tell patients that their doctor was called to an emergency, when pilots tell passengers that the plane is waiting to be cleared for gate departure, when work crews place a sign on the road warning to expect delays during a certain period of time, and when amusement parks place signs in the queue telling customers the waiting time from that point in line, this information makes waiting customers much more patient because they know that a delay will occur and the reasons for the delay. Consequently, they are much more willing to stay in line, remain satisfied, and complete the service.

Group Customers Together

Customers would much rather wait together (and commiserate) in waiting lines, than wait alone. Customers act to alleviate their own and others' anxieties, fears, and problems while waiting in line by talking to each other, sharing concerns, and helping out if possible. This sense of togetherness reduces perceived waiting times and may even add enjoyment to the waiting experience. Companies should think of ways to create or encourage group waiting instead of solo waiting such as closer seating, single queues instead of multiple queues, and use of numbered tickets so people don't have to stand in line.

Design a Fair Waiting System

"Taking cuts" in line is something that can cause significant irritation to others waiting in line, particularly if it is seen as unfair. In an emergency room, most people waiting will likely accept that others coming into the queue later might be taken care of first (the queue discipline is most-critical-first-served). Alternately, taking cuts in a long queue at a retail store or amusement park could result in grumbling and shouting from those already waiting in line. Whenever the queue discipline is something other than first-come-first-served, managers need to be aware of the potential problems this causes and take steps to reduce the feeling of unfairness or segment customers such that the queue discipline is not obvious. Examples include physically separating customers such as in first class versus economy class seating on airplanes, taking names and group sizes at a restaurant while concealing the list, and putting up signs like "six items or less" at checkout stands. In many cases, customers will understand and accept the reasons for using a particular queue discipline if they are informed of it. The next concern of service response logistics is the management of distribution channels.

Managing Distribution Channels

This segment of service response logistics describes several distribution channels and strategies a service can use to deliver their services and products to customers. Table 12.2 lists a number of distribution alternatives for a retail store, a bank, an auto repair facility, and a university. Many of these distribution alternatives are the traditional ones everyone is used to seeing; however, services today are experimenting with other nontraditional distribution channels as customer preferences and habits change, demographics change, technology changes, and competition changes.

Some distribution channels have revolutionized the way services do business. For instance, ATMs, debit cards, and the Internet have completely changed the financial services industry; many customers almost never set foot inside a bank or stockbroker's office. Today, many people have come to expect these things, and many services have responded.

Other distribution strategies have arisen because new technologies made them possible, and because customers were asking for them. In the grocery industry, Amazon.com's new grocery delivery service AmazonFresh, promises next-day delivery of

Table 12.2	**Service Distribution Channels**
SERVICE	**DISTRIBUTION CHANNEL**
Retail Store	• Free standing • Mall • Internet • Mail order
Bank	• Main/headquarters • Free standing branches • Sites in malls • Sites in retail locations • ATMs • Internet • Telephone
Auto Repair Business	• Free standing • Attached to retailer (Wal-Mart) • Franchised outlets • Mobile repair van
University/College	• Public • Private • Specialized/General • Traditional/Adult education • Main campus • Branches • Internet • Day/Evening • Television

groceries to customers in Seattle, Washington. Even though grocery home delivery businesses have failed in the past, materials handling technologies such as robotics and refrigerated totes and the deep pockets of Amazon give it a good chance of succeeding this time around.[22] Several of the distribution channel alternatives and issues facing services today are discussed next.

Eatertainment, Entertailing, and Edutainment

As service distribution concepts change, new words have been coined to describe these concepts. **Eatertainment** is the combination of restaurant and entertainment elements. Many of these services incorporate elements of local culture or history into their design themes and offer the capabilities of eating, drinking, entertainment, and shopping all in one venue. Sports-themed restaurants such as the ESPN Zone, the jungle-themed restaurant Rainforest Café, and Buddakan, an Asian-fusion restaurant in Atlantic City, New Jersey, where the dining room is a re-created Chinese town square, complete with a giant golden Buddha and a star-filled sky, are all examples of eatertainment facilities.[23]

Entertailing refers to retail locations with entertainment elements. Many shopping malls are designed today to offer entertainment such as ice skating, rock climbing, and amusement park rides. Metreon, in San Francisco, is a high-tech electronics-themed complex with an IMAX theater, virtual reality games, and a 3-D facility. Toy stores such as Toys "R" Us are designed around centers within the stores to allow customers to try out and play with toys. Entertailing developments are designed to hold customers longer than the typical 45 minutes, perhaps up to 3 or 4 hours. Owners are finding that these customers spend almost twice as much as the typical retail customer on merchandise and services.

Museums, parks, and a host of service providers are getting into the act with **edutainment** or **infotainment** to attract more customers and increase revenues. Edutainment combines learning with entertainment to appeal to customers looking for substance along with play. The Web site www.thegoodfoodfight.com allows visitors to fling food at moving targets while educating them about healthy foods. In the U.S., state and national park employees entertain and inform tourists with indigenous animal lectures and shows, or campfire stories in the evenings. Theme parks such as Legoland in San Diego offer attractions that combine fun and education aimed at the two- to twelve-year-old audience. Finally, television shows such as Sesame Street and software aimed at teaching math and foreign languages in an engaging way also fall into this category.

Franchising

Franchising allows services to expand quickly into dispersed geographic markets, protect existing markets, and build market share. When the owners have limited financial resources, franchising is a good strategy for expansion. Franchisees are required to invest some of their own capital, while paying a small percentage of sales to the franchiser in return for the brand name, start-up help, advertising, training, and assistance in meeting specific operating standards. Many services such as fast-food restaurants, accounting and tax businesses, auto rental agencies, beauty salons, clothing stores, ice cream shops, motels, and many other small service businesses use franchising as a strategy for growing and competing.

Control problems are one of the biggest issues in franchising. Franchisors periodically perform financial and quality audits on the franchisees along with making frequent visits to facilities to assure that franchisees are continuing to comply with operating standards of the company. The idea of control, however, is something that some new franchisors are experimenting with. The Massachusetts-based Wings Over chicken wing franchise chain, for instance, lets franchisees make changes to their stores in order to lend an element of uniqueness to each restaurant. The franchise in Washington, D.C. is called Wings Over Washington D.C.; several in Florida offer raspberry chipotle wing sauce; and in college towns, many Wings Over restaurants don't open until 4:00 pm and they close at 3:00 or 4:00 am. This gives franchisees the flexibility to compete with local businesses. It also is viewed as a way to attract franchisees, that have a large number of businesses to select from. Since 2003, more than 900 new concepts have begun franchising in the U.S. and as of 2007 there were approximately 800,000 franchised businesses operating in the U.S. in more than 80 industries.[24]

International Expansion

The search for larger and additional markets has driven services to expand globally. Since the world today has become essentially borderless because of the Internet and other communication media, more freedom of movement, greater use of common currencies, and the expansion that has already taken place, services today compete in a global economy.

Global service expansion most likely means operating with partners who are familiar with the region's markets, suppliers, infrastructure, government regulations, and customers. For instance, when McDonald's opened its first restaurant in Moscow, an entire food supply chain had to be designed and implemented. McDonald's had to train farmers to produce the type and quality of crops needed to run the business, and then find a market for the excess food produced (they help to supply food to Moscow hotels and embassies).[25]

China's service sector is emerging as a key driver of the Chinese economy—the service sector has now surpassed agriculture in terms of contribution to annual GDP, and is growing annually by 14.5 percent. Consequently, many foreign services are looking to become involved in Chinese markets. For instance, U.S. knowledge services, network services, and financial services have been busy setting up operations in China. In fact, between 2001 and 2005, U.S. foreign direct investment flows from services setting up in China were $3 billion.[26]

Exposure to foreign currency exchange rate fluctuations can also pose a problem for firms, requiring them to use financial hedging strategies to reduce exchange rate risk. Firms can operate in several different countries to offset currency problems, since economic downturns in one country can often be offset by positive economic conditions in other countries.

Language barriers, cultural problems and the varying needs of different regional cultures also must be addressed when expanding. Local management must be allowed to vary services, signage, and accompanying products to suit local tastes. Restaurants, for instance, typically add local favorites to menus to increase acceptability. Companies must become familiar with language translations in order to properly change the wording on signs and advertisements to increase readability and understanding. The Coca-Cola name in China was initially rendered as "ke-kou-ke-la" on thousands of signs before it was found that the meaning of the phrase was either "bite the wax tadpole" or "female horse stuffed with wax" depending on the dialect. Coke personnel then had to study 40,000 characters to find the phonetic equivalent "ko-kou-ko-le," which translated into "happiness in the mouth." Similarly, Japan's second largest tourist agency, Kinki Nippon Tourist Co., felt compelled to change its

U.S. name after they began getting requests from American customers for unusual sex-oriented tours.[27]

Internet Distribution Strategies

Internet-based "dot-com" companies exploded on the scene during the latter part of the 1990s, pushing the NASDAQ to historic highs and promising to enrich anyone with an idea, good or bad, with which he/she could create a Web site that would generate revenues on the Internet. E-commerce was touted as the coming trillion dollar revolution in retailing, but as it turned out, many of the dot-com companies of the 2000 time period are gone today. Still, Internet retailing is growing faster than traditional retailing. By the first quarter of 2007, e-commerce accounted for $31.5 billion in U.S. retail sales, or approximately 3 percent of total U.S. retail sales. This reflects an increase of more than 18 percent from the previous year's same quarter, and far exceeds the growth rate in overall retail sales.[28]

One of the primary advantages of the Internet is its ability to offer convenient sources of real-time information, integration, feedback, and comparison shopping. Individual consumers use Internet search engines to look for jobs, find and communicate with businesses, find the nearest movie theater, find products, sell things, and barter goods. And they can do all this in the privacy of their homes. Americans conducted 6.8 billion online searches in October 2006, for example.[29] Businesses, too, use the Internet to communicate, find and then purchase items from suppliers, and sell or provide goods and services to individual consumers and other businesses. Today, most businesses either have a Web site or are thinking about building one. Many individuals also have their own Web sites, since domain names can be purchased for as little as $10 per year. Many retailers today sell products exclusively over the Internet (a *pure strategy*), while others use it as a supplemental distribution channel (a *mixed strategy*).

The **pure Internet strategy** can have several distinct advantages over traditional brick-and-mortar services. They can become more centralized reducing labor, capital, and inventory costs, while using the Internet to decentralize their marketing efforts to reach a vastly distributed audience of business or individual consumers. Amazon.com falls into this category. Today, though, the **mixed Internet strategy** of combining traditional retailing with Internet retailing seems to be emerging as the stronger business model. Firms such as JCPenney sell items in retail outlets and also sell items from Internet and store catalogs. Customers can either pick up their purchases at the store or have them delivered. Southwest Airlines was the first airline to establish a home page on the Internet, and today approximately 50 percent of its passenger revenue is generated by online bookings via their industry leading Web site, www.southwest.com.

Developing good customer service capabilities can be challenging, though. JCPenney representatives, for instance, must be able to perform customer service functions over the Internet, in-person, and via mail and telephone. Companies are addressing this problem by developing sophisticated **customer contact centers**. These centers integrate their Web site and their traditional call center to offer 24/7 support where customers and potential customers can contact the firm and each other using telephone, e-mail, chat rooms, and e-bulletin boards. These contact centers allow firms to serve a large number of geographically dispersed customers with a relatively small number of customer service agents.

Just as services have to be concerned with managing service capacity and waiting lines, firms must also invest management efforts in designing the necessary distribution channels to compete in today's marketplaces. The final element of the service response logistics discussion affects all elements of the service itself and the way it is distributed, and that is the management of service quality. Although this topic was initially addressed in Chapter 8, the quality management topics geared strictly toward services need further discussion, and this topic is presented below.

Managing Service Quality

For services, quality occurs during the service delivery process and typically involves an interaction between a customer and a service employee. Customer satisfaction with the service depends not only on the ability of the firm to deliver what customers want, but on the customers' perceptions of the quality of the service received. When customer expectations are met or exceeded, the service is deemed to possess high quality and when expectations are not met, the perception of quality is poor. In a survey of hundreds of consumers, Brady and Cronin found that when consumers perceived that firms were customer-oriented, their satisfaction and perceptions of service quality were higher.[30] Thus, service quality is highly dependent upon the ability of the firm's employees and service systems to satisfy customers, and on the varying expectations of the customers themselves. Because of this variable nature of customer expectations, services must continually be monitoring their service delivery systems using the tools described in Chapter 8 while concurrently observing, communicating with, and surveying customers to adequately assess and improve quality.

The Dimensions of Service Quality

Some of the more-quoted studies of service quality are those done by Drs. Parasuraman, Zeithaml, and Berry.[31] Studying a number of different services, they identified **five dimensions of service quality** generally used by customers—reliability, responsiveness, assurance, empathy, and tangibles. Reliability was consistently reported in their study as the most important quality dimension.

- *Reliability.* consistently performing the service correctly and dependably.
- *Responsiveness.* providing the service promptly and in a timely manner.
- *Assurance.* using knowledgeable, competent, courteous employees who convey trust and confidence to customers.
- *Empathy.* providing caring and individual attention to customers.
- *Tangibles.* the physical characteristics of the service including the facilities, the servers, equipment, and other customers.

Using their survey, the three researchers were able to identify any differences occurring between customer expectations in the five dimensions and customer perceptions of what was actually received during a service encounter. These differences were referred to as service quality "gaps," and can thus be used to highlight areas in need of improvement for services.

Organizations can develop criteria relating to the five service quality dimensions and then collect data using customer comment cards or mailed surveys, on customers' satisfaction with each of the quality dimensions, to measure overall service quality performance. Table 12.3 presents criteria that might be used in each of the five quality dimensions. When weaknesses or gaps are encountered in any of the performance criteria, managers can institute improvements in the areas indicated.

World-class service companies realize they must get to know their customers and they invest considerable time and effort gathering information about their needs and

Table 12.3	Examples of Service Quality Criteria
SERVICE QUALITY DIMENSION	**CRITERIA**
Reliability	• billing accuracy • order accuracy • on-time completion • promises kept
Responsiveness	• on-time appointment • timely callback • timely confirmation of order
Assurance	• skills of employees • training provided to employees • honesty of employees • reputation of firm
Empathy	• customized service capabilities • customer recognition • degree of server-customer contact • knowledge of the customer
Tangibles	• appearance of the employees • appearance of the facility • appearance of customers • equipment and tools used

expectations. This information is then used to design services and delivery systems that satisfy customers, capture market share, and create profits for the firm. These organizations understand that one of the most important elements affecting long-term competitiveness and profits is the quality of their products and services relative to their competitors. For example, research by Canadian consulting firm Service Quality Measurement Group found that customer satisfaction dropped by 15 percent for each callback a customer must make to a contact center. In addition, higher first-call resolution was found to result in lower contact center operating costs, fewer defecting customers, and higher employee satisfaction.[32]

Recovering from Poor Service Quality

There will undoubtedly, from time to time, be occasions when even the best organizations' products and services do not meet a customer's expectations. In most cases, quick recovery from these service failures can keep customers loyal and coming back, and may even serve as good word-of-mouth advertising for the firm, as customers pass on their stories of good service recoveries. Most important, when service failures do occur, firms must be able to recover quickly and forcefully to satisfy customers. This involves empowering front-line service personnel to identify problems and then provide solutions quickly and in an empathetic way.

Good services offer guarantees to their customers and empower employees to provide quick and meaningful solutions when customers invoke the guarantee. In the

U.S., the great majority of retailers offer money-back guarantees if customers are not satisfied and about half offer low-price guarantees where customers are refunded the price difference for a period of time after purchase.[33] In many cases, solutions to guarantee problems are designed into the process and become part of the service firm's marketing efforts. To be effective, guarantees should be unconditional, easy to understand, and easy to implement. Firms that anticipate where service failures can occur, develop recovery procedures, train employees in these procedures, and then empower employees to remedy customer problems can assure they have the best service recovery system possible.

SUMMARY

Services constitute a large and growing segment of the global economy. Managing the supply chains of services is thus becoming an important part of an overall competitive strategy for services. Since service customers are most often the final consumers of the services provided, successfully managing service encounters involves managing productive capacity, managing waiting lines, managing distribution channels, and managing service quality. These four concerns are the foundations of service response logistics and were the primary focus of this chapter.

Service companies must accurately forecast demand, design capacity to adequately meet demand, employ waiting line systems to serve customers as quickly and efficiently as possible, utilize distribution systems to best serve the firm's customers, and then take steps to assure service quality and customer satisfaction throughout the service process. Provided that managers have selected a good location, designed an effective layout, hired, trained, and properly scheduled service personnel, and then employed effective service response logistics strategies, firms and their supply chains should be able to maintain competitiveness, market share, and profitability.

KEY TERMS

arrival pattern, 422

balking, 423

Baumol's disease, 405

capacity utilization, 417

chase demand strategy, 417

closeness desirability rating, 410

cost leadership strategy, 406

customer contact centers, 434

demand management, 416

demand source, 422

differentiation strategy, 407

distribution channels, 416

eatertainment, 432

edutainment, 432

entertailing, 432

facilitating products, 410

First and Second Laws of Service, 429

five dimensions of service quality, 435

focus strategy, 408

infotainment, 432

mixed Internet strategy, 434

multiple channel queuing system, 424

multiple phase queuing system, 424

multiple-factor productivity, 404

perceived waiting times, 428

pure Internet strategy, 434

pure services, 403

queue discipline, 424

queue management, 417

queuing systems, 421

reneging, 423

service bundle, 408

service capacity, 416

service delivery systems, 408

service layout strategies, 409

service quality, 414

service response logistics, 416

single-factor productivity, 404

state utility, 403

waiting times, 416

Wal-Mart effect, 405

walk-through service audits, 409

DISCUSSION QUESTIONS

1. Is your university a *pure service*? Explain.

2. Why is the service sector in the U.S. and other highly developed economies growing so much more rapidly than the manufacturing sector?

3. Describe the primary differences between goods and service firms.

4. Give an example of a single-factor productivity measure and a multiple-factor productivity measure. Using the formula for productivity, describe all the ways that firms can increase productivity. Which can be described as risky?

5. Define *Baumol's disease* and the *Wal-Mart effect*, and how they affect service-oriented economies like the U.S. economy.

6. Discuss the primary issues in the management of global services.

7. What are the three generic strategies that services use to compete? Give examples.

8. When customers purchase a service, they are actually getting a bundle of service attributes. List and describe these attributes.

9. Provide some examples of *front-of-the-house* and *back-of-the-house* service operations.

10. What are some things service firms can do to monitor customer satisfaction?

11. Why are service locations so important?

12. Discuss the principle design objectives for service layouts.

13. How do supply chain management activities differ between services and manufacturing companies? In what ways are supply chain management activities alike?

14. What are the four concerns of *service response logistics*?

15. Define *service capacity* and provide three examples of service capacity not listed in the text.

16. Define *capacity utilization*. What is an ideal utilization? Can utilization ever be greater than 100 percent? Explain.

17. Describe how you would use a level and a chase demand capacity utilization strategy.

18. What are some alternatives to hiring and laying-off workers to vary service capacity as demand varies?

19. Can customers be used to provide extra service capacity? Explain.

20. Describe some demand management techniques that are used when demand exceeds capacity, and when capacity exceeds demand.

21. How can firms make use of excess capacity?

22. What are the two elements managers must pay attention to, when managing wait times, so as to minimize waiting in line?

23. What are the primary elements to consider when designing any queuing system?

24. Define the terms *balking* and *reneging*.

25. What type of queuing system does a three channel, four phase system refer to?

26. Explain and give examples of Maister's First and Second Laws of Service.

27. If you have designed an effective queuing system, why is it still necessary to practice waiting time management on some occasions?

28. What are the distribution channel alternatives for a weather service? A souvenir shop? A marriage counselor?

29. Describe the important issues in the international expansion of services.

30. Describe and give examples of a *pure Internet distribution strategy* and a *mixed Internet distribution strategy*. Find your examples on the Internet.

31. How is service quality related to customer service and satisfaction?

32. Describe the five dimensions of service quality for a dentist's office, how performance in these dimensions might be measured, and how recoveries might be handled for failures in each of the service quality dimensions.

INTERNET QUESTIONS

1. Search the Internet for examples of eatertainment, entertailing, and edutainment.

2. Search the Internet for new franchise concepts and report on several.

INFOTRAC QUESTIONS

Access http://academic.cengage.com/infotrac to answer the following questions:

1. Search on the term "McDonald's carbon footprint" or "McDonald's green initiatives" and write a report on this firm's efforts.

2. Write a paper on Wal-Mart's location and layout strategies.

PROBLEMS

1. Write the general formula for labor productivity at a bank for example, and describe all the ways that service productivity can be increased. Which would be the most desirable way to increase productivity? Why?

2. For the office layout shown below and the accompanying trip and distance matrices, determine the total distance traveled per day. Find another layout that results in a lower total distance traveled per day.

Management (1)	Production (2)	Engineering (3)	Reception (4)
Files (5)	Accounting (6)	Purchasing (7)	Sales (8)

INTERDEPARTMENTAL TRIPS PER DAY

	(2)	(3)	(4)	(5)	(6)	(7)	(8)
(1)	6	5	2	1	7	6	15
(2)		12	4	5	2	10	5
(3)			2	9	2	10	8
(4)				18	12	4	2
(5)					0	0	0
(6)						6	14
(7)							6

DISTANCES BETWEEN DEPARTMENTS (meters)

	(2)	(3)	(4)	(5)	(6)	(7)	(8)
(1)	15	30	45	10	20	35	50
(2)		15	30	20	10	20	35
(3)			15	40	20	10	20
(4)				60	50	30	10
(5)					10	30	50
(6)						20	40
(7)							20

3. For the office layout shown in problem number 2, determine the closeness desirability rating using the rating table below. Treat the hallway as if it doesn't exist (i.e., the Production and Accounting Departments touch each other). Can you find a more desirable layout? How could you use both the distance traveled and the closeness desirability in assessing the layout alternatives? Can you find a layout resulting in relatively good scores using both types of criteria?

CLOSENESS DESIRABILITY BETWEEN DEPARTMENTS

	(2)	(3)	(4)	(5)	(6)	(7)	(8)
(1)	2	2	−1	0	1	3	3
(2)		3	0	0	0	3	1
(3)			0	2	0	2	3
(4)				3	1	2	2
(5)					2	2	1
(6)						0	2
(7)							1

4. Oana's Cat Care needs help in her grooming business as shown below for the 5-day workweek. Determine a full- and part-time work schedule for the business using the fewest number of workers.

	MONDAY	TUESDAY	WEDNESDAY	THURSDAY	FRIDAY
Workers Required	2	3	3	4	5

5. Given an average service rate of 12 customers per hour, what is the probability the business can handle all the customers when the average arrival rate is 10 customers per hour? Use the Poisson distribution to calculate the probabilities for various customer arrivals.

6. With an average service rate of 12 customers per hour and an average customer arrival rate of 10 customers per hour, calculate the probability that actual service time will be less than or equal to 6 minutes.

7. Stella can handle about 10 customers per hour at her one-person comic book store. The customer arrival rate averages about six customers per hour. Stella is interested in knowing the operating characteristics of her single channel, single phase queuing system.

8. How would Stella's queuing system operating characteristics change for the problem above, if she added another cashier and increased her service rate to 20 customers per hour?

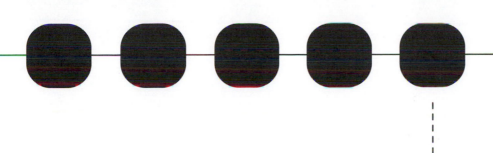

Part 5

Integration Issues in Supply Chain Management

Chapter 13

SUPPLY CHAIN PROCESS INTEGRATION

Those who work alone can only accumulate, but those who collaborate intelligently can multiply.[1]

In one way, when you look at it, folks have been collaborating forever, ever since they've done business with another company. However, the nature of doing business together has gone through some fundamental and very interesting shifts.[2]

Learning Objectives

After completing this chapter, you should be able to

- Discuss the overall importance of process integration in supply chain management.
- Describe the advantages of, and obstacles to, process integration.
- Understand the important issues of internal and external process integration.
- Understand the role played by information systems in creating information visibility along the supply chain.
- Describe the various processes requiring integration along the supply chain.
- Understand the various causes of the bullwhip effect and how they influence process integration.
- Discuss the various issues associated with supply chain security and risk.

Chapter Outline

Introduction

The Supply Chain Management Integration Model

Obstacles to Process Integration Along
  the Supply Chain

Managing Supply Chain Risk and Security

Summary

Supply Chain Management in Action	*Process Integration at ViewSonic*

ViewSonic has won numerous industry awards for its visual display products, which include plasma and LCD screens and monitors. But the California-based company would have difficulty selling those innovative products without the strong relationships it maintains with a global network of distributors and retailers.

Jordan Beseiso, ViewSonic's manager of global business-to-business integration, says the company's adoption of the Gentran Integration Suite (GIS) from Sterling Commerce helps keep those relationships, as well as ViewSonic's balance sheet, intact. The key feature of GIS, from Beseiso's perspective, is the centralized partner-management capability, which delivers a single interface for ViewSonic employees to monitor business processes and navigate reports and statistics in near-real time. It also offers insight as to where and how processes can be improved. "The partner-management capabilities are important for us," says Beseiso. "We add and execute key business processes while maintaining our existing staff levels. This allows creating new revenue opportunities without incurring additional resource expenses."

"Leveraging IT strength enables a company to improve enterprise and supply chain performance by tightly integrating and monitoring key business processes," says Russell Scherwin, director of global product marketing, B2B Solutions, with Sterling Commerce. Ken Vollmer, principal analyst with Massachusetts-based Forrester Research says Sterling Commerce has improved GIS in recent years to meet manufacturers' demand for more integrated business solutions. "Today, [GIS] has a fully functional, integration-centric business process management suite that enables users to first set up, and then monitor, business processes," Vollmer says.

What that means for ViewSonic is rather than focus on the underlying technology, it can tie different systems together, model processes, and focus on refining business issues, says Beseiso. That approach gives ViewSonic a competitive edge by offering customers, that global network of distributors and retailers, maximum flexibility when they place, check, or change orders.

For instance, GIS enabled ViewSonic to establish a fully automated order-to-cash process. The highly integrated supply chain allows near-real time purchase order modification, shipment notification, and electronic invoicing. When inventory requirements change or product lines shift, original purchase orders, and subsequent invoicing, can be modified to meet market demand while eliminating fragmented, data-transfer processes conducted via fax or e-mail.

"It used to take months to meet electronic requests from major retailers," Beseiso says. "Now we meet these requests in less than a week. In one case, we quickly met the electronic transaction demands of a new customer, and consequently secured millions of dollars in additional sales."

Source: Fulcher, J. "ViewSonic Gets Clearer Picture of Business Process Management with Sterling Commerce Integration Suite." *Manufacturing Business Technology,* 25, no. 8 (2007): 47. © Reed Business Information. Used with permission.

Introduction

The ultimate goal in supply chain management is to create value for the services and products provided to end-customers, which in turn, will benefit the firms in the supply chain network. To accomplish this, firms in a supply chain must first integrate their process activities internally, and then with their trading partners. Throughout this textbook, the integration of key business processes along the supply chain has been a recurring theme. The term **process integration** means sharing information and coordinating resources to jointly manage a process. We have been introducing and discussing the various processes and issues concerning this time-consuming and somewhat daunting task throughout the text, and have been alluding to the idea that key processes must be somehow coordinated, shared, or integrated among the supply chain members. In this chapter, some of these issues will be revisited.

In addition, the advantages, challenges, methods, and tools used to achieve process integration both within organizations and among supply chain trading partners will be discussed. Today, process integration remains a significant problem for many organizations. In a 2006 survey of U.S. manufacturers, 34 percent of responding companies stated they had no process integration at all with their suppliers, and 30 percent had no integration with their customers.[3]

Specifically, this chapter discusses the key business processes requiring integration, the impact of integration on the bullwhip effect, the importance of internal and external process integration in supply chain management, issues of supply chain risk and security that come about as information is shared and products moved significant distances, and the important role played by information technology (IT), such as ViewSonic's integration software use in the Supply Chain Management in Action profile, in making data and communications available throughout a supply chain.

Process integration can be an extremely difficult task because it requires proper training and preparedness, willing and competent trading partners, trust, compatible information systems, and potentially a change in one or more organizational cultures. However, the benefits of collaboration and information sharing between trading partners can be significant: reduced supply chain costs, greater flexibility to respond to market changes, less supply chain safety stock, higher quality levels, reduced time to market, and better utilization of resources. It is hoped that this chapter will allow readers to recall and consider all the topics of the previous chapters, their contributions to successful supply chain management, and the means by which collaboration, information sharing, and process integration must occur to make supply chain management a core competitive strength.

The Supply Chain Management Integration Model

Figure 13.1 presents a supply chain integration model, starting with the identification of key trading partners, the development of supply chain strategies, aligning the strategies with key process objectives, developing internal process performance measures, internally integrating these key processes, developing external supply chain performance measures for each process, externally integrating key processes with supply chain partners, extending process integration to second-tier supply chain participants, and then finally, reevaluating the integration model periodically. Each of the elements in the model is discussed next.

Identify Critical Supply Chain Trading Partners

For each of the firm's products and services, it is important to identify the critical or **key trading partners** that will eventually enable the successful sale and delivery of end products to the final customers. At least initially, including a large number of supply chain businesses will be extremely difficult and cumbersome, particularly as the firm

| **Figure 13.1** | **The Supply Chain Integration Model** |

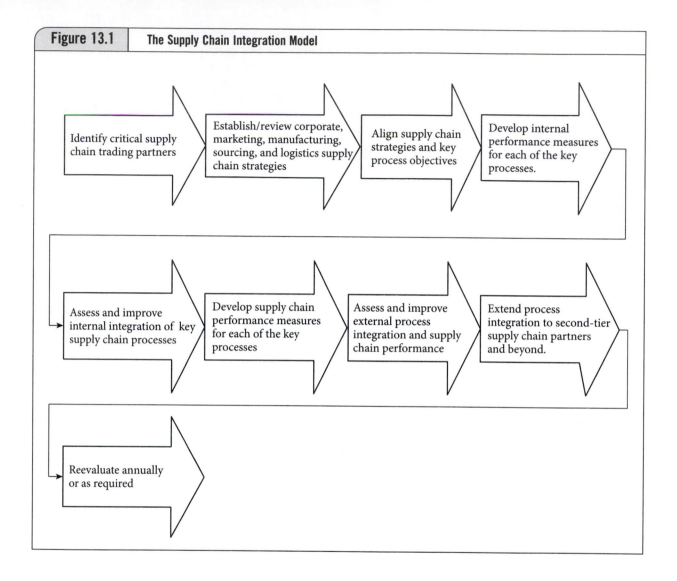

moves out to second- and third-tier suppliers and customers. Identifying only the primary trading partners allows the firm to concentrate its time and resources on managing important process links with these companies, enabling the supply chain to perform well. Including other nonessential or supporting businesses will prove counterproductive in terms of successful supply chain management. In a landmark supply chain paper by Lambert, Cooper, and Pagh, they define primary or key supply chain members to be "all those autonomous companies or strategic business units who actually perform operational and/or managerial activities in the business processes designed to produce a specific output for a particular customer or market."[4]

Depending on where within a supply chain the focal firm is located (close to its key suppliers, close to end-product customers, or somewhere in between), the structure of the network of primary trading partners will vary. Mapping the network of primary trading partners is something that should be done to help the firm decide which businesses to include in their supply chain management efforts. For instance, a firm with many key suppliers and customers will most likely limit the number of integrative processes the firm can successfully manage, leading to fewer tier-2 relationships. Coordinating processes with its key suppliers was seen as so important by IBM, for example, that in 2006 it moved its global procurement headquarters to Shenzhen China from the U.S. to be closer to their many important Chinese suppliers.[5]

Review and Establish Supply Chain Strategies

On an annual basis, management should identify the basic supply chain strategies associated with each of their firm's products and services. If an end product is competing based on quality, then supply chain members should also be using strategies consistent with delivering high quality products at competitive price and service levels. Product strategies should then translate into internal functional policies regarding the types of parts purchased and suppliers used, the manufacturing processes employed, the designs of the products manufactured, the warranty and return services offered, and potentially the amount of outsourcing employed. In each of these areas, policies should be geared toward supporting the overall strategy of the supply chain (in this case, high quality).

Similarly, if end products are competing primarily on the basis of cost, then strategies and functional policies among each of the supply chain participants must be consistently aimed at achieving low cost as intermediate products and services are purchased, produced, and moved along the supply chain. When competition, technology, and customer requirements change, management must also adjust supply chain and internal strategies to remain competitive.

Align Supply Chain Strategies with Key Process Objectives

Once the primary strategy has been identified for each of the supply chain end products, managers need to identify the important processes linking each of the supply chain partners and establish process objectives to assure that resources and efforts are effectively deployed within each firm, to support the end-product strategy. The key processes and the methods used to integrate and manage process links among supply chain partners will vary based on the internal structure of each firm, the prevailing economic conditions in the marketplace, the degree to which **functional silos** exist in any of the trading partners, and the nature of existing relationships within the supply chain. In some cases, it may be best to integrate only one key process with a trading partner, while with other partners, more processes will be integrated.

Based on the research of Lambert, Cooper, and Pagh, eight processes have been identified as important supply chain business processes. These **key supply chain processes** are shown in Table 13.1. A process can be defined as a set of activities designed to produce a product or service for an internal or external customer. A discussion of each of these processes follows.

Customer Relationship Management

The **customer relationship management (CRM)** process provides the firm with the structure for developing and managing customer relationships. As discussed in Chapter 10, key customers are identified, their needs are determined, and then products and services are developed to meet their needs. Over time, relationships with these key customers are solidified through the sharing of information, the formation of cross-company teams

Table 13.1	The Eight Key Supply Chain Business Processes[6]
PROCESS	**DESCRIPTION**
Customer Relationship Management	Identifying key customer segments, tailoring product and service agreements to meet their needs, measuring customer profitability and the firm's impact on customers.
Customer Service Management	Providing information to customers such as product availability, shipping dates, order status; administering product and service agreements.
Demand Management	Balancing customer demand with the firm's output capacity; forecasting demand and coordinating with production, purchasing, and distribution.
Order Fulfillment	Meeting customer requirements by synchronizing the firm's marketing, production, and distribution plans.
Manufacturing Flow Management	Determining manufacturing process requirements to enable the right mix of flexibility and velocity to satisfy demand.
Supplier Relationship Management	Managing product and service agreements with suppliers; developing close working relationships with key suppliers.
Product Development and Commercialization	Developing new products frequently and getting them to market effectively; integrating suppliers and customers into the process to reduce time to market.

to improve product design, delivery, quality, and cost, the development of shared goals, and finally, improved performance and profitability for the trading partners along with agreements on how to share these benefits. The firm should monitor the impact of customer relationship management efforts on their financial statements as well as on customer satisfaction levels.

Customer Service Management

The **customer service management process** is what provides information to customers while also providing ongoing management of any product and service agreements between the firm and its customers. Information can be provided through a number of communication channels including Web sites, personal interactions, information system linkages, and printed media. Objectives and policies are developed to assure proper distribution of products and services to customers, to adequately respond to product and delivery failures and complaints, and to utilize the most effective means of communication to coordinate successful product, service, and information deliveries. The process also includes methods for monitoring and reporting customer service performance, allowing firms to understand the extent to which their management efforts are achieving the process objectives.

Demand Management

The **demand management process** is what balances customer demand and the firm's output capabilities. The specific demand management activities include forecasting demand, and then utilizing techniques to vary capacity and demand within the purchasing, production, and distribution functions. Various forecasts can be used, based on the time frame, the knowledge of the forecaster, the ability to obtain **point of sale information**, and the use of forecasting models contained in many ERP systems. The next step is to determine how to synchronize demand and productive capacity. As was discussed in Chapters 5 and 12, a number of effective techniques exist to smooth demand variabilities and increase or decrease capacity when disparities exist between demand and supply.

Contingency plans must also be ready for use when demand management techniques fail or when forecasts are inaccurate. Performance measurement systems can prove quite useful here to increase the accuracy of forecasts, and to track the success of various demand management activity implementations.

Order Fulfillment

The **order fulfillment process** is the set of activities that allows the firm to fill customer orders while providing the required levels of customer service at the lowest possible delivered cost. Thus, the order fulfillment process must integrate the firm's marketing, production, and distribution plans to be effective. More specifically, the firm's distribution system must be designed to provide adequate customer service levels, and their production system must be designed to produce at the required output levels, while marketing plans and promotions must consider the firm's output and distribution capabilities. Related order fulfillment issues are the location of suppliers, the modes of inbound and outbound transportation used, the location of production facilities and distribution centers, and the system used for entering, processing, communicating, picking, delivering, and documenting customer orders. The order fulfillment process must integrate closely with customer relationship management, customer service management, supplier relationship management, and returns management to assure that customer requirements are being met, customer service levels are being maintained, suppliers are helping to minimize order cycle times, and customers are getting undamaged, high quality products.

Manufacturing Flow Management

The **manufacturing flow management process** is the set of activities responsible for making the actual product, establishing the manufacturing flexibility required to adequately serve the markets, and designing the production system to meet cycle time requirements. To be effective, manufacturing flow management activities must be interfaced with the demand management and customer relationship management processes, using customer requirements as inputs to the process. The supply chain and manufacturing flow process must change to maintain firm competitiveness, as customers and their requirements change. As shown in Chapter 8, the flexibility and rapid response requirements in many supply chains results in the firm's use of lean systems in order to continue to meet customer requirements.

Manufacturing flow characteristics also affect supplier requirements. For instance, as manufacturing batch sizes and lead time requirements are reduced, supplier deliveries must become smaller and more frequent, causing supplier interactions and supplier relationships to potentially change. The importance of an adequate material planning system should become evident here, as customer requirements must be translated into production capabilities and supplier requirements. As with other processes, a good set of performance metrics should also be utilized to track the capability of the manufacturing flow process to satisfy demand.

Supplier Relationship Management

The **supplier relationship management process** defines how the firm manages its relationships with suppliers. As was discussed in Chapters 2, 3, and 4 of this textbook, firms in actively managed supply chains seek out small numbers of the best performing suppliers and establish ongoing, mutually beneficial, close relationships with these suppliers in order to meet cost, quality, and/or customer service objectives for key materials, components, and products. For other nonessential items, firms may use reverse

auctions, bid arrangements, or catalogs to select suppliers. Activities in this process include screening and selecting suppliers, negotiating product and service agreements, managing suppliers, and then monitoring supplier performance and improvement. Some companies may have a cross-functional team to manage suppliers' progress toward meeting the firm's current and long-term requirements and establishing records of performance improvement over time, while other suppliers may be managed little or not at all, depending on supply chain, company, or product requirements. Supplier relationship management personnel routinely communicate with production personnel to obtain feedback on supplier and purchased item performance, and with marketing personnel for customer feedback. In addition, suppliers are frequently contacted for new product development and performance feedback purposes.

Product Development and Commercialization

The **product development and commercialization process** is responsible for developing new products to meet changing customer requirements and then getting these products to market quickly and efficiently. In actively managed supply chains, customers and suppliers are involved in the new product development process to assure that products conform to customers' needs and purchased items meet manufacturing requirements. Activities in the product development and commercialization process include methods and incentives for generating new product ideas, the development of customer feedback mechanisms, the formation of new product development teams, assessing and selecting new product ideas based on financial impact, resource requirements, and fit with existing manufacturing and logistics infrastructure, designing and testing new product prototypes, determining marketing channels and rolling out the products, and finally, assessing the success of each new product. Successful new product development hinges on the involvement of external customers and suppliers, and of internal manufacturing, marketing, and finance personnel.

Returns Management

The **returns management process**, discussed earlier in Chapter 9, can be extremely beneficial for supply chain management in terms of maintaining acceptable levels of customer service and identifying product improvement opportunities. Returns management activities include environmental compliance with substance disposal and recycling, composing operating and repair instructions, troubleshooting and warranty repairs, developing disposition guidelines, designing an effective reverse logistics process, and collecting returns data. Returns management personnel frequently communicate with customers and personnel from customer relationship management, product development and commercialization, and supplier relationship management during the returns process.

One of the goals of returns management is to reduce returns. This is accomplished by communicating return and repair information to product development personnel, suppliers, and other potential contributors to any returns problems, to guide the improvement of future product and purchased item designs. Logistics services may also be included in the returns feedback communication loop.

For each of the eight processes identified above, objectives or goals must be developed to help guide the firm toward their supply chain strategy. In addition, consistent objectives within each functional area of the firm, for each process, help to integrate the processes internally, as well as focus efforts and firm resources on the supply chain strategy. For instance, if the supply chain strategy is to compete using low pricing, marketing objectives for the customer relationship management process

might be to find cheaper delivery alternatives, develop vendor managed inventory (VMI) accounts, and to automate the customer order process. Production objectives might be to develop bulk packaging solutions consistent with the modes of transportation and distribution systems used, to increase mass production capabilities, and to identify the lowest total cost manufacturing sites for specific products, while purchasing objectives might be to identify the cheapest materials and components that meet specifications and to utilize reverse auctions whenever possible. Firms should similarly progress through each of the key processes using teams of employees from each function to develop process objectives.

Develop Internal Performance Measures for Key Process Effectiveness

As alluded to in each of the key processes above (and to be discussed at greater length in Chapter 14), procedures and metrics must be in place to collect and report internal performance data for the eight processes. Before companies can measure performance among supply chain partners, they must first build good internal performance measurement capabilities across functions. This can prove troublesome, given that in a recent survey of Canadian manufacturing firms, only approximately 50 percent were found to have reasonably well-developed performance measurement systems.[7] Performance measures need to drive a consistent emphasis on the overall supply chain strategy and corresponding process objectives. In order to assure that processes are supporting the supply chain strategy, performance should be continuously measured using a set of metrics designed for each process.

Continuing the discussion from the previous section where competing based on low pricing was the supply chain strategy, performance measures for the customer relationship management process would need to be designed for each of the firm's functional areas. The responsibility for designing these measures can also be assigned to the team developing objectives for each of the functional areas. Because the objectives in this case are cost driven, the performance measures should reflect this as well. For the customer relationship management process, performance measures in marketing might be the average delivery cost, the number of new VMI accounts, the average cost of ordering and carrying inventories for the new VMI accounts, and the number of new automated order systems during the period of time studied. For production, performance measures might be the average packaging cost per order, the average daily output capability for each product, and the average unit cost per order. For purchasing, the performance measures for the customer relationship management objectives might be the average purchasing cost for each of the items purchased and the percentage of time that reverse auctions were used during the period of time studied. Performance measures would similarly be designed for each of the key processes and their corresponding functional objectives. In this way then, firms have the capability to track their progress toward meeting each of its objectives for each of the key processes.

Assess and Improve Internal Integration of Key Supply Chain Processes

Successful supply chain management requires process coordination and collaboration internally between the firm's functional areas as well as externally, between the firm and its trading partners. Achieving process integration within the firm requires a transition from the typical functional silos to one of teamwork and cooperation across all business functions. Internal integration has been shown to provide significant benefits for the firm. In a survey of 500 U.S. organizations, interdepartmental relationships were found to result in reduced cycle times and fewer stockouts.[8] To achieve internal integration, personnel must have management support, resources, and empowerment to make meaningful organizational changes to foster the type of cooperation necessary to support the overall supply chain strategy. The formation of cross-functional teams to develop the key process objectives and accompanying performance measures is a good starting point in achieving internal process integration.

The primary enabler of integration though, is the firm's ERP system. In Chapter 6 the importance and capabilities of ERP systems was described, along with some of the various software applications or modules that are used today. ERP systems provide a view of the entire organization, enabling decision-makers within each function to have information regarding customer orders, production plans, work-in-process and finished goods inventory levels, outbound goods in transit, purchase orders, inbound goods in transit, purchased item inventories, and financial and accounting information. ERP systems thus link business processes and facilitate communication and information sharing between the firm's departments. Because the key business processes overlay each of the functional areas, the firm eventually becomes process oriented rather than functionally oriented, once ERP systems are deployed. It is this visibility of information across the organization that allows processes to become integrated within the firm.

When assessing current internal integration of key processes, firms should first develop an understanding of the **internal supply chain** of an organization. Internal supply chains can be complex, particularly if the firm has multiple divisions and global organizational structures. Thus, firms should assess the makeup of the teams used in setting process objectives and performance measures—do they include representatives from each of the organization's divisions or business units? These cross-functional teams should adequately represent the firm's internal supply chain.

Once the firm has an understanding of their internal supply chain, they can begin to assess the level of information access across the internal supply chain. Does the firm have a single, company-wide ERP system, linking all functional areas? Are all of the firm's **legacy systems** linked to their ERP system? How easy is it to extract the information needed to make effective decisions? Are **data warehouses** being used to collect data from the various divisions of the firm? Firms that are successfully integrating key business processes are using global ERP systems and data warehouses to make better, informed decisions. Data warehouses store information collected from ERP and legacy systems in one location, such that users can extract information as needed, analyze it, and use it to make decisions.

A globally linked ERP system allows the firm to use a common database from which to make product, customer, and supplier decisions. Information is captured once, reducing data input errors; information is available in real time, eliminating delays throughout the organization as information is shared; and finally, information is visible throughout the organization—all transactions taking place can be seen and accessed by everyone on the system. As the firm moves away from legacy systems and moves toward the fully integrated ERP system, as organization-wide cross-functional teams are created to link key processes to the supply chain strategy, and as process performance is monitored and improved, the firm will become more focused on managing key supply chain processes in an integrated fashion.

Develop External Supply Chain Performance Measures for the Key Processes

As was done earlier for internal performance measures, the firm should also develop external performance measures to monitor the links with trading partners in the key supply chain management processes. And, as with the creation of internal performance measures, teams composed of members from a number of primary trading partners should be created to design these measures to be consistent with the overall supply chain strategy.

Continuing with the low cost supply chain strategy example, trading partners should decide on monitoring a number of cost-oriented measures that are averaged across the member firms for each of the key supply chain processes. For the customer relationship management process, examples might include the average delivery cost, rush order cost, VMI carrying cost, finished goods safety stock costs, returned order costs, and spoilage costs. Inbound and outbound logistics costs in particular have come under much greater scrutiny during the past few years, because of sharply rising fuel costs. From 2004 to 2005, for example, diesel fuel prices increased by 33 percent in the U.S.[9] Fuel prices have thus placed increased pressure on trading partners to find cheaper ways to transport goods in a timely fashion, and this can be particularly problematic for supply chains following a low-cost strategy. External performance measures should align with internal performance measures, but may vary based on purchasing, production, distribution, customer service, and other variations across the participating firms. The topic of external performance measures is discussed further in Chapter 14.

Assess and Improve External Process Integration and Supply Chain Performance

Over time, firms eliminate poorly performing suppliers as well as unprofitable customers and try to concentrate efforts on developing beneficial relationships and strategic alliances with their remaining suppliers and customers. Building, maintaining, and strengthening these relationships is accomplished through use of external process integration. As process integration improves among supply chain partners, so too does supply chain performance. When firms have achieved a reasonably good measure of internal process integration, they are ready to move on to externally integrating key supply chain processes with trading partners.

Supply chain members must be willing to share sales and forecast information, along with information on new products, expansion plans, new processes, and new marketing campaigns in order to ultimately satisfy end-customers and maximize profits for the entire supply chain membership. Focusing on process integration will enable firms to collaborate and share this information. Again, as with internal process integration, the teams formed to design and organize process performance measures should be viewed as a key resource for external process integration. These teams can set and revise supply chain process objectives, and the type of information that must be shared to achieve the objectives. Once the performance metrics are designed for each of the processes, they can be monitored to identify lack of process integration and supply chain competitive weaknesses. Firms should thus periodically, jointly assess their levels of process performance and integration, and collaborate on methods to improve both.

Once again, the way information is communicated plays an extremely important role in external process integration. Today, connecting buyers and suppliers via the Internet is the way supply chains are becoming integrated. More generally termed **knowledge-management solutions**, Internet applications tied to desktop applications enable real-time collaboration and flow of information between supply chain partners, the ability to "see" into suppliers' and customers' operations, faster decision making, and the collection of supply chain performance metrics. "Today's competitive landscape is defined by companies that are best-in-class in managing their extended end-to-end supply chain," says Lorenzo Martinelli, executive vice-president of E2Open, a California-based provider of supply chain management software.[10]

© 1999 Ted Goff

"You have a meeting on biznow.com,
a contract to ftp, a virtual conference,
and a chat to give on smithville.edu."

Supply chain communication and Internet technologies have a number of issues to deal with including handling the flows of goods and information between companies, negotiation and execution of contracts, managing supply and demand problems, making and executing orders, and handling financial settlements, all with a high level of security. To date, though, few standards have been widely adopted. A large number of companies are becoming involved in creating Web-based collaborative infrastructures that can accommodate these communication applications using legacy systems and ERP applications. SAP, for example, is making an enterprise Web portal a central part of its knowledge management product strategy, while Microsoft is focusing its efforts on desktop applications.[11]

Extend Process Integration to Second-Tier Supply Chain Partners

As supply chain relationships become more trusting and mature, and as the supply chain software used to link supply chain partners' information systems evolves and becomes widely used and relied upon, the tendency will be to integrate processes to second-tier partners and beyond. Today, supply chain software suppliers are developing systems that integrate more easily with other applications, allowing trading partners to exchange ever-more complex or detailed information on contracts, product

e-Business Connection

Supply Chain Visibility at Solectron

California-based Solectron Corp. makes extensive use of a supply chain visibility capability from Kinaxis to better serve the needs of customers such as Massachusetts-based Teradyne, the world's largest designer and manufacturer of automatic test equipment. Solectron supplies Teradyne with contract electronics manufacturing services following Teradyne's decision in 2000 to outsource manufacturing.

The Kinaxis supply chain visibility capability, called RapidResponse, is dubbed a "glass pipeline" by Kinaxis CTO Dave Haskins. "When a company outsources manufacturing to an electronics manufacturing services company, it loses visibility to some of the supply chain links that it had before—such as purchase commitments that tier-one suppliers are placing on their tier-two suppliers, for example. As a result, the response time to answer queries from customers can deteriorate, because—compared to when manufacturing was in-house—it takes much longer to get answers back from the contract manufacturer. The RapidResponse pipeline restores that visibility," he says.

Essentially an ERP-diagnostic series of data feeds from along the supply chain—drawing together information such as inventory levels, work-in-progress, forecasts, outstanding orders, and backlogs—the collaborative relationship that RapidResponse enables between Solectron and its customers is a close one. According to Beth McKone, Solectron VP of worldwide site program management, "The information flow takes place in a moment. We're using an application to create a virtual enterprise that combines aspects of the customer and ourselves."

Take a scenario in which a supplier has an interruption in production, McKone adds, such as a fire or a major machine breakdown. "I can run a simulation, as can Teradyne, allowing us to predict what might happen. Together we can make decisions about what we're going to do about the delays," she says. "With both of us sharing the information about demand and supply, we're seeing a bigger picture—and making better decisions based on that picture."

Previously, asserts Robert Kenney, a supply chain manager for Teradyne, it took up to 4 days to aggregate incoming supply chain information—sometimes leading to erroneous assumptions. "Because of that delay, we were making the wrong decisions. We had inventory out of position within the pipeline. We couldn't see it and we couldn't move it, which caused tremendous delays to our customers." Now, just as Solectron can respond more quickly to demand changes from Teradyne, so too can Teradyne respond more quickly to its customers—in just a day, in fact, a reduction from up to 14 days beforehand.

The greater the scope of the solution—in terms of the customer-supplier linkages that Solectron embraces—the greater the resilience to supply chain shocks. To combat unforeseen component shortages, notes Kathleen Ward, Solectron's director of demand management, Solectron can divert supplies of components from one plant—and one customer contract—to another plant and another customer contract if necessary. It's not a frequent occurrence, but one that is occasionally very useful. "Of course, we do an analysis to determine the impact of shifting those materials from the originally intended customer, and make sure we have conversations with the originally intended customer—as well as the supplier—before anything happens," Ward stresses.

Source: Wheatley, M. "Reality Trumps Perfection." *Manufacturing Business Technology,* 25, no. 2 (2007): 1. Used with permission.

designs, forecasts, sales, purchases, and inventories. Using these linkages, companies can, in real time, work with suppliers and customers to compare design ideas, forecasts and order commitments, determine supply/demand mismatches, and analyze supplier performance.

Every major software developer today is trying to make its supply chain tools easier to integrate with existing systems and gather data anywhere along a firm's supply chain. One development is the **radio frequency identification tag (RFID),** discussed earlier in Chapters 7 and 9. These microchip devices can be attached to pallets or cases to relay information on the products' whereabouts as they move through the supply chain. Thus, a firm's supply chain system can access real-time inventory information and instigate a replenishment order as inventories are drawn down.

The prices of RFID tags vary greatly depending on whether they are *active* or *passive*. **Passive RFID tags** don't contain a power source and require power from a tag reader and cost perhaps $0.20 each, while **active RFID tags** draw power from an internal battery and are currently priced in the $50 range. Both are finding applications. The passive variety are placed on pallets, cases, and even units of product and are used in many warehousing environments; today they are being used by suppliers complying with Wal-Mart's requirement of RFID tags on shipments. The much more costly active tags are being used in hospitals to track the whereabouts of IV pumps, EKG carts, and other expensive mobile equipment so that they will never be misplaced. The U.S. Marines, for example, also use active tags to track container loads on international shipments. The Marines' vision is to have tags talk directly to logistics databases via network access points that will then communicate information to other locations via satellite.[12]

Prior to the development of these supply chain software applications, integrating processes beyond first-tier suppliers and customers was somewhat more difficult and time consuming. As discussed in Chapter 4, firms can develop relationships with their second-tier suppliers, and then insist that their direct suppliers use these suppliers. They can also work closely with their key direct suppliers to solve second-tier supplier problems, and help them in turn, to better manage their direct suppliers. To stay on the competitive edge, firms today must use a combination of information system linkages and old-fashioned customer and supplier teamwork to identify and manage second-tier relationships along the supply chain.

Reevaluate the Integration Model Annually

In light of the dramatic and fast-paced changes occurring with the development of supply chain communication technologies and the frequent changes occurring with new products, new suppliers, and new markets, trading partners should revisit their integration model annually, to identify changes within their supply chains and to assess the effect these changes are having on integration efforts. New suppliers may have entered the scene with better capabilities, more distribution choices, and better resources. Alternatively, perhaps the firm may be redesigning an older product, requiring different purchased components or supplier capabilities. Another possibility is the firm may be moving into a new foreign market, potentially requiring an entirely different supply chain. These examples are common and should cause firms to reevaluate their supply chain strategies, objectives, processes, performance measures, and integration levels. In what may appear to readers as this textbook's favorite company, Wal-Mart is a great example of a firm that continuously reevaluates what its many supply chains are doing and how these activities influence total costs.

Global Perspective

Wal-Mart's Drive to Green Its Supply Chains

Wal-Mart wants its suppliers to save the company money and live cleaner. The retail behemoth is partnering with the British nonprofit group Carbon Disclosure Project on a new program to audit the energy consumption and carbon emissions of seven product categories throughout their supply chains, including the manufacturing and distribution of consumer goods.

Following up on environmental projects such as its initiative to reduce packaging and sharply improve the fuel efficiency of its private truck fleet, the new effort is being pitched as something to establish the retailer's environmental bona fides. But it will definitely save them money. "One of the major reasons why companies are interested in the green supply chain and sustainability is that they realize [carbon and energy waste] is an expense," said Patrick Penfield, assistant professor of supply chain management at Syracuse University. "If you really look underneath it, it's about cost savings. It's not about saving the environment."

Wal-Mart is big enough that it may be able to save truckloads of money and help save the planet, too. Last year, the world's biggest retailer asked its 60,000 suppliers worldwide to reduce their use of packaging by 5 percent by 2008—a move the company said was equivalent to removing 667,000 metric tons of carbon dioxide from the air and 213,000 trucks from the road, and which would save Wal-Mart $3.4 billion.

Wal-Mart is also doubling the fuel economy of its trucks to save 60 million gallons of diesel fuel a year by 2015, and has pledged to make its stores more energy efficient by cutting electricity use 20 percent, or 3.5 million megawatt hours, by 2013. Andrew Winston, co-author of "Green to Gold," and founder of consulting firm Winston Eco-Strategies, said Wal-Mart's new initiative with the Carbon Disclosure Project goes beyond most companies' efforts of trying to map their own carbon footprint to extending the effort to partners throughout the supply chain. "In the larger sense, the greening of business, this is a fairly monumental effort," he said.

Wal-Mart has said its operations in the U. S. produce more than 15 million metric tons of carbon dioxide. Jim Stanway, senior director of the retailer's global supply chain initiatives, says the company has an even larger indirect impact through its suppliers, producing perhaps 200 million metric tons of carbon dioxide.

The company held a supplier conference at its Bentonville, Arkansas, headquarters on the environment and Winston, who attended, said he heard only a relatively small amount of grousing from suppliers about being pushed around by their largest customer. "Companies are realizing this is a tremendous opportunity," he said. When it comes to energy and emissions reductions in transportation, Penfield said it might be easier to extract savings than sometimes believed. The question is the number of variables: truck fuel consumption and emissions are more easily measured than the impact of warehouses.

Wal-Mart's pilot with the Carbon Disclosure Project, a Britain-based not-for-profit advocacy group of institutional investors representing a combined total of $41 trillion in assets, is just the beginning. "I think we're going to see a whole bunch of things that sort of seem obvious all throughout the economy," Winston said.

Source: Hoffman, W. "Who's Carbon-Free?" *Traffic World* (October 22, 2007): 1. Used with permission.

They are partnering now with various organizations in an effort to further green their supply chains, with the objectives of reducing carbon emissions and their associated costs. The Global Perspective profile discusses these efforts.

Obstacles to Process Integration Along the Supply Chain

A number of factors can impede external process integration along the supply chain, causing information distortion, longer cycle times, stockouts, and the **bullwhip effect**, resulting in higher overall costs and reduced customer service capabilities. Managers can identify these obstacles and take steps to eliminate them, resulting in improved profitability and competitiveness for the supply chain's members. Table 13.2 summarizes these obstacles. Each of them are discussed next.

The Silo Mentality

Too often, firms do not consider the impact of their actions on their supply chains, long-term competitiveness and profitability. An "I win, you lose" **silo mentality** can be evidenced when using the cheapest (or hungriest) suppliers, paying little attention to the needs of customers, and assigning few resources to new product and service design. Particularly with firms involved in global supply chains, silo mentalities can crop up, stemming from cultural differences. The U.K. auto firm Rover is a case in point. In the 1980s, Rover formed a partnership with Japan-based Honda to provide products for its new model program. The arrogance of Rover managers and the lack of a learning culture at Rover prevented them from realizing any benefits from the partnership. Later, when the German firm BMW bought Rover, communications with German managers and political in-fighting was even worse. The managerial problems which surfaced with Chrysler and Daimler-Benz, leading to dissolution of that partnership, were similar.[13]

Table 13.2	Obstacles to Supply Chain Integration
OBSTACLE	**DESCRIPTION**
Silo mentality	Failing to see the big picture, and acting only in regard to a single department within the firm, or a single firm within the supply chain.
Lack of supply chain visibility	The inability to easily share or retrieve trading partner information in real time, as desired by the supply chain participants.
Lack of trust	Unwillingness to work together or share information because of the fear that the other party will take advantage of them or use the information unethically.
Lack of knowledge	Lack of process and information system skills, and lack of knowledge regarding the benefits of SCM among management and other employees, within the firm and among partners.
Activities causing the bullwhip effect:	
Demand forecast updating	Using varying customer orders to create and update forecasts, production schedules, and purchase requirements.
Order batching	Making large orders for goods from suppliers on an infrequent basis to reduce order and transportation costs.
Price fluctuations	Offering price discounts to buyers, causing erratic buying patterns.
Rationing and shortage gaming	Allocating short product supplies to buyers, causing buyers to increase future orders beyond what they really need.

Eventually, lack of internal or external collaboration will create quality, cost, delivery timing, and other customer service problems that are detrimental to supply chains. In fact, Mr. Wayne Bourne, vice president of logistics and transportation at electronics retailer Best Buy, noted in an interview that the most significant obstacle to overcome in supply chain management was the silo mentality that exists in companies.[14] Internally, the silo effect can present itself among department personnel. The transportation manager, for instance, may be trying to minimize total annual transportation costs while inadvertently causing customers' safety stocks to increase due to delivery inconsistencies, leading to shortages and deteriorating customer service levels.

To overcome the silo mentality, firms must strive to align supply chain goals and their own goals and incentives. Functional decisions must be made while considering the impact on the entire firm's profits and those of the supply chain members. Performance reviews of managers should include the ability of their department to integrate processes internally and externally, and in meeting overall supply chain goals. Outside the firm, managers must work to educate suppliers and customers regarding the overall impact of their actions on their supply chains and the end-customers. This should be an important part of the supply chain partnership creation and management process. In addition, suppliers should be annually evaluated and potentially replaced if their performance vis-à-vis supply chain objectives do not improve.

Lack of Supply Chain Visibility

Lack of **information visibility** along the supply chain is also cited as a common supply chain process integration problem. In a recent survey of 1500 pharmaceutical manufacturers, only one third thought that their IT systems were providing adequate information visibility, even though most already had spent millions on ERP systems, advanced planning systems, and other technologies.[15] According to an AMR Research report, long lead times, high logistics costs, and lack of information visibility were the top three issues complicating foreign trade with Asian suppliers.[16]

If trading partners have to carve out data from their information systems and then send it to one another where it then has to be uploaded to other systems prior to the data being shared and evaluated, the extra time can mean higher inventories, higher costs, and lost end-customers in a supply chain. This is the primary problem that supply chain software producers are working to overcome today.

Most of the information visibility applications available today allow users to share data among third-party business applications having advanced event management and process integration capabilities. Keeping track of cargo containers for ocean carriers is one such area where supply chain visibility is creating big improvements for the parties involved. For every 100 incoming containers at ports, for instance, approximately 45 go out loaded, leaving revenue-generating backhauls on the table. Better supply chain visibility in this case can lead to a better match of loads and containers. International Asset Systems and Trinium Technologies has created a joint venture to create a shipping container data hub linking shipment data from inbound and outbound truckers and ocean carriers, to increase backhaul opportunities.[17]

As businesses expand their supply chains to accommodate foreign suppliers and markets, and as outsourcing of manufacturing and logistics services continues, the need to discover tools which extend real-time information to trading partners increases. "It's not good enough to just take the order," says Beth Enslow of Massachusetts-based research company Aberdeen Group. "Now you have to provide a continuous stream of information about its status, feasibility, and total cost to customers and partners throughout the world. You don't want customers receiving unexpected transportation expenses or delays in shipments—or worse, receiving them without you knowing about it."[18]

RFID technology can add tremendous real-time information visibility capabilities to supply chains. Users can determine the exact location of any product, anywhere in a supply chain, at any time. Further, RFID tags can capture more accurate, specific, and timely data than barcodes, while reducing or eliminating data collection labor time and errors. An RFID tag attached to an automobile seat or engine, for example, can be used to gather and exchange work-in-process data. When a shipment of roses drops below a safe temperature, an RFID system can alert packers to pull those cartons and send them to a closer destination. When a thief tries to break in to a shipping container, an RFID-controlled monitor can send an alert to every supply chain partner who needs the information. These are all applications of RFID technology. "When you have bad data, you make bad decisions," says Kaushal Vyas, director of product development at Georgia-based Infor, a business software provider. "You must be able to source and mine data from all the different places in real time, so you can focus on the exceptions that you need to manage in order to boost your performance."[19]

Lack of Trust

Successful process integration between trading partners requires trust, and as with the silo mentality and lack of information visibility, trust is seen as a major stumbling block in supply chain management. Trust develops over time between supply chain partners, as each participant follows through on promises made to the other businesses. Even though this sounds cliché, relationships employing trust result in win-win, or win-win-win for the participants. Boeing's 787 Dreamliner, debuted in July of 2007, was the most successful airline launch ever—it resulted in orders for 710 airplanes from 50 companies. Playing a central role in the success of this airliner were Boeing's 70 supplier-partners, who are supplying close to 70 percent of the airplane's parts and assemblies. The trust underlying the partnerships is clearly evident in the fact that Boeing also relied on these suppliers to perform detailed engineering and testing of many of the components supplied for the airliner.[20]

Unfortunately, old-fashioned company practices and purchasing habits won't change overnight. Until managers understand that it is in their firms' best interests to trust each other and collaborate, supply chain management will be an uphill battle. Organizations like the medical treatment innovator Mayo Clinic build a collaborative culture by hiring professionals with collaborative attitudes and a common set of deeply held values regarding care for patients. At computing giant IBM, CEO Sam Palmisano transformed an extremely hierarchical culture based on individualism, to one of collaboration by organizing online town meetings involving tens of thousands of IBM employees and dozens of trading partners. Collaborative projects are resulting from these meetings. IBM reinforces collaboration with "thanks awards," which are t-shirts, backpacks and other similar gear, emblazoned with the IBM logo, and given by IBM employees.[21]

While reciprocal sharing of information among supply chain partners is growing in acceptance, many companies still have a long way to go. "We are early in the cycle, maybe in the second inning," says David Smith, head of human performance practice at Accenture, a global technology services consulting firm. "Companies are beginning to attack it. Very few are getting it right." As a matter of fact, in a 2006

Accenture global survey of 250 executives, 42 percent said knowledge capture and sharing was a significant-to-severe challenge.[22]

Some useful advice for creating collaboration and trust are summed up nicely in an article appearing in *CIO* magazine, a business journal for IT and other business executives. They recommended six ways of "getting to yes."[23]

1. *Start small*—Begin by collaborating on a small scale. Pick a project that is likely to provide a quick return on investment for both sides. Once you can show the benefits of trust and collaboration move to larger projects.

2. *Look inward*—The necessary precondition for establishing trust with outside partners is establishing trust with internal constituents. Break down the barriers to internal communication and integration.

3. *Gather 'round*—The best way to build trust is to meet face-to-face, around a table. Listen to objections, find out the agendas, and spring for lunch. Then do it all over again, as people leave and as management changes.

4. *Go for the win-win*—Collaboration is a new way of doing business, where the biggest companies don't bully their partners, but instead help create an environment that optimizes business for all supply chain members.

5. *Don't give away the store*—No one has to share all of their information. Some information should remain proprietary. The simple exchange of demand, purchase, and forecast information goes a long way.

6. *Just do it*—One of the best ways to build trust is to simply start sharing information. If all goes well, success breeds trust, allowing partners to progress to bigger things.

Lack of Knowledge

Companies have been slowly moving toward collaboration and process integration for years, and it is just within the past few years that technology has caught up with this vision, enabling process integration across extended supply chains. Getting a network of firms and their employees to work together successfully requires managers to use subtle persuasion and education to get their own firms and their trading partners to do the right things. The cultural, trust, and process knowledge differences in firms are such that firms successfully managing their supply chains must spend significant time influencing and increasing the capabilities of their own employees as well as those of their trading partners.

Training of supply chain partner employees is also known as **collaborative education** and can result in more successful supply chains and higher partner returns. As technologies change, as outsourcing increases, and as supply chains are expanded to foreign sources and markets, the pressure to extend software and management training to trading partners increases. Farm and construction equipment manufacturer John Deere, for example, has established a global learning and development center specifically for training its key suppliers. Retailer J.C. Penney partners with the Retail Compliance Council to train suppliers on how best to ship products to Penney's distribution centers.[24]

Change and information sharing can be threatening to people; they may fear for their job security, particularly if outsourcing accompanies process integration. In addition, as firms construct their supply chain information infrastructure, they may find themselves with multiple ERP systems, a mainframe manufacturing application, and desktop analysis and design software, all of which need to be integrated both internally and externally. Thus, firms must realize that the people to be using the systems must be involved early on, in terms of the purchase decision, the implementation process, and in training.

For all organizations, successful supply chain management requires a regimen of on-going training. When education and training are curtailed, innovation cannot occur, and innovation fuels supply chain competitiveness. Poor decision making and other human errors can have a rippling effect in supply chains, causing loss of confidence and trust, and a magnification of the error and correction cost as it moves through the supply chain. Industry trade shows, conferences, and expos such as the Sensors Expo and Conference, the Symposium on Purchasing and Supply Chain Management, or the U Connect Conference can also be valuable sources of learning, exchanging ideas, and gathering new information about supply chain management.[25]

Activities Causing the Bullwhip Effect

As discussed in Chapter 1 of this textbook, the bullwhip effect can be a pervasive and expensive problem along the supply chain, and is caused by a number of factors that supply chain members must control. Recall that even though end-item demand may be relatively constant, forecasts of end-item and trading partner demand and the corresponding orders from suppliers as we move up the supply chain can become amplified; causing what is termed the bullwhip effect. These variations in demand cause problems with capacity planning, inventory control, and workforce and production scheduling, and ultimately result in lower levels of customer service, greater levels of safety stock, and higher total supply chain costs. In an early publication on the bullwhip effect, Dr. Hau Lee and his associates identified four major causes of the bullwhip effect.[26] These causes and the methods used to counteract them are discussed below.

Demand Forecast Updating

Whenever a buying firm places an order, the supplier uses that information as a predictor of future demand. Based on this information, suppliers update their demand forecasts and the corresponding orders placed with their own suppliers. As lead times grow between orders placed and deliveries, then safety stocks also grow and are included in any orders as they pass up the supply chain. Thus, fluctuations are magnified as orders vary from period to period, and as the review periods change, causing frequent **demand forecast updating**. These are major contributors to the bullwhip effect.

One solution to this problem is for the buyer to make their actual demand data available to their suppliers. Better yet, if all point-of-sale data is made available to the upstream tiers of suppliers, all supply chain members can then update their demand forecasts less frequently, using actual demand data. This real demand information also tends to reduce safety stocks among supply chain members, generating even less variability in supply chain orders. Thus, the importance of supply chain information visibility can again be seen.

Using the same forecasting techniques and buying practices also tends to smooth demand variabilities among supply chain members. In many cases, buyers allow some of their suppliers to observe actual demand, create a forecast, and determine the resupply schedules, a practice known as **vendor managed inventory** (discussed in Chapter 4). This practice can generally reduce inventories substantially.

Reducing the length of the supply chain can also reduce the bullwhip effect, by reducing the number of occasions where forecasts are calculated. Examples of this are Dell Computers, Amazon.com, and other firms who bypass distributors and resellers and sell directly to consumers. Firms can thus see actual end customer demand, resulting in much more stable and accurate forecasts.

Finally, reducing the lead times from order to delivery will reduce the bullwhip effect. Developing just-in-time ordering and delivery capabilities results in smaller, more frequent orders being placed and delivered, more closely matching supply to demand patterns.

Order Batching

In a typical buyer/supplier scenario, demand draws down existing inventories until a reorder point is reached wherein the buyer places an order with the supplier. Inventory levels, prior delivery performance, and the desire to order full truck loads or container loads of materials may cause orders to be placed at varying time intervals. Thus, the supplier receives an order of some magnitude, then at some indeterminate future time, another order is received from the buyer, for some quantity potentially much different in size from the prior order. This type of **order batching** amplifies demand variability, and adds to the use of safety stock, creating the bullwhip effect.

Another type of order batching can occur when salespeople need to fill end-of-quarter or end-of-year sales quotas, or when buyers desire to finish year-end budget allocations. Salespeople may generate production orders to fill future demand and buyers may make excess purchases to spend budget money. These erratic, periodic surges in consumption and production also increase the bullwhip effect. If the timing of these surges is the same for many of the firm's customers, the bullwhip effect can be severe.

As with forecast updating, information visibility and use of more frequent and smaller order sizes will tend to reduce the order batching problem. When suppliers know that large orders are occurring because of the need to spend budgeted monies, for instance, they will not revise forecasts based on this information. Further, when using automated or computer-assisted order systems, order costs are reduced, allowing firms to order more frequently. To counteract the need to order full truck loads or container loads of an item, firms can order smaller quantities of a variety of items from a supplier, or use a freight forwarder to consolidate small shipments, to avoid the high unit cost of transporting at less-than-truck load or less-than-container load quantities.

Price Fluctuations

When suppliers offer special promotions, quantity discounts, or other special pricing discounts, these price fluctuations result in significant **forward buying** activities on the part of buyers, who are stocking up to take advantage of the low price offers. Forward buying occurs between retailers and consumers, between distributors and retailers, and between manufacturers and distributors due to pricing promotions at each stage of a supply chain, all contributing to erratic buying patterns, inaccurate forecasts, and consequently the bullwhip effect. If these price discounts become commonplace, firms will stop buying when prices are undiscounted, and buy only when the discount prices are offered, even further contributing to the bullwhip effect. To deal with these surges in demand, manufacturers may have to vary capacity by scheduling overtime and undertime for employees, finding places to store stockpiles of inventory, paying more for transportation, and dealing with higher levels of inventory shrinkage as inventories are held for longer periods.

The obvious way to reduce the problems caused by fluctuating prices is to eliminate price discounting among the supply chain's members. Manufacturers can reduce forward buying by offering uniform wholesale prices to its customers. Many retailers have adopted **everyday low prices** (EDLP), while eliminating sales or promotions that cause forward buying. Similarly, buyers can negotiate with their suppliers to offer EDLP, while curtailing promotions.

Rationing and Shortage Gaming

Rationing can occur when demand exceeds a supplier's finished goods available, and in this case, the supplier may allocate product in proportion to what buyers ordered. Thus, if the supply of goods is 75 percent of the total demand, buyers would be allocated 75 percent of what they ordered. When buyers figure out the relationship between their orders and what is supplied, they tend to inflate their orders to satisfy their real needs. This strategy is known as **shortage gaming**. Of course, this further exacerbates the supply problem, as the supplier and in turn its suppliers, struggle to keep up with these higher demand levels. When, on the other hand, production capacity eventually equals demand and orders are filled completely, orders suddenly drop to less than normal levels, as the buying firms try to unload their excess inventories. This has occurred occasionally in the U.S. and elsewhere around the world, for instance, with gasoline supplies. As soon as consumers think a shortage is looming, demand suddenly increases as people top-off their tanks and otherwise try to stockpile gasoline, which itself creates a deeper shortage. When these types of shortages occur due to gaming, suppliers can no longer discern their true demand, and this can result in unnecessary additions to production capacity, warehouse space, and transportation investments.

One way to eliminate shortage gaming is for sellers to allocate short supplies based on the demand histories of its customers. In that way, customers are essentially not allowed to exaggerate orders. And once again, the sharing of capacity and inventory information between a manufacturer and its customers can also help to eliminate customers' fears regarding shortages, and eliminate gaming. Also, sharing future order plans with suppliers allows suppliers to increase capacity if needed, thus avoiding a rationing situation.

Thus, it is seen that a number of rational decisions on the part of buyers and suppliers tend to cause the bullwhip effect. When trading partners use the strategies discussed above to reduce the bullwhip effect, the growth of information sharing, collaboration, and process integration occurs along the supply chain. Firms that strive to share data, forecasts, plans, and other information can significantly reduce the bullwhip effect.

Managing Supply Chain Risk and Security

As supply chains grow to include more foreign sources and markets, there is a corresponding increase in supply chain disruptions, caused by weather and traffic delays, infrastructural problems, political problems, and fears of, or actual, unlawful or terrorist-related activities. For example in just the last few years there have been dockworker strikes along the U.S. west coast, fuel protests in the U.K., subprime mortgage losses among global financial institutions, massive recalls of Chinese toys containing lead paint, collapsing bridges, widespread fires, tsunamis, airplane crashes, car-bombs, and suicide bombs. Besides the obvious impact on life and limb, these events add elements of greater financial and customer service risk to global supply chains and the need for enhanced security to mitigate risk.

So, although lengthening supply chains may have resulted in cheaper labor and material costs, and better product quality, it has also resulted in higher security costs and greater levels of risk, potentially leading to deteriorating profit and customer service levels. Managing risk and security along the supply chain is discussed in detail below.

Managing Supply Chain Risk

In 2006, Ken Landis, senior strategy principal at Deloitte Consulting in New York, discussed the idea of **supply chain risk management** with representatives from 25 leading U.S. corporations and found that not one of them was managing supply chain risks in any disciplined, coherent manner. Supply chain risk refers to the risk of supply disruptions caused by any number of factors such as the weather, political upheavals, and customs delays. Ultimately, his suggestion was to add the job function, Chief Risk Officer, to the global firm's job structure.[27] In a recent study commissioned by Rhode Island-based commercial insurer Factory Mutual Insurance Co., the three biggest threats facing companies through 2009 according to 500 North American and European company executives were competition, supply chain disruptions, and property-related risks.[28] In yet another study completed in 2006 by global management consulting company Accenture, 73 percent of the responding companies had experienced supply chain disruptions within the past 5 years, and more than half had said the effect on customers was moderate to significant. These and other studies point to the fact that as more and more firms penetrate new and emerging markets, supply chain risk is increasing, yet little is being done to manage or reduce these risks.

A number of steps have been suggested for managing supply chain risk, and several good examples exist, which highlight successful supply chain risk management. Table 13.3 describes these risk management activities, and they are discussed here.

Increase Safety Stocks and Forward Buying

If the firm fears a supply disruption, it may choose to carry some level of safety stock to provide the desired product until a suitable substitute supply source can be

Table 13.3	Activities Used to Manage Supply Chain Risk[29]
RISK MANAGEMENT ACTIVITY	**DESCRIPTION**
Increase safety stocks and forward buying	Can be costly. A stopgap alternative.
Identify backup suppliers and logistics services	Can create ill-will with current partners; requires additional time and relationship building.
Diversify the supply base	Use of suppliers from geographically dispersed markets to minimize the impacts of disruptions.
Utilize a supply chain IT system	Collection and sharing of appropriate information with supply chain partners.
Develop a formal risk management program	Identifies potential disruptions and the appropriate responses.

found. If the purchased item is readily available from other sources, the desired level of safety stock may be relatively small. On the other hand, if the item is scarce, if the supply disruption is likely to be lengthy, or if the firm fears a continued and lengthy price increase, it may decide to purchase large quantities of product, also known as **stockpiling** or forward buying. Safety stocks and forward buying should only be viewed as temporary solutions, however, because they can both dramatically increase inventory carrying costs, particularly for firms with large numbers of purchased items.

In some cases, though, stockpiling may be viewed as the only short-term solution for managing risk. In 2006, many organizations opted to stockpile the influenza drug Tamiflu to prepare for a potential avian influenza pandemic, because shortages of the drug worldwide had already been experienced. In the U.S., for example, 300 firms along with the government itself had already been engaged in significant stockpiling by the summer of 2006. Since then, supplies of antiviral drugs have increased, and the practice of stockpiling has decreased.[30]

Identify Backup Suppliers and Logistics Services

Another very simple strategy for guaranteeing a continuous supply of purchased items and logistics services is to identify suppliers, transportation and warehousing services, and other third-party services to use in case the preferred supplier or service becomes unavailable. This topic was discussed in relation to the use of sole or single sources in Chapter 2. The disadvantage of this strategy is that it requires additional time to find and qualify sources and to build value-enhancing relationships. In addition, it may tend to damage existing supplier or logistics provider relationships. The backup source may see limited value in the relationship if they are providing only a small percentage of total demand, their price for the goods or services will likely be higher, and the existing firm may view the use of backup companies as a signal that their "piece of the pie" will continue to shrink. In addition, use of multiple sources may allow proprietary designs or technologies to be copied, creating yet additional risk.

Backup or emergency sourcing and multiple sourcing, though, may be a sound strategy in specific cases. During the 2002 U.S. west coast dockworker strikes, air-freight capacity quickly ran out, causing freight rates to skyrocket and firms unable to move freight quickly. Firms that had already entered into contracts for emergency airfreight service, though, were able to maintain operations during the port disruptions.[31] Sainsbury's, a U.K. supermarket chain, uses multiple suppliers for the many products it buys, as part of their business continuity plan, established in response to events such as the Irish Republican Army's bombing campaigns in the 1990s, the Y2K computer bug, the 2001 fuel shortage, and the foot-and-mouth disease outbreaks in the U.K. In addition, they work closely with key suppliers to assure that they too have business continuity plans.[32]

Diversify the Supply Base

Madagascar, one time provider of half of the world's vanilla supply, saw Cyclone Hudah destroy 30 percent of the country's vanilla bean vines in 2000. In addition, a political problem in Madagascar caused their primary port to be closed for many weeks in 2002. These two events caused vanilla prices to skyrocket for an extended period of time until growers in other countries could increase their capacities. Buyers with vanilla supply contracts in multiple countries were able to avoid some of this pricing problem. Eventually, the market for vanilla became more diversified, creating a situation whereby vanilla buyers today have more vanilla sources from which to select outside of Madagascar.[33] The supply of liquid natural gas, LNG, is at risk, because much of the supply of LNG comes from plants in Arabian Gulf countries and Russia. LNG consumers are thus busy trying to diversify their purchases of LNG from other countries such as Norway, Algeria, and Libya. Further, new plans for construction of LNG shipping and receiving facilities, additional LNG vessels, and LNG regasification facilities will eventually allow for diversification of LNG supply and transportation services.[34] An earthquake in Japan in 2007 halted automobile production at a number of the country's car plants because they were all buying piston rings from Riken, which had sustained damage from the earthquake.[35]

In all of the examples above, concentrating purchases with one supplier was seen as increasing supply risk, although purchasing the same or similar products from geographically dispersed suppliers could have the effect of spreading and hence reducing the risk of supply disruptions from political upheavals, weather-related disasters, and other widespread supply problems, buyers must also consider the impact of a geographically dispersed supply base on other supply chain risks. Although potentially reducing the risk associated with geographic supply disruptions, the use of suppliers in multiple countries exposes buyers to additional political, customs clearance, exchange rate, and security risks.

Utilize a Supply Chain IT System

Chapter 6 discussed the importance of a supply chain communication and information system. Today, as firms expand their supply chains, they find customs clearance requirements and paperwork to be more detailed and complicated than ever. Complying with these regulations requires information and data visibility among supply chain participants and involvement by all key supply chain partners. Accurate data transmissions, as discussed in Chapter 6, can also aid in the reduction of stock-outs and the bullwhip effect caused by forecasting and order inaccuracies, and late deliveries, which also pose significant risk and cost to supply chains.

Information systems should be designed so as to help mitigate supply chain risk. As stated by Julian Thomas, head of the supply chain advisory department at global auditing and advisory firm KPMG, "Risk should be on the agenda and as you build your systems, you need to put in place systems to monitor and evaluate risk continuously."[36] Retail farm and ranch chain Tractor Supply, headquartered in Tennessee, is a good example of a firm making use of information technologies to support flexible and quick decision making to reduce risk. For example, they use an on-demand transportation management system (TMS), an ERP system, and a voice-picking solution for their distribution centers. "In 2005, transportation capacity was really tight after Hurricane Katrina hit, but the way our TMS is configured we have the ability to escalate carrier service from low-cost to high-cost providers and sometimes when all the carriers in a market were taken, we had to take carriers in from another market," says Mike Graham, vice president of logistics at Tractor Supply. "We also have the flexibility within our DC network to react quickly if there is an event and move stores from one DC to another."[37]

Develop a Formal Risk Management Program

By far the most proactive risk management activity is to create a formal risk management plan encompassing the firm and its supply chain participants. Risk management should become an executive-level priority. Potential risks should be identified and prioritized, and appropriate responses should be designed, which will minimize the disruption to the supply chain. In addition, mechanisms should be developed to recover quickly, efficiently, with minimal damage to the firm's reputation and customer satisfaction. Finally, performance measures need to be developed to monitor the firm's ongoing risk management capabilities.

As mentioned in the opening paragraph of this section, a supply chain risk manager or director position should be created to oversee and coordinate the firm's risk management efforts. The risk manager provides guidance and support to department managers, is the interface between the firm and its trading partner risk managers, and possesses the knowledge to adequately identify, prioritize, and provide a plan to reduce risks. In 2005, Tractor Supply, mentioned earlier, developed a disaster recovery plan as part of its overall risk management strategy. One year later, their Waco, Texas, distribution center was struck by a tornado in the evening, leaving two to three inches of water standing in the facility and product scattered across the landscape for miles. By the time logistics VP Mike Graham made it to his office the next day, plans were already in place to repair the damage, and within several hours all of the customers served by the Waco distribution center were linked to other facilities. "We did not miss a delivery the following week and May is actually a peak season for us," said Mr. Graham.[38]

A small piece of advice from Richard Sharman, a partner in KPMG's risk advisory services group, for developing risk management plans is given here: "Companies almost need to ask themselves the stupid questions to think about the full spectrum of business risks, and how they would manage them." Another factor is to know who the firm is doing business with, to assure they are using an appropriate labor force, complying with product safety guidelines, and generally using practices that fit with the firm's reputation. "Know you partner. There is no substitute for that," says Brian Joseph, partner at global business consultant PricewaterhouseCoopers.[39] When outsourcing to firms in foreign locales, it is also necessary to have adequate quality controls in place, and require suppliers to report periodically to the firm to assure their products meet design requirements. And finally, according to Stuart Winn, senior vice president of New York-based Marsh Risk Consulting, risk management activities must answer the question, "What does it take for the retail brand and company to survive?"[40]

Managing Supply Chain Security

As supply chains become more global and technologically complex, so does the need to secure them. **Supply chain security management** is concerned with reducing the risk of intentionally created disruptions in supply chain operations including product and information theft and activities seeking to endanger personnel or sabotage supply chain infrastructure. The crash of Pan Am Flight 103 in Lockerbie, Scotland in 1998 not only tragically illustrated the weaknesses of airline security systems at the time, but it also exposed the dependency of entire supply chains on each member's security capabilities. Pan Am's security processes did not fail in permitting a bomb onto Flight 103—it was Malta Airlines' security system that allowed the luggage carrying the bomb into the baggage handling system.[41] In the U.S., the attacks of September 11, 2001, were a wakeup call to many businesses to begin assessing their needs for supply chain security systems. Prior to that time, most executives were aware that their operations might be vulnerable to security problems; however, most firms (as well as governments) chose to put off improving security practices.

The notion that a supply chain is only as secure as its weakest link is illustrated in the Pan Am example above. It is therefore necessary today for firms to manage not only their own security but the security practices of their supply chain partners as well. Eventually, as supply chains and relationships with trading partners mature, security management will be recognized as an important supply chain process. Supply chain security, though, is an extremely complex problem—security activities begin at the factory where goods are packaged and loaded, and then include the logistics companies transporting goods to ports, the port terminals and customs workers, the ocean carriers, the destination ports and customs workers, additional transportation companies, distribution centers and workers, and the final delivery companies. And connecting all of these participants are various information systems, which also need to be protected.

Security management collaboration should include, for example, contractual requirements for secure systems, "standards of care" for movement and storage of products as they move along the supply chain, and the use of law enforcement officials or consultants in security planning, training, and incident investigation. James G. Liddy, internationally recognized expert on security, CEO of Virginia-based security firm Liddy International, and son of famous Watergate burglar and talk-show host G. Gordon Liddy, says "Focus on what your real vulnerabilities are and have in place a safety-and-preparedness plan for all hazards. When you enhance your safety procedures and integrate them into your security you create efficiencies."[42]

Table 13.4 describes four increasing levels of supply chain security system preparedness, and these are described below.

Basic Initiatives

At the most basic level, security systems should include procedures and policies for securing offices, manufacturing plants, warehouses, and other physical facilities, and should provide security for personnel, computing systems, and freight shipments. Managers should consider use of security badges and guards, conducting background checks on applicants, using anti-virus software and passwords, and using shipment tracking technologies.

Today, cargo theft is one of the biggest problems facing global supply chains, and some of the basic security approaches can be used to reduce this threat. Loss estimates in the U.S. are tagged at $10 billion to $30 billion per year. And technology and lack of downside risk has enabled thieves to be more sophisticated and daring than ever before. Stolen goods can be moved to a warehouse, off-loaded, repackaged, re-manifested and placed on another vehicle before the theft is even discovered and reported. The

Table 13.4	Supply Chain Security System Response[43]
LEVEL OF SECURITY SYSTEM RESPONSE	**DESCRIPTION**
Basic initiatives	Physical security measures; personnel security; standard risk assessment; basic computing security; continuity plan; freight protection.
Reactive initiatives	Larger security organization; C-TPAT compliance; supply base analysis; supply continuity plan; limited training.
Proactive initiatives	Director of security; personnel with military or government experience; formal security risk assessment; advanced computing security; participation in security groups.
Advanced initiatives	Customer/supplier collaboration; learning from the past; formal security strategy; supply chain drills, simulations, exercises; emergency control center.

existence of online marketers and auction sites even further facilitates the movement and sale of stolen merchandise.[44] Wal-Mart represents a very good example of a network of complex global supply chains—their systems process more than 11 million data transfers daily, and their annual worldwide product losses top $3 billion.[45]

Corruption is another potential problem organizations must begin to manage. In a recent study of corruption, the German-designed Transparency International Corruption Index was used to determine the degree of corruption existing in a number of countries. The scale ranged from 0 (highly corrupt) to 10 (no corruption). The index combined price, business, and political corruption. The U.S. was found to have an index rating of 7.6, while Switzerland had a rating of 9.1. On the other end of the scale, the three most corrupt countries were found to be Nigeria, Malaysia, and Indonesia.[46]

Reactive Initiatives

Reactive security initiatives represent a somewhat deeper commitment to the idea of security management compared to basic initiatives, but still lack any significant efforts to organize a cohesive and firm-wide plan for security management. Many firms in this category have implemented security systems in response to the terrorist attacks of September 11, 2001. These initiatives include becoming **C-TPAT compliant**, an assessment of suppliers' security practices, developing continuity plans for various events, and implementing specific training and education programs.

C-TPAT stands for *Customs-Trade Partnership Against Terrorism*, and refers to a partnership between U.S. Customs, the International Cargo Security Council (a U.S. nonprofit association of companies and individuals involved in transportation), and Pinkerton (a global security advising company, headquartered in New Jersey), whereby companies agree to improve security in their supply chain in return for "fast lane" border crossings. This includes conducting self-assessments of the firm's and its partner facilities and updating security policies to meet C-TPAT security requirements, and then completing a C-TPAT application. U.S. Customs and Border Protection states that non-participants are six times more likely to receive a security-related container inspection at U.S. border crossings.[47]

A number of government initiatives also fall into the reactive category, and some argue that not enough is being done to assure global freight security. Mike Mitre, director of port security for the International Longshore and Warehouse Union, headquartered in San Francisco, is worried that port security is just not strong enough. Mitre explains, "Congress is heavily lobbied by large terminal operators and shippers who say anything that slows commerce or cargo delivery is not acceptable." In addition, in the U.S., some 80 percent of U.S. shipping terminals are owned and operated by foreign entities, further complicating port security.[48]

Proactive Initiatives

Proactive security management initiatives venture outside the firm to include suppliers and customers, and also include a more formalized approach to security management within the firm. Security activities occurring among firms in this category include the creation of an executive-level position such as Director of corporate security, the hiring of former military, intelligence, or law enforcement personnel with security management experience, a formal and comprehensive approach to assess the firm's exposure to security risks, the use of cyber-intrusion detection systems and other advanced information security practices, the development of freight security plans in collaboration with third-party logistics services (3PLs), and the active participation of employees in industry security associations and conferences. Home Depot, for example, uses a computer risk modeling approach to assess their supply chains' vulnerabilities and design appropriate security measures. "We look at 35 global risk elements and one of those is threat of terrorism," explains Benjamin Cook, senior manager for global trade service for Home Depot. "We use that technique to help us roll out a strategy that is most appropriate to the country we are sourcing from."[49]

Massachusetts-based life Insurance company MassMutual wanted to ensure the security of their IT system, spread across a dozen applications, including their Web site, as well as the 12 million business and individual customer accounts they managed. They named a vice-president of information security to direct their information security efforts, and they put in place a 50-person security group that included an internal consulting team with specific security item experts, an engineering team that supported firewalls, a security assurance team that analyzed security monitoring devices, and a team responsible for identity management. Finally, they purchased a security management software application to help their security team quickly assess and prioritize risks. It creates an aggregate risk score for each application and system that MassMutual uses to determine which risks need to be addressed first.[50]

Advanced Initiatives

Firms with advanced security management systems are recognized as industry leaders with respect to their security initiatives. Activities within this category include full collaboration with key suppliers and customers in developing quick recovery and continuity plans for supply chain disruptions, consideration of past security failures of other firms in developing a more comprehensive and effective security system, the design of a complete supply chain security management plan which is implemented by all key trading partners, the undertaking of exercises designed to train participants and test the resilience of the supply chain to security disruptions, and the use of an emergency control center to manage responses to unexpected supply chain disruptions.

Industry security leaders such as Michigan-based Dow Chemical see supply chain security as simply good business. As Henry Ward, director of transportation security and safety at Dow offers, "We view security as one of the steps we take to make sure we remain a reliable supplier of goods to the marketplace." Dow's efforts to improve supply chain visibility and security led to a 50 percent improvement in the time it takes to identify and resolve trade transit problems, and a 20 percent inventory reduction at receiving terminals. Dow uses RFID and a global positioning system (GPS) to track large intermodal containers as they move from North America to Asia. Dow also sees collaboration with governments and its supply chain partners as crucial to their success. "We take an integrated approach to supply chain security, which means we look at it holistically," says Ward.[51]

As described in this final section, supply chain participants are pulled from opposing objectives: one is to reduce supply chain costs and improve freight handling speed to improve competitiveness and profits; the other is to manage the risk and cost of security breaches. Unfortunately, as supply chains venture into countries in search of cheaper sources and implement practices to reduce transit times, the security risks grow. Tim Manahan, a vice-president at supply management software provider Procuri, admits, "Very few companies have effective supply chain security systems in place, either for monitoring security issues, or for reacting to problems." Managers and government representatives understand the problem much better today than 10 years ago, and hopefully, this is beginning to lead to better management of risk and security.

SUMMARY

In this chapter, the topic of integrating processes within the firm and among supply chain partners was discussed, including the steps required to achieve internal and external process integration, the advantages of doing this, and the obstacles to overcome. Process integration should be considered the primary means to achieving successful supply chain management, but it is the one thing most firms struggle with when setting out to manage their supply chains. For without the proper support, training, tools, trust, and preparedness, process integration most likely will be impossible to ever fully achieve.

The supply chain integration model provides the framework for integrating processes first within the firm, and then among trading partners, and this model served as the foundation of the chapter. The role played by performance measures in assessing and improving integration was also discussed. Finally, a discussion of supply chain risk and security management outlined the need for firms and their trading partners to collaborate in developing effective strategies for assessing the risk of supply chain disruptions, and implementing solutions.

KEY TERMS

active RFID tags, 458

bullwhip effect, 460

C-TPAT compliant, 472

collaborative education, 463

customer relationship management (CRM), 449

customer service management process, 450

data warehouses, 454

demand forecast updating, 464

demand management process, 450

everyday low prices, 466

forward buying, 465

functional silos, 449

information visibility, 461

internal supply chain, 454

key supply chain processes, 449

key trading partners, 447

knowledge-management solutions, 456

legacy systems, 454

manufacturing flow management process, 451

order batching, 465

order fulfillment process, 451

passive RFID tags, 458

point of sale information, 450

process integration, 447

product development and commercialization process, 452

radio frequency identification tag (RFID), 458

rationing, 466

returns management process, 452

shortage gaming, 466

silo mentality, 460

stockpiling, 468

supplier relationship management process, 451

supply chain risk management, 467

supply chain security management, 470

vendor managed inventory, 464

DISCUSSION QUESTIONS

1. What does *process integration* mean, and why is it difficult to achieve?

2. What makes a supplier or customer a key or primary supply chain partner? Describe why it is important to begin supply chain management efforts with only these companies.

3. What are the eight key supply chain business processes, and why are they important?

4. Is it necessary to have internal performance measures for each of the supply chain business processes? Why or why not?

5. Which should come first—internal integration or external integration? Why?

6. Why is an ERP system important for both internal and external process integration? What other IT considerations are there?

7. Think of some supply chain (external) performance measures for several of the eight key supply chain business processes, assuming the overall strategy is superior customer service.

8. What are *knowledge management solutions*, and how can they support a firm's supply chain integration efforts? Give some examples.

9. Why is lack of trust an obstacle to supply chain management? How can we overcome this obstacle?

10. How can RFID tags improve a firm's ability to manage supply chains?

11. Define the *bullwhip effect* and describe how it influences supply chain integration, or how integration affects the bullwhip effect.

12. What are some things firms must overcome to achieve supply chain process integration? What is the difference between supply chain management and supply chain process integration?

13. How can firms minimize the impact of the items listed in question 12?

14. Define the term *collaborative education* and explain what this has to do with supply chain management.

15. Describe an incidence either personally or at work, where you have been involved in shortage gaming.

16. What is the difference between *supply chain risk management* and *supply chain security management*? Which do you think is most important?

17. What types of supply chains are most likely to be affected by risk and security problems? Why?

18. List some steps firms can take to reduce supply chain risk and increase security.

INTERNET QUESTIONS

1. Go to the Institute for Supply Management Web site, www.ism.ws, and find the listing for the latest ISM Annual International Supply Management Conference. Then find the Conference Proceedings and report on a paper that was presented regarding a topic covered in this chapter.

2. Find the Web sites of several supply chain security and risk assessment firms and report on their specialties and management experience.

 INFOTRAC QUESTIONS

Access http://academic.cengage.com/infotrac to answer the following questions:

1. Search on the term "Customs-Trade Partnership against Terrorism" or C-TPAT, and write a paper on the history of C-TPAT and how it is being used today.

2. Search on the term "supply chain security problems" and write a report on several current problems and how they are being addressed.

Chapter 14

PERFORMANCE MEASUREMENT ALONG THE SUPPLY CHAIN

A metric is just a number. The question involves how to use data from the metric to diagnose processes and make improvements over time.[1]

Today, leading supply chain managers increasingly recognize that SCM is not just about reducing costs, but more importantly about enhancing business value. To that end, these leaders understand the importance of aligning the capabilities and the performance metrics of their suppliers with those of their customers.[2]

Learning Objectives

After completing this chapter, you should be able to

- Describe why firms need to measure and assess performance.
- Discuss the merits of financial and non-financial performance measures.
- List a number of traditional and world-class performance measures.
- Describe how the Balanced Scorecard and the SCOR models work.
- Describe how to design a supply chain performance measurement system.

Chapter Outline

Supply Chain Management in Action   *How HP Measures Supplier Performance*

When Hewlett-Packard began outsourcing its manufacturing facilities, it knew it had to clearly define what was expected of its suppliers. The only way to make sure product quality met requirements was by clearly defining what the metrics for measurement were. By forming a concrete set of standards regarding product technology, quality, responsiveness, delivery, cost, and environmental impact, HP has been able to weed out noncompliant suppliers, and drive performance higher in others.

Back when most of HP's manufacturing facilities were based in Western Europe and the U.S., it was easier to easier to focus solely on the quality of supplier performance. As HP increasingly outsourced its manufacturing facilities to what Bonnie Nixon-Gardiner, global program manager of supply chain social and environmental responsibility, terms the "higher risk geographies" in Asia, Eastern Europe, and Central America, that changed. The need for all aspects of supplier performance, including environmental and labor concerns, to be clearly measured and defined became a new priority.

In countries like China, where Nixon-Gardiner says more than 80 percent of HP's products are manufactured, there are government laws regulating environmental, ethical, and worker safety requirements. "But the laws on paper are not always regulated by governmental agencies to the degree or frequency that they should be, and that's a big concern for a company like HP," she says. "So that's where we've had to really step in and make sure that these things are being paid attention to and integrated into the supplier's overall management system."

Nixon-Gardiner began benchmarking the labor and environmental compliance practices of companies in other sectors, such as oil, gas, and food, just to learn "what went well, what didn't go well in these other sectors," she says. "Quite frankly, one of the real areas of concern was the metrics and clear measurements; communications about how suppliers can be successful and how they're measured. They hadn't really been developed, and I didn't feel that there were successful systems put in place nor solid decision-making methods in these areas."

The company uses a scorecard system to measure its suppliers—with responsiveness and delivery lumped in one category. In addition to quarterly business reviews, suppliers are told to expect regular on-site audits, which vary in frequency depending on what they make and how they are performing. If a supplier is deemed "high-risk" by HP, Nixon-Gardiner says they can expect up to four audits in a year. In the cases where a supplier's labor or environmental practices are cause for concern, HP performs additional audits on the supplier's management system to see if there is potential for change. "If we don't receive action within a couple of weeks," she says, "we will begin to change the business relationship. If they present a risk for us and lose, then we all lose. We're working hard to help them understand that as partners of ours, they need to increase their competencies in this space, they need to commit and they need to recognize this is the right thing to do, it's good for business," she says.

Source: Varmazis, M. "How HP Measures Supplier Performance and Compliance." *Purchasing*, 135, no. 13 (2006): 47–49. Used with permission.

Introduction

This chapter discusses the role and importance of performance measurement for both the firm and its supply chains. The old adage, "you can't improve what you don't measure" is certainly true for firms as well as their supply chains. In fact, a report by the Conference Board of Strategic Performance Management found that companies using performance measurement were more likely to achieve leadership positions in their industry and were almost twice as likely to handle a major change successfully.[3] Although several types of performance measures were discussed or suggested in earlier chapters of this textbook, firms need to develop an entire system of meaningful performance measures to become and then remain competitive, particularly when managing supply chains is one of the imperatives.

Performance measurement systems vary substantially from company to company. For example, many firms' performance measures concentrate solely on the firm's costs and profits. Although certainly important, managers must realize that making decisions while relying on cost-based or financial performance alone gives the manager no indication of the underlying causes of financial performance. Designing standards and then monitoring performance of the many activities that indirectly or directly influence financial performance can provide much better information for decision-making purposes.

Even for companies such as Wal-Mart that rely on low prices to attract customers, cost performance alone is not enough to guarantee success without assuring that products are also available when needed, and at acceptable levels of product quality. Attaining world-class competitive status requires managers to realize that making process decisions to create or purchase products and services customers want and then to distribute them in ways that will satisfy customers, requires careful monitoring of cost, quality, and customer service performance among all key supply chain trading partners. Achieving adequate performance and then continually improving on these measures, is what firms must take aim at. Using an adequate system of performance measures allows managers to pursue that vision. Unfortunately, many firms and their supply chains today are not adequately measuring process performance. According to a survey of Canadian manufacturing firms in 2006 for instance, just 50 percent of the firms had even moderately well-developed performance measurement systems.[4] In some cases, organizations are busy measuring everything in sight, and in so doing, they make poor measurements, measure the wrong things, measure things that only make the firm look good, and occasionally these actions can even prove dangerous. Managers need to realize the importance of creating a good set of performance measures, and this is the objective of this chapter.

When managing supply chains, assessing the performance of several tiers of suppliers and customers further complicates an already formidable performance measurement problem. With supply chains, the performance system must become much larger, and is complicated by a range of relationships, trust, and interactions. Performance at the end-product level depends on adequate performance among the primary trading companies along the supply chain. Thus, performance measures must be visible and communicated to all participating members of the supply chain while managers continue to collaborate to achieve results that allow all supply chain members to plan ahead and benefit. Indeed, it will most likely be the case that some member costs will be higher than otherwise would be the case, to permit supply chains to offer what end-customers want. It is only through cooperation and shared planning and benefits, that an effective supply chain-wide performance measurement system can be designed.

This chapter will discuss the basics of performance measurement including cost-based and other traditional measurements, and then move on to discuss the more effective measurement systems typical of world-class organizations. From there, the discussion will move into measuring the performance of supply chains. Finally, the Balanced Scorecard and the SCOR model methods of performance measurement that are being utilized effectively in supply chain settings will be presented and discussed.

Viewing the Supply Chain as a Competitive Force

The eventual and ultimate goal of a supply chain is to successfully deliver products and services to end-customers. Traditionally, to meet customer service requirements, firms along the supply chain would simply load their retail shelves, warehouses, and factories with finished goods. Today, though, this strategy would ultimately lead to inventory carrying costs and product prices so high that firms would no longer be competitive. For firms and their supply chains to be effective, customers along the supply chain and the end-product users must be satisfied. Thus, firms must invest time and effort understanding end-customers and supply chain partners, and then adjust or acquire supply chain competencies to satisfy the needs of these customers. To obtain the resources to accomplish these tasks, top managers must become involved, and support the firm's improvement efforts. Ultimately, well-designed performance measurement systems within each supply chain partner and integrated throughout the supply chain must be implemented to control and enhance the capabilities of these firms and thus the supply chain. Management efforts to evaluate the firm and its employees using performance measurement systems that either have no effect or adversely affect the supply chain will ultimately fail in their supply chain management efforts.

Understanding End-Customers

As discussed in Chapter 10, companies must make efforts to segment customers based on their service needs, then design a delivery network to meet the needs of those customers. In other words, instead of taking a one-size-fits-all approach to product design and delivery, firms and their supply chains need to look at each segment of the markets they serve and determine the needs of those customers. Companies must look at customer segment needs such as:

- the variety of products required;
- the quantity and delivery frequency needed;
- the service level desired;
- the product quality desired; and
- the pricing of products.

Obviously, depending on the range of customers the company and its supply chains serve, there will be multiple customer groups, a range in products desired, along with various quantities and delivery needs, product availability and response time needs, product quality demanded, and prices that customers are willing to pay. German company Henkel, for instance, known for its Duck brand duct tape, provides benefits to the customers of retailers such as Home Depot by designing, branding, and marketing household products as the result of analyzing household buying habits and trends.

Henkel uses focus groups, expert advisory panels, and a consumer hotline to capture consumer ideas. This way, they can build brand loyalty, provide benefits to their retail customers, and suggest new products to their supply chain partners.[5]

Understanding Supply Chain Partner Requirements

Once firms understand end-customer needs, the next step is determining how best their supply chains can satisfy those needs. Supply chain strategies must consider the potential trade-offs existing between the cost, quality, quantity, and service requirements mentioned above. For instance supply chain responsiveness (meeting due date, lead-time, and quantity requirements, providing high levels of customer service) can come at a cost. To achieve the desired level of responsiveness, companies along the supply chain may also have to become more responsive, potentially requiring investments in additional capacity and faster transportation. Likewise, supply chain quality or reliability (providing customers with the desired levels of product quality) may require investments in newer equipment, better technology, and higher quality materials and components among participants in the supply chain.

Conversely, increasing supply chain efficiency (enabling retailers to offer lower prices for goods) creates the need among supply chain partners to make adjustments in their production and delivery capabilities that will lower costs. This may include using slower transportation modes, buying and delivering in larger quantities, and reducing the quality of the parts and supplies purchased. Ultimately, firms within supply chains must collaborate and decide what combination of customer needs their supply chains will provide, both today and in the long term.

Adjusting Supply Chain Member Capabilities

With these capability requirements understood, supply chain members can then audit their capabilities and those of their supply chain partners to determine if what they do particularly well is consistent with the needs of the end-customers and other supply chain trading partners. Some companies may be well positioned to supply the desired levels of cost, quality, and customer service performance, although others may not be as well positioned. Matching or adjusting supply chain member capabilities with customer requirements can be a very difficult task, particularly if the communication and cooperation levels among companies are not excellent, or if companies are serving multiple supply chains and customer segments requiring a different set of capabilities.

In many cases, a dominant company within the supply chain (Wal-Mart for instance) can use their buying power to leverage demands for supplier conformance to their supply chain requirements. As customer tastes and competition change over time, supply chains can reassess and redesign their strategies for meeting customer requirements and remaining competitive. Use of the Internet for instance has become a significant part of many firms' competitive strategies, allowing firms to offer much greater product variety and convenience than ever before.

Matching supply chain capabilities to end-customer requirements means that firms and their supply chain partners must be continually reassessing their performance with respect to these changing end-customer requirements. This brings us back to the importance of performance measures and their ability to relay information regarding the performance of each member within the supply chain, along with the performance of the supply chain vis-à-vis their end-customers. Now, more than ever before, successful supply chains are those that can continue to deliver the right combination of cost, quality, and customer service as customer needs change. Weaknesses in any of these areas can mean loss of competitiveness and profits for all members along the supply chain. Today, the best supply chain performers are more responsive to customer needs, quicker to anticipate changes in the markets, and much better at controlling costs, resulting in greater supply chain profits. The next section discusses traditional performance measures.

Traditional Performance Measures

Most performance measures used by firms today continue to be the traditional cost-based and financial statistics reported to shareholders in the form of annual report, balance sheet, and income statement data. This information is relied upon by potential investors and shareholders to make stock transaction decisions, and forms the basis for many firms' performance bonuses. Unfortunately, financial statements and other cost-based information don't necessarily reflect the underlying performance of the productive systems of an organization, and as most people witnessed with companies such as Texas energy company Enron and Mississippi-based long distance phone company WorldCom a few years ago, cost and profit information can be hidden or manipulated to make performance seem far better than it really is. Enron claimed revenues of $111 billion in 2000. That year, *Fortune* magazine named Enron "America's Most Innovative Company." The following year high-profile managers left the company, Enron declared bankruptcy, their fraudulent corporate and accounting practices became public, and by 2004 it had become one of the costliest bankruptcy cases in U.S. history. Thousands of employees lost everything, executives ended up in jail, and the Arthur Andersen accounting company was dissolved.[6]

As illustrated above, decisions that are made solely to maximize current stock prices don't necessarily mean the firm is performing well or will continue to perform well into the future. Business success depends on the firm's ability to turn internal competencies into products and services that customers want, while providing desired availability, quality, and customer service levels at a reasonable price. **Financial performance measures**, although important, cannot adequately capture a firm's ability to excel in these areas.

Use of Organization Costs, Revenue, and Profitability Measures

These might at first glance seem to be useful types of performance measures, but several problems are associated with using costs, revenues, and profits to gauge a firm's performance. Windfall profits have been occurring for the past few years in the oil industry, as prices have risen due to demand increases and supply interruptions. Consequently, firms such as airline companies and other transportation companies have experienced much higher costs and reductions in profits. Similarly, many tourist destinations such as Las Vegas were hit hard after September 11, 2001, causing hotels to report much lower occupancies and profits in the following months. The profits and losses shown were not the result of something the firms did or did not do particularly well; they were caused for the most part by uncontrollable environmental conditions. Thus, changes in cost and profit statistics may not accurately reflect the true underlying capabilities of firms.

Another problem with the use of costs, revenues, or profits as performance measures is the difficulty in most cases, to attribute cost, revenue, or profit contributions to the various functional units or specific processes of the organization. Many departments and units are interdependent and share costs, equipment, labor, and revenues, making it extremely difficult to split out costs and revenues equitably. Additionally, using cost as a departmental or business unit performance measure can result in actions that actually raise costs for the organization. For example, rewarding the purchasing department for minimizing their purchasing costs might increase product return rates and warranty repair costs due to low cost but poor quality part purchases. Minimizing transportation costs might also look great on financial reports, but result in late deliveries and lower customer service levels, causing a loss of customers. Finally, the practice of allocating overhead costs based on a department's percentage of direct labor hours causes managers to waste time trying to reduce direct labor hours to reduce overhead cost allocations when today, direct labor accounts for only a small fraction of total costs. In essence, these overhead costs merely get transferred somewhere else in the firm, leaving the organization no better off, and perhaps in worse shape due to the loss of valuable labor resources.

© 2000 Ted Goff

"We need to cut down on productivity, quality and customer service to save money."

Use of Performance Standards and Variances

Establishing **standards for performance** for comparison purposes can be particularly troublesome and in some cases, even damaging to an organization. Establishing output standards like 1000 units/day or productivity standards like 10 units/labor hour establishes an ultimate goal that can drive employees and managers to do whatever it takes to reach their goals, even if it means producing shoddy work or "cooking" the books. Additionally, once goals are actually reached, there is also no further incentive to improve any further.

When standards are not reached, a **performance variance** is created, which is the difference between the standard and actual performance. When organizations hold managers up to performance standards which then create performance variances, managers can be pressured to find ways to make up these variances, resulting in decisions that may not be in the long-term best interests of the firm. Decisions such as producing to make an output quota regardless of current finished goods inventory levels, or purchasing unneeded supplies just to use up department budgets are examples of things that can happen when performance standards are applied without considering the true performance benefits to the organization. When applied at the functional level, these standards act to reinforce the idea of **functional silos**. Departments are then assessed on meeting functional standards instead of optimizing firm or supply chain performance.

Use of Firm-Wide Productivity and Utilization Measures

Firm-wide **total productivity measures** or **single factor productivity measures** such as output/(costs of labor + capital + energy + material), or output/(cost of labor), are potentially useful but have the same problems as the use of revenues, costs, and profits for performance measures. These measures, although allowing firms to view the effect of one or any number of the firm's inputs (such as the cost of labor) on the firm's outputs (such as units produced), do not allow the firm to determine the actual performance of any of the resources behind these elements. Decisions made to increase productivity may prove to actually increase a firm's costs and reduce quality or output in the long term, ultimately reducing productivity. For example, a business unit might be tempted to produce at output levels greater than demand, to increase productivity, which also increases inventories and inventory carrying costs. Or managers might be inclined to lay off workers and buy the cheapest materials to decrease input costs and thus maximize their productivity ratios, without considering the effect on the firm's quality, customer service, and employee morale. In these ways, productivity measures can prove to be damaging. Example 14.1 provides a look at calculating productivity, and the problems that can arise when making decisions based solely on productivity.

Labor and machine utilization can be shown as (actual units produced)/(standard output level) or (actual hours utilized)/(total hours available). These performance measures, when used alone, can encourage the firm once again to reduce labor levels until everyone is overworked, causing queues of work or customers to develop, morale to suffer, and quality and customer service levels to erode. Additionally, using the measures discussed above, there is a tendency to continue producing and adding to inventory just to keep machines and people busy. Less time is spent doing preventive maintenance, training, and projects that can lead to greater performance and profits in the future. Although it is obviously beneficial to meet demand and keep labor costs at optimal levels, maximizing utilization can prove to be very expensive for firms.

Thus, the emphasis on overall performance in terms of generalized criteria such as the firm's financial, output, productivity, or utilization characteristics does not tell the entire story. Although it certainly is important for firms to possess financial strength and high levels of productivity and factory utilization, these measures do not tell a detailed story of the firm's performance. Using general and internally focused measures like these do not give any clues as to specific problems that may exist, or how to go about solving the problems. Managers are left to guess at what types of actions are needed and have no way of knowing if any corrections made actually had the intended effect. What is needed is a set of detailed performance measures throughout the organization and extending to supply chain partners that are consistent with firm and supply chain strategies, allow managers to find root causes of performance failures, and finally, lead managers to problem solutions.

Example 14.1   Productivity Measures at Boehm's Ski Emporium

Bob and Marcia Boehm's company makes top-of-the-line custom snow skis for high-end ski shops as well as their own small retail shop, and employs 15 other employees. Bob has been adamant about finding a way to increase productivity, because their sales have been flat for the past two seasons. Given the information shown below, he has calculated the single factor and total productivity values as:

Labor productivity $= 1000$ skis/10,800 hours $= 0.093$ skis per labor hour

Material productivity $= 1000$ skis/$18,000 $= 0.056$ skis per dollar of materials

Lease productivity $= 1000$ skis/$24,000 $= 0.042$ skis per lease dollar

INPUTS AND OUTPUTS	LAST YEAR
Skis produced	1000
Labor hours	10,800
Materials purchased	$18,000
Lease payments	$24,000

He calculates their total productivity by multiplying the labor hours by their average wage of $17 per hour, and finds:

Total productivity $= 1000$ skis/$[10,800(\$17) + \$18,000 + \$24,000]$

$= 0.0044$ skis per dollar

So, Bob figures he can get some great improvements in productivity by finding a low-cost supplier, moving to a cheaper location, and laying-off 6 workers (reducing his workforce by 40 percent), making his new single factor productivities:

Labor productivity $= 1000$ skis/10,800(.6) hours $= 0.154$ (a 66 percent increase)

Material productivity $= 1000$ skis/$12,000 $= 0.083$ (a 48 percent increase)

Lease productivity $= 1000/\$18,000 $= 0.056$ (a 33 percent increase),

and his new total productivity:

Total productivity $= 1000$ skis/$[10,800(\$17)(.6) + \$12,000 + \$18,000]$

$= 0.0071$ skis per dollar (a whopping 61 percent increase!)

Consequently, Bob talked Marcia into making the changes for the coming year. Unfortunately, they went out of business in 6 months due to poor quality materials, a bad location, and overworked, low-morale employees.

Traditional performance measures also tend to be short-term oriented. To maximize profits next quarter, firms may expend considerable effort on delaying capital investments, selling assets, denying new project proposals, contracting out work, and leasing instead of purchasing equipment. These actions, although reducing short-term costs, can also significantly reduce a firm's ability to develop new products and remain competitive. New product research, new technology purchases, new facilities, and newly trained people all enhance the capabilities of the firm and position it to keep up with ever-changing customer requirements, but these things all initially worsen the performance measures discussed above. Without this infusion of ideas and capital expenditures though, firms will ultimately perform poorly.

On the other hand, world-class organizations realize that long-term competitive advantage is created when firms' strategies are geared toward continually meeting and exceeding customer expectations of product and service cost, quality, dependability, flexibility, and innovation. These firms realize that investments to improve the firms' capabilities in these areas will eventually bear fruit and enable the firms to be successful in the long term. Effective performance measurement systems link current operating characteristics to these long-term strategies and objectives.

World-Class Performance Measurement Systems

Businesses respond to increased competitive pressures by attempting to develop and maintain a distinctive competitive advantage, creating the need to develop effective performance measurement systems linking firm strategy to operating decisions. Performance criteria that guide a firm's decision making to achieve strategic objectives must be easy to implement, understand, and measure; they must be flexible and consistent with the firm's objectives; and they must be implemented in areas that are viewed as critical to the success of the firm. Wisconsin-based Briggs & Stratton Corp., a small engine manufacturer, has been using an enterprise-wide performance monitoring system for a number of years to help them attain the company's vision of producing low-cost, high-volume, good-quality products. More than 1500 company users from various departments view and analyze different performance metrics applicable to their side of the business. The company has saved millions of dollars, for instance, by correcting quality problems identified from monitoring warranty claims and costs.[7]

Thus, an **effective performance measurement system** should consist of the traditional financial information for external reporting purposes along with tactical-level performance criteria used to assess the firm's competitive capabilities while directing its efforts to attain other desired capabilities. Finally, a good performance measurement system should include measures of *what is important to customers*. These measures will vary by company and through time as strategic changes occur to the firm, its products, and its supply chains.

Developing World-Class Performance Measures

Creating a set of **world-class performance measures** involves the following steps:[8]

- Identify the firm's strategic objectives.
- Develop an understanding of each functional area's role and the required capabilities for achieving the strategic objectives.
- Identify internal and external trends likely to affect the firm and its performance over time.
- For each functional area, develop performance measures that will describe each area's capabilities.
- Document current performance measures and identify changes that must be implemented to improve performance.
- Assure the compatibility and strategic focus of the performance measures to be used.
- Implement the new performance system.
- Periodically reevaluate the firm's performance measurement system as competitive strategies, products, and customers change.

In this way, world-class firms can establish strategically oriented performance criteria among each of the functional areas of the firm within the categories of quality, cost, and customer service, and then revisit these measures as problems are solved, competition and customer requirements change, and as supply chain and firm strategies change. Table 14.1 lists a number of performance measures that might be used in different functional areas of the firm to satisfy objectives, enhance the value of the firm's products and services, and increase customer satisfaction. As firms become more proactive in managing their supply chains, performance measures must be incorporated into this effort. The next section discusses performance measurement in a supply chain setting.

Supply Chain Performance Measurement Systems

Performance measurement systems for supply chains must effectively link supply chain trading partners to achieve breakthrough performance in satisfying end-users. At the local or interfirm level, performance measures similar to the ones presented in Table 14.1 are required for world-class performance. In a collaborative supply chain setting, these measures must overlay the entire supply chain to assure that firms are all contributing to the supply chain strategy and the satisfaction of end-customers. In successful supply chains, members jointly agree on a supply chain performance measurement system. The focus of the system should be on value creation for end-customers, since customer satisfaction drives sales for all of the supply chain's members. Although challenging to implement, supply chains are indeed pulling it off. In a major study by the Massachusetts-based Performance Measurement Group that looked at firms and their supply chains from 1995 to 2000, the top supply chain performers were found to be leading the way in a number of areas, shown here:[9]

- High levels of responsiveness and flexibility—average supply chain performance improved by 65 percent.
- High levels of efficiency—average total supply chain management costs fell by 27 percent, and cash-to-cash cycle time fell by 18 percent.
- Use of the Internet to fundamentally alter communications among trading partners—orders placed via the Internet were quickly replacing telephone, mail, and fax orders. The Internet was also used to transmit shipment, order, and inventory status.
- Perfect order fulfillment as the new definition of reliability—perfect order fulfillment (complete, on-time, and damage-free orders) increased by 5 percent.

Thus, leading supply chains are achieving superior customer service levels at competitive prices, and their performance is improving continuously each year.

Electronics retailer Best Buy has been busy for several years now transforming its operations to allow consumer demand to drive its supply chains. Termed **demand-driven supply networks**, the idea is to design supply chains with enough flexibility to respond quickly to changes in the marketplace. One of the cornerstones of Best Buy's supply chain transformation is performance measurement. They have installed an integrated business intelligence system that provides internal users and supply chain members with visibility into its business performance, allowing users to view financial and other performance data and perform trend analyses, for example. Problems can be quickly identified and remedied to reduce costs and improve sales.[10]

Table 14.1	World-Class Performance Measures

CAPABILITY AREAS	PERFORMANCE MEASURES
Quality	1. No. of defects per unit produced and per unit purchased 2. No. of product returns per units sold 3. No. of warranty claims per units sold 4. No. of suppliers used 5. Lead time from defect detection to correction 6. No. of work centers using statistical process control 7. No. of suppliers who are quality certified 8. No. of quality awards applied for; No. of awards won
Cost	1. Scrap or spoilage losses per work center 2. Average inventory turnover 3. Average setup time 4. Employee turnover 5. Average safety stock levels 6. No. of rush orders required for meeting delivery dates 7. Downtime due to machine breakdowns
Customer Service	**Flexibility** 1. Average number of labor skills 2. Average production lot size 3. No. of customized services available 4. No. of days to process special or rush orders **Dependability** 1. Average service response time or product lead time 2. % of delivery promises kept 3. Average no. of days late per shipment 4. No. of stockouts per product 5. No. of days to process a warranty claim 6. Average no. of hours spent with customers by engineers **Innovation** 1. Annual investment in R&D 2. % of automated processes 3. No. of new product or service introductions 4. No. of process steps required per product

Supply Chain Environmental Performance

Environmental sustainability has been somewhat of a recurring theme throughout this textbook, and as consumers, governments, and business leaders begin to address the need for protecting the environment and reducing greenhouse gas emissions, the demand for products and services will change, along with regulations influencing how supply chains operate. As a result, supply chain performance must begin to include assessments of environmental performance.

Ultimately, **green supply chain management** (GSCM) is the objective of an effective supply chain environmental performance system. The reach of GSCM extends across the organization and its trading partners, and includes the processes involved in purchasing, manufacturing and materials management, distribution, and reverse logistics. GSCM should promote the sharing of environmental responsibility along the supply chain in each of these areas, such that environmentally sound practices predominate, and adverse effects to global environments are minimized.[11] U.S. retail chain Mervyns, for example, recently completed a system-wide lighting retrofit to reduce energy consumption. They partnered with Sylvania Lighting Services and Studio Three Twenty One to design and provide energy efficient lighting for their retail locations. The new system requires an average of 73 fewer lamps for each store, provides a brighter environment, and will eliminate 65 million pounds of carbon dioxide and 1.8 million milligrams of airborne mercury emissions. "We have launched a green initiative and will be looking across the organization and supply chain to see how we can improve our environmental performance and business at the same time," says Rob Lucacher, environmental and energy manager at Mervyns.[12]

The design of an effective green supply chain performance system should be discussed by all key supply chain members and be compatible with existing performance monitoring systems. As discussed in earlier chapters, the ISO 14000 environmental management standards, typically associated with one organization's environmental compliance, can be a good starting point for building a green supply chain strategy among supply chain partners. Supply chain members are all beginning to realize that green supply chains are not only becoming a requirement, but they also provide cost savings, additional profits, and cheaper prices to the supply chain members and end-product customers. For these reasons, use of environmental sustainability assessments is a concept that is gaining in popularity. Today, software is available that enables companies to analyze the **carbon footprint** of their supply chains and then evaluate design configurations and various options for reducing total carbon emissions. In many cases, this will also mean lower costs. In a recent survey, 49 percent of the companies that were actively taking steps to reduce their carbon footprint cited "good business" as the prime reason for their environmental efforts.[13]

Automaker General Motors, for example, plans to reduce its energy use worldwide by 10 percent by 2010. They use an Internet system that receives, validates, and stores energy use data, tracks billing accuracy, and allows users to monitor the usage and cost data through various tracking tools. They work with Suppliers Partnership for the Environment (a joint concern of automakers, suppliers, and the U.S. Environmental Protection Agency) that seeks to improve environmental performance while reducing cost throughout the automobile supply chains. Nissan has also recently announced their Nissan Green Program 2010, which focuses on reducing carbon dioxide emissions and exhaust emissions, and accelerating recycling efforts throughout its supply chains.[14] The Global Perspective feature profiles Office Depot's green supply chain initiatives.

Specific Supply Chain Performance Measures

To achieve the type of performance alluded to in this chapter, specific measures must be adopted by supply chain trading partners such that performance can be further aligned with supply chain objectives. A number of these are listed below.[15]

Global Perspective

Office Depot's Green Supply Chain Initiatives

For Office Depot, environmental stewardship is a multifaceted commitment encompassing all parts of the company, from the supply chain and internal operations to business and consumer markets. "Our environmental vision involves a holistic strategy to increasingly buy green, be green and sell green," said Yalmaz Siddiqui, environmental strategy advisor at Office Depot, which operated 1186 stores in North America and another 369 units around the globe as of 2006.

The chain has an array of ambitious programs in place related to its green buying and selling objectives, from buying papers from certified well-managed forests and buying greener office products for internal use to selling green products to contract and retail customers and delivering innovative green solutions to online shoppers. Its Green Book catalog, launched in six countries in five languages in 2006, included 6000 environmentally preferable products. "The catalog is designed as a communications vehicle and purchasing vehicle for our business or customers," Siddiqui said. "It has lots of pages dedicated to tips on going green."

The chain reduced electricity consumption by approximately 66 million kilowatt-hours in 2006 as a result of energy-efficiency and conservation efforts in its stores and warehouses. The reduction translated into an avoidance of more than $6.2 million in utility costs in the 1 year alone. "The results cemented our belief that being green also means saving green, in terms of dollars," Siddiqui said. "Many companies deny investment in environmental activities because they look at it only as an expense. But that's not the case. We have shown that there are investments in green technologies that deliver a strong ROI."

A number of initiatives contributed to the chain's energy reduction, including the installation of sensors to automatically turn off lighting when restrooms and break rooms are unoccupied, and high-efficiency HVAC systems. In addition, the chain completed an energy-management system upgrade that allows for tracking of energy usage and trends from a central location, setting of temperatures for all locations, identification of energy-related anomalies, and control notification by alarm when anomalies (for example, lights left on overnight) occur. The system allows corporate headquarters to get real-time data on store energy use across the nation in order to optimize energy use. "It gives us better scheduling and monitoring ability," said Ed Costa, VP construction, Office Depot. "It also gives us a lot more flexibility so that we can be more proactive with regard to energy use."

But perhaps most significant was the completion of a T5 high-output fluorescent lighting retrofit across all its stores. "While it was the combination of investments we made in lighting, HVAC and the like that provided us with the energy cost savings and greenhouse gas reduction, the T5 retrofit was the single most dramatic investment we made to deliver the environmental benefits," Siddiqui said.

On the transportation side, Office Depot has made significant improvements. The chain has been replacing its oversized diesel-powered delivery trucks with fuel-efficient, ultra-low emission Sprinter cargo vans for the past several years. It has realized additional cost and fuel-consumption savings by using a sophisticated software program for custom deliveries (it arranges routes to maximize deliveries while minimizing distance traveled and time). The same software is being used to plan the delivery of products from distribution centers.

Office Depot's efforts to green its transport fleet and distribution operations have aided its greenhouse gas reduction strategy. So has its recent membership in the Carbon Disclosure

Project. It also participates in the Business Roundtable's Climate Resolve program and the Environmental Protection Agency's (EPA) Green Power partnership, purchasing renewable energy credits (RECs) equal to 12 percent of its total electricity consumption. "Our greenhouse gas reduction strategy is a three-phase program that will continue to unfold during the next several years," Siddiqui said.

In Phase 1, the chain completed the implementation of the first round of its store efficiency and conservation efforts, finished a carbon footprint for North American operations and transportation, and purchased RECs, which it will continue to do.

In Phase 2, it will complete a carbon footprint for its European operations and look beyond the quick wins of the first round of efficiency upgrades for other opportunities.

"We will also explore investments in renewable energy infrastructure, which will likely include solar," Siddiqui said. As part of Phase 3, the chain will develop a strategy that looks more globally, setting global greenhouse gas reduction goals.

As to future environmental goals, Office Depot does not have a quantitative target. "Our goal is one of continuous improvement," Siddiqui said. "You need to look at green as a continuum and disaggregate it, breaking up environmental issues into specific program areas. Ultimately, the most effective path to sustainability is to take small steps."

Source: Wilson, M. "Office Depot's Green Rx." *Chain Store Age,* 83, no. 10 (2007): 45–46.
Reprinted by permission from *Chain Store Age,* October 2007. Copyright Lebhar-Friedman, Inc. 425 Park Ave., NY, NY 10022.

1. *Total Supply Chain Management Costs*: the costs to process orders, purchase materials, purchase energy, comply with environmental regulations, manage inventories and returns, and manage supply chain finance, planning, and information systems. Leading supply companies are spending 4-5 percent of sales on supply chain management costs, while the average company spends approximately 5-6 percent.

2. *Supply Chain Cash-to-Cash Cycle Time*: the average number of days between paying for raw materials and getting paid for product for the supply chain trading partners (calculated as inventory days of supply + days of sales outstanding − average payment period for material). This measure shows the effect of lower inventories on the speed of cash moving through firms and the supply chain. Top supply chain companies have a cash-to-cash cycle time of approximately 30 days, which is far less than the average company. These trading partners no longer view "slow-paying" as a viable strategy.

3. *Supply Chain Production Flexibility*: the average time required for supply chain members to provide an unplanned, sustainable 20 percent increase in production. The ability for the supply chain to quickly react to unexpected demand spikes while still operating within financial targets provides tremendous competitive advantage. One common supply chain practice is to maintain stocks of component parts locally for supply chain customers, to quickly respond to unexpected demand increases. Average production flexibility for best-in-class supply chains is from 1 to 2 weeks.

4. *Supply Chain Delivery Performance*: the average percentage of orders for the supply chain members that are filled on or before the requested delivery date. In the top performing supply chains, delivery dates are being met from

94-100 percent of the time. For average firms, delivery performance is approximately 70-80 percent. Updating customers on the expected delivery dates of orders is becoming a common e-service for many supply chains.

5. *Supply Chain Perfect Order Fulfillment Performance*: the average percentage of orders among supply chain members that arrive on-time, complete, and damage-free. This is quickly becoming the standard for delivery performance and represents a significant source of competitive advantage for top-performing supply chains and their member companies.

6. *Supply Chain e-Business Performance*: the average percentage of electronic orders received for all supply chain members. In 1998, just 2 percent of all firms' purchase orders were made over the Internet. By 2007, for example, office supply retailer Staples said that 90 percent of their orders came in electronically. Additionally, use of e-procurement can save up to 90 percent of the administrative costs of ordering.[16] Today, supply chain companies are investing heavily in e-based order-receipt systems, marketing strategies, and other forms of communication and research using the Internet.

7. *Supply Chain Environmental Performance*: the percentage of supply chain trading partners that have become ISO 14000 certified; the percentage of supply chain trading partners that have created a director of environmental sustainability; the average percentage of environmental goals met; the average number of policies adopted to reduce greenhouse gas emissions; and the average percentage of carbon footprints which have been offset by sound environmental practices. Although these performance indicators may certainly vary by supply chain and industry, the measures here will provide a good starting point for collaboration on supply chain environmental performance.

When combined with the world-class performance measures of Table 14.1, the measures shown above help global supply chain trading partners align themselves with supply chain strategies, creating competencies that lead to dominant positions in their markets. Perhaps most important, this type of performance has translated into approximately 75 percent higher profits when compared to the average company.[17]

The Balanced Scorecard

The **balanced scorecard** (BSC) approach to performance measurement was developed by Drs. Robert Kaplan and David Norton and representatives from a number of companies in 1992, as a way to align an organization's performance measures with its strategic plans and goals, while allowing a firm to move away from reliance on merely financial measures, thus improving managerial decision making.[18]

Also referred to as simply **scorecarding**, it has become a widely used model with some 80 percent of large U.S. businesses either using it or having previously used it and a smaller but growing percentage of European businesses using it. Many companies have reported notable successes with the use of the BSC including Mobil Oil, Tenneco, Brown & Root, AT&T, Intel, Allstate, Ernst & Young, and KPMG Peat Marwick.[19] According to Shell Canada's human resource director John Hofmeister, "It gives us better and better alignment (between all operating units) and focuses attention on what's important and on results. In addition, the group's reward structure is linked directly to the scorecard."[20] Additionally, in a survey of 1000 global members of the

Institute of Management Accountants, 61 percent of the companies using BSC reported improvements in bottom-line financial results.[21]

There are some indications though, that BSC use can be problematic, expensive, and even unsuccessful. Research from the U.S.-based benchmarking company Hackett Group indicated that although 82 percent of their company database reportedly used scorecards, only 27 percent of the systems were considered "mature." They concluded that most companies were having difficulty taking BSC from concept to reality. John McMahan, senior advisor at Hackett Group said, "Most companies get very little out of scorecards because they haven't followed the basic rules that make them effective." For example, in the U.S., the average number of measures used is a very high and often confusing 132, although Kaplan and Norton suggest use of 20 to 30 measures.[22] In addition, consultants are used in many cases to help map the organization's strategy and its effect on performance, and to assist in selecting performance measures. Further, information systems may have to be modified, sometimes at great expense, to supply the information necessary for the scorecards. Other weaknesses in the BSC include its inability to show what one's competitors are doing; exclusion of employee, supplier, and alliance partner contributions; and its reliance on top-down measures.[23]

Nevertheless, the BSC is widely used in helping organizations track performance and identify areas of weakness. Scorecarding is designed to provide managers with a formal framework for achieving a balance between nonfinancial and financial results across both short-term and long-term planning horizons. The **balanced scorecard framework** consists of four perspectives as shown in Figure 14.1:

- *Financial Perspective*—measures that address revenue and profitability growth, product mix, cost reduction, productivity, asset utilization, and investment strategies. Traditional financial measures are typically used.
- *Internal Business Process Perspective*—focuses on performance of the most critical internal business processes of the organization including quality, new product development, flexibility, innovative elements of processes, and time-based measures.
- *Customer Perspective*—measures that focus on customer requirements and satisfaction including customer satisfaction ratings, reliability and responsiveness, customer retention, new customer acquisition, customer valued attributes, and customer profitability.
- *Learning and Growth Perspective*—measures concentrating on the organization's people, systems, external environment, and including retaining and training employees, enhancing information technology and systems, employee safety and health, and environmental sustainability issues.

These perspectives are all linked together through performance measures within each of the four areas. Measurements are developed for each goal in the organization's strategic plan and include both outcome measures and the performance drivers of those outcomes. In doing this, senior managers can channel the specific set of capabilities within the organization toward achieving the firm's goals. A properly constructed scorecard should support the firm's strategy, and consist of a linked series of measures that are consistent and reinforcing. By developing suitable performance measures in each of the perspectives, firms can detect problem areas before they become significant, trace the problem to its root causes, and make improvements to alleviate the problem.

The process of developing a BSC begins with defining the firm's strategy. Once the firm's strategy is understood and agreed upon by senior managers, the next step

---

Figure 14.1 | **The Balanced Scorecard Framework[24]**

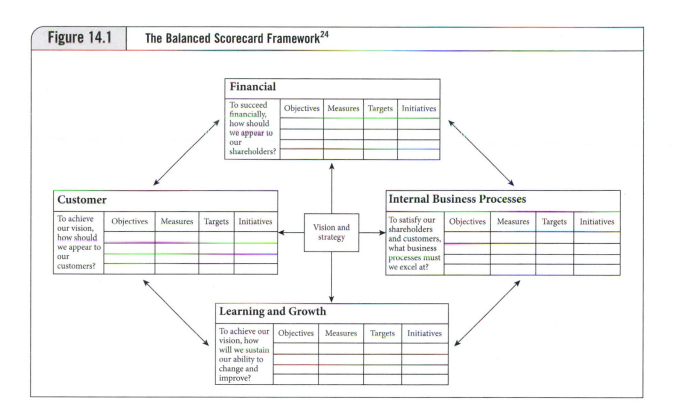

is to translate the strategy's goals into a system of relevant performance measures. Each of the four perspectives in the BSC require four to seven performance measures, resulting in a scorecard with approximately two dozen measures relating to one single strategy. As alluded to above, the potential for failure does exist if firms are not clear about what they are hoping to achieve and are not focused on ensuring that the best scorecards with the right performance measures linked to firm strategies are used.

The BSC can be also be utilized by firms in a collaborative supply chain setting by expanding the internal perspective of the scorecard to include interfunctional and partnership perspectives that characterize the supply chain. In this way, for instance, the firm's employees are motivated to view their firm's performance vis-à-vis the success of the entire supply chain. Supply chain-oriented performance measures such as the ones described earlier can thus be added to the more internally focused measures traditionally used in a balanced scorecard, to help the firm as well as their supply chains meet their objectives.

Balanced scorecards are being used in the government sector too, with many positive outcomes. One example is the U.S. Economic Development Administration (EDA). The EDA has used the BSC to help develop a world-class performance measurement system. After adoption of the BSC approach, they aligned the organization around a common set of goals, improved the quality of their investments, enhanced efficiencies, and created higher quality jobs. In 2004 they exceeded their target for new investment partners and improved their private sector investment leverage ratio by 500 percent. Today they are recognized as one of the U.S. government's top performers.[25]

Web-Based Scorecards

Today, a number of software applications are available to help design scorecards, which also link via the Web to a firm's enterprise software system. Web-based balanced scorecard applications are also sometimes referred to as **dashboards**. These enable users to retrieve data easily from enterprise resource planning (ERP) databases and also enable wide access by users at many locations, while providing desired security features. Today, dashboards are being used to track "big picture" corporate objectives as well as core process performance and more tactical, detailed data. Use of these **Web-based scorecards** provide managers to see real-time progress toward organizational milestones and help to ensure that decisions remain in sync with the firm's overall strategies.

---

e-Business Connection	*Hilton's Long Time Use of Web-Based Balanced Scorecards*

There was a time when California-based Hilton Hotels Corp. tracked performance metrics with the standard electronic spreadsheet, updated monthly. But almost 10 years ago, the hospitality company decided to automate the process to achieve better real-time measurements and instant companywide access. Hilton chose a Web-based balanced scorecard application from CorVu Corp. which tracks five key "value drivers" at its 2300 properties, including operational effectiveness, revenue maximization, customer loyalty, brand management and employee training.

Adhering to the classic graphical representation of dashboards, Hilton's scorecards gauge these drivers across three color zones: green, indicating achievement of goals; yellow for slightly below goal; and red for well below goal. Goals are set against industry standards and competitors' performances. "Our approach has been if you can't measure it, you can't manage it," said Romy Bhojwani, VP-asset management at Hilton. "And the fact that you can pull up a graphical interface and look at an individual hotel or an entire division and see performances across all those drivers is a tremendous improvement over the past."

Individual hotel managers have access to their own properties' dashboards, and can drill down to view causes of poor performance. Regional managers and higher executives can do the same by region or different Hilton brands.

According to Hilton, the system encourages a focus on both short- and long-term drivers of success; cultivates teamwork (because each hotel property is assessed as a whole); makes performance reviews more objective; and encourages sharing of best practices.

"Because many of Hilton's properties are franchised, and not owned by Hilton itself, the dashboards dramatically demonstrate to the actual property owners the value of the Hilton relationship," Bhojwani said. A separate set of dashboards measures the performance of the company's vendors.

Bhojwani said that the scorecards do more than depict performance. They also drive action. "As a result of the scorecards, it is a very fair statement to say we have operating margins across all our hotels about 300 basis points above our competitive set," he said.

Source: Hosford, C. "Hilton's Dashboards Graphically Depict Five 'Value Drivers' at Hotel Properties." *BtoB,* 91, no. 17 (2006): 18. Used with permission.

Virtually all accounting applications for example, provide BSC capabilities, including applications offered by Microsoft, SAP, IBM, and Oracle. These applications are becoming very popular. According to a 2005 survey by The Data Warehousing Institute, an education and certification organization headquartered in Washington, 74 percent of the respondents stated they used dashboards or were in the process of implementing them.[26] California-based Hilton Hotels has been using a Web-based BSC for a number of years now. A discussion of their experiences appears in the e-Business Connection feature.

The SCOR Model

One of the more recognized methods for integrating supply chains and measuring trading partner performance is use of the **Supply Chain Operations Reference (SCOR) model** developed in 1996 by supply-chain consulting firms Pittiglio Rabin Todd & McGrath and AMR Research. These firms also founded the Supply-Chain Council, a nonprofit global organization currently with a membership of approximately 1000 firms, to manage the SCOR model. Today, the Supply-Chain Council has international chapters in North America, Europe, China, Japan, Australia/New Zealand, South East Asia, Brazil, and Southern Africa.[27] Their members continuously review and update the SCOR model for use by the membership and others who can purchase the model software. The SCOR model integrates the operations of supply chain members by linking the delivery operations of the seller to the sourcing operations of the buyer, as shown in Figure 14.2.

The SCOR model is used as a supply chain management diagnostic, benchmarking, and process improvement tool by manufacturing and service firms in a variety of industries around the globe. Some of the more notable firms to have success using the SCOR model include Intel, IBM, 3M, Cisco, Siemens, and Bayer. Striving for the best telecommunications supply chain, Alcatel used SCOR metrics following the economic downturn of 2001 to measure and benchmark its performance. Major improvements were realized in delivery performance, sourcing cycle time, supply chain management cost, and inventory days of supply.[28]

The SCOR model separates supply chain operations into five process categories—plan, source, make, deliver, and return, as described below:[29]

- *PLAN*—Demand and supply planning including balancing resources with requirements; establishing/communicating plans for the supply chain;

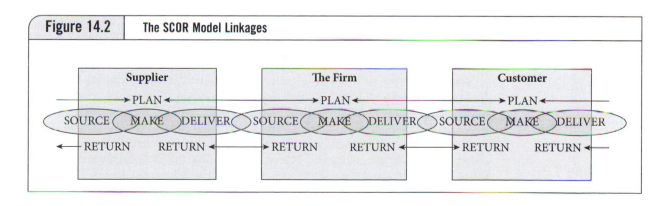

Figure 14.2 | **The SCOR Model Linkages**

management of business rules, supply chain performance, data collection, inventory, capital assets, transportation, and regulatory requirements.

- *SOURCE*—Sourcing stocked, make-to-order, and engineer-to-order products including scheduling deliveries, receiving, verifying, and transferring product, authorizing supplier payments, identifying and selecting suppliers, assessing supplier performance, managing incoming inventory and supplier agreements.
- *MAKE*—Make-to-stock, make-to-order, and engineer-to-order production execution including scheduling production activities, producing, testing, packaging, staging, and releasing product for delivery, finalizing engineering for engineer-to-order products, managing work-in-process, equipment, facilities, and the production network.
- *DELIVER*—Order, warehouse, transportation, and installation management for stocked, make-to-order, and engineer-to-order product including all order management steps from order inquiries and quotes to routing shipments and selecting carriers, warehouse management from receiving and picking to loading and shipping product, invoicing customer, managing finished product inventories and import/export requirements.
- *RETURN*—Returns of purchased materials to suppliers and receipt of finished goods returns from customers including authorizing and scheduling returns, receiving, verifying, and disposition of defective or excess products, return replacement or credit, and managing return inventories.

There are three standardized levels of process detail in the SCOR model. At Level 1, users select appropriate process categories from the SCOR configuration toolkit to represent their supply chain and select from 13 performance attributes as shown in Table 14.2. In Level 2, the SCOR processes are further described by process type. Within each process type are process categories that users specify. The process types and categories are shown in Table 14.3. In Level 3, process flow diagrams are defined with process elements or specific tasks for each of the process categories established in Level 2, showing inputs, process elements, and outputs. In addition, specific performance measures are identified for each of the process elements within the flow diagrams. Some example measures are shown in Table 14.4. Best practices can also be identified at this level. Finally, implementation of supply chain management practices within the company occurs at Level 4 and beyond.

As can be seen in the tables, implementing the SCOR model is no simple task and requires a significant investment of time and communication within the firm and among supply chain partners. But the firms who use the model find it very helpful. For instance, Mr. Joe Williams, Director of Global Productivity at Mead Johnson Nutritionals, a division of Bristol-Myers Squibb, says the SCOR model is playing a big role in helping their unit measure its supply chain performance against other companies. But getting those measurements "is a big job," he said. "SCOR is definitive in some respects and open to interpretation in others."[30]

Thus, as can be seen by the information presented here, the SCOR model is used to describe, measure, and evaluate supply chain configurations. The model is designed to enable effective communication, performance measurement, and integration of processes between supply chain members. A standardized reference model helps management focus on management issues, serving internal and external customers, and instigate improvements along the supply chain. Using the SCOR software, virtually any supply chain can be configured, evaluated, and benchmarked against best practices, leading to continuous improvements and sustainable competitive advantage for

Table 14.2	SCOR Level 1 Performance Categories and Attributes
PERFORMANCE CATEGORY	**PERFORMANCE ATTRIBUTE**
Reliability	1. Delivery performance 2. Fill rates 3. Perfect order fulfillment
Responsiveness	1. Order fulfillment lead times
Flexibility	1. Supply chain response times 2. Production flexibility
Cost	1. Supply chain management cost 2. Cost of goods sold 3. Value-added productivity 4. Warranty cost or returns processing cost
Assets	1. Cash-to-cash cycle time 2. Inventory days of supply 3. Asset turns

Table 14.3	SCOR Level 2 Process Types and Categories		
SCOR PROCESS TYPE	**CHARACTERISTICS**	**PROCESS CATEGORY**	
Planning	Processes that align expected resources to meet expected demand requirements.	P1: Plan supply chain P2: Plan source P3: Plan make P4: Plan deliver P5: Plan return	
Execution	Processes triggered by planned or actual demand that changes the state of material goods. These are Source (S1-3), Make (M1-3), Deliver (D1-3), and Return (R1-3) processes.	S1: Source stocked product S2: Source MTO product S3: Source ETO product M1: Make-to-stock M2: Make-to-order M3: Engineer-to-order	D1: Deliver stocked product D2: Deliver MTO product D3: Deliver ETO product R1: Return defective product R2: Return MRO product R3: Return excess product
Enable	Processes that prepare, maintain, or manage information or relationships on which planning and execution processes rely. Enable processes are EX1-9.	EX1: Establish and manage rules EX2: Assess performance EX3: Manage data EX4: Manage inventory EX5: Manage capital assets EX6: Manage transportation EX7: Manage supply chain configuration EX8: Manage regulatory compliance EX9: Process specific elements (align SC/financials, supplier agreements)	

Note: X = P,S,M,D,R

Table 14.4	SCOR Level 3 Performance Categories and Measures

PROCESS ELEMENT: SCHEDULE PROCESS DELIVERIES	
PERFORMANCE ATTRIBUTE CATEGORIES	**MEASURES**
Reliability	• % schedules generated within supplier's lead time • % schedules changed within supplier's lead time
Responsiveness	• Average release cycle of changes
Flexibility	• Average days per schedule change • Average days per engineering change
Cost	• Product management and planning costs as a % of product acquisitions costs
Assets	No measures identified

the supply chain's participating members. At Nabisco, for instance, the SCOR model is used to link two separate foods divisions. Its U.S. Foods Division ships to warehouses, whereas its Biscuits Division ships directly to retail outlets. They also use SCOR to see if their handling of returns is keeping up with the industry best practices.[31]

Recently, two additions have been made to the SCOR model, that are meant to help further integrate supply chains: the **Customer Chain Operations Reference model (CCOR)** and the **Design Chain Operations Reference model (DCOR)**. Part of the difficulty of using the SCOR model is that does not address the processes of sales and marketing, some aspects of service, and support processes such as human resources and technology development. In response to this, the CCOR model defines the customer part of the supply chain as the integration of Plan, Relate, Sell, Contract, Service, and Enable processes. Further, the DCOR model defines the design portion of the supply chain as the integration of Plan, Research, Design, Integrate, Amend, and Enable processes.[32]

SCORmark is the newest tool of the Supply-Chain Council, which allows member firms to benchmark performance against selected peer companies, using a benchmarking portal at the Supply-Chain Council's Web site. Benchmark data is supplied by the American Productivity and Quality Center, a Houston-based nonprofit research organization. The *SCORmark* portal removes cost barriers for members to obtain accurate and timely benchmark reports. "Our members are now able to use the defined metrics in the SCOR model to set corporate strategy and accurately analyze performance gaps," says Thomas Phelps, the Supply-Chain Council's chairman.[33]

SUMMARY

Measuring the performance of companies and their supply chains is critical for identifying underlying problems and keeping end-customers satisfied in today's highly competitive, rapidly changing marketplaces. Unfortunately, many firms have adopted performance measurement systems that measure the wrong things and are thus finding it difficult to achieve strategic goals, and align their goals with those of the other supply chain members and the supply chain as a whole. Good performance measures allow firms to improve processes and can turn mediocre supply chains into world-class supply chains that benefit all of its members.

Financial performance, although important to shareholders, is argued to provide too little information regarding the firm's ability to provide products and services that satisfy customers. Thus, use of measures that say something about the firm's product quality, productivity, flexibility, and customer service capabilities have begun to be used successfully in many organizations. World-class organizations realize how important it is to align strategies with the performance of their people and processes, and performance measurement systems give these firms a means for directing efforts and firm capabilities toward what the firm is trying to do over the long haul—meet strategic objectives and satisfy customers.

As was discussed throughout the chapter, performance measurement systems should be a mix of financial, nonfinancial, quantitative, qualitative, process-oriented, environmentally-oriented, and customer-oriented measures that effectively link the actions of the firm to the strategies defined by the firm's executive managers. Firms trying to manage their supply chains have an added layer of performance measurement requirements—measures must be added that link the operations of member firms as well as linking the actions of the firms to the competitive strategies of the supply chain. Several performance measurement models were presented and discussed in the chapter which have been successfully used in supply chains to monitor and link supply chain members' performance—namely the Balanced Scorecard and the Supply Chain Operations Reference models.

KEY TERMS

balanced scorecard, 491

balanced scorecard framework, 492

carbon footprint, 488

customer chain operations reference model (CCOR), 498

dashboards, 494

demand-driven supply networks, 486

design chain operations reference model (DCOR), 498

effective performance measurement system, 485

environmental sustainability, 487

financial performance measures, 481

functional silos, 483

green supply chain management, 488

performance variance, 482

scorecarding, 491

single factor productivity measures, 483

standards for performance, 482

supply chain operations reference (SCOR) model, 495

total productivity measures, 483

Web-based scorecards, 494

world-class performance measures, 485

DISCUSSION QUESTIONS

1. Do you think there is a relationship between performance measurement and a firm's competitiveness and profitability? Explain.

2. What do customers have to do with good performance measures?

3. How should performance measures be viewed from a supply chain perspective?

4. In building supply chain competencies, what are the trade offs that must be considered?

5. What risk do managers take when they view their firm's performance solely in financial terms?

6. List some of the traditional performance measures and describe their value in today's competitive climate.

7. Discuss the use of performance standards and performance variances. Do schools and universities use them? How can they be damaging to the organization?

8. What is the difference between a *total productivity measure* and a *single-factor productivity measure*? Provide an example.

9. List some single-factor and total productivity measures for a restaurant; a quick-change oil garage; and an overnight delivery service.

10. **Problem:** Cindy Jo's Hair Salon is concerned about their rising costs of supplies, energy, and labor, so they are considering investing in better equipment, which hopefully will reduce the time required to perform most hair styles as well as resulting in better perceived quality by their customers. They predict that the added investment will increase output levels as well as reduce energy costs, because some of the new equipment (hair dryers) use less electricity. Using the following information, determine the current and expected single-factor and total productivity measures. What other items should be considered, before making this capital investment? Do you think the increase in output will overcome the capital costs?

INPUTS AND OUTPUTS	CURRENT (THIS YEAR)	EXPECTED (NEXT YEAR)
Hairstyles per week	250	300
Labor costs per week	$960	$1010
Energy costs per week	$400	$350
Material costs per week	$300	$325
Capital investment	$0	$12,000

11. What are the advantages and disadvantages of using labor utilization as a performance measure? Do these same arguments apply to machine utilization?

12. How could you increase labor productivity without increasing labor utilization?

13. Using the formulas provided for utilization, calculate the utilization of your classroom.

14. What do you think a good labor utilization would be for a factory and a restaurant?

15. How do world-class performance measures differ from financial performance measures?

16. Using the steps suggested for developing performance measures, create several world-class performance measures for a hotel's front-desk area; maintenance department; room service personnel.

17. How should a firm extend their performance measures to include other supply chain members?

18. What are *demand-driven supply networks* and what role do performance measures play in these networks?

19. Why should supply chains begin using green performance measures? Provide some examples of green supply chain performance measures.

20. What is a *carbon footprint* and how can firms reduce theirs?

21. What is *perfect order fulfillment*? *Cash-to-cash cycle time*?

22. Describe the four perspectives of the Balanced Scorecard. How is this model different from a set of world-class performance measures?

23. What are the steps in developing a Balanced Scorecard?

24. How is a scorecard different from a dashboard?

25. What are the five process categories of the SCOR model and which one do you think is most important?

26. Describe what happens as a firm progresses through the three standardized levels of process detail in the SCOR model.

27. Which model do you think is best suited to measure supply chain performance—the Balanced Scorecard or the SCOR? Why?

INTERNET QUESTIONS

1. Go to the U.S. Bureau of Labor Statistics on the Internet at www.bls.gov, and report on the labor and total productivity of the U.S. and of other countries listed. How does the U.S. stack up?

2. Go to www.economagic.com and look at utilization numbers for U.S. manufacturers. What is it now? What have the trends been for the past 10 years?

3. Go to the Ritz-Carlton Web site (www.ritzcarlton.com) and see if you can find performance measures that are used in the company.

INFOTRAC QUESTIONS
Access http://academic.cengage.com/infotrac to answer the following questions:

1. Find current examples of firms that are using Balanced Scorecards and the SCOR model and report on their success.

2. What are the current environmental performance issues in your area? Discuss the companies that are performing well regarding these issues.

Appendix 1
Areas Under the Normal Curve

This table gives the area under the curve to the left of x, for various Z scores, or number of standard deviations from the mean. For example, in the figure, if $Z = 1.96$, the value .97500 found in the body of the table is the total shaded area to the left of x.

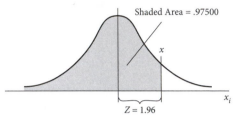

Shaded Area = .97500

x

x_i

$Z = 1.96$

Z	.00	.01	.02	.03	.04	.05	.06	.07	.08	.09
.0	.50000	.50399	.50798	.51197	.51595	.51994	.52392	.52790	.53188	.53586
.1	.53983	.54380	.54776	.55172	.55567	.55962	.56356	.56749	.57142	.57535
.2	.57926	.58317	.58706	.59095	.59483	.59871	.60257	.60642	.61026	.61409
.3	.61791	.62172	.62552	.62930	.63307	.63683	.64058	.64431	.64803	.65173
.4	.65542	.65910	.66276	.66640	.67003	.67364	.67724	.68082	.68439	.68793
.5	.69146	.69497	.69847	.70194	.70540	.70884	.71226	.71566	.71904	.72240
.6	.72575	.72907	.73237	.73536	.73891	.74215	.74537	.74857	.75175	.75490
.7	.75804	.76115	.76424	.76730	.77035	.77337	.77637	.77935	.78230	.78524
.8	.78814	.79103	.79389	.79673	.79955	.80234	.80511	.80785	.81057	.81327
.9	.81594	.81859	.82121	.82381	.82639	.82894	.83147	.83398	.83646	.83891
1.1	.86433	.86650	.86864	.87076	.87286	.87493	.87698	.87900	.88100	.88298
1.2	.88493	.88686	.88877	.89065	.89251	.89435	.89617	.89796	.89973	.90147
1.3	.90320	.90490	.90658	.90824	.90988	.91149	.91309	.91466	.91621	.91774
1.4	.91924	.92073	.92220	.92364	.92507	.92647	.92785	.92922	.93056	.93189
1.5	.93319	.93448	.93574	.93699	.93822	.93943	.94062	.94179	.94295	.94408
1.6	.94520	.94630	.94738	.94845	.94950	.95053	.95154	.95254	.95352	.95449
1.7	.95543	.95637	.95728	.95818	.95907	.95994	.96080	.96164	.96246	.96327
1.8	.96407	.96485	.96562	.96638	.96712	.96784	.96856	.96926	.96995	.97062
1.9	.97128	.97193	.97257	.97320	.97381	.97441	.97500	.97558	.97615	.97670
2.0	.97725	.97784	.97831	.97882	.97932	.97982	.98030	.98077	.98124	.98169
2.1	.98214	.98257	.98300	.98341	.98382	.98422	.98461	.98500	.98537	.98574
2.2	.98610	.98645	.98679	.98713	.98745	.98778	.98809	.98840	.98870	.98899
2.3	.98928	.98956	.98983	.99010	.99036	.99061	.99086	.99111	.99134	.99158
2.4	.99180	.99202	.99224	.99245	.99266	.99286	.99305	.99324	.99343	.99361
2.5	.99379	.99396	.99413	.99430	.99446	.99461	.99477	.99492	.99506	.99520
2.6	.99534	.99547	.99560	.99573	.99585	.99598	.99606	.99621	.99632	.99643
2.7	.99653	.99664	.99674	.99683	.99693	.99702	.99711	.99720	.99728	.99736
2.8	.99744	.99752	.99760	.99767	.99774	.99781	.99788	.99795	.99801	.99807
2.9	.99813	.99819	.99825	.99831	.99836	.99841	.99846	.99851	.99856	.99861
3.0	.99865	.99869	.99874	.99878	.99882	.99886	.99889	.99893	.99896	.99900
3.1	.99903	.99906	.99910	.99913	.99916	.99918	.99921	.99924	.99926	.99929
3.2	.99931	.99934	.99936	.99938	.99940	.99942	.99944	.99946	.99948	.99950
3.3	.99952	.99953	.99955	.99957	.99958	.99960	.99961	.99962	.99964	.99965
3.4	.99966	.99968	.99969	.99970	.99971	.99972	.99973	.99974	.99975	.99976
3.5	.99977	.99978	.99978	.99979	.99980	.99981	.99981	.99982	.99983	.99983
3.6	.99984	.99985	.99985	.99986	.99986	.99987	.99987	.99988	.99988	.99989
3.7	.99989	.99990	.99990	.99990	.99991	.99991	.99992	.99992	.99992	.99992
3.8	.99993	.99993	.99993	.99994	.99994	.99994	.99994	.99995	.99995	.99995
3.9	.99995	.99995	.99996	.99996	.99996	.99996	.99996	.99996	.99997	.99997

Appendix 2
Answers to Selected End-of-Chapter Problems

Chapter 2

1. 8%
3. 5 times
5. a. 5,500 units, $69,000
   b. buy, $4,000
   c. make, $2,000

Chapter 3

1. The weighted score is 89. Supplier is classified as a Certified Vendor.

Chapter 4

23. 50,000 second-tier suppliers

Chapter 5

2. a. 72,567
   b. 71,980
   C. 71,058

Chapter 6

1. a. Chase production strategy

Month	Jan	Feb	Mar	Apr	May	Jun
Demand	2000	3000	5000	6000	6000	2000
Production	2000	3000	5000	6000	6000	2000
Ending inventory	0	0	0	0	0	0
Workforce	20	30	50	60	60	20

1. b. Level production strategy

Month	Jan	Feb	Mar	Apr	May	Jun
Demand	2000	3000	5000	6000	6000	2000
Production	4000	4000	4000	4000	4000	4000
Ending inventory	2000	3000	2000	0	−2000	0
Workforce	40	40	40	40	40	40

Note: −2000 indicates backlog of 2000 in May

3. ATP: D

Week	1	2	3	4	5	6	7	8
Model B								
MPS BI = 20	20	0	20	20	0	20	20	20
Committed customer orders	10	10	10	10	10	0	0	10
ATP:D	20	0	10	0	0	20	20	10

Chapter 7

1. 13.7 times
3. EOQ = 26.18615 (rounded to 5 decimal places)
   Annual holding cost = annual order cost = $11,456.44
   Total annual inventory cost = $3,022,912.88 (including product cost)

7. Safety stock = 117.6 units, statistical reorder point = 767.6 units
9. Safety stock = 1,470 units, statistical reorder point = 4,470 units

Chapter 8

2. $T \approx 3$.
3. a. DPMO = 23,214 per million rentals.
   b. slightly less than 3.5
4. b. $\overline{\overline{X}} = 99.2$ and $R = 8.4$
   c. $UCL_x = 105.3$, $LCL_x = 93.1$, $UCL_R = 19.2$, $LCL_R = 0$
6. a. $\overline{P} = .1167$
   b. $\sigma_P = .1015$
   c. UCL = 0.42; LCL = 0.

Chapter 9

14. $S_2 = 12,728$ units total for the 3 warehouses; and 7348 units total for one warehouse.

Chapter 10

9. $NPV_A = \$2,639$; $NPV_B = \$2,362$; $NPV_C = \$3,018$

Chapter 11

2. Site A has the highest total weighted score of 84.5 and is the selected site.

Chapter 12

2. 5545 m/day; then put Depts. 4 and 5 closer together (switch 5 and 8); new distance = 3805 m/day.
3. 19 points; try switching Depts. 5 and 8.
4. 2 full-time and 3 part-time workers to fill the requirements.
6. Probability = 0.7
7. $L_s = 1.5$ customers; $L_q = 0.9$ customer
8. $P_0 = 1/(1+.6+.18(1.43)) = 0.538$; $L_q = .538 (.36(.3)/2(.7^2))$
   $= .059$ customer

Chapter 14

10. Current total productivity = 250/$1660 = 0.151 haircuts/dollar
    Expected total productivity = 300/$1685 = 0.178 haircuts/dollar (an 18% increase)

Glossary

A

80/20 rule Originates from Pareto theory, which suggests that most of a firm's problem "events" (80%) are accounted for by just a few (20%) of the problems. Can be applied to other areas, too, like ABC inventory control, which says that 80 percent of the inventory dollars come from 20 percent of the inventory items.

ABC inventory control system A useful technique for determining which inventories should be managed more closely and which others should not (A-items are most important).

ABC inventory matrix Used to identify whether a firm's physical inventory matches its inventory usage. It is derived by plotting an ABC analysis based on inventory usage classification on the vertical axis and an ABC analysis based on physical inventory classification on the horizontal axis.

acceptance sampling A statistical screening technique that can be used to determine whether or not a shipment will be accepted, returned to the supplier, or used for billback purposes when defects are fixed or units are eliminated by the buyer.

active RFID tags An RFID tag that is equipped with an onboard power supply to power the integrated circuits and broadcast its signal to the reader.

aggregate production plan (APP) A long-range production plan; it sets the aggregate output rate, workforce size, utilization, inventory, and backlog levels for a plant.

air carriers One of the five modes of transportation (airliners).

airline security Protecting airlines against terrorist attacks and other illegal activities.

analytic SRM This allows the company to analyze the complete supplier base.

application service providers Companies that offer Web site services for a fee, such as self-serve reverse auction Web sites.

applistructure A term used to describe the merger of enterprise application and infrastructure technology.

arrival pattern The frequency with which customers arrive at a business.

Association of Southeast Asian Nations (ASEAN) An economic and geo-political organization created in 1967 and today comprises the following countries in the Southeast Asian region: Brunei, Cambodia, Indonesia, Laos, Malaysia, Myanmar, the Philippines, Singapore, Thailand, and Vietnam.

The primary objective of ASEAN is to promote economic, social, and cultural development of the region through cooperative programs.

assignable variations These are process variations that can be traced to a specific cause. Assignable variations are created by causes that can be identified and eliminated and thus become the objective of statistical process control efforts.

attribute data Yes/no kinds of data. These indicate the presence of some attribute such as color, satisfaction, workability, or beauty (for instance, determining whether or not a car was painted the right color, if a customer liked the meal, if the light bulb worked, or if the dress was pretty).

automation Transactional processes between an organization and its suppliers.

available-to-promise (ATP) quantity The uncommitted portion of a firm's planned production. It is used to promise new customer orders.

B

backsourcing Bringing back in-house some activities which had been previously outsourced. Also called insourcing.

backward vertical integration This term refers to acquiring upstream suppliers.

balanced scorecard A management system developed in the early 1990s by Robert Kaplan and David Norton that helps companies to continually refine their vision and strategy. The balanced scorecard uses a set of measures to provide feedback on internal business performance in order to continually improve strategic performance.

balanced scorecard framework Refers to the method used to complete the balanced scorecard (the types of data used).

balking Refusing to join the queue once it is seen how long it is.

barter The complete exchange of goods and/or services of equal value without the exchange of currency. The seller can either consume the goods and/or services or resell the items.

Baumol's disease For most services, automation can be a troublesome issue, and the labor content per unit of output can be quite high relative to manufactured goods. These two things can lead to a declining productivity growth rate as a nation's economy becomes less manufacturing-oriented and more service-oriented.

benchmarking The practice of copying what other businesses do best; studying how things are done well in other firms to potentially make use of the same methods.

best-of-breed solution Picks the best application or module for each individual function when implementing an ERP system.

bid bonds Bonds posted by bidders to ensure that the successful bidder will fulfill the contract as stated.

bill of materials (BOM) An engineering document that shows an inclusive listing of all component parts and assemblies making up the final product.

billback penalty A fee charged back to the supplier for services or products not received by the customer.

blank check purchase order This is a small value purchase order with a signed blank check attached, usually at the bottom of the purchase order.

blanket order release A form used to release a specific quantity against a pre-negotiated blanket purchase order.

blanket purchase order A purchase order that covers a variety of items and is negotiated for repeated supply over a fixed time period, such as quarterly or yearly.

breakbulk When large quantity shipments are broken down so that items can be combined into specific customer orders, and then shipped out.

breakeven analysis A technique that uses the fixed and variable costs to determine the quantity where the total costs are equal between two or more alternatives. It is a handy tool for computing the cost-effectiveness of sourcing decisions, when cost is the most important criterion. Breakeven occurs when revenues equal fixed plus variable costs. Can also refer to when one cost curve intersects another.

breakeven model See breakeven analysis.

bullwhip effect A term referring to ineffective communication between buyers and suppliers and infrequent delivery of materials, combined with production based on poor forecasts along a supply chain that results in either too little or too much inventory at various points of storage and consumption. Simply, it causes an amplification of the variation in the demand pattern along the supply chain.

business cycle Alternating periods of expansion and contraction in economic activity.

business clusters According to Dr. Michael Porter, "clusters are geographic concentrations of interconnected companies and institutions in a particular field. Clusters encompass an array of linked industries and other entities important to competition."

business process reengineering (BPR) This seeks to create a systematic, automated approach to change management through assessments of current processes, design of better processes using modeling techniques, implementation of the new processes, and continuing performance assessments.

Buy American Act It mandates U.S. government purchases and third-party purchases that utilize federal funds to buy domestically produced goods, if the price differential between the domestic product and an identical foreign-sourced product does not exceed a certain percentage amount.

C

C-charts A statistical process control technique that is used to monitor the total number of defects per unit.

C-TPAT compliant An assessment of suppliers' security practices, developing continuity plans for various events, and implementing specific training and education programs.

call centers or **customer contact centers** Customer service departments that integrate all of the methods customers can use to contact a business, including telephone, mail, comment cards, email, and Web site messages and chat rooms.

capacity This refers to a firm's labor and machine resources.

capacity planning A hierarchical planning process that is used to determine the capacity needed for a specific production level.

capacity requirements planning (CRP) A short-range capacity planning technique that is used to check the feasibility of the material requirements plan.

capacity utilization A ratio equal to (capacity used/capacity available) per period; used to indicate the level at which the firm utilizes its available capacity.

carbon footprint A firm's or supply chain's total carbon emissions.

carbon-neutral When a firm can offset the carbon footprint of its operations, by planting trees for instance.

cause-and-effect diagrams (also called **fishbone diagrams** or **Ishikawa diagrams**) This can be used to aid in brainstorming and isolating the causes of a problem. Typically there are four causes of problems (the 4-Ms).

cause-and-effect forecasting This assumes that one or more factors (independent variables) are related to demand and, therefore, can be used to predict future demand.

centralized–decentralized purchasing structure A hybrid purchasing structure that is centralized at the corporate level, but decentralized at the individual business unit level.

centralized purchasing A single purchasing department, usually located at the firm's corporate office, makes all the purchasing decisions for the entire corporation.

change management An organized approach to manage the change from the current state to the desired state.

channel equity The value for a firm embodied in its distribution channel.

channel integration Collaborating with, or taking over suppliers and customers (vertical channel integration); or doing the same with competitors (horizontal channel integration).

chase demand strategy This strategy is used when the amount of capacity varies with demand. See also chase production strategy.

chase production strategy A production strategy that produces to match the sales quantity during each production period.

check sheet A sheet listing a number of potential problems which receive a check mark every time the problem occurs.

Civil Aeronautic Act of 1938 Promoted the development of the air transportation system, air safety, and airline efficiency by establishing the Civil Aeronautics Board to oversee market entry, establish routes with appropriate levels of competition, develop regional feeder airlines, and establish reasonable rates. The Civil Aeronautics Administration was also established to regulate air safety.

class rates These are transportation rates based on the particular class of the product transported—some products have higher published class rates than others.

clickstream The things that a specific customer clicks on, when visiting a Web site.

closed-loop MRP An MRP-based manufacturing planning and control system that incorporates the aggregate production plan, the master production schedule, the material requirements plan, and the capacity requirements plan.

closeness desirability rating A scale used to rate how desirable it is to have two departments close together. The objective is to design a layout that maximizes the desirability rating for the entire office.

co-managed inventories A somewhat more collaborative form of VMI. Can also refer to JIT II.

co-sourcing Co-sourcing refers to the sharing of a process or function between internal staff and an external supplier. Also referred to as **selective sourcing,** or partial outsourcing.

coal slurry Pulverized coal that is suspended in water.

collaboration Working together with suppliers and customers on various activities.

collaborative education Training of supply chain partner employees.

collaborative negotiations Also referred to as **integrative negotiations.** Both sides work together to maximize the joint outcome, or to create a win-win result.

collaborative planning, forecasting, and replenishment (CPFR) According to the Voluntary Interindustry Commerce Standards (VICS) Association, "Collaborative Planning, Forecasting and Replenishment (CPFR®) is a business practice that combines the intelligence of multiple trading partners in the planning and fulfillment of customer demand. CPFR links sales and marketing best practices, such as category management, to supply chain planning and execution processes to increase availability while reducing inventory, transportation and logistics costs."

collaborative relationships Supply chain companies work together, creating collaborative relationships, or win-win relationships.

collaborative transportation management Logistics providers and shippers working together and sharing forecasting, planning, and replenishment information to optimize transportation vehicle usage.

commodity rates Rates that apply to minimum quantities of specified products that are shipped between two specified locations.

common carriers Transportation providers that offer services to all shippers at published rates, between designated locations.

Common Market of Eastern and Southern Africa (COMESA) COMESA is a customs union established to foster economic growth among the member countries of Angola, Burundi, Comoros, Entrea, Ethiopia, Kenya, Lesotho, Malawi, Mauritius, Rwanda, Sudan, Swaziland, Tanzania, Uganda, Zaire, Zambia, and Zimbabwe.

competitive bidding A process whereby suppliers offer bid prices to buyers, to get business. The purchase contract is usually awarded to the *lowest priced bidder,* determined to be a responsive and responsible supplier by the buyer.

concurrent engineering Designing the manufacturing process or service delivery system simultaneously with the design of the product.

consolidation warehouses Warehouses that collect large numbers of LTL shipments from nearby regional sources of supply, then deliver in TL or CL quantities to a manufacturer.

consumer's risk When a buyer accepts a shipment of poor-quality units because the sample *did* meet the acceptance standard, this is termed consumer's risk and results in a type-II error.

consumer survey forecast A questionnaire is developed that seeks input from customers on important issues such as future buying habits, new product ideas, and opinions about existing products. The survey is administered through telephone, mail, Internet, or personal interviews. Data collected from the survey are analyzed using statistical tools and judgments, to derive a set of meaningful results.

container-on-flatcar (COFC) One form of intermodal transportation; standardized shipping containers are transported via rail flatcar, and can also be placed on a truck chassis and on an ocean-going container ship.

continuous improvement Constantly seeking improvements in all processes. The cornerstone of TQM and Six Sigma quality efforts.

continuous review system An inventory management system where the physical inventory levels are counted on a continuous or daily basis.

contract carriers These are for-hire carriers like common carriers; however, they are not bound to serve the general public.

Contracts for the International Sale of Goods (CISG) A set of rules established by the United Nations to govern the international transactions in goods.

contributor factory It plays a greater strategic role than a server factory by getting involved in product development and engineering, production planning, making critical procurement decisions, and developing suppliers.

control charts These monitor process variabilities, and then collect and plot sample measurements of the process over time. The means of these sample measures are plotted on the control charts.

corporate purchasing cards A credit card issued to authorized employees to purchase goods, usually small value purchases, directly from suppliers without the need to go through the purchasing department.

cost-of-service pricing It is used when carriers desire to establish prices that vary based on their fixed and variable costs.

cost leadership strategy This requires a large capital investment in automated, state-of-the-art equipment, significant efforts in the areas of controlling and reducing costs, doing things right the first time, standardizing services, and aiming marketing efforts at cost-conscious consumers.

counterpurchase It is a trade arrangement whereby the original exporter either buys or finds a buyer to purchase a specified amount of unrelated goods and/or services from the original importer.

countertrade Global sourcing may involve countertrade, in which goods and/or services of domestic firms are exchanged for goods and/or services of equal value or in combination with currency from foreign firms. This type of arrangement is sometimes used by countries where there is a shortage of hard currency or as a means to acquire technologies.

critical-to-quality (CTQ) characteristics Identify customers and their service or product requirements critical to achieving customer satisfaction.

cross-docking A continuous replenishment logistics process at a distribution center, where incoming goods are sorted and/or consolidated, and then shipped out to their final destinations, without the need to store the goods. Cross-docking generally takes place within 24 hours, sometimes less than an hour, after shipment arrivals and is used to replenish high-demand inventories.

cross-selling This occurs when customers are sold additional products as the result of an initial purchase.

customs brokers They move international shipments through customs for companies as well as handle the necessary documentation required to accompany the shipments.

customer chain operations reference (CCOR) model The CCOR model defines the customer part of the supply chain as the integration of Plan, Relate, Sell, Contract, Service, and Enable processes.

customer churn The rate at which customers leave or stop using the firm.

customer contact centers or call centers Customer service departments that integrate all of the methods customers can use to contact a business, including telephone, mail, comment cards, e-mail, and Web site messages and chat rooms.

customer defection analysis Analyzing why customers stop using a particular business.

customer lifetime value Assigning a profit figure to each customer by summing the margins of all the products and services purchased over time, less the cost of marketing to and maintaining that customer, such as the costs of direct mail and sales calls and the service costs for each customer. Additionally, the firm forecasts future purchased quantities, profit margins, and marketing costs for each customer, discounts these back to the current date, and then adds this projected profit quantity to the current profit amount.

customer relationship management (CRM) To manage the firm's customer base so that customers remain satisfied and continue to purchase goods and services.

customer service The provision of information, help, and/or technical support to customers in a way that meets or exceeds customer expectations.

customer service management process This provides information to customers while also providing ongoing management of any product and service agreements between the firm and its customers.

customer value The value that customers place in the products they buy.

Customs-Trade Partnership Against Terrorism (C-TPAT) program A partnership between U.S. Customs, the International Cargo Security Council (a U.S. non-profit association of companies and individuals involved in transportation), and Pinkerton (a global security advising company, headquartered in New Jersey), whereby companies agree to improve security in their supply chain in return for "fast lane" border crossings.

cycle counting A commonly used technique in which physical inventory is counted on a periodic basis to ensure that physical inventory matches current inventory records.

cyclical variations These are wavelike movements (in demand) that last longer than one year and are influenced by macroeconomic and political factors.

D

dashboards Web-based balanced scorecard applications.

data warehouses Information system structures used to store data that was collected from the various divisions of the firm.

decentralized–centralized purchasing structure A hybrid purchasing structure that is decentralized at the corporate level, but centralized at the individual business unit level.

decentralized purchasing This is where individual, local purchasing departments, such as at the plant or field-office level, make their own purchasing decisions.

deep-sea transportation Ocean-going shipping vessels, primarily carrying containers.

defects per million opportunities (DPMO) A Six Sigma quality metric.

Delphi method forecast A qualitative forecasting method in which a group of experts are surveyed during several rounds to gain consensus on future events. Group members do not physically meet and thus avoid the scenario where one or a few experts could dominate a discussion.

demand-driven supply networks The idea is to design supply chains with enough flexibility to respond quickly to changes in the marketplace.

demand forecast updating Changing the method used to calculate the forecast.

demand management A set of activities that range from determining or estimating the demand from customers through converting specific customer orders into promised delivery dates to help balance demand with supply.

demand management process This balances customer demand and the firm's output capabilities.

demand source The customer arrivals are referred to as the demand source.

demand time fence A firmed planning segment is also known as the demand time fence, used with the MRP application, and it usually stretches from the current period to a period several weeks into the future.

Department of Defense (DOD) This is a major public procurement entity in the United States.

Department of Transportation Act In 1966, the Department of Transportation Act created the Department of Transportation (DOT) to coordinate the executive functions of all government entities dealing with transportation related matters.

dependent demand The internal demand for parts based on the demand of the final product in which the parts are used.

design chain operations reference (DCOR) model Defines the design portion of the supply chain as the integration of Plan, Research, Design, Integrate, Amend, and Enable processes.

differentiation strategy This is based on creating a service that is considered unique.

direct costs Costs that are directly traceable to the unit produced, such as the amount of materials and labor used to produce a unit of the finished good.

direct offset This usually involves coproduction, or a joint venture, and exchange of related goods and/or services.

distribution center A warehouse that forms outbound specific product assortments which are then shipped to the customer.

distribution channels Defines the way products and services are delivered to customers.

distribution network The design of the distribution system.

distribution requirements planning (DRP) A time-phased finished goods inventory replenishment plan in a distribution network.

distributive negotiations When the negotiating objective is to seek an outcome that favors primarily one side's interests.

E

e-procurement Electronic or computerized purchasing system.

early supplier involvement (ESI) Involving key suppliers during the product design and development stage to take advantage of their knowledge and technologies.

eatertainment The combination of restaurant and entertainment elements.

economic manufacturing quantity (EMQ) or production order quantity (POQ) A variation of the classic EOQ model, used to determine the most economical number of units to produce.

economic order quantity (EOQ) model The classic independent demand inventory system that computes the optimal order quantity to minimize total inventory costs.

economies of scale As the number of units purchased, produced, or transported increases, the cost per unit decreases.

edutainment The combination of learning with entertainment to appeal to customers looking for substance along with play.

effective performance measurement system It consists of the traditional financial information for external reporting purposes along with tactical-level performance criteria used to assess the firm's competitive capabilities while directing its efforts to attain other desired capabilities.

efficient consumer response (ECR) Another term referring to JIT. ECR concepts are intended to make the firm more flexible and responsive to customer requirements and changes.

electronic data interchange (EDI) A computer-to-computer exchange of business documents such as purchase orders, order status inquiries and reports, promotion announcements, and shipping and billing notices.

electronic invoice presentment and payment (EIPP) Sending and receiving invoices and payments online, represents one of the most commonly used B2B transactions, and it is designed to create greater efficiencies among the companies using the technology.

electronic product code (EPC) A widely used RFID standard managed by the EPC-global, Inc.

enterprise resource planning (ERP) A packaged business software system that lets a company automate and integrate the majority of its business processes, share common data and practices across the enterprise, and produce and access information in a real-time environment.

entertailing It refers to retail locations with entertainment elements.

European Union (EU) A European international trade organization designed to reduce tariff and nontariff barriers among member countries. Set up after the Second World War, the European Union was officially launched on May 9, 1950, with France's proposal to create a European federation consisting of six countries: Belgium, Germany, France, Italy, Luxembourg, and the Netherlands. A series of accessions has resulted in a total of 27 member states in 2007. Currently, the EU has three candidate countries of Croatia, Former Yugoslav Republic of Macedonia, and Turkey.

environmental management system (EMS) The practices of a firm in trying to reduce environmental waste, and improve environmental performance.

environmental sustainability The need to continually protect the environment and reduce greenhouse gas emissions.

event-based marketing The idea with event-based marketing is to offer the right products and services to customers at the right time.

everyday low prices Keeping prices as low as possible to reduce the need to have promotions, which leads to more bullwhip effect.

expediting The act of contacting the supplier to speed up an overdue shipment.

exception rates These are published rates that are lower than class rates for specific origin-destination locations or volumes.

exempt carriers These are for-hire carriers, but they are exempt from regulation of services and rates.

F

facilitating products Facilitating products such as computers, furniture, and office supplies that are not part of the services sold, but rather consumed inside the firm, and these materials must also be managed.

Federal Acquisition Regulation (FAR) The primary set of rules issued by the U.S. government to govern the process through which the government purchases goods and services.

Federal Acquisition Streamlining Act (FASA) A federal act signed by President Clinton in October 1994 to remove many restrictions on government purchases that do not exceed $100,000.

Federal Aviation Act of 1958 Replaced the Civil Aeronautics Administration with the Federal Aviation Administration (FAA) and gave the FAA authority to prescribe air traffic rules, make safety regulations, and plan the national airport system.

financial performance measures Performance measures which concentrate on cost, profits, and sales figures.

finished goods Completed products ready for shipment.

First and Second Laws of Service David Maister proposed these: *Rule #1: Satisfaction = perception – expectation. Rule #2: It is hard to play catch-up ball.*

first-tier customers The firm's direct customers.

first-tier supplier A firm's direct supplier.

fishbone diagrams These can be used to aid in brainstorming and isolating the causes of a problem.

five dimensions of service quality They refer to reliability, responsiveness, assurance, empathy, and tangibles.

five-Ss The original five-Ss came naturally, from Toyota, and were Japanese words relating to industrial housekeeping. The idea is that by implementing the five-Ss, the workplace will be cleaner, more organized, and safer, thereby reducing processing waste and improving productivity.

fixed costs These are independent of the output quantity.

fixed order quantity models Independent demand inventory models that use fixed parameters to determine the optimal order quantity to minimize total inventory costs.

flow diagrams These use annotated boxes representing process action elements and ovals representing process wait periods, connected by arrows to show the flow of products or customers through the process.

FOB destination pricing When products are purchased from a supplier, they may quote a price that includes transportation to the buyer's location.

FOB origination prices The buyer may decide to purchase goods and supply their own transportation to the shipping destination; in this case, the supplier quotes are lower.

focal firm The firm used in an example; the subject firm.

focus strategy This incorporates the idea that a service can serve a narrow target market or niche better than other firms that are trying to serve a broad market.

follow-up A proactive act to contact the supplier to ensure on-time delivery of the goods ordered.

forecast bias It measures the tendency of a forecast to be consistently higher (negative bias) or lower (positive bias) than the actual demand.

forecast error It is the difference between actual quantity or demand and the forecast.

foreign freight forwarders These services move goods for companies from domestic production facilities to foreign customer destinations, using surface and air transportation and warehouses. They consolidate small shipments into larger TL, CL, or container shipments, decide what transportation modes and methods to use, handle all of the documentation requirements, and then disperse the shipments at their destination.

foreign trade zones (FTZs) These are secure sites within the U.S. under the supervision of the U.S. Customs Service. These are where materials can be imported duty-free as long as the imports are used as inputs to production of goods that are eventually exported.

forward buying Activities on the part of buyers, who are stocking up to take advantage of the low price offers.

forward vertical integration This term refers to acquiring downstream customers.

fourth-party logistics provider (4PL) Also termed a lead logistics provider, a 4PL manages all of a firm's worldwide 3PL providers.

freight forwarders They consolidate a large number of small shipments to fill entire truck trailers or rail cars that transport items at truckload or carload prices.

Free and Secure Trade Program (FAST) U.S. Customs' security program; the overall goal is to ensure the security of international supply chains and international trucking in particular. To participate in FAST, motor carriers must become C-TPAT certified and their commercial drivers must complete an application and undergo a background check.

functional products MRO items and other commonly purchased items and supplies. These items are characterized by low profit margins, relatively stable demands, and high levels of competition.

functional silos Departments in a firm that are only concerned with what is going on in their department, and not what is in the best interests of the firm.

G

general freight carriers They carry the majority of goods shipped in the U.S. and include common carriers.

General Services Administration (GSA) A U.S. federal agency that is responsible for most federal purchases. It is based in Washington, D.C. and has 11 regional offices throughout the U.S.

global supply chains Supply chains with foreign trading partners.

granger laws The granger laws in the 1870s made Congress realize the impact of railroad monopolies.

green development This is used to describe environmentally friendly development.

green logistics A philosophy of understanding and working to reduce the ecological impact of logistics in both the forward and reverse supply chain.

green purchasing Also termed green sourcing and sustainable procurement, when purchasing personnel include environmental considerations and human health issues when making purchasing decisions.

green reverse logistics programs These programs include reducing the environmental impact of certain modes of transportation used for returns, reducing the amount of disposed packaging and product materials by redesigning products and processes, and making use of reusable totes and pallets.

green sourcing See green purchasing.

green supply chain management Extends the concept of green logistics to include activities related to environmentally responsible product design, acquisition, production, distribution, use, reuse, and disposal by partners within the supply chain.

H

high-speed trains Typically passenger trains that are averaging approximately 70 miles per hour, although top speeds can reach 120 miles per hour.

holding or **carrying costs** The costs incurred for holding inventory in storage.

hybrid centralized distribution system A system using IT applications to combine a more decentralized warehousing system with a central control of stocks.

hybrid purchasing organization A firm that uses either a centralized–decentralized or decentralized–centralized purchasing structure.

I

ICC Termination Act of 1995 The Interstate Commerce Commission was eliminated.

implosion A DRP logic where demand information is gathered from the of field distribution centers and aggregated in the central warehouse, and eventually passed onto the manufacturing facility.

import broker A firm that is set up to import goods for customers for a fee. An import broker does not take title to the goods.

import merchant A firm that imports and takes title to the goods, and then resells the goods.

incoterms (International Commercial Terms) A uniform set of rules created by the International Chamber of Commerce to simplify international transactions of goods with respect to shipping costs, risks, and responsibilities of the buyer, seller, and shipper.

indented bill of materials The multilevel bill of materials can also be presented as an indented bill of materials.

independent demand The demand for final products and service parts. It has a demand pattern that is affected by trends, seasonal patterns, and general market conditions.

indirect costs These are those that cannot be traced directly to the unit produced, and they are synonymous with manufacturing overhead.

indirect offset This involves exchange of goods and/or services unrelated to the aerospace or defense sector.

industrial buyers Buyers with a primary responsibility of purchasing raw materials for conversion purposes.

information visibility The degree that information is communicated and made available to various constituents.

infotainment Also called edutainment; combines learning with entertainment to appeal to customers looking for substance along with play.

insourcing To begin performing in-house some activity that was formerly outsourced.

integrated logistics When two companies share logistics processes.

integration Provides a view of the supply chain that spans multiple departments, processes, and software applications for internal users and external partners.

integrative negotiations Win-win negotiations.

intermediately positioned strategy This places warehouses midway between the sources of supply and the customers.

intermodal marketing companies (IMCs) These are companies that act as intermediaries between intermodal railroad companies and shippers.

intermodal transportation Two or more modes of transportation are combined to deliver a shipment of goods.

internal supply chain An organization's network of internal suppliers and its internal customers. Internal supply chains can be complex, particularly if the firm has multiple divisions and organizational structures around the globe.

international purchasing Buying raw materials from overseas suppliers. It is also referred to as global sourcing.

Interstate Commerce Act of 1887 The 1887 act created the Interstate Commerce Commission (ICC), required rail carriers to charge reasonable rates, to publish rates, file them with the ICC and make these available to the public, and prohibited discriminatory practices (charging some shippers less than others for the same service). The act also prohibited agreements between railroads to pool traffic or revenues.

inventory costs The purchase cost, order cost, and carrying cost.

inventory turnover This shows how many times a firm's inventory is utilized and replaced over an accounting period, such as a year.

inventory turnover ratio or inventory turnovers A widely used measure to analyze how efficiently a firm uses its inventory to generate revenue.

inventory visibility The ability of supply chain companies to see inventory quantities of the various members.

invitation for bid (IFB) A request for qualified suppliers to submit bids for a contract. Suppliers are asked to bid, given certain opening and closing dates of the bid. The basis for awarding a contract is preset and binding.

Ishikawa diagram Also called fishbone diagram; a tool for brainstorming causes of problems.

ISO 9000 A series of management and quality assurance standards in design, development, production, installation, and service developed by the International Organization for Standardization (ISO).

ISO 14000 A family of international standards for environmental management developed by the International Organization for Standardization (ISO).

J

JIT warehousing As firms develop their supply chain management capabilities, items will be moving more quickly through inbound and outbound warehouses and distribution centers. These warehouses and distribution centers will thus have to develop more JIT capabilities, like cross-docking.

jury of executive opinion forecast A qualitative forecasting method in which a group of experts collectively develop a forecast.

Just-in-Time (JIT) Originally associated with Toyota managers like Mr. Taiichi Ohno along with his kanban system, JIT encompasses continuous problem solving to eliminate waste. Today it is also referred to as lean.

Just-in-Time (JIT) production system Also called the Toyota Production System and the lean production system.

K

kaizen A Japanese word for continuous improvement.

kanban A Japanese word for "card," it is a visual tool—often a card in a rectangular vinyl envelope—used in lean production.

keiretsu relationships These involve partnership arrangements, between buyer and supplier.

key suppliers The firm's most important, strategic suppliers.

key supply chain processes The eight processes which are most important to integrate in the supply chain.

key trading partners They eventually enable the successful sale and delivery of end products to the final customers.

knowledge-management solutions Internet applications tied to desktop applications enable real-time collaboration and flow of information between supply chain partners.

L

lag capacity strategy A reactive approach that adjusts capacity in response to demand.

lead capacity strategy A proactive approach that adds or subtracts capacity in anticipation of future market condition and demand.

lead factory A source of product and process innovation and competitive advantage for the entire organization.

lead logistics provider (LLP) Also termed a 4PL, the lead logistics provider manages all of the firm's 3PLs.

lead management Using a lead management tool allows sales reps to follow prescribed sales tactics when dealing with sales prospects or opportunities, to aid in closing the deal with a client.

lean layouts Layouts that reduce wasted movements of workers, customers, and/or work-in-process (WIP), and achieve smooth product flow through the facility.

lean manufacturing See lean production.

lean production Organizing work and analyzing the appropriateness of currently operating machines, warehouses, and systems to fit a lean process flow. The goals are to reduce production throughput times and inventory levels, cut order lead times, increase quality, and improve customer responsiveness with fewer people and other assets.

lean Six/lean Six Sigma A new term used to describe the melding of lean production and Six Sigma quality practices.

lean supply chain relationships When the focal firm, its suppliers, and its customers begin to work together to identify customer requirements, remove waste, reduce cost, and improve quality and customer service, this marks the beginning of lean supply chain relationships.

legacy MRP system A broad label used to describe an older information system that usually works at an operational level to schedule production within a single facility.

legacy systems A firm's existing software applications.

legal forms of transportation For-hire transportation service companies are classified legally as either common, contract, exempt, or private carriers.

less-than-truckload (LTL) carriers Carriers move small packages or shipments that take up less than one truckload, and the shipping fees are higher per hundred weight (cwt) than TL fees, since the carrier must consolidate many small shipments into one truckload, then break the truckload back down into individual shipments at the destination for individual deliveries.

level production strategy A production strategy that uses a constant output rate and capacity while varying inventory and backlog levels to handle the fluctuating demand pattern.

leveraging purchase volume An obvious benefit is the concentration of purchase volume to create quantity discounts, less-costly volume shipments, and other more favorable purchase terms.

line haul rates These are the charges for moving goods to a non-local destination, and these can be further classified as *class rates, exception rates, commodity rates,* and *miscellaneous rates.*

linear trend forecast A forecasting method in which the trend can be estimated using simple linear regression to fit a line to a time series of historical data.

load brokers Also referred to as transportation brokers, they bring shippers and transportation companies (mainly truckers) together. The load broker is legally authorized to act on the shipper's or carrier's behalf and typically these companies are hired because of their extensive knowledge of the many transportation alternatives available or the many shippers needing transportation.

logistics audit With the passage of time, logistics characteristics all tend to change, requiring firms to periodically audit their logistics system with the objective of finding an optimal mix of both cost and service.

M

maintenance, repair, and operating (MRO) supplies These materials and supplies are used when producing the products but are not parts of the products.

make or buy (materials or components) This is a strategic decision that can impact an organization's competitive position.

make-to-order manufacturing firms These firms make custom products based on orders from customers, resulting in long lead times and higher unit costs.

make-to-stock manufacturing firms These are firms which typically emphasize immediate delivery of off-the-shelf, standard goods at relatively low prices compared to the chase strategy.

manufacturing cells These are designed to process similar parts or components, saving duplication of equipment and labor, as well as centralizing the area where units of the same purchased part are delivered.

manufacturing flow management process The set of activities responsible for making the actual product, establishing the manufacturing flexibility required to adequately serve the markets, and designing the production system to meet cycle time requirements.

manufacturing resource planning (MRP-II) An outgrowth and extension of the closed-loop MRP system.

market dominance The firm with the dominant position in the market, selling the most units of product.

market positioned strategy This locates warehouses close to customers, to maximize distribution service and to allow the firm to generate transportation economies by using TL and CL deliveries to each warehouse location.

master production schedule (MPS) A medium-range plan and is more detailed than the aggregate production plan.

match or tracking capacity strategy A moderate strategy that adjusts capacity in small amounts in response to demand and changing market conditions.

material requirements planning (MRP) A software application that has been available since the 1970s; it performs an analysis of the firm's existing internal conditions and reports back what the production and purchase requirements are for a given finished product manufacturing schedule.

material requisition (MR) An internal document initiated by the material user to request materials from the warehouse or purchasing department.

mean absolute deviation (MAD) An indicator of forecast accuracy based on an average of the absolute value of the forecast errors over a given period of time. The measure indicates, on average, how many units the forecast is off from the actual data (we cannot determine if the forecasting model is over or under forecasting).

mean absolute percentage error (MAPE) An indicator of forecast accuracy based on the true magnitude of the forecast error. The monthly absolute forecast error divided by actual demand is summed, then divided by the number of months used in the forecast to derive an average, and lastly multiplied by 100. The measure indicates, on average, what percent the forecast is off from the actual data.

mean square error (MSE) An indicator of forecast accuracy. The forecast errors are squared and then summed and divided by the number of periods to determine the mean square error. The measure penalizes large errors more than small errors.

merchants Firms that buy goods in large quantities for resale purposes. Wholesalers and retailers are examples of merchants.

micro-purchases Government purchases of $2,500 and below.

miscellaneous rates These apply to contract rates that are negotiated between two parties and to shipments containing a variety of products (in this case, the rate is based on the overall weight of the shipment).

mixed Internet strategy Combining traditional retailing with Internet retailing seems to be emerging as the stronger business model.

motor carriers Trucks.

Motor Carrier Act of 1935 Brought motor carriers under ICC control, thus controlling entry into the market, establishing motor carrier classes of operation, setting reasonable rates, requiring ICC approval for any mergers or acquisitions, and controlling the issuance of securities.

muda A Japanese word meaning waste or anything that does not add value.

multiple channel queuing system Multiple servers acting in parallel is referred to as a multiple channel queuing system.

multiple-factor productivity These inputs can be represented by the sum of labor, material, energy, and capital costs.

multiple phase queuing system Multiple servers acting in series is referred to as a multiple phase queuing system.

multiple regression forecast A forecast technique using multiple regression.

N

naïve forecast A forecasting approach where the actual demand for the immediate past period is used as a forecast for next period's demand.

natural variations Also termed environmental or white noise; when variations are random with no specific cause.

non-vessel operating common carriers (NVOCC) They operate very similarly to international freight forwarders, but normally use scheduled ocean liners.

nontariffs These are import quotas, licensing agreements, embargoes, laws, and other regulations imposed on imports and exports.

North American Free Trade Agreement (NAFTA) It began on January 1, 1994, and will eventually remove most barriers to trade and investment among the U.S., Canada, and Mexico.

O

Ocean Shipping Reform Act of 1998 The requirement for ocean carriers to file rates with the Federal Maritime Commission came to an end with this act.

offset This is an exchange agreement for industrial goods and/or services as a condition of military-related export. It is also commonly used in the aerospace and defense sectors.

offshore factory This manufactures products at low cost with minimum investment in technical and managerial resources.

on-demand CRM Outsourced or externally hosted on-line CRM services.

open-end purchase order A purchase order that covers a variety of items and is negotiated for repeated supply over a fixed time period, such as quarterly or yearly. Additional items and expiration dates can be renegotiated in an open-end purchase order.

open-source CRM products Free on-line CRM applications and user forums.

operating exposure The risk caused by fluctuating exchange rates, affecting production, warehousing, purchasing, and selling price.

opportunities for a defect to occur (OFD) The number of activities or steps in a process. Used in the DPMO calculation.

optimization Process and decision-making optimization occurs through enhanced analytical tools such as On-Line Analytical Processing (OLAP) tools. Determines the optimal number of units to produce, store, or purchase, among other things.

option overplanning Raising the final requirements of component parts beyond

100 percent in a super bill of materials to cover uncertainty.

order batching When small orders are combined into one large order this amplifies demand variability, adds to the use of safety stock, creating the bullwhip effect.

order costs The direct variable costs associated with placing an order with the supplier.

order cycle The activities involved in ordering and receiving purchased items.

order fulfillment process The set of activities that allows the firm to fill customer orders while providing the required levels of customer service at the lowest possible delivered cost.

outsource This occurs when a firm purchases materials or products instead of producing them in-house.

outpost factory The outpost factory is set up in a location with an abundance of advanced suppliers, competitors, research facilities, and knowledge centers to get access to the latest information on materials, components, technologies, and products.

P

P-charts These monitor the *percent defective* in each sample.

Pareto analysis A graphic technique that prioritizes the most frequently occurring problems or issues. The analysis recommends that problems falling into the most frequently occurring category be assigned the highest priority and managed closely.

Pareto charts These are useful for many applications, are based on the work of Vilfredo Pareto, a nineteenth-century economist.

passive RFID tags RFID tags that are without internal power source, but require power from a tag reader.

payment bonds Bonds posted by the bidders to protect the buyer against any third-party liens not fulfilled by the successful bidder.

perceived waiting times Customers perceive the wait time to be much longer or shorter than it really is.

perfect order fulfillment Orders arriving on time, complete, and damage free.

performance bonds Bonds posted by the bidders to guarantee that the work done by the successful bidder meets specifications and is completed in the time specified.

performance scorecards Refers to Balanced Scorecards or other forms of scorecarding, where a formal approach to develop performance measures is undertaken.

performance variance The difference between the standard and actual performance.

periodic review system This reviews physical inventory at specific points in time.

petty cash This is a small cash reserve maintained by a midlevel manager or clerk.

piggyback A transportation term referring to the loading of shipping containers or truck trailers on a rail flatbed car (also known as container-on-flat-car (COFC) and trailer-on-flat-car (TOFC)).

pipeline carriers One of the five modes of transportation—carries oil, natural gas, coal slurry and other liquids/gases.

place utility This is created when customers get things delivered to the desired location.

planned order releases The bottom line of an MRP part record. It designates when the specific quantity is to be ordered from the supplier or to begin being processed. These quantities also determine the gross requirements of the dependent or "children" parts going into this higher level part or product.

planning factor It shows the number of units of a specific component required to make one unit of a higher-level part.

planning time fence The *tentative segment* is also known as the planning time fence, and it typically stretches from the end of the firmed segment to several weeks farther into the future.

point of sale information Cash register sales data.

poka-yoke Error- or mistake-proofing.

posttransaction After the sale.

posttransaction costs Customer service costs that occur after the sale.

pretransaction Before the sale.

price break point The minimum quantity required to receive a quantity discount.

private carrier A form of transportation owned by a company, such as a fleet of trucks, which is used to ship that company's goods only.

private warehouses These refer to warehouses that are *owned by the firm storing the goods*.

process diagrams This tool is the necessary first step to evaluating any manufacturing or service process.

process integration This refers to sharing information and coordinating resources to jointly manage a process.

process map A drawing showing how products or people flow through a process.

procurement credit cards Also known as corporate purchasing cards. A credit card issued to authorized employees to purchase goods, usually small value purchases, directly from suppliers without the need to go through the purchasing department.

producer's risk When a buyer rejects a shipment of good-quality units because the sample quality level *did not* meet the acceptance standard, this is termed producer's risk.

product development and commercialization process This is responsible for developing new products to meet changing customer requirements and then getting these products to market quickly and efficiently.

product family It consists of different products that share similar characteristics, components, or manufacturing processes.

product positioned strategy It locates warehouses close to the sources of supply, to enable the firm to collect various goods and then consolidate these into TL or CL quantities for shipment to customers.

production kanban A visual signal used to trigger production of certain components.

profit-leverage effect A purchasing performance measure that measures the impact of a change in purchase spend on a firm's profit before taxes, assuming gross sales and other expenses remain unchanged.

public procurement or public purchasing It refers to the management of the purchasing and supply management function of the government and nonprofit sector, such as educational institutions, charitable organizations, and the federal, state, and local governments.

public warehouse An independent warehouse that is operated as a for-profit business.

pull system An operating system where synchronized work takes place only upon authorization from another downstream user in the system rather than strictly to a forecast.

purchase order (PO) A contractual commercial document issued by the buying firm to a supplier, indicating the type, quantities and agreed prices for products or services that the supplier will provide to the buying firm.

purchase requisition An internal document initiated by the material user to request the purchasing department to buy specific goods or services.

purchasing spend Amount spent by an organization in buying goods and services.

pure Internet strategy Selling goods or services strictly over the Internet.

pure services This offers little or no tangible products to customers.

Q

qualitative dimensions Non-quantitative assessments, such as closeness desirability, when assessing how close to position departments in a layout.

quality-of-life factors Those issues that contribute to "a feeling of well-being, fulfillment, or satisfaction resulting from factors in the external environments."

quantity discount model or **price break model** One variation of the classic EOQ model, wherein purchase price is allowed to vary with the quantity purchased.

queue discipline The discipline describes the order in which customers are served.

queue management To deal with excess customers.

queuing systems The processes used to align, prioritize, and serve customers.

quick response (QR) Another term for JIT.

R

R-chart This is used to track sample ranges, or the variation of the measurements within each sample.

radio frequency identification (RFID) A technology that enables huge amounts of information to be stored on chips (called tags) and read at a distance by readers, without requiring line-of-sight scanning.

radio frequency identification tag The chips used to store information about a specific product or carton using RFID.

rail carriers Trains.

Railroad Revitalization and Regulatory Reform Act Commonly known as the 4-R Act, it was passed in 1976 and made several regulatory changes to help the railroads.

Railway Passenger Service Act Passed in 1970, creating Amtrak.

random variations These are due to unexpected or unpredictable events such as natural disasters (hurricanes, tornadoes, fire), strikes, and wars.

rationing This can occur when demand exceeds a supplier's finished goods available, and in this case, the supplier may allocate product in proportion to what buyers ordered.

raw materials These are defined as unprocessed purchased inputs or materials for manufacturing the finished goods.

Reed-Bulwinkle Act In 1948, gave groups of carriers the ability to form rate bureaus or conferences wherein they could propose rate changes to the ICC.

relationship marketing or permission marketing An extension of target marketing.

regional trade agreements Trade agreements between countries, as in the EU.

reneging It refers to leaving the line before completing the service.

reorder point (ROP) The lowest inventory level at which a new order must be placed to avoid a stockout during the order cycle time period.

request for proposal (RFP) A formal request for a project or product proposal issued by the buyer to qualified suppliers. The use of RFPs allows the supplier to develop part specifications based on their own knowledge of the materials and technology needed.

request for quotation (RFQ) A formal request for pricing from a supplier; commonly used when the purchasing requirements are clear.

resource requirements planning (RRP) A long-range capacity planning module, is used to check whether aggregate resources are capable of satisfying the aggregate production plan.

responsible bid One that is capable and willing to perform the work as specified.

responsive bid This is a submitted bid that conforms to the invitation to bid.

return on assets (ROA) A financial measure, calculated as after-tax income divided by total assets.

return on investment (ROI) A financial ratio, calculated as after-tax income divided by total investment.

returns management process How product returns are managed. This can be extremely beneficial for supply chain management in terms of maintaining acceptable levels of customer service and identifying product improvement opportunities.

returns management systems Developing and implementing efficient methods for transporting and storing returns while seeking to recover some value, if possible, from the returned items. Returns management activities include environmental compliance with substance disposal and recycling, composing operating and repair instructions, troubleshooting and warranty repairs, developing disposal guidelines, designing an effective reverse logistics process, and collecting returns data.

reverse auctions An on-line bidding arrangement whereby suppliers try to underbid each other to win a purchase order.

reverse logistics activities A unique form of inbound logistics where returned goods are properly disposed with an attempt to recover some of their original value.

right-to-work laws "...secures the right of employees to decide for themselves whether or not to join or financially support a union."

risk pooling It describes the relationship between the number of warehouses, inventory, and customer service, and it can be explained intuitively as follows: when market demand is random, it is very likely that higher-than-average demand from some customers will be offset by lower-than-average demand from other customers.

RO-ROs *Roll-on-roll-off* containerships; these allow truck trailers and containers to be directly driven on and off the ship, without use of cranes.

rough-cut capacity plan (RCCP) This is used to check the feasibility of the master production schedule.

running sum of forecast errors (RSFE) A measure of forecast bias, that is, whether the forecast tends to be consistently higher or lower than actual demand.

S

sales activity management The use of a sales activity management tool reduces errors and improves customer satisfaction and productivity.

sales agent The authorized sales representative of an overseas supplier to assist the supplier to conduct business in a foreign country.

sales force automation (SFA) Products are used for documenting field activities, communicating with the home office, and retrieval of sales history and other company-specific documents in the field.

sales force composite forecast When field sales personnel are asked to estimate their customers' purchases for the period in question. These are then summed, to achieve the forecast.

sales order Supplier's offer to sell goods and services at the supplier's terms and conditions.

sales territory management These tools allow sales managers to obtain current information and reporting capabilities regarding each salesperson's activities on each customer's account, total sales in general for each sales rep, their sales territories, and any ongoing sales initiatives.

scorecarding Refers to Balanced Scorecard or some other form of performance measure design technique using a scorecard.

seasonal variations These show peaks and valleys that repeat over a consistent interval such as hours, days, weeks, months, years, or seasons.

second-tier suppliers and customers These are the suppliers' suppliers and the customers' customers.

segment customers Placing customers in a behavioral class, such as males/females, age brackets, and profitability, so as to better design marketing campaigns for each segment.

selective sourcing Also referred to as co-sourcing, and refers to the sharing of a process or function between internal staff and an external provider.

server factory A server factory is set up primarily to take advantage of government incentives, minimize exchange risk, avoid tariff barriers, and reduce taxes and logistics costs to supply the regional market where the factory is located.

service bundle A bundle of attributes when purchasing services, including the explicit service itself, the supporting facility, facilitating goods, and implicit services. Successful services are designed to deliver this bundle of attributes in the most efficient way, while still satisfying customer requirements.

service capacity The number of customers per day the firm's service delivery systems *are designed to serve,* although it could also be some other period of time such as customers per hour or customers per shift.

service delivery systems These fall along a continuum with mass-produced, low-customer-contact systems at one extreme (such as ATMs) and highly customized, high-customer-contact systems at the other (such as an expensive beauty salon).

service layout strategies Work in combination with location decisions to further support the overall business strategies of differentiation, low cost, or market focus. Office layouts tend to be departmentalized; commercial airliner layouts segment customers; casino layouts are designed to get customers in quickly and then keep them there by spacing out the attractions; and self-serve restaurant buffet layouts are designed to process customers quickly.

service level The in-stock probability.

service quality It includes many elements —for example, because of health and safety concerns, pharmacies are under intense pressure to provide high quality services to customers.

service response logistics The management and coordination of the organization's activities that occur while the service is being performed.

setups The activities required to change products on an assembly-line.

setup costs This is used in place of order costs to describe the costs associated with setting up machines and equipment to produce a batch of product.

seven Rs rule Having the *right* product, in the *right* quantity, in the *right* condition, at the *right* place, at the *right* time, for the *right* customer, at the *right* cost.

seven wastes A term that encompasses things such as excess wait times, inventories, material and people movements, processing steps, variabilities, and *any other non-value-adding activity.*

Shipping Act of 1984 This act allowed ocean carriers to pool or share shipments, assign ports, publish rates, and enter into contracts with shippers.

shippers' associations Non-profit membership cooperatives which make domestic or international arrangements for the movement of members' cargo.

shortage gaming This means when buyers figure out the relationship between their orders and what is supplied, they tend to inflate their orders to satisfy their real needs.

sigma drift It posits that process variations will grow over time, as process measurements drift off target.

silo effect This causes the firm to be reactive and short-term-goal oriented. At this stage, no internal functional integration is occurring.

silo mentality See silo effect.

simple exponential smoothing forecast This is a sophisticated weighted moving average forecasting technique in which the forecast for the next period's demand is the current period's forecast adjusted by a fraction of the difference between the current period's actual demand and forecast. This approach requires less data than the weighted moving average method because only two data points need to be used.

simple linear regression forecast It is equivalent to the trend forecast. The difference is that the x variable is no longer time but an explanatory variable of demand.

simple moving average forecast This uses historical data to generate a forecast and works well when the demand is fairly stable over time.

simplification This refers to reduction of the number of components, supplies, or standard materials used in the product or process during product design.

single factor productivity measures Various output measures divided by a single input measure, such as labor cost.

single integrator solution An ERP system that uses all the desired applications from the same vendor.

single source Buying from one supplier when multiple suppliers are available.

Six Sigma This stresses a commitment by the firm's top management to enable the firm to identify customer expectations and excel in meeting and exceeding those expectations. A type of TQM method devised by Motorola.

software-as-a-service model (SaaS model) Also referred to as an application service provider or ASP. Perhaps as many as 50 percent of all CRM programs are now designed and maintained for clients by ASPs. In many cases, firms do not have the time, knowledge, or infrastructure to buy and build an effective CRM program, so they use Internet on-demand CRM services provided by an ASP. These providers also offer high levels of data security, which many firms find very attractive.

sole sourcing This typically refers to the situation when the supplier is the *only available source.*

source factory A source factory has a broader strategic role than an offshore factory, with plant management heavily involved in supplier selection and production planning.

sourcing Purchasing.

Southern Common Market (MERCOSUR) A regional trade agreement among Argentina, Brazil, Paraguay, and Uruguay, formed in March 1991.

specialized carriers These transport liquid petroleum, household goods, agricultural commodities, building materials, and other specialized items.

square root rule This rule suggests that the system average inventory (impacted by adding warehouses to the system) is equal to the old system inventory times the ratio of the square root of the new number of warehouses to the square root of the old number of warehouses.

Staggers Rail Act of 1980 This act was aimed at improving finances for the rail industry.

standards for performance Specific performance requirements or objectives set by top management.

statistical process control (SPC) This allows firms to visually monitor process performance, compare the performance to desired levels or standards, and take corrective steps quickly before process variabilities get out of control and damage products, services, and customer relationships.

state utility State utility, meaning that services do something to things that are owned by the customer.

stockless buying or **system contracting** This is an extension of the blanket purchase order.

stockpiling To set aside or hoard purchased items, if it is thought that prices will soon increase.

strategic 3PL alliances Partnerships with third-party logistics providers.

strategic alliance development Improving the capabilities of key trading partners.

strategic partnerships These are trading partner relationships.

strategic sourcing Enables companies to strategically analyze how they source products and services to improve cost, quality, delivery, performance, and competitive advantage.

strategic supplier alliances Creating partnerships with key suppliers.

subcontracting Entering into a contractual agreement with a supplier to produce goods and/or services according to a specific set of terms and conditions.

super bill of materials Another type of bill of materials is the super bill of materials, which is useful for planning purposes.

supplier certification Defined by the Institute of Supply Management as "an organization's process for evaluating the quality systems of key suppliers in an effort to eliminate incoming inspections."

supplier co-location Also referred to as JIT II®. Placing a supplier's employee within the firm, performing purchasing activities. A type of VMI.

supplier development The efforts of a buying firm to improve the capabilities and performance of specific suppliers to better meet its needs.

supplier evaluation This is one of the key activities in supplier management—determining the capabilities of suppliers.

supplier management One of the most crucial issues within the topic of supply management—getting suppliers to do what you want them to do.

supplier partnerships A commitment over an extended time to work together to the mutual benefit of both parties, sharing relevant information and the risks and rewards of the relationship.

supplier relationship management (SRM) An umbrella term that includes "extended procurement processes, such as sourcing analytics (e.g., spend analysis), sourcing execution, procurement execution, payment and settlement, and—closing the feedback loop—supplier scorecarding and performance monitoring." Accenture defines SRM as "the systematic management of supplier relationships to optimize the value delivered through the relationship over their life cycle."

supplier relationship management process A process by which the firm manages its relationships with suppliers.

supply base or supplier base This refers to the list of suppliers that a firm uses to acquire its materials, services, supplies, and equipment.

supply base rationalization Also referred to as supply base reduction—getting rid of poorly performing suppliers.

supply base reduction See supply base rationalization.

supply base optimization See supply base rationalization.

supply chain A network of companies which supply each other until a final product is produced.

supply chain integration Collaborating with or sharing key supply chain process activities with supply chain trading partners.

supply chain management (SCM) The integration of key business processes regarding the flow of materials from raw material suppliers to the final customer.

Supply Chain Operations Reference (SCOR) model This was developed in 1996 by supply chain consulting firms Pittiglio Rabin Todd & McGrath and AMR Research, to formalize the attainment of supply chain management.

supply chain performance measurement Determining the performance of an entire supply chain.

supply chain risk management Managing the risks in supply chains, such as weather and political risks.

supply chain security management It is concerned with reducing the risk of intentionally created disruptions in supply chain operations including product and information theft and activities seeking to endanger personnel or sabotage supply chain infrastructure.

supply chain visibility The ability of supply chain members to see what is happening to inventories up and down the supply chain.

supply management The identification, acquisition, access, positioning, and management of resources the organization needs or potentially needs in the attainment of its strategic objectives.

surety bonds Bonds posted by bidders to ensure that the successful bidder will accept the contract.

sustainable development A development that meets the needs of the present without compromising the ability of future generations to meet their own needs.

sustainable procurement Also referred to as green purchasing.

sustainability Environmental responsibility.

system nervousness It is defined as a situation where a small change in the upper-level production plan causes a major change in the lower-level production plan.

T

target marketing Targeting specific customer segments, with respect to promotional efforts.

tariff This is an official list or schedule showing the duties, taxes, or customs imposed by the host country on imports or exports.

third-party logistics services (3PLs) For-hire outside agents that provide transportation and other services including warehousing, document preparation, customs clearance, packaging, labeling, and freight bill auditing.

threshold costs It is defined as the firm's variable costs, and the ICC determined whether the firm was in a market dominant position (absence of market competition).

time series forecasting This forecast is based on the assumption that the future is an extension of the past, thus, historical data can be used to predict future demand.

time utility This is created when customers get products delivered at precisely the right time, not earlier and not later.

total cost of ownership or **total cost of acquisition** This includes the unit price of the material, payment terms, cash discount, ordering cost, carrying cost, logistical costs, maintenance costs, and other more qualitative costs that may not be easy to assess.

total productivity measures Measure of total outputs divided by total inputs.

tracking signal This is a tool used to check the forecast bias.

trade secrets Proprietary information owned by the firm—financial, business, scientific, technical, economic, or engineering information, including patterns, plans, compilations, programmed devices, formulas, designs, prototypes, methods, techniques, processes, procedures, programs, or codes, whether tangible or intangible.

trading companies They put buyers and sellers from different countries together and handle all of the export/import arrangements, documentation, and transportation for both goods and services.

trailer-on-flatcar service/TOFC service This offers point-to-point pick-up and delivery service using motor carriers and flatcars that carry truck trailers.

transactional SRM Enables an organization to track supplier interactions such as order planning, order payment, and returns. The volume of transactions involved may result in independent systems maintained by geographic region or business lines. Transactional SRM tends to focus on short-term reporting.

Transportation Act of 1920 The act instructed the ICC to ensure that rates were high enough to provide a fair return for the railroads each year.

Transportation Act of 1940 Further extended the Interstate Commerce Act of 1887, establishing ICC control over domestic water transportation.

Transportation Act of 1958 Established temporary loan guarantees to railroads, liberalized control over intrastate rail rates, amended the rule of rate making to ensure more intermodal competition, and clarified the differences between private and for-hire motor carriers.

transportation brokers They bring shippers and transportation companies (mainly truckers) together.

transportation deregulation Laws that sought to reduce government regulation in the transportation industry, allowing market forces to dictate services offered.

transportation intermediaries For-hire agencies that bring shippers and transportation providers together.

transportation management systems Applications allow firms to select the best mix of transportation services and pricing to determine the best use of containers or truck trailers, to better manage transportation contracts, to rank transportation options, to clear customs, to track fuel usage and product movements, and to track carrier performance.

transportation security Providing protection to transportation companies against unlawful activities such as terrorism.

traveling requisition A material requisition that is used for materials and standard parts that are requested on a recurring basis.

trend variations These represent either increasing or decreasing movements over time and are due to factors such as population growth, population shifts, cultural changes, and income shifts. Common trends are linear, S-curve, exponential, or asymptotic.

Toyota Production System A methodology created by Toyota Motor Co. in the 1950s. The idea is to make best use of an organization's time, assets, and people in all processes in order to optimize productivity. Also known as JIT and lean systems.

Type-I error When a process is mistakenly thought to be out of control and an improvement initiative is undertaken unnecessarily.

Type-II error When a process is thought to be exhibiting only natural variations and no improvement is undertaken, even though the process is actually out of control.

U

U.S. Baldrige Quality Award This was signed into law on August 20, 1987, and is named in honor of then U.S. President Reagan's Secretary of Commerce, who helped draft an early version of the award, and who was tragically killed in a rodeo accident shortly before the award was enacted.

Uniform Commercial Code (UCC) Governs the purchase and sale of goods.

V

value engineering Using various design techniques to reduce production and usage costs as much as possible, so as to maximize profitability.

value-of-service pricing Carriers price their services at competitive levels the market will bear.

variable costs They vary as a function of the output level.

variable data These are measurable, such as weight, time, and length (as in the weight of a box of cereal, the time to serve a customer, or the length of a steel girder).

vendor managed inventory A progressive partner-based approach to controlling inventory and reducing supply chain costs. Customers provide information to the key supplier, including historical usage, current inventory levels, minimum and maximum stock levels, sales forecasts, and upcoming promotions, who then takes on the responsibility and risk for planning, managing, and monitoring the replenishment of inventory. The supplier may even own the inventory until the product is sold.

vertically integrated firm A firm whose business boundaries include one-time suppliers and/or customers.

virtual inventory Feeding inventory information into one shared database.

visibility Information and process flows in and between organizations. Views are customized by role and aggregated via a single portal.

W

waiting times Time spent by customers who are waiting for service.

Wal-Mart effect This postulates that the booming growth in information technology has allowed many big-box retailers such as Wal-Mart to realize large productivity growth rates.

walk-through service audits These should also be performed by management, covering service system attributes from the time customers initially encounter the service until they leave.

warehouse management systems The proper storage and movement of inventory and minor manufacturing such as assembly or labeling activities within the warehouse, and movement of shipments onto the transportation carrier.

water carrier A ship.

Web-based CRM CRM applications that are available on-line.

Web-based scorecards These provide managers to see real-time progress toward organizational milestones and help to ensure that decisions remain in sync with the firm's overall strategies.

Web site self-service Self-service applications on a company's Web site.

weighted-factor rating model A method commonly used to compare the attractiveness of several locations along a number of quantitative and qualitative dimensions.

weighted moving average forecast It allows greater emphasis to be placed on more recent data to reflect changes in demand patterns.

withdrawal kanban A visual signal to indicate a container of parts can be moved from one work cell to another.

work-in-process (WIP) This describes materials that are partially processed but not yet ready for sales.

world-class performance measures Performance measures used by world-class firms.

World Trade Organization (WTO) The only international organization dealing with the rules of trade between nations. Its functions include administering the WTO agreements, providing a forum for trade negotiations, handling trade disputes, monitoring national trade policies, providing technical assistance and training programs for developing countries, and cooperating with other international organizations.

X

$\bar{x}$**-chart** This is used to track the central tendency of the sample means.

Z

zone of rate freedom Allows carriers to charge fees over their variable costs, up to a set limit.

References

CHAPTER 1

Burgess, R. "Avoiding Supply Chain Management Failure: Lessons from Business Process Reengineering." *International Journal of Logistics Management,* 9, no. 1 (1998): 15–24.

Chopra, S. and P. Meindl. *Supply Chain Management: Strategy, Planning, and Operation.* Upper Saddle River, NJ: Prentice Hall, 2001.

Frazelle, E. *Supply Chain Strategy: The Logistics of Supply Chain Management.* New York: McGraw-Hill, 2002.

Hammer, M. and J. Champy. *Reengineering the Corporation.* London: Nicholas Brealey, 1993.

Handfield, R. B. and E. L. Nichols. *Introduction to Supply Chain Management.* Upper Saddle River, NJ: Prentice Hall, 1999.

Lambert, D. M., M. C. Cooper, and J. D. Pagh. "Supply Chain Management: Implementation Issues and Research Opportunities." *International Journal of Logistics Management,* 9, no. 2 (1998): 1–19.

Lee, H. L., V. Padmanabhan, and S. Whang. "Information Distortion in a Supply Chain: The Bullwhip Effect." *Management Science,* 43, no. 4 (1997): 546–58.

Simchi-Levi, D., P. Kaminsky, and E. Simchi-Levi. *Designing and Managing the Supply Chain.* New York: McGraw-Hill, 2000.

Stevens, G. C. "Integrating the Supply Chain." *International Journal of Physical Distribution and Logistics Management,* 19, no. 8 (1989): 3–8.

Tan, K. C. "A Framework of Supply Chain Management Literature." *European Journal of Purchasing and Supply Management,* 7, no. 1 (2001): 39–48.

Webster, S. *Principles & Tools for Supply Chain Management.* New York: McGraw-Hill/Irwin, 2008.

CHAPTER 2

Burt, D. N., D. W. Dobler, and S. L. Starling. *World Class Supply Management: The Key to Supply Chain Management,* 7th ed. New York, NY: McGraw-Hill/Irwin, 2003.

Leenders, M. R., P. F. Johnson, A. E. Flynn, and H. E. Fearon. *Purchasing and Supply Management,* 13th ed. New York, NY: McGraw-Hill/Irwin, 2006.

Monczka, R., R. Trent, and R. Handfield. *Purchasing and Supply Chain Management,* 3rd ed. Cincinnati, OH: Southwestern Publishing, 2005.

Prahalad, C. K. and G. Hamel. "The Core Competence of the Corporation." *Harvard Business Review,* 68, no. 3 (1990): 79–91.

Wisner, J. D. and K. C. Tan. "Supply Chain Management and Its Impact on Purchasing." *Journal of Supply Chain Management,* 36, no. 4 (2000): 33–42.

CHAPTER 3

Austin, J. *The Collaboration Challenge: How Non-profits and Businesses Succeed Through Strategic Alliances,* San Francisco, CA: Jossey-Bass Publishers, 2000.

Avery, S. "At Boeing, Supplier Collaboration Takes Off." *Purchasing,* 136, no. 13 (October 18, 2007): 44.

Baglieri, E., R. Secchi, and S. Croom. "Exploring the Impact of a Supplier Portal on the Buyer–Supplier Relationship. The Case of Ferrari Auto." *Industrial Marketing Management,* 36, no. 7 (October 2007): 1010.

Clarke, E. "Let's Work Together." *Supply Management,* 12, no. 15 (July 19, 2007): 26–29.

Greenhalgh, L. *Managing Strategic Relationships: The Key to Business Success.* New York: The Free Press, 2001.

Grieco, Jr., P., M. Gozzo, and J. Claunch. *Supplier Certification: Achieving Excellence.* Miami: PT Publications, Inc., 1998.

Gunasekaran, A., C. Patel, and E. Tirtiroglu. "Performance Measures and Metrics in a Supply Chain Environment." *International Journal of Operations & Production Management,* 21, no. 1/2 (2001): 71–87.

Han, B., S. Chen, and M. Ebrahimpour. "The Impact of ISO 9000 on TQM and Business Performance." *The Journal of Business and Economic Studies,* 13, no. 2 (fall 2007): 1–23.

Maass, R., J. Brown, and J. Bossert. *Supplier Certification: A Continuous Improvement Strategy.* Milwaukee, WIS: ASQC Press, 1990.

McIvor, R. and M. McHugh. "Partnership Sourcing: An Organization Change Management Perspective." *Journal of Supply Chain Management* (summer 2000): 12–20.

Mieghem, V. *Implementing Supplier Partnerships.* Upper Saddle River, NJ: Prentice Hall, 1995.

Moon, M. and L. Bonney. "An Application of the Investment Model to Buyer-Seller Relationships: A Dyadic Perspective." *Journal of Marketing Theory and Practice,* 15, no. 4 (fall 2007): 335 (13 pages).

Morgan, J. "New Survey Finds Big Gap Between Rhetoric and Reality." *Purchasing* (November 15, 2001), www.manufacturing.net/pur/.

Morgan, J. "Performance Measurement: New Competitive Importance!" *Purchasing* (February 8, 2002), www.manufacturing.net/pur/.

Parsons, A. "What Determines Buyer–Seller Relationship Quality? An Investigation from the Buyer's Perspective." *Journal of Supply Chain Management,* 38, no. 2 (spring 2002): 4–12.

Petros Sebhatu, S. and B. Enquist. "ISO 14001 as a Driving Force for Sustainable Development and Value Creation." *The TQM Magazine,* 19, no. 5 (2007): 468.

Sarkis, J. and S. Talluri. "A Model for Strategic Supplier Selection." *Journal of Supply Chain Management,* 38, no. 1 (winter 2002): 18–28.

Speckman, R., L. Isabella, and T. MacAvoy. *Alliance Competence: Maximizing the Value of Your Partnerships.* New York: John Wiley & Sons, 2000.

Spina, G. and G. Zotteri. "The Implementation Process of Customer-Supplier Partnership: Lessons from a Clinical Perspective." *International Journal of Operations & Production Management,* 20, no. 10 (2000): 1164–82.

Underhill, T. *Strategic Alliances: Managing the Supply Chain.* Tulsa, OK: Pennwell Publishing Company, 1996.

CHAPTER 4

Anderson, M. and P. Katz. "Strategic Sourcing." *International Journal of Logistics Management,* 9, no. 1 (1998): 1–13.

Burt, D., D. Dobler, and S. Starling. *World Class Supply Management: The Key to Supply Chain Management,* 7th ed. New York: McGraw-Hill/Irwin, 2003.

Kaplan, N. and J. Hurd. "Realizing the Promise of Partnerships." *Journal of Business Strategy,* 23, no. 3 (2002): 38–42.

Lummus, R., R. Vokurka, and K. Alber. "Strategic Supply Chain Planning." *Production and Inventory Management Journal,* 39, no. 3 (1998): 49–58.

Simchi-Levi, D., P. Kaminsky, and E. Simchi-Levi. *Designing and Managing the Supply Chain: Concepts, Strategies, and Case Studies,* 2nd ed. New York: McGraw-Hill/Irwin, 2003.

Vonderembse, M. "The Impact of Supplier Selection Criteria and Supplier Involvement on Manufacturing." *Journal of Supply Chain Management,* 35, no. 3 (1999): 33–39.

CHAPTER 5

Foote, P. S. and M. Krishnamurthi. "Forecasting Using Data Warehousing Model: Wal-Mart's Experience." *Journal of Business Forecasting Methods & Systems,* 20, no. 3 (fall 2001): 13–17.

Gilliland, M. "Is Forecasting a Waste of Time?" *Supply Chain Management Review* (July 1, 2002); available from http://www.scmr.com/article/CA237922.html.

"Global Commerce Initiative Recommended Guidelines for CPFR Version 2.0"; available from http://www.vics.org/committees/cpfr/voluntary_v2/CPFR_Tabs_061802.pdf.

Goeke, R. J. and R. H. Faley. "Leveraging the Flexibility of Your Data Warehousing." *Communications of the ACM,* 50, no. 10 (October 2007): 107–111.

Haugen, K. J. "Using Spreadsheets to Forecast Product Needs." *NAPM Insights* (November 1, 1994): 32; available from http://www.ism.ws.

Jain, C. L. "Benchmarking Forecasting Errors." *Journal of Business Forecasting,* 25, no. 4 (winter 2006/2007): 18–21.

Jain, C. L. "Benchmarking Forecasting Models." *Journal of Business Forecasting,* 25, no. 4 (winter 2006/2007): 14–17.

Jain, C. L. "Benchmarking Forecasting Practices in America." *Journal of Business Forecasting,* 25, no. 4 (winter 2006/2007): 9–13.

Jain, C. L. "Benchmarking Forecasting Software and Systems." *Journal of Business Forecasting,* 25, no. 4 (winter 2006/2007): 28–30.

Jain, C. L. "Benchmarking New Product Forecasting." *Journal of Business Forecasting,* 25, no. 4 (winter 2006/2007): 22–23.

Jain, C. L. "Questions to Ask When Reviewing the Benchmarking Data." *Journal of Business Forecasting,* 25, no. 4 (winter 2006/2007): 4–7.

Lapide, L. "Demand Management Revisited." *Journal of Business Forecasting,* 25, no. 3 (fall 2006): 17–19.

Makridakis, S., S. Wheelwright, and R. Hyndman. *Forecasting Methods and Applications.* New York: John Wiley & Sons, 1998.

Portougal, V. "Demand Forecast for a Catalog Retailing Company." *Production and Inventory Management Journal* (first/second quarter 2002): 29–34.

"The Evolution of CPFR." Syncra Systems Inc. (June 2003); available from http://hosteddocs.ittoolbox.com/MJ091004.pdf.

Smith, L. "West Marine: A CPFR Success Story." *Supply Chain Management Review* (March 1, 2006); available from http://www.scmr.com/article/CA6317964.html.

CHAPTER 6

Chase, R. B., F. R. Jacobs, and N. J. Aquilano. *Operations Management for Competitive Advantage,* 11th ed. Boston, MA: McGraw-Hill/Irwin, 2006.

Chopra, S. and P. Meindl. *Supply Chain Management,* 2nd ed. Upper Saddle River, NJ: Prentice Hall, 2004.

Duffy, R. J. and M. Gorsage. "Facing SRM and CRM." *Inside Supply Management,* 13, no. 8 (August 2002): 30–37.

Fogarty, D. W., J. H. Blackstone, and T. R. Hoffmann. *Production and Inventory Management,* 2nd ed. Cincinnati, OH: South-Western Publishing Co., 1991.

Monk, E. F. and B. J. Wagner. *Concepts in Enterprise Resource Planning,* 2nd ed. Boston, MA: Course Technology, 2005.

Simchi-Levi, D., P. Kaminsky, and E. Simchi-Levi. *Designing and Managing the Supply Chain: Concepts, Strategies, and Case Studies,* 2nd ed. Boston, MA: McGraw-Hill/Irwin, 2003.

Vollmann, T. E., W. L. Berry, D. C. Whybark, and F. R. Jacobs. *Manufacturing Planning and Control for Supply Chain Management,* 5th ed. Boston, MA: McGraw-Hill/Irwin, 2005.

CHAPTER 7

Chase, R. B., F. R. Jacobs, and N. J. Aquilano. *Operations Management for Competitive Advantage,* 11th ed. Boston, MA: McGraw-Hill/Irwin, 2006.

EPCglobal. "EPCglobal Tag Data Standards Version 1.3 Ratified Specification." EPCglobal Inc., March 8, 2006.

EPCglobal. "The EPCglobal Architecture Framework EPCglobal Final Version 1.2." EPCglobal Inc., September 10, 2007.

Fogarty, D. W., J. H. Blackstone, and T. R. Hoffmann. *Production & Inventory Management,* 2nd ed. Cincinnati, OH: South-Western Publishing Co., 1991.

Hax, A. and D. Candea. *Production and Inventory Management.* Englewood Cliffs, NJ: Prentice Hall, Inc., 1984.

Krajewski, L. J., L. P. Ritzman, and M. J. Malhorta. *Operations Management: Process and Value Chains,* 8th ed. Reading, MA: Prentice Hall, 2007.

Vollmann, T. E., W. L. Berry, D. C. Whybark, and F. R. Jacobs. *Manufacturing Planning and Control for Supply Chain Management,* 5th ed. Boston, MA: McGraw-Hill/Irwin, 2005.

CHAPTER 8

Burt, D. N., D. W. Dobler, and S. L. Starling. *World Class Supply Management: The Key to Supply Chain Management,* 7th ed. New York: McGraw-Hill, 2003.

Crosby, P. B. *Quality Is Free.* New York: McGraw-Hill, 1979.

Crosby, P. B. *Quality Without Tears.* New York: McGraw-Hill, 1984.

Deming, W. E. *Out of the Crisis.* Cambridge, MA: MIT Center for Advanced Engineering Study, 1986.

Evans, J. R. and W. M. Lindsay. *The Management and Control of Quality,* 4th ed. Cincinnati, OH: South-Western, 1999.

Heizer, J. and B. Render. *Principles of Operations Management,* 4th ed. Upper Saddle River, NJ: Prentice Hall, 2000.

Jacobs, F. and R. Chase. *Operations and Supply Management: The Core.* New York: McGraw-Hill/Irwin, 2008.

Juran, J. and A. Godfrey. *Juran's Quality Handbook.* New York: McGraw-Hill, 2000.

Krajewski, L., L. Ritzman, and M. Malhotra. *Operations Management: Processes and Value Chains,* 8th ed. Upper Saddle River, NJ: Pearson/PrenticeHall, 2007.

Lucier, G. and S. Seshadri. "GE Takes Six Sigma Beyond the Bottom Line." *Strategic Finance,* 82, no. 11 (2001): 40–46.

Smith, G. *Statistical Process Control and Quality Improvement.* New York: Macmillan, 1991.

Vokurka, R. J. and R. R. Lummus. "The Role of Just-in-Time in Supply Chain Management." *International Journal of Logistics Management,* 11, no. 1 (2000): 89–98.

CHAPTER 9

Bloomberg, D. J., S. LeMay, and J. B. Hanna. *Logistics.* Upper Saddle River, NJ: Prentice Hall, 2002.

Coyle, J. J., E. J. Bardi, and C. J. Langley. *The Management of Business Logistics,* St. Paul: West.

Lambert, D. M., J. R. Stock, and L. M. Ellram. *Fundamentals of Logistics Management.* New York: McGraw-Hill, 1998.

Sampson, R. J., M. T. Farris, and D. L. Shrock. *Domestic Transportation: Practice, Theory, and Policy,* 5th ed. Boston: Houghton Mifflin, 1985.

Stock, J. R. and D. M. Lambert. *Strategic Logistics Management,* 4th ed. New York: McGraw-Hill, 2001.

CHAPTER 10

Barnes, J. G. *Secrets of Customer Relationship Management.* New York, NY: McGraw-Hill, 2001.

Bergeron, B. *Essentials of CRM: A Guide to Customer Relationship Management.* New York, NY: John Wiley & Sons, 2002.

Bloomberg, D. J., S. LeMay., and J. B. Hanna. *Logistics.* Upper Saddle River, NJ: Prentice Hall, 2002.

Dychè, J. *The CRM Handbook: A Business Guide to Customer Relationship Management.* Upper Saddle River, NJ: Addison-Wesley, 2002.

Fitzsimmons, J. and M. Fitzsimmons. *Service Management for Competitive Advantage.* New York, NY: McGraw-Hill, 1994.

Lawrence, F. B., D. F. Jennings., and B. E. Reynolds. *eDistribution.* Mason, OH: South-Western, 2003.

Metters, R., K. King-Metters., and M. Pullman. *Successful Service Operations Management.* Mason, OH: South-Western, 2003.

CHAPTER 11

Arend, M. "Manufacturing Is on the Move." *Site Selection* (November 2002); online edition; available from www.siteselection.com.

Barnes, N. G., A. Connell, L. Hermenegildo, and L. Mattson. "Regional Differences in the Economic Impact of Wal-Mart." *Business Horizons* (July/August 1996): 21–25.

Barros, A. I. *Discrete and Fractional Programming Techniques for Location Models*. Dordrecht: Kluwer Academic Publishers, 1998.

Beckmann, M. J. *Lectures on Location Theory*. Berlin, New York: Springer-Verlag, 1999.

Bolton, J. and E. Chu. "Global Sourcing for High Performance: Leading Practices and the Emerging Role of International Procurement Organizations in China" (November 22, 2006); available from http://www.accenture.com/Countries/Netherlands/Research_and_Insights/By_Industry/Consumer_Goods_and_Services/GlobalSourcingHighPerformance.htm.

Brown, G. and A. McMahon. "The MATRIX: Here's the Smartest Way to Compare Factors and Narrow Your Location Choices." *Business Facilities* (April 2002); available from http://www.facilitycity.com/busfac/bf_02_04_cover.asp.

Clapp, D. "Making the Move: A Paradigm Shift in the Far East." *Business Facilities* (September 2002); available from http://www.facilitycity.com/busfac/bf_02_09_move.asp.

Clapp, D., M. E. McCandless, and K. Khan. "The World's Most Competitive Locations." *Business Facilities* (September 2001); available from http://www.facilitycity.com/busfac/bf_01_09_cover.asp.

Devan, J. E. Carr, I. Ho, S. Yiannouka, and J. A. Pantangc. "Doing Business in China: A McKinsey Survey of Executives in Asia." *The McKinsey Quarterly* (March 7, 2007); available online at http://www.mckinseyquarterly.com/Strategy/Globalization/Doing_business_in_China_A_McKinsey_Survey_of_executives_in_Asia_1887_abstract.

Drezner, Z. and H. W. Hamacher. *Facility Location: Applications and Theory*. Berlin: Springer-Verlag, 2004.

Ferdows, K. "Making the Most of Foreign Factories." *Harvard Business Review* (March–April 1977): 73–88.

Greenhut, M. L. *Location Economics: Theoretical Underpinnings and Applications*. Aldershot, UK; Brookfield, VT: Edward Elgar Publishing Limited, 1995.

Hack, G. D. *Site Selection for Growing Companies*. Westport, CT: Quorum Books, 1999.

Hagel, J. III and M. Singer. "Unbundling the Corporation." *Harvard Business Review* (March–April 1999): 133–41.

Jensen, K. and G. Pompelli. "Manufacturing Site Location Preferences of Small Agribusiness Firms." *Journal of Small Business Management,* 40, no. 3 (July 2002): 204–18.

Khan, K. "Project Persuasion." *Business Facilities* (July 2000); available from http://www.facilitycity.com/busfac/bf_02_07_cover.asp.

Lee, H. Y. H., V. M. R. Tummala, and R. C. M. Yam. "Manufacturing Support for Hong Kong Manufacturing Industries in Southern China"; available from http://www.ism.ws/ResourceArticles/2000/winter00p35.cfm.

MacCormack, A., D. Lawrence, J. Newmann III, and D. B. Rosenfield. "The New Dynamics of Global Manufacturing Site Location." *Sloan Management Review* (summer 1994): 69–79.

MacKay, S. "The New Rules for G7 Site Selection." *Business Facilities* (September 2002); available from http://www.facilitycity.com/busfac/bf_02_09_cover.asp.

Magretta, J. "The Power of Virtual Integration: An Interview with Dell Computer's Michael Dell." *Harvard Business Review* (March–April 1998): 72–84.

Mallot, J. "Quality of Life: How to Know It When You See It." *Business Facilities* (September 2002); available from http://www.facilitycity.com/busfac/bf_02_11_cover2.asp.

Porter, M. "Clusters and Competition: New Agenda for Companies, Government, and Institutions."*Harvard Business School Press Chapter* (June 7, 1999).

Porter, M. "Clusters and the New Economics of Competition." *Harvard Business Review* (November 1, 1998): 77–90.

Rufinni, F. "The New Face of Logistics: Technology and e-Commerce Have Reshaped the Horizons of Today's Largest Distribution Hubs." *Business Facilities* (September 2002); available from http://www.facilitycity.com/busfac/bf_02_09_special1.asp.

Scott, B. R. *Country Analysis in a "Global Village."* Harvard Business School Note #9-701-073 (January 12, 2001).

"Taming the Dragon: Mastering China's Growth Dynamics" (July 2005); available from http://www.accenture.com/Global/Netherlands/Research_and_Insights/policy_And_Corporate_Affairs/TamingTheDragonDynamics.htm.

CHAPTER 12

Anderson, D., D. Sweeney, and T. Williams. *An Introduction to Management Science*. Mason, OH: South-Western, 2003.

Davis, M., N. Aquilano, and R. Chase. *Fundamentals of Operations Management*. New York: McGraw-Hill, 1999.

Drazen, E., R. Moll, and M. Roetter. *Logistics in Service Industries.* Oak Brook, IL: Council of Logistics Management, 1991.

Fitzsimmons, J. and M. Fitzsimmons. *Service Management for Competitive Advantage.* New York: McGraw-Hill, 1994.

Heizer, B. and B. Render. *Principles of Operations Management.* Upper Saddle River, NJ: Prentice Hall, 2001.

Markland, R., S. Vickery, and R. Davis. *Operations Management.* Mason, OH: South-Western, 1998.

Metters, R., K. King-Metters, and M. Pullman. *Successful Service Operations Management.* Mason, OH: South-Western, 2003.

Rodriguez, C. *International Management: A Cultural Approach.* Mason, OH: South-Western, 2001.

Taha, H. A. *Operations Research: An Introduction.* Upper Saddle River, NJ: Prentice Hall, 2003.

Taylor, B. *Introduction to Management Science.* Upper Saddle River, NJ: Prentice Hall, 2002.

CHAPTER 13

Chopra, S. and P. Meindl. *Supply Chain Management: Strategy, Planning, and Operation.* Upper Saddle River, NJ: Prentice Hall, 2001.

Croxton, K. L., S. J. Garcia-Dastugue, D. M. Lambert, and D. S. Rogers. "The Supply Chain Management Processes." *International Journal of Logistics Management,* 12, no. 2 (2001): 13–36.

Handfield, R. B. and E. L. Nichols. *Supply Chain Redesign: Transforming Supply Chains into Integrated Value Systems.* Upper Saddle River, NJ: Prentice Hall, 2002.

Lambert, D. M., M. C. Cooper, and J. D. Pagh. "Supply Chain Management: Implementation Issues and Research Opportunities." *International Journal of Logistics Management,* 9, no. 2 (1998): 1–19.

Simchi-Levi, D., P. Kaminsky, and E. Simchi-Levi. *Designing and Managing the Supply Chain.* New York: McGraw-Hill/Irwin, 2003.

CHAPTER 14

Evans, J. R. and W. M. Lindsay. *The Management and Control of Quality.* Mason, OH: South-Western, 2002.

Kaplan, R. S. and D. P. Norton. "Linking the Balanced Scorecard to Strategy." *California Management Review,* 39, no. 1 (1996): 53–79.

Metters, R., K. King-Metters, and M. Pullman. *Successful Service Operations Management.* Mason, OH: South-Western, 2003.

Nicholas, J. M. *Competitive Manufacturing Management.* New York: McGraw-Hill, 1998.

Wisner, J. D. and S. E. Fawcett. "Linking Firm Strategy to Operating Decisions Through Performance Measurement." *Production and Inventory Management Journal,* 32, no. 3 (1991): 5–11.

Endnotes

CHAPTER 1

1. Mishra, D. "Optimizing the Supply Chain." *Dealerscope,* 49, no. 2 (2007): 26.

2. Quayle, M. "Purchasing and Supply Chain Management." *Information Management,* 19, no. 1/2 (2006): 1–3.

3. Carbone, J. "Supply Chain Manager of the Year: Steve Darendinger Champion of Change." *Purchasing,* 135, no. 13 (2006): 37.

4. Reprinted with permission of the publisher, the Institute for Supply Management™, "Glossary of Key Purchasing and Supply Terms" (2000).

5. Courtesy of the Supply-Chain Council.

6. Listed in the Council of Supply Chain Management Professionals' glossary of terms, www.cscmp.org.

7. Zieger, A. "Don't Choose the Wrong Supply Chain Partner." *Frontline Solutions,* 4, no. 6 (2003): 10–14.

8. Tan, K. C., S. B. Lyman, and J. D. Wisner. "Supply Chain Management: A Strategic Perspective." *International Journal of Operations and Production Management,* 2, no. 6 (2002): 614–31.

9. U.S. Census Bureau information found at http://www.census.gov/prod/2006pubs/am0531gs1.pdf, and transportation and inventory carrying cost information found in Cooke, J. "Logistics Costs Under Pressure." *Logistics Management* (July 1, 2006) online article at www.logisticsmgmt.com/article/CA6352889.html.

10. Keith, O. and M. Webber. "Supply-Chain Management: Logistics Catches Up with Strategy." *Outlook* (1982), cit. Christopher, M. G. *Logistics, The Strategic Issue.* London: Chapman and Hall, 1992.

11. Shaw, A. *Some Problems in Market Distribution.* Cambridge, MA: Harvard University Press, 1915.

12. Smith, J. "The Adam Smith of Supply Chain Management." *World Trade,* 19, no. 9 (2006): 62.

13. Avery, S. "Supply Chain Management Is Key to Meeting Requirements of Demanding Customers." *Purchasing,* 136, no. 1 (2007): 56.

14. Hill, S. "Taming the Beast," *MSI,* 20, no. 5 (2002): 38–44.

15. Carbone. "Supply Chain Manager of the Year."

16. Smith. "The Adam Smith of Supply Chain Management."

17. Mishra. "Optimizing the Supply Chain," 1.

18. Hannon, D. "3PL Helps Fashion Retailer Turnaround Its Supply Chain." *Purchasing,* 135, no. 17 (2006): 24.

19. Mishra, D. "Everyone's Business." *Dealerscope,* 48, no. 13 (2006): 164–5.

20. Mishra. "Everyone's Business."

21. Mejza, M. C. and J. D. Wisner. "The Scope and Span of Supply Chain Management." *International Journal of Logistics Management,* 12, no. 2 (2001): 37–55.

22. Anonymous. "Meeting Compliance Mandates Requires a Good Look at the Shop Floor." *Manufacturing Business Technology,* 25, no. 2 (2007): 16.

23. Field, A. "China Imposes 'Green' Rules." *Journal of Commerce,* 8, no. 8 (February 26, 2007): 40–41.

24. Lamming, R. and J. Hampson. "The Environment as a Supply Chain Management Issue." *British Journal of Management,* 7, Special Issue (1996): S45–62.

25. McLinden, S. "Always Low Energy." *National Real Estate Investor,* 49, no. 2 (2007): 16.

26. Hoffman, W. "CEOs Catch Logistics." *Traffic World* (March 6, 2006): 1.

27. Copyright © 1994 President and Fellows of Harvard College (the Beer Game board version) and © 2002 The MIT Forum for Supply Chain Innovation (the Beer Game computerized version). Interested students can visit http://beergame.mit.edu to learn more about the Beer Game and to play the computerized version of the game. Students can also read Hammond, J. H. "The Beer Game: Board Version," Harvard Business School case #9-694-104, rev. October 27, 1999 for more information.

CHAPTER 2

1. Anonymous. "Top CPOs." *Purchasing,* 135, no. 16 (November 2, 2006): 44–45.

2. Carbone, J. "Knock, Knock." *Purchasing,* 136, no. 4 (March 15, 2007): 24.

3. Carbone, J. "Electronics Design: Involve Buyers!" *Purchasing,* 131, no. 5 (March 21, 2002): 27.

4. "Statistics for Industry Groups and Industries: 2005." *Annual Survey of Manufactures,* U.S. Census Bureau (November 2006): 1.

5. ISM Glossary of Key Supply Management Terms, www.ism.ws, accessed October 15, 2007.

6. Tan, K. C. and R. Dajalos. "Purchasing Strategy in the 21st Century: E-Procurement." *Practix: Best Practices in Purchasing & Supply Chain Management,* 4, no. 3 (2001): 7–12.

7. Tan and Dajalos. "Purchasing Strategy in the 21st Century."

8. World Trade Organization. "World Trade 2006: Prospects for 2007." *WTO Press Release* # 472 (April 12, 2007).

9. Hornbeck, J. F. "CRS Report for Congress—NAFTA at Ten: Lessons from Recent Studies." Congressional Research Service, The Library of Congress, Order code RS21737 (February 13, 2004).

10. Case, S. and D. Arnold. "Greening Federal Purchasing." *Government Procurement* 13, no. 4 (August 2005): 18–26.

CHAPTER 3

1. "Doing Business with Boeing." The Boeing Company; available from http://www.boeing.com/companyoffices/doingbiz/index.html.

2. Quote from Michael Dempsey, vice president of global direct procurement, Bowes, P. "Supplier Relationship Management: Pathways to Convergence." *Purchasing* (April 5, 2007), http://www.purchasing.com/article/CA6429358.html?text=srm.

3. "ISM Glossary of Key Supply Management Terms: Supplier Partnership." Institute of Supply Management.

4. Stundza, T. "Ford Has a Better Idea." *Purchasing* (September 7, 2006).

5. Ohmae, K. "The Global Logic of Strategic Alliances." *Harvard Business Review* (March–April 1989): 143–52.

6. Lewis, Jordan D. *Trusted Partners: How Companies Build Mutual Trust and Win Together.* New York, NY: The Free Press, 1999, p. 7.

7. "Buyers Target Strategic Partners." *Purchasing* (April 5, 2001),www.manufacturing.net/pur/.

8. "Supplier Selection & Management Report," March 2002, Institute of Management and Administration (IOMA).

9. Stephen R. Covey, Stephen R. Covey Quotations, Stephen R. Covey Sayings—Famous Quotes and Famous Sayings Network Web site.

10. MacDonald, M. "Managing Change: A Matter of Principle." *Supply Chain Management Review* (January/February, 2002),www.manufacturing.net/scm/.

11. Atkinson, W. "Whirpool's Procurement Takes the Lead in Outsourcing." *Purchasing Magazine Online* (March 1, 2007).

12. Drab, D. "Economic Espionage and Trade Secret Theft: Defending Against the Pickpockets of the New Millennium." August 2003, Xerox Corporation; available from http://www.xerox.com/downloads/wpaper/x/xgs_business_insight_economic_espionage.pdf.

13. Drab. "Economic Espionage and Trade Secret Theft."

14. Hannon, D. "Best Practices: Hackett Group Outlines the World-Class Procurement Organization." *Purchasing* (December 8, 2006).

15. "Designed to Differentiate: How Procurement Leaders Are Using Supplier Relationship Management to Achieve High Performance." Accenture, 2006; available from http://www.accenture.com/NR/rdonlyres/40BC378B-C7C5-4ED4-8825-881334D9F318/0/SRM__survey_final.pdf.

16. Babineaux, F. M. "Measuring Supplier Performance (How to Get What You Measure and Other Intentional Consequences)." 87th Annual International Supply Management Conference, 2002 International Conference Proceedings, May 2002, Institute of Supply Management Web site.

17. "ISM Glossary of Key Supply Management Terms: Total Cost of Ownership." Institute of Supply Management.

18. Kelly, K. M. "Lessons from the Toy Aisle." *Automotive Design & Production*, 119, no. 10 (October 2007): 8.

19. Finstad, R. "Total Recall: A Flawed System of Trade." *Far Eastern Economic Review,* 70, no. 9 (November 2007): 46–50.

20. Stundza, T. "Top Suppliers Get Awards, Business." *Purchasing* (November 16, 2006); available from http://www.purchasing.com/article/CA6389588.html

21. "Honeywell E-Business Case Study Supply Line"; available from http://www.honeywell.com/eventures/announcement_details.jsp?rowID=2&docID=16&catID=13.

22. "Glossary of Key Supply Management Terms: Supplier Certification," Institute of Supply Management Web site.

23. "Supplier Certification: A Continuous Improvement Strategy." Tompkins Associates—M-49, www.tompkinsinc.com.

24. The ISO Survey—2005; available from http://www.iso.org/iso/survey2005.pdf.

25. Han, B., S. K. Chen, and M. Ebrahimpour. "The Impact of ISO 9000 on TQM and Business Performance." *The Journal of Business and Economic Studies,* 13, no. 2 (fall 2007): (1:25 pages).

26. The ISO Survey—2005.

27. Sebhatu, S.P. and B. Enquist. "ISO 14001 as a Driving Force for Sustainable Development and Value Creation." *The TQM Magazine,* 19, no. 5 (2007): 468.

28. Handfield, R. B., D. R. Krause, T, V. Scannell, and R. M. Monzka. "Avoid the Pitfalls in Supplier Development." *Sloan Management Review* (winter 2000): 37–49.

29. Stundza. "Top Suppliers Get Awards, Business."

30. Handfield, Krause, Scannell, and Monzka, "Avoid the Pitfalls in Supplier Development."

31. "Supplier Continuous Quality Improvement Program"; available from https://supplier.intel.com/static/quality/scqi/FINAL_SCQI_Brochure.pdf.

32. "Supplier Continuous Quality Improvement Program."

33. Porter, A, M. "Just the Facts." *Purchasing* (April 18, 2002), www.manufacturing.net/pur/.

34. Stundza. "Top Suppliers Get Awards, Business."

35. Phillip Morris USA—Our Initiatives & Programs: Supplier Recognition Program; available from http://www.philipmorrisusa.com/en/our_initiatives/suppliers_guidelines_programs/supplier_recognition_program.asp.

36. "Fifty-Five 2006 World Excellence Awards Presented to Ford's Global Suppliers," The Ford Motor Company; available from http://media.ford.com/newsroom/release_display.cfm?release=25874.

37. "Intel Honors 44 Companies with Preferred Quality Supplier Award"; available from http://www.intel.com/pressroom/archive/releases/20070327corp_a.htm.

38. "Hormel Foods Corporation Announces Supplier Awards." (September 27, 2006); available from http://www.hormelfoods.com/newsroom/press/20060927a.aspx.

39. Stundza. "Top Suppliers Get Awards, Business."

40. Barling, B. "The Five Tenets of SRM." *AMR Research* (June 10, 2002), www.amrresearch.com.

41. "Effective Supplier Relationship Management—Accenture Researches the Correlation with High Performance Business"; available from: http://www.accenture.com/Countries/South_Africa/About_Accenture/Newsroom/News_Releases/EffectiveHPBusiness.htm.

42. "A Study of Emerging Issues and Cutting-Edge Knowledge." SAS Institute Inc.; available from http://www.sas.com/solutions/sci/special_report.pdf.

43. "Survey—Supply Chain Management." *Financial Times (London),* June 20, 2001, p. 6.

44. "A Study of Emerging Issues and Cutting-Edge Knowledge." SAS Institute Inc.; available from http://www.sas.com/solutions/sci/special_report.pdf.

45. Barling. "The Five Tenets of SRM."

46. O'Rourke, B. "Manage Supplier Relationships for Repeatable, Sustainable ROI." *Inside Supply Chain Intelligence–A Study of Emerging Issues and Cutting-Edge Knowledge,* pp. 22–26, SAS Institute Inc.; available from http://www.sas.com/solutions/srm/report.html.

47. O'Rourke. "Manage Supplier Relationship for Repeatable, Sustainable ROI.

48. "Supplier Relationship Management (SRM): The SupplyWorks Answer to Accelerating Competitive Advantage." *Business Matters #2,* A Series of Manufacturing SRM Business Briefs from SupplyWorks, Inc., May 2001.

49. "Customer Success: From Purchasing to Profits—SAS Uses Its Own SAS® Supplier Relationship Management to Drive Strategic Sourcing." SAS; available from http://www.sas.com/success/sas_srm.html.

50. Smith, V. C. "Supplier Relationship Management and Procurement: Driving Value Through Best Practices." 2006 ASUG/SAP Benchmarking Study, http:www.sap.com.

CHAPTER 4

1. Quote by Paul Cousins, professor of supply chain management at Manchester Business School. Found in Bradley, A. "Purchasers Urged to be Strategic." *Supply Management,* 11, no. 22 (2006): 12.

2. Quote from Tony English, managing director at Purcon, a purchasing consultancy. Found in Ellinor, R. "Interims Cash in on Demand Boost." *Supply Management,* 11, no. 15 (2006): 13.

3. Ellinor, R. "Taking a Larger Slice of the Market." *Supply Management,* 11, no. 1 (2006): 15.

4. Mytton, G. "Purchasers Progress in Pay League." *Supply Management,* 11, no. 12 (2006): 7.

5. Ellinor, R. "Huge Demand for Top Purchasers." *Supply Management,* 11, no. 15 (2006): 11.

6. Fisher, M. "What Is the Right Supply Chain for Your Product?" *Harvard Business Review,* 75, no. 2 (1997): 105–16.

7. Snell, P. "Chrysler Ups Spend on Low-Cost Sourcing." *Supply Management,* 12, no. 5 (2007): 8.

8. Adapted from: Lummus, R., R. Vokurka, and K. Alber. "Strategic Supply Chain Planning." *Production and Inventory Management Journal,* 39, no. 3 (1998): 49–58.

9. Morrissey, H. "Be a Top Flight Customer." *Supply Management,* 11, no. 17 (2006): 30.

10. See, for example, Simpson, P., J. Siguaw, and S. White. "Measuring the Performance of Suppliers: An Analysis of Evaluation Processes." *Journal of Supply Chain Management,* 38, no. 1 (2002): 29–41; Wisner, J. and K. Tan. "Supply Chain Management and Its Impact on Purchasing." *Journal of Supply Chain Management,* 36, no. 4 (2000): 33–42.

11. Anonymous. "Nu Horizons Awarded Lockheed's STAR Supplier Award." *FinancialWire* (August 30, 2006): 1.

12. Simpson, Siguaw, and White. "Measuring the Performance of Suppliers," 29–41.

13. Trent, R. and R. Monczka. "Achieving World-Class Supplier Quality." *Total Quality Management,* 10, no. 6 (1999): 927–38.

14. The interested reader is invited to navigate the ISO Web page: www.iso.org.

15. Kelly, K. "Overcoming Negative Quality Stereotypes at Chrysler." *Automotive Design & Production,* 118, no. 2 (2006): 54.

16. For more information, see the Goldman Environmental Prize Web page: www.goldmanprize.org.

17. For more information about ISO certifications, see Web page: www.iso.org.

18. Anonymous. "Getting Leaner—Ahead of the Pack: Suppliers Adjust to New Packaging Priorities." *Retailing Today* (fourth quarter 2006): 16.

19. Snell, P. "Struggle with Sustainability." *Supply Management,* 11, no. 23 (2006): 7.

20. For more information about the Institute for Supply Management, see Web page: www.ism.ws.

21. Ellinor, R. "Costing the Earth." *Supply Management,* 12, no. 2 (2007): 24.

22. Snell, P. "Struggle with Sustainability".

23. Anonymous. "Getting Leaner—Ahead of the Pack."

24. For more information, see the TerraChoice Web page: www.terrachoice.com.

25. Case, S. "Fighting Global Warming: Government Purchasers Play an Important and Growing Role." *Government Procurement,* 15, no. 1 (2007): 18.

26. For more information, see www.capsresearch.org.

27. Whitten, D. and D. Leidner. "Bringing IT Back: An Analysis of the Decision to Backsource or Switch Vendors." *Decision Sciences,* 37, no. 4 (2006): 605–22.

28. Atkinson, W. "Chevron Leverages Buyers in Outsourcing Decisions." *Purchasing,* 135, no. 5 (2006): 20.

29. Forth, K. "Insourcing to Improve Output." *FDM,* 78, no. 5 (2006): 30–35.

30. Whitten and Leidner. "Bringing IT Back."

31. Bailor, C. "Making a Clear Connection." *Customer Relationship Management,* 9, no. 5 (2005): 30–35.

32. Purdum, T. "VMI: Size Matters." *Industry Week,* 256, no. 3 (2007): 19–20.

33. Shister, N. "Applying the ideas of the Wal-Marts of the World to Smaller Companies." *World Trade,* 19, no. 3 (2006): 26–29.

34. Albright, B. "No More Label Worries." *Frontline Solutions,* 3, no. 9 (2002): 54.

35. Varmazis, M. "Dow Leverages Vendor-Managed Inventory for Office Supplies." *Purchasing,* 136, no. 2 (2007): 40.

36. Thompson, V. *Ignited.* Upper Saddle River, NJ: Financial Times Prentice Hall, 2007.

37. Atkinson, W. "Does JIT II Still Work in the Internet Age?" *Purchasing,* 130, no. 17 (2001): 41–42.

38. Anonymous "Chrysler Embarks on 'Most Advanced Supplier Co-Location Project'." *MSI,* 22, no. 11 (2004): 48.

39. Deierlein, B. "JIT: Zero Tolerance for Late Deliveries." *Fleet Equipment,* 26, no. 1 (2000): 36–39.

40. Avery, S. "Linking Supply Chains Saves Raytheon $400 Million." *Purchasing,* 130, no. 16 (2001): 27–31.

41. See, for example, Langfield-Smith, K. and D. Smith. "Management Control Systems and Trust in Outsourcing Relationships." *Management Accounting Research,* 14, no. 3 (2003): 281–307; Ertel, D. "Alliance Management: A Blueprint for Success." *Financial Executive,* 17, no. 9 (2001): 36–41.

42. Dyer, J., P. Kale, and H. Singh. "How to Make Strategic Alliances Work." *Sloan Management Review,* 42, no. 4 (2001): 37–43.

43. Park, S. and J. Hartley. "Exploring the Effect of Supplier Management on Performance in the Korean Automotive Supply Chain." *Journal of Supply Chain Management,* 38, no. 2 (2002): 46–52.

44. Anonymous "Before Implementation: Know Where You're Going." *Logistics Management* (November 2004): 24–25.

45. Fosdick, G. and M. Uphoff. "Adopting Cross-Industry Best Practices for Measurable Results." *Healthcare Executive,* 22, no. 3 (2007): 14–19.

46. See, for instance, Andersen, B., T. Fagerhaug, S. Randmael, J. Schuldmaier, and J. Prenninger. "Benchmarking Supply Chain Management: Finding Best Practices." *Journal of Business and Industrial Marketing,* 14, no. 5/6 (1999): 378–89; Carr, A. and L. Smeltzer. "The Relationship among Purchasing Benchmarking, Strategic Purchasing, Firm Performance, and Firm Size." *Journal of Supply Chain Management,* 35, no. 4 (1999): 51–60; Trent and Monczka. "Achieving World-Class Supplier Quality," 927–38; Ellram, L., G. Zsidisin, S. Siferd, and M. Stanly. "The Impact of Purchasing and Supply Management on Corporate Success." *Journal of Supply Chain Management,* 38, no. 1 (2002): 4–17.

47. Hoffman, W. "3PLs Maturing Fast." *Traffic World* (November 27, 2006): 1.

48. Anonymous "Radar Screen." *Journal of Commerce* (February 5, 2007): 1.

49. Verespej, M. "Logistics' New Look? It's Now Service." *Frontline Solutions,* 3, no. 6 (2002): 24–33.

50. Biederman, D. "A Matter of Trust." *Journal of Commerce* (April 9, 2007): 1.

51. Giunipero, L. and D. Pearcy, "World-Class Purchasing Skills: An Empirical Investigation." *Journal of Supply Chain Management,* 36, no. 4 (2000): 4–13.

CHAPTER 5

1. "Profitably Manage Your Customer Demand," White Paper, i2 Technologies, Inc. (October 2001); available from http://www.i2.com/web505/media/9E16A575-18D3-47B0-A0B734EA8DCC5691.pdf.

2. ISM Report on Business Web site: http://www.ism.ws/ISMReport/content.cfm?ItemNumber=10743&navItemNumber=12944.

3. The Institute for Supply Management. *Manufacturing and Non-Manufacturing Report on Business.* The Institute for Supply Management (May 2007).

4. Ibid.

5. Fisher, M., J. Hammond, W. Obermeyer, and A. Raman. "Making Supply Meet Demand in an Uncertain World." *Harvard Business Review* (May–June 1994): 83–93.

6. "PlayStation Sales Zoom." *New York Times,* March 7, 2000.

7. Pham, A. "Sony to Cut Game Workers in U.S." *Los Angeles Times,* June 7, 2007, p. C.3.

8. Wingfield, N. "Sony Cut PlayStation 3 Price to Lift Sales." *Wall Street Journal,* July 9, 2007.

9. Phillips, M. "The Afternoon Report: The iPhone Weekend." Online Edition, *Wall Street Journal,* July 2, 2007.

10. Cheng, R. "Apple Takes Hit on AT&T's iPhone Sales." *Wall Street Journal,* July 25, 2007, p. B4.

11. Knox, N. "A380 Makes Massive Debut." *USA Today;* available from www.usatoday.com/money/biztravel/2005-01-16-a380-usat_x.htm.

12. Armstrong, D. "Airbus A380's Arrival Brings Immense Questions." *San Francisco Chronicle,* March 19, 2007; available from http://sfgate.com/cgi-bin/article.cgi?f=/c/a/2007/03/19/BUGGVONSL916.DTL.

13. Annett, T. "The Afternoon Report: Air-Show Business." Online Edition, *Wall Street Journal,* June 18, 2007.

14. Fisher, Hammond, Obermeyer, and Raman, "Making Supply Meet Demand."

15. Jain, C. L. "Forecasting Process at Wyeth Ayerst Global Pharmaceuticals." *The Journal of Business Forecasting* (winter 2001–2002): 3–4, 6.

16. Jain, C. L. "Benchmarking Forecasting Models." *The Journal of Business Forecasting,* 25, no. 4 (winter 2006/2007): 14–17.

17. Lawrence, M., M. O'Conner, and B. Edmundson. "A Field Study of Forecasting Accuracy and Processes." *European Journal of Operational Research,* 22, no. 1 (April 1, 2000): 151–60.

18. Global Commerce Initiative Web site: http://www.gci-net.org.

19. VICS Collaborative Planning, Forecasting and Replenishment (CPFR): An Overview, May 18, 2004.

20. Ibid.

21. Smith, L. "West Marine: A CPFR Success Story"; available from www.scmr.com/article/CA6317964.html.

22. Ibid.

23. "CPFR Pilot Project Overview." VICS CPFR; available from www.cpfr.org/documents/ pdf/07_4_0_CPFR_pilot_Overview.pdf.

24. Jain, C. L. "Benchmarking Forecasting Practices in America." *The Journal of Business Forecasting,* 25, no. 4 (winter 2006/2007): 9–13.

25. i2 Technologies Web site; available from http://www.i2.com.

26. "Profitably Manage Your Customer Demand." White Paper, i2 Technologies, Inc. (October 1, 2001).

27. "The Next Wave of Supply Chain Advantage: Collaborative Planning, Forecasting, and Replenishment." Industry Directions Inc. and Syncra Systems, Inc. (April 2000); available from http://www.industrydirections.com/pdf/CPFRPublicReport.pdf.

28. Uchneat, J. "CPFR's Woes Not Related to Trust." *Computerworld* (July 22, 2002); available from www.computerworld.com/news/2002/story/0,11280,72834,00.html.

29. Wal-Mart "Exceeding Customer Expectations"; available from www.walmartstores.com/wmstore/wmstores/Mainabout.jsp?BV_SessionID=@@@@0340977454.1067474232@@@@&BV_EngineID=ccccadcjjgkkfhmcfkfcfkjdgoodglh.0&pagetype=about&template=DisplayAllContents.jsp&categoryOID=−8276&catID=−8242.

30. Johnson, A. H. "A New Supply Chain Forged." *Computerworld* (September 30, 2002); available from www.computerworld.com/industrytopics/retail/story/0,10801,74647,00.html.

31. Goeke, R. J. and R. H. Faley. "Leveraging the Flexibility of Your Data Warehousing." *Communications of the ACM,* 50, no. 10 (October 2007): 107–111.

32. Troy, M. "When Hurricanes Strike … Landfall Could Mean Windfall." *Retailing Today,* 46, no. 9 (June 4, 2007): 4–33.

33. Jain, C. L. "Benchmarking Forecasting Software and Systems." *The Journal of Business Forecasting,* 25, no. 4 (winter 2006/2007): 28–30.

34. "i2 Demand Collaboration." i2 Web site; available from www.i2technologies.com/web505/media/CBF9A153-1181-4C3A-822EA9C6F7C94B3E.pdf.

CHAPTER 6

1. Field, A. M. "Stretching the Limits of ERP." *Journal of Commerce,* 8 (January 2007): 76–78.

2. Aberdeen Group. *The ABCs of ERP: An Executive Primer.* Boston, MA: Aberdeen Group, Inc., August 2004.

3. www.gnc.com/corp/index.jsp?page=history, August 17, 2007.

4. www.logility.com, August 17, 2007.

5. Fogarty, D. W., J. H. Blackstone, and T. R. Hoffmann. *Production and Inventory Management,* 2nd ed. Cincinnati, OH: South-Western Publishing Co., 1991.

6. Anonymous. "New Technology." *Management Sciences* 46, no. 10 (October 2002): 24–8.

7. Zygmont, J. "Mixmasters Find an Alternative to All-in-One ERP Software." *Datamation* (February 1, 1999); available from http://itmanagement.earthweb.com/erp/article.php/608181.

8. Turbide, D. "ERP Outlook: Your Company's Needs Make a Difference." *APICS Magazine,* 17, no. 7 (July/August 2007): 15.

9. Roberto, M. "ERP Enters Age of Infrastructure." *Manufacturing Business Technology,* 25, no. 7 (July 2007): 24–25.

10. Curt, B. "The ERP Edge." *Multichannel Merchant,* 3, no. 7 (July 2007): 50–54.

11. Roberto. "ERP Enters Age of Infrastructure."

12. Jutras, C. *The ERP in Manufacturing Benchmark Report.* Boston, MA: Aberdeen Group, Inc., August 2006, pp. 1–31.

13. Roberto. "ERP Enters Age of Infrastructure."

CHAPTER 7

1. Dibenedetto, B. "Putting VIM in VMI: Retailers Can Gain an Edge Through Vendor-managed Inventory." *Journal of Commerce,* 8, no. 6 (February 12, 2007): 34–35.

2. Wal-Mart Stores, Inc. Annual Report on Form 10-K for the Fiscal Year Ended January 31, 2007.

3. Target Corp. Annual Report on Form 10-K for the Fiscal Year Ended February 3, 2007.

4. Sears Holdings Corporation. Annual Report on Form 10-K for the Fiscal Year Ended February 3, 2007.

5. http://www.epcglobalinc.org/home, accessed September 24, 2007.

6. Anonymous. "Wal-Mart, DOD Start Massive RFID Rollout; Is Everybody Ready?" 5, no. 1 (January 2005): 1, 10–12.

7. Songini, M. L. "Procter & Gamble: Wal-Mart RFID Effort Effective." *ComputerWorld,* 41, no. 9 (February 26, 2007): 14.

8. http://en.wikipedia.org/wiki/Image:EPC-RFID-TAG.jpg, accessed October 7, 2007. (Wikimedia Commons is a freely licensed media file repository).

9. Narsimhan, S., D. W. McLeavey, and P. Billington. *Production Planning and Inventory Control,* 2nd ed. Upper Saddle River, NJ: Prentice Hall, 1995.

CHAPTER 8

1. Quote by Dr. Karl Manrodt, Georgia Southern University, in Kerr, J. "What Does 'Lean' Really Mean?" *Logistics Management,* 45, no. 5 (2006): 29–33.

2. Quote by Mr. Charles King, director of continuous process improvement at Connecticut-based Kaman Industrial Technologies, in Trombly, R. "Running Lean, Running Strong." *Industrial Distribution,* 91, no. 8 (2002): 53–55.

3. For histories of lean and the Toyota Production System see, for instance, Becker, R. "Learning to Think Lean: Lean Manufacturing and the Toyota Production System." *Automotive Manufacturing & Production,* 113, no. 6 (2001): 64–65; Dahlgaard, J. and S. Dahlgaard-Park. "Lean Production, Six Sigma Quality, TQM and Company Culture." *TQM Magazine,* 18, no. 3 (2006): 263–77.

4. Information on the Ford manufacturing system was found at www.lean.org.

5. Manivannan, S. "Error-Proofing Enhances Quality." *Manufacturing Engineering,* 137, no. 5 (2006): 99–105.

6. Nakamoto, M. and J. Reed. "Toyota Claims Global Top Spot from GM." *FT.com* (April 24, 2007): 1.

7. Womack, J., D. Jones, and D. Roos. *The Machine That Changed the World.* New York, NY: Maxwell Macmillan International, 1990.

8. Ben-Tovim, D., J. Bassham, D. Bolch, and M. Martin. "Lean Thinking Across a Hospital: Redesigning Care at the Flinders Medical Centre." *Australian Health Review,* 31, no. 1 (2007): 10–15.

9. Anonymous. "A Small Company Makes Big Gains Implementing Lean." *Management Services,* 50, no. 3 (2006): 28–31.

10. Kerr. "What Does 'Lean' Really Mean?"

11. Forger, G. "Trends in Distribution, Warehousing, and Manufacturing." *Modern Materials Handling,* 62, no. 1 (2007): 1.

12. Kerr. "What Does 'Lean' Really Mean?"

13. Hill, W. and W. Kearney. "The Honeywell Experience." *ASQ Six Sigma Forum Magazine,* 2, no. 2 (2003): 34–38.

14. Campbell, K. "The Endless Journey." *Plant Engineering,* 60, no. 8 (2006): 51.

15. Anonymous. "Tool for Productivity, Quality, Throughput, Safety." *Management Services,* 50, no. 3 (2006): 16–18; Becker, J. "Implementing 5S: To Promote Safety & Housekeeping." *Professional Safety,* 46, no. 8 (2001): 29–31.

16. Marks, J. "Wal-Mart Sharpens Direct Sourcing Focus." *Home Textiles Today,* 27, no. 41 (2006): 1.

17. Shaw, M. "Customers Drive End-Product Attributes, Technology Choices at MeadWestvaco Mill." *Pulp Paper,* 78, no. 1 (2004): 40.

18. Caulk, S. "Warehouse Changes Are Just in Time." *Purchasing Today* (March 2000 Supplement).

19. Gourley, C. "What's Driving the Automotive Supply Chain?" *Warehouse Management,* 5, no. 10 (1998): 44–48.

20. DiBenedetto, B. "Thinking Lean." *Journal of Commerce* (May 21, 2007): 1.

21. Varley, P. "All-Inclusive Deal." *Supply Management,* 4, no. 21 (1999): 40–41.

22. Aaron, L. J. "From Push to Pull: The Supply Chain Management Shift." *Apparel Industry Magazine,* 59, no. 6 (1998): 58–59.

23. Anonymous. "Improvements Drilled Through." *Works Management,* 59, no. 10 (2006): 38–39.

24. Gourley, C. "What's Driving the Automotive Supply Chain?" *Warehousing Management,* 5, no. 10 (1998): 44–48.

25. Deming, W. *Out of the Crisis.* Cambridge, MA: MIT Press, 1993.

26. King, A. and M. Lenox. "Lean and Green? An Empirical Examination of the Relationship Between Lean Production and Environmental Performance." *Production and Operations Management,* 10, no. 3 (2001): 244–56.

27. Beazant, G. "Lean, Green Driving Machine." 19, no. 12 (2006): 34–35.

28. Blanchard, D. "Diagnosis: Green and Lean." *Industry Week,* 255, no. 9 (2006): 13.

29. Smith, M. "Going Green Drives Sales." *Printing Impressions,* 49, no. 10 (2007): 60–61.

30. Phillips, E. "Six Sigma: The Breakthrough Management Strategy Revolutionizing the World's Top Corporations." *Consulting to Management,* 13, no. 4 (2002): 57–59.

31. Information about Six Sigma and sigma drift can be found at multiple locations, for example, www.isixsigma.com, or www.wikipedia.org/Six_Sigma.

32. Arnheiter, E. and J. Maleyeff. "Research and Concepts: The Integration of Lean Management and Six Sigma." *TQM Magazine,* 17, no. 1 (2005): 5–18.

33. Blanchard. "Diagnosis: Green and Lean."

34. See, for example, *CRN* (June 4, 2007): 12 and Phillips. "Six Sigma."

35. "Business Brief—Primary PDC Inc.: Joint Bankruptcy Plan Filed to Dissolve Former Polaroid." *Wall Street Journal* (January 17, 2003): B-3.

36. "Six Sigma and Lean: A Marriage in the Making." *Business Credit,* 108, no. 10 (2006): 35.

37. McClenahen, J. "Where Lean Is on Target." *Industry Week,* 255, no. 10 (2006): 36.

38. Harbert, T. "Lean, Mean, Six Sigma Machines." *Electronic Business,* 32, no. 6 (2006): 38–42.

39. Byrne, G., D. Lubowe, and A. Blitz. "Using a Lean Six Sigma Approach to Drive Innovation." *Strategy and Leadership,* 35, no. 2 (2007): 5–9.

40. "Mattel Issues New Massive China Toy Recall." August 14, 2007, www.msnbc.msn.com/id/20254745.

41. Sharrock, R. "Road to Gold." *Industrial Engineer,* 39, no. 5 (2007): 44–48.

42. Butman, J. and J. Roessner. "An Immigrant's Gift: The Life of Quality Pioneer Joseph M. Juran." PBS Documentary Video, produced by Howland Blackiston, copyright WoodsEnd, Inc.

43. Baldrige information was obtained from the official Web site: www.nist.gov.

44. ISO information was obtained from the organization's Web site: www.iso.org.

45. Information found in the Web site: www.ge.com/sixsigma.

46. Descriptions found in the Web sites: www.isixsigma.com, www.asq.org, and www.xlp.com.

47. Adapted from: Table 27 of the ASTM STP 15D ASTM *Manual on Presentation of Data and Control Chart Analysis,* © 1976 American Society for Testing and Materials, Philadelphia, PA.

CHAPTER 9

1. Cassidy, W. "Next-Day Is Now." Charles Hammel, president of Pitt Ohio Express, in, *Traffic World* (April 18, 2005): 1.

2. Hannon, D. "Put the Umbrellas Away, the Sky Is not Falling." Eric Starks, president of logistics consulting firm FTR Associates of Indiana, in *Purchasing,* 136, no. 10 (2007): 78.

3. Council of Logistics Management, http://www.clm1.org/mission.html (February 12, 1998).

4. Hasbrouck, E. "FAQ About Airline Bankruptcies." *The Practical Nomad,* found at www.hasbrouck.org/articles/bankruptcy.html.

5. "Swift Currents, Debris Slow Recovery Effort," August 13, 2007; found at http://www.npr.org.

6. Rohman, R. "Regional LTLs Stake Out New Turf." *Logistics Management,* 42, no. 2 (2002): 33–36.

7. Belman, D. L. and K. A. Monaco "The Effects of Deregulation, De-unionization, Technology, and Human Capital on the Work Lives of Truck Drivers." *Industrial & Labor Relations Review,* 54, no. 2A (2001): 502–24.

8. "Acela Express, USA," found at www.railway-technology.com/projects/amtrak/.

9. Macklem, K. "Is There a Fast Train Coming?" *MacLean's,* 116, no. 8 (2003): 24–25; Hood, C. "Biting the Bullet: What We Can Learn from the Shinkansen." *Electronic Journal of Contemporary Japanese Studies* (May 23, 2001): Discussion paper No. 3.

10. "The World's Top Cargo Airlines." *Traffic World* (January 15, 2007): 1; Hannon, D. "Shippers Leverage Air Cargo as Global Sourcing Extends Supply." *Purchasing,* 136, no. 5 (2007): 25–27.

11. Hibbert, L. "Out of the Backwater." *Professional Engineering,* 15, no. 7 (2002): 26–27; British Waterways publication, "New Freight on Inland Waterways," found at www.british-waterways.co.uk/images/BWFBroc1_tcm6-71390.pdf.

12. Singhj, B. "The World's Biggest Ship." *The India Tribune* (online edition), July 11, 1999, www.tribuneindia.com/1999/99jul11/sunday/head3.htm.

13. Information found at en.wikipedia.org/wiki/Container_ship.

14. BNSF Web site: www.bnsf.com.

15. Atlantic Container Line Web site: www.aclcargo.com.

16. "AMR Posts Q4 Upside Surprise; Southwest Air's Profit Drops on Fuel Costs." *Seeking Alpha,* (January 18, 2007), www.transport.seekingalpha.com/article/24419.

17. BBC news item, "U.S. Airline Security Chief Quits," April 9, 2005, www.news.bbc.co.uk.

18. Boyd, J. and J. Gallagher. "Taking Aim at Transportation." *Traffic World* (April 9, 2007): 1; Keane, A. "Order of the Day: Secure Surface Transportation." *Traffic World* (December 18, 2006): 1; Natter, A. "Tracking Mexican Trucks." *Traffic World* (July 2, 2007): 1; Phillips, Z. "Fish Story." *Government Executive,* 39, no. 7 (2007): 39–43; Smith, C. "Seeking Pipeline Security." *Oil & Gas Journal,* 105, no. 7 (2007): 15.

19. Jerman, R. E. and R. D. Anderson. "Regulatory Issues: Shipper versus Motor Carrier." *Transportation Journal,* 33, no. 3, (1994): 15–23.

20. Mueller, G. and A. Mueller. "Warehouse Demand and the Path of Goods Movement." *Journal of Real Estate Portfolio Management,* 13, no. 1 (2007): 45–55.

21. Feare, T. "Jazzing Up the Warehouse." *Modern Material Handling,* 56, no. 7 (2001): 71–72.

22. Terreri, A. "The Course to Outsource." *Warehousing Management,* 8, no. 9 (2001): 35–38.

23. Maister, D. H. "Centralization of Inventories and the 'Square Root Law'." *International Journal of Physical Distribution and Materials Management,* 6, no. 3 (1976): 124–34.

24. Schipper, R. "Centralized vs. Distributed Warehousing in Europe: From Make-Hold-Sell to Sell-Source-Deliver." *World Trade,* 13, no. 1 (2000): 64–66.

25. Hoover, E. M. *The Location of Economic Activity.* New York: McGraw-Hill, 1948.

26. Warnenburg, C.M., trans. and P. Hall, ed., *von Thunen's Isolated State.* Oxford: Pergamon Press, 1966.

27. Friedrich, C. J. trans., *Alfred Weber's Theory of the Location of Industries.* Chicago: University of Chicago Press, 1929.

28. Greenhut, M. L. *Plant Location in Theory and in Practice.* Chapel Hill, NC: University of North Carolina Press 1956.

29. Richardson, H. L. "Make Time an Ally." *Transportation and Distribution,* 36, no. 7 (1995): 46–52.

30. Fabey, M. "Changing Trade Winds." *Traffic World,* 263, no. 8 (2000): 41–42.

31. MacDonald, A. "How Companies Choose and Manage 3PLs." *World Trade,* 20, no. 2 (2007), 18–24.

32. Hannon, D. "GM Hatches Plan to Cut 70 Days from Order Cycle Time." *Purchasing,* 130, no. 13 (2001): 61–62.

33. Schulz, J. "GM Buys Out Vector SCM, Brings Logistics Back In-House." *Logistics Management Online,* August 1, 2006; www.logisticsmgmt.com/index.asp?layout=articlePrint&articleID=CA6365036.

34. Hoffman, W. "The Greening of Logistics." *Traffic World* (June 25, 2007): 1–2.

35. Hoffman. "The Greening of Logistics."

36. Kerr, J. "What's the Right Role for Global 3PLs?" *Logistics Management,* 45, no. 2 (2006): 51–54

37. See, for example, Abshire, R. D. and S. R. Premeaux. "Motor Carrier Selection Criteria: Perceptual Differences Between Shippers and Carriers." *Transportation Journal,* 31, no. 1 (1991): 31–35; Bardi, E. J., P. K. Bagchi, and T. S Raghunathan. "Motor Carrier Selection in a Deregulated Environment." *Transportation Journal,* 29, no. 1 (1989): 4–11; Foster, J. R. and S. Strasser. "Carrier\Modal Selection Factors: The Shipper \Carrier Paradox." *Transportation Research Forum,* 31, no. 1 (1990): 206–12; and Murphy, P. R., J. M. Daley, and P.K. Hall. "Carrier Selection: Do Shippers and Carriers Agree, or Not?" *Transportation Research,* 33E, no. 1 (1997): 67–72.

38. Kerr. "What's the Right Role for Global 3PLs?"

39. Richardson, H. L. "A Shift in Freight Forwarding." *World Trade,* 16, no. 2 (2003): 22–26.

40. Obtained from the Red Book Web site: www.redbooktrucking.com.

41. Information obtained from www.ams.usda.gov/tmd/shipping/existing.htm.

42. Richardson, H. L. "Intermodal Update: Industry Is Meeting Customer's Demands." 16, no. 4 (2003): 40–41.

43. Kerr, J. "3 Key Software Trends." *Logistics Management,* 43, no. 3 (2004): 53–55.

44. McCrea, B. "TMS Steps Out of the Shadows." *Logistics Management,* 46, no. 2 (2007): 53.

45. Anonymous. "Frozen Gourmet Sees Double-Digit Growth with SmartTurn." *Frozen Food Age,* 55, no. 12 (2007): 25.

46. Anthes, G. H. "Refurnishing the Supply Chain." *Computerworld,* 38, no. 23 (2004): 39–40

47. Witt, C. "LES Is More (Important)." *Material Handling Management,* 59, no. 4 (2004): 28–32.

48. Sullivan, L. "Hey, Wal-Mart, a New Case of Pampers Is on the Way." *InformationWeek,* (January 23, 2006): 28.

49. Trebilcock, B. "Managing Returns with WMS." *Modern Materials Handling,* 59, no. 10 (2004): 33–36.

50. Morton, R. "Measuring a Supply Chain from End to End." *Logistics Today,* 47, no. 6 (2006): 1–2.

51. McCrea, B. "Metrics Take Center Stage." *Logistics Management,* 45, no. 1 (2006): 39–41.

52. Mejza, M. C. and J. D. Wisner "The Scope and Span of Supply Chain Management." *The International Journal of Logistics Management,* 12, no. 2 (2001): 37–56; K. C. Tan. and J. D. Wisner. "A Comparison of the Supply Chain Management Approaches of U.S. Regional and Global Businesses." *Supply Chain Forum,* 2, no. 2 (2001) 20–28.

53. Dutton, G. "Collaborative Transportation Management." *World Trade,* 16, no. 2 (2003): 40–43.

54. Wresch, W. and S. Fraser. "Managerial Strategies Used to Overcome Technological Hurdles: A Review of E-Commerce Efforts Used by Innovative Caribbean Managers." *Journal of Global Information Management,* 14, no. 3 (2006): 1–15.

55. Varon, E. "To Bill or Not to Bill (on-line): Digital Invoicing Is the Next Big Step in e-Business Transactions." *CIO,* 16, no. 3 (2002): 91–94.

56. BNSF's Web page is www.bnsf.com.

57. Hannon, D. "Transportation Tech Helps Companies Buy and Sell Globally." *Purchasing,* 131, no. 10 (2002): 37–38.

58. Hickey, K. "The Road Less Traveled." *Traffic World* (January 27, 2003): 19–20.

59. Arntzen, B. "Fulfillment Partners in the Internet-Driven Supply Chain." *Transportation & Distribution,* 41, no. 11 (2000): S19–S22.

60. Rosencrance, L. "Shippers Face Automation Task for Customs Deadline." *Computerworld,* 37, no. 4 (2003): 10.

61. NTE's Web page is www.nte.net.

62. Hannon, D. "Proposed Customs Regulations Weigh on Air Freight Market." 132, no. 3 (2003): 35–37.

63. Russell, S. "'Robust' Security for Crossborder Trucking." *Traffic World* (July 2, 2007): 1.

64. Anonymous. "Meeting the Challenge." *Logistics Management,* 41, no. 8 (2002): 59–60.

65. U.S. Dept. of Commerce Web site: http://www.ita.doc.gov/td/oetca/staff.html.

66. U.S. Dept. of Commerce Foreign-Trade Zones Board Web site: http://ia.ita.doc.gov/ftzpage/index.

67. NAFTA information was obtained from the U.S. Trade Representative Web site: www.ustr.gov.

68. Morton, R. "NAFTA Revisited." *Logistics Today,* 48, no. 4 (2007): 1–2.

69. Lawrence, D. "China Issues Food, Toy Recall Rules to Tighten Safety." *Bloomberg.com News* (August 31, 2007), www.bloomberg.com/apps/news?pid=20601080&sid=asUaOAct_vrc&refer=asia.

70. Morton, R. "Turning a Negative into a Positive." *Logistics Today,* 48, no. 1 (2007) 18–19.

71. More information on this case can be found at http://web.indstate.edu/recycle/9505.html.

72. Trowbridge, P. "A Case Study of Green Supply-Chain Management." *Greener Management International* (autumn 2001): 121–35.

CHAPTER 10

1. Dickie, J. "Fueling the CRM Engine." Quote by Jim Dickie, a partner with CSO Insights, a CRM research firm, in *Customer Relationship Management,* 11, no. 4 (2007): 10.

2. Beasty, C. "Feedback Mountain." Esteban Klosky, senior research director at Gartner, a supply chain management research company, in *Customer Relationship Management,* 11, no. 2 (2007): 28–32.

3. Dickie, J. "Fueling the CRM Engine." *Customer Relationship Management,* 11, no. 4 (2007): 10.

4. Nairn, A. "CRM: Helpful or Full of Hype?" *Journal of Database Marketing,* 9, no. 4 (2002): 376–82.

5. Jackson, J. "Breaking News: A CRM Success Story." *Customer Relationship Management,* 11, no. 1 (2007): 45.

6. Dychè, J. *The CRM Handbook: A Business Guide to Customer Relationship Management,* Upper Saddle River, NJ: Addison-Wesley, 2002.

7. Bergeron, B. *Essentials of CRM: A Guide to Customer Relationship Management,* New York, NY: John Wiley & Sons, 2002.

8. Ragins, E. J. and A. J. Greco. "Customer Relationship Management and e-Business: More than a Software Solution." *Review of Business,* 24, no. 1 (2003): 25–30.

9. Cavusgil, S. T. "Extending the Reach of e-Business." *Marketing Management,* 11, no. 2 (2002), 24–29.

10. Morphy, E. "Global CRM Market to Surpass $11 Billion by 2008." *CRM Daily.com* (August 2, 2004); Morphy, E., "Studies: Customers Number One in 2002." *CRM Daily.com* (November 29, 2001), www.crm-daily.com.

11. Dickie, "Fueling the CRM Engine."

12. Anonymous. "NMA @ 10: Secrets of Success." *New Media Age* (June 16, 2005): 18.

13. Chilton, D. "CRM Masters." *Marketing,* 111, no. 21 (2006): S19–20.

14. Bailor, C. "Clicking the Tires." *Customer Relationship Management,* 10, no. 8 (2006): 43.

15. Bailor, C. "Elder Effect." *Customer Relationship Management,* 10, no. 11 (2006): 36–40.

16. Creamer, M. "Seeking to Clear the Clutter." *TelevisionWeek,* 26, no. 15 (2007): 188.

17. Tungate, M. "The Man from MySpace." *Campaign* (September 29, 2007): 36.

18. Anonymous. "Case Study: KBC Achieves Success in Cross-Selling." *Life Insurance International* (January, 2007): 9.

19. Liddle, A. J. "Haddad Group Pleased by Changing Face of Card Program." *Nation's Restaurant News,* 37, no. 2 (2003): 47.

20. Ragins, E. J. and A. J. Greco. "Customer Relationship Management and e-Business: More than a Software Solution." *Review of Business,* 24, no. 1 (2003): 25–30.

21. Nadeem, M. "How e-Business Leadership Results in Customer Satisfaction and Customer Lifetime Value." *The Business Review, Cambridge,* 6, no. 1 (2006): 218–24.

22. Bailor, C. "Not Fade Away." *Customer Relationship Management,* 11, no. 2 (2007): 22–26.

23. Collieer, S. "Another Way to Look at 'Member Value'." *Credit Union Magazine,* 73, no. 1 (2007): 9A.

24. Arnold, M. "Interactive Forces." *Medical Marketing and Media,* 41, no. 11 (2006): 36–39.

25. Hosford, C. "AmerisourceBergen Saves with Automated Sales Info." *B to B,* 91, no. 13 (2006): 18.

26. Shaprio, R. D. and J. L. Heskett. *Logistics Strategy: Cases and Concepts.* St. Paul, MN: West Publishing Co., 1985.

27. McCartney, S. "The Middle Seat: A Report Card on the Nation's Airlines." *The Wall Street Journal* (February 6, 2007): D1.

28. Levin, G. "The Viability of Virtual Queuing Tools." *Call Center Magazine,* 19, no. 10 (2006): 29.

29. Anonymous. "Special Report: Telemarketing's True Calling." *Marketing Week* (September 21, 2006): 39.

30. Klie, L. "Satisfaction with Automation Increases Only Slightly." *Speech Technology,* 12, no. 5 (2007): 10–11.

31. Ali, S. "Leadership (A Special Report): If You Want to Scream, Press … Do Call Centers Have to Be So Infuriating?" *The Wall Street Journal* (October 30, 2006): R4.

32. Wisner, J. D. and W. J. Corney. "Comparing Practices for Capturing Bank Customer Feedback." *Benchmarking: An International Journal,* 8, no. 3 (2001): 240–50.

33. Anonymous. "Net Threat Rising." *Consumer Reports,* 70, no. 9 (2005): 12–18.

34. Many of these references can be found at the American CRM Directory, or www.american-crm-directory.com.

35. Dychè. *The CRM Handbook.*

36. Goldenberg, B. "A CRM Initiative's Bermuda Triangle." *Customer Relationship Management,* 11, no. 5 (2007): 10.

37. Fitzgerald, M. "CRM Made Simple; New Software to Supercharge Your Sales." *Inc. Magazine,* 29, no. 1 (2007): 46.

38. See www.netsuite.com for more information.

39. More on Oracle CRM applications can be found at www.oracle.com.

40. See www.microsoft.com/dynamics for more information.

41. Levine, C. "The Trouble with Customer Data." *Wall Street & Technology,* 25, no. 1 (2007): 32.

42. Burns, M. "Third Annual CRM Survey." *CA Magazine,* 139, no. 10 (2006): 18.

CHAPTER 11

1. "Taming the Dragon: Mastering China's Growth Dynamics" (July 2005); available from www.accenture.com/Global/Netherlands/Research_and_Insights/policy_And_Corporate_Affairs/TamingTheDragonDynamics.htm.

2. "Honda Chooses Indiana for US$400 mil. Factory"; available from www.globalinsight.com/SDA/SDADetail6236.htm.

3. Burt, J. "Toyota Picks Tupelo, Mississippi for Plant" (February 27, 2007); available from www.thecarconnection.com/Auto_News/Daily_Auto_News/Toyota_Picks_Tupelo_Miss_For_Plant.S173.A11977.html.

4. Poe, J. "Fueling the Economy: Government Leaders in the South Liberally Use Taxpayer Funds to Attract Lucrative Auto Plants 2001 Southern Economic Survey." *The Atlanta Journal - Constitution* (April 8, 2001).

5. Ritzler, K. "It's Official: Honda Picks Alabama for Auto Plant." *The Atlanta Constitution* (May 7, 1999).

6. Poe. "Fueling the Economy."

7. Shirouzu, N. and R. Brooks. "South Korea's Hyundai Motor Chooses Alabama Site for Firm's First U.S. Plant." *Wall Street Journal* (April 2, 2002).

8. Clapp, D. "Success Stories: Teamwork Drives Hyundai to Alabama!" *Business Facilities* (August 2002); available from www.facilitycity.com/busfac/bf_02_08_cover.asp.

9. Poe. "Fueling the Economy."

10. Baird, C. "Unions on the Run." *Government Union Review and Public Policy Digest,* 20, no. 2 (2002).

11. "Taming the Dragon."

12. Porter, M. "Clusters and the New Economics of Competition." *Harvard Business Review* (November–December 1998).

13. American Honda Motor Company Web page: available from www.hondacorporate.com.

14. Aron, L. J. "Clicks and Bricks Meet Head On in the Software/IT Location Revolution." *Site Selection Online* (May 2000); available from www.siteselection.com/features/2000/may/software.

15. Anders, G. "Virtual Reality: Web Firms Go on Warehouse Building Boom." *Wall Street Journal(September* 8, 1999).

16. 2001 Amazon.com Annual Report; available from http://212.180.4.141/swim/files/us/US0231351067_01_Amazon_Com_Annual_Report_2001_0.42_Mo.pdf.

17. 2006 Amazon.com Annual Report.

18. Anders. "Virtual Reality."

19. "Amazon Coming to Nevada." *Las Vegas Review – Journal* (January 8, 1999).

20. Foley, J., S. Konicki, and G. V. Hulme. "Amazon's IT Agenda." *Information Week* (November 6, 2000).

21. Katz, F. "Amazon Shuts Down McDonough Facility 442 Jobs Affected by Sudden Move." *The Atlanta Constitution* (January 31, 2001).

22. 2006 Amazon.com Annual Report.

23. 2006 Amazon.com Annual Report.

24. Acohido. "Amazon Posts Gain, Boosts Outlook." *USA Today* (January 24, 2003).

25. Brody, B. "Site Selection for the 21st Century... and Beyond." *Business Facilities* (April 2001); available from www.facilitycity.com/busfac/bf_01_04_cover1.asp 2.

26. Shah, J. B. "Fedex's Hub of Supply Chain Activity—At Its Own Operation, the Logistics Company Has Made an Art Out of the Science of Supply Chain Management." *EBN* (April 30, 2001).

27. Ferdows, K. "Making the Most of Foreign Factories." *Harvard Business Review* (March–April 1997): 73–88.

28. Ferdows. "Making the Most of Foreign Factories."

29. Ferdows. "Making the Most of Foreign Factories."

30. Ferdows. "Making the Most of Foreign Factories."

31. "Foreign Investment in China" (February 2007); available from http://uschina.org/info/forecast/2007/foreign-investment.html. Bolton, J. and E. Chu. "Global Sourcing for High Performance: Leading Practices and the Emerging Role of International Procurement Organizations in China" (November 22, 2006); available from http://www.accenture.com/Countries/Netherlands/Research_and_Insights/By_Industry/Consumer_Goods_and_Services/GlobalSourcingHighPerformance.html; "Taming the Dragon."

32. "Foreign Investment in China."

33. "Taming the Dragon."

34. Bolton and Chu. "Global Sourcing for High Performance."

35. "Foreign Investment in China."

36. Hofstede, G. "Cultural Dimensions"; available from www.geert-hofstede.com.

37. Hofstede, G. "Cultural Dimensions for China"; available from www.geert-hofstede.com/hofstede_china.shtml.

38. Farrell, D. and A. J. Grant. "China's Looming Talent Shortage." *The McKinsey Quarterly,* no. 4, (2005)

39. "Foreign Investment in China."

40. Zeng, C. "China's unions emboldened by Wal-Mart success" (August 24, 2006); available from/www.atimes.com/atimes/China_Business/HH24Cb03.html.

41. People's Daily Online Editor's Note; available from http://english.people.com.cn/zhuanti/Zhuanti_473.htm.

42. Acohido. "Amazon Posts Gain, Boosts Outlook."

43. "Foreign Investment in China."

44. "Regional Trade Agreements and the Multilateral Trading System." Document 103/226 final EN (November 27, 2002) Commission on Trade and Investment Policy, ICC; available from www.iccwbo.org/home/statements_rules/statements/2002/Regional%20trade%20agreements_multilateral%20trading%20system.asp.

45. "The European Union at a Glance, Member States of the EU"; available from http://europa.eu/abc/european_countries/index_en.htm.

46. "Key Facts and Figures about Europe and the Europeans 2006"; available from http://europa.eu/abc/keyfigures/index_en.htm.

47. "NAFTA: A Strong Record of Success" (March 22, 2006); available from www.ustr.gov/Trade_Agreements/Regional/NAFTA/Fact-Sheets/Section_Index.html.

48. "The EU Relations with MERCOSUR"; available from www.europa.eu.int/comm/external_relations/mercosur/intro.

49. ASEAN Secretariat; available from www.aseansec.org.

50. Clapp, D., M. E. McCandless, and K. Khan. "The World's Most Competitive Locations." *Business Facilities* (September 2001); available from www.facilitycity.com/busfac/bf_01_09_cover.asp.

51. IMD *World Competitiveness Yearbook;* available from www.imd.ch/research/publications/wcy/announcing.cfm.

52. "Global Competitiveness Report 2006–2007"; available from www.weforum.org/en/initiatives/gcp/Global%20Competitivenss%20Report/index.htm.

53. World Competitiveness Report, Methodology and Principles of Analysis; available from www.imd.ch/research/publications/wcy/upload/methodology.pdf.

54. IMD *World Competitiveness Yearbook;* available from www.imd.ch/research/publications/wcy/index.cfm.

55. "Global Competitiveness Report 2006–2007."

56. Grier, P. "An Economic Vision: Silicon States." *Christian Science Monitor,* 91, no. 61 (February 24, 1999).

57. 2006 Amazon.com Annual Report.

58. Brody. "Site Selection for the 21st Century."

59. Clapp, D. "A Paradigm Shift in the Far East." *Business Facilities* (September 2002); available from www.facilitycity.com/busfac/bf_02_09_move.asp.

60. Krauss, C. "Halliburton Moving C.E.O. From Houston to Dubai." *New York Times,* March 12, 2007.

61. Ghosh, A. and S. L. McLafferty. *Location Strategies for Retail and Service Firms.* Lexington, MA: Lexington Books, 1987.

62. "The Supercenter Era: 1992 to 2002." *DSN Retailing Today* (August 6, 2002): 27–31.

63. Markham, V. and N. Steinzor. "U.S. National Report on Population and the Environment" (2006); available from /www.cepnet.org/documents/USNatlReptFinal.pdf.

64. "NAFTA 5 Years Report—Encouraging Environmental Protection"; available from www.ustr.gov/naftareport/encouraging.htm.

65. "Trade and Environment." World Trade Organization; available from www.wto.org/english/tratop_e/envir_e/environment.pdf.

66. "Trade and Environment."

67. Pope, B. "China Versus Mexico." *Ward's AutoWorld* (June 1, 2006); available from www.wardsautoworld/ar/auto_china_vs_mexico.

68. "Report Seeks Reality Behind Number of Engineering Graduates"; available from www3.nsta.org/main/news/stories/nsta_story.php?news_story_ID=52016.

69. Poe. "Fueling the Economy."

70. Clapp. "A Paradigm Shift in the Far East."

71. Noorbakhsh, F., A. Paloni, and A. Youssef. "Human Capital and FDI Inflows to Developing Countries: New Empirical Evidence." *World Development,* 29, no. 9 (2001): 1593–610.

72. "Right-to-Work States"; available from www.nrtw.org/rtws.htm.

73. Malkin, E. "Manufacturing Jobs Are Exiting Mexico." *New York Times* (November 5, 2002).

74. Donnelly, R. "Dealing with the Rising Sun"; available from www.mexconnect.com/mex_/travel/bzm/bzmjapan.html.

75. Rolling Blackout; available from http://en.wikipedia.org/wiki/Rolling_blackout.

76. "New Plants Help Ease Energy Shortage"; available from www.newsgd.com/news/china1/200606060036.htm.

77. "Call Centers." Outsourcing International LLC; available from www.outsourcingintl.com/call.htm.

78. Mallot, J. "Quality of Life: How to Know It When You See It." *Business Facilities* (November 2002); available from www.facilitycity.com/busfac/bf_02_11_cover2.asp.

79. Mallot. "Quality of Life."

80. Lindquist, D. and A. Cearley. "U.S. Exec Abducted in Tijuana" (April 7, 2006); available from www. signonsandiego.com/news/mexico/tijuana/20060407-9999-7m7kidnap.html.

81. "We Turn Information into a Competitive Advantage"; available from www.mappinganalytics.com/company/about-us.html.

82. "We Turn Information into a Competitive Advantage."

83. Porter. "Clusters and the New Economics of Competition."

84. "Business Clusters in the UK—A First Assessment"; available from www.dti.gov.uk/clusters/map/graphics/forintro.pdf.

85. Brody, B. "High-Tech Clusters Span the Globe." *Business Facilities* (March 2001); available from www. facilitycity.com/busfac/bf_01_03_global.asp.

86. Executive Summary, Strategic Review 2007; available from www.nasscom.in/Nasscom/templates/NormalPage.aspx?id=50856.

87. Porter. "Clusters and the New Economics of Competition."

88. Grier. "An Economic Vision."

89. United Nations Division for Sustainable Development; available from www.un.org/esa/sustdev/.

90. CSD-15 Chairman's Summary; available from www.un.org/sustdev/.

91. The United Nations Framework Convention on Climate Change; available from http://unfcc.int/essential_background/convention/items/2627.php.

92. Kyoto Protocol Reference Manual on Accounting of Emissions and Assigned Amounts; available from http://unfcc.int/kyoto_protocol/items/2830.php.

93. Kyoto Protocol; available from http://unfcc.int/kyoto_protocol/items/2830.php.

94. "Sustainable Development"; available from http://en.wikipedia.org/wiki/Sustainable_development.

CHAPTER 12

1. Gentry, C. "Merry Customer Service." *Chain Store Age,* 83, no. 1 (2007): 76.

2. Jill Bossi, senior vice president in supply chain management, Bank of America, in Siegfried, M. "One on One." *Journal of Supply Chain Management,* 40, no. 4 (2004): 2–3.

3. Howells, T., K. Barefoot, and B. Lindberg. "Annual Industry Accounts: Revised Estimates for 2003–2005." *Survey of Current Business,* 86, no. 12 (2006): 45–55.

4. Zainulbhai, A. "A Vision for India in 2020: Freer, Better, Bigger." *Business Today,* January 14, 2007, p. 226.

5. Blackstone, B. "Is Productivity Growth Back in Grips of Baumol's Disease?" *Wall Street Journal,* August 13, 2007, p. A2.

6. Geier, R. "Get Flexible." *Best's Review,* 107, no. 10 (2007): 77–79.

7. Anonymous. "India Calling Vodafone." *Global Agenda,* 12 (February 2007): 1.

8. Uhlfelder, E. "A Safer Way to Cope with Emerging Market Perils." *Financial Times,* January 15, 2007, p. 7.

9. Porter, M. *Competitive Strategy: Techniques for Analyzing Industries and Competitors.* New York, NY: The Free Press, 1980.

10. Anonymous. "Southwest Airlines CEO." *Aviation Week & Space Technology,* 165, no. 16 (2006): 18.

11. Elan, E. "Operators Warm to Idea of Saving Energy and Money by Reducing Greenhouse Gas Emissions." *Nations' Restaurant News,* 41, no. 18 (2007): 4–6.

12. Bailor, C. "Buying Into the Customer Experience." *Customer Relationship Management,* 11, no. 6 (2007): 15.

13. Hoffman, W. "Building the Little Guy." *Traffic World* (September 3, 2007): 1.

14. Anonymous. "Supplier Relationships Prove Invaluable to Purchasing at UNICCO Service Co." *Purchasing,* 136, no. 10 (2007): 102.

15. Anonymous. "Toyota Honors Ryder with 2006 Excellent Award for Value Improvement." *Traffic World* (May 1, 2007): 1.

16. Vecchione, A. "Eight Steps to Reaching High Performance." *Drug Topics,* 151, no. 3 (2007): 47.

17. Cullen, S. "How to Tell If You're Receiving Quality Copier Service." *Office Solutions,* 23, no. 6 (2006): 21–24.

18. Drazen, E. L., R. E. Moll, and M. F. Roetter. *Logistics in Service Industries.* Oak Brook, IL: Council of Logistics Management, 1991, pp. 34.

19. Maister, D. "The Psychology of Waiting Lines." *The Service Encounter,* edited by J. A. Czepiel, M. R. Solomon, and C. F. Surprenant, Lexington, MA: Lexington Books, D.C. Heath & Co., 1985.

20. Maister. "The Psychology of Waiting Lines."

21. Ruggless, R. "Which Wich Chain Has Expansion, Streamlined Operations in the Bag." *Nation's Restaurant News,* 39, no. 38 (2005): 30.

22. Andel, T. "Can Amazon Succeed at Grocery Delivery?" *Modern Materials Handling,* 62, no. 9 (2007): 15.

23. Glazer, F. "The New Dinner Theater." *Nation's Restaurant News,* 41, no. 5 (2007): 138.

24. Flandez, R. "New Franchise Idea: Fewer Rules, More Difference." *Wall Street Journal,* September 18, 2007, p. B4.

25. Byrne, H. "Welcome to McWorld." *Barron's,* 74, no. 35 (1994): 25–28.

26. Britton, E. and V. Rossi. "The Future of China's Service Sector." *The China Business Review,* 34, no. 3 (2007): 42–47.

27. Hoffman, G. "On Foreign Expansion." *Progressive Grocer,* 75, no. 9 (1996): 156.

28. Chamberlain, D., C. Stambaugh, and T. Miller. "A Better System: The Streamlined Sales Tax Project." *Journal of Government Financial Management,* 56, no. 3 (2007): 48–54.

29. Pinkerton, J. and A. Gray. "Retail in a Google World." *Dealerscope,* 49, no. 1 (2007): 46–51.

30. Brady, M. K. and J. J.Cronin, Jr. "Customer Orientation: Effects on Customer Service Perceptions and Outcome Behaviors." *Journal of Service Research,* 3, no. 3 (2001): 241–51.

31. See, for instance, Parasuraman, A., V. A. Zeithaml, and L. L. Berry. "SERVQUAL: A Multiple-Item Scale for Measuring Consumer Perceptions of Service Quality." *Journal of Retailing,* 64, no. 1 (1988): 12–40; Parasuraman, A., V. A. Zeithaml, and L. L. Berry. "Conceptual Model of Service Quality and Its Implications for Future Research." *Journal of Marketing,* 49 (fall, 1985): 41–50.

32. Levin, G. "Measuring the Things That Matter." *Call Center Magazine,* 20, no. 3 (2007): 24.

33. McWilliams, B. and E. Gerstner. "Offering Low Price Guarantees to Improve Customer Retention." *Journal of Retailing,* 82, no. 2 (2006): 105.

CHAPTER 13

1. Quote attributed to Joachim Milberg, CEO of BMW, in Wilding, R. "Playing the Tune of Shared Success." *Financial Times* (November 10, 2006): 2.

2. Quote by Andrew McGlasson, distribution global marketing director for integration software maker Infor, in Perriello, B. "The Seamless Supply Chain." *Industrial Distribution,* 96, no. 10 (2007): 26.

3. Blanchard, D. "Too Many Supply Chains Are Failing to Integrate." *Industry Week,* 255, no. 11 (2006): 45–46.

4. Lambert, D. M., M. C. Cooper, and J. D. Pagh. "Supply Chain Management: Implementation Issues and Research Opportunities." *International Journal of Logistics Management,* 9, no. 2 (1998): 1–19.

5. Siu, S. "CargoSmart Ltd." *Journal of Commerce* (January 8, 2007): 1.

6. These processes are discussed in detail in Lambert, Cooper, and Pagh. "Supply Chain Management," and in Croxton, K. L., S. J. Garcia-Dastugue, D. M. Lambert. "The Supply Chain Management Processes." *International Journal of Logistics Management,* 12, no. 2 (2001): 13–36.

7. Henri, J. "Are Your Performance Measurement Systems Truly Performing?" *CMA Management,* 80, no. 7 (2006): 31–35.

8. Wilding, R., "Playing the Tune of Shared Success," *Financial Times* (November 10, 2006): 2.

9. Blanchard, D. "How to Fight the High Cost of Moving Freight." 255, no. 10 (2006): 18–19.

10. DiBenedetto, B. "Thinking Lean." *Journal of Commerce* (May 21, 2007): 1.

11. Neal, H. "The Rebirth of Knowledge Management." *Manufacturing Business Technology,* 24, no. 10 (2006): 38–41.

12. See for instance, Andel, T. "RFID: The Only Thing Passive about the Marines." *Modern Materials Handling,* 62, no. 8 (2007): 61; Fink, R., J. Gillett, and G. Grzeskiewicz. "Will RFID Change Inventory Assumptions?" *Strategic Finance,* 89, no. 4 (2007): 34–39; Joch, A. "'Active' Assistance." *Hospitals & Health Networks,* 6, no. 3 (2007): 36–37.

13. Lester, T. "Masters of Collaboration—How Well Do U.K. Businesses Work Together." *Financial Times,* (June 29, 2007): 8.

14. Trunick, P. "It's Crunch Time." *Transportation & Distribution,* 43, no. 1 (2002): 5–6.

15. Geller, S. "The Pharmaceutical Industry Looks to Reduce Waste by Getting Lean." *Pharmaceutical Technology,* 31, no. 3 (2007): 130.

16. Purdum, T. "Hitting a Moving Target." *Industry Week,* 256, no. 2 (2007): 14–15.

17. Hoffman, W. "Linking the Chain." *Traffic World* (April 23, 2007): 1.

18. Beasty, C. "The Chain Gang." *Customer Relationship Management,* 11, no. 10 (2007): 32–36.

19. Field, A. "Sound the Alarm." *Journal of Commerce* (May 7, 2007): 1.

20. Avery, S. "At Boeing, Supplier Collaboration Takes Off." *Purchasing,* 136, no. 13 (2007): 1.

21. Maccoby, M. "Creating Collaboration." *Research Technology Management,* 49, no. 6 (2006): 60–62.

22. Roberts, B. "Counting on Collaboration." *HRMagazine,* 52, no. 10 (2007): 47–51.

23. Paul, L. "Suspicious Minds: Collaboration Among Trading Partners Can Unlock Great Value." *CIO,* 16, no. 7 (2003): 74–82.

24. Maylett, T. and K. Vitasek. "For Closer Collaboration, Try Education." *Supply Chain Management Review,* 11, no. 1 (2007): 58.

25. Information about these annual conferences can be found in the Web sites: www.sensorsexpo .com, www.ism.ws, and www.uconnect.gs1us.org.

26. Lee, H. L., V. Padmanabhan, and S. Whang. "The Bullwhip Effect in Supply Chains." *Sloan Management Review,* 38, no. 3 (1997): 93–102.

27. Stern, S. "The Supply Chains that Could Bind Unsuspecting Managers." *Financial Times* (November 28, 2006): 10.

28. Hofmann, M. "Financial Executives Rate Top Challenges Through 2009." *Business Insurance,* 41, no. 21 (2007): 4–5.

29. Field, A. "How 'Free' Is Free Trade?" *Journal of Commerce* (December 18, 2006): 1–3; Kline, J. "Managing Emerging Market Risk." *Logistics Management,* 46, no. 5 (2007): 41–4; Swaminathan, J. and B. Tomlin. "How to Avoid the Risk Management Pitfalls." *Supply Chain Management Review,* 11, no. 5 (2007): 34–43.

30. Esola, L. "Employers Questioned on Pandemic Drug Plan." *Business Insurance,* 40, no. 49 (2006): 4–5.

31. Swaminathan and Tomlin. "How to Avoid the Risk Management Pitfalls."

32. Anonymous. "Supply Disruption Discussed." *Business Insurance,* 37, no. 22 (2003): 17.

33. Swaminathan and Tomlin. "How to Avoid the Risk Management Pitfalls."

34. Anonymous. "Supply Diversity Cuts Risk Exposure." *Oil & Gas Journal,* 105, no. 17 (2007): 65–68.

35. Tieman, R. "It's About Common Sense." *Financial Times* (September 10, 2007): 5.

36. Tieman. "It's About Common Sense."

37. Anonymous. "Flexing Supply Chain Muscle." *Chain Store Age,* 83, no. 9 (2007): 10A.

38. Tiemen. "It's About Common Sense."

39. Felsted, A. "Lessons from Barbie World." *Financial Times* (September 10, 2007): 1.

40. Anonymous. "Mitigating Risks." *Chain Store Age,* 83, no. 9 (2007): 14A.

41. Rice, J. "Rethinking Security." *Logistics Management,* 46, no. 5 (2007): 28.

42. Terreri, A. "How Do You Balance Shipment Speed with a Secure Supply Chain?" *World Trade,* 19, no. 11 (2006): 18–22.

43. Rice, J. "Rethinking Supply Chain Security." *Logistics Management* (May 1, 2007).

44. Anderson, B. "Prevent Cargo Theft." *Logistics Today,* 48, no. 5 (2007): 37–38.

45. McCourt, M. "Supply Chains: Get a Global View and Find the Weakest Link." *Security,* 44, no. 8 (2007): 8.

46. Purtell, D. and J. Rice. "Assessing Cargo Supply Risk." *Security Management,* 50, no. 11 (2006): 78–84.

47. See, for example, the Web site: www.cargosecurity.com/ncsc/education-CTPAT.asp.

48. Terreri. "How Do You Balance Shipment Speed with a Secure Supply Chain?"

49. Terreri. "How Do You Balance Shipment Speed with a Secure Supply Chain?"

50. Greenemeier, L. "Mass Mutual Gets Control of Its Security Data." *InformationWeek* (September 17, 2007): 108–109.

51. Michel, R. "Profit from Secure Supply Chains." *Manufacturing Business Technology,* 24, no. 11 (2006): 1.

CHAPTER 14

1. Quote from Julie Fraser, principal at Industry Directions, in "MESA Moves Metrics Framework to the Next Level of Operational Improvements." *Manufacturing Business Technology,* 25, no. 1 (2007): 44.

2. Lummus, R., S. Melnyk, R. Vovurka, L. Burns, and J. Sandor. "Getting Ready for Tomorrow's Supply Chain." *Supply Chain Management,* 11, no. 6 (2007): 48–53.

3. Adams, B. L. "Performance Measures and Profitability Factors of Successful African-American Entrepreneurs: An Exploratory Study." *Journal of American Academy of Business,* 2, no. 2 (2003): 418–24.

4. Henri, J. "Are Your Performance Measurement Systems Truly Performing?" *CMA Management,* 80, no. 7 (2006): 31–35.

5. Blackwell, R. D. and K. Blackwell. "The Century of the Consumer: Converting Supply Chains into Demand Chains." *Supply Chain Management Review* (fall, 1999): 22–32.

6. Fusaro, P. and R. Miller. *What Went Wrong at Enron: Everyone's Guide to the Largest Bankruptcy in U.S. History.* Hoboken, NJ: Wiley, 2002.

7. Katz, J. "Beyond the Executive Branch." *Industry Week,* 256, no. 1 (2007): 20A.

8. Adapted from: Nicholas, J. M. *Competitive Manufacturing Management.* New York: McGraw-Hill, 1998; Wisner, J. D. and S. E. Fawcett. "Linking Firm Strategy to Operating Decisions Through Performance Measurement." *Production and Inventory Management Journal,* 32, no. 3 (1991): 5–11.

9. Geary, S. and J. P. Zonnenburg. "What It Means to Be Best in Class." *Supply Chain Management Review* (July 2000): 42–50.

10. Mishra, D. "Feeding Best Buy." *Dealerscope,* 48, no. 12 (2006): 82.

11. Hervani, A., M. Helms, and J. Sarkis. "Performance Measurement for Green Supply Chain Management." *Benchmarking,* 12, no. 4 (2005): 330–54.

12. Wilson, M. "Spotlight on Savings." *Chain Store Age,* 83, no. 9 (2007): 84.

13. DiBenedetto, B. "The Color of Money." *Journal of Commerce* (June 25, 2007): 1.

14. Brandt, D. "No Vroom for Pollution." *Industrial Engineer,* 39, no. 9 (2007): 34–35.

15. Adapted from: Geary and Zonnenburg. "What It Means to Be Best in Class."

16. Varmazis, M. "What to Look for in Online Office Supply Catalogs." *Purchasing,* 136, no. 11 (2007): 33.

17. Geary and Zonnenburg. "What It Means to Be Best in Class."

18. See, for example, DeBusk, G. and A. Crabtree. "Does the Balanced Scorecard Improve Performance?" *Management Accounting Quarterly,* 8, no. 1 (2006): 44–48; Kaplan, R. S. and D. P. Norton. "The Balanced Scorecard—Measures That Drive Performance." 70, no. 1 (1992): 71–79; Lester, T. "Measure for Measure, the Balanced Scorecard Remains a Widely Used Management Tool." *Financial Times* (October 6, 2004): 6; and Lawson, R., W. Stratton, and T. Hatch. "Scorecarding in the Public Sector: Fad or Tool of Choice?" *Government Finance Review,* 23, no. 3 (2007): 48–52.

19. Chow, C. W., D. Ganulin, K. Haddad, and J. Williamson. "The Balanced Scorecard: A Potent Tool for Energizing and Focusing Healthcare Organization Management." *Journal of Healthcare Management,* 43, no. 3 (1998): 263–80.

20. Lester. "Measure for Measure, the Balanced Scorecard Remains a Widely Used Management Tool."

21. DeBusk and Crabtree. "Does the Balanced Scorecard Improve Performance?"

22. Lester. "Measure for Measure, the Balanced Scorecard Remains a Widely Used Management Tool."

23. Alsyouf, I. "Measuring Maintenance Performance Using a Balanced Scorecard Approach." *Journal of Quality in Maintenance Engineering,* 12, no. 2 (2006): 133–43.

24. Kaplan, R. S. and D. P. Norton. "Linking the Balanced Scorecard to Strategy." *California Management Review,* 39, no. 1 (1996): 53–79.

25. Bush, P., "Strategic Performance Management in Government: Using the Balanced Scorecard." *Cost Magazine,* 19, no. 3 (2003): 24–31.

26. Stephens, T. Jr. "Drive Your Business Performance: Getting Started with Digital Dashboards." *Catalyst* (July/August 2007): 22–24.

27. Interested readers can visit www.supply-chain.org for more information about the Supply-Chain Council.

28. Taken from the online proceedings of the Supply-Chain World—Latin America 2002 conference, Mexico City, Mexico (www.supplychainworld.org/la2002/program.html).

29. Printed with permission from the Supply-Chain Council, www.supply-chain.org.

30. Stedman, C. "Users Eye Standard for Supply Chain." *Computerworld News* (June 1, 1998) issue. Web page: www.computerworld.com/news/1998.

31. Saccomano, A. "Keeping SCOR." *Traffic World,* 255, no. 13 (1998): 27–28.

32. Bolstorff, P. "How to Make Your Supply Chain More Valuable." *Logistics Today,* 46, no. 6 (2005): 19–21.

33. DiBenedetto, B. "Keeping SCOR." *Journal of Commerce* (April 23, 2007): 1.

Author Index

Subject Index